*Acclaim for* **RANDALL KENNEDY**'s

# INTERRACIAL INTIMACIES

"Brave. . . . Celebrates the way desire and family intimacy have defied and evaded state power."
— *The New York Times Book Review*

"A riveting account of interracial sex and kinship in America. . . . Extend[s] the debate over what a multiracial society should look like." — *San Francisco Chronicle*

"Using the personal stories of couples and families across the United States, Kennedy illustrates the personal consequences of evolving laws and mores." — *Chicago Sun-Times*

"[A] probing look at interracial relationships. . . . While much of the book examines legal issues, [Kennedy] uses anecdotes and pop culture references that make it lively and compelling."
— *The Hartford Courant*

"Clear and accessible. . . . Trace[s] this country's laws, customs and myths surrounding interracial relationships. . . . Will surely be the subject of some passionate discussions."
— *The Atlanta Journal-Constitution*

"[A] comprehensive, well-argued history of race in the sexual and familial imagination of Americans, beginning in the slave era and continuing to today's 'destructive' practice of race matching in contemporary adoptions." — *Minneapolis Star Tribune*

RANDALL KENNEDY

# INTERRACIAL INTIMACIES

Randall Kennedy is the author of *Nigger: The Strange Career of a Troublesome Word* and *Race, Crime, and the Law.* He received his undergraduate degree from Princeton and his law degree from Yale. A Rhodes Scholar, he served as a law clerk to Supreme Court Justice Thurgood Marshall. He is a professor at Harvard Law School and lives in Dedham, Massachusetts.

ALSO BY RANDALL KENNEDY

*Race, Crime, and the Law*

*Nigger: The Strange Career of a Troublesome Word*

# INTERRACIAL INTIMACIES

*Sex, Marriage, Identity, and Adoption*

## RANDALL KENNEDY

*Vintage Books*

*A Division of Random House, Inc.*

*New York*

FIRST VINTAGE BOOKS EDITION, JANUARY 2004

*Copyright © 2003 by Randall Kennedy*

All rights reserved under International and Pan-American Copyright Conventions.
Published in the United States by Vintage Books, a division of Random House, Inc.,
New York, and simultaneously in Canada by Random House of Canada Limited,
Toronto. Originally published in hardcover in the United States by Pantheon Books,
a division of Random House, Inc., New York, in 2003.

Vintage and colophon are registered trademarks of Random House, Inc.

Grateful acknowledgment is made to the following for permission to reprint
previously published material: HarperCollins Publishers, Inc.: Excerpt from
*The Collected Poems of Sterling A. Brown* edited by Michael S. Harper.
Copyright © 1980 by Sterling A. Brown. Reprinted by permission
of HarperCollins Publishers, Inc.

The Library of Congress has cataloged the Pantheon edition as follows:
Kennedy, Randall
Interracial intimacies: sex, marriage, identity, and adoption / Randall Kennedy.
p. cm.
Includes bibliographical references and index.
1. Interracial Marriage—Law and legislation—United States.    2. Miscegenation—
Law and legislation—United States.    3. Interracial adoption—United States.
I. Title.
KF511.K46 2003        346.73016—DC21        2002072786

Vintage ISBN: 0-375-70264-4

*Book design by Johanna S. Roebas*

www.vintagebooks.com

Printed in the United States of America
10   9   8   7   6   5   4   3   2   1

*This book is dedicated to my dutiful, wise, loving parents,*
*Henry Harold Kennedy Sr. and Rachel Spann Kennedy.*

# Contents

# INTERRACIAL
# INTIMACIES

# Introduction

Jacqueline Henley's aunt turned her niece over to the custody of the New Orleans Department of Welfare on October 1, 1952, because she was becoming darker by the day and some of the neighbors had complained that "the child possibly was a nigger."[1] Jacqueline was not yet two years old.[2]

Jacqueline's mother, a white woman named Ruby Henley, had endured a tough life. Wed for the first time at thirteen, she had married at least twice more and given birth to four children prior to Jacqueline. Henley was a thirty-two-year-old ailing divorcée when Jacqueline was born, on November 2, 1950, at the New Orleans Charity Hospital. Soon after the birth Henley was stricken with a brain tumor that left her paralyzed and unable to speak. On October 11, 1952, she died in the city's Home for Incurables.

During Henley's two years of incapacitation, her sister, Mrs. Carol Lee Henley McBride, cared for Jacqueline. There is reason to believe that she did so with fondness; a social worker who was involved in the case recalls that she showed her niece genuine affection.[3] Carol McBride, however, was married and had nine children of her own. She also had misgivings about keeping Jacqueline in her household because, in her view, the baby was "too dark" compared to the other children, who were all "fair."[4] Within a matter of months, Jacqueline's darkening coloration had become a source of intense gossip in the McBrides' all-white neighborhood. Carol McBride knew it would be only a matter of time before things turned ugly, so she surrendered Jacqueline to city authorities, who declared her to be an abandoned child. They then placed her in foster care with a Negro family.[5]

Before long, Robert and Lillie Mae Green, a childless Negro couple who had been married for seventeen years, expressed an interest in adopting Jacqueline. She stayed with the Greens for two or three weeks, during which time their tentative desire to adopt her bloomed into a settled commitment to do so.[6] The Greens were an attractive couple— responsible, secure, energetic, and intelligent. Mr. Green held two jobs, including one as an officer in a labor union. Mrs. Green was a school-teacher.[7] The Greens, like Carol McBride, encountered resistance from friends and neighbors on account of Jacqueline's color. Her skin was noticeably lighter than theirs; it was a very light brown, or what many southerners described as "yaller." The Greens, by contrast, were "brown-skinned" people. Color consciousness among African Americans was acute in many communities in the 1950s, particularly New Orleans. The Greens heard through the neighborhood grapevine that some of their relatives, friends, and acquaintances felt they should adopt a child darker than Jacqueline. A complicated stew of sentiments nourished this opinion. One ingredient was prejudice against light-skinned blacks—a mainly defensive or retaliatory reaction to the long-standing hierarchy within African American circles that privileged those with lighter skin.[8] Another element was the feeling that it was better for blacks to adopt brown-skinned children because they stood a lesser chance of being adopted than lighter-skinned children. Thus, the Greens could redistribute opportunities more equitably by investing their love in a "brown" rather than a "yaller" child. A third notion was that a darker child would constitute a better match for this particular household because observers would be more likely to think that the Greens were the child's "real"—that is, flesh-and-blood, biological—parents.

The Greens dismissed all of these objections. They liked and wanted Jacqueline. But there was a hitch: when the baby was born, Louisiana's Bureau of Vital Statistics had registered her as a white person.[9] Since she looked white and her mother was white, officials at the hospital had taken it as a given that her father was, too.

The darkening of Jacqueline's skin as she aged belied that initial assumption. But the resulting ambiguity surrounding Jacqueline's racial identity posed a dilemma for a legal system that demanded everyone be assigned a racial station that he or she would then occupy for life. Officials at the Department of Welfare would have allowed the Greens to adopt Jacqueline but for the "problem" of her racial status.[10] That difficulty, however, constituted an insuperable legal impediment in that Louisiana law expressly required rigid racial matching in adoption, permitting people to adopt only children of their own race. Just as Louisiana law in the 1950s mandated racial separation in trains, schools, housing, and circuses, so, too, did it decree racial separation in adoption. The same segregationist logic that prevented individuals from marrying interracially also banned couples from adopting interracially.[11] The Department of Welfare was willing to let the Greens raise Jacqueline without officially adopting her, but Mrs. Green did not like that idea, so she and her husband tried another approach. They obtained legal counsel and petitioned the Louisiana Bureau of Vital Statistics to change Jacqueline's racial designation from "white" to "colored." The civil servant with whom they had to deal was one Naomi Drake, "an autocrat [who] was for fifteen years the arbiter of who was black and who was white."[12] Drake was so obsessed with keeping individuals in their "correct" racial place that she systematically investigated birth certificates for babies designated as "white" but whose names were common among blacks. If her genealogical investigation revealed that a baby had any African or African American ancestors, she would certify him or her as colored, notwithstanding the objections by the infant's distraught parents. Between 1960 and 1965, Drake held in abeyance at least 4,700 applications for birth certificates and 1,100 for death certificates. During her tenure in office (1949–1965), thirty-eight petitions for reclassification were filed against her bureau in state court. In the overwhelming majority of cases, petitioners sought to alter their racial designation from black to white; the Greens were unusual, if not unique, in seeking a change in the opposite direction. In another sense, though, the Greens were like most of the other petitioners: they failed to change Drake's mind.* When the Bureau of Vital

---

*Drake patrolled the race line with fervor. In 1964 Larry Lillie Toledano succeeded in persuading a court to order the Bureau of Vital Statistics to issue a new birth cer-

Statistics refused to reclassify Jacqueline, the Greens sued. The lawyer to whom they turned for assistance was Fred J. Cassibry, a white attorney who often represented Mr. Green's labor union. Cassibry immediately fobbed the case off onto Burton Klein, a young, inexperienced attorney.

Klein urged Judge Paul E. Chasez to overturn the determination made by Naomi Drake and the Bureau of Vital Statistics. He noted that Mrs. McBride and her white neighbors had believed Jacqueline to be a Negro, and emphasized the Department of Welfare's initial decision to place the little girl with Negroes for foster care and to match her with Negroes for adoption.[13] He also presented "scientific" testimony from Arden R. King, a professor of anthropology at Tulane University. After examining Jacqueline's skin, eyes, nose, hair, lips, ears, skull, and anal pit, King concluded that it was "extremely probable that the child is a mixture . . . of a white mother and of a father who [was of] anywhere from five-eighths to one-fourth Negro ancestry."[14] King qualified his opinion, however, in two respects. He said that given the state of the science of racial identification, he was unable to declare absolutely that Jacqueline was a Negro; at present he could speak only in terms of probabilities. He added that when Jacqueline got older and her body was more fully developed, he would be in a better position to determine her race definitively.[15]*

---

tificate listing him as white. Drake complied with the court's order by crossing out the word "colored" on Toledano's original certificate and writing over it, in red ink, the word "white." She also noted on the document that it had been altered pursuant to court order. Toledano subsequently argued, of course, that Drake's mode of compliance had cast a pall over his claim to whiteness. The Court of Appeals of Louisiana declined to order Drake to alter her response. See *Toledano v. Drake,* 161 So. 2d 339 (La. Ct. App. 1964). The same court later suggested that it had been wrong to uphold Drake's action; see *Cline v. City of New Orleans,* 207 So. 2d 856, 859 (La. Ct. of App. 1968).

Eventually Drake's racial obsession would contribute to her undoing. In 1965 bureau officials fired her for a long litany of infractions, including insubordination and mistreatment of colleagues and members of the general public. See Virginia R. Dominguez, *White by Definition: Social Classification in Creole Louisiana* (1986), 36–45; Calvin Trillin, "American Chronicles Black or White," *New Yorker,* February 24, 1986.

*At the time of Jacqueline Henley's ordeal, Louisiana law followed the "one-drop

Klein identified the man whom he believed to be Jacqueline's bio-logical father, a Negro laborer named Herbert Stanton. Strong circum-stantial evidence supported this conclusion. On the witness stand, Stanton testified that he had met Ruby Henley at a "colored bar," Lena's, where she worked as a barmaid.[16] Stanton conceded that he had sometimes shared a drink with Henley and that he had written to her when she took a trip to Detroit. One letter that Klein introduced into evidence read, in part, "You know that I'll always love you" and "I wish you was home I miss you so." The letter was signed "with love, Rock"—Stanton's nickname.[17] Still, Stanton insisted that he could not possibly have fathered Jacqueline because he had never been "inti-mate" with her.[18]

In rebuttal, Klein elicited testimony from Mr. Green that on the first day of trial, Stanton—ignorant of Mr. Green's identity—had offhand-edly mentioned to him that he had been Henley's lover and had once sent her to Michigan to have an abortion.[19]* Stanton, however, denied

---

rule," under which any trace of African ancestry—no matter how remote—was suf-ficient to make a person a Negro. This rule did not apply to the descendants of Native Americans and Filipinos. Although in the late nineteenth century these groups had typically been subjected to the same Jim Crow segregationist treatment as Negroes, by the 1920s Louisiana courts were treating non-Negro people of color differently from—that is, better than—blacks. The Louisiana legal system was will-ing to accept some sorts of coloredness within the family of whiteness, but it drew the line at a single Negro ancestor.

Thus, in *Green v. City of New Orleans,* everything turned on whether or not Jacqueline Henley had any trace of Negro blood. If it could be proved beyond doubt that she did, then she would be entitled to reclassification. But if there was any doubt at all as to her racial origins—if there was a chance, for instance, that her father was an Indian or a Filipino rather than a Negro—then the bureau's original label would stick.

For an excellent analysis of the Louisiana courts' response to the question "Who is a Negro?," see Dominguez, *White by Definition* (1986), 23–55. See also F. James Davis, *Who Is Black? One Nation's Definition* (1991); Charles S. Mangum Jr., *The Legal Status of the Negro* (1940), 1–17; Gilbert Thomas Stephenson, *Race Distinction in American Law* (1910), 12–25; Christopher A. Ford, "Administering Identity: The Determination of 'Race' in Race-Conscious Law," *California Law Review* 182 (1994): 1231; and "Who Is a Negro?," *University of Florida Law Review* 11 (1958): 235.

*The cirumstances under which Stanton made the damning admission are revealing. The law and custom of Jim Crow segregation threw Stanton and Green together for

having made this statement and again denied having had any intimate association with Henley. Reminiscing forty years later, Klein would recall that Stanton had been "scared to death" of publicly admitting he had had sex with a white woman.[20] After all, he was testifying in a courtroom in Jim Crow Louisiana, surrounded by white men, including law-enforcement officials; any admission that he, a black man, not only had been sexually involved with a white woman but also had gotten her pregnant would have been a direct affront to their sensibilities.

Stanton was so scared, in fact, that he even claimed not to have been aware that Ruby was white, as the following colloquy from Klein's cross-examination indicates:

> Q. [Was] she a white woman?
> A. I wouldn't know, sir. I don't know.
> . . .
> Q. Did she have white skin?
> A. Well, a lot of people have light skin and not be white. I never asked—had occasion to ask her her color.[21]

Stanton's reply to Klein's question was more apposite than he may have realized. Some "colored" people do indeed have "white" skin. But Stanton was not aiming here to provide enlightenment on the mysteries of racial labeling; rather, he was seeking to shrug off the volatile charge that he had intentionally had sex with a woman whom he *knew* to be white.

Notwithstanding Stanton's evasive answers, Judge Chasez ruled against the Greens in a decision that was subsequently affirmed by the Court of Appeals of Louisiana. While acknowledging that in civil cases,

---

a few minutes as partners in a cooperative venture: they bumped into each other while seeking a toilet. Unable to find any men's room not reserved for whites, they were forced to leave the courthouse and wander through the surrounding French Quarter in search of relief. According to Mr. Green, it was the spirit of camaraderie the two developed during this brief sojourn that inspired Stanton's casual acknowledgment of his affair with Ruby Henley. See Record, *Green v. City of New Orleans*, No. 337–854 (1955) at 31–33. This material is on file at the Harvard Law School Library, Interracial Intimacies Collection. Information on this episode is also derived from my interviews in June 1998 with Burton Klein and Lillie Mae Green.

as a general rule, a mere preponderance of the evidence was sufficient to prevail,[22] the appellate court observed that this was no ordinary civil dispute. This was a suit over a child's racial classification, an issue of "transcendent importance" that was "vital to the general public welfare."[23] Quoting a Louisiana Supreme Court decision affirming an earlier refusal to alter a racial classification, the court of appeals insisted that "the registration of a birthright must be given as much sanctity in the law as the registration of a property right."[24] Thus, for a petitioner to be entitled to a change in racial classification, "there must be no doubt at all."[25] Although Professor King had stated that it was "extremely probable" that Jacqueline was a Negro, the court chose to focus on the small sliver of possibility that she was not. In doing so, it echoed the opinion of Judge Chasez, who had cited in his ruling Professor King's inability to prove beyond all doubt that Jacqueline "was the issue of a white person and a person of the negro race."[26]* Concluding that the evidence presented was inadequate to quell all doubts, the Court of Appeals affirmed the trial judge's refusal to order the Bureau of Vital Statistics to reclassify Jacqueline, though it left the door open for a reconsideration of her racial status at a later date, when her physical development might offer a more secure foundation for the determination of her "real" racial identity.[27]

The decision was not unanimous. Although Judge George Janvier agreed with his colleagues about the law applicable to the case, he differed with them on the facts to which that law applied. Judge Janvier

---

*The possibility that Jacqueline's father might have been a man of color other than a Negro had concerned Judge Chasez throughout the trial. At one point during Professor King's testimony, the judge had interjected his doubts:

> The direst question is whether or not you can positively state that this child is white or an admixture of Negro and white, and be positive about that, as against any other mixture? . . . If this child was a Filipino and white child . . . it would not be Negroid; if it was Syrian and a white connection . . . it would not be a Negro . . . if it were Mongolian, Jap, Chink or a Chinaman or any of those persons of the Mongoloid races, it would not be white and Negro. [*Green v. City of New Orleans,* No. 337–854 (La. Dist. Ct. Aug. 22, 1955), on file at Harvard Law School Library, Interracial Intimacies Collection.]

maintained that there was "no doubt at all that the little girl in question is a Negress."[28] He further remarked that if Judge Chasez's order was allowed to stand, it would "result in the most unfortunate situation that the little girl registered as white will continue to associate with Negroes . . . and yet she will be unable to marry a Negro since, being registered as a white person, miscegenation laws will make such marriage impossible."[29] Finally, Judge Janvier lamented that Jacqueline "will labor under the embarrassment of socially associating only with Negroes who will no doubt taunt her with being registered as 'white.'"[30] Unlike his colleagues, this judge paid primary attention to the real-world perception of Jacqueline and considered how the court's ruling would affect her future treatment, by society in general and by the state in particular. In his view, the case should not have turned on an abstract inquiry into Jacqueline's racial identity; after all, that had already been determined by her aunt's neighbors, who, on discerning a speck of Negro ancestry, had pronounced her a "nigger." Rather, the case should have centered on a pragmatic appraisal of which classification would best suit Jacqueline, given that those closest to her perceived her to be a Negro. Despite her official designation as a white person, everyone—including state officials—seemed to have proceeded on the assumption that she was black. Authorities had placed her with Negro families for foster care and, with special permission, enrolled her in Negro public schools. Since she was being given the Negro treatment anyway, Judge Janvier reasoned, fairness dictated that she be registered as a Negro so she could be adopted, freely marry "her own kind," and escape the racial limbo to which she had been consigned by the tragic circumstances surrounding her birth.

Within the limits of segregationist logic, the two judges responsible for the final decision of the Louisiana Court of Appeals went about their task conscientiously. As they saw it, each of the three pieces of evidence presented by Klein allowed for at least some uncertainty as to Jacqueline's "race," as defined by the prevailing mores of 1950s Louisiana. As to Mrs. McBride and her neighbors, they claimed no expertise in racial identification, and there existed little basis for deferring to their perception. As to Stanton, the Greens had failed to present any evidence that decisively linked him parentally with Jacqueline.

Even if he had been sexually intimate with Henley, that did not mean he had impregnated her; some other man might have fathered her child. And as to the anthropologist witness, Professor King, the court of appeals rightly viewed his scientific pretensions with skepticism. The judges' cautionary notes on the precariousness of efforts to determine race "scientifically" were much more sensible than the pseudoscientific claims of the professor.[31] It may even be argued that in this case, the Louisiana judiciary acted with solicitude in protecting Jacqueline's classification as a white person. Throughout American history, individual whites have lost their privileged racial status merely by associating too closely with blacks, and it would have come as no surprise if such a fate had befallen Ruby Henley and her daughter in the courts of Jim Crow Louisiana. Ruby had worked in a colored bar and had obviously been quite friendly with "Rock" Stanton. Segregationist Louisiana judges might predictably have been indifferent to the fate of a racially ambiguous child born out of wedlock to a lower-class, divorced white barmaid who had fraternized with Negroes. But in fact, as we have seen, the judges were not at all indifferent; on the contrary, they were notably concerned. Similarly, white supremacist judges might be expected to have stood as watchful sentries eager to protect the white community from colored "infiltration." In this case, though, the judges were being asked not to bar the door of white racial purity to an infiltrator but rather to let an insider *out,* by permitting a racially ambiguous but officially white child to be reclassified as a Negro. This they were unwilling to do. Instead, the judges defended the child's legal right to whiteness, adopting the perspective of the attorney who had been appointed by the court to represent Jacqueline's best interests. Strenuously attacking the proposed reclassification, guardian ad litem Frank J. Stich Jr. had asserted that "to change the race of this very young child now . . . from white to colored, would not only be premature . . . but would be grossly unjust to the child who has her life before her."[32]*

---

*This argument resonated even with Mrs. Green, at least in retrospect. Reflecting upon the case in 1998, she held that there was a lot to be said for the court's preservation of Jacqueline's official whiteness, since in the 1950s "things were so bad for blacks." She also said that at the time of the lawsuit, she had worried that if she and

That the court's resolution of the controversy arguably showed concern for Jacqueline within the limits of segregationist logic does nothing to mitigate the cruel absurdity of that logic. Its ascendancy meant that not so long ago, as a matter of law, Louisiana (among other states) prohibited any child from being adopted by an adult not of the same race. The state believed, in other words, that it was better for a child to be reared in an institution, no matter how bad, than to be adopted into a family of a different race, no matter how good. In this particular case, moreover, after preventing Jacqueline's adoption by loving, capable black adults who wanted to embrace her as their own, state officials relegated her to a blacks-only orphanage and kept her in a segregated Negro school. Thus, though the lingering "taint" of color had been insufficient to persuade judges to order a formal reclassification, the perception of racial contamination gave other color-obsessed authorities license to deny the child the benefits of *both* her legal "whiteness" and her apparent "coloredness." Their actions cast her—for a while, at least—into a terrible limbo in the depths of the black-white racial divide.

*Green v. City of New Orleans* serves as a useful point of entry into the subjects explored in this book, which looks at the ways in which interracial intimacy has shaped and in turn been affected by laws and custom in the United States. *Green* is a rather obscure case, one that does not figure prominently, if it figures at all, in the curricula of courses in American history, family law, constitutional law, or the law of race relations.[33] The same may be said of many of the other cases examined here. But their very obscurity stands as the predicate for one of my major purposes, which is to assist in moving interracial intimacy to center stage as a necessary focus of inquiry for anyone seriously interested in understanding and improving American society.

---

her husband were to prevail, they might be confronted decades later by a daughter who felt that her parents had wrongly "made her into a Negro." (Interview with Lillie Mae Green, New Orleans, Louisiana, June 1998.)

Interracial intimacy and its many ramifications are far more central to American life than many people appreciate or are willing to acknowledge. Its influence begins with the material basis of human existence: the body. Interracial intimacy—or more specifically, in this context, heterosexual interracial intimacy—has affected, through reproduction, key physiological markers in American society, including skin pigmentation, nose width, lip breadth, and hair texture. Appraisals of Jacqueline Henley's physiognomy played a significant role in deciding who would be permitted to raise her, but not so many generations earlier, such judgments had had even more dramatic consequences, determining whether racially ambiguous persons of unknown parentage would be free or consigned to slavery.*

Although most Americans continue to use a vocabulary of race consisting of unalloyed primary colors—white, black, red, and yellow— the country's population is in fact already what racial purists have long feared it might become: a people characterized by a large measure of

---

*At the turn of the eighteenth century in North Carolina, for example, a twelve-year-old white girl playing in a barn found a baby boy who was believed to be just days old. According to a court report, she took him home and treated him humanely but claimed him as her slave. He was "of a colour between black and yellow, and had a prominent nose" (*Gober v. Gober*, 2 N.C. [Haywood] 170 [1802]). When the foundling got older, he sued for his freedom in court and prevailed. The court concluded, however, that the same presumption should not attach "to mulattoes or persons of mixed race; for if one of that description be in fact descended from a free woman, he is also free; and where the fact cannot be proved, the chance of a descent from a free mother is equal to that of his having descended from a slave and black mother, but free father. In such a case . . . the conclusion must proceed on probabilities; and if there are circumstances indicating that the mother was a white woman rather than a black one, the jury should find in favor of his freedom."(ibid.) The court presumed that every black person was a slave.

As we saw in *Green*, courts have historically looked to a variety of physical markers as determinants of race. In an 1806 case concerned with whether a family should be deemed free or slave, a court in Virginia maintained that "nature has stampt upon the African and his descendants two characteristic marks, besides the difference of complexion, which often remain visible long after the characteristic of colour either disappears or becomes doubtful; a flat nose and woolly head of hair" (*Hudgins v. Wright*, 11 Va. [1 Hen. & M.] 134, 139 [1806]). See also *Daniel v. Guy*, 23 Ark 50, 51 (1861): "No one who is familiar with the peculiar formation of the Negro foot can doubt but that inspection of that member would ordinarily afford some indication of the race."

racial admixture, or what many have referred to distastefully as "mongrelization." This trend is, furthermore, accelerating. Interracial dating, sex, and marriage are steadily increasing, as is the number of children born of interracial unions. This development has prompted observers to speak either approvingly or despairingly of the "creolization" or "browning" or "beiging" of America.

Race has—and has long had—a massive presence in the sexual imaginations of Americans. This is attested to by countless speculations regarding racial differences in sexual practices and the size of genitalia. Such impressions have been expressed in scientific journals and fictional narratives, in paintings and motion pictures, in songs and jokes. By the eighteenth century in Europe, according to one historian, "the sexuality of the black, both male and female, [had become] an icon for deviant sexuality in general."[34] Leading European intellectuals elaborated upon perceived racial distinctions in sexual physiognomy, sensibility, and appetite, claiming, among other things, that black men were endowed with larger penises and greater sexual energy than white men, and that black women were blessed (or cursed) with a sexual primitivism that manifested itself in distinctively protruding buttocks. These ideas seeped into the consciousness of Americans of all races and, alongside observations originating on American shores, contributed to a racial folklore that is still in existence, still growing, and still remarkable in its reach.[35]

The shadow cast by race on sexual notions, experiences, and feelings is apparent at every level of the culture. It emerges in the work of such varied and distinguished writers as Jean Toomer, William Faulkner, James Baldwin, Richard Wright, Alice Walker, and Gayl Jones, all of whom have explored and imaginatively depicted ways in which racial conflict can enter sexual life.[36] In popular culture, the race-sex connection announces its presence in countless jokes, typified by a punch line in an episode of the television situation comedy *The Nanny*. An elderly and virtually blind Jewish white woman in a nursing home falls in love with a black man played by the blind singer Ray Charles. When the woman's relatives inform her of the man's race, she grins slyly and says, "So that explains it."[37] The joke, of course, depends upon the audience's familiarity with the stereotype of the black man as sexual stud. This stereotype has long figured in folk humor and professional comedy routines. In her compilation of African American folklore, for example, Daryl Cumber Dance includes the tale of the "Fornication Contest":

> It was generally known that a Black nigger could outfuck a white man. But this particular white man did not believe it, and his friends didn't believe it.
>
> So they had a fucking contest: the Master fucking a white wench, and the nigger fucking a nigger wench. And the scorekeepers keeping score.
>
> The white man fucked her twelve times and fell away—couldn't do no more. The nigger went right on fucking. When they got to twenty-four times, the scorekeepers got confused. One said it was twenty-four; the other said twenty-five. There was an argument.
>
> The nigger said, "No need to argue and fuss. I will start over again."[38]*

In Mel Brooks's film *Blazing Saddles* (1974), a white woman schemes to have sex with the black hero. When she succeeds, the bedroom is enveloped in darkness. The viewer can see nothing and no one, and can hear only the rustling of sheets. Suddenly the woman exclaims excitedly, "It's true, it's true!" What she believes she has verified is that black men really do have greater staying power and larger penises than white men.†

---

*This theme has been dramatized in countless ways. For a notable variation, see Melvin Van Peebles's film *Sweet Sweetback's Baadasss Song* (1971).

†In *My Secret Garden: Women's Sexual Fantasies* (1973), Nancy Friday asserts that "the most loaded question in the contemporary bedroom after 'What are you thinking about?' is 'Have you ever made it with a black man/woman?'" Friday explains that in her estimation, while "most white women haven't [actually had interracial sex,] in their fantasies they do, and everything that worked against it ever happening in reality adds mileage to the fantasy" (p. 171). While a number of Friday's white correspondents share fantasies involving blacks (ibid., 13, 173–75, 295), it is the

In pornography the race-sex connection is a frequent motif. A whole genre of X-rated videos is dedicated to titillating those who presumably derive special pleasure from watching the interracial sexual activities depicted in such films as *Whose Dat Girl?, I Am Curious Black, White Chicks Can't Jump,* and *Let Me Tell Ya 'bout White Chicks.*\* Long Dong Silver is a reflection of this fascination. A character in video pornography, he is a black man with an enormously long penis who caricatures the stereotype of the hypersexual Negro.† When Supreme Court Justice Clarence Thomas was accused in his 1991 confirmation hearing of enjoying pornography, cultural literacy at the elite level suddenly required knowledge of Long Dong Silver, and his moniker has since become part of the common lexicon.‡

---

author herself who explores the matter with the most enthusiasm, noting at one point that

> size is the real power of the black-man fantasy. . . . [The fantasist wants] to feel more, to have more novelty and experience under her belt, thanks to the life-enhancing mythical prick and promise of the sexy black man. . . . In fantasy, the 'big' black man promises to take us to that final exploration of sex, the most absolute orgasmic time it is humanly possible to experience. And then, forever after, at least we'll have known what "it" is "all about." [Ibid., 171–72.]

See also Friday's *Women on Top: How Real Life Has Changed Women's Sexual Fantasies* (1991) and *Forbidden Flowers: More Women's Sexual Fantasies* (1975).

\*An Internet search in June 2003 using the search term "interracial sex" yields hundreds of thousands of Web sites, the vast majority of which market pornography. Representative sites include "Abe's Interracial Sex Orgy: hardcore pics of interracial sex"; "Interracial Vampires: black vampires seek young white victims for interracial hardcore sex"; and "Porno Interracial Sex: hardcore interracial sex pictures of blacks and whites."

†In addition to my own recollection of the film, I depend here upon the information offered in Jane Mayer and Jill Abramson, *Strange Justice: The Selling of Clarence Thomas* (1994), 107. An Internet search for "Long Dong Silver" in June 2003 brings up more than fifteen thousand entries.

‡In the most bizarre judicial confirmation battle in the history of the United States, Professor Anita Hill accused then-Judge Clarence Thomas of having harassed her sexually when she worked under his supervision at the Equal Employment Opportunity Commission. She claimed, among other things, that he had regaled her with lurid summaries of pornographic movies he had watched. See U.S. Senate Committee on the Judiciary, *Nomination of Judge Clarence Thomas to Be Associate Justice of the Supreme Court of the United States: Hearing Before the Senate Committee on*

In *Notes on the State of Virginia* (1787), Thomas Jefferson explicitly compared what he perceived to be the distinct erotic natures of whites, blacks, and Native Americans. Writing in derogation of Negro men, Jefferson asserted that while "they are more ardent after their female . . . love seems with them to be more an eager desire, than a tender delicate mixture of sentiment and sensation."[39] The anxieties surrounding such comparisons have often poisoned American society, inspiring both horrific conduct and rationalizations for that conduct. If, as Jefferson and other patriarchs persuaded themselves, African American men merely "desired" rather than "loved," then there was no reason to feel troubled about breaking up slave marriages in pursuit of increased profits. And if, as folklore had it, the sexual voraciousness of African American women rendered them positively insatiable, there was little reason to protect them and every reason to doubt their claims of abuse: "If she was *that* lascivious—well, a man could not sincerely be blamed for succumbing against overwhelming odds."[40]

Sexual anxieties have prompted intensive policing of the race line by a wide variety of means—from antimiscegenation laws to lynchings. The desire to suppress sexual competition was one of the forces that long kept blacks out of the running for top placings in beauty contests and leading roles in major motion pictures. Many sectors of white America demanded a monopoly on the societal valorization of sexual attractiveness. Thus, while overweight, rag-wearing black mammies (usually played by Hattie McDaniel or Louise Beavers) were acceptable on Hollywood's big screen, love interests portrayed by alluring black starlets—until recently—were not.[41]

The pervasiveness of racial complexes in American sexual history

---

*the Judiciary,* 102d Cong., First Session, 1991, pt. 4, statement and testimony of Anita F. Hill. Judge Thomas adamantly denied "each and every single allegation . . . that suggested in any way that [he had] had conversations of a sexual nature or about pornographic material with Anita Hill, that [he had] ever attempted to date her, that [he had] ever had any personal sexual interest in her, or that [he had] in any way ever harassed her" (ibid., 157). Judge Thomas suggested that in addition to being untrue, the charges against him contributed to the degradation of African American men by mirroring and reinforcing "racist, bigoted stereotypes . . . that are impossible to wash off" (ibid., 202).

would be difficult to exaggerate. They reside like booby traps even in terrain set aside especially for pleasure. In 1992 Miriam DeCosta-Willis, Reginald Martin, and Roseann P. Bell edited a pioneering volume entitled *Erotique Noire/Black Erotica*. Disappointed by the paucity of blacks included either as writers or as subjects in previous anthologies of erotica, the editors of *Erotique Noire* compiled a large store of stories, poems, essays, and memoirs intended to celebrate African American sexual expressiveness. The preface to the anthology, however, a piece ("Fore/Play") written by Ntozake Shange, opens on a far from celebratory note. Shange observes that *Erotique Noire* is being published "thirty-seven years since Emmett Till's slaughter," that to obtain respectability, black people have had "to combat absurd phantasmagoric stereotypes about [their] sexuality," and that "rape and rapists are intimately connected to the culture's unconscious perception and prescriptions for people of color."[42] All of these statements are true, as the following pages will document. But the fact that Shange was moved to make them at the outset of a collection of contemporary African American erotica is a telling indication of just how racially embattled many blacks feel, even when it comes to the subject of sexual joy.

Legions of legislators, judges, prosecutors, police officers, and other officials have attempted to prevent interracial amalgamation. Between the 1660s and the 1960s, forty-one colonies or states enacted racial laws regulating sex or marriage.* In a substantial number of these jurisdictions, authorities sought to protect the bloodlines of the white population from people besides African Americans: Native Americans, Asiatic Indians, West Indians, Hindus, and people of Chinese, Japanese, Korean, and Filipino ancestry were among the groups variously designated as threats to the racial integrity of whites, and thus barred from marrying them. Blacks, however, were targeted in *every* instance in which authorities imposed racial bans, a vivid confirmation of Alexis de Tocqueville's theory that the Negro occupies a uniquely stigmatized niche in American society.[43]

Over four centuries, authorities offered a range of justifications for

---

*See pages 214–43.

antimiscegenation laws, including the supposed obligations to respect nature, to follow God's directions, to prevent the contamination of whites, to protect the distinct (albeit lesser) character of colored peoples, and to avoid the propagation of "mixed breeds," which were thought to be sterile and otherwise inferior to "pure" stocks. Affirming the conviction of a defendant who had married across racial lines, the Virginia Court of Appeals held in 1878 that

> the purity of public morals, the moral and physical development of both races, and the highest advancement of our cherished southern civilization, under which two distinct races are to work out and accomplish the destiny to which the Almighty has assigned them on this continent—all require that they should be kept distinct and separate, and that connections and alliances so unnatural that God and nature seem to forbid them, should be prohibited by positive law, and be subject to no evasion.[44]

Affirming the constitutionality of an enhanced punishment for interracial (as opposed to intraracial) fornication,* the Supreme Court of Alabama declared in 1881 that a greater penalty would serve as a necessary deterrent to a crime that would result in "the amalgamation of the two races, producing a mongrel population and a degraded civilization, the prevention of which is dictated by a sound public policy affecting the highest interests of society and government."[45] In 1959 a

---

*Under the challenged law, "if any man and woman live together in adultery or fornication, each of them must, on the first conviction of the offence, be fined not less than one hundred dollars, and may also be imprisoned . . . or sentenced to hard labor for the county for not more than six months." For subsequent offenses, the penalty increased to a maximum of two years' imprisonment or hard labor. By contrast, Alabama law provided that "if any white person and any negro, or the descendant of any negro to the third generation, inclusive, though one ancestor of each generation was a white person, intermarry or live in adultery or fornication, each of them must, on conviction, be imprisoned . . . or sentenced to hard labor . . . for not less than two nor more than seven years" (*Pace v. Alabama,* 106 U.S. 583 [1883]). This statute gave rise to the poignantly named *Love v. The State,* 124 Ala. 82 (1899), in which a white man was convicted of living in adultery with a Negro woman.

judge demonstrated the staying power of these ideas by justifying Virginia's prohibition against interracial marriage in the following terms: "Almighty God created the races white, black, yellow, malay and red, and he placed them on separate continents. And but for the interference with his arrangement there would be no cause for such marriages. The fact that he separated the races shows he did not intend for the races to mix."[46]

Disputes over interracial intimacy have figured prominently in some of the most momentous controversies in American history. In his infamous opinion in Dred Scott v. Sandford (1857),[47] Chief Justice Roger B. Taney argued that laws prohibiting interracial marriage reflected that the Founding Fathers had never intended for blacks, even those who were free, to become citizens of the United States. Such laws, he wrote, were evidence of a "perpetual and impassable barrier erected between the white race and the one which [whites] had reduced to slavery . . . and which they looked upon as so far below them in the scale of created beings that intermarriages between white persons and negroes and mulattoes were regarded as unnatural and immoral, and punished as crimes."[48*]

The very term "miscegenation"—combining the Latin words *miscere* ("to mix") and *genus* ("race")—was coined during the presidential campaign of 1864, while the Civil War was still raging. Seeking to provoke outrage and mislead white public opinion, Northern opponents of Abraham Lincoln published and distributed a pamphlet suggesting that Lincoln and his Republican party encouraged interracial marriage. This was hardly the first time that racists had played the miscegenation card

---

*Prior to the abolition of Negro slavery, white supremacists frequently warned that *any* concessions made to African Americans would quickly escalate into the apocalypse of racial amalgamation. In 1804 a white Pennsylvanian inveighed against permitting blacks to vote on the ground that doing so would lead inevitably to intermarriage. Posing a rhetorical question that has since become a cliché, he asked, "Would thee be very contended to have a negro for thy daughter's husband, a negress for thy son's wife, and in short have them assimilated into thy family as well as the general and state governments[?]" (quoted in David H. Fowler, *Northern Attitudes Towards Interracial Marriage: Legislation and Public Opinion in the Middle Atlantic States of the Old Northwest, 1780–1930* [1987], 100).

against the Great Emancipator: during the legendary senatorial debates between Lincoln and Stephen A. Douglas, the latter repeatedly charged Lincoln with being an advocate of racial equality and condoning interracial marriage. In response Lincoln pointed out that it was in the slave states, not the free ones, that interracial sex flourished and multiracial children abounded. Lincoln protested, moreover, "that counterfeit logic which concludes that, because I do not want a black woman for a *slave* I must necessarily want her for a wife."[49]*

During Lincoln's presidency, his enemies continued to assert that he wanted to encourage or even compel interracial social relations. Complaining that his Emancipation Proclamation transformed the War for the Union into a "nigger crusade," parodists concocted a "Black Republican Prayer" to debase the president's image in the eyes of whites to whom the idea of interracial intimacy was abhorrent:

> May the blessings of Emancipation extend throughout our unhappy lands and the illustrious, sweet-scented Sambo nestle in the bosom of every Abolition woman, that she may be quickened by the pure blood of the majestic African, and the Spirit of amalgamation shine forth in all its splendor and glory, that we may become a regenerated nation of half-breeds and mongrels, and the distinction of color be forever consigned to oblivion, and that we may live in bonds of fraternal love, union and equality with the Almighty Nigger, henceforth, now and forever. Amen.[50]

---

*In the fourth debate Lincoln stated,

> I am not, nor ever have been in favor of bringing about in any way the social and political equality of the white and black races [applause]. . . . I am not nor ever have been in favor of making voters or jurors of negroes, nor of qualifying them to hold office, nor to intermarry with white people; and I will say in addition to this that there is a physical difference between the white and black which I believe will for ever forbid the two races living together on terms of social and political equality. [Abraham Lincoln, *Speeches and Writings, 1832–1858* (Library of America, 1989), 636–37.]

After the Civil War, when Congress was debating means of uprooting slavery, nullifying *Dred Scott,* and elevating the legal status of African Americans, a constant refrain sounded by opponents of reform was that racial equality would threaten state antimiscegenation laws. As one student of the Reconstruction period has observed, "The spectre of miscegenation was . . . a bugaboo which the [white] southerners in Congress and their northern sympathizers overworked at every opportunity. It became the *reductio ad absurdum* of the congressional debates. Whenever anyone proposed measures for the protection of Negro rights, the cry 'Do you want your daughter to marry a Negro?' was raised."[51]

The reply typically offered was that, of course, no self-respecting white man would permit (much less encourage) his daughter to marry a Negro. But most reformers maintained that nothing in the new federal constitutional amendments or related civil rights legislation would interfere with local antimiscegenation laws, so long as such statutes treated all races equally. They argued that if both whites and people of color were prohibited from marrying or having sex across race lines, there could be no justifiable basis for complaint because all persons would then be subject to the same treatment under the law.[52]

During the reaction against Reconstruction, white supremacists exploited fears of interracial intimacy as perhaps *the* major justification for subverting the civil and political rights that had been granted to blacks, and *the* major reason for confining blacks to their degraded "place" at the bottom of the social hierarchy. This argument had been previously rehearsed with respect to free blacks during the Age of Slavery. Hence, in 1834 some white New Yorkers objected to blacks' being allowed to celebrate Emancipation Day (the commemoration of the state's enactment of a law providing for the gradual abolition of slavery), on the ground that Negro men would go "parading the streets with their canes and dandy dresses seeking white wives."[53] In 1841 a number of white Ohioans opposed permitting blacks to testify in court against whites because it would "tend to an equality of the races and promote their intermarriage."[54] In the Age of Jim Crow, such arguments remained potent, notwithstanding the reforms of Reconstruction. "Everyone knows," Justice Harlan observed in his famous 1896 dissent in *Plessy v. Ferguson* that segregation on railroads "had its origin in the purpose, not so much to exclude white persons from railroad cars occupied by blacks, as to exclude colored people from coaches occupied by . . . white persons."[55] That purpose was aimed at protecting whites, and most particularly white women, from the perceived contamination that would ensue from close physical proximity to Negroes (other than servants, concubines, and other subordinates, that is). Defending the segregation statute at issue in *Plessy*, the *New Orleans Times Democrat* posited that a white man "who would be horrified at the idea of his wife or daughter seated by the side of a burly negro in the parlor of a hotel or at a restaurant cannot see her occupying a crowded seat in a car next to a negro without the same feeling of disgust." W. W. Wright spoke for many whites when he warned, "Do away with the social and political distinctions now existing, and you immediately turn all the blacks and mulattoes into citizens, co-governors, and acquaintances: and acquaintances . . . are the raw material from which *are manufactured friends, husbands and wives*. The man whom you associate with is next invited to your house, and the man whom you invite to your house is the possible husband of your daughter, whether he be black or white."[56]

Fears of interracial intimacy, and especially interracial marriage, constituted an emotional and psychological seedbed from which sprouted all manner of efforts to distance blacks and subordinate them. Through segregation, disfranchisement, and the brutality used to effectuate these policies, whites sought to shield themselves from unwanted associations with people whom they considered their racial inferiors. In *An American Dilemma* (1944), Gunnar Myrdal rightly maintained that an "amalgamation doctrine" was integral to "the white man's theory of color caste."[57]* Embodying the belief—indeed, the insistence—that

---

*For Myrdal, the essential elements of "the white man's theory of color caste" were as follows:

(1) The concern for "race purity" is basic in the whole issue; the primary and essential command is to prevent amalgamation; the whites are determined to utilize every means to this end.

blacks and whites should be prevented from intermarrying, "this doctrine," according to Myrdal,

> more than anything else, gives the Negro problem its unique-
> ness among other problems of lower status groups, not only in
> terms of intensity of feelings but more fundamentally in the
> character of the problem. . . . Not only in the South but often
> also in the North the stereotyped and hypothetical question is
> regularly raised without any intermediary reasoning as to its
> applicability or relevance . . . [:] "Would you like to have your
> sister or daughter marry a Negro?"[58]

In Myrdal's view, an appreciation of the centrality of the legal or customary proscription of interracial marriage was the key to grasping the
peculiar nature of American race relations.

In the middle years of the twentieth century, segregationists consistently linked sex and marriage with race, regularly invoking the
prospect of interracial marriage as their political trump card. One vivid
example of antimiscegenation demagoguery in the era immediately prior
to *Brown v. Board of Education* was the book *Separation or Mongrelization: Take Your Choice* (1947), authored by Senator Theodore G.
Bilbo of Mississippi. The period just following *Brown* saw the publication of Tom P. Brady's *Black Monday* (1955), which asserted that the
attack on racial segregation in the public schools was aimed not at
attaining equity in education but rather at fostering racial amalgamation. And anyway, whatever the reformers' real motivation, Brady suggested, "you cannot place little white and negro children in classrooms
and not have integration. They will sing together, dance together, eat

---

(2) Rejection of "social equality" is to be understood as a precaution to
hinder miscegenation and particularly intermarriage.

(3) The danger of miscegenation is so tremendous that the segregation and
discrimination inherent in the refusal of "social equality" must be
extended to nearly all spheres of life. There must be segregation and
discrimination in recreation, in religious services, in education, before
the law, in politics, in housing, in stores, and in breadwinning. [Gunnar
Myrdal, *An American Dilemma: The Negro Problem and Modern
Democracy* (1944; twentieth-anniversary edition, 1962), 1:58.]

together and play together. They will grow up together and the sensitivity of the white children will be dulled. Constantly the negro will be endeavoring to usurp every right and privilege[,] which will lead to intermarriage."[59]

While the National Association for the Advancement of Colored People (NAACP) opposed antimiscegenation laws and lobbied against their spread, it did not aggressively challenge the Jim Crow marriage altar. Fearful of inciting a greater white backlash than it already faced, the organization tried instead to obtain racial justice in areas of perceived greater priority, including public schooling, voting, and the administration of criminal law.* Some champions of African American advancement also felt that any active challenge to antimiscegenation laws would be seen as a manifestation of blacks' supposed desire not only to be equal to whites but also to be intimate with them, or even to *become* white themselves†—suppositions that have long galled many

---

*Cloyte M. Larsson, editor of *Marriage Across the Color Line* (1965), makes the point nicely. Commenting on blacks' reluctance to confront antimiscegenation laws, he writes: "Defend interracial marriage on principle! Principle costs too much. . . . First things *do* come first. Survival comes first. Food. Clothing. Jobs. Shelter. Recreation. Creature comforts. But interracial marriage? That is for the few. The very few." Ibid. at vii–viii.

For a contrasting view, see Hannah Arendt, "Reflections on Little Rock," in *The Portable Hannah Arendt,* ed. Peter Baehr (2000), 236: "The right to marry whoever one wishes is an elementary human right compared to which 'the right to attend an integrated school, the right to sit where one pleased on a bus [and] the right to go into any hotel . . . regardless of one's skin or color or race' are minor indeed. Even political rights, like the right to vote . . . are secondary to the inalienable human rights to 'life, liberty, and the pursuit of happiness' proclaimed in the Declaration of Independence; and to this category the right to home and marriage unquestionably belongs."

†Tom P. Brady maintained, for example, that "the American negro, like any intelligent white man, knows his weaknesses and . . . realizes that he can ameliorate these inherent deficiencies by intermarriage, just as the strain of a long horn can be improved by being bred with a white-faced Hereford" (*Black Monday* [1955], 66–67). Elsewhere in his diatribe, Brady claimed that the grand goal of the Negro civil rights leadership was "the passing of the Negro" en masse (ibid., 64, internal quotations omitted).

This idea has deep roots. Writing in the 1830s, Alexis de Tocqueville remarked that "The Negro makes a thousand fruitless efforts to insinuate himself among men who repulse him. . . . Having been told from infancy that his race is naturally infe-

African Americans.[60] In fact, substantial numbers of blacks have always been hostile to interracial marriage, viewing black participants in such matches as racial defectors. These considerations help to explain why it was not until 1967, near the end of the civil rights movement, that the Supreme Court finally invalidated all remaining antimiscegenation laws.*

Since then the environment for interracial intimacy has changed dramatically and for the better. Indicative of this change was an incident that occurred in the spring of 2000, when George W. Bush, at a crucial moment in his campaign for the Republican presidential nomination, paid a highly publicized visit to Bob Jones University in South Carolina. During that visit he offered no criticism of the institution's prohibition against interracial dating.† Amid the controversy that ensued—itself a positive development—not a single nationally prominent public figure

---

rior to that of the whites, he assents to the proposition and is ashamed of his own nature. . . . [I]f it were in his own power, he would willingly rid himself of everything that makes him what he is" (*Democracy in America* [Phillips Bradley, ed., 1945]: 334). For reactions to these sentiments that call upon blacks to inculcate a deeper group solidarity and pride and to eschew intimacy with whites, see pages 109–23.
*See pages 272–77.
†Until 1971 Bob Jones University excluded black students altogether. From 1971 to 1975 it accepted a small number of blacks, and beginning in 1975 it permitted unmarried blacks to enroll but prohibited interracial dating and marriage. University policy furthermore decreed that "students who are members of or affiliated with any group or organization which holds as one of its goals or advocates interracial marriage will be expelled" (see *Bob Jones Univ. v. United States*, 461 U.S. 574, 580, [1983]). In 1976 the Internal Revenue Service revoked Bob Jones's tax-exempt status, a move that led to protracted litigation during which the university enjoyed the support of, among others, Trent Lott and Ronald Reagan. See *Bob Jones Univ. v. United States;* Meyer G. Freed and Daniel D. Polsby, "Race, Religion, and Public Policy: *Bob Jones University v. United States*," *Supreme Court Review*, 1983, p. 1 (Philip B. Kurland, Gerhard Casper, and Dennis J. Hutchinson, eds.).
According to university officials, the prohibition on interracial dating was instituted in the mid-1950s to deal with a white-Asian liaison to which the parents of the Asian student strongly objected. The same officials insist that the prohibition did not evince any hostility toward blacks or interracial couples per se but was instead animated by a desire to oppose cultural trends that were repugnant to the university's

came forward to defend Bob Jones's policy. Public opinion not only forced Bush to distance himself (albeit belatedly) from Bob Jones but even prompted the notoriously stubborn and reactionary administration of that school to drop its ban.[61]*

The racial demographics of dating and marriage demonstrate, however, the continued power of racial selectivity within most Americans' personal lives. On the Internet and in newspapers and magazines across the country, people openly and self-consciously deploy racially discriminatory advertising in their search for romantic companionship,† placing ads like the following:

> Warm, genuine, fun, attractive SWPF, 39, N/S, enjoys Ritz movies, live music, NPR, sailing, biking, running, and adventurous dining. ISO attractive S/DWPM, 32–50, for LTR.

> Successful, financially secure, handsome, wise, kind WWM, 55, 5'10", 165 lbs, physician, loves tennis, cooking, slow danc-

---

fundamentalist Christian values. See "The Truth About Bob Jones University," available at www.bju.edu (Aug. 1, 2000).

*Even after dropping its ban on interracial dating and marriage, Bob Jones continued to stigmatize such relationships by announcing that any student wishing to date or marry across racial lines must first obtain parental permission. See "Bob Jones U. Requires Parental Permission for Interracial Dating," Washington Post, March 8, 2000.

†The idea of using advertisements to search for romantic partners is nothing new, and attention has long been paid to the racial character of such ads. In the 1830s several newspapers smeared abolitionists by charging that their publications ran advertisements on behalf of individuals looking for spouses of a different race from their own. On July 8, 1834, for example, the New York Times published the following notice:

> A gentleman of color of first rate education, literary tastes and appointments, genteel figure and amiable manner, advertises in an evening paper that he is ready to receive proposals from any white young lady who is so far willing to discard her prejudices as to amalgamate with a descendant of the nobility of the ancient kingdom of Congo. When one gets windward of him, he is one of the sweetest fellows in the land—especially in cool weather. . . . Communications are to be directed post paid to the Editor of the Liberator. [Quoted in Elise Virginia Lemire, "Making Miscegenation: Discourses of Interracial Sex and Marriage in the United States, 1790–1865" (Ph.D. diss., Rutgers University, 1996).]

ing. Seeking intelligent, humorous, very attractive, kind SWF, 40–50.

Tall (5'11"), pretty RN, 49, loves animals, jazz, books, nature, surf, astronomy. Seeks single, white, professional male, 40–55, who's on the road less traveled.

When Harry Met Sally: Young, attractive, 5'4", Chinese NY female, professional, cute, warm, funny, seeks Chinese professional NY guy, 5'8" plus, likes tennis and swimming, 32–36, in law, medicine, arts, or education.

SWM, 39, 5'4", physically fit, attractive, financially secure, seeks educated, outgoing, and adventurous SWF for friendship and LTR. Interests include bicycling, jogging, camping, hiking, and touring New England.

Winter Wonderland: attractive, outgoing, intelligent, compassionate, warm SWPF, 50, slim, loves outdoor adventures, skating, cross-country skiing. Seeks romantic SWPM, 48–55, to enjoy the season's adventures.[62]*

---

*Many people who place ads for companionship do not employ racial signs in describing either themselves or the type of person for whom they are searching. Others, however, use racial signals as a way of facilitating cross-racial liaisons, as the following ads attest:

  *Columbia, S.C.* Honest, attractive, childless, physically fit, and college-educated professional SBCF, 27. Seeking SWM, 25–35, with similar qualities for LTR, possibly marriage.

  *Elwood, Ind.* . . . White, 58 y/o woman, nurse . . . blonde, blue eyes, young & free thinker. Looking for 55–70 y/o black man, N/S/D/A, w/ good sense of humor, to enjoy retirement.

  *Gastonia, N.C.* SBM, 6 ft. 210 lbs., stocky build, N/S, no children, enjoy music, church, sports. ISO SWF, 25–40, for friendship, maybe more.

Indeed, there exist whole agencies dedicated to bringing together people who want to pursue interracial romance. One such agency, located in Chicago, has the interesting name Color-Blind, Inc.—Inter-Racial Dating Service.

The racial selectivity seen in personal ads highlights several important problems. One has to do with the idea of "racial discrimination." People often make statements that sweepingly condemn *all* racial discrimination, including—or perhaps especially—affirmative-action programs intended to assist racial minorities. Professor Alexander Bickel, for instance, asserted in 1975 that "discrimination on the basis of race is illegal, immoral, unconstitutional, inherently wrong, and destructive of democratic society."[63] And Professor William van Alstyne insisted in 1979 that "one gets beyond racism by getting beyond it now: by a complete, resolute, and credible commitment never to tolerate in one's own life—or in the life or practices of one's government—the differential treatment of other human beings by race. . . . In all we do in life, whatever we do in life, to treat any person less well than another for being black or white or brown or red, is wrong."[64] But the context of personal ads makes manifest the need to discriminate among discriminations. Not all discriminations are the same; they stem from different motives and are used to attain different goals.* The differences are hard to discern because racially discriminatory personals, like other forms of racial discrimination, are opaque. We see the racial signals but not the motives behind them. Wanting to obtain a clearer picture of what moves people to use racial signifiers in their search for companionship, I wrote to a number of people who had taken out racially discriminatory personal ads and asked them to explain their strategy.† While I

---

*There is a school of thought that holds that all racial distinctions are the same—that morally, Jim Crow segregation and affirmative action are equivalently bad, and that racial discrimination is racial discrimination, "plain and simple" (see, e.g., *Adarand Constructors, Inc., v. Pena,* 515 U.S. 200, 240–41 [1995] [concurring opinion of Justice Clarence Thomas). This is a simple-minded notion, akin to suggesting that all killing is the same, whether it is done to impose tyranny or to resist it. The "all discrimination is the same" assertion "would equate a law that made black citizens ineligible for military service with a program aimed at recruiting black soldiers," much as it "would disregard the differences between a 'No Trespassing' sign and a welcome mat" (ibid. at 245 [dissenting opinion of Justice John Paul Stevens]). For an acknowledgment of this point by a jurist who disapproved of affirmative action, see Judge Thomas Gee's opinion in *Weber v. Kaiser Aluminum & Chem. Corp.,* 611 F.2d 132, 133 (5th Cir. 1980), distinguishing between a "mistaken" ruling and an "evil" one.
†I solicited responses from people who placed personal ads in *Boston Magazine, New York* magazine, *The Washingtonian, Harvard Magazine,* and *Interrace.*

never heard from the overwhelming majority of the people to whom I wrote, I did receive a few responses. The first person who answered gave racist reasons for including whiteness among the traits he desired. He believed that whites—or, to use his terminology, "Aryans"—were superior to others and needed to band together to combat what he saw as the worldwide antiwhite conspiracy.* Another correspondent wrote that she had been unaware that her advertisement was racially discriminatory; she renounced it and said that she would change its wording in the future.† Several respondents referred to past personal experiences, among them one woman who declared, "I prefer Jewish men. There is a culture, a history, a sense of humor, a way of looking at things that we have in common. There is less to have to explain to him (Jewish mothers, worries, etc.)."[65]

Most of my correspondents claimed that they used racial signals as an efficient method of preselecting people with whom they might be compatible. As one wrote impatiently:

> Doesn't it seem obvious [that] people with similar ethnic and cultural backgrounds are more likely to possess the characteristics desired? . . . Sure, people of different backgrounds can be good for each other, just like lots of people from the same background cannot get along. The benefit of similar backgrounds is that there is a commonality that will be one less problem [in], for example, raising children, or dealing with

---

*Vowing that he would "have no woman other than a White woman," this correspondent complained that "all Western governments [have] deliberately instituted policies to reduce the power of Whites in their own countries[,] . . . suppress White identity movements or sentiments of any kind, and encourage miscegenation." Whites, he maintained, "are truly *arya,* best." See Personals Advertising Questionnaire Material (hereafter, Personals Material), in the Interracial Intimacies Collection, on file at the Harvard Law School Library.
†"I just automatically put ["single white male" in the ad]. . . . I believe I was wrong to say I am only interested in single white men. . . . When I wrote the ad, I honestly wasn't deliberately trying to discriminate (although it came out that way)" (Personals Material).

families. The probability is just lower when there are basic differences like race and religion.[66]*

When a man actually guided by this motivation states that he is in search of, say, a white woman with certain qualities, he does not mean to express hostility toward, or disrespect for, women who do not possess those traits.† Nor is he necessarily declaring a lack of interest in all but white women. He is simply indicating his belief that by deploying racial signals, he will be more successful in gathering quickly a pool of candidates among whom he may find an enjoyable romantic partner. He is essentially engaged in racial profiling.

Some of my correspondents confided that their racial signals evidenced an aesthetic or erotic preference. An advertiser in *The Washingtonian* stated: "I don't like my women 'dark,' meaning [with] dark hair, dark eyes, dark skin, because I am a Middle Easterner, and dark women remind me of my sisters. So I like the white, white blonde, etc. I confess in the name of science, yes, my motive was 'sex.'"[67]‡ Others cited a desire to avoid social disapproval. A retired New York City police officer

---

*Another correspondent wrote:

> For a long-term, intimate, romantic companionship I believe that my most likely contentment is with someone of my own race. In my experience there has been greater spiritual, emotional, psychological, and physical compatibility with someone of my own race. I have experienced some of those four ingredients with men of another race, but not all four. At fifty-six years of age, and with about thirty-eight relationships behind me, I have completed my own research project! Perhaps many people simply use the SWPF or SWPM descriptors because they're frequently used, but my choice was careful and thoughtful [Personals Material].

†It is important to consider, however, that even when people are trying their best to be candid, they often cannot fathom their own motives. While my correspondents may have truly believed that they were using racial signals only for purposes of dating efficiency, they may also have been motivated by unconscious prejudices. See Charles R. Lawrence, "The Id, the Ego, and Equal Protection: Reckoning with Unconscious Racism," 39 *Stanford Law Review* 317 (1987).
‡Another respondent wrote, "Why African-American? I think it is a preference, just like some people prefer fish over meat . . ." (Personals Material).

noted that he had restricted his search to white women because his going out with a black woman would have caused great stress between him and his "Archie Bunker neighbors." "I was looking," he wrote, "to make life easier."[68] Some of my correspondents justified their racially discriminatory ads in terms of their desire to affiliate themselves with "their own people." They wanted to maintain and pass on to their future progeny certain traditions, beliefs, rituals, and social networks, and they thought they could do this best, or only, with partners whose racial background was similar to their own. Jews expressing a preference for other Jews constituted the most frequent manifestation of this tendency.*

While the great majority of Americans claim to disapprove of racial discrimination, I doubt that most object to the idea of individuals' preferring to date or marry persons they perceive as racially identical to themselves. Many Americans talk of wanting to create a society in which racial boundaries have disappeared and race no longer matters to anyone. At the same time, though, many of these same people either organize themselves implicitly or explicitly around racial signposts or

---

*An advertiser in *Boston Magazine* wrote that her "strong preference [was] to meet someone Jewish" because she wanted "to have a 'Jewish' family (i.e., one that enjoys our religious and cultural history, and celebrates our holidays. . . . I want to pass these things on to children because I have always enjoyed being Jewish and find the religion to be quite interesting and moving both intellectually and emotionally)" (Personals Material). A considerable amount of ink has been devoted to the high incidence of Jewish-Gentile dating and marriage and what it might mean for the future of Jewry. See, for example, Elliot Abrams, *Faith or Fear: How Jews Can Survive in a Christian America* (1997); Alan M. Dershowitz, *The Vanishing American Jew: In Search of Jewish Identity for the Next Century* (1997).

Some may find it strange and perhaps disquieting to see Jews denoted here as a "race," for Jewish people are now commonly viewed as a religious or ethnic subgroup of "whites." This illustrates just how slippery and protean the idea of race can be as a conceptual sorter of human beings. See Karen Brodkin, *How Jews Became White Folks and What That Says About Race in America* (1998).

In 1987 counsel for the Anti-Defamation League of B'nai B'rith argued before the Supreme Court that even though Jews were not members of a scientifically distinct "race," they should nonetheless receive the protection against racial discrimination provided by the Civil Rights Act of 1866 (*Landmark Briefs and Arguments of the Supreme Court of the United States,* vol. 172, *Constitutional Law 1986 Term Supplement,* eds. Philip B. Kurland and Gerhard Casper [1988], 14–15). The Supreme Court agreed (*Shaare Tefila Congregation v. Cobb,* 481 U.S. 615 [1987]).

support others who do—hence the existence and popularity of innumerable African American, Asian American, and white ethnic social or self-help organizations. Which ideal of the "good society" do we want to develop: the cosmopolitan one that evinces negligable attachment to inherited racial solidarities or the pluralistic one that encourages personal and communal identification along racial lines? There is no better point of departure for sorting out the type of racial community we really want than the subject of interracial intimacies. The issues it raises test uniquely the contours of our deepest beliefs and intuitions, fears and hopes about race, race relations, and the American future. Yet intimate association typically receives far less attention than other racial topics; all too predictably, for example, it was accorded hardly a mention during the forums that constituted President William Jefferson Clinton's "Conversation on Race" in 1997. Americans are interested in interracial intimacy, but they rarely undertake systematic examinations of it. This is true even in academia. In a classroom a lively discussion always ensues when students are asked whether race can properly be used as a criterion for sorting applicants for schooling, housing, or employment. The debate will immediately be muted, however, if a further question is posed: Is race a legitimate criterion for choosing a partner for romance or marriage? This book had its origins in just such an exchange. A few years ago, during a class at Harvard Law School, a student declared that he opposed affirmative action because he rejected *all* racial discriminations. I asked him if he would condemn a friend who indicated in a personal ad that he or she was looking for a romantic partner of a given race. Before my question students had been straining to jump into the discussion; after it there were stretches of awkward silence. The present study results from my efforts to understand, overcome, and transform that silence. Statutes, judicial opinions, presidential directives, and voluminous commentary prepare us to assess racial discrimination in employment, housing, public accommodations, and the administration of criminal justice. By contrast, relatively few sources give us guidance in evaluating racial discrimination in the choice of friends, dates, or spouses.[69]

In these pages, in addition to conveying basic information, I hope to persuade readers to take positions on matters that implicate fundamental beliefs and aspirations. I urge the rejection of racial idolatry and racial authoritarianism of every stripe. In the United States, worship of whiteness has been the most common and most poisonous type of racial idolatry. It has taken many forms, from reserving for whites places of power and honor; to holding aloft light skin, straight hair, thin lips, and narrow noses as indicia of beauty; to discouraging inter-racial sex, marriage, and adoption. Although in recent decades the idolatry of whiteness has been strongly challenged and substantially undermined, it remains a force in American culture.

Many African Americans have sought to counter white racial pride with black racial pride, and white racial power with black racial power. White racial narcissism began the destructive spiral and is far more potent than black reactions, which are essentially defensive and compensatory responses to white aggression.[70] Victims of oppression are nonetheless quite capable of hurting themselves and others through specious beliefs and mistaken actions. Among the most influential opponents of interracial intimacy are blacks who see it as a capitulation to white dominance. Asserting that blacks need to feel a greater sense of racial obligation to themselves as a collective, that on the ground of racial kinship they ought to prefer one another to others, and that interracial intimacy constitutes a divisive diversion, significant numbers of African Americans oppose black participation in interracial dating, marriage, or adoption (especially when the others involved are white). The controversy over the last of these—interracial adoption—is especially telling. It offers the most vivid example of the mischief that can be caused by the self-defeating resentfulness sometimes harbored by beleaguered minorities. For over three decades the most effective organized foe of interracial adoption has been the National Association of Black Social Workers (NABSW). Comprised largely of child-welfare officials, the NABSW has at times eerily echoed the rhetoric of white segregationists, asserting that individuals "belong" on a racial basis to and with "their own," that interracial families are necessarily inferior to "normal" (meaning racially homogeneous) ones, and that those who believe in the ability of empathy and love to overcome racial barriers are *at best* dangerously naive. Yet the "expertise" of the NABSW has been accorded weighty and respectful deference by journalists, policymakers, judges, and others. Correspondingly narrow and invidious racial views can of course be found among whites, but few, if any, predominantly white organizations expressing sentiments analogous to those put forward by the NABSW would be permitted the same leeway or allowed the same influence. Indeed, they would almost certainly be condemned, as was Bob Jones University.[71]

The primary targets of my campaign against racial idolatry and racial authoritarianism are state-supported discouragements of interracial intimacy. The most conspicuous of these—laws prohibiting interracial sex and marriage—have been leveled. Others, however, continue to wreak havoc upon the most delicate of human associations. I am thinking here of the judges who wrongly punish women involved in interracial intimacies by depriving them of parental custody of their children, often at the urging of angry ex-husbands.* I am thinking of the child-welfare officials who prefer or even require that adoptive parents be of the same race as prospective adoptees, and who prevent or delay for long periods adoptions by those perceived to be of the "wrong" race.† I am also thinking of legislators who empower bureaucrats with the authority to require prospective adoptive parents to parrot racial notions that are deemed to display "cultural competency"—on pain of being denied a child with whom the parental candidates have fallen in love.‡

As I seek to persuade readers to eschew state-supported racial separatism in its various manifestations, I also urge that we all embrace a positive ideal: a cosmopolitan ethos that welcomes the prospect of genuine, loving interracial intimacy. This does not mean that we should blind ourselves to racial realities. As a matter of brute fact, race matters greatly in all areas of American life. But a fact does not dictate the proper response to its existence. The prominence of race in our society does not mean that individuals must or should continue to use race as a factor in choosing their intimate affiliations. We are free to restructure and improve the society we have inherited, and we should do so. For now, one way to accomplish that is to view racial discrimination of *any*

---

*See pages 372–77, 380–86.
†See pages 402–48.
‡See pages 441–46.

sort, even in the most intimate spheres of our lives, as a cause for concern, a matter worthy of worry, something that requires careful justification. I want this book to provoke readers to rethink their casual and unreflective reliance on racial distinctions in their private affairs. I am not asserting that all racial distinctions are the same. There is a huge difference between a sign saying "White folks welcome!" and "White folks stay out!" I am saying, though, that acting on the basis (or even partly on the basis) of racial difference, even for well-intentioned and valuable ends, is a weighty and tricky decision that should always occasion a sober second thought.

Even more strenuously, I argue that state and federal officials should be allowed neither to prevent nor to discourage the free flow of intimate associations across racial lines.* I therefore oppose race matching in adoption and foster care, as I object to kindred policies such as "cultural-competency" screening for adults who seek to adopt or offer foster care interracially. I favor any arrangement designed to place parentless children in the arms of able and caring adults as quickly as possible, without regard to race.† I concede that efforts to effectuate this vision of society must be limited in recognition of important and worthy competing values. It would be a mistake, for instance, for the government either to expressly encourage interracial intimacy directly or to prohibit individuals from exercising racial discrimination in their search for companionship. It would be likewise misguided to forbid prospective adoptive parents to indicate the race of the child they wish to adopt. Just as racial justice is a weighty concern, so, too, are privacy and prudent limits on state power. That is why much of this book makes an appeal not to legislatures or to courts but rather to those diffuse but influential governors of all our actions: individual conscience and public opinion.

Americans are becoming increasingly multiracial in their tastes, affections, and identities. The rates of interracial dating, marriage, and adop-

---

*Indian tribes—the third governmental sovereign in American government—require a limiting exception to the argument I press; see pages 480–518.
†See pages 402–46.

tion are inching, and in some places rocketing, upward.* This trend is, in my view, a positive good. It signals that formal and informal racial boundaries are fading. I am not suggesting here that interracial relationships are better than intraracial ones; nor am I suggesting that the existence of an interracial relationship necessarily indicates that those involved are free of ugly racial sentiments. Malignant racial biases can and do reside in interracial liaisons. But against the tragic backdrop of American history, the flowering of multiracial intimacy is a profoundly moving and encouraging development, one that lends support to Frederick Douglass's belief that eventually "the white and colored people of this country [can] be blended into a common nationality, and enjoy together . . . the inestimable blessings of life, liberty, and the pursuit of happiness."[72]

The subject of interracial intimacy bristles with complexity and paradox, mystery and drama; that is why scores of novelists, playwrights, lyricists, and filmmakers have been and continue to be drawn to it. Here as in so many other areas, however, the strangeness of reality provides stiff competition for the imagination's flights. A good example is the tale with which I began this introduction, the account of the Greens' attempt to adopt Jacqueline Henley. The Louisiana appellate court's resolution of her case easily could have been the sad end of the story. But neither Jacqueline nor the Greens nor the attorneys who represented them were destroyed when that court delivered its judgment. Soon after Jacqueline was remanded to the care of the St. John Berchmans Asylum, a Catholic institution for colored orphans, a Negro family in Chicago expressed an interest in adopting her. It is unclear how she came to their attention; perhaps they read about her in a cover story in *Jet* magazine—"The Dixie Orphan Whites Won't Have, Negroes Can't Adopt"—highlighting the cruel irony of her plight. In any event, Roi and Alice Ottley succeeded in bringing her to live with them in

---

*See pages 123–29.

Chicago. Unwilling though they were to allow a black couple to adopt Jacqueline within the state, Louisiana authorities were apparently agreeable to the idea of her being adopted by a black couple outside of it: the Ottleys adopted the child and renamed her Lynne.* She grew up in affluent, racially mixed neighborhoods in Chicago and Washington, D.C., attended Fisk University, became an ophthalmological technician, twice married black men, and raised three children. In the 1980s she moved back to the New Orleans area. Today she evinces no bitterness regarding the controversy that surrounded her early years, nor any interest in pursuing her biological familial roots. She is profoundly appreciative of those who, absent any blood ties, lovingly raised, nurtured, and educated her.[73]

Mr. and Mrs. Green journeyed to Oregon after the disappointment of their failed lawsuit and from there adopted a boy born in Korea, the child of a Korean mother and an unknown African American father who was almost certainly a member of the United States armed services. The Greens returned to New Orleans with their son, raised him to adulthood, and continued to remain active, public-spirited members of their community. Mr. Green is now deceased, but Mrs. Green still lives in New Orleans. In connection with research conducted for this book, she was reintroduced to the person she had known as Jacqueline.[74] Burton Klein became a prosperous attorney and is a well-known and respected member of the New Orleans bar.[75] The lawyer who handed him the Greens' case, Fred J. Cassibry, became a United States district court judge. On March 24, 1972, Judge Cassibry struck down the law that had prevented the Greens from adopting Jacqueline two decades earlier.[76]

---

*Roi Ottley was a distinguished journalist who worked for the *Amsterdam News*, the *Pittsburgh Courier*, and *PM* before becoming, in 1953, the *Chicago Tribune*'s first black reporter and columnist. He published several works of nonfiction, including *The Lonely Warrior: The Life and Times of Robert S. Abbott* (1955) and *Inside Black America* (1943), which won, among other citations, the Peabody Award. He also wrote a novel, *White Marble* (1965), about an interracial marriage; edited by his wife and published posthumously (he died in 1960), the book was dedicated to his daughter. See Jenifer W. Gilbert, Roi Ottley, American National Biography Online (Feb. 2000), at http://www.anb.org.articles/16/16-01243.html.

---

The chapters that follow seek to describe and assess the beliefs, customs, laws, and institutions that shaped the fight over Jacqueline Henley's future, and continue to affect race relations in the most intimate spheres of Americans' lives. I do not claim to cover comprehensively the territory of interracial intimacies. All too little is said here about gay and lesbian relationships, for example, or about cross-racial encounters beyond the black-white frontier. This book, therefore, cannot rightfully be termed definitive. I merely hope that it will contribute something useful to American culture by synthesizing much of what is currently known about interracial intimacy, particularly its regulation by legal institutions, noting gaps in our knowledge that warrant research, and advancing a viewpoint and ethos intended to nourish the better features of American multiracial democracy.

ONE

# In the Age of Slavery

### White Men/Black Women

Slavery constituted the principal backdrop against which whites and blacks encountered one another for over two hundred years, from the 1660s to the 1860s.[1] The overwhelming majority of slave owners were white, and the overwhelming majority of slaves, black.* There was probably more black-white sex during this period than at any other time (thus far) in American history.[2] Most of it was unwanted sex, stemming from white males' exploitation of black women—the subject of many pages to come.† But what about mutually desired sex or what I refer to as sexual intimacy? Some commentators insist that there can have been no such thing as sexual intimacy between a black enslaved

---

*Some Indians were enslaved, most often following defeat in battle. See Thomas D. Morris, *Southern Slavery and the Law 1619–1860* (1996), 19–21. Some "whites" were also enslaved insofar as the definition of whiteness in certain states permitted a sizable portion of African ancestry and slave status was matrilineal. Throughout much of the nineteenth century, for example, Virginia law labeled as "white" anyone who was less than one fourth "black." This legal definition allowed a person to be both legally "white" and a slave if his or her mother was a slave. See Lucia Stanton and Dianne Swann-Wright, "Bonds of Memory: Identity and the Hemings Family," in Jan Lewis, Peter S. Onuf, and Jane E. Lewis, eds., *Sally Hemings and Thomas Jefferson: History, Memory, and Civic Culture* (1999), 161–64. See also Ariela J. Gross, "Litigating Whiteness: Trials of Racial Determination in the Nineteenth-Century South," 108 *Yale Law Journal* 109 (1998).

†See pages 162–77.

woman and any white man—a slave owner or overseer or even a mere stranger—because mutually desired sex requires *choice,* a power denied to slaves by bondage. According to this view, slavery created an extreme dependency that precluded the possibility of chosen as opposed to unwanted sex. As a result, *all* of the sex that took place between enslaved women and white men constituted some form of sexual assault. Professor Angela Davis is among those who make this argument. Criticizing the notion that a slave woman could consent to have sex with a master, Davis maintains that "there could hardly be a basis for 'delight, affection and love' as long as white men[,] by virtue of their economic position, had unlimited access to Black women's bodies."[3] Proponents of this view are right to stress the cruel coerciveness of slavery.* While the specifics of bondage varied widely over time and from place to place, the condition itself always endowed masters with despotic personal power over their human property.

A vivid illustration of slavery's despotism is *State v. Mann,*[4] an 1829 decision in which the North Carolina Supreme Court reversed the conviction of a white man who had been prosecuted for criminally assaulting a female slave. John Mann had shot a leased slave named Lydia when, for reasons that are unclear, she ran away from him and refused to stop. Writing for the court, Judge Thomas Ruffin declared that under common law, the intentional wounding of a slave by a master did not rise to the level of a crime. In explaining the court's conclusion, Ruffin described the terrible core of American racial slavery with eloquent, if chilling, clarity. The slave, he observed, was "one doomed

---

*A small number of blacks also owned slaves. Sometimes their slave "ownership" merely represented efforts to free relatives or other loved ones in jurisdictions that prohibited the emancipation of slaves; such purchases were thus effectively manumissions. In other instances, though, blacks owned slaves for the same reasons as their white counterparts, motivated by the desire to make a lucrative investment, to acquire prestige, or to free themselves from drudgery. I have come across no literature discussing the sexual exploitation of black slaves by black masters. This sort of abuse is virtually certain to have occurred, however, given what we know about the sexual misuse of power by people throughout world history. The place to begin exploration of this thinly documented subject is Michael P. Johnson and James L. Roak's superb book *Black Masters: A Free Family of Color in the Old South* (1984).

in his own person, and his posterity, to live . . . without the capacity to make anything his own, and to toil that another may reap the fruits."[5] Absent legislation, masters should be permitted to discipline slaves in whatever way they saw fit, because, Ruffin asserted, "we cannot allow the right of the master to be brought into discussion in the Courts of Justice. The slave, to remain a slave, must be made sensible, that there is no appeal from his master; that his power is in no instance, usurped; but is conferred by the laws of man at least, if not by the law of God."[6] It was good policy, Judge Ruffin insisted, for courts to refrain from criminalizing even cruel and unreasonable battery on slaves by their owners, for the only thing that could create the obedience that slavery required was "uncontrolled authority over the body."[7] "The power of the master," he postulated, "must be absolute, to render the submission of the slave perfect."[8]

The slave system *failed*, however, to perfect the domination that Ruffin envisioned. It *failed* to bind the slaves so tightly as to deprive them of all room to maneuver. It *failed* to wring from them all prohibited yearnings. Slavery was, to be sure, a horribly oppressive system that severely restricted the ambit within which its victims could make decisions. But slavery did not extinguish altogether the possibility of choice. It was that possibility which endowed slaves with moral responsibility then, and which renders them susceptible to moral assessment today. It is precisely because they made wrong choices, albeit in excruciating circumstances, that slave informants who betrayed other slaves can appropriately be condemned. Similarly, it is because enslaved rebels made right choices in difficult situations that they can now be applauded. In the next chapter, in a discussion focusing on the sexual exploitation of enslaved African American women, we shall meet Harriet Jacobs, a slave who experienced tremendous suffering at the hands of a wickedly lecherous master.* Jacobs left a wonderful memoir that tells us how, even in the midst of her terrible predicament, she was able to make important decisions. She decided, for example, to resist her

---

*See pages 164–68.

master's advances, and she chose to have sex with a different white man, whose children she bore, because for her "it seem[ed] less degrading to give one's self than to submit to compulsion."[9] As a keen observer wrote over a century later, "One might be tempted to characterize [Jacobs] as a victim of her circumstances. But she repeatedly demonstrated her ability to transform the conditions of her oppression into the preconditions of her liberation and that of her loved ones."[10]

Harriet Jacobs was not alone in exercising self-expression and self-assertion from within a position of enslavement. Bondage severely limited the power—including the sexual power—of slaves. But it did not wholly erase their capacity to attract and shape affectionate, erotic attachments of all sorts, including interracial ones.[11] In a hard-to-quantify but substantial number of cases, feelings of affection and attachment between white male masters and their black female slaves somehow survived slavery's deadening influence.* The great difficulty, in any particular instance, lies in determining whether sex between a male master and a female slave was an expression of sexual autonomy or an act of unwanted sex. The truth is that most often we cannot know for sure, since there exists little direct testimony from those involved, especially the enslaved women. There is good reason to presume that most of the sex between masters and slaves was unwanted by the latter, who were forced into accepting it by subtle threats or brute violence. Coerced sex was a widespread, feared, and traumatic aspect of enslavement. This is hardly surprising, for it would be difficult to construct a context more conducive to sexual exploitation than American racial slavery. Masters *owned* slaves and largely dictated the conditions under which they toiled. They could assign troublesome individuals backbreaking tasks or reward favorites with less burdensome duties. They could break up enslaved families or keep them together. They could condemn the living children or future progeny of slaves to bondage or hold out the possibility of emancipating them in return for satisfying service. We may get some sense of the imbalance of power by considering that today, even though sexual harassment has been outlawed in many settings, some

---

*The effect of slavery and other forms of racial hierarchy on same-sex desires or relationships is a subject much in need of investigation.

bosses continue to impose unwanted sexual attention on their subordinates. Slave masters constituted the ultimate bosses. But perhaps no analogy to a contractual employment relationship can sufficiently convey the inherent coerciveness of slavery; a better analogue may be the prison guard who lords it over incarcerated women.[12] After all, in addition to facing brutal sexual assaults, women inmates commonly face subtler forms of compulsion, often in the guise of coercive offers.[13] Yet slaves were even more vulnerable than inmates to sexual exploitation. A master's control over the fate of a slave woman's children and other kinfolk was a much more powerful tool than anything at the disposal of a prison guard. Furthermore, slaves were prohibited from testifying against masters,[14] and almost all American jurisdictions failed even to recognize as a crime the rape of a slave.[15]

We can be sensitive to the plight of enslaved women, however, and still acknowledge that consensual sex, prompted by erotic attraction and other mysteries of the human condition, has occurred between subordinates and superiors in even the most barren and brutal settings. Evidence of consensual sexual intimacy within the confines of bondage is found in the unusual solicitude shown by certain masters toward slaves with whom they had sex and by whom they sired children. Freeing a slave mistress or the offspring of such a union, acknowledging paternity of or assuming financial responsibility for a slave's children, marrying a former slave—all of these are potentially telltale signs of affection.

Drawing inferences from such conduct is a hazardous undertaking. Some slaveholders did not view manumission as a sign of affection; on the contrary, perceiving bondage to be a positive good for slaves as well as masters, they deemed emancipation an act of cruelty. One such master was James Henry Hammond, a governor of South Carolina who owned nearly 150 slaves. At least two of their number, a mother and a daughter, were mistresses by whom he probably sired children. In a letter requesting that his son by his legal (white) wife care for these women and their offspring in the event of his death, Hammond declared, "I cannot free these people & send them North. It would be cruelty to them. Nor would I like that any but my own blood should own as slaves my own blood. . . . Do not let . . . any of my children or possible children be the Slaves of Strangers. Slavery *in the family* will be their happiest earthly condition."[16]*

Nor was every master's conduct toward the child he sired necessarily indicative of the conditions under which that child had been conceived. David Dickson was a rich white Georgian who attentively raised, educated, and supported Amanda America Dickson, the daughter he fathered by one of his many slaves. It would be a mistake, however, to read into his relationship with Amanda's mother the tender solicitude that Dickson showered upon his daughter. According to a careful scholarly study, as well as the oral tradition of the black side of the Dickson family, Amanda was conceived by rape one day in 1849, when her forty-year-old father decided to initiate sexually a thirteen-year-old slave girl to whom he took a sudden fancy as she worked in his fields.[17]

More generally, though, and given the indifference, hostility, and denial typically displayed by white men who had sex with slaves, acknowledgments of a sexual partner or of the offspring of a sexual liaison may be regarded as unusual acts that probably betokened some variety of tender attachment.[18] The more evident such acts of acknowledgment were in any specific case, the more confident we can be in describing the relationship as "intimate." That adjective may surely be applied, for example, to the relationship between Thomas Bell, a white businessman, and Mary Hemings, one of Thomas Jefferson's many slaves. In the 1780s, Jefferson leased Hemings to Bell, who fathered two children by her. Several years into the leasing arrangement, Hemings asked Jefferson to sell her and her two children to Bell; after Jefferson did so, Hemings, Bell, and their children openly lived together, and Hemings adopted Bell's last name.†

---

*Two other facts are of interest here. First, Hammond's son was likely also involved sexually with one or more of his father's slave mistresses. Second, the governor's political career was ruined when it became public knowledge that he had sexually fondled four of his nieces, the daughters of his influential brother-in-law Wade Hampton II. See Drew Gilpin Faust, *James Henry Hammond and the Old South: A Design for Mastery* (1982).

†There is little doubt that Bell was Hemings's "master/lover." It seems, however, that he never freed her. See Annette Gordon-Reed, *Thomas Jefferson and Sally Hemings: An American Controversy* (paperback ed., 1998), 136.

Mary Hemings had given birth to four children prior to her association with

Another intimate relationship united Thomas Wright, a prosperous landowner in Prince Edward County, Virginia, and Sylvia, one of his slaves.[19] The two began living together in the late 1770s, and though they never married (such a marriage would have violated Virginia law), Wright never hid the nature of their companionate relationship from others. They lived, neighbors recalled, "as man and wife."[20] Wright freed his mistress's two children by a fellow slave (born before Wright purchased her) as well as the four children they had together, whom he also assisted financially.

In yet another case, Ralph Quarles, a prosperous Virginia plantation owner and military hero of the Revolutionary War, entered into an intimate association with Lucy Langston, a black woman who had become his slave in settlement of a debt. Langston bore four children by Quarles, all of whom he emancipated along with their mother, and all of whom he carefully provided for financially. In 1834, after Quarles and Langston both died following brief illnesses, they were buried side by side, pursuant to instructions left in his will.*

The court reports of the slave states furnish scores of similar examples of white men who sought to help their black mistresses and children escape the deprivations imposed upon them by enslavement and racism.[21] More than any other state, Louisiana provides an abundant array of such cases.[22] Douglass Wilkins, for instance, left a will in which he emancipated his slave mistress, Leonora, and acknowledged their two sons. He also willed a $150 annuity to Leonora, bequeathed the sum of $5,000 to the sons, and stipulated that "as soon as [the

---

Thomas Bell, whom Thomas Jefferson praised as a man "remarkable for his integrity" (quoted in Lucia Stanton, "Monticello to Main Street: The Hemings Family and Charlottesville," *Magazine of Albermarle County History* 55 [1997]: 75, 97). Jefferson gave one of these children to his sister on her marriage, and another to his daughter on hers. When Jefferson sold Hemings to Bell, the transaction also included two children, a boy and a girl, both fathered by Bell himself (Stanton, "Monticello to Main Street," 99–100).

*The youngest of the Quarles-Langston children was John Mercer Langston, who graduated from Oberlin College, served as the founding dean of the Howard University School of Law, and represented Virginia in the United States House of Representatives. See William Cheek and Aimee Lee Cheek, *John Mercer Langston and the Fight for Freedom 1829–65* (1989).

boys] shall be old enough to be separated from their mother, my executors shall send them to some State of the Union in which slavery is not tolerated, to be instructed in reading, writing and arithmetic, and in some mechanical art or trade."[23] It appears that his wishes were carried out. Like Wilkins, Elisha Crocker left the bulk of his estate to his mistress and former slave—Sofa—and the children she had borne him, whom he formally acknowledged. Crocker's white brothers and sisters challenged his will on the ground that under state law, he had had no right to bequeath to his concubine and illegitimate children any more than one quarter of his property. His siblings, of course, wanted the remainder for themselves. They prevailed insofar as the Supreme Court of Louisiana agreed with their reading of the relevant law and transferred to them three quarters of their brother's estate. Nevertheless, Crocker's mistress and three children received what he had most wished for them to have: their freedom and at least some share of the inheritance that would grant them a large measure of independence.[24] In a third case, Jean-Baptiste Lagarde, an overseer, purchased a slave woman named Adelaide and her daughter Amelia from his employer and treated them as free. In short order Adelaide gave birth to a second daughter, Cydalize, and then contracted cholera and died. Lagarde was almost certainly the father of both Amelia and Cydalize. After their mother's death, he paid a free woman of color, Marie Louise Audat, to raise the girls as her own, a beneficent act that surely hinted at paternal solicitude. Lagarde did not, however, emancipate his daughters. No one knows why he failed to do so, though Professor Judith Kelleher Schaefer has speculated that it may have had something to do with his marrying a white woman after Adelaide died—a woman who perhaps harbored ill will toward her husband's children. Whatever his reasons, Lagarde's omission would have serious consequences, as the slave status of Amelia and Cydalize survived their father's death. Although he had apparently intended to send his daughters to live with his sister in France, he died before he could effectuate this wish. Labeled as slaves, the two girls were included in his estate and auctioned off at a probate sale. Luckily for them, Audat purchased the girls and subsequently ensured that they were formally emancipated.[25]

The cases recounted above all had relatively happy endings. In other instances, however, laws designed to discourage interracial intimacy frustrated efforts on the part of white men to provide for women and children who were deemed by authorities to reside on the other side of the color line. William Adams Jr. lived openly with a slave named Nancy and fathered two children by her. In his will, Adams ordered his executor to free Nancy and give her his watch and furniture. He also left two gifts of $1,000 each to their children. Alongside Adams's illegitimate colored family, though, was a legitimate white one, and after Adams died, his white son challenged his will. Under Louisiana law, no one could bequeath more than one tenth of his net worth to a concubine—meaning, in effect, that if the value of a slave mistress exceeded 10 percent of the total estate, she could not be freed. This rule spelled disaster for Nancy, who was valued at $1,000, while the value of the rest of Adams's estate, excluding her, was put at just $4,750. Since her slave price exceeded the one-tenth limitation, the Louisiana Supreme Court ruled that Nancy could not be freed and hence could not receive the other gifts that Adams had sought to bestow upon her, as slaves were legally prohibited from inheriting anything at all. Adams's white son thus became the owner of his father's black concubine and possibly her children as well.[26]

A second case also vividly illustrates how attempts by white men to provide for their enslaved black mistresses could run aground on the material or emotional demands of their white wives, lovers, friends, or heirs. Erasmus R. Avart's black mistress, Marie, was someone else's slave. Avart stipulated in his will that upon his death, his executor should purchase Marie and their son and free them. He drew up his will at a dramatic moment: after wounding himself and before dying of the wound. Although Marie's master was willing to sell, no sale occurred because Avart's heirs objected. Marie sued the executor and the heirs. The heirs argued that the will was invalid because Avart had been of unsound mind when he signed it. As proof of his insanity they cited his evident affection for Marie; he had, they claimed, been "consumed with passion" for her. On other grounds the white heirs ultimately prevailed.[27]

*Sally Hemings and Thomas Jefferson*    The most famous episode of interracial sexual intimacy prior to the Civil War involved Thomas Jefferson and Sally Hemings.[28]* Although many historians long dismissed the possibility of such an affair, the evidence overwhelmingly points to a sexual relationship that produced multiple children. Even the Thomas Jefferson Memorial Foundation now allows that there is a "high probability" that Jefferson sired all of Hemings's children.[29] Although Jefferson knew Hemings practically from her birth in Virginia, the two became acquainted in France in 1787, when Jefferson was forty-four and Hemings thirteen or fourteen. He was then the United States ambassador to France, and she was one of the many slaves attached to his estate. A widower who had promised his dying wife that he would never marry again, Jefferson was, at that point, the father of two surviving children. When he insisted that his younger daughter, Polly, join him in Paris, Sally Hemings was dispatched to accompany her. Little is known about Hemings's life in Paris (or anywhere else, for that matter), but her son Madison Hemings would later maintain that when the Jeffersons returned to Virginia in 1789, his mother was carrying the first of the several children she would bear for her master, the principal author of the Declaration of Independence and third president of the United States. Madison Hemings also reported being told by his mother that she and Jefferson had reached an agreement whereby she would

---

*Another prominent politician whose interracial sexual dealings generated a good deal of publicity was Richard M. Johnson, vice president of the United States under President Martin Van Buren. Johnson had several black slave mistresses, one of whom bore him two daughters whom he subsequently educated, supported financially, and married off to white men. Inveighing against the prospect of Johnson's becoming vice president, a New England newspaper asked disgustedly, "How would it look in the eyes of civilized Europe and the world, to see the Vice President and his yellow children, and his wooly headed wife, in the city of Washington, mingling in all the giddy mazes of the most fashionable and reputable society in the country?" (quoted in Thomas Brown, "The Miscegenation of Richard Mentor Johnson as an Issue in the National Election Campaign of 1835–1836," *Civil War History* 39 [1993]: 5, 7. See also Werner Sollors, "Presidents, Race, and Sex," in Jan Lewis, Peter S. Onuf, and Jane E. Lewis, eds., *Sally Hemings and Thomas Jefferson: History, Memory, and Civic Culture* (1999).

leave Paris for Virginia on the condition that he promise to emancipate any children born of their relationship.[30]

The circumstantial evidence for Jefferson's paternity includes the following: he and Sally Hemings were in the same place in the time periods when she must have gotten pregnant; Hemings never conceived a child in Jefferson's absence; Hemings's children bore a striking resemblance to Jefferson; he allowed two of them to run away from Monticello and made no effort to recapture them, and he formally freed two others; a detailed, internally consistent statement by Madison Hemings recounts his mother's identification of Thomas Jefferson as Madison's father and the father of his siblings; and friends of Jefferson's noted privately that he had a slave mistress. Finally, the result of DNA testing is consistent with the circumstantial evidence that Jefferson sired Sally Hemings's children.

Before proceeding, I would like to make it clear that hereafter I will treat the sexual relationship of Thomas Jefferson and Sally Hemings as historical "fact." Even if one approaches the issue with a rather strong presumption against the veracity of the allegation, sufficient probative evidence has been introduced to rebut that presumption. Is there any possibility that there was no sexual association between the two? Yes, there is some such possibility.* But the same is true with respect to other "facts" that historians *never* dispute—for example, the "fact" that Jefferson fathered the daughters of his wife, Martha Wayles Skelton Jefferson. It is simply assumed that he was their biological as well as their legal father, though we know from countless other cases that wives' extramarital sexual activity may call such presumptions into question. I do not mean to impugn Martha Jefferson's fidelity; I merely wish to point out that if historians were as exacting in describing Jefferson's marriage as some have been in writing of his relationship with

---

*Although many commentators have promoted the notion that DNA testing proved definitively that Thomas Jefferson sired Sally Hemings's children, the testing did not in fact yield wholly conclusive results. It established only that *some* Jefferson—not necessarily Thomas Jefferson—was a male ancestor of the Hemings line. See Thomas Jefferson Memorial Foundation, *Report of the Research Committee on Thomas Jefferson and Sally Hemings* (2000) (www.monticello.org).

Sally Hemings, they might assert that it is only "likely" that he sired his legitimate "white" children.

Scholars should, of course, be careful in their labeling and assessment of facts. Much of the resistance to accepting the reality of a Jefferson-Hemings affair, however, has its roots not in any scholarly punctiliousness but rather in the urge to protect Thomas Jefferson's reputation from a charge that is perceived as being particularly pernicious. Why is it, though, that allegations of interracial sex should seem so much more damning than charges regarding other aspects of the man's conduct—for example, the indisputable fact that he owned, sold, and gave as gifts numerous human beings? For several of the most influential participants in the debate over the Jefferson-Hemings relationship, the answer lies in an aversion to interracial sex. Interestingly enough, that very aversion once *fueled* assertions of the affair. The allegation that Jefferson had sired children by Hemings was first publicly aired by the journalist James Callender, writing in Jefferson's own day. If not for Callender's persistence, the rumor might well have sunk into obscurity, as have so many other rumors accurately associating prominent white men with black paramours. But Callender's background and motivations also seemed to justify the eagerness and effectiveness with which many observers have dismissed his charge. In the 1790s, Federalist authorities had successfully prosecuted him for publishing harsh rhetorical attacks against Jefferson's political enemies. When Jefferson became president, he took steps to ease the financial hardship that the prosecution had inflicted upon Callender. Jefferson, though, refused Callender's demand to be appointed to a patronage post. This rebuff infuriated Callender and turned him into a vindictive foe who would announce in a Richmond, Virginia, newspaper, on September 1, 1802, that Thomas Jefferson "keeps, and for many years past has kept, as his concubine, one of his own slaves. Her name is SALLY. . . . By this wench sally, our president has had several children. . . . Behold the favorite, the first born of republicanism! The pinnacle of all that is good and great! In the open consummation of an act which tends to subvert the policy, the happiness, and even the existence of this country!"[31]

Denyers of Callender's allegation have stressed his personal animus against Jefferson. Even those who are animated by vengeance, however, can offer accurate information about people they wish to destroy. A vengeful fellow, Callender was also a resourceful journalist who had a good record of reporting the essential truth of the stories he broke.

Ironically, aversion to interracial intimacy was a sentiment that Callender had in common with some of those who have most detested him down the years. Often overlooked by historians is the fact that Callender's exposé of the Jefferson-Hemings affair stemmed not only from his antipathy toward the man but also from a deep-seated racism that prompted him to oppose all manifestations of black-white interracial intimacy. After moving to Richmond, for instance, he led a campaign to ban "black dances"—that is, gatherings at which white men consorted with black women. Later he exposed white men who attended the theater with black women. In "outing" Jefferson, Callender was thus pursuing both a personal vendetta and an ideological project to which he was strongly committed. Charging Jefferson with miscegenation enabled Callender to tap into and nourish a strain of racist folklore that equated amalgamation with something akin to bestiality.

It is precisely because miscegenation has long been so stigmatized that some of Jefferson's defenders have responded to the allegations of his affair with Sally Hemings with such sustained indignation. This indignation often emerges in what has become the principal defense against the allegation: the so-called character defense. Under this theory, Jefferson is absolved of wrongdoing because essential features of his character supposedly render inconceivable his participation in the alleged affair. Jefferson's granddaughter Ellen Coolidge mounted a version of this defense when she remarked that "there are such things, after all, as moral impossibilities."[32] Another version is offered by Professor Douglas L. Wilson, who objects to the miscegenation charge on the ground that

> it doesn't fit Jefferson. If he did take advantage of Hemings and her children over a period of twenty years, he was acting completely out of character and violating his own standards of honor and decency. For a man who took questions of morality and honor very seriously, such a hypocritical liaison would have been a constant source of shame and guilt. For his close-

knit family, who worshiped him and lived too near to him to have been ignorant of such an arrangement, it would have been a moral tragedy of no small dimensions.[33]

A third iteration of the character defense, and probably the most influential, was propounded by Jefferson's leading biographer, Dumas Malone. "The charges of a sexual relationship with Sally Hemings," Malone maintained, "are distinctly out of character, being virtually unthinkable in a man of Jefferson's moral standards and habitual conduct. . . . It is virtually inconceivable that this fastidious gentleman whose devotion to his dead wife's memory and to the happiness of his daughters and grandchildren bordered on the excessive could have carried through a period of years a vulgar liaison which his own family could not have failed to detect."[34]

Championing the character defense does not require embracing a belief that interracial intimacy would have morally disgraced Jefferson. One might think that a Jefferson-Hemings affair was a moral impossibility because he never would have had sex outside of marriage or had sex with a servant (regardless of race). Absent from the most influential recent proponents of the character defense are explicit statements of revulsion against miscegenation. Still, at the level of informal discourse and in the implicit messages of ostensibly nonracial arguments, there resides the active belief, still widespread, that interracial sexual affection is shameful and thus a type of misconduct that must at all costs be cleared from Jefferson's record. The reason some of Jefferson's defenders have so tirelessly attempted to refute allegations of a liaison between him and Hemings is that interracial sexual relationships have long been viewed as morally dirtying. Jeffersonians who have been willing to accept the reality of all manner of other rumored peccadilloes have therefore refused to entertain even the possibility that Jefferson engaged in a long-term, perhaps affectionate sexual relationship with a black slave woman. Consider the case of Dumas Malone.[35] He bitterly denounced Fawn Brodie's *Thomas Jefferson: An Intimate History* (1974), which was, until recently, the primary scholarly work positing as true a Jefferson-Hemings sexual affair. Several years later he lobbied the Columbia Broadcasting System (CBS) to cancel a planned mini-series based on Barbara Chase-Riboud's 1979 fictional portrayal of a Jefferson-Hemings romance. Yet by 1984 even Malone had to concede that sex between Jefferson and Hemings "might have happened once or twice."[36] Unwilling to admit the barest possibility of an emotionally serious relationship between his hero and Hemings, Malone preferred to posit the alternative of an emotionally barren one-night stand.

Typically, the character defense of Jefferson displays a pietistic exceptionalism that obscures the horror of slavery. Thus, moved by empathy with Jefferson's *white* relatives, one writer suggests that a Jefferson-Hemings relationship "would have been a moral tragedy of no small dimensions" for them, and hence something that the great man would have avoided.[37] Professor Annette Gordon-Reed, however, aptly challenges this attitude:

> Why should we assume for a moment that the Jeffersons . . . could live in the midst of the slave system and not be touched by some of the more common circumstances it spawned? . . . To write of [the Jefferson-Hemings affair] as though it would have amounted to some special horror unknown in the annals of southern history misleads as to the extent of the contradictions and complexities of antebellum southern life.[38]

Master-slave sex was rife in the social circles of the white Virginia elite. Sally Hemings's mother, Betty Hemings, was the daughter of a slave woman and her master, as was Sally herself. Her father—and the father of five other children borne by Betty Hemings—was John Wayles, Jefferson's widely respected father-in-law. It was not at all unusual for a master to be sexually involved with one or more of his slaves; that was one of the widely indulged prerogatives of ownership.

Some denyers of the Jefferson-Hemings connection assert that such an affair would have been out of character for the Virginia statesman because he abhorred the idea of miscegenation with Negroes and found blacks physically unattractive.[39] It is true that Jefferson expressed disgust for black-white interracial sex: Amalgamation, he averred, "produces a degradation to which no lover of his country, no lover of excellence in the human character, can innocently consent."[40] It is also true that he perceived blacks to be inferior to whites in terms of beauty as well as intelligence. Stressing the importance of color, Jefferson wrote:

> Is it not the foundation of a greater or less share of beauty in the two races? Are not the fine mixtures of red and white, the expressions of every passion by greater or less suffusions of colour in the one, preferable to that eternal monotony which reigns in the countenances, that immoveable veil of black which covers all the emotions of the other race? Add to these, flowing hair, a more elegant symmetry of form, and their own judgment in favour of the whites declared by their preference of them, as uniformly as is the preference of the Oran-ootan for the black women over those of his own species. The circumstance of superior beauty, is thought worthy of attention in the propagation of our horses, dogs, and other domestic animals, why not in that of man?[41]

Jefferson's having sex with a woman of African ancestry, however, is not at all irreconcilable with his espousing racist views. Sally Hemings, whose biological father and grandfather were both white, was described as a light-skinned Negro with long, flowing hair. Her appearance may well have offset Jefferson's aesthetic biases; after all, he carefully distinguished blacks from mulattoes and other, more mixed Negro strains, judging the latter more appealing. In any case, moreover, sex often involves more than "looks." A person may be less than captivated by certain of his or her partner's features but extremely aroused by others; and even the most powerful figures sometimes compromise their quest for the ideal to enjoy "flawed" bedmates who minister well to compelling desires. That Jefferson was racist does not mean he was incapable in all circumstances of appreciating the humanity of blacks. Like many racists, he made exceptions for individual Negroes while supporting policies that expressed contempt for African Americans as a whole. Many white supremacists have similarly abjured white-black miscegenation *in general* even as they enjoyed it *in particular* with their own black paramours.*

Invoking the character defense, Virginius Dabney has written that "it would indeed have been the height of hypocrisy for a man who entertained [antiblack, antimiscegenationist] views and expressed them over most of his adult life to have sired mulatto children."[42] Obviously, though, the specter of hypocrisy failed to dissuade Jefferson from engaging in conduct at odds with his stated beliefs. The principal draftsman of the Declaration of Independence was, after all, a slaveholder!†

The character defense makes much of Jefferson's devotion to the memory of his dead wife. No one has suggested, however, that his sex-

---

*Examples abound. As a young man in the 1920s, Strom Thurmond sired a child by a black maid employed by his parents. (See Jack Bass and Marilyn W. Thompson, *Ol' Strom: An Unauthorized Biography of Strom Thurmond* [1998], 272–88.) Later, as a governor and United States senator, Thurmond would staunchly defend segregation. The story of his interracial involvement was kept alive by a black oral tradition that a number of commentators dismissed as mere myth, though they never expended much effort to determine whether or not there was any truth to the persistent whispers (see, e.g., Nadine Cohodas, *Strom Thurmond and the Politics of Southern Change* [1993], 481). Just as rumors about Jefferson and Hemings were discredited by the status or dubious motivation of certain sources, so, too, were rumors of Thurmond's interracial paternity tainted by their publication in the notorious girlie magazine *Penthouse* and in the pages of a small local South Carolina newspaper edited by a man who detested Thurmond. Although the woman identified as Thurmond's daughter denies the claim, Jack Bass and Marilyn Thompson compellingly argue that the rumors are true. The circumstantial evidence they adduce, abetted by the absence of a denial by the senator, is sufficiently persuasive, I believe, to allow Thurmond's paternity to be categorized as a "fact." One of the strongest pieces of evidence in support of this conclusion is the otherwise inexplicable financial assistance that Thurmond provided to the woman during her college years.

†Just as there are different sorts of racism, so, too, are there different sorts of sex. The discussion in the text presupposes a type of sex based on a substantial degree of mutual appreciation by both parties. Some sex, though, is almost wholly unilateral and exploitative, with one participant—man or woman—seeking only self-satisfaction. Where that kind of sex was involved, there would have been no tension between enslavement and sexual pleasure. It would have made perfect (albeit horrible) sense for a racist master to satisfy his sexual desires with slaves, just as he satisfied his financial ambitions with them.

ual interest in women died with her; on the contrary, the biographers all agree that when he was in Paris, he showed considerable romantic inter-est in Maria Cosway, a married Englishwoman. Why is it that in the biographical literature, Jefferson's feelings for Cosway are portrayed as being "in character" while his "supposed" attraction to Hemings is labeled "out of character"? One reason is that several influential arbiters of the Jeffersonian image have *themselves* found Cosway much more appealing than Hemings. The notion of a Jefferson-Hemings affair, one commentator has disapprovingly noted, requires believing that Jefferson "would turn his back on the delectable Cosway . . . to seduce a markedly immature, semi-educated, teenage virgin, who stood in a peculiarly personal relationship to him, both as slave, and as half-sister to his dead wife, and as the companion and almost sister to his young daughters."[43] Vladimir Nabokov would have loved this sentence for its naïveté.[44] Thomas Jefferson, like many other experienced and respectable widowers of his day (and ours), might well have been intrigued by the prospect of an affair with "a markedly immature . . . teenage virgin." But inasmuch as some observers have thought it implausible that the great Thomas Jefferson could become smitten by a mere sixteen-year-old, we need to consider how elite white men in the United States in the early nineteenth century perceived teenage girls and, more specifically, whether they regarded romantic relationships with girls of that age as being morally permissible.* While this is not the place for a comprehensive assessment, it bears noting that James Madison fell in love with a fifteen-year-old when he was thirty-one,

---

*In eighteenth-century Virginia the age of consent was ten. See "History of the Changes in the Law on the Age of Consent," *Virginia Law Review* 81, 82 (1924).

When nineteenth-century reformers moved to raise the age of consent in certain jurisdictions, white supremacists resisted, claiming that young black women of loose morals would thereby be empowered to menace innocent but legally vulnerable white men. See Leslie K. Dunlap, "The Reform of Rape Law and the Problem of White Men: Age-of-Consent Campaigns in the South, 1885–1910," in Martha Hodes, ed., *Sex, Love, Race: Crossing Boundaries in North American History* (1999), 352.

The age of consent in several states remains quite young; in South Carolina and Arkansas, for example, it is fourteen. See S.C. Const. Ann. Art. III, Stat. 33 (1999); Ark. Stat. Ann. Stat. 5-14-103 (1999).

that Jefferson himself served as a go-between for that couple, and that Madison and his young love went so far as to set a date for marriage before the teenager broke Madison's heart by rejecting him in favor of a boy her own age.[45] Jefferson in particular might well have found Sally Hemings a more suitable romantic partner than Maria Cosway. Cosway was already married when they met, whereas Hemings was unattached. And Cosway might well have demanded marriage as the price for an ongoing sexual relationship—a demand that would have forced Jefferson to rethink the deathbed promise he had made to his wife. Hemings, for her part, likely asked for nothing more than freedom for any children she might bear Jefferson. As for Cosway's "delectability," there were certain less savory aspects of her personality that some observers seem to have overlooked in their haste to pronounce her so much more appealing than Sally the slave. Perhaps up close the Englishwoman was not so "delectable" after all. Two years after her flirtation with Jefferson in Paris, Cosway abandoned her infant child and her husband to run off with another man.[46]

Long ignored or maligned by writers (Callender, for one, described her as a slut "as common as pavement"),[47] Sally Hemings has more recently been reimagined as beautiful, resourceful, intelligent, and, despite her slave status, influential—in short, an able rival for a racially privileged white woman.[48] "She owned [Jefferson]," declares the narrator of Barbara Chase-Riboud's popular novel Sally Hemings, "just as surely as he owned her."[49] In this view, Sally Hemings was, among other things, a liberator who succeeded over the course of a lifetime in achieving something granted to few enslaved women: she elevated her children from bondage to freedom.*

## Black Men/White Women

Sexual intimacies in the slavery era also involved white women and black men.[50] Consider, for example, the case of Nell Butler and Negro Charles, a couple who wed in Maryland in 1681.[51] He was a slave, the human property of a prominent white family, and she was an inden-

---

*Others have depicted Hemings differently. In his novel ARC D'X (1993), Steve Erickson casts her as the victim of brutal and repeated acts of rape.

tured servant, bound for a term of years to the third Lord Baltimore. According to witnesses, Lord Baltimore tried to dissuade Butler from going through with her wedding plans, mindful that under Maryland law, any white woman who married a slave not only became a slave herself for as long as her husband lived, but also bequeathed permanent servitude to her children.* But Butler refused to be deterred, supposedly exclaiming that she would rather marry and go to bed with Negro Charles than with Lord Baltimore himself.

Little is known about the marriage of Butler and Charles. While we have some sense of the ardor with which the bride-to-be embraced their impending union, and know that Butler and Charles would produce three or four children, the groom's feelings and voice are wholly absent from the record. Nevertheless, more is known about their relationship than about most intimacies between black men and white women in the age of slavery. After all, officially discouraged though it was, the Butler-Charles marriage did constitute an open, publicly recognized covenant. By contrast, many other couplings involving black men and white women were covert, illicit affairs.

Divorce proceedings also reveal interracial liaisons between white women and black men during the slavery era.[52] In 1806, for instance, after a year of marriage, a white man named William Howard discovered that his wife, Elizabeth, was engaged in "the most brutal and licentious connections, having no regard to persons of color." Howard claimed to have found his wife one evening "undressed and in bed" with Aldredge Evans, "a man of color." When she continued "to pursue her accustomed vicious and licentious course of life," he sought a divorce.[53] For the first years of their marriage, also in the early 1800s,

---

*After the marriage of Nell Butler and Negro Charles, the Maryland legislature changed the law relating to the status of free wives of slaves and their children. Revision of the law was instigated by the fact that it prompted some masters actually to force or encourage marriage between free women—often free *white* women—and enslaved men in order to increase the value of the masters' estates. The new law declared that if a marriage between a male slave and a "freeborn English or white woman" who was a servant had been coerced or even merely permitted by the woman's master, the woman was to be released from servitude and her children born free. See Martha Hodes, *White Women, Black Men: Illicit Sex in the Nineteenth-Century South* (1997), 29.

Elizabeth and John Dever seemed to be a rather typical young, white, happily married couple. That illusion was smashed, however, when Dever petitioned to divorce his wife on the ground that she "suckled at her breast an infant bearing the most certain marks of a colored father."[54] In 1823 an elderly white man named Lewis Bourne sought to divorce his young wife, Dorothea, whom he accused of associating with black men in their community. He further charged that she had been sexually intimate with at least one of them: Edmond, a neighbor's slave. Several witnesses confirmed Bourne's allegations, with one reporting that Dorothea kept "the company of negro slaves as often or perhaps oftener than any other company."[55] Bourne's brother testified that he had caught his sister-in-law in bed with her paramour; another man swore that the two lovers lived together "almost as man and wife."[56] A neighbor noted that Dorothea's children were "colored," and Edmond's owner asserted that his slave was definitely the father of her youngest child.[57] Dorothea Bourne had moved out of her husband's house and into a separate dwelling located on the far edge of his property, an arrangement that one neighbor believed Lewis Bourne had consented to so that his wife "might have it in her power to have uninterrupted intercourse" with Edmond.[58] A county sheriff had subsequently informed Bourne, however, that he would be legally and financially responsible for any children born to his wife, even if they were the product of an adulterous relationship. That information appears to have been what finally spurred the cuckold to seek a divorce.

Bourne and other white men like him often hesitated to turn to officials for marital relief. In some cases, the hesitancy seems to have sprung from a belief in the virtue and wisdom of forgiveness. Thus, Isaac Fouch wrote that even after catching his wife in bed with a free black man on several occasions, he had continued to hope "that she might yet be reclaimed"; it was only when that hope was repeatedly dashed that he petitioned for divorce.[59]* In other instances, embarrassment was the likely cause of reluctance, for a man who sought a divorce was essentially making a public confession that he had been unable to

---

*In Virginia, Richard Hall charged that his wife, Sarah, had begun a sexual relationship with a black man before their 1829 marriage and given birth to a racially mixed

manage his wife properly. And even more devastating to a white man's honor, of course, was admitting that his wife found a black man preferable to him as a sexual partner.[60]

Pursuing a divorce was a cumbersome, time-consuming, and expensive process.[61] In Virginia between 1803 and 1848, for example, a complete divorce on grounds of adultery could be granted only by the state legislature. The outcome, moreover, was uncertain even in cases that appeared strongly to favor the petitioner. Lewis Bourne's petition, for instance, was unsuccessful, perhaps because the Virginia assemblymen feared that Dorothea Bourne and her children would become public wards and thus a drain on taxpayers.* Permitting divorce was a matter of discretion, and the authorities empowered to sever marriages typically did so only in an exceedingly narrow range of circumstances, in which the petitioner was deemed faultless, the defendant egregiously wrong, and the marriage beyond repair. In the almost half-century for which the Virginia legislature handled divorce, an appreciable proportion of the divorce petitions filed—one researcher estimates 9 percent— included accusations of interracial adultery, the majority of them made by husbands against wives.[62] Of the 153 petitions *granted* during that period, twenty-seven (or just over 17 percent) contained such allegations.[63] Of the twenty-three men who cited interracial adultery in their petitions, sixteen (or just under 70 percent) were granted divorces.†

Over the state line, in North Carolina, the judicial responses to two

---

baby six months after their wedding. Yet it was not until 1838, after Sarah Hall had borne two more racially mixed children, that her husband sought to divorce her. See Joshua D. Rothman, "'To Be Freed from That Curse and Let at Liberty': Interracial Adultery and Divorce in Antebellum Virginia," *Virginia Magazine of History and Biography* 106 (1998): 443, 457.

*See Martha Hodes, *White Women, Black Men: Illicit Sex in the Nineteenth-Century South* (1997), 83.

†Some students of the subject maintain that "racism successfully and consistently overcame the law's powerful biases towards the promotion of matrimony" (Michael Grossberg, *Governing the Hearth: Law and the Family in Nineteenth-Century America* [1985], 126). More persuasive is the proposition that racial sentiment, albeit important, was only one of several influential factors that decision makers weighed. After all, as Joshua Rothman argues, if the racial factor had been as decisive as some insist, it would follow "that men leveling [well-supported accusations of interracial infidelity] would have received their divorces almost automatically" ("'To Be Freed

divorce petitions filed in 1832 shed some light on contemporary attitudes regarding interracial intimacy between white women and black men. Marville Scroggins claimed that he had been living "in uninterrupted harmony" with his wife, Lucretia, for nearly five months when her "infidelity and fraud . . . [were] manifested by an occurrence which admitted of neither explanation or palliation, and dissipated all hopes of happiness"[64]—in short, Lucretia Scroggins gave birth to what appeared to be a mulatto child. Marville Scroggins promptly petitioned for divorce. After a judge denied his petition, he appealed to the North Carolina Supreme Court. That court expressed sympathy for Scroggins in an opinion written by Justice Ruffin (author of the *Mann* decision discussed earlier in this chapter). The bench, Ruffin noted, was

> entirely sensible of the peculiar character of this case, produced by the odious circumstances of color. It appeals powerfully to the prejudices, the virtues, and vices of our nature. The stigma in our state of society is so indelible, the degradation so absolute, and the abhorrence of the community against the offender, and contempt for the husband so marked and inextinguishable, that the Court has not been able, without a struggle, to follow those rules which their dispassionate judgment sanctions.[65]

In the end, however, the justices unanimously agreed to uphold the lower court's decision to deny Scroggins's request for a divorce.

Ruffin maintained that it was in the best interests of the institution of marriage that couples understand that once they married, they would be unable to exit except under a very few narrow and closely policed circumstances. The state, Ruffin explained, permitted divorce only in the event of impotency that existed at the outset of the marriage and continued to persist afterward; in the event that one party deserted the marriage and lived in adultery outside of it; or in the event that the marriage violated prohibitions against incest. He believed that by making divorce virtually unattainable otherwise, the state encouraged people to be more thoughtful and prudent in their choice of a spouse *before* marriage, and more accepting *afterward* of a bond from which there was no escape. If the door to divorce was opened any wider, Ruffin feared that the parties to a marriage would expect too much of each other, become too unforgiving, and be too quick to call an end to a difficult relationship. Only by resolutely impressing upon couples the indissolubility of marriage could the courts and the state adequately impart to them "the necessity of mutual forbearance, of submitting to slight inconveniences, overcoming antipathies and contributing to the enjoyments of each other."[66] Echoing his assertion in *Mann* that slaves benefitted from a legal regime in which they possessed no legally enforceable rights against their masters, Ruffin now defended the general unavailability of divorce, arguing that, as humans, "we reconcile ourselves to what is inevitable. Experience finds pain more tolerable than it was expected to be; and habit makes even fetters light."[67] In marriage, he asked, "is it not wiser, better, kinder to the parties themselves and their issue . . . to make their union so intimate, so close, and so firm, that no discoveries of concealed defects . . . could rend it asunder?"[68] The lower court had been right to deny the petition, Ruffin declared, because mere concealment of prenuptial defects ought not to be permitted to serve as the predicate for undoing a marriage. Marville Scroggins claimed that his wife had defrauded him, and that her moral character and physical condition were not what he had believed them to be when he consented to marry her. Ruffin countered that in the context of marriage, at least, mere concealment did not rise to the level of fraud, for "it is not to be expected that the parties will declare their own defects . . . [or] publish their shame."[69] He was concerned about the potential consequences if dissatisfied spouses were permitted to obtain divorces on the ground that they had been duped during premarital courtship. If that claim were allowed in Scroggins's case, said Ruffin, then the *next* dissatisfied spouse could assert that *he* had consented to marry only because he was "young and inexperienced, hurried on by impetuous passion, or that he was in his dotage, and [that] advantage [was] taken of the lusts of his imagination, which were stronger than his understanding."[70] In sum, Ruffin intoned, "there is, in general, no safe rule but this: that persons who marry agree to take each other *as they are.*"[71]*

Soon after *Scroggins,* the North Carolina Supreme Court issued another opinion in a divorce case that likewise turned on an alleged interracial affair. Jesse Barden claimed that though he had known at the time of their marriage that his wife had previously given birth to a child, he had believed, based on her representations, that the child was his. He had subsequently discovered, however, that the child was *not* his but instead the issue of a black man. When a judge dismissed his petition for divorce, Barden sought appellate review. The outcome in the just-decided *Scroggins* might have suggested that this appeal stood little chance of succeeding; after all, the complaints were remarkably similar: in both, white husbands sought divorces on the ground of fraud after their white wives gave birth to children sired by black men. All of the arguments Ruffin had articulated to justify withholding a divorce from Marville Scroggins applied about equally well to the claim of Jesse Barden. The results, however, differed. In *Barden v. Barden,*[72] the North Carolina Supreme Court reversed the trial court's dismissal of the aggrieved husband's petition. The court instructed the trial judge to give the husband a chance to prove that his wife's child was of mixed blood; that he and his wife were both white; that he had believed at the time of his marriage that his wife's child was his; that such belief had been created by the misrepresentations of his wife; and that at the time of their marriage, the baby had not so obviously been the offspring of an African American man that a person of ordinary diligence and intelligence would have realized that the child was at least partly colored. If

---

*Ruffin added that the North Carolina judiciary had also been right to deny a divorce to Marville Scroggins on yet another, even narrower reading of the law. Scroggins said he had been deceived. But in Ruffin's view, the man had almost certainly been aware that his wife was not a virgin when he married her, for circumstances indicated that he himself had engaged in premarital sexual intercourse with her. That being so, Ruffin observed, Scroggins's disgrace had been "voluntarily incurred" because "he who marries a wanton, knowing her true character, submits himself to the lowest degradation." The court concluded that Marville Scroggins had been a "criminal accessary to his own dishonor, in marrying a woman he knew to be lewd." *Scroggins v. Scroggins,* 14 N.C. (3 Dev.) at 542, 546, 547.

the husband could prove all of these propositions, the court ruled, he was entitled to a divorce. Ruffin acceded to this decision, though only reluctantly: he voiced his own opinion that Barden should have been denied a divorce for the same reason as Scroggins. But he noted that his colleagues discerned a significant difference between the two cases: whereas Scroggins never alleged that he had married his wife in order to consecrate their premarital sex and to legitimate the baby she said was his, Barden did make those claims. Scroggins had wed his wife *before* she delivered and was thus viewed by the justices as having accepted the risk that her child had been sired by someone else. By contrast, Barden had waited to marry until *after* his fiancée delivered and *after* he saw the child. In the court's view, it would have been unfair to make Barden bear completely the risk that his fiancée was lying, inasmuch as he had given definite indications that he was willing to marry her only in the event that she gave birth to *his* child. Although Ruffin agreed to join the decision opening the door to a possible divorce, he stressed that under the court's ruling, it was by no means clear that after trial the husband would prevail.

*Free Blacks and Interracial Intimacy*    Interracial intimacy played a prominent role in the development of the free black community during the age of slavery. A substantial portion of that community was comprised of individuals who had been born to enslaved mothers and freed by their white fathers, or born to black fathers (slave or free) and free white mothers. For the most part, free colored people socialized among themselves or with slaves, but with some frequency they also found themselves entangled intimately with whites. This topic is in need of considerable excavation; our knowledge of it is spare and imprecise. A couple of controversies, however, offer at least a glimpse of some of what was happening in that era. In Montgomery County, Alabama, in 1847, an elderly free Negro named Girard Hansford filed for divorce from his wife, Maria George, the mixed-race daughter of a white woman, charging her with adultery. He had forgiven his young bride for previous sexual indiscretions, but he reached his breaking point when she admitted that her last child had been sired by a white man, and announced that she intended for any future children to be fathered by white men as well. To add insult to injury, the white man who had cuckolded Hansford attempted to support the child he had fathered. In making his case, Hansford explained to the court that "it would not do for [the] family to be raised in one part white and well-supported by their fathers and the other colored and poor."[73]

In Cambell County, Virginia, in 1816 Robert Wright, a slaveholding farmer, asked the General Assembly to grant him a divorce.[74]* He said that his wife, Mary Godsey, had committed adultery and deserted him by running off with another man. Godsey was white and Wright colored. One of the ironies of Robert Wright's predicament was that in petitioning the General Assembly to pass a statute granting him a divorce, he was seeking the dissolution of a marriage that, under existing law, should have been deemed illicit in the first place under Virginia's antimiscegenation statute. Far from trying to hide his racially mixed lineage, Wright proudly described himself in his petition as "a free man of color."[75] He plainly felt that he was entitled to the assembly's understanding and solicitude, as did at least fifty of his white neighbors, who endorsed his request for a divorce and attested to his good standing in their community. The interracial character of Wright's relationship with Godsey did have some effect on public reaction to their marriage. For one thing, the county clerk had never recorded it. Although no one can know for sure what accounts for the absent record, a knowledgeable observer has speculated that the minister who officiated may have destroyed the wedding certificate in an effort to insulate himself from legal liability in the event that the authorities decided to enforce the statute against interracial marriage.[76] Much more striking, though, is how accepting local whites apparently were, including Mary's mother, who expressly consented to the marriage of her underage daughter. There is, moreover, no evidence that anyone publicly objected at any point to Mary Godsey's marriage to Robert Wright.

Godsey was not the only white woman with whom Wright was intimate. After the General Assembly declined to grant him a divorce from

---

*Recall that we earlier encountered Thomas Wright, Robert's doting and slave-owning father; see page 47.

Godsey, he took up with another white woman, Polly Davidson. Whereas before none of Wright's white neighbors had complained about his domestic arrangement, the affair with Davidson brought forth expressions of disgruntlement; according to some witnesses, her status as Wright's "concubine" rendered her "notorious in the neighbourhood."[77] These objections, however, seemed to have stemmed not from the interracial character of their relationship but rather from its open flouting of norms prohibiting adultery. With virtual unanimity, the white community surrounding Robert Wright "behaved as if interracial marriage was normal and . . . the legislation prohibiting miscegenation in Virginia did not or should not exist."[78] By contrast, a substantial part of that same community openly disapproved of Wright's living with another woman while he was still married. To these neighbors, unlawful adultery mattered more than unlawful miscegenation.

A detailed description of the extent and character of interracial sexual intimacy in antebellum America must await further research. Especially needed are studies focusing on life in the North.[79] We do know enough, however, to state definitively that the consensual crossing of racial boundaries with respect to sex was more common than conventional historical understandings have suggested. Correcting such misunderstandings will require us to pay closer attention to the fact that legal formalities, while significant, do not always mirror social conduct. People married across the color line, for example, even when laws prohibited them from doing so. We will also have to jettison the habit of reading history backward, inscribing onto past eras subsequent developments. Given the militance with which white supremacists condemned sex between black men and white women in the late nineteenth century and throughout much of the twentieth, some have supposed that such violent antipathy must have been present earlier as well. There were jurisdictions in 1860, though, where an interracial couple stood a much better chance of raising a family together than would the same couple in the same place in 1910 or, for that matter, in 1950. In a fascinating study of free blacks in antebellum Alabama, Professor

Gary B. Mills uncovered eighty-three long-term interracial relationships, of which approximately half involved white women and free colored men. In none of these cases did he find evidence that any community action was taken against the couple. In a substantial number of cases, moreover, white husbands permitted their wives to keep mulatto children who had obviously been sired by colored paramours—children who subsequently appear to have been generally accepted into the white community.[80] These anecdotes do not change the overall fact that most whites heartily disapproved of interracial intimacy. That is precisely why the image of miscegenation became such a potent weapon of propaganda, widely used against persons or groups susceptible to being portrayed as friends of the Negro. As Leonard L. Richards has observed, "Throughout the ante-bellum period, anti-abolitionists repeated no charge with greater pertinacity than that of amalgamation, and none could more effectively stir up the rancor and the brutality of the mob."[81] It is important to keep in mind, however, that, as we have seen, interracial intimacy bloomed on occasion even in the era of slavery, and thus even in the least nurturing of soils.

TWO

# From Reconstruction to
# Guess Who's Coming to Dinner?

*From Emancipation to the Renewal of White Supremacy*
History crammed extraordinary change into the period between 1865 and 1900. Especially important were three key developments. The first was the abolition of slavery in the aftermath of the Civil War. Under slavery the sexual lives of the vast majority of blacks were under the direct control of white masters. Emancipation enabled former slaves to put some distance between themselves and whites. With their families now granted legal recognition, they struggled mightily to avoid situations in which black women would have to labor outside their own households under the supervision of white men. The result of this effort was a marked decline in both interracial sexual coercion and interracial intimacy.[1] The second significant development was Reconstruction, which heralded the emergence of federal statutory and constitutional laws stipulating that governments must treat all persons equally, regardless of their race. This radical notion meant that states could no longer lawfully bar people on a racial basis from testifying, owning property, entering into contracts, sitting on juries, voting, or holding office (though in practice, racial exclusions continued to flourish). In a few instances, reformers even succeeded in temporarily repealing or invalidating antimiscegenation laws. The third key development was the collapse of Reconstruction, after which Militant Negrophobia halted the movement toward racial equality.

During these pendulum swings, sexual and particularly marital intimacy remained primarily an intraracial affair, with whites seeking companionship with whites and blacks with blacks. Nevertheless, racially heterodox relationships, if rare, did exist. In the 1870s in Fort Mill, South Carolina, for instance, twenty-five to thirty white women lived with colored husbands.[2] In Georgia, the Halls—Carrie (a white woman) and Sandy (a black man)—were finally married. In a letter in 1867, pleading for assistance from the Freedman's Bureau, Carrie wrote that she was "very much attached to this colored gentleman" and that she wished "to choose him for [her] companion and husband through life," for "he was the only one on earth that [she] desired for a husband." The only thing that prevented them from being "one of the happiest couples in the world," she added, were the threats made against them by whites.[3] In Mississippi, an Ohio-born planter who would later become the sheriff of Yazoo County said to his brother, "Look me in the eye, ole polecat, I am anxious to see how you take it— there, steady now! . . . God willing, I am going to marry a 'nigger' schoolmarm."[4] In the same state, a former slave owner married his former slave mistress, insisting to an army chaplain that he had already "married her in the sight of God."[5]

The North, too, saw its share of black-white marriages. In his 1899 book *The Philadelphia Negro,* W. E. B. DuBois reported that he had identified thirty-three mixed marriages in a single Philadelphia ward and speculated that there might be as many as 150 in the city as a whole. The ever observant DuBois was able to wring some useful information from his small sample. He found that most of the mixed marriages were between black men and white women and that a striking number of these women were foreign-born.* He also found it to be untrue, at least in Philadelphia, that the only people drawn to interracial marriage were the lumpen proletariat or dregs of society, a claim often voiced by opponents of amalgamation. Rather, he discovered that

---

*Twenty-nine of the white spouses in the thirty-three mixed marriages were women. Fifteen of these had been born abroad: six in Ireland, three in England, two each in Scotland and Germany, and one each in Canada and Hungary. See W. E. B. DuBois, *The Philadelphia Negro: A Social Study* (1899), 361–63.

the bulk of mixed marriages involved members of the respectable "laboring classes, and especially . . . servants, where there is the most contact between the races."[6]

Little is known about these racially mixed couples—how they met, for example, or how they entertained; how family, friends, and strangers related to them; how they dealt with social ostracism; how they perceived one another and their common situation. A partial exception is the marriage of Frederick Douglass and Helen Pitts, which commenced on January 24, 1884, in Washington, D.C.[7] The bride was a forty-six-year-old white woman with deep roots in America; by lineage she was entitled to membership in the Colonial Dames of America and the Daughters of the American Revolution. A graduate of the Mount Holyoke Seminary and briefly a teacher at the Hampton Institute, Pitts was active in the women's rights movement. She and Douglass had known each other since the 1870s, when they were introduced by her uncle, his next-door neighbor; the friendship deepened after he hired her as his secretary during the period when he served as the recorder of deeds for the District of Columbia.

The marriage was Pitts's first and Douglass's second. His first wife, Anna Murray Douglass, was a free-born, dark-skinned African American woman who had helped him escape from bondage. Her death in 1882 ended a relationship that had lasted almost forty-four years and produced five children. At the time of his second marriage, the sixty-six-year-old Douglass was the most famous and respected African American in the nation. The founder and editor of the *North Star* newspaper, the author of three memoirs, and the deliverer of numerous oft-quoted speeches ("If there is no struggle, there is no progress"), Douglass had been a major voice of abolitionism, a stalwart friend of feminism, and a strong ally of Irish resistance to English rule.

The Douglass-Pitts marriage was controversial. Pitts's father, himself a committed abolitionist, refused to give it his blessing, and her brother would not have anything to do with the couple. Although the reason for the male Pittses' objection is not altogether clear, it seems likely that race played a primary role in their disapproval. Regarding other whites, however, such speculation is entirely unnecessary, as they made the racial cast of their opposition plain. A paper in Virginia, for example, called Douglass a "lecherous old African Solomon," and the marriage "a deliberate challenge to the Caucasian race."[8]

Members of Douglass's family also opposed the marriage. For one thing, whether it was a cause or a result of that antipathy, he kept secret from them his plans to wed. For another, they viewed his selection of a white woman for his second wife as a repudiation of his black kin.[9] That perception was shared by a substantial number of black Americans. The black journalist T. Thomas Fortune noted that "the colored ladies take [Douglass's marriage] as a slight, if not an insult, to their race and their beauty," and maintained that "big colored men, like big white men, owe some deference to the prejudices of the people they represent."[10] As Booker T. Washington explained in his biography of Douglass:

> The fact that his second wife . . . was a white woman caused something like a revulsion of feeling throughout the entire country. His own race especially condemned him, and the notion seemed to be quite general that he had made the most serious mistake of his life. Just how deep-seated was the sentiment of white and black people alike against amalgamation has never been so clearly demonstrated as in this case.[11]

A dispatch published in a black-owned newspaper aptly captures the tenor of the hurt: "Fred Douglass has married a red-head white girl. . . . Goodbye, black blood in that family. We have no further use for him. His picture hangs in our parlor, we will hang it in the stables."[12]*

Contributing to the vehemence of the outcry may have been the knowledge that Douglass had had a succession of white women confidantes with whom he was emotionally and probably also sexually intimate. One was the German-born journalist Ottilie Assing, who called

---

*Mary Church Terrell (1863–1954), a founder of the National Association of Colored Women, reported that due to the uproar over Douglass's marriage, she herself decided early in life that she would never marry a white man. See Mary Church Terrell, *A Colored Woman in a White World* (1940), 93.

herself Douglass's "natural wife." Assing had expected Douglass to marry her upon the expiration of a suitable interval following his first wife's death. When he married Pitts instead, Assing committed suicide.[13]

Douglass and Pitts resolutely defended their marriage.* "Love came to me," Helen Pitts later declared, "and I was not afraid to marry the man I loved because of his color."[14] For his part, Douglass scoffed at the protestations of whites who opposed interracial marriage on the basis of a professed wish to preserve racial purity. What they typically objected to, he observed, was "not a mixture of the races, but honorable marriage between them."[15] Douglass himself occasionally made light of the simplifications people resorted to when urging "whites" and "blacks" to stick to their "own." Highlighting the extent to which amalgamation had already become an irreversible fact of American life, he puckishly told one audience, "My first wife, you see, was the color of my mother, and my second wife the color of my father. . . . I wanted to be perfectly fair to both races."[16]

Emphasizing his independence from communal tyrannies in general, Douglass stressed that his own sense of self-respect precluded him from truckling to illegitimate demands, whatever the complexion of those making them. Writing to his old friend Elizabeth Cady Stanton,

---

*Francis J. Grimké, the presiding minister of the Fifteenth Street Presbyterian Church in Washington, D.C., married Douglass and Pitts and later justified their union in the pages of the *Journal of Negro History* ("The Second Marriage of Frederick Douglass," *Journal of Negro History* 19 [1934]: 324). Like Douglas, Grimké was the son of an enslaved black woman and a white man, in this case Henry Grimké, a lawyer and businessman. Grimké acknowledged Francis and the two other sons he sired by his slave mistress. (Two of Henry's sisters, Angelina and Sarah, had long been leading figures in the national abolitionist movement.) In his will, Henry Grimké directed his white son, Montague Grimké, to care generously for his colored half brothers. Despite the fact that Montague ignored this instruction, putting the boys to work in his own household and sending the law after one of them when he ran away, two of the colored Grimké brothers eventually managed to attain elite status in American society. Francis graduated from the Princeton Theological Seminary and went on to preside over one of the country's most well-established black congregations; Archibald attended Harvard Law School and became a successful attorney. Both men actively supported the National Association for the Advancement of Colored People. See Gerda Lerner, *The Grimké Sisters from South Carolina: Rebels Against Slavery* (1967), 358–66.

he explained, "I would never have been at peace with my own soul or held up my head among men had I allowed the fear of popular clamor to deter me from following my convictions as to this marriage. I should have gone to my grave a self-accused and a self-convicted moral coward."[17]

Even as Douglass and Pitts exercised their prerogatives within the relatively safe confines of Washington, D.C., white racists elsewhere were rolling back many of the achievements won during Reconstruction.[18] The ascendancy of racial reactionaries led to the exclusion of African Americans from voting, jury service, or any other form of participation in governance. Businesses and unions kept blacks out of "white" jobs and relegated them to the lowest-paying, least prestigious, and most menial positions—so-called Negro jobs. Segregation laws separated whites from blacks in schools, in hospitals, in cemeteries, in taxis, in telephone booths, at water fountains, in lavatories, at restaurants, and in hotels. In some courthouses, authorities insisted that blacks and whites use different Bibles for the taking of oaths. Whites entered the homes of blacks by the front door, but blacks were expected to use the back door at white people's houses. Blacks were supposed to show whites deference when speaking to them, by calling them "Mr." or "Mrs." or "Miss"; whites, by contrast, were expected to address blacks casually or by their first names or as "boy" or "girl," regardless of their age or station. White men frequently resorted to extralegal violence to enforce Jim Crow etiquette, especially the unwritten rule that black men must take care to avoid white women. The most lethal of the terroristic weapons used against blacks was lynching, a phenomenon we will examine later.*

Reconstruction's egalitarian spirit had posed challenges to antimiscegenation laws, but these challenges were typically short-lived. South Carolina's history is instructive in this regard. Prior to the Civil War, the state had declined to prohibit interracial marriage, but immediately following the abolition of slavery, white authorities enacted an antimiscegenation statute. Reformers removed this barrier in 1868, only to see it

---

*See pages 192–95.

be reenacted in 1879.* In 1895 white supremacists embedded the prohibition in the state constitution, where it remained for 103 years.

In spite of Reconstruction, the racialized sexual hierarchy of the antebellum era soon reasserted itself, albeit on a much diminished scale. White men continued to enjoy privileged access to black women, as Jim Crow custom generally permitted such pairings not only for sexual purposes but also as the nucleus of stable, family-like relationships. According to journalist Ray Stannard Baker, "White men in many communities, often prominent judges, governors, wealthy planters, made little or no secret of the fact that they had a negro family as well as a white family."[19] White society required, however, that white men refrain from formally acknowledging these connections or displaying openly any serious, sentimental interracial attachment. While relations between white men and black women could be approved of, or at least tolerated, as sexual exercise or comic diversion, a white man faced sanctions if he revealed genuine feeling for a black lover or children. Making this point, the authors of the anthropological study *Deep South* (1941) repeated a story told to them in the 1930s in Natchez, Mississippi. When the house of a white man's Negro mistress caught on fire, the man was among the crowd that gathered to watch.

> His wife was standing right beside him but I guess he didn't know or didn't care. Anyway he broke through the crowd and called out, "Let me in to save my children!" He went into the house and came out with all those little black children. Well, his wife just left him; she never went back to him. He had grown-up white children too. Nobody had anything to do with him after that.[20]

---

*The same dynamic led to revisions of existing antimiscegenation laws in Alabama and Mississippi. Alabama changed its laws to render all interracial marriages null and void, while Mississippi increased the punishment for the violation of its prohibition on interracial marriage: persons engaging in such unions, the state declared, could be confined to the penitentiary for life. See Alabama Constitution of 1865, art. 4, sec. 31; Miss. Session Laws ch. 4, sec. 3 (1865). See also Peter W. Bardaglio, *Reconstructing the Household: Families, Sex, and the Law in the Nineteenth-Century South* (1995), 179.

Professor John Dollard has theorized that the opprobrium visited upon such revelations likely resulted in the camouflaging of loving attachments. Describing the intersection of race and sex in Indianola, Mississippi, in 1935–36, Dollard observed that "the dehumanization of sexuality is often only official; warm and lasting personal relationships occur behind the facade. Social pressure tends to force any genuine love affair between white man and Negro woman under ground, since being lovers openly would tend to legitimate their relationship and would thus challenge caste arrangements."[21] Reliable evidence in support of this formulation is scant, but here and there records survive of words or deeds that did seem to suggest that real affection could persist even as couples accommodated a regime that made the forthright display of interracial love a shocking provocation. The authors of *Deep South* quoted a black source, the longtime mistress of a white man, as saying, "I love Jim's daddy [her son's white father], 'n Jim's daddy loves me. Nothing else matters. We were boy and girl sweethearts 'n we're sweethearts today. So the rest of the world can just go by. . . . I feel I'm living a great deal more decently with a union based on love than some who are married before the law."[22]

The annals of litigation reveal other instances of forbidden intimacies. In one 1944 case, a white man named Ben Watts had decided that he wanted to leave his estate to his black housekeeper and sexual partner, Nazarine Parker.[23] He directed his attorney to prepare a will that would accomplish this, warning that his relatives would surely attack the validity of the bequest after his death. As predicted, Watts's relatives did contest his will. They argued that Parker had exercised undue influence over him and that his will therefore failed to reflect his true wishes.* Disputing that charge, Watts's executor testified that his client

---

*In *Smith v. DuBose,* 78 Ga. 413 (1887), the white relatives of David Dickson attempted to prevent his massive estate, one of the richest in Georgia, from passing by bequest into the hands of Amanda Dickson, his illegitimate daughter by a slave (see page 46). They claimed, among other things, that Amanda and her mother had exercised undue influence over David Dickson and had also defrauded him. The relatives lost. The former slave and her children, themselves all fathered by white men, thereby obtained control of an estate valued at half a million dollars. See Kent

"was a man of very sound mind," "a man of strong determination,"[24] a man who could not be easily swayed from his judgment. As to his motive for wanting to bequeath his estate to Parker, the executor reported that Watts had said, "I want to leave what I have for this Negro woman that has been taking care of me all the time. . . . All my own people have ever done for me was to borrow money and never pay it back."[25] A jury nevertheless found in favor of Watts's relatives. One justice of the Alabama Supreme Court agreed with this outcome, maintaining that the jurors had been within their authority in concluding that Watts's bequest had arisen from an impaired mental or emotional state. Justice Bouldin asserted that what he assumed to be the sexual relationship between Watts and his housekeeper constituted "a continuous felony" under state law, one that deprived the deceased of "respect on the part of friends and neighbors of his own race"[26] and subjected his blood relatives to humiliation. Bouldin's opinion even went so far as to insinuate that Watts's apprehension of these adverse consequences had perhaps driven him over the edge, adding that in any event, there existed sufficient evidence to permit a jury to credit this theory if it so chose.

A majority of the justices, however, disagreed with their colleague. They reversed the jury's disposition of the case and insisted that further proceedings be initiated, giving Parker another chance at receiving the inheritance Watts had wanted her to have. The justices in the majority went out of their way to condemn the relationship. "It is reprehensible enough," they declared, "for a white man to live in adultery with a white woman, thus defying the laws of both God and man, but it is

---

Anderson Leslie, *Woman of Color, Daughter of Privilege: Amanda America Dickson, 1849–1893* (1995), 919–25.

There are several other cases on record in which disappointed whites likewise claimed that only insanity, undue influence, or fraud could possibly account for the decision of their white relatives to favor people of color in their wills. As in Ben Watts's case, such claims were often rejected by the courts. See, e.g., *Jolliffe v. Fanning & Phillips*, 44 S.C.L. (10 Rich.) 186 (1856); *Farr v. Thompson*, 25 S.C.L. (Chev.) 37 (1839). See also Adrienne D. Davis, "The Private Law of Race and Sex: An Antebellum Perspective," *Stanford Law Review* 51 (1999): 221, 261–326.

more so, and a much lower grade of depravity, for a white man to live in adultery with a Negro woman."[27] They also took pains to express sympathy for Watts's disinherited family; according to the court, one contributing factor in Watts's posthumous rejection of his relatives had been their criticism of what the justices described as his "disgraceful way of life."[28] But in the end, the court majority found it impossible to believe that Watts had lacked adequate capacity to convey his true desires. The deceased, they concluded,

> chose the evil way. But whatever may be said in condemnation of his manner of life, and however disgraceful and reprehensible it may have been, the courts must not lose sight of the fact that his accumulated estate . . . was his own; and it is clearly shown from this record, beyond the peradventure of a doubt, that he wanted this estate to go to Nazarine Parker.[29]

The Alabama Supreme Court abhorred the fact that Ben Watts had carried on an apparently affectionate sexual relationship with his black housekeeper for many years in violation of state law. Even more abhorrent to it, however, was the prospect of courts failing to effectuate the prerogatives of property owners.

*The Case of Jack Johnson*   In Jim Crow America, those who crossed the race line in matrimony typically worked hard to keep their heads down, anxious to avoid unwanted attention even in locales where interracial unions were lawful. One very conspicuous exception to this rule was John Arthur Johnson, better known as Jack Johnson.[30] No individual in American history has created more commotion through his choice of marital partners. This effect stemmed in part from Johnson's unique status as the first black professional heavyweight boxing champion.* Even more upsetting to some observers than his dominance in

---

*Johnson won the title in 1908. Promoters scoured the country for a "great white hope" who could beat him, and finally succeeded in coaxing Jim Jeffries, a former heavyweight champion, out of retirement for one last fight. The Johnson-Jeffries bout, on July 4, 1910, began with a rendition of "All Coons Look Alike to Me," but

the ring, however, were his exploits outside it. A remarkable pugilist, he was also a redoubtable sexual athlete who surrounded himself with professional sexpots, many of whom were white. He preferred white women, explaining late in life, "I could love a colored woman, but they never give me anything. Colored women don't play up to a man the way white girls do. No matter how colored women feel towards a man, they don't spoil him and pamper him and build up his ego. They don't try to make him feel like he's somebody."[31]

Although Johnson treated all of his sexual conquests shabbily, race had an undeniable impact—in certain ways a negative one—on his behavior toward his white paramours. "If there was love in his attitude toward white women," one biographer has observed, "there was also hate": "Capable of tenderness at one moment, he could be mean and cruel at the next. . . . He gave expensive gifts, then took them back. He made love to his white women, but he also beat them up. At once, he wished to elevate and defile them."[32] Johnson thrice married white women. He met Etta Terry Duryea at a racetrack in 1909 and began living with her soon after. That arrangement by no means gave Duryea a monopoly on Johnson's amorous attention, however. When he traveled, he frequently took along one or two experienced prostitutes in addition to his live-in mistress. Although the other women generally stayed in different hotels than the couple, Duryea periodically encountered them, and such incidents served only to vex further an already troubled relationship. Beyond his philandering, Johnson also beat Duryea, once so badly that she had to be hospitalized. Still, she married him, though she had no reason to believe that such a contract would substantially change his conduct. Two years into the marriage, she killed herself. Although the precise reasons for her suicide are unclear, it is likely that alongside the abuse she suffered at her husband's hands, a sense of isolation contributed to her despondency. "I am a white woman and tired of being a social outcast," she reportedly told a maid.

---

it ended in another victory for Johnson. The champion was ultimately defeated in 1915 in a bout that many have suspected was fixed. See Randy Roberts, *Papa Jack: Jack Johnson and the Era of White Hopes* (1983), 109.

"All my misery comes through marrying a black man. Even the negroes don't respect me. They hate me."[33]

Soon after Duryea's death, a concatenation of events turned Johnson into what Professor Kevin Mumford has described as "the central sexual and racial scapegoat of his era."[34] His wife's suicide put him on the defensive. One white editorialist commented that it showed "how sharp is the line that runs between the races" and how "limited was Jack Johnson's so-called 'conquest of the white race.' He whipped competitors in the prize ring . . . but he could not extend the conquest to those achievements that lie in the province of sentiment and affection."[35] The notoriety attendant on this tragedy would pale, though, in comparison with what was soon to follow: a federal prosecution for sexual immorality, in a case closely intertwined with Johnson's second marriage to a white woman.

After Duryea died, Johnson began to keep company on a regular basis with one Lucille Cameron. Although only eighteen when she was introduced to the boxer at his saloon, the Café de Champion, Cameron was already an experienced prostitute. She had worked at a brothel in Minnesota before relocating to Chicago, where she met Johnson through the good offices of two other "sporting women." Soon she became his primary (but by no means exclusive) sexual partner, an ornament that he pointed to in support of his claim that given his prominence, money, and appeal, he could "get" all the white women he wanted. Unsurprisingly, antagonists who resented his behavior sought revenge. One of them was Cameron's mother, who accused Johnson of having criminally abducted her daughter. Pursuant to her complaint, the federal government arrested him for violating a federal statute—the White Slavery Act of 1910, also known as the Mann Act—prohibiting the transportation of a woman or girl across state lines for purposes of prostitution. Under ordinary circumstances, the federal government would not have sought to imprison a man simply for hiring a prostitute. But this was no ordinary case. This was the case of a highly publicized black man who had already made himself obnoxious to many whites, not only by becoming successful but by openly consorting with a virtual harem of white women.

Despite the government's best efforts, Cameron never appeared as its star witness against her lover. Authorities jailed her to keep her isolated while she testified before a grand jury, but on her release, she returned to Johnson, who in short order married her. Whether he did so merely to keep her from talking or for other, more sentimental reasons is unknown. In either case it did not solve his legal problems, for even before the marriage eliminated its principal witness, the government had already mobilized a desperate search for other women who might testify against him. The prosecutors found several such, the most damning of them being yet another white prostitute, named Belle Schreiber. Her testimony was especially damaging insofar as it was both unusually detailed (she proffered the exact dates when and places where she had had sex with Johnson across the country) and sensationally lurid, portraying a promiscuous sexuality that flew in the face of the racial and sexual conventions of the era. When Schreiber mentioned that she had become pregnant by Johnson, her casual tone indicated that for her, "pregnancy was merely an occupational hazard, much like a cut eye for a boxer."[36]* The only part of her testimony that was directly relevant to the charges against Johnson was her claim that he had paid for her to travel from Pittsburgh to Chicago, where she had set herself up in an apartment to sell sex. Apparently that was enough for the jury of twelve white, male, churchgoing midwesterners, several of whom had openly expressed a dislike for Negroes; they voted to convict.

There was tremendous fallout from the case. Johnson himself would eventually serve a one-year prison term (after having fled the country to avoid incarceration). For many blacks, it was yet another instance of white racism bringing down a strong black man who refused to kowtow to insulting conventions. Others, however, saw Johnson as a disreputable, irresponsible, dangerous embarrassment.

---

*Johnson had met Schreiber at the Everleigh Club, a prestigious brothel in Chicago. Unable to buy her services there because the club's owners rigorously enforced a color bar, Johnson had enticed her and two of her colleagues to join him and an associate at a nearby hotel. Later at least nine prostitutes at the club were dismissed for having sexual relations with Johnson; four of them would testify against him. Randy Roberts, *Papa Jack* (1983), 72–73.

Particularly objectionable to these blacks was the boxer's obvious hankering for white women—and prostitutes, at that—which they saw as a sign of deficient racial pride rather than heroic defiance. After Johnson's arrest on charges of violating the Mann Act, the black-run Philadelphia *Tribune* published a headline that read: JACK JOHNSON, DANGEROUSLY ILL, VICTIM OF WHITE FEVER.[37] Around the same time, a black writer for the Birmingham *Exchange* asserted that every "race-loving Negro . . . must indefatigably denounce Johnson's debased allegiance with the other race's women."[38]

Almost without exception, whites who participated in the discussion denounced Johnson. A sportswriter for the *Police Gazette* branded him as "the vilest, most despicable creature that lives. . . . He has disgusted the American public by flaunting in their faces an alliance as bold as it was offensive."[39] An editorialist for the *Beaumont* (Texas) *Journal* suggested that his "obnoxious stunts . . . are not only worthy of but demand an overgrown dose of Southern 'hospitality'"[40]—by which he meant, of course, lynching. The governor of Virginia called Johnson's matrimonial history "a desecration of one of our most sacred rites."[41] The governor of New York attacked it as "a blot on our civilization."[42] The governor of South Carolina plaintively asked, "If we cannot protect our white women from black fiends, where is our boasted civilization?"[43]

Other politicians also got into the act, offering concrete political proposals as well as heated rhetoric. Representative Seaborn A. Roddenberry of Georgia proposed a constitutional amendment stipulating that marriage between "persons of color and Caucasians . . . [be] forever prohibited."[44] In making his argument, Roddenberry articulated the racial views then dominant in the white South. He lauded his home region's solution to "the negro problem," noting that where he came from, relations between the races were such that

> no African within all of Dixie land carries in his heart the hope
> or cherishes in his mind the aspiration that he can ever lead
> there to the altar of matrimony a woman of Caucasian blood.
> With all the impositions we are alleged to have placed upon this
> inferior race, such is our harmony, such is the fellowship

between the blacks and the whites of the South, such is the
black's respect for the superiority of his former master, that [he]
would commit self-destruction before [he] would entertain the
thought of matrimony with a white girl beneath southern
skies.[45]

By contrast, Roddenberry charged, race relations in the North had
reached a perilous pass, epitomized by the harrowing reality that in certain states the law permitted "a white girl of this country [to be] made
the slave of an African brute . . . by the form of a marriage ceremony."[46] Such authorization was terrible for whites, the congressman
declared, because it made them vulnerable to an infusion of "kinky-
headed blood." "Let this condition go on if you will," he warned. "At
some day, perhaps remote, it will be a question always whether or not
the solemnizing of matrimony in the North is between two descendants
of our Anglo-Saxon fathers and mothers or whether it be of a mixed
blood descended from the orang-utan trodden shores of far-off
Africa."[47] The lack of interdiction against intermarriage in the North
was bad for blacks as well, he argued, because such matches would succeed only in tempting them to take liberties that would prompt a justifiably brutal response. In Roddenberry's words:

> We can do no greater violence, we can offer no more ill-fated
> injustice, to the negro in this land than to let our statutes permit
> him to entertain the hope that at some future time he or his off-
> spring, or she or her offspring, may be married to a woman or a
> man of the white race. It will bring conflicts in the coming
> years—black, dark, gruesome, and bloody. . . . This slavery of
> white women to black beasts will bring this Nation to a conflict
> as fatal and as bloody as ever reddened the soil of Virginia or
> crimsoned the mountain paths of Pennsylvania.[48]

It was "repulsive and averse to every sentiment of pure American
spirit, . . . abhorrent and repugnant to the very principles of a pure
Saxon government," and "destructive of moral supremacy" to permit

by law "the sombre-hued, black-skinned, thick-lipped, bull-necked, brutal-hearted African" to wed a white woman, Roddenberry insisted. He therefore urged his colleagues to "uproot and exterminate now this debasing, ultrademoralizing, un-American, and inhuman leprosy."[49]

"There is no racial antipathy in this,"[50] Roddenberry assured his audience on the floor of the United States House of Representatives. Rather, it was the simple truth that

> no blacker incubus ever fixed its slimy claws upon the social body of this Republic than the embryonic cancer of Negro marriage to white women in certain parts of our country. . . . No more voracious parasite ever sucked at the heart of pure society, innocent girlhood, or Caucasian motherhood than the one which welcomes and recognizes the sacred ties of wedlock between Africa and America.[51]

This last bit of rhetoric drew a round of applause.

### Interracial Intimacy During the Decline of Jim Crow

Between 1920 and 1950, white public opinion continued overwhelmingly to oppose interracial marriage. Gunnar Myrdal found that among white southerners, the proscription against interracial marriage and sexual intercourse constituted the racial discrimination of greatest importance, and thus the one most in need of defense. According to Mydral, "even a [white] liberal-minded Northerner of cosmopolitan culture and with a minimum of conventional blinds will, in nine cases out of ten, express a definite feeling against amalgamation."[52]

An important exception to this rule was the anomalous microcosm that was the Communist party. Like virtually all other predominantly white institutions, the Democratic and Republican parties ostracized Negroes. By contrast, the Communist party devoted a sizable portion of its resources to the active recruitment of Negro members.[53] Within the party, too, blacks were frequently treated with a respect that was notably lacking elsewhere; in 1932, for example, James W. Ford, a Negro, was the Communists' nominee for the vice presidency of the

United States. In terms of sheer numbers, the U.S. Communist party was always quite small, counting a mere 27,000 members in 1935, of whom approximately 11 percent were black. In that 1932 election, the Communist ticket of William Foster (running for president) and James Ford garnered just 102,221 votes, in contrast to the 883,990 votes tallied by the Socialist party and the millions more cast for the Democratic and Republican candidates.[54] The influence of the Communist party, however, far exceeded its tiny official membership. In large measure because of its attractiveness to certain high-profile intellectuals, artists, unionists, and politicians, the party and its suppression had a wide-ranging impact.

In practice, the Communist party's rhetorical egalitarianism often ran up against stubborn racial biases within its own ranks. The party was, moreover, quite willing to subordinate the struggle for racial justice to other perceived imperatives when its leaders, taking their orders from Joseph Stalin, so directed. Still, as even its harsher critics have conceded, the Communist party was singular in its outreach to blacks.[55] Some Communists were eager to display interracial affection as a way of proving the purity of their ideological allegiance to the class struggle. It was this impulse, in part, that prompted one observer to note that white women Communists in particular "went out of their way to demonstrate how serious the Party was in eliminating . . . barriers between the two races."[56] Some commentators have even insisted that the Communists consciously deployed white women as "bait" to attract black men. Whether and to what extent such charges reflected anti-Communist animus, antimiscegenation sentiment, and/or reality remains unclear. What we *do* know is that a substantial proportion of the minuscule cadre of blacks prominent within Communist party circles (typically men) married across racial lines.[57] (Examples include James Ford, William Patterson, Benjamin Davis Jr., Harry Haywood, Henry Winston, and Abner Berry.)[58] Some black female comrades protested, and a group in Harlem even went so far as to request that party leaders henceforth ban interracial marriage. Although that petition was denied, officials did respond in a fashion that revealed the remarkable nature of the party's engagement with problems posed by multiracial organizing.

To encourage fraternization between white men and black women at party social affairs in Harlem, organizers offered dancing lessons to the men so they would feel comfortable on the dance floor.[59]*

Other sectors of the Left also boasted an appreciable number of black-white interracial couples. Ewart and Eugenia Guinier were just one notable example. As a black labor leader and political activist in New York City, Guinier was friendly with the Communist movement; later he would be appointed the first head of Afro-American Studies at Harvard University. Lani Guinier, his daughter, would be a prominent civil rights attorney before becoming the first tenured black woman on the faculty of Harvard Law School.[60] Richard Wright, the author of *Black Boy* (1937) and *Native Son* (1940), was first a Communist and later an anti-Communist Socialist. In 1945 a black woman wrote Wright a letter chastising him for marrying a white woman. In his journal he responded, "I did not marry a white woman. I married the woman I loved. . . . I live but once on this earth and I'll be damned if I'll live according to some narrow and crazy race doctrine."[61]† Conrad Lynn, a black attorney, broke with the Communist party but remained on the Left. In his autobiography, Lynn recounts how he once proposed to a white woman whose father then solemnly promised to kill him in the event of a marriage; with that, the two "decided to remain boyfriend and girlfriend." Lynn subsequently asked another white woman to marry him, whereupon *her* stricken parents sent her off to

---

*Professor Mark Naison writes that interracial sexual intimacies and tensions within the Communist movement in Harlem gave rise to an array of jokes, with some black comrades speaking of the "ass struggle replacing the class struggle" (*Communists in Harlem During the Depression* [1983], 281).

Lampooning "the breakdown of Communism among [Negroes]," Roi Ottley wrote that "the bait is beat. . . . The Ofay [white] gals are very seedy, frowsy and sad-looking. . . . The Emancipated Mose [Negro man], when he goes adventuring for a wife, is seeking a woman who has, along with other things, pulchritude" (*Amsterdam News,* September 15, 1934).

†Before he married Ellen Poplowitz, Wright had proposed to two black women. The first refused his overture, and he broke off the engagement to the second when he learned, upon applying for a marriage license with her, that she suffered from congenital syphilis. See Hazel Rowley, *Richard Wright: The Life and Times* (2001).

Scotland to distance her from him. Upon her return, however, she and Lynn were wed.[62]

To most white Americans, interracial marriage was a bizarre heresy that generated both curiosity and abhorrence. In a 1958 Gallup poll—the first in which Gallup gauged public opinion regarding interracial marriage—only 4 percent of whites questioned approved of marriage between blacks and whites. In the South, 99 percent of whites disapproved.[63] Elaborating on the character, function, and consequences of popular repugnance with regard to black-white intermarriage, Gunnar Myrdal maintained that it served to define "the Negro group in contradistinction to all in the non-colored minority groups in America and all other lower class groups."[64] For the stalwart opponent of intermarriage, Myrdal observed,

> the boundary between Negro and white is not simply a class line which can be successfully crossed by education, integration into the national culture, and individual economic advancement. The boundary is fixed. It is not a temporary expediency during an apprenticeship in the national culture. It is a bar erected with the intention of permanency.[65]

Confirming Myrdal's formulation, Professor Paul R. Spickard has noted that the "bulk of White Americans were just as horrified at the thought of interracial marriage in 1950 as they had been in 1900 or 1850."[66] Statutes in thirty states punished those who married across racial lines, and even the U.S. government, while it never enacted a federal antimiscegenation law, discouraged the practice as a matter of policy. During and immediately after World War II, commanding officers in the armed services routinely denied black servicemen permission to marry white girlfriends abroad.* In one instance, a black member of

---

*Henry Stimson, President Franklin Roosevelt's secretary of war, supported the continued segregation of the armed forces and confided to his diary that in his view, "certain radical leaders of the colored race" were using the war crisis to obtain "race equality and interracial marriages" (Stimson diary entry for June 24, 1943, quoted in Richard M. Dalfiume, "The 'Forgotten Years' of the Negro Revolution," *Journal of American History* 55 [1968]: 90, 106). On the panic that overtook some white

the U.S. Air Force sought, with her parents' consent, to marry his white English sweetheart, who was pregnant with his child. His request was initially granted by his immediate superiors, then subsequently denied by higher authorities.[67] On appeal, the air force bureaucracy refused to budge, informing the petitioner that "the policy of this headquarters regarding mixed marriages has not been changed. Such marriages are considered to be against the best interests of the parties concerned and of the service."[68] Nor was this the only means the military used to quash mixed marriages. Black soldiers who applied for permission to marry white women were often sent far away from their units, confined to base, or assigned extra duties in an effort by the brass to preclude or at least discourage any continuation of "troublesome" relationships.*

Of the unofficial pressures brought to bear on interracial intimacies, perhaps the most powerful was the prospect of disappointing or angering parents, siblings, and other relatives. Many students of race relations support Joseph Golden's assertion that, in the absence of governmental prohibition, it is "the family which, more than other institutions, assumes the responsibility for preventing miscegenation."[69] In some cases in which fear of familial disapproval was insufficient to prevent such a marriage, it was nonetheless sufficient to cause the parties to keep their marriage a secret. One white woman who had secretly married a Negro faced a crisis on the death of her mother: she wanted to attend the funeral with her husband, yet not divulge the interracial character of her marriage to her other relatives. She "solved" the problem by persuading her husband to pose as her chauffeur.[70] Others sim-

---

officials in England and the United States at the thought of sexual relations occurring between white English women and Negro American soldiers during World War II, see Graham Smith, *When Jim Crow Met John Bull: Black American Soldiers in World War II Britain* (1987).

*In the 1950s, when they returned to the United States from tours of duty abroad, black servicemen who had married white European women were transferred from military units stationed in jurisdictions that prohibited interracial marriages. See *U.S. News and World Report,* October 11, 1957, p. 110.

In 1965 the comptroller general's office refused military death benefits to the black wife of a deceased white soldier because they had been wed in a state that prohibited interracial marriage. See David E. Seidelson, "Miscegenation Statutes and the Supreme Court," *Catholic University Law Review* 15 (1966): 156, 157.

ply dropped out of the lives of their kinfolk and former friends. In Chicago, in 1940, a white woman broke off all communication with her family; they would not see her again for another thirty years, though they lived in the same city. She had married a black man and, fearful of her relatives' reaction, vanished from their world: "I'd much rather they didn't know where I am than know the truth," she said.[71] Those who did reveal their interracial engagements, marriages, and pregnancies often had to face parents who would plead with, cajole, entice, or threaten them, or take whatever other action might seem likely to undo what they perceived to be a looming tragedy. When the writer Hettie Jones informed her parents that she had married a black man (LeRoi Jones, now known as Amiri Baraka) and was pregnant by him, her father volunteered to accompany her to Mexico so she could get a quick divorce and an abortion. When she declined his offer (really a demand), he tearfully told her never to call him or her mother again.[72]* A recurrent theme in the accounts of white women involved in interracial unions consisted in the tendency of their parents, relatives, and friends to behave as if weddings were really funerals.[73] Often, opposition to interracial marriages stemmed from sheer prejudice. Sometimes it was based on apprehension that news of a child's racial deviancy would damage the social standing of the entire family. Some parents also objected out of concern that their beloved sons or daughters were imprudently pursuing relationships that would only bring them grief. Inasmuch as racial prejudice against blacks constituted a heavy burden, many white parents sought to dissuade their children from attaching themselves to partners who would weigh them down with that load. Such fears were well founded. Opportunities for employment, housing, and public accommodations were routinely closed even to the white partners in interracial relationships. E. W. Crutchfield, for example, lost her job as a cashier after her boss discovered that she was

---

*Hettie Jones also relates that immediately after her wedding, she, her husband, and another couple—two of their closest friends—pooled their money to rent an apartment together. After a large deposit had been put down on a place, the parents of one of those friends paid the couple *not* to move in with Jones and her husband. See Hettie Jones, *How I Became Hettie Jones* (1990), 64. For more on the Jones family, see pages 112–14.

married to a Negro. Louise Woods was dismissed from her position in a drugstore when her interracial marriage was found out. And Dorothy Garrett was fired from her job as a garment-factory supervisor after she was seen at a baseball game with her black spouse.[74] To avoid trouble, partners in interracial marriages often assumed as low a profile as possible, which meant eschewing large public weddings and announcements, strictly separating home life from work life, and engaging in various sorts of "passing." Traveling through Wyoming, one couple, Scipio and Virginia Highbaugh, stopped at a motel for the night, asked for a room, and were told that while Mrs. Highbaugh would be welcome, her driver would have to sleep in the car.[75] Because of that and other, similar incidents, Mrs. Highbaugh admitted, she and her husband "just don't go places. Before we go out to eat or to drive anywhere, we always ask ourselves—is there a possibility we'll be turned down?"[76]

Discouraging, too, was the hostility shown by police. In the recollections of interracial couples, episodes of police harassment—almost always involving white officers—abounded. Bitterest of all were memories of policemen treating as prostitutes the women partners in interracial couples. Writing in the early 1960s, one Elaine Neil reported that when she and her black husband moved into an apartment house in New York City against the wishes of its white residents, angry neighbors retaliated by telling the police that the couple were running a drug and prostitution ring, a charge that eventually led to a prosecution (though not a conviction) despite an absence of substantial evidence.[77] On Coney Island, a white man walking with his black wife was set upon by a gang of white thugs. When the wife ran to the police for help, they accused her of being a prostitute and refused to provide any assistance.[78] In 1962, in San Francisco, police harassed Melba Pattillo and her white husband.* According to Pattillo, the first thing one of the officers said to her husband was, "Where'd you pick up this nigger whore[?]"[79] When her husband objected and noted that he himself was

---

*Pattillo was one of the nine blacks who, as teenagers in the fall of 1958, had desegregated Central High School in Little Rock, Arkansas—one of the most dramatic moments of the Civil Rights Revolution. See Melba Pattillo Beals, *White Is a State of Mind: A Memoir* (1999).

a military policeman, the officer merely redoubled his racist taunting: "You're a cop and you're popping this nigger bitch? You ought to be ashamed of yourself, son."[80] Is it any wonder that the white spouse of a Negro husband remarked, "I feel like an innocent criminal"?[81]

### Interracial Intimacy Onstage, in Film, and Through Music

Popular culture has been another domain in which authorities have sought to enforce customary prohibitions against interracial intimacy. In an effort to make *Othello* palatable to white Americans, for example, producers, directors, and actors have repeatedly altered characterizations, costuming, makeup, and even dialogue. In the eighteenth century, white actors in the title role wore black makeup. This practice bothered some patrons, among them Abigail Adams, who complained that because of "the sooty appearance of the Moor," she could "not separate the African color from the man, nor prevent that disgust and horror which filled my mind every time I saw [Othello] touch the gentle Desdemona."[82] In deference to such sentiments, many theater managers began to lighten Othello so as to lessen the shock occasioned by even a make-believe Negro's sexual involvement with a white woman.[83] When Edwin Booth (brother of John Wilkes Booth, future assassin of Abraham Lincoln) played Othello in the 1850s, he "sought to expunge from the play any taint of miscegenation by becoming the lightest-skinned Othello ever, thus eliminating visually any liaison between a black man and a white aristocrat's daughter."[84] Booth went so far as to don a turban and wield a scimitar to assure his audiences that Othello was "Arabian not African."[85]*

---

*Other whites joined Booth in negating the very idea of Othello as a Negro. In 1869 Mary Preston wrote, for example, that in studying the play "I have always *imagined* its hero to be a *white* man. . . . Shakespeare was too correct a delineator of human nature to have coloured Othello *black,* if he had personally acquainted himself with the idiosyncrasies of the African race. We may regard, then, the daub of black upon Othello's portrait as . . . one of the few erroneous strokes of the great master's brush, the *single* blemish on a faultless work. Othello *was* a *white* man!" Quoted in *A New Variorum Edition of Shakespeare,* vol. VI, *Othello,* second ed., Horace Howard Furness, ed. (1877).

The first black actor to play Othello in a major American venue before mixed audiences was Paul Robeson.* In 1942, Robeson and a white director, Margaret Webster, decided to stage the play in New York City. None of the theater owners Webster approached was willing to take the risk, however; by her account, "They were just plain scared of the issues which the production would raise."[86] Webster and Robeson were able to secure venues only in summer theaters out of town. After the interracial staging of the play received enthusiastic reviews at the Brattle Theater in Cambridge, Massachusetts, and the McCarter Theater in Princeton, New Jersey, the Theater Guild agreed to sponsor a Broadway production that would go on to attract international attention. Still, even in the 1940s, the mere dramatization of interracial intimacy—in a work by now three and a half centuries old, no less—was enough to offend the sensibilities of many Americans.† In his memoirs, Conrad Lynn tells of going to see Robeson star in *Othello* in the spring of 1945, accompanied by a black soldier from Sparta, Georgia. When Robeson, as the Moor, seized the throat of white Desdemona, Lynn's

---

*Although the American-born black actor Ira Aldridge won acclaim for his portrayal of Othello in Europe in the 1830s, he never performed in his native land. As the real-life husband of a white wife and lover of a white mistress, he constituted what many nineteenth-century white Americans regarded as an absolute monstrosity. See Tilden G. Edelstein, "Othello in America: The Dream of Racial Intermarriage," in J. Morgan Kousser and James M. McPherson, eds., *Region, Race, and Reconstruction: Essays in Honor of C. Vann Woodward* (1982), 188.

†During the period under discussion, other plays and musicals dramatizing interracial sex or marriage included Eugene O'Neill's *All God's Chillun Got Wings* (1924) and Richard Rodgers and Oscar Hammerstein II's *South Pacific* (1948). See Joyce Flynn, "Melting Plots: Patterns of Racial and Ethnic Amalgamation in American Drama Before Eugene O'Neill," *American Quarterly* 38 (1986): 417; Andrea Most, "'You've Got to Be Carefully Taught': The Politics of Race in Rodgers and Hammerstein's 'South Pacific,'" *Theatre Journal* 52 (2000): 307; Michael Sturma, "*South Pacific* . . . Film in Context," *History Today* 8 (1997): 25. During the tour, the interracial character of the cast prompted some ugly reactions. In a Boston hotel, as Robeson rode an elevator arm in arm with the white actress Uta Hagen, who played the role of Desdemona, another white woman suddenly spat in Hagen's face—clearly displeased by what she perceived to be an interracial couple. In fact, Robeson did become romantically involved with Hagen. See Martin B. Duberman, *Paul Robeson: A Biography* (1988), 286–94.

companion became terror-stricken and rushed out of the theater, exclaiming, "He can't do that to that white woman! Let me get out of here!"[87]

Struggles over depictions of interracial intimacy have also shaped the production of motion pictures. In the 1920s, for example, the pioneering black director Oscar Michaux constantly encountered resistance from local censors who insisted that he delete from his films depictions of interracial intimacy. His *Symbol of the Unconquered* centers on a land speculator's romantic involvement with a colored woman who is passing for white. The Chicago Board of Censors (in the person of its lone black member) permitted Michaux to screen his film in that city but required him to cut "all scenes of colored man holding white girl's hand."[88]* When Michaux adapted Charles W. Chesnutt's novel *House Behind the Cedars,*† he again ran up against the censors. The book and film concern the marriage and near-marriage of whites to light-skinned Negroes who are passing for white.‡ Refusing to approve Michaux's application for permission to show the film, the Virginia Board of Censors ruled that "whatever its good points, [*House Behind the Cedars*] should not be displayed in this state—especially in negro [movie] houses for which it is intended—since [the movie] contravenes the spirit of the recently enacted anti-miscegenation law which has put Virginia in the forefront as a pioneer in legislation aimed to preserve the integrity of the white race."[89] Only by removing all subtitles indicating interracial intimacies—in other words, amputating any verbalized expression, in this silent film, of the story Chesnutt intended to tell— was Michaux able to obtain the required licenses from state authorities.

---

*In 1915 the Supreme Court held that films fell outside the protection of the First Amendment and could therefore be subject to local and state censorship (*Mutual Film Corp. v. Indus. Comm'n of Ohio,* 236 U.S. 230 [1915]). In 1951 the Court reversed itself, ruling that "motion pictures are a significant medium for the communication of ideas" and thus deserving of protection under the First Amendment (*Joseph Burstyn Inc. v. Wilson,* 343 U.S. 495, 501 [1952]). On Michaux's many battles with film censors, see Charlene Regester, "Black Films, White Censors: Oscar Michaux Confronts Censorship in New York, Virginia, and Chicago," in Francis G. Couvares, ed., *Movie Censorship and American Culture* (1996).

†For more on Chesnutt's wonderful novel, see pages 321–22.

‡For more on passing, see pages 281–338.

In Hollywood's early years, film moguls titillated the public's yearnings for exotic eroticism by allowing white actors and actresses on-screen trysts with Native Americans, East Indians, or Polynesians—but never African Americans.* The suppression of black-white intimacy in films reflected the moguls' assessment of what white audiences would enjoy or tolerate. It also represented an effort, on the part of Hollywood, to preempt government censorship with self-censorship. The 1927 predecessor to what would in 1934 become the Motion Picture Production Code listed "miscegenation (sex relationships between the white and black races)" among "those things which . . . shall not appear in pictures produced by [members of the Motion Picture Association of America—that is, the major film studios], irrespective of the manner in which they are treated."[90]† In the 1950s the ban on depictions of black-white interracial intimacy began to erode. Darryl Zanuck's 1957 production *Island in the Sun* was an important milestone in this process. A drama about politics and racial conflict on a Caribbean island, the film featured two of the most significant black entertainers of the century, Harry Belafonte and Dorothy Dandridge. *Island in the Sun* hints rather broadly that Belafonte's character is intimately involved with a white woman played by Joan Fontaine. Dandridge's character, by way of contrast, is explicitly shown as having an affair with a white man played by John Justin. Although Zanuck tried

---

*A few foreign films explored black-white interracial intimacy. In a 1931 French film, *Le Blanc et Le Noir,* a white, childless, married woman sends for a singer whom she has never seen but whose voice she enjoys. In a darkened room, he slips into bed with her and makes her pregnant. After she delivers, she is kept ignorant of the fact that her baby is partly colored; finally, unbeknownst to her, her cuckolded husband, determined to save their marriage, replaces the baby with a white infant in need of a home. *Variety,* that Bible of Hollywood deals, gossip, and mores, announced that while *Le Blanc et Le Noir* had gone over "big" in Paris, "in America, no audience would stand for it"—a claim that went untested, since the film never found a U.S. distributor. See Thomas Cripps, *Slow Fade to Black: The Negro in American Film, 1900–1942* (1977), 212.

†Other prohibited subjects or items included "pointed profanity," "any licentious or suggestive nudity," "any inference of sexual perversion," "ridicule of the clergy," and "willful offense to any nation, race, or creed." See Gerard Gardner, *The Censorship Papers: Movie Censorship Letters from the Hays Office, 1934 to 1968* (1987), 213.

to delete a part of the film in which the audience can actually hear an endearment spoken by Justin to Dandridge, the actors succeeded in saving it. Belafonte and Fontaine did not fare as well. During the filming of one scene, the extraordinarily handsome Belafonte held Fontaine with a sensual closeness that would have let any observer know that their characters were well on their way to sexual intimacy, if not already there. Moviegoers, however, did not get to see that brief but powerful sign of passion, as it was edited out of the final cut. At no point in the film, moreover, do either of the interracial couples kiss. Curiously, advertisements for *Island in the Sun* contradicted the movie's very theme and essence by picturing the blacks and whites separately, as if they belonged to two distant and wholly exclusive worlds.[91]

Another strategy that filmmakers employed to depict interracial intimacy without scandalizing white audiences had only white actors enacting the tabooed affairs. In *Kings Go Forth* (1958), for example, Frank Sinatra and Tony Curtis portray two white American soldiers who fall in love with a woman who, unknown to them, is partly black. Dorothy Dandridge wanted to be cast as the love interest but was turned down; instead, the role went to the white actress Natalie Wood. In *Night of the Quarter Moon* (1959), a woman gets engaged to a wealthy white man and then "confesses" that despite her appearance, she is partly black; again, a white actress played the role. The same was true of the 1959 version of *Imitation of Life,* in which a Negro woman passing for white marries an unsuspecting white man: here, too, a white actress was cast in the lead. Directors and producers believed that by staging depictions of interracial affairs using white actors, they could forestall the alienation and anger of disapproving white moviegoers. By only *pretending* to show such intimacies on-screen, they could explore new racial territory without risking a white consumer rebellion. If anyone charged them with corrupting American morals by portraying miscegenation, they could respond by explaining that it was all make-believe, that in actuality no color line had been crossed.

Enemies of interracial intimacy also policed popular music; their principal targets were rhythm and blues and rock 'n' roll. "Sensuous Negro music," Asa Carter insisted, eroded "all the white man has built through his devotion to God."[92] As leader of the segregationist North Alabama Citizens Council, Carter proclaimed in 1956 that "the basic heavy beat of Negroes . . . appeals to the very base of man," bringing out his "animalism and vulgarity."[93] In Norfolk, Virginia, police arrested the black singer Larry Williams after he violated racial custom by jumping offstage to dance with white female fans—a transgression that was viewed with special alarm inasmuch as he had stripped off his shirt before making his leap.[94] At a whites-only concert in Birmingham, Alabama, white supremacists beat up the featured star of the program, the Negro singer Nat "King" Cole. They were angry in general at what they rightly perceived to be the subversive influence of black music on white youth, and they were angry in particular at Cole because he had previously appeared onstage with a white singer named June Christy. The white-supremacist magazine *The Southerner* had just reprinted a publicity photograph showing Cole seated at a piano with Christy standing close by, her hands resting on his shoulders. The author of the accompanying article asked:

> How close are the Coles and the innumerable Negro enter-
> tainers bringing the white girl to the Negro male? How many
> negroes have been encouraged to make advances to white girls
> and women, by the constant strumming of such propaganda
> into their minds? . . . You have seen it, the fleeting leer, the look
> that stays an instant longer [than it should] . . . the savagery,
> now, almost to the surface.[95]

The protests of southern white segregationists were echoed in other parts of the country. The *New York Times* quoted a psychiatrist in Hartford, Connecticut, as saying that rock 'n' roll was a "tribalistic and cannibalistic" style of music that was tantamount to "a communicable disease."[96] The Very Reverend John Carroll cautioned his Boston flock against the insidious seductions of rock 'n' roll, claiming that it "inflames and excites youth like jungle tom-toms."[97] And when Alan Freed's *The Rock 'n' Roll Dance Party* accidentally aired a shot of the Negro singer Frankie Lymon dancing with a white girl, thirteen Columbia Broadcasting System (CBS) affiliates immediately dropped the television show, which the network canceled soon afterward.*

### The Post–World War II Loosening
### of the Black-White Interracial-Intimacy Taboo

Even as strong pressures inhibited displays of interracial intimacy in the decades preceding the civil rights revolution, powerful countercurrents were nourishing prospects for a freer social environment. Social controls have always been harder to impose and maintain in urban than in rural areas. Thus, when massive numbers of blacks moved from the countryside to the city in 1900–1950, they almost automatically enlarged their spheres of personal autonomy. Similarly, since other parts of America tended to be less racially oppressive than the South, the massive emigration of blacks northward and westward expanded and enhanced possibilities for interracial intimacy.

World War II facilitated change as well. For one thing, Nazism gave racism a bad name; Hitler's Nuremberg laws cast a pall over America's Jim Crow legislation.† But the war itself also made a difference because, like other armed conflicts in which blacks participated, it emboldened African Americans. Having braved bullets abroad, many black veterans were determined upon their return home to confront white supremacy in all its guises—not excluding the taboo against intimacy between black men and white women. And while sociological, technological, legal, and cultural changes were freeing up race relations, a similarly broad array of influences was relaxing gender roles and sexual mores. These included the advent of more accessible and reliable modes of contraception and treatments for gonorrhea and syphilis, the sexual libertarianism reflected in Hugh Hefner's *Playboy*, the large increase in the number of women in the workforce, and the huge growth of colleges and universities, all of which pushed Americans toward greater social permissiveness and individual autonomy.[98]

---

*For an acerbic but nonetheless hilarious parody of efforts to maintain the color line on a televised rock 'n' roll dance show, see John Waters's film *Hairspray* (1988). See also his book *Crackpot: The Obsessions of John Waters* (1986), 88–100.
†On Nazi laws prohibiting Jews from marrying non-Jews, see pages 242–43.

Against this backdrop, more and more people crossed racial lines to marry. Useful data on the incidence of interracial marriage have long been (and remain) scarce. Still, it can be stated with confidence that after declining from the early decades of the twentieth century to around 1940, the number of black-white intermarriages has been gradually rising ever since.[99] Among the relatively small set of largely anonymous individuals involved in such marriages, some have stood out because of their wealth, status, celebrity, or achievement. The Negro entertainers Lena Horne, Dorothy Dandridge, Eartha Kitt, and Pearl Bailey all married white men.[100] Quite a few prominent black male entertainers also married across the race line. Almost all of them echoed the sentiment voiced by the singer Chubby Checker when he wed the winner of the Miss Holland and Miss World beauty contests: "I hope my people understand," he declared, "that I am not marrying Catherine because she's white. How was I to know that I would fall in love?"[101]

Perhaps the most highly publicized of the celebrity interracial marriages was that between the black entertainer Sammy Davis Jr. and the white Swedish film star May Britt.[102] From the start, public opinion intruded on the relationship. Davis had joined his friends Frank Sinatra and Peter Lawford in avidly campaigning for the Democratic party nominee, John F. Kennedy, in the 1960 presidential campaign. Fearing that his marrying Britt before the election might spur angry whites to express their disapproval by voting against Kennedy, Davis postponed his nuptials. Once Kennedy had been elected, however, he failed to reciprocate Davis's loyalty. Mindful of strongly held antipathies to interracial marriage, the president-elect arranged for Davis to be conspicuously absent from the inaugural festivities.[103]

For months after their wedding, Davis and Britt were together only episodically and furtively, and always under the protection of bodyguards, because they kept receiving death threats. Later Davis would express regret that his wife had been caught "in the prison of [his] skin."[104] Also problematic, if less immediately alarming, were the expectations heaped upon the Davises by well-wishers who essentially deputized them to be ambassadors of racial enlightenment. The rabbi who married them, for example, announced that their differing racial backgrounds rendered them "a symbol . . . of the success that must come from such unions. If you are true to the story of your love then your social role in our times will be an important one. Important for the future of the amity of races."[105] Although made with the best of intentions, such extravagant claims imposed on the couple a weight that, alongside their individual foibles, strained the relationship. After nine years and three children, the marriage ended in divorce.

### Interracial Sex and the Civil Rights Movement

During the 1960s many white and black activists who joined together to fight for social justice also had sex with one another. Some fell in love. A few even embarked on marriages.* Marian Wright, the first black woman to become a member of the Mississippi bar, met her future husband, Peter Edelman, while testifying about racism and poverty before a Senate committee on which sat Edelman's boss, Senator Robert F. Kennedy.[106] The distinguished black writer Alice Walker married the white civil rights attorney Mel Leventhal.[107] Charlayne Hunter-Gault, who desegregated the University of Georgia, secretly married her white classmate Walter Stovall; after the marriage became public, Georgia's governor condemned it as "a shame and a disgrace."[108] Her parents expressed disappointment, while his went into mourning, calling the elopement "the end of the world."[109] Neighbors agreed, dropping by the Stovalls' house to offer condolences. In a speech she gave in 1988 at the University of Georgia's graduation ceremony, Hunter-Gault paid a moving tribute to her former husband. Speaking of their decision to marry, she observed:

> We both took the leap, and he unhesitatingly jumped into
> my boat with me. He gave up going to the movies because he
> knew I couldn't get a seat in the segregated theaters. He gave up

---

*On interracial romances and marriages that had their origins in service in the Peace Corps, see Jonathan Zimmerman, "Crossing Oceans, Crossing Colors: Black Peace Corps Volunteers and Interracial Love in Africa, 1961–1971," in Martha Hodes, ed., *Sex, Love, Race: Crossing Boundaries in North American History* (1999), 514.

going to the Varsity because he knew they would not serve me—although he said at the time it was because the chili dogs tasted funny. We married, despite the uproar we knew it would cause, because we loved each other. And while we are now both happily married to other people that we love . . . the reason our marriage didn't work out certainly wasn't because either of us lacked the courage to try in a time of sea changes. I salute Walter for his courage and for continuing to be a good father to our daughter and one of my best friends and collaborators.[110]

In the famous Mississippi Freedom Summer Project of 1964, interracial sex proliferated as hundreds of white volunteers traveled south to assist black civil rights workers in registering black voters, teaching black children, and publicizing the racist horrors of the segregation regime in its death throes.[111] In that remarkable campaign, young whites and blacks attempted to live together as equals in a manner unprecedented in American history. Whereas the Communist movement had been led by whites, the movement in the 1960s for African American liberation was predominantly black in both its leadership and its following. The prevalence of interracial sex in the Freedom Summer Project had much to do with age—the volunteers were for the most part unmarried people in their early twenties—but it also had something to do with the setting. Free of parental supervision (in some cases for the first time), the activists had easy access to potential sexual partners and were operating in perilous conditions that facilitated mutual feelings of dependence and yearnings for comfort. Interracial sex was also encouraged by their aim to erase white racism both in the world and within themselves. As Professor Doug McAdam has observed, many volunteers viewed their activism as the living embodiment of freedom and equality, "the 'beloved community' that would serve as a model of . . . a true egalitarian society."[112] Thus inspired, some openly and joyfully welcomed interracial sex because of its very status as a dangerous taboo in racist America. For these young adults, interracial sex became "conclusive proof of their right to membership in the 'beloved community.'"[113] The sex itself, as one participant would remark years later, "was considered not so much license as one more small expression of a liberation that was taking place on all fronts."[114] There was, to be sure, an ugly underside to this, as whites and blacks alike sometimes manipulated emotions and vulnerabilities in exploitative and hurtful ways in order to scratch various emotional itches. White women sampled the black male body that was the subject of such envy and fear, while black men tried the white female body they had been warned to avoid. The activist-intellectual Stoughton Lynd once noted that "every black [civil rights worker] with perhaps a few exceptions counted it as a notch on his gun to have slept with a white woman—as many as possible."[115]* Notwithstanding eruptions of sexual opportunism, the interracial solidarity of the activists constituted one of the most praiseworthy developments in American history. At a time when racist violence posed a dire threat because of thuggery that was openly condoned by state officials, the heroes and heroines of Freedom Summer challenged Jim Crow etiquette at every level, including the realm of intimate associations.

Threatened on their home turf, segregationists attempted to transform interracial sexual affection among civil rights activists into a discrediting myth by portraying the protests as nothing more than a cover for wild promiscuity. Following Martin Luther King Jr.'s successful campaign to portray the brutality of racial exclusion from voting in Selma, Alabama, in the spring of 1965, Albert Persons, a stringer for *Life* magazine, published *The True Selma Story*. The book offered numerous testimonials by whites and some (unnamed) blacks about the supposed erosion of all sexual compunction among civil rights activists. Persons quoted Deputy Sheriff V. B. Bates as saying, "I saw white females . . . building up their sexual desires with Negro males. After a few minutes of necking and kissing the Negro male would lead them off into the Negro housing project. I watched this procedure many, many times."[116] Another of Persons's witnesses was Nettie Adams, whom he

---

*According to Professor Doug McAdam's interviews with project participants, "the heaviest volume of sexual activity . . . involved black men . . . and white women. There was also considerable activity between the white male and female volunteers, but a great deal less so involving white males and black females, and black males and black females" (*Freedom Summer* [1988], 95).

identified as an employee of the Montgomery Police Department. According to Persons, Adams recalled:

> This one particular couple on the lawn of St. Margaret's [Hospital] was engaged in sexual relations, a white woman [a skinny blond] and a Negro man. After they were through, she wiggled out from beneath him and over to [another man]. . . .[117]

An anonymous black resident of Montgomery was said to have told Persons, "I saw numerous instances of boys and girls of both races hugging and kissing and fondling one another openly in the church. On one occasion I saw a Negro boy and a white girl engaged in sexual intercourse on the floor of the church. [O]ther boys and girls stood around and watched, laughing and joking."[118]

It is difficult to know what to make of such statements. Perhaps they are accurate representations of what the persons quoted *believed* they witnessed; or perhaps they are distortions stemming from a desire to curry favor with their interviewer, a need to vent personal anger or frustration, or a compulsion to discredit the civil rights activists for ideological reasons. Much less obscure is the motivation driving Persons, whose book is an obvious example of tendentious propaganda. As one critic has aptly observed, Persons's aim was to identify and pillory the categories of people he saw as the principal "enemies of the [white] South: outside agitators, horny white women . . . and rapacious black men."[119]

The sexual fears, resentments, and anxieties of segregationists did take their toll. On the evening of March 25, 1965, in Selma, a car full of Ku Klux Klansmen became enraged when they saw a white woman and a black man, most likely civil rights organizers, standing together in a pose suggestive of sexual intimacy. The success of the well-publicized protest march from Selma to Montgomery earlier in the day had already put the Klansmen in an ugly mood. Seeing an open display of interracial sexual affection—and between a white woman and a black man, no less—sent them into a homicidal fury. The driver of the car sped toward the couple but swerved away when one of his passengers (who also happened to be an FBI informant) warned him that there was a military jeep nearby. A little later, the Klansmen spotted another example of what they considered to be illicit race "mixing": an automobile with a white woman at the wheel and a young black man sitting in the front seat beside her.

After chasing the car for about twenty miles, the Klansmen pulled up alongside it and shot into it at close range. The passenger survived; the driver died. Her name was Viola Liuzzo, and she was perhaps the lone white woman murdered on account of civil rights activism during the 1960s.

Lest it be thought that Down South was the exclusive repository of vicious racial hatred, it should be noted that in Detroit, in the days following Liuzzo's funeral, hooligans burned a cross in front of her family home, threw rocks at her daughter (a first-grader), and called her sons "nigger lovers" at school. Her husband, moreover, was besieged by obscene telephone calls and hate mail, much of it from angry white northerners who believed that the Klansmen had been right, that Mrs. Liuzzo had been romantically linked with the black man in her car, and that therefore she had gotten what she deserved.[120]

### 1967: The Pivotal Year

Although a large majority of whites continued to disapprove of interracial marriage throughout the 1960s—in 1964, 60 percent of adult whites polled declared their support for antimiscegenation laws—the matrimonial color bar eventually suffered the same fate as all the other customs and laws of segregation. Nineteen sixty-seven was the key year—the year Guy Smith and Peggy Rusk got married, the year of the Supreme Court's decision in *Loving v. Virginia,* the year in which Hollywood's most talked-about film was *Guess Who's Coming to Dinner?*

Suggestive of a new openness regarding interracial intimacy was the marriage of Peggy Rusk, the white daughter of sitting United States Secretary of State Dean Rusk, to Guy Smith, a black man. Ms. Rusk was only eighteen at the time, but by then she and Smith had already been "going together" for four years. Unlike many interracial couples, this one received considerable parental backing, from both sets of parents. Although at the time some news reports indicated that he had offered his resignation to president Lyndon B. Johnson (who was said to have declined it), Rusk himself asserted in his memoir that he had merely informed the president of the impending wedding.[121] In any event, the secretary of state walked his daughter down the aisle, offered no hint of apology for or regret over her marital choice, and received considerable public applause for his conduct. Ten years earlier, it would have been inconceivable for one of the nation's weekly news magazines conspicuously to champion an interracial marriage, but on September 29, 1967, *Time* did just that, running a photo of the Rush-Smith newlyweds on its cover and praising their union as "a marriage of enlightenment."[122]

The most consequential of the year's developments was *Loving v. Virginia,* the aptly named United States Supreme Court decision that invalidated state antimiscegenation statutes. Later, we will take a closer look at *Loving* and the courtroom struggles that preceded it.* For now, we need note only that *Loving* withdrew from states the authority to prohibit marriages on racial grounds.

In *Guess Who's Coming to Dinner?,* the third key milestone of 1967, Hollywood finally produced and celebrated a mass-market film that showed interracial intimacy in a sympathetic light.[123] The film details a day in the life of Joey Drayton (played by Katharine Houghton), a twenty-three-year-old white woman who brings home the man she loves to meet her parents; the two of them are eager to marry, following a whirlwind ten-day romance in Hawaii. The object of Joey's affections is Dr. John Prentice (played by Sidney Poitier), a thirty-seven-year-old internationally renowned specialist in tropical diseases who just happens to be black. The elder Draytons are affluent, liberal Unitarians who have raised their daughter to believe that distinctions should not be made between people on a racial basis; when her fiancé walks in through the front door, however, their views on race are unexpectedly tested. Mrs. Drayton (played by Katharine Hepburn) is so moved by Joey's obvious happiness that she rather quickly gives the wedding plans her blessing. It takes her husband (played by Spencer Tracy) a little longer, concerned as he is about the difficulties the couple and their future children will surely face, but ultimately he, too, consents.

---

*See pages 259–77.

Directed by Stanley Kramer, *Guess Who's Coming to Dinner?* was clearly intended to make a dramatic artistic and social statement. As some critics recognized, however, the film is laughably sentimental. *Newsweek*'s Joseph Morgenstern succinctly described Joey Drayton and John Prentice as "a pair of pop ups from some children's book on tolerance." Moreover, he quipped, "what those two propose is no interracial marriage but an unprecedented crossbreeding of nobility, intellect, and virtue."[124] According to the film critic for *Time* magazine, "Kramer's new film bravely sets out to face the problem of [opposition to interracial marriage], but ends up merely offering a great big heaping tablespoon of sugar to help the medicine go down."[125] Even more dismissive was Andrew M. Greeley, writing in *The Reporter.* "Love generally doesn't conquer very much," he mused, "and it certainly cannot conquer the dishonest, tasteless, and meretricious view of the race problem on which *Guess Who's Coming to Dinner?* is based."[126]

Kramer's cloying sentimentality reaches its apogee in his treatment of white racism: he whitewashes it. The most villainous white person depicted in the film is a smarmy, gossipy woman who purports to console Mrs. Drayton in light of the impending family "tragedy." Kramer could have done something interesting by making the disapproving foil someone with authority over the Draytons—a boss, for example, or even the spouse of a boss. That sort of pressure is what many people in the real world face if they or their sons or daughters deviate radically from accepted social norms. But in *Guess Who's Coming to Dinner?,* Mrs. Drayton is the *gossip's* boss. Wealth and influence are thus conjoined with racial liberalism to eliminate any on-screen impediment to Stanley Kramer's vision of proper racial politics.

Some critics also complained about Kramer's presentation of John Prentice, charging that he seemed to be nothing less than a combination of Jonas Salk, Albert Schweitzer, and Charles Drew.[127] Kramer countered that the logic of the plot demanded that Prentice be extraordinary; after all, he had to win the love of a well-to-do, idealistic, beautiful young woman who undoubtedly must have had her choice of desirable suitors. And Prentice's exceptional good looks, the director added, served to accentuate the race issue. In sum, he said, the character's singular worth and appeal eliminated the possibility that his prospective in-laws could object to the marriage on any basis other than a racial one.[128] Alternative or supplemental interpretations are, of course, conceivable. One is that Kramer made Dr. Prentice a paragon of intelligence, charm, honesty, fidelity, and respectfulness in order to make him *acceptably* exceptional. An ordinary Negro would have represented more of a racial challenge to social convention, if only because there are so many more ordinary Negroes than there are Dr. Prentices. That Kramer was seeking, whether consciously or unconsciously, to avoid alarming white theatergoers is also suggested by the way he chose to handle the sexual component of the Drayton-Prentice relationship. To ensure that Poitier's character would be suitably acceptable to whites, Kramer kept the film's erotic temperature notably low. Accordingly, the audience learns early on that Prentice has refrained from sleeping with his fiancée, despite *her* desire for premarital sex. The explanation Drayton offers is that he wants to hold off on sexually consummating their romance until he is sure that they will, in fact, be married—a certainty that is conditioned on her parents' *un*conditional blessing. If Poitier was allowed to display more sexuality in *Guess Who's Coming to Dinner?* than Belafonte had been permitted in *Island in the Sun,* that sexuality was nonetheless kept tightly under wraps. In only one scene—during their taxi ride to Drayton's home—is the couple shown kissing on-screen. And that shot is exceedingly brief.

Contrary to the claims that have occasionally been made for it,[129] *Guess Who's Coming to Dinner?* was by no means the first movie to present a positive perspective on interracial intimacy. A year earlier, Larry Peerce had directed *One Potato, Two Potato,* a film about the dispute that ensues when a white divorcé seeks custody of his daughter after his white ex-wife marries a black man. *One Potato, Two Potato* is both artistically superior to *Guess Who's Coming to Dinner?* and considerably more revealing sociologically. It illuminates features of the social landscape—such as sexual competition between white and black men—that *Guess Who's Coming to Dinner?* avoids. But *One Potato, Two Potato* was an "art film" that reached only a relatively small audience and is now largely forgotten. By contrast, *Guess Who's Coming to*

*Dinner?* was an immensely popular, financially successful film whose title remains instantly recognizable. That such a film could present the prospect of a white-black interracial marriage not as a menace or a mistake or a tragedy but rather as an expression of virtuous love makes it a landmark in American social history.

# THREE

# From Black-Power Backlash to the New Amalgamationism

## Black-Power Backlash

By and large, African Americans fall into three camps with respect to white-black interracial marriage. One camp views it as a positive good that decreases social segregation; encourages racial open-mindedness; increases blacks' access to enriching social networks; elevates their status; and empowers black women in their interactions with black men.[1]

A second camp is agnostic, seeing interracial marriage simply as a private choice that individuals should have the right to make. Professor Cornel West, for example, after noting that "more and more white Americans are willing to interact sexually with black Americans *on an equal basis,*" has maintained that he himself "view[s] this [development] as neither cause for celebration nor reason for lament."[2]* This is probably the predominant view among blacks. It allows those who espouse it simultaneously to oppose antimiscegenation laws and to disclaim any personal desire to marry across racial lines. Many African Americans are attracted to this position because, among other things, it helps to refute a not infrequent assumption among whites that is deeply annoying to blacks: the notion that blacks, particularly those who are accomplished, attractive, and ambitious, would like nothing better than to be intimate with whites, or even, if it were possible, to *become* white themselves. The pressure of this assumption prompted a writer who called

---

*West proceeds, however, to soften his expressed indifference somewhat by rhapsodizing that "anytime two human beings find genuine pleasure, joy, and love, the stars smile and the universe is enriched" (*Race Matters* [1993; reprint, 1994], 122).

himself Mordechai to declare in 1827, in the pages of *Freedom's Journal,* the nation's first black newspaper, "I am not covetous of sitting at the table of [the white man], to hold him by his arm in the streets—to marry his daughter . . . nor to sleep in his bed—neither should I think myself honoured in the possession of all these favours."[3] A hundred and thirty-seven years later, Charles H. King restated the point in the *Negro Digest.* Asserting that "'Miss Anne' [a generic white woman] does not fall into the category of our present needs," King insisted (and entitled his essay), "I Don't Want to Marry Your Daughter."[4]

A third camp repudiates interracial marriage on the ground that black participation in it constitutes an expression of racial disloyalty; implies disapproval of fellow blacks; impedes the perpetuation of black culture; weakens the African American marriage market; and fuels racist mythologies, especially the fiction that blacks lack pride of race.[5] While black opposition to intermarriage has always been a powerful and constant undercurrent, it was largely suppressed prior to the mid-1960s in order to accentuate protest against antimiscegenation laws, which most black enemies of mixed marriage also opposed. Periodically, however, blacks' latent objections did erupt. In 1949, after Walter White, the Negro secretary of the NAACP, divorced his black wife (the mother of his two children) and married a white woman from South Africa, the *Norfolk* [Virginia] *Journal and Guide* spoke for many blacks in suggesting that a "prompt and official announcement that [White] will not return to his post . . . is in order."[6]* Much of the anger over this obviously very personal decision stemmed from fear that segregationists would seize on the marriage as "proof" that what Negro civil rights activists really wanted was not mere "equality" but sex with white women. Also contributing to the anger was the widespread sense that White's actions sent the message that in his eyes, at least, no Negro woman was good enough for him.†

---

*For more on Walter White, see pages 287–89.
†Although White escaped ouster, he lost influence within the NAACP in part as a consequence of the controversy over his second marriage. See Nathan Patrick Tillman Jr., "Walter Francis White: A Study in Interest Group Leadership" (Ph.D. diss., University of Wisconsin, 1961), 141–70.

By the late 1960s, with the burden of de jure racial stigmatization having been considerably lightened, increasing numbers of blacks felt emboldened to air their disapproval of mixed marriages. As "We Shall Overcome" gave way to "Black Power," the rejection of interracial intimacy gained in prestige and prominence. Concern with improving the image of blacks in the minds of whites yielded to the cultivation of a deeper allegiance to racial solidarity—an allegiance that many blacks perceived as being incompatible with interracial intimacy.* Thus, even while the African American social reformer George Wiley dedicated himself to the struggle for racial justice as a leading figure in the Congress for Racial Equality (CORE) and the founder of the National Welfare Rights Organization (NWRO), his marriage to a white woman earned him the scorn of many black activists. In 1972, when he addressed a rally in Washington, D.C., on African Liberation Day, a group of black women heckled him with the taunting chant "Where's your white wife? Where's your white wife?" When he attempted to focus his remarks specifically on the situation of black women, the heckling continued unabated, though the chant changed to "Talking black and sleeping white."[7]† Other politically active blacks with white spouses faced similar pressures; among their number were James Farmer, a founder of CORE,[8] and the tenacious activist Julius Hobson.[9] Julius Lester was a longtime member of the Student Non-violent Coordinating Committee (SNCC) and the author of one of the most arrestingly entitled books of that flamboyant era, *Look Out Whitey! Black Power's Gon' Get Your Mama* (1968). For many black activists, however, Lester's writings and ideas were decidedly less significant a measure of his commitment to the cause of African American advance-

---

*In the early 1970s, opposition to interracial intimacy also manifested itself in denunciations of interracial adoption. For a discussion of this topic, see pages 393–98; 402–46.

†In the poem "Niggers Are Scared of Revolution," the black nationalist group the Last Poets scoffed at fellow blacks whom they perceived as insufficiently committed to challenging the white establishment. A repeated target of the Last Poets' ire were "niggers [who] shoot sharp glances at white women," and "niggers" who sighed, "Oooooh white thighs. Oooh white thighs." See Abiodur Oyewole, Umer Bin Hassan, with Kim Greene, *On a Mission: Selected Poems and History of the Last Poets* (1996), 61–64.

ment than was his choice of a white woman to be his wife. To them his marriage bespoke hypocrisy. Ridiculing Lester, a black woman wrote in a letter to the editor of *Ebony* that only a fool would regard him as a trustworthy leader. After all, she charged, he could not even "crawl out of bed" with whites.[10]

The "sleeping white" critique embarrassed a wide variety of individuals, as distinctions between the personal and the political evaporated. At many colleges and universities, black students ostracized other blacks who dated (much less married!) whites. A black student who wanted to walk around "with a blonde draped on his arm" could certainly do so, a student leader at the University of Washington told St. Clair Drake; "All we say," the student continued, "is don't try to join the black studies association."[11] Drake, a leading African American sociologist, himself ran up against this bias: by his account, when he revisited his old high school in 1968, the black student union refused to have anything to do with him because he was involved in an interracial relationship. Likewise shunned, and for the same reason, was Drake's classmate Charles V. Hamilton, the coauthor, with Stokely Carmichael, of *Black Power: The Politics of Liberation in America* (1967).[12]

In some instances, black opposition played a role in the dissolution of interracial marriages. One dramatic example was the breakup of Everett LeRoi Jones (now known as Amiri Baraka) and Hettie Jones.[13] LeRoi Jones was born to middle-class black parents in Newark, New Jersey, in 1934. For two years he attended Howard University, which he detested. After serving in the air force for three years, he moved to New York in 1957 and joined the Beat community in Greenwich Village. He worked for *Record Changer* magazine and launched his literary career as a coeditor of *Yugen,* an avant-garde journal that published work by William Burroughs, Gregory Corso, Allen Ginsberg, Jack Kerouac, Charles Olson, and Jones himself. His coeditor was his future wife, Hettie Cohen, a woman of Jewish parentage who had grown up in suburban New York and attended Mary Washington, the women's college of the University of Virginia. Jones and Cohen were married in 1958. His parents accepted the marriage easily, while hers were so horrified by it that they broke off all contact with their daughter.

For a time, the marriage was, according to Hettie Jones, a happy and loving one. But eventually the pressures of bohemian penury, the demands of two children, and infidelities by both husband and wife (including a relationship in which LeRoi Jones had a baby by another woman, who also happened to be white) began to take their toll. Also burdening the marriage were Jones's political activities and ambitions: as the black protest movement gathered steam in the early 1960s, he aimed to become an important figure in it. At the same time, his career as a writer was blossoming. He wrote well-regarded poetry, social and political essays, and an important book, *Blues People* (1963), on the history of African American music. What made LeRoi Jones a celebrity, however, and ensured him a niche in American literary history, was his two-act play *The Dutchman,* which premiered in New York City on March 24, 1964.

In *The Dutchman,* a reticent, bookish, middle-class black man named Clay meets a white temptress named Lula in a New York subway car. The play consists mainly of their verbal combat. Angered by Clay's refusal to dance with her, Lula taunts him:

> Come on, Clay. Let's rub bellies on the train. . . . Forget your social-working mother for a few seconds and let's knock stomachs. Clay, you liver-lipped white man. You would-be Christian. You ain't no nigger, you're just a dirty white man.[14]

And Clay responds in kind:

> Tallulah Bankhead! . . . Don't you tell me anything! If I'm a middle-class fake white man . . . let me be. . . . Let me be who I feel like being. Uncle Tom. Thomas. Whoever. It's none of your business. . . . I sit here, in this buttoned-up suit, to keep myself from cutting all your throats. . . . You great liberated whore! You fuck some black man, and right away you're an expert on black people. What a lotta shit that is.[15]

But Lula has the last word, so to speak, when she suddenly stabs Clay to death. Her fellow passengers throw his body out of the subway car and disappear. Alone, Lula takes her seat again. When another Negro man enters the car, she begins anew her lethal routine.

Although Jones was situated in a predominantly white, bohemian milieu when he wrote *The Dutchman,* he had already begun to embrace the idea that it was primarily blacks—indeed, exclusively blacks—to whom he should be addressing his art. Increasingly successful, he was also becoming increasingly radical in his condemnation of white American society. Asked on one occasion by a white woman what whites could do to help solve the race problem, Jones replied, "You can help by dying. You are a cancer. You can help the world's people with your death."[16] Outrageous as this statement would have been coming from anyone, it was even more startling in being directed at a white woman by an African American who was himself married to a white woman. Jones, though, was by no means alone in living within this particular paradox. He noted in his autobiography that at one point he and some other black intellectuals had objected to the presence of white radicals in an organization they were trying to establish. "What was so wild," he recalled, "was that some of us were talking about how we didn't want white people on the committee . . . but we were all hooked up to white women. . . . Such were the contradictions of that period of political organization."[17] The more prominent Jones became, the more he was accused of hypocrisy. The cultural critic Stanley Kauffmann, for example, asserted that he was an exemplary figure in "the tradition of the fake."[18] Stung by such charges, infatuated by black nationalist rhetoric, inspired by the prospect of re-creating himself, and bored by a disappointing marriage, LeRoi Jones in 1965 divorced his wife, Hettie, in preparation for waging war on behalf of the Black Nation.*

---

*In 1970, having changed his name to Amiri Baraka, the former LeRoi Jones wrote:

The Leftists have reintroduced the white woman for the precise purpose of stunting the [black] nation. . . . Must it be our fate to be the police dogs of "revolutionary white boys," egged on by Sheena . . . the blond jungle queen[?] . . . As long as any *thing* separates the black man and the black woman from moving together, being together, being absolutely in tune, each doing what they are supposed to do, then the nation will never re-emerge. [Amiri Baraka, *Raise Race Rays Raze: Essays Since 1965* (1971), 153.]

Throughout the Black Power era, substantial numbers of African Americans loudly condemned black participation in interracial marriage, especially with whites, deeming it to be racial betrayal. Joyce Blake searingly articulated this sentiment in a 1968 letter to the editor of the *Village Voice:*

> It really hurts and baffles me and many other black sisters to see our black brothers(?) coming down the streets in their African garbs with a white woman on their arms. It is fast becoming a standard joke among the white girls that they can get our men still—African styles and all. . . .
>
> It certainly seems to many black sisters that the Movement is just another subterfuge to aid the Negro male in procuring a white woman. If this be so, then the black sisters don't need it, for surely we have suffered enough humiliation from both white and black men in America.[19]

The argument that intermarriage is destructive of racial solidarity has been, as we have seen, the principal basis of black opposition over the years. Another objection is that it robs black women of black men who should be their "natural" partners, thus weakening the position of black women in the marriage market. Lula Miles advanced this idea in an August 1969 letter to the editor of *Ebony.* Responding to a white woman who had expressed bewilderment at black women's anger, Ms. Miles wrote, "Non-sister wonders why the sight of a black man with a white woman is revolting to a black woman. . . . The name of the game is 'competition.' Non-sister, you are trespassing!"[20] Miraonda J. Stevens reinforced the point the following month in a letter of her own, predicting that "in the future there aren't going to be enough nice black men around for us [black women] to marry."[21]

The "market" critique of interracial marriage has had a long history. In 1929 Palestine Wells, a black columnist for the *Baltimore Afro-American,* wrote, "I have a sneaking suspicion that national intermarriage will make it harder to get husbands. A girl has a hard time enough getting a husband, but methinks 'twill be worse. Think how awful it would be if all the ofay girls with a secret hankering for brown skin men could openly compete with us."[22] Forty-three years later, Katrina Williams echoed Wells's remarks. "The white man is marrying the white woman," she noted. "The black man is marrying the white woman. [W]ho's gonna marry me?"[23] Behind Pickens's anxious question resided more than demographic facts regarding the pool of black men available for marriage. There was, too, the perception (or the fear) that many African American men believed, first, that white women were relatively more desirable than black women, and second, that black women themselves were downright *un*attractive. Again the pages of *Ebony* offered vivid testimony: "Let's just lay all phony excuses aside and get down to the true nitty, nitty, NITTY-GRITTY and tell it like it really is," Mary A. Dowdell wrote in 1969. "Black males hate black women just because they are black. The whole so-called Civil Rights Act was really this: 'I want a white woman because she's white and I not only hate but don't want a black woman because she's black.' . . . The whole world knows this."[24]

Decades later, African American hostility to interracial intimacy would remain widespread and influential. Three examples are revealing. The first is *Jungle Fever* (1991). Directed by Spike Lee and set in New York City in the early 1990s, the movie focuses on an unhappy interracial affair. Flipper Purify is an ambitious, college-educated black architect who lives in Harlem with his colored wife and their young daughter. Angie Tucci, a young white woman, works for Purify as a secretary. Educated only through high school, she lives in Bensonhurst with her father and brothers, all of whom are outspoken racists. One evening when Purify and Tucci stay late at the office, business concerns are superseded by erotic longings tinged with racial curiosity. He has never been sexually intimate with a white woman, and she has never been sexually intimate with a black man. They bridge that gap in their experience by sexually exploring each other right then and there on a chair and drafting table. Afterward, they both stupidly confide in indiscreet friends who carelessly reveal their secret. Angie Tucci's father throws her out of the family home after viciously beating her for "fucking a nigger." Flipper Purify's wife, Drew, kicks him out, too. Purify and Tucci move into an apartment together, but the arrangement quickly falls apart under the pressure of their own feelings of guilt and uncertainty and the strong disapproval they encounter from blacks and whites alike.[25]

A second expression of contemporary black opposition to interracial intimacy is Lawrence Otis Graham's 1995 essay "I Never Dated a White Girl."[26] Himself educated at Princeton University and Harvard Law School in the 1980s, Graham sought to explain why "black middle class kids . . . [who are] raised in integrated or mostly white neighborhoods, [and] told to befriend white neighbors, socialize and study with white classmates, join white social and professional organizations and go to work for mostly white employers," are also warned by their parents and friends, "'Oh, and by the way, don't ever forget that you are black, and that you should never get so close to whites that you happen to fall in love with them.'"[27]* Graham did more than merely describe this reaction, however; he also justified it, in a candid polemic that might as well have been entitled "Why I Am *Proud* That I Never Dated a White Girl."

A third example is "Black Men, White Women: A Sister Relinquishes Her Anger," an essay by the novelist Bebe Moore Campbell. Recounting the moment when she and her girlfriends spied a handsome black celebrity escorting a white woman at a trendy Beverly Hills restaurant, Campbell reminisced:

> In unison, we moaned, we groaned, we rolled our eyes heavenward. We gnashed our teeth in harmony and made ugly faces. We sang "Unmph! Unpph! Umph!" a capella style, then shook our heads as we lamented for the ten thousandth time the perfidy of black men and cursed trespassing white women

---

*In a memoir about his struggles with interracial intimacy, Brent Staples recalled his grandmother telling him, "Boy, you bet' not bring me no white girl, you hear?" ("The White Girl Problem," *New York Woman*, March 1989). Likewise, Diane Weathers reported that on the day she left home for college, her grandmother admonished her, "Don't come back to this house with a white man" ("White Boys," *Essence*, April 1990).

who dared to "take our men." . . . Before lunch was over I had a headache, indigestion, and probably elevated blood pressure.[28]*

In each of these works, three themes recur. The first is the burden of the past—the feeling that certain brutal facts of history should dissuade African American men and women from entering into intimate relations with whites.† For some black women, the key inhibiting collective memory is of white men raping their kind with impunity.‡ For some black males, the painful counterpoint is the image of the lynchings inflicted on African American men accused of sexual misconduct with white women—another subject we will deal with at length later.§ Explaining why he had never dated a white girl, Graham cited as a primary reason "the ghost of Emmitt Till,"[29] the black youngster from Chicago who was murdered in Mississippi in 1955 for whistling at a white woman.# Graham was aware that, fortunately, black men of his generation were much less vulnerable than their predecessors. But partly in homage to those who had gone before him, Graham himself

---

*Surveying women's perceptions of stressful phenomena, a psychologist at the University of Michigan found in the late 1990s that among her black respondents, the sight of black-white interracial couples constituted the second most often cited source of anxiety, ahead of economic worries but behind a perceived deficiency of personal time. According to the researcher, many black women "see an increase in interracial couples as a decrease in their chances of finding a partner" (quoted in Richard Morin, "Unconventional Wisdom: New Facts and Hot Stats from the Social Sciences," *Washington Post*, June 29, 1997).

†Melba Pattillo Beals recalled that when she informed her mother she had married a white man, the immediate response was "How can you marry a white man after all the pain white folks have caused you?" (*White Is a State of Mind: A Memoir* [1999], 159).

‡See pages 162–69.

§See pages 192–99.

#For more on Till, see pages 203–5.

In *Jungle Fever*, when Flipper Purify brings his white lover home to meet his parents, his elderly father is far from approving. A retired minister from Georgia, he lectures the couple on the exploitation of enslaved women by white masters who grabbed "every piece of black poontang [they] could lay [their] hands on." He then regales them with images of lynchings passively observed by white women standing on racial pedestals, who dreamed of what it would be like to have "one of them big black bucks that their husbands were so desperately afraid of."

consciously declined to cross racial boundaries that would have been physically hazardous for his forebears to traverse

A second recurrent idea is that racial pride and loyalty demand that blacks, especially the more successful among them, marry other blacks. Of particular significance in *Jungle Fever* is that the protagonist is an *affluent* and *highly educated* black man. It is precisely because he has "made it" that other black characters in the film—to the approbation of many black filmgoers—are so caustic in condemning his interracial affair. This argument holds that, having been assisted by the communal efforts of African Americans, successful blacks must, in all fairness, "give back" to that community. And one crucial way for them to do that is to make themselves available personally, as spouses, to other blacks. Given the plummeting marriage rate within African American communities, some even contend that this is an essential act of solidarity.* Relating how he and his friends regularly engage in "race checking," Graham confided:

> We flip through glowing profiles [about successful blacks] in *People, Ebony,* or *Business Week* quietly praising the latest black trailblazer and role model. Then we look for what we consider the final determinant of this person's black identity—that thing that will allow us to bestow our unqualified appreciation. We look for the litmus test of loyalty to the race: the photo of the person's spouse or significant other.[30]†

Many black critics of interracial marriage see it as a diversion that siphons off valuable human resources that black communities can ill

---

*According to Professor Halford Fairchild, "For black men to date and marry white women in the face of our lingering debt to each other is irresponsible. The brother who dates or marries interracially has sold out. We have a responsibility to each other. We are under siege. We are at war. To sleep with the enemy is treason, racial treason" (quoted in Lynn Norment, "Black Men/White Women: What's Behind the Furor," *Ebony,* Nov. 1994, p. 50).

†The "litmus test" employed by Graham and his friends is widespread and intergenerational. Writer Jake Lamar noted that his mother "kept a mental shit list of black celebrities who had white wives or girlfriends" (*Bourgeois Blues: An American Memoir* [1991], 156).

afford to lose. Only a small percentage of the black men who marry do so interracially; in 1999 just 7 percent of married black men had non-black wives.[31] But given the relative paucity of marriageable black men as a consequence of poverty, imprisonment, and other factors, a substantial number of black women feel acutely this loss of potential black mates. In 1992 researchers found that for every three black unmarried women in their twenties, there was only one unmarried black man whose earnings rose above the poverty level.[32] In view of the realities facing black women, resentful disparagement of interracial marriage should come as no surprise.[33] "In a drought," Bebe Moore Campbell wrote, "even one drop of water is missed." Moreover, "for many African American women," she continues, "the thought of black men, particularly those who are successful, dating or marrying white women is like being passed over for the prom by the boy of their dreams, causing them pain, rage, and an overwhelming sense of betrayal and personal rejection."[34]* Compiling a roster of prominent blacks either married to or otherwise romantically involved with whites—Clarence Thomas (justice of the Supreme Court of the United States), Henry Louis Gates (chairman of Afro-American Studies at Harvard University), Quincy Jones (stellar musician), Franklin A. Thomas (former president of the Ford Foundation), John Edgar Wideman (prominent

---

*As Denan Miller and Nick Chiles explain it,

> Any brother who shows up to the ball with someone who looks like the original Cinderella is gonna get called out by the sistahs—or at least talked about after the party's over. And that goes for every sistah, from the one who's physically repulsed by the sight of a white girl wrapped around a brother to those of us who are down with the "Color Doesn't Matter Committee." No matter how repressed or progressive we are when it comes to matters of the heart, we all think the same thing when we see her and him together: Either brotherman has that self-hating identity complex thing happening, or he thinks black girls are somehow inferior to Cindy. [*What Brothers Think, What Sistahs Know: The Real Deal on Love and Relationships* (1999), 83.]

See also Aliona L. Gibson, *Nappy: Growing Up Black and Female in America* (2000), 104–17. Gibson's discussion of interracial relationships is contained in a chapter entitled "Ultimate Insult."

novelist), Orlando Patterson (professor of sociology at Harvard University), and Wilbert Tatus (editor of the *Amsterdam News*)*—Graham voiced disappointment that so many of "our most talented role models" had made choices that were, or could be plausibly interpreted as, "a means to dissociate . . . from the black race."[35] When a prominent black person "turns out to be married to a white mate," Graham averred, "our children say, 'Well, if it's so good to be black, why do all my role models date and marry whites?' . . . As a child growing up in the 'black is beautiful' 1970s," he declared, "I remember asking these questions."[36]

Anticipating the objection that his championing of race matching within marriage constituted a sort of "reverse racism" that was itself no less evil than antiblack bigotry, Graham noted that his beliefs were aimed neither at keeping the races separate nor at assigning a status of superiority to one group over another. Rather, it was his desire, he said, to develop "solutions for the loss of black mentors and role models at a time when the black community is overrun with crime, drug use, a high dropout rate, and a sense that any black who hopes to find . . . career success must necessarily disassociate himself from his people with the assistance of a white spouse."[37] Seeking to spotlight the systematic consequences of decisions typically defended as innocent assertions of individual autonomy, Graham maintained:

> It's not the discrete decision of any one of these individuals that makes black America stand up and take notice. It is the cumulative effect of each of these personal decisions that bespeaks a frightening pattern for an increasingly impoverished and wayward black community. The cumulative effect is that the very blacks who are potential mentors and supporters of a financially and psychologically depressed black community are

---

*This list could be supplemented by the addition of James Baldwin, Bayard Rustin, Harry Belafonte, Benny Carter, Diahann Carroll, Ward Connerly, Michael Jackson, James Earl Jones, Martin Kilson, Jamaica Kincaid, Audre Lorde, Thurgood Marshall Jr., Michael K. Powell, Richard Pryor, Paul Robeson, Paul Robeson Jr., Diana Ross, Shelby Steele, and William Julius Wilson.

increasingly deserting the black community en masse, both physically and emotionally.[38]

A third theme here is that blacks involved in interracial relationships generally suffer from a noxious combination of self-centeredness and self-denigration. The self-centeredness manifests itself in what might be described as conspicuous consumption of whiteness. In *Jungle Fever*, on-screen critics of Flipper Purify say mockingly that blacks like him are no longer satisfied with obtaining light-skinned colored women as their trophies; nowadays, these critics aver, the Flipper Purifys of Afro-America demand "the real thang"—"Miss Anne," a white female trophy—as the emblematic signature of their prowess.* The self-denigration is revealed, so the theory goes, in a yearning for whiteness that necessarily implies a belittling of blackness. Graham, for one, pushed this point hard, asserting that there existed, in many highly visible interracial relationships between black men and white women, a notable asymmetry in which the men were outstanding and the women mediocre. He was frustrated, he wrote, at seeing accomplished blacks aggressively pursuing unaccomplished whites.[39]† Various characters in

---

*An arresting articulation of the idea of the white woman as trophy was offered by Frantz Fanon, a black Martinican anticolonialist theoretician. Fanon, who himself married a white woman, declared that when his "restless hands caress . . . white breasts, they grasp white civilization and dignity and make them [his]" (*Black Skin, White Masks* [1967], 63; see also David Macey, *Frantz Fanon: A Biography* [2001]).

†The notion that in interracial marriages, black men may in fact trade superior educational or economic attainments for the racial prestige provided even by less accomplished white women was posited as a plausible hypothesis by the distinguished sociologist Robert K. Merton. We should expect, Merton maintained, the pairing of lower-class white women with upper-class Negro men in situations in which "the Negro male exchanges his higher economic position for the white female's higher caste status." See "Intermarriage and the Social Structure: Fact and Theory," in Milton L. Barron, ed., *The Blending American: Patterns of Intermarriage* (1972), 28. See also Kingsley Davis, "Intermarriage in Caste Societies," *American Anthropologist* 43 (1941): 388. Merton's hypothesis is probably the single most fervently discussed theoretical contribution to the sociology of intermarriage. See, e.g., Zhenchao Quien, "Breaking the Racial Barriers: Variations in Interracial Marriage Between 1980 and 1990," *Demography* 34 (1997): 263, 273 (presenting data consistent with the hypothesis); Ernest Porterfield, *Black and White Mixed Marriages* (1978), 86–97 (suggesting that the data do not support Merton's hypothesis); Thomas P. Monahan,

*Jungle Fever* make similar observations. Drew Purify's black girl-friends, commiserating with her, note that it is all too typical that her husband would fall for a white secretary who has not even been to college—in contrast to his wife, a sophisticated, college-educated manager. Purify's brother, Gator, says much the same thing, but with a comedic spin that compares the physical attributes of certain categories of black and white women. Upon meeting Angie, Gator pulls his brother aside and compliments him on his lover's attractiveness. In that sense alone, she is unusual, he says, because while the black women who go out with white men are almost always "slammin'," the white women whom black men date are usually homely—not Penthouse Pets, Gator complains, but outhouse pets.*

## The New Amalgamationism

Despite continued opposition to interracial marriage from various quarters, the general situation for people involved in interracial intimacies has never been better. For the most part, the law prohibits officials from taking race into account in licensing marriages, making child-custody decisions, and arranging adoptions.† Moreover, across the country, public opinion now permits interracial intimacies to be pursued and enjoyed with unparalleled levels of freedom, security, and support. This trend will almost certainly continue; polling data and common observation indicate that younger people tend to be more lib-

---

"The Occupational Clan of Couples Entering into Interracial Marriages," *Journal of Comparative Family Studies* 7 (1976): 175 (also disputing Merton's conclusions).

*Nicole Bouchet recounts that in the 1990s, in a college class on feminist theory, an African American woman professor proffered the following impression of the sort of white women whom black men usually dated or married: "uneducated, unattractive, trailer-park trash that white men don't want anyway" ("On the Contrary," *Interrace*, no. 43 [1998]).

In the first novel written by an African American woman, Harriet E. Wilson's *Our Nig; or, Sketches from the Life of a Free Black* (1859), a pathetic black man, Jim, desires to marry an ill-educated, impoverished, unattractive woman whose principal appeal for him resides in her whiteness. While wooing this woman, Jim says, revealingly, "I's black outside, I know, but I's got a white heart inside" (*Our Nig; or Sketches from the Life of a Free Black* [1859; reprint, 1983]).

†An important exception is the Indian Child Welfare Act. For more on this, see pages 480–518.

eral on these matters than their elders.[40] Thus, despite the black-power backlash and the remnants of white hostility to "race mixing," the most salient fact about interracial intimacies today is that those involved in them have never been in a stronger position, or one in which optimism regarding the future was more realistic.

Dramatic evidence of this is offered by the career of one of the most controversial figures in recent American history: Justice Clarence Thomas, the ultraconservative black jurist whom President George Bush nominated in 1991 to fill the Supreme Court seat being vacated by Thurgood Marshall.* Extraordinary conflict surrounded both the senatorial hearings on his confirmation—during which Thomas's professional and personal suitability for the post was sharply challenged—and the close vote that ultimately put him on the Court.[41] Little negative comment surfaced publicly, however, regarding the nominee's marriage to a white woman, Virginia Lamp.† Notable, too, was that among Thomas's most fervent backers were former segregationists and their ideological descendants. Among these, the most evocative and prominent was Strom Thurmond. A founder of the influential Dixiecrat movement, a proponent of massive resistance to *Brown v. Board of*

---

*Thurgood Marshall, the first black Supreme Court justice, could himself be said to have entered into an interracial marriage when he wed his second wife, Celia Suyat, a Hawaiian of Filipino ancestry. (His first wife, an African American, died in 1954.) At the time of his remarriage, Marshall was the legendary director of litigation for the NAACP, whose leadership worried about the potential fallout. In fact, there was none. (See Juan Williams, *Thurgood Marshall: American Revolutionary* [1998], 243–44.) The relatively uncontroversial nature of the Marshall-Suyat marriage may reflect the sense of many onlookers that it was not really cross-racial, as the new Mrs. Marshall was sufficiently colored to count as a Negro.

†The negative comments that did surface tended to come from blacks. Professor Russell Adams of the Howard University Department of Afro-American Studies, for example, was quoted as remarking that Thomas's "marrying of a white woman is a sign of his rejection of the black community." Likewise, Barbara Reynolds, a black columnist for *USA Today,* noted of Thomas, "Here's a man who's going to decide crucial issues for the country and he has already said no to blacks; he has already said if he can't paint himself white he'll think white and marry a white woman." See Laura Blumenfeld, "The Nominee's Soul Mate; Clarence Thomas's Wife Shares His Ideas. She's No Stranger to Controversy. And She's Adding to His," *Washington Post,* September 10, 1991.

*Education,* and an opponent of the nomination of Thurgood Marshall, Thurmond had once fought desegregation at every turn.* Yet he and many of his fellow conservatives now enthusiastically supported Clarence Thomas. Given the intensity with which such racial traditionalists had always resisted interracial intimacy, their endorsement of a black Supreme Court nominee who was married to a white woman constituted a significant landmark in American race relations.

Two dissenting opinions have been advanced here. The first holds that white conservatives' acceptance of Thomas was an anomaly, based narrowly on his open dissociation from the mainstream of black politics, and as such reflected no substantive change in that group's racial sentiments. Proponents of this argument contend that Thomas is seen by many conservative whites as an "honorary white" and thus no real challenge to white racial hegemony. They further argue that white racism has not so much diminished as become more sophisticated, eschewing the primitive one-drop rule and embracing instead a subtle situational concept of race that employs factors other than skin color and ancestry as guides to ascription. According to this view, many of Thomas's white supporters consciously or unconsciously "whiten" him because of his ultraconservative political opinions. The second dissent asserts that little can be made of the conservative embrace of Thomas because the social meaning of racial intermarriage has itself been transformed. No longer seen as a threat to the established racial order, such marriages have become acceptable, comforting, and even attractive to dominant elites insofar as they camouflage what remains in essence a white-supremacist pigmentocracy. Those who take this view maintain that in the eyes of many whites, the white wife on the arm of a Negro husband is a sign that the man is safe and wants to assimilate. There is some evidentiary basis for this speculation. For instance, when asked how she had felt about the marriage of her niece to Clarence Thomas, one of Virginia Lamp's aunts responded, "He was so nice, we forgot he

---

*For Thurmond's own experience with interracial intimacy and the difficulties encountered in obtaining such information, see page 57.

was black." Thomas treated her niece so well, this aunt continued, that "all of his other qualities made up for his being black."[42]

Nevertheless, considering the vehemence with which, until recently, most whites have disparaged interracial intimacies, and particularly mixed marriage, even mere tolerance is a notably historic departure. The Thomas-Lamp union was one of a total of approximately 177,000 black-white marriages in America in 1987.[43]* In 1960 there were about 51,000 black-white married couples in the United States; in 1970, 65,000; in 1980, 121,000; in 1991, 213,000; and in 1998, 330,000. In other words, between 1960 and 2000, black-white mixed marriages increased more than sixfold. But not only are mixed marriages becoming more numerous; they are also becoming more common among people who are younger and more fertile. Previously, participants in such marriages tended to be older than other brides and grooms. Frequently they were veterans of divorce, embarking on second or third marriages.[44] In recent years, though, interracial couples have been marrying at younger ages than their pioneering predecessors, and have shown a greater inclination to raise children and pursue all of the other "normal" activities that married life offers.

---

*In one sense, the Thomas-Lamp alliance followed the pattern of most black-white interracial marriages: 121,000—or 68 percent—were between black men and white women. Similarly, of the 330,000 such marriages in 1998, 210,000—or 64 percent—involved black husbands and white wives (U.S. Bureau of the Census, 1999). The striking gender differential in blacks' involvement in interracial marriage dates back at least to the 1950s. See Porterfield, *Black and White Mixed Marriages,* 85–98; David M. Heer, "The Prevalence of Black-White Marriage in the United States, 1960 and 1970," *Journal of Marriage and the Family* 36 (1974): 246. Lately, however, an increasing number of black women have also begun to marry across racial lines. In 1980, of 121,000 black-white marriages, 27,000 were between white males and black females; in 1991 the figure was 75,000 out of 231,000. In 1998, in 330,000 black-white couples, there were 120,000 black wives (United States Census Bureau, "MS-3 Interracial Married Couples: 1760 to Present," January 7, 1999). See also Maria P. P. Root, *Love's Revolution: Interracial Marriage* (2001), 179–88. For journalistic explorations of this phenomenon, see Pamela Johnson, "The Color of Love," *Essence,* July 2002; Laura B. Randolph, "Black Woman/White Man: What's Goin' On?," *Ebony,* March 1989; Dorothy Tucker, "Guess Who's Coming to Dinner Now?," *Essence,* April 1987; Shawn D. Lewis, "Black Woman/White Man: The 'Other' Mixed Marriage," *Ebony,* January 1978.

Given the low historical baselines against which trends today are measured, it is easy to exaggerate the scope of black-white marital integration. It should therefore be stressed that mixed marriages remain remarkably rare, comprising a mere .6 percent of the total marriages in 1998, for instance, when 330,000 couples out of 55,305,000 overall had one black and one white partner. Moreover, blacks' racial isolation on the marriage market appears to eclipse that of other people of color. The percentages of Native Americans and Asian Americans marrying whites are much larger than the percentage of blacks doing the same.* Professor Nathan Glazer is correct, then, in stating that "blacks stand out uniquely among the array of ethnic and racial groups in the degree to which marriage remains within the group."[45] Among the complex reasons for this social isolation are aggregate subjective evaluations of marriageability, beauty, personality, comfort, compatibility, and prestige that favor certain groups over others. At the dawn of the twenty-first century, a wide array of social pressures continue to make white-black marital crossings more difficult, more costly, and thus less frequent than other types of interethnic or interracial crossings.

Still, even taking into account the peculiar persistence of the black-white racial divide, the trajectory of this form of miscegenation is clear: through turbulent times and in the face of considerable opposition, the number of black-white marriages has been increasing consistently (albeit slowly) for at least forty years. Reinforcing this growth is the fact that interracial marriage has become compatible with lofty ambitions across a variety of fields—not only entertainment but government service, scholarship, the philanthropic sector, business, and the professions. The Thomas-Lamp marriage is indicative of this trend. So, too,

---

*"Over 93 percent of whites and of blacks marry within their own groups, in contrast to about 70 percent of Asians and of Hispanics and less than one-third of American Indians." Roderick J. Harrison and Claudette E. Bennett, "Racial and Ethnic Diversity," in Reynolds Farley, ed., *State of the Union: America in the 1990s—Vol. Two: Social Trends* (1995), 165.

When people of Latino and Asian ancestry marry exogamously, "their spouses are very likely to be white; interracial marriages in the United States [have seldom] involved the mixing of two minority groups" (Ibid.).

are the unions of William Cohen (former senator from Maine and secretary of defense in the Clinton administration) and his black wife;[46]
Peter Norton (inventor of widely used computer software) and his
black wife;[47]* and Franklin Raines (former director of the Office of
Management and Budget and chief executive officer of Fannie Mae)
and his white wife.[48] Furthermore, despite the substantial influence of
the black-power backlash, some African Americans whose positions
make them directly dependent upon black public opinion have managed to marry whites without losing their footing. A good example is
Julian Bond, the chairman of the board of directors of the NAACP,
whose wife is white.

There are other signs, too, that black-white interracial romance has
become more broadly accepted and even, in certain contexts, quite
fashionable. One such indicator is advertising. Advertisers seek to persuade people to buy goods and services by increasing awareness of
them and associating them with imagined pleasures. In the past, advertisers targeting general audiences with the lure of romance have typically—indeed, overwhelmingly—used couples of the same race. But
these days, at least occasionally, interracial couples are being deployed
as enticements to shop at Nordstrom's, Club Monaco, or Wal-Mart, or
to purchase furniture from IKEA, jeans from Guess, sweaters from
Tommy Hilfiger, cologne from Calvin Klein, shampoo from Procter &
Gamble, or watches from Gucci.[49]

Television programming also signals important changes in sexual attitudes. Prior to the 1960s, portrayals or even insinuations of
black-white interracial romance were virtually nonexistent on TV.
The November 22, 1968, episode of the popular science-fiction series
*Star Trek* marked a breakthrough in showing a kiss shared by the leg-

---

*Reflecting on his marriage, Peter Norton once mused, "Other than sex itself, why
do you want to spend your life in the company of a woman as opposed to a best male
friend? Part of the answer has to do with the wonderful, bizarre, inexplicable differences between male psychology and female psychology. Well, in the same vein, why
would you want to spend your life with a person from the same ethnic background?
You miss the frisson" (quoted in David Owen, "The Straddler," *The New Yorker,*
January 30, 1995).

endary (white) Captain James T. Kirk and (black) Lieutenant Uhura. Remarkably, however, the characters were not portrayed as actively *wanting* to kiss each other; instead they were *forced* to do so by a villain who captured Kirk's vessel, the starship *Enterprise,* and usurped the will of its crew.[50] Not until 1975 did network television portray a married black-white couple, Tom and Helen Willis, who occupied a prominent place on the popular sitcom *The Jeffersons.* The show, a spinoff of Norman Lear's *All in the Family,* was about an eponymous black family whose patriarch, the hardworking but obnoxious George Jefferson, was obsessed with upward mobility, or what the theme song referred to as "movin' on up." The Willises lived in the same expensive apartment building as the Jeffersons. Although George constantly taunted the couple, calling them zebras, the families ultimately merged when the Jeffersons' son married the Willises' daughter.* Since the 1970s, depictions of interracial intimacies have remained rare on commercial television, though they do surface occasionally. In 1989 the short-lived *Robert Guillaume Show* presented viewers with a romance between a divorced black marriage counselor and his white secretary. The following year, the upstart Fox television network reluctantly aired *True Colors,* a situation comedy centered on the marriage of a black dentist (with two teenage sons) and a white schoolteacher (with a live-in mother and a teenage daughter). According to the show's creator, executives at the three older networks (ABC, CBS, and NBC) expressly stated that they were afraid the interracial marriage would alienate potential advertisers and dissuade at least some local affiliates from broadcasting the program.[51] Notwithstanding cold feet at the top, writers have in the last decade or so succeeded in convincing television executives to air more entertainment fare featuring, or at least noting the existence of, interracial intimacy. Indeed, several of the most

---

*Roxie Roker, the black actress who played Helen Willis, was herself married to a white man. The popular musician Lenny Kravitz is their son. See Lynn Norment, "Am I Black, White, or in Between?," *Ebony,* August 1995; "Roxie Roker, 66, Who Broke Barrier in Her Marriage on TV's *Jeffersons,*" *New York Times,* December 6, 1995.

popular and influential shows of the 1990s portrayed transracial romances.[52] Sometimes the racial aspect of the relationship was highlighted, as in *L.A. Law*'s dramatization of a black lawyer feeling that he must choose between his white lover and his job as an elected representative of a mainly black constituency. Sometimes it was ignored, as on *Ally McBeal*, where race matters seldom if ever arose in conversations between the white woman attorney and the black male physician with whom she was infatuated. On occasion, on-screen interracial relationships failed. The producers of *ER*, for example, terminated a romance between a black male doctor and a white colleague, not in deference to viewer opposition but because the black actor involved objected. He complained that whereas his character had always been obnoxious in his dealings with black women, he was now being shown as sympathetic in his treatment of the white woman. On other programs, interracial romance was permitted to blossom. In 1994, for example, on *In the Heat of the Night*, the white sheriff of a town in the Deep South married a black woman on-screen,* and in 1997, a network production of *Cinderella* paired a black actress in the title role with a Filipino Prince Charming, to great popular acclaim.†

In some venues, nonfictional portrayals of interracial intimacy have been sensationally negative, as on confessional talk shows that, for a while at least, uniformly depicted transracial relationships as troubled,

---

*Denise Nicholas, who played the character whom the sheriff married, actively shaped the public image of her role, particularly with respect to the interracial relationship. Nicholas felt that the characters "should either break [the relationship] off or get married because oftentimes, historically, interracial relationships were back-alley affairs, hidden and lied about, particularly in the South. It became really important to me that the [characters] do something dignified; I didn't want my character to be cheap" ("Denise Nicholas and Carroll O'Connor Wed on TV Drama 'In the Heat of the Night,'" *Jet*, May 9, 1994). It should be recalled that the basis for the television series was the film of the same name (1967), which featured a thoroughly bigoted white sheriff (played by Rod Steiger, in an Academy Award–winning performance).

†ABC's hugely successful musical production starred Brandy as Cinderella and Paolo Montalban as the prince. Taking the role of Prince Charming's mother, the queen, was a black actress, Whoopi Goldberg, while the king was played by a white actor, Victor Garber. See Veronica Chambers, "The Myth of Cinderella," *Newsweek*, November 3, 1997; "Cinderella TV Music Special Produces Spectacular Rating for ABC," *Jet*, November 24, 1997.

weird, or pathological.* In other contexts, however, televison programs have acknowledged the gamut of personalities and emotions to be found among those who happen to be involved in interracial intimacies. In the fall of 1999, the Public Broadcasting System (PBS) aired *An American Love Story*, a ten-hour documentary film by Jennifer Fox that chronicled the lives of an interracial family: Bill Sims, a black man, Karen Wilson, a white woman, and their two daughters, Cecily and Chaney.[53] Wilson and Sims first met in 1967, at a resort where he was playing piano in a rhythm-and-blues band and she was vacationing with her parents. He was the son of a cleaning woman and a steelworker who was also a Baptist minister; her father was a machinist, and her mother was a grocery clerk. When their courtship began, Bill was eighteen and Karen seventeen. Neither set of parents objected to the relationship, and both urged the couple to marry after Wilson got pregnant (though they in fact did not do so until the child was six years old).

Whites in Wilson's hometown of Prospect, Ohio, strongly condemned her romance with Sims. Her supposed friends ostracized the couple, and the local sheriff jailed Sims on several occasions for no other reason than to harass him. In 1972 they moved with their baby daughter to Columbus, but even in this larger, less isolated locale, they encountered overt hostility. They suspected bigots of killing their dog and setting their car afire in a successful campaign to frighten them away. They moved again, this time to Flushing, New York, where they hoped to find a more open-minded community.

Over the years, the Wilson-Sims family subsisted largely on Karen's reliable earnings as a manager, supplemented by Bill's spotty wages as, among other things, a carpenter, mail carrier, and musician. At the price of some tedium, *An American Love Story* shows its subjects engaged in all the quotidian tasks of daily life—cooking, cleaning, resting, seeking comfort, venting frustration—that have little or nothing to do with

---

*Such depictions were no accident. When television producers sought guests for these programs, they advertised for people who had had *bad* experiences in or on account of interracial relationships. It was this bias that gave rise to episodes such as "Woman Disowned by Her Family for Dating a Black Man" on *Jenny Jones* and "Blacks and Blondes: White Girls Dating Black Guys for Sex, Style, and Status" on *Geraldo*.

racial differences. It also shows them facing various nonracial crises, including Karen's hysterectomy and Bill's alcoholism. Almost inevitably, though, racial difficulties surface to menace the couple and their children. Among the most poignant segments of the series are wrenching scenes from Cecily's years as an undergraduate at Colgate College, where tyrannical black classmates tell her, essentially, that if she wants to be their friend, she must refuse to join a predominantly white sorority and, more generally, defer to their black-separatist sensibilities. She declines their terms, and they retaliate; she is hurt. Throughout, the television audience is privy to the conflict.*

The creators of *An American Love Story* wanted to document an interracial marriage that spanned the final decades of the twentieth century. Its subjects, for their part, wanted to change perceptions through education; this ambition constituted the principal explanation offered by the Sims-Wilson clan for permitting their family life to be examined in such a public manner. Education was also the primary aim cited by the program's director, Jennifer Fox, a white woman who credited her own love affair with a black man with opening her eyes to important areas of American life to which she had previously been blind.†

On the big screen, too, recent years have seen an increase in both the number and the quality of depictions of interracial intimacy.[54] There was a time, not so long ago, when the scarcity of such portrayals made keeping track of them easy; now, because of their increasing numbers and variety, that task is much more difficult. True, the fear of an adverse audience response can still cause cautious film producers to suppress interracial romance, not only through their choice of projects but even in their handling of plot points. In John Grisham's novel *The*

---

*Several months after *An American Love Story* aired, Cecily Wilson married a white union organizer whom she had met on a blind date. See "Weddings: Cecily Wilson, Gregory Speller," *New York Times*, May 7, 2000.

†Fox has stated that she was surprised by some of her relatives' negative reactions to her interracial relationship, and surprised, too, by the regularity of the racial mistreatment her black lover suffered. In retrospect, she observes, "it was almost like I was deluded or something; I thought I was living in a different world than I was living in" (quoted in Paula Span, "Modern Family Life in Black and White: PBS Documentary Chronicles an Interracial Marriage," *Washington Post*, September 9, 1999).

*Pelican Brief* (1992), for instance, the protagonists become lovers, but in the screen version (1993), there is no romance; the relationship remains resolutely platonic. The reason for this alteration is obvious: the male lead is played by a black actor (Denzel Washington), and the female lead by a white actress (Julia Roberts). There are, moreover, scores of other examples of black actors apparently being singled out for Hollywood's cold-shower treatment lest they mirror real-life interracial erotic excitement. Prominent among these desexualized roles are Will Smith's character in *Men in Black* (1997) and Wesley Snipes's in *Murder at 1600* (1997). This approach led one wag to remark, in reference to *The Bone Collector* (1999), that the only way Denzel Washington would ever be shown "getting the girl" was if he played a man paralyzed from the waist down. That being said, a number of major motion pictures released in the past decade have followed actors and actresses of all complexions in their pursuit of sexual pleasures across color lines, and have done so with a boldness that probably would not have been tolerated in the environment that generated *Guess Who's Coming to Dinner?* Examples include the explicit erotic grapplings of Lawrence Fishburne and Ellen Barkin in *Bad Company* (1995), Wesley Snipes and Natassia Kinski in *One Night Stand* (1997), Reese Witherspoon and Bookeem Woodbine in *Freeway* (1996), Warren Beatty and Halle Berry in *Bulworth* (1998), Tom Cruise and Thandie Newton in *Mission Impossible 2* (2000), Julia Stiles and Sean Patrick Thomas in *Save the Last Dance* (2000), and Halle Berry and Billy Bob Thornton in *Monster's Ball* (2001).* In increasing numbers of films, moreover, interracial intimacy has been emerging as simply one part of a larger story in which racial difference is of little or no significance. This is an important development because presuming the normalcy of interracial intimacy—treating it as "no big deal"—may be more subversive of traditional norms than stressing the racial heterodoxy of such relationships. Although examples of this presumption can be found in several films (e.g., *Pulp Fiction* [1994], *Cruel Intentions* [1999], and *Mystery*

---

*Two excellent coming-of-age films that evoke the hazards and rewards of teenage interracial dating in the 1950s are Robert De Niro's *A Bronx Tale* (1993) and Barry Levinson's *Liberty Heights* (2000).

*Men* [1999]), the most significant was the blockbuster *The Bodyguard* (1992), which starred Kevin Costner and Whitney Houston.

Literature comprises yet another forum in which negative depictions of interracial intimacies are being supplemented by positive portrayals, though the former continue to dwarf the latter.[55] White racist writers have long condemned miscegenation as both unnatural and disgusting. Writing under the pseudonym Oliver Bolokitten, Jerome B. Holgate authored *A Sojourn in the City of Amalgamation, in the Year of Our Lord, 19 __* (1835), a novel that envisions a future in which intermarriage is rife. In Holgate's dystopia, white abolitionists associate on intimate terms with blacks, even though their very senses alert them to the danger of their doing so, causing them to retch constantly in reaction to the supposedly foul odors given off by the Negroes. Disregarding their physical repulsion, the white amalgamationists not only persist in their own interracial socializing but also force their children to associate with blacks, even to the extent of drugging resistant daughters.[56] Following in Holgate's footsteps have come many other opponents of miscegenation, similarly racist and similarly mediocre as literary artists. One of these was Gertrude Atherton, author of *Senator North* (1900), a novel in which a white man commits suicide upon learning that the woman he has married is distantly related to African Americans. Another was William Pierce, author of *The Turner Diaries* (1978), an apocalyptic vision of a future in which Christian white supremacists prevail over their enemies, including blacks, Jews, Latinos, and other whites who have disgraced themselves by associating with their racial inferiors. Pierce enthusiastically depicts the murder of white women who are killed on account of their sexual intimacy with black men.

Black writers, too, have used literature to attack miscegenation. We have already noted the work of LeRoi Jones in this context.* There are others as well. In *'Sippi* (1967), John Oliver Killens portrays interracial intimacy as an infantile phase that many black men go through before taking on the serious responsibilities of racial loyalty and leadership. Rejecting a white woman who expects him to marry her, the hero of

---

*See pages 113–14.

'*Sippi* declares that "marrying the white man's daughter is not a part of the Black Power program"—a jilting that the narrator approvingly describes as "sweet revenge."[57]* Cecil Brown's *The Life and Loves of Mr. Jiveass Nigger* (1969) offers plenty of interracial sex but no interracial love. "It is a tragedy," the novel's protagonist asserts, "if a black man lets himself love something in a white woman, just as it is if a man lets himself get fucked by another man."[58] Set in Copenhagen, Denmark, in the 1960s, Brown's novel chronicles the shenanigans of a group of black gigolos who service white women. The main character, George Washington, has fled to Scandinavia in order "to get the White Bitch out of his system by wallowing in whiteness until he could live without it."[59] One of the white women he encounters there is the American consul, who pays Washington and other black men for their sexual attention and is so badly beaten by one of them that she is rendered sterile.

Writers of all hues have turned to depictions of interracial romance to highlight the depth and persistence and perniciousness of racism. Although some of these authors may have had no objection themselves to interracial intimacy, they nonetheless portrayed it in ways likely to be viewed by most readers as frightening. In the novels and stories (*Light in August* [1932]; *Absalom, Absalom!* [1936]; *Go Down, Moses* [1942]) of William Faulkner, for example, interracial intimacy emerges repeatedly as a problem—a problem, moreover, surrounded by shame, misery, ostracism, violence, and death. Other novelists (most of them considerably less skilled than Faulkner) have also highlighted trouble and tragedy in interracial intimacies. Thus, in Anna Dickenson's *What Answer?* (1868), the white English wife of a Negro man dies in childbirth after a race riot drives them from their home in Philadelphia. Years later, the couple's daughter marries a white man, only to be murdered with him in the New York draft riots of 1863. In Albion Tourgee's *Toinette* (1874), a former slave master is struck blind when he decides to propose to the woman who was once his slave mistress. In Lillian

---

*The jilted white woman is a racist unaware of her prejudice. "I gave you my pure white body," she fumes at her former beau, "and you're entirely ungrateful about it. I mean, I even overlooked the fact that you were black" (John Oliver Killens, '*Sippi* [1967], 341).

Smith's *Strange Fruit* (1944), a black woman's brother kills her white lover, an act that provokes a white mob to murder a wholly innocent African American bystander. In Chester Himes's *The Primitive* (1953), a black man and a white woman become intimate not because they feel a healthy attraction to each other but because they are driven by pathological expediency. He is impelled, like an addict, to sleep with a white woman; as for her, "only when sleeping with a Negro could she feel secure in the knowledge that she wasn't dirt." To add to the misery, the man senselessly kills the woman.* In James Baldwin's *Another Country* (1962), a white woman who has become sexually involved with a black man has a nervous breakdown; her black lover commits suicide. In Ann Fairbairn's *Five Smooth Stones* (1966), the hero, a black lawyer-activist, marries his white girlfriend and is almost immediately done in by a vengeful bigot.† In *I Want a Black Doll* (1967), Frank Hercules's principal characters have deep feelings of affection for each other but still fail to surmount the racial difficulties that divide them: "They knew ecstasy but never achieved union; never became one, were always straining towards but never really touching each other, were always a Negro man and a white woman."[60] Buffeted by doubts within and hostility without, their life together falls apart. He poisons their relationship with mistaken suspicions that she is seeing another man—a white man. She tries to abort their baby and dies in the process. In Ernest Gaines's *The Auto-*

---

*Chester Himes once pronounced interracial sexual relationships "battlefields of racial antagonism" (quoted in Jonathan Little, "Definition Through Difference: The Tradition of Black-White Miscegenation in American Fiction" [Ph.D. diss., University of Wisconsin–Madison, 1988], 254). His novels offered dismaying reports from that front; see, e.g., *If He Hollers Let Him Go* (1943), *Lonely Crusade* (1947), *The Third Generation* (1954), and *Pinktoes* (1961).

†Further illustrating the doom that supposedly shadows interracial marriages is an anguished alcoholic character in *Five Smooth Stones,* who passes for white for a time at Vassar College before dropping out. She is the daughter of a frightfully unhappy interracial couple who either committed suicide together or killed each other. For an account of a real episode of passing at Vassar, see pages 294–95. Of the novels mentioned here, Fairbairn's was one of the most popular in its day, though now it has been largely forgotten. A Book-of-the-Month Club selection, it sold more than a million copies and went through ten printings. Its author wrote under a pseudonym; her real name was Dorothy Tate. See Marcia Press, "That Black Man–White Woman Thing: Images of an American Taboo" (Ph.D. diss., Indiana University, 1989), 141.

*biography of Miss Jane Pittman* (1971), a white man kills himself because the colored woman he loves refuses, for racial reasons, to marry him. In Calvin Hernton's *Scarecrow* (1974), the black protagonist kills his white wife. In sum, for many writers miscegenation has been the har-binger of mayhem, misery, and death—the very symbol of destructive intimacy.

Distinctly undeveloped is the literary tradition that portrays inter-racial relationships that are at least potentially rewarding. Pioneering contributions to this tradition include Lydia Maria Child's *A Romance of the Republic* (1867), William Dean Howells's *An Imperative Duty* (1892), Sinclair Lewis's *Kingsblood Royal* (1947), and Willard Savoy's *Alien Land* (1949). In spite of their more benevolent attitude, however, these novels share a striking feature: they all involve "black" figures who look "white," a characteristic that attenuates the challenge posed by their marriages. In *A Romance of the Republic,* the colored women who wed across the race line can and do pass as white for much of their lives. Similarly, the putatively colored man who marries white is actu-ally white himself, having been raised as a slave by mistake. *An Impera-tive Duty* centers on a woman who was raised as white and learned about her colored ancestry only as an adult. While the white man who becomes her husband is aware of her racial heritage, she continues to hold herself out as white to everyone else. In *Alien Land,* the colored protagonist looks white and passes for white after his marriage. In *Kingsblood Royal,* the central character, who used to be a white racist, publicly identifies himself as colored, transforms his thinking, and becomes a champion of the rights of colored people—as does his white wife, who has herself been a complacent bigot. Still, his situation is hardly that of an ordinary black man: of one thirty-second colored ancestry, he is very much a voluntary Negro.

The attempt to compile a list of novels, stories, or plays in which interracial romance or marriage is portrayed in a positive light, and whose characters are explicitly perceived as colored, makes for an instructive exercise. The rarity of such writings underlines the degree to which miscegenation and its representations have been discouraged. In *Subdued Southern Nobility* (1882), an anonymous novelist crafted a story featuring a Negro woman who happily marries a northern white man, and in *Hearts of Gold* (1896), J. McHenry Jones brought to life a wealthy, educated white woman who happily marries a black man.[61] Then, in the late 1960s, Frank Yerby eschewed the black-power backlash at that time in vogue. In *Speak Now* (1969), he created an interracial couple who, for once, did not have to endure the horrible scourges imposed upon so many of their literary predecessors traversing the color bar. Nor are their racial identities ambiguous, or their characterizations too angelic to credit. The white woman protagonist is initially a bigot, but she evolves. Her affair with the black man whom she grows to love corrects her racist upbringing. Just as she rejects the racial chauvinism of disapproving whites, so, too, does her husband reject that of disapproving blacks. Asked tauntingly whether he has any race pride, Yerby's protagonist answers in the negative. Maintaining that "a biological accident is hardly sufficient motive for self-congratulation," he declares that the only race in which he takes pride "is the human race."[62]

Yerby chose to situate his couple outside of the United States, setting their story in France—suggesting, perhaps, that in the late 1960s, at least, America was still too toxic to permit the healthy growth of an interracial affair. That affair does grow, and bloom; it promises the couple a future, as the novel ends on a determinedly optimistic note:

> Quite suddenly they both knew it was going to work. To go on. In spite of everything. That even after it did go flat, become routine, descended to the level of boredom all marriages get to, sooner or later, even if it went bad in any of the ten thousand different ways most legally sanctioned matings do, they'd hold on, endure, cling to one another. . . . They would be very careful of each other, until that care became a condition of living, and . . . a means of preserving the tenderness they now felt.[63]

Since the publication of *Speak Now,* a tiny procession of black writers has also approvingly depicted interracial love stories. Barbara Chase-Riboud (*Sally Hemings* [1979]) and Charles Johnson (*The Oxherding Tale* [1982]) did so in innovative novels that envision loving interracial relationships in the era of slavery—thereby rejecting the dogma that bondage rendered impossible authentic love between masters and slaves.* Probing but ultimately approving portraits of inter-racial relationships set in more recent times include Dorothy West's *The Wedding* (1995) and Stanley Crouch's *Don't the Moon Look Lonesome* (2000).

Sandra Kitt has written a series of novels notable for their tender portrayal of people whose search for companionship takes them across racial lines. In Kitt's *The Color of Love* (1995) and *Close Encounters* (2000), black women fall in love with white policemen. In Eric Jerome Dickey's *Milk in My Coffee* (1998), a young black man whose office is adorned with a photograph of Malcolm X becomes joyfully involved with a white woman he meets during a shared cab ride. The work of both Kitt and Dickey has been categorized as "popular fiction" as opposed to "serious literature"—a label that has limited these writers' artistic and intellectual influence, insofar as their efforts have been largely ignored by academics, intellectuals, and the major book reviews. Nevertheless, the fact that their books have been widely disseminated on the mass market indicates some confidence on the part of profit-minded publishers that a broad audience is open to enjoying interracial love stories.

One of the most memorable of the novels championing interracial relationships is also one of the most neglected. Ann Allen Shockley's *Loving Her* (1974) is the story of Renay Lee, a black woman who flees her abusive black husband, Jerome. Jerome raped Renay on a date when they were both college students; impregnated by the assault, she married him out of fear, ignorance, and desperation. After several years of an increasingly hellish existence punctuated by her husband's cruel sale of her treasured piano, Renay, young daughter in tow, leaves her marriage and moves in with Terry, a white woman with whom she proceeds to fall in love. The escape revives Renay; suddenly "there was life in life now, and love in its moments."[64] But tragedy awaits her: Jerome abducts their daughter, gets drunk, and crashes his car, killing the child. Distraught, Renay leaves Terry, then quickly returns to forge a union that Shockley unabashedly embraces: "Two as one, one as two, waiting for the morning, which promised to be even better than the night."[65]

---

*See pages 41–49.

Shockley audaciously challenges the black-power backlash by treating with respect both the interracial and the lesbian aspects of the Renay-Terry relationship. Many black opponents of interracial intimacy have also been critics of gay and lesbian sexuality.[66]* Some have even gone so far as to claim that gay-lesbian sexuality is foreign to authentic black culture, and that black gays and lesbians have merely succumbed to white sexual degeneracy. Shockley's counter-attack on such views is unsparing. She searingly debunks patriarchal black nationalism by picturing Renay as Jerome's slave. Even more provocatively, she imagines a black woman who finds greater sexual pleasure with her white female lover than with her black male husband. Shockley thus simultaneously subverts marriage, the presumed superiority of heterosexuality, the supposed primacy of black male sexual prowess, and the taboo against interracial sex. In college bull sessions, Renay's black friends "would wonder how Lena Horne and Pearl Bai-

---

*Recalling his struggle to come out to his black family, activist-intellectual Keith Boykin wrote:

> Over the phone, I told my sister I was gay and she accepted it very sup-portively. Her most intrusive question about my boyfriend was predictable. "Is he black or white?" she asked. "White," I sheepishly responded. That simple question led me to examine whether my family would react more favorably to my being involved with a black man than with a white woman. Homosexual and interracial relationships raise many of the same concerns to black families, including continuation of the family, humilia-tion of the family, and commitment to the race. A black man who dates only men raises the specter of the extinction of the family name, potentially causes embarrassment to the family, and often suggests an irresponsible disregard for the need to create strong black families. Dating a white woman raises similar concerns, compromising the racial purity of the fam-ily and the couple's offspring. Black homosexuals dating each other raises concerns too, but at least [it] suggest[s] some appreciation of the beauty within the race; it does not seem as much an abandonment of blackness as does interracial dating. The shared racial identity develops a much stronger family bond than any presumed identity based on sexual orientation. I never polled my family members, but ultimately I decided that some would be more disturbed by my dating a white woman, while others would be more upset by my dating a black man. This confusion helped me realize that I had to live my life for myself, not for my family. [*One More River to Cross: Black and Gay in America* (1996), 22–23.]

ley could wake up in the morning to white faces beside them. But now she knew: you can't confine love to color."[67]*

Perhaps the most potent influence in creating new possibilities for interracial intimacy is that wielded by individuals engaged in (or born of) transracial dating, marriage, and parenting.[68] This population, numbering in the hundreds of thousands, exhibits tremendous variety. One generalization that can properly be made about it, however, is that it is becoming increasingly vocal. There was a time, not so long ago, when the vast majority within this group sought invisibility; now, by contrast, many of its members seek recognition and are establishing or joining advocacy organizations devoted to publicizing their views and institutionalizing their presence. Announcing the formation of the Association of Multi-Ethnic Americans (AMEA) in November 1988, Carlos Fernandez declared:

> We who embody the melting pot . . . stand up, not merely as neutrals in interethnic conflicts, but as intolerant participants against racism from whatever quarter it may come. . . . We are the faces of the future. Against the travails of regressive interethnic division and strife, we can be a solid core of unity bonding the peoples of all cultures together in the common course of human progress.[69]

People involved in interracial intimacies used to voice quiet requests for simple protection against intimidation and violence. Now their demands are becoming more ambitious. One of these has to do with racial labeling. Many interracial couples object to standardized forms that compel them to designate their children either merely "black" or merely "white."[70] Similarly, many who identify themselves as "mixed"— or "mulatto" or "half-and-half" or "multiracial"—bridle at classificatory

---

*Other fictional explorations of interracial same-sex romance include Timothy Murphy, *Getting Off Clean* (1997), Steven Corbin, *Fragments That Remain* (1993), and Wallace Thurman, *Infants of the Spring* (1932).

regimes that impose singular racial identifications, as if everyone must be *only* white *or* black *or* Latino *or* Asian (etc., etc.). Prior to the census of 2000, the United States Census Bureau counted individuals according to that assumption. But after a good deal of prodding by AMEA and similar groups, the bureau decided to broaden the menu boxes available for indicating racial affiliation. Rather than being limited to only one box, respondents are now authorized to check whatever boxes they deem applicable, though the census bureau continues to decline to offer a separate "multiracial" box.* One complaint leveled against the traditional "check one box" regime is that it fosters confusion and inaccuracy—describing as "black," for example, people who are also partly white or partly Native American or partly Asian. Susan Graham, the (white) founder of Project RACE (Reclassify All Children Equally) notes that her "child has been white on the U.S. Census, black at school, and multiracial at home, all at the same time."[71] Beyond the issue of statistical inaccuracy, the system has more personal ramifications, in that it compels mixed individuals to select for recognition only one aspect of their composite background, and thereby subordinate all the other aspects.

The census bureau's multiple-box-checking initiative addresses some but by no means all of the objections raised by critics.† Some contend that even the option of checking several boxes indicates, in effect, that multiracial individuals are only parts of other communities, rather than constituent members of a distinct multiracial community of their own.[72] Some observers protest, moreover, the continuation of *any*

---

*Although they failed to persuade the United States Census Bureau to offer the "multiracial" box for the 2000 census, multiracialist reformers have succeeded in convincing a number of state governments—including those of Georgia, Illinois, Florida, Indiana, Michigan, and Ohio—to require that such a box be provided on state forms that collect racial data. They have also managed to convince several important private institutions, among them Harvard University, to add a "multiracial" category alongside the other, more familiar and established, choices. See Tanya Kateri Hernandez, "'Multiracial' Discourse: Racial Classifications in an Era of Color-Blind Jurisprudence," *Maryland Law Review* 57 (1998): 97, 98 n. 4.

†When the racial-classification issue was decided for the 2000 census, the person in charge of the supervisory agency was Franklin Raines, a black man married to a white woman. Franklin and Wendy Raines had two children who themselves faced this classification dilemma. See Julia Malone, "Facing the Racial Question: More Categories in the Census," *The Atlanta Journal and Constitution*, October 15, 1997.

racial scheme of classification, however it may be supplemented or repackaged.[73] Whatever one may think of the ideas propounded by these various dissidents,[74] it is clear that they are flexing their political muscles as never before and affecting hearts and minds in fundamental ways. They are not content to accept inherited conventions but insist instead on adding their own preferences to America's cultural mix. Professor Maria P. P. Root has demanded a Bill of Rights for racially mixed people, which would include the rights to identify one's race differently in different situations, to change one's racial identity over a lifetime (and more than once), to have loyalties to and identifications with more than one racial group, and to be able freely to choose whom to befriend and love.[75] The winner of the 1995 Miss USA beauty pageant objected to being pegged as "black." "If people are going to know me," Chelsi Smith explained, "it's important for them to know that I'm black and white and that it hasn't been a disadvantage."[76] Tiger Woods likewise does not enjoy being referred to as the first "black" or "African American" golf superstar, believing that those labels obscure other aspects of his ancestry that are just as important to him. He has therefore coined the term "'Cablinasian'—[for] Caucasian, Black, Indian, Asian"— to describe himself.* The coinage has proved controversial.† Many people, mainly blacks, have accused him of wanting to flee an African

---

*Woods made his views known on Oprah Winfrey's television show soon after he won the prestigious Masters golf tournament. See Greg Couch, "Woods: I'm More Than Black," *Chicago Sun-Times,* April 22, 1997, p. 1.

†In a satirical essay entitled "The Mulatto Millennium," Danzy Senna facetiously defined "Cablinasian" thus:

> A rare exotic breed found mostly in California. This is the mother of all mixtures. . . . A show mulatto, with great performance skills, the Cablinasian will be whoever the crowd wants him to be, and can switch at the drop of a dime. Does not, however, answer to the name Black. . . . Note: If you spot a Cablinasian, please contact the Benetton Promotions Bureau. [In Claudine Chiawei O'Hearn, ed., *Half and Half: Writers on Growing Up Biracial and Bicultural* (1998), 26.]

For a powerful defense of Woods's position, see Gary Kamiya, "Cablinasian like Me," Salon.com, April 1997. For a critique, see Leonard Pitts, "Is There Room in This Sweet Land of Liberty for Such a Thing as 'Cablinasian'? Face It, Tiger: If They Say You're Black, Then You're Black," *Baltimore Sun,* April 29, 1997.

American identity that whites will impose upon him regardless of his preferences. ("When the black truck comes around," one observer quipped, "they're gonna haul his ass on it.")[77] Such reactions notwithstanding, the real point here is that Root, Smith, Woods, and tens of thousands more like them have felt sufficiently self-assured to speak up, and have received substantial support in doing so. Their conduct mirrors and strengthens a new force in America: the will of people engaged in or born of multiracial relationships, who have begun to insist upon public recognition of the full complexity of their lives.

Across the country, scores of interracial support groups have sprung up, among them MOSAIC (Multiethnics of Southern Arizona in Celebration), A Place for Us (North Little Rock, Arkansas), I-Pride (Interracial Intercultural Pride, Berkeley, California), MASC (Multiracial Americans of Southern California, Los Angeles, California), F.C. (Families of Color) Communiqué (Fort Collins, Colorado), Interracial Family Alliance (Augusta, Georgia), Society for Interracial Families (Troy, Michigan), 4c (Cross Cultural Couples & Children, Plainsboro, New Jersey), the Interracial Club of Buffalo, the Interracial Family Circle of Washington, D.C., and HONEY (Honor Our New Ethnic Youth, Eugene, Oregon). On college campuses, students can join organizations such as FUSION (Wellesley), Kaleidoscope (University of Virginia), Students of Mixed Heritage and Culture (SMHAC, Amherst), Half 'n' Half (Bryn Mawr), and Mixed Plate (Grinnell). These groups offer forums in which people can meet others in their situation, disseminate relevant information, debate, and organize. Although most of these organizations lack deep roots, many display a vigor and resourcefulness that suggest they will survive into the foreseeable future. They stem from and represent a community in the making. It is a community united by a common demand that the larger society respect and be attentive to people who either by descent or by choice fall outside the conventional racial groupings—people who are partners in interracial couples, parents of children whose race is different from their own, and children whose race differs from their parents'. The members of this community want whites to cease viewing them as products or agents of an alarming mongrelization. They want blacks to stop regarding them as inauthentic and unstable in-betweeners. They want security amid the

established communities from which they have migrated. They want to emerge from what the writer Lise Funderberg has aptly called the "racial netherworld."[78] They want to enjoy interaction with others without regret or fear, defensiveness or embarrassment. They want respect.

The community arising from interracial intimacies is rent by all manner of divisions. While some of its partisans trumpet pride in their identity,* others urge the dampening of such sentiments, fearful that pride will inevitably degenerate into chauvinism—especially in a society in which lighter-skinned hybrids have often been seen as superior to their darker-skinned relatives.[79] Where some voice unequivocally a desire to inculcate a strong sense of multiracial peoplehood, others question the wisdom of creating new racial groups.[80] The most salient feature of this nascent and fractious community, however, is a new sense of assertive self-confidence—a heady feeling that transracial affiliations are, for the first time in American history, being rightly appreciated as valuable resources. An editorial in the spring 2000 issue of *Mavin*, a magazine of "the mixed race experience," is indicative of this spirit. The 2000 census, wrote *Mavin*'s editor in chief, Matt Kelley, is finally granting the mixed race community "institutional recognition":

> Up until now we have been a one- or two-generation-only community. . . . But now, having gained some form of institutional legitimacy, we may perpetuate [ourselves]. . . . We have an opportunity to take advantage of our collective resources and improve discourse both within and outside our fledgling community. That is a social and political cause worth organizing for.[81]

---

*A letter published in *Spectrum*, the newsletter of the Multiracial Americans of Southern California (MASC), flatly stated, "Like it or not, racially mixed people are the most beautiful people of all." See Lisa Jones, *Bulletproof Diva: Tales of Race, Sex and Hair* (1994), 59. Similarly prideful is Carlos A. Fernandez's remark that the multiracial community "is uniquely situated to confront racial and interethnic issues because of the special experiences and understanding we acquire in the intimacy of our families and our personalities" ("Testimony of the Association of Multi-ethnic Americans Before the Subcommittee on Census, Statistics, and Postal Personnel of the U.S. House of Representatives," in Naomi Zack, ed., *American Mixed Race: The Culture of Microdiversity* [1995]).

Among the publications supported by and aimed at the emerging community of politically self-conscious multiracial people—particularly those whose affiliations bridge the black-white racial divide—one of the most informative was *Interrace*. Candace Mills, a black woman, and Gabe Grosz, her white husband, started the magazine in 1989. According to them, *Interrace*

> proudly celebrates racial diversity and colorblind love. We cele-
> brate the interracial family, the interracial child and adult, and
> the interracial couple. We celebrate freedom. Freedom of the
> pursuit of happiness as every individual sees it, not as society as
> a whole sees it. . . . *Interrace Magazine* is not a white only,
> black only, hispanic only, or asian only magazine. *Interrace
> Magazine* is a people magazine. A magazine for all people
> involved in interracial relationships and for the beautiful off-
> spring they create![82]*

A low-budget *Ebony* for the multiracial community, *Interrace* was an irregular quarterly that performed a variety of functions. First of all, it served as a mirror, feeding the hunger of multiracial individuals and

---

*Mills and Grosz met in 1980, when she was a fifteen-year-old student and track star at a public high school in Los Angeles, and he was a twenty-eight-year-old teacher and track coach. Two years later, they became sexually intimate. Her parents found out and pressed for a criminal prosecution. Grosz was convicted of illegal sexual intercourse with a minor, put on three years' probation, and ordered to stay away from Mills until she was eighteen. Two weeks after Mills graduated from high school, she and Grosz were married; eventually they became parents. See *Interrace,* November/December 1989, pp. 15–20; November/December 1992, p. 2; July/August 1990, pp. 9–10.

Mills was clearly the dominant figure in running the magazine. (Grosz's name appeared on the masthead for several years but dropped off it as of the May 2000 issue.) Explaining why she started *Interrace* at a time when she had little money and no publishing experience, Mills states, "[I] wanted my biracial daughter (then 5 years old) to have a magazine of her own, one that would positively and truthfully explore interracial relationships and multiracial identity. . . . I was young and ambitious and obsessed with my desire to make a difference" (*Interrace,* spring 2000, p. 2). It seems, sadly, that *Interrace* has ceased publication.

families to see themselves as part of the social landscape.[83] Accordingly, many of the magazine's pages were given over to photographs of inter-racial couples, mixed-race children, and multiracial family gatherings.* Second, it offered a sounding board for those who wished to relate experiences stemming from their interracial relationships. A 1994 arti-cle entitled "When Your In-Laws Drive You Crazy!," by Henry Rubin, described numerous instances of in-laws objecting to marriages on racial grounds.[84] In one particularly sad case history, a black man noted that members of his white fiancée's family had shot at him, beaten him, poured sugar into his gas tank, and slashed his tires. Rubin's own expe-rience with the subject came through his white Jewish mother's disap-proval of his marriage to a (presumably Christian) Puerto Rican. Like many features in *Interrace*, the piece ended by emphasizing the po-tential of bigotry to give way to enlightenment, and injustice to re-demption. "With a little patience and a lot of understanding," Rubin promised, "many in-law problems can be handled successfully."[85] His mother, for example, overcame much of her prejudiced disapproval of his wife, managing a transformation that undoubtedly encouraged his conclusion that "if you are persistent and are committed to your inter-racial relationship then the rewards will surely come your way."[86] *Interrace* constantly served a cheerleading function, self-consciously striving to boost the morale of its constituency. Seeking to rebut the sus-picion that interracial intimacies produce misfits and attract mainly weirdos, the magazine highlighted likable people of accomplishment, including Dan O'Brien (an Olympic track and field star and the biracial adopted son of a white couple), Eartha Kitt (a biracial entertainer who has been romantically involved with a number of white men), Peggy Lipton (a white actress, best known for her role on the television series *The Mod Squad*, who was married to the black musical impresario

---

*Seeking material and an audience for a book of photographs and stories, *Inter-race* maintained in an advertisement that "you and your spouse can be included in . . . *The Greatest Love: A Celebration of Interracial Marriage*, which will portray the beauty and joy of interracial marriage. Please send us one or two wedding photos that best capture the joy of the moment." See back cover of *Interrace* 46 (1999).

Quincy Jones), and Marian Wright Edelman (the black founder of the Children's Defense Fund who married a white man in Virginia soon after the *Loving* decision).[87]

In an effort to refute still-prevalent beliefs that interracial intimacies are doomed to unhappiness and failure, *Interrace* profiled smiling, vigorous, enraptured couples who had managed to stay together for substantial periods of time. In 1993, for instance, it introduced readers to Charlene McGrady (black), Doug Fearn (white), and Hannon Fearn (mixed) of West Chester, Pennsylvania. Describing their experience, McGrady commented, "We've never felt any overt condemnation. . . . We think this is because we don't walk around with a defensive posture. . . . We know we belong together and act it! . . . Our marriage is happy, secure and thriving, and not all that different from any other marriage with children."[88] To drive the point home, McGrady concluded her testimony, "I didn't know I could be so happy."[89]

Later that same year, *Interrace* ran another "Success Story," this one about the China family: William China, a black man from South Carolina; Mary China, a white woman from New Jersey; William's child from a previous marriage (to a black woman); and the two children William and Mary had together. The interracial character of the Chinas' marriage had drawn some unwanted attention—opposition to it, for example, had probably prompted one employer to wrongly fire Mary—but by and large the Chinas expressed satisfaction with their lot and high hopes for their future. Believing that "true love *really* is color blind!," Mary China delightedly celebrated the love she felt for her husband and the love he felt for her.[90]

In 1994 *Interrace* profiled the Smith family: a black man, a white woman, and their three highly accomplished children. In 1992 one of the Smith children had received a bachelor of arts degree, the second her degree in medicine, and the third a degree in law. With a measure of both pride and resentment, Maurice Smith contended that "there will be no made-for-TV movie about my family nor will you see us center-stage on a talk show."[91] Keen to counter endlessly repeated tales of woe, Smith noted that he and his wife had been married for twenty-nine years, and that both sets of in-laws had embraced the marriage from the start.

Steve and Ruth White (he is white and she is black) had a harder time of it than the Smiths. When they first contemplated getting married, in 1980, the minister of their church was opposed on racial grounds, as were Steve's parents.* Steve White recalls his father declaring, "You really must have hated us to do this. Birds can fall in love with fish but not get married to them." His mother cried and reminded him, among other things, that her best friend had been robbed by a black person.[92] Steve and Ruth got married anyway and went on to create an apparently happy home, write a self-published book about their experience (*Free Indeed: An Autobiography of an Interracial Couple*), and found an interracial support group, A Place for Us.[93]

Insisting that "dreams can come true and that people can be different and yet still be the same," Darryl Anderson, a white man, informed the *Interrace* community in 1994 that he and his black wife had gotten their start as a married couple at a small-town Wisconsin wedding that was well attended by contingents from both families. He recounted how "the reception turned into a big party and a true mixture of two cultures. . . . Everyone, both young and old, had the time of their lives, dancing Polkas and Waltzes and finishing the evening with the Electric Slide."[94]

*Interrace* also advertised dating services and cruises and ran personals intended to facilitate interracial romance.† Here it reached

---

*There were other, nonracial factors that might have justified parental caution or skepticism, notably the fact that Ruth already had three children by previous unstable relationships. But those did not comprise the primary basis for the opposition voiced by Steve's parents; racial difference did. See Tia L. Daniel, "An Overview of Historical Amalgamationists and the Modern Amalgamationist Impulse" (third-year paper, Harvard Law School, 1998), 40 (on file at Harvard Law School Library, in the Interracial Intimacies Collection).

†The following are representative of the personals that appeared in *Interrace*:

SBM, 34, in-shape, educated, professional, financially secure with a sense of humor. Seeks honest, sincere, affectionate woman of any race who desires meaningful relationship.

Are you the right woman for me? Blue-collar SWM, honest down-to-earth. Enjoys day trips, walks on the beach and movies. Seeks same in Caribbean, African, or black American woman.

beyond the mere defense of the right to choose, and supported individuals who expressed a *preference* for men or women of a different race from themselves. Responding retrospectively to a black professor who had asserted offhandedly that black men typically dated or married the uneducated or unattractive white women whom white men passed over, Nicole Bouchet adopted the risky strategy of using herself as a rebuttal witness. Maintaining that she was well educated, at least moderately attractive, and representative of a substantial cadre of white women, Bouchet testified:

> For the past six years, I have been in an interracial relationship with a black man. For as long as I can remember, I have more readily preferred black men. There is nothing pathological about this attraction. All people have preferences. Some people prefer blondes or redheads, larger women—I prefer black men. It's as simple as that. If it is not pathological for white men to prefer white women with bronzed skin and long blond hair, then why can't I prefer black men? Why does something have to be wrong with me?[95]

Finally, *Interrace* assumed an advisory role, publishing articles intended to help with some of the recurrent difficulties that bedevil those involved in transracial relationships. In 1991, for instance, Sarah Farmer offered advice on dealing with racists.[96] Her article chronicled how she, a white adoptive mother of a black girl, had gradually learned to control her anger when confronting people who referred to her as a "nigger lover." Initially, Farmer recalled, her outrage would overcome her ability to respond coherently, but crucial assistance from her daughter had enabled her to take a more reasoned approach. "Now when I am called a nigger-lover," she wrote, "I simply reply, 'No, I am not a

---

Classy 44-year-old SWF looking to have fun with a tall, handsome, romantic African American gentleman.

Attractive SBF, 28 y/o, ISO honest, open-minded, down-to-earth single Latino or white male for LTR leading to marriage.

See *Interrace Singles*, no. 3 (1999), pp. 35, 37.

nigger-lover, I am a mother. And by the way her name is Jessy. And you can call me Ms. Farmer.' Then I flash an ear-to-ear smile and walk away. . . . No more ranting or raving. Just the simple facts."[97]

Pepper Fisher, a white man, recommended a strategy that he and his black wife used:[98] they bent over backward, he explained, to give the benefit of the doubt to those around them. To illustrate what he saw as the virtue of this strategy, he described two episodes. In the first, he and his wife and their son stopped at a fried-chicken restaurant near their small town, fifty miles from Seattle, Washington. (His in-laws were probably the only black family in the town, he noted in an aside.) When Fisher entered the restaurant with his family, he noticed a woman staring at them. He disregarded her:

> Nothing unusual about it, I told myself. Here we are, Black woman, White man, beautiful kid, small town, bound to happen. Her curiosity is natural, and I learned years ago that a little extra attention from people is just one of the things that come with the interracial territory. Besides, it rarely lasts long because good manners usually kick in and people soon realize that overt rubbernecking is a little invasive.[99]

On this occasion, though, the woman kept staring, and her mouth dropped open. Offended, Fisher stepped over to her and scolded peremptorily, "Don't stare." He immediately regretted his action, however, realizing that

> there were no winners, only losers. My wife [let] out a groan, which made me feel even worse, and before the girl behind the counter could say "ISTHATFORHEREORTOGO," I was sorry I had opened my big mouth.[100]

Later that evening, his wife told him she had been embarrassed by his pettiness, adding "that if the woman was behaving rudely [he] should have just turned away and gone about [his] business."[101] He agreed. After all, he reasoned, the woman might just have been preoccupied with difficulties of her own and gazing blankly into space. And in any event, even if she had been disturbed by his family's presence, he "shouldn't have made her problem into our problem. The world is full of bad attitudes. It's pointless and self-destructive to go head to head with everyone you run into."[102]

To reinforce this conclusion, Fisher related a second story. Years earlier, during a dinner at another restaurant, an elderly white woman seated at the next table had stared at him and his wife. They were just about to confront the woman "when the old gal reached out and touched my wife gently on the arm and said, 'I just want to tell you that you are so beautiful.'" The two women chatted for a few minutes, during which time the elderly woman implicitly communicated that she was "quietly pulling for [them]." The lesson to be learned, Fisher averred, echoing his wife, was that mixed couples simply had to be patient, diplomatic, and willing to assume good motives on the part of others. Interracial couples "can't go around conking people over the head to get their respect. We have to earn that over time, through the example set by ourselves and our children. . . . We're like ambassadors from the tiny nation of interracial love."[103]

This patient, conciliatory, almost self-abnegating approach was by no means the only or even the dominant one touted in *Interrace*. More typical was advice to be vocal, direct, militant. "Interracial couples and families," Sandy Carillo maintained in 1992, "should no longer feel and carry on as if discretion is the key to survival in a racist society. If we don't make ourselves seen and heard, then how can we really expect for others to learn to accept us and our choices as normal and as natural as theirs?"[104]

People involved in interracial relationships have lately begun to produce a burgeoning body of memoir literature detailing their experiences, ideas, and sentiments.* These works reflect a new self-confidence and security, a belief on the part of their authors that they have something unusual and uplifting to share with the world, a sense that many

---

*See, e.g., Rebecca Walker, *Black, White Jewish: Autobiography of a Shifting Self* (2001); Jane Lazarre, *Beyond the Whiteness of Whiteness: Memoir of a White Mother of Black Sons* (1997); James McBride, *The Color of Water: A Black Man's Tribute to His White Mother* (1997); Gregory Howard Williams, *Life on the Color Line* (1995); Lise Funderburg, *Black, White, Other: Biracial Americans Talk About Race and Identity* (1994); Walt Harrington, *Crossings: A White Man's Journey into Black America* (1992); Hettie Jones, *How I Became Hettie Jones* (1990); Patrick Huber, *Two Races Beyond the Altar* (1976).

existing understandings of interracial intimacies are mired in mislead-
ing and derogatory stereotypes, and a conviction that the old imagery
of interracial intimacy is unlikely to change absent determined intervention. Lamenting "the virtual absence . . . of a written tradition from
and about people who have crossed the color line," Maureen T. Reddy
wrote in *Crossing the Color Line* (1994) that

> interracial couples begin not as inheritors of a tradition, but as
> pioneers. Each of us begins at the very beginning, with few but
> negative guides. If we go looking for information . . . we find
> mainly cautionary tales of tragedy and loss, written from a per-
> spective we cannot share. Portrayed mostly from the outside,
> by both black and white observers, we find our relationships
> treated as sick manifestations of deep-seated racial myths or
> rebellions against our families, backgrounds, cultures: the
> black partner is in flight from blackness, a victim of internal-
> ized racism[, while the] white partner is running from banality,
> in search of the exotic. These stereotypes are so ingrained in all
> of us in the United States that, for *both* blacks and whites, there
> is an automatic presumption of underlying pathology in inter-
> racial relationships.[105]

In retracing what she saw as her "journey towards an internalized
understanding of race and racism as the white wife of a black husband
and the white mother of black children," Reddy emphasized the positive aspects of her unusual racial position. To her, racial difference
enriched much more than it burdened her marriage. Describing her
partnership with her husband, Doug, Reddy noted that

> contrary to what one might expect from the received wisdom,
> none of the very few problems Doug and I have had in our mar-
> riage have been caused by a racial gap between us. In fact, I think
> we have had fewer misunderstandings of any kind than do most
> couples, because from the beginning we knew that the external
> pressures on us would be enormous and that we would have to
> keep the inner strength to deal with them together. In other words,
> inside our marriage, racial differences have worked *for* us.[106]

Even more than marrying across racial lines, interracial parenting reportedly brought Reddy extraordinary joy and enlightenment. Raising a black son, she wrote with an air of gratitude and exhilaration, "awakened me from ⁞ . . . a delusion of colorlessness."[107] She acknowledged encountering difficulties: bigoted landlords, insulting motel clerks, spurious "friends." But her book's central message is overwhelmingly upbeat: "Living as a racial bridge," Reddy claimed, could be "wonderfully freeing and endlessly instructive."[108]

*Love in Black and White: The Triumph of Love over Prejudice and Taboo* (1992), a memoir by Gail and Mark Mathabane, also offers important documentation of the emergent assertiveness of individuals involved in interracial relationships. Gail Mathabane is a white American from a comfortably middle-class family. Her husband is a black South African who was born into poverty during the apartheid era but escaped it by dint of luck, hard work, unusual talent (as a student and as a tennis player), and the generosity of the American tennis star Stan Smith, who, during a tour of South Africa, recognized and nurtured Mark's potential. Gail and Mark met in 1984 in New York City, where both were attending the Columbia Graduate School of Journalism. Their book details the challenges they faced in marrying across the race line, and expresses their shared sense that ultimately they made the right decision. Gail first had to overcome a residue of prejudice and fear left over from her upbringing. In that context, one incident from her childhood outside Austin, Texas, constituted a defining moment: a black boy forcibly kissed her, and when she told a girlfriend about it, the friend responded with horror, "You let that nigger *kiss* you?"[109] Within days, Gail was being called a "nigger lover," despite her insistence that she had neither invited nor welcomed the black boy's attention.* Not long after that, Gail's family moved to a suburb of Minneapolis, Minnesota, where, notwithstanding the relative scarcity of blacks, she developed an acute wariness of black men. Seeking to explain the source of this anxi-

---

*According to Gail, while "dating Mexicans was fine, even 'cool' . . . if a white girl did so much as speak for more than five minutes with a black boy she was labeled an NL (nigger lover). Blacks and whites never touched each other, never danced together, never came in close contact with each other except through sports, like

ety, her memoir mentions, among other things, two experiences that left a lasting impression on her. One was hearing stories about Negro pimps who lured white girls from their homes and turned them into prostitutes. The other was attending a concert given by the rock musician Prince. She was shocked by his aggressive sexuality and by the appreciation shown him by the predominantly black audience. Frightened, she concluded that blacks possessed a dangerous sexual energy and that "any white girl who dated a black boy was throwing herself away." After all, she wondered, "who, in her right mind, would give up all her white friends and the love of her family for a black boy?"[110]

A stint at Brown University in the early 1980s helped Gail become more independent and cosmopolitan. Important influences on her thinking during this period were some people of color with whom she became friendly and a Lebanese girlfriend whose preference in male companionship ran strongly to blacks. Gail's maturation, however, by no means precluded the emergence of some significant anxieties when she became seriously involved with Mark. Anticipating resistance from her father, Gail avoided telling him about their relationship for a long while. At one point, her fear that her continued association with Mark might alienate her permanently from her family, friends, and professional ambitions caused her to suspend their romance for about five months. But more than her relatives, it was her own doubts that held her back and kept her from committing to a love that would jeopardize deeply entrenched assumptions. She confessed, for example, that during a weekend visit with an interracial couple on Long Island, New York, she was overcome one evening by a realization that was like "a stab in [her] heart."[111] She had realized, she recalled, "that I wanted a baby with pink cheeks and blue eyes. . . . I wanted what many of us want: a child that reminds us of ourselves as we once were."[112]

The Mathabanes' memoir suggests that initially, Mark faced fewer internal and external obstacles than Gail in pursuing their romance. It was he who pushed them toward marriage. After they married, however, Mark consciously distanced himself from Gail, at least in public.

---

football and wrestling" (Mark Mathabane and Gail Mathabane, *Love in Black and White: The Triumph of Love over Prejudice and Taboo* [1992], 30).

His autobiography *Kaffir Boy* (1986) had become a best-seller and catapulted him into prominence; aware that many blacks in America and elsewhere would react with disappointment and anger to his interracial marriage, he tried to keep it as inconspicuous as possible. For a time, he discouraged Gail from attending his lectures, particularly the ones he gave before black audiences. Once, when she did come to a lecture, he became angry with her. By his account,

> She was the only white at the table of black students who treated me to dinner. . . . Their faces did not conceal their shock on hearing me introduce her as my wife. There were awkward silences, gaps in the conversation, and I could tell many of the students were offended and wondered how she could possibly relate to the issues of race they were discussing.[113]

Afterward, he told Gail that she had exhibited an embarrassing ignorance of African American history and would never understand how it felt to be permanently victimized by racial discrimination. He even questioned whether he had done the right thing in marrying her, given the feelings of so many within the black community.

Despite the various challenges that confronted them, Mark and Gail Mathabane succeeded in marrying, staying together, and creating a family that was soon supplemented by two children, whom they smilingly clutch in the photo that graces the cover of their book. Breaking free of the tethers that constrained them required firm action: Gail had to inform her father that he must accept her love for Mark or risk losing her affection, and Mark had to stop attempting to mollify his readers who opposed interracial marriage. Declining any longer to relegate Gail to the shadows, he "came out" regarding their relationship by placing their wedding photo in a prominent spot in his book *Kaffir Boy in America* (1989). As he later explained, "I was fed up with playing games with my emotions [and] with hurting a woman whose love for me was unqualified."[114] Speaking on their own behalf and on behalf of other interracial couples, Gail and Mark Mathabane have asserted proudly that they are "living proof that blacks and whites do not have to hate each other," "that racial harmony can become a reality," and that all the many things that separate blacks and whites "can be replaced by trust, cooperation, mutual respect, and even love."[115]

As a rule, amalgamationists do not restrict their claims for interracial intimacy's benefits merely to the individuals involved; they also declare, more broadly, that black-white interracial intimacy can be an engine of positive social transformation. The idea of deploying intermarriage programatically is by no means novel. Thomas Jefferson, Patrick Henry, and other white American statesmen proposed that intermarriage between whites and Indians be encouraged as a way of peacefully appropriating the Indians' land and humanely civilizing "the noble savages." These proposals envisioned, at base, the whitening of the red people as a "solution" to the "Indian problem."[116] A few commentators have advanced a similar strategy for "curing" the "Negro problem." Franz Boas suggested in 1921, for example, that

> the greatest hope for the immediate future lies in a lessening of the contrast between negroes and whites. . . . Intermixture will decrease the contrast between extreme racial forms. . . . In a race of octoroons, living among whites, the color question would probably disappear. . . . It would seem, therefore, to be in the interest of society to permit rather than restrain marriages between white men and negro women. It would be futile to expect that our people [white] would tolerate intermarriages in the opposite direction.[117]

Forty years later, Norman Podhoretz would remark that "the wholesale merger of the two races is the most desirable alternative for everyone concerned. . . . The Negro problem can be solved in this country in no other way."[118] Boas and Podhoretz were both considered racial liberals—indeed, racial radicals—when they wrote the statements quoted above. At the same time, they were also pessimistic accommodationists insofar as they believed that white racism could never be comprehensively transformed without a prior whitening of the black population.

Such proposals have received little attention. They would, if noticed, offend simultaneously those whites who loathe the prospect of race mixing and those blacks who despise the idea of "whitening" themselves and their descendants through intermarriage in order to avoid or accommodate antiblack prejudice. Refusing to see blackness as a taint, the latter reject any policy or theory premised on the necessity of systematic racial bleaching.*

Another brand of amalgamationism encourages interracial intimacy as a bilateral as opposed to a unilateral process. Its proponents urge a mutual blending rather than a mere extinguishment of blackness, and regard interracial intimacy as a positive good for whites as well as blacks. Among the leading partisans of this approach is Michael Lind.[119] Proclaiming with approval that "a mongrelized population will eventually complement our already-mongrelized culture—and not a moment too soon," Lind argues that removing the race line in intimate affairs is an essential precursor to erasing it everywhere else:

> If people discriminate on the basis of physical race when it comes to the most fundamental matters—sex and reproduction— they can hardly be expected to overlook physical race in a thousand lesser areas of social life. They will not forget they are white or black when it comes to voting or hiring, only to suddenly remember they are white or black when it comes to sex and marriage. Race-consciousness cannot be turned on and off. . . . Either it is very strong, or it is very attenuated, with respect to *all* matters, intimate and public, profound and trivial.[120]

An outspoken and distinguished African American amalgamationist is Professor Orlando Patterson.[121]† A champion of transracial free trade

---

*For a satirical critique of plans to address racism by getting rid of blackness, see George Schuyler's *Black No More* (1931), discussed on pages 344–51.
†Another noteworthy African American amalgamationist, Joseph R. Washington Jr. maintained:

> We can and we must create conditions whereby every American home anticipates with high expectations the possibility of welcoming into the family a black or white sister, brother, daughter, or son, though this may be

in intimacy in general, Patterson lauds the benefits of interracial marriage in particular. He maintains that interracial marriage typically makes accessible to those involved valuable new sources of "cultural capital," including advice, know-how, and social networks. "When we marry," he has written, "we engage in an exchange of social and cultural dowries potentially far more valuable than gold-rimmed china."[122]* In making his case, Patterson points to the upward mobility of Jews and Japanese Americans (both groups with much higher levels of intermarriage than blacks) and to the remarkable success of certain black men who have ignored racial custom by enjoying white paramours.† He

---

a reality for only a precious few. It is sheer rhetoric to proclaim the American dream and espouse the American creed without at the same time affirming the goodness and desiring the possibility of brotherhood and sisterhood in black and white within the immediate or very near family. [*Marriage in Black and White* (1972; 1993), 326.]

*According to Patterson:

When one marries into another ethnic group, one greatly expands one's social network. Every spouse brings a cultural dowry of social networks and cultural capital in the form of childrearing patterns, and it is to reap this rich harvest of social and cultural capital that Americans [other than black Americans] are busily intermarrying with each other, fully exploring . . . their "ethnic" options. [Orlando Patterson, *The Ordeal of Integration: Progress and Resentment in America's "Racial" Crisis* (1997), 195.]

†Patterson writes that "Afro-American men have disproportionately relied on Euro-American lovers to provide them with a link to networks and cultural information that are critical for their success. This pattern goes all the way back to Booker T. Washington and Frederick Douglass" (*Ordeal of Integration,* 197). Furthermore, he claims that "the recent exposé of the late Ron Brown's complicated love affair with [a Euro-American] on whom he depended heavily for counsel, funds, and contacts, is merely the tip of a long, historical iceberg" (ibid.).

That Douglass and Brown both engaged in interracial love affairs is clear. (For information on Douglass, see pages 72–75; for information on Brown, see Steven Holmes, *Ron Brown: An Uncommon Life* [2000], and Peter J. Boyer, "Ron Brown's Secrets," *The New Yorker,* June 9, 1997.) Patterson probably errs, however, with respect to Washington. He offers no source for his comment, and Louis R. Harlan's comprehensive biography of Washington contains no reference to any interracial liaisons (*Booker T. Washington: The Making of a Black Leader, 1856–1901* [1972]; *Booker T. Washington: The Wizard of Tuskegee, 1901–1915* [1983]). In 1911 a white woman in New York City caused a furor by accusing Washington of address-

maintains that there are at least two lessons to be drawn from the evidence: "If you want in, you marry in. And if you are from a group with impoverished social networks, you have even more reason to do so."[123] He claims that the dissolution of the informal racial boundaries that divide the marriage market would redound especially to the benefit of black women, by alleviating, to an appreciable extent, the marriage squeeze that afflicts them with special force due to the paucity of marriageable black men. Patterson envisions large numbers of white men who will increasingly become open to the possibility of marrying black women—if such women will simply give them a chance. He observes, moreover, that even a relatively small incursion by black women into the ranks of marriageable white men would substantially enlarge that former group's marital options. After all, if just one in five of the nonblack male population came a-courting, black women would see an immediate doubling of the potential pool of spouses available to them.[124] According to Patterson, this would be a good thing not only because it would make marriage more accessible to those black women desirous of it, but also because the presence of larger numbers of white (and other) suitors would strengthen the hand of black women in their dealings with black men. As Patterson sees it, by forswearing nonblack suitors, many black women have senselessly put themselves at the mercy of black men, who have exploited their market position by declining to be as accommodating as they might have to be in the face of greater competition.[125]

Finally, Patterson argues that widespread intermarriage is necessary to the full integration of blacks into American life. He agrees with Calvin Hernton's assertion that intermarriage is "the crucial test in determining when a people have completely won their way into the mainstream of any given society."[126] He therefore urges blacks, particularly African American women, to renounce doctrines that militate against interracial intimacy. Higher rates of intermarriage, he counsels, "will complete the process of total integration as [blacks] become to other Americans not only full members of the political and moral com-

---

ing her in a familiar fashion ("Hello, sweetheart" was the alleged salutation). There is good reason, however, to doubt her word (see Harlan, *Wizard of Tuskegee*, 379–404).

munity, but also people whom 'we' marry. When that happens," he avers, "the goal of integration will have been fully achieved."[127]

Some may question whether higher rates of interracial marriage will do and signify as much as Patterson and other amalgamationists contend. The history of race relations in racially divided societies elsewhere offers ample evidence that racial hierarchy can coexist alongside high rates of miscegenation and even intermarriage. In considering "the uncertain legacy of miscegenation," Professor Anthony W. Marx has noted that despite considerable race mixing and a formal repudiation of racism, Brazil nonetheless constructed and retains "an informal racial order that [discriminates] against blacks and browns."[128] Contrary to optimistic projections, miscegenation did not so much ensure upward mobility for dark Brazilians as reinforce a myth of mobility. That myth has undergirded a pigmentocracy that continues to privilege whiteness. A similar outcome is possible in the United States. Various peoples of color—Latinos, Asians, Native Americans, and light-skinned Negroes—could well intermarry with whites in increasingly large numbers and join with them in a de facto alliance *against* darker-skinned Negroes, who would thus remain racial outcasts even in a more racially mixed society. We cannot merely assume that increased rates of interracial marriage will propel the society beyond the grip of racial conflict.* Historically, though, at least in the United States, openness to interracial marriage has been a good barometer of racial enlightenment in thought and practice. As a general rule, those persons, institutions, and communities that have been most welcoming of interracial marriage (and other intimate interracial associations) are also those that have most determinedly embraced racial justice, a healthy respect for diverse desires, and a belief in the essential oneness of humanity.

---

*Michael Lind warns, for example, that "shifting patterns of racial intermarriage suggest that the [coming years] may see the replacement of the historic white-black dichotomy in America with a troubling new division, one between beige and black" ("The Beige and the Black," *New York Times Magazine*, August 16, 1998). See also Roger Sanjek, "Intermarriage and the Future of Races in the United States," in Steven Gregory and Roger Sanjek, eds., *Race* (1994).

# FOUR

# *Race, Racism, and Sexual Coercion*

## *Black Women, White Men, and Sexual Coercion*

In an essay entitled "Sleeping with the Enemy," Audrey Edwards explained that before she could even consider the possibility of dating a white man, she first had to confront a painful aspect of the American past. "Of all the ways a white man can get to know a black woman," she wrote, "fucking is clearly the route he has taken most. Sex blazes through the landscape of America's racial history as hot and heavy as the lash of slavery." It is slavery, "with its legacy of rape . . . that has traditionally defined and colored much of black women's relationships with white men." And it is largely for that reason, Edwards concluded, that "black women do not easily factor white men into the equation of desirables when seeking men to mate and marry. . . . There is too much dirty water under the bridge for us to find the white man a likely turn-on."[1] Such attentiveness to the sexual element of racial subordination is by no means atypical among politically self-conscious African Americans.* The subject has long vexed a wide range of black artists, intel-

---

*Nor have African Americans been alone in studying, publicizing, and condemning racist sexual abuse perpetrated by white men. White abolitionists addressed the subject. The most famous and influential treatment was Harriet Beecher Stowe's *Uncle Tom's Cabin* (1852). Richard Hildreth's abolitionist novel *The Slave* (1836) contains a scene in which an enslaved woman struggles with a man—her master and father— who drags her toward his bed: "She looked him in the face, as well as her tears could allow her. . . . 'Master—Father,' she cried, 'what is it you would have of your own

lectuals, and activists.[2] The sexual abuse of enslaved women was a constant refrain, for example, in Frederick Douglass's indictment of bondage:

> More than a million women, in the Southern States . . . are, by the laws of the land, and through no fault of their own, assigned to a life of revolting prostitution. . . . Youth and elegance, beauty and innocence are exposed for sale upon the auction block; while villainous monsters stand around, with pockets lined with gold, gazing with lustful eyes upon their prospective victims. . . . Every slaveholder is a party, a guilty party, to this awful wickedness.[3]

Similarly, a black delegate to the 1868 Arkansas Constitutional Convention complained that "the white men of the South have been for years indulging in illicit intercourse with colored women, and in the dark days of slavery this intercourse was largely forced upon the innocent victims."[4] W. E. B. DuBois, for his part, declared that he would never forgive the white South's "wanton and continued and persistent insulting of the black womanhood which it sought and seeks to prostitute to its lusts."[5]* Recounting the horrors of slavery, the poet Sterling Brown wrote:

> They broke you like oxen
> They scourged you

---

daughter?'" (vol. 2, p. 9). Attacking slavery, a white minister began an 1858 speech by declaiming that while "we [northerners] send to prison. . . . our violators of female chastity . . . our abductors of young girls from their homes and parents . . . the South sends to Congress her ruffians who commit rape . . . her violators of wives, sellers of maidens . . . whippers of women" (the Reverend W. G. Brownlow and the Reverend A. Pryne, *Ought American Slavery to Be Perpetuated?: A Debate Held at Philadelphia* [1858], 223). See also Melton A. McLaurin, *Celia: A Slave* (1991); Susan Brownmiller, *Against Our Will* (1975).

*This was a subject to which DuBois would return repeatedly. In *The Souls of Black Folk* (1903; reprint, 1996), he decried the "red stain of bastardy which two centuries of systematic legal defilement of Negro women [have] stamped upon [blacks]" (p. 107).

They branded you
They made your women breeders
They swelled your numbers with bastards.[6]

Malcolm X noted at the beginning of his famous autobiography that he had "learned to hate every drop of that white rapist's blood" that ran through his veins.[7] Sexual exploitation is salient, too, in Professor Patricia Hill Collins's *Black Feminist Thought*. "Freedom for Black women," she asserted, "has meant freedom *from* White men, not the freedom to choose White men as lovers and friends." Moreover, she observed, "given the history of sexual abuse of Black women by White men, individual Black women who choose White partners become reminders of a difficult history. . . . Such individual liaisons aggravate a collective sore spot because they recall historical master/slave relationships."[8]

The most powerful exposé of the racial and sexual exploitation of enslaved women is that offered by Harriet A. Jacobs in her *Incidents of the Life of a Slave Girl—Written by Herself* (1861).[9]* This extraordi-

---

*Several distinguished scholars have questioned whether Jacobs's memoir can properly be seen as a testamentary record documenting real facts. Most notably, Professor John W. Blassingame doubted the credibility of Jacobs's account, suggesting that her account was "too melodramatic: miscegenation and cruelty, outraged virtue, unrequited love, and planter licentiousness appear on practically every page" (*The Slave Community: Plantation Life in the Antebellum South* [1972; rev. and enl. ed., 1979], 373; see also Elizabeth Fox-Genovese, *Within the Plantation Household: Black and White Women of the Old South* [1988], 372–96).

I agree with Professor Blassingame's call for care in the use of autobiographies as documentary evidence. As he noted, few people (more likely none!) "are able to tell the *whole* truth about themselves. Almost inevitably they exaggerate the difficulties they faced and make themselves more heroic than they were in real life. The unconscious plays tricks on the conscious; some things are . . . too painful to recall or to reveal to others." The autobiographical literary form, moreover, posed special problems for black people as "they contemplated the hostile audience to which they were addressing themselves. Could they really strip themselves bare before white America?" (ibid., 368).

Despite the doubts that have been voiced as to its authenticity or accuracy, however, I view *Incidents in the Life of a Slave Girl* as a reliable memoir as opposed to a historical novel. My reliance is based largely on Professor Jean Fagan Yellin's prodi-

nary memoir is a veritable catalog of the devastations that bondage inflicted upon the intimate lives of slaves.[10] Born a slave in 1813 in Edenton, North Carolina, Jacobs was given at the age of eleven to a three-year-old whose father, Dr. James Norcom,* sought to seduce the young servant as soon as she entered early womanhood. According to Jacobs, when she turned fifteen, "my master began to whisper foul words in my ear. Young as I was, I could not remain ignorant of their import. . . . He tried his utmost to corrupt the pure principles my grandmother had instilled. He peopled my young mind with unclean images."[11]

When she resisted his sexual advances, "He told me that I was made for his use, made to obey his command in *every* thing; that I was nothing but a slave, whose will must and should surrender to his."[12]† Jacobs insisted that she had avoided the fate her master envisioned for her. Although he had numerous sexual dalliances with other slave women, by whom he consequently sired several children (some of whom he subsequently sold), he never possessed Jacobs sexually. He did succeed, however, in making her miserable through his constant attempts, by means of bribery and threats, to force her to give in to his sexual overtures. Jacobs got a brief glimpse of happiness when a free black man asked her to marry him, but her master quickly squelched this possibility by refusing to sell her, denying her permission to wed, and threatening the man who had dared to propose to her: "'Never let me hear that fellow's name mentioned again,'" he warned Jacobs. "'If I ever know of your speaking to him, I will cowhide you both; and if

---

gious archival research, which has overwhelmingly confirmed Jacobs's main claims. See the preface to Harriet A. Jacobs, *Incidents in the Life of a Slave Girl, Written by Herself* (1861; edited and with an introduction by Jean Fagan Yellin, 1987), vii.

*Incidents* has inspired a substantial library of commentary. See, for example, Deborah M. Garfield and Rafia Zefer, eds., *Harriet Jacobs and* Incidents in the Life of a Slave Girl: *New Critical Essays* (1996); Jennifer Fleischner, *Mastering Slavery: Memory, Family, and Identity in Women's Slave Narratives* (1996).

*In Jacobs's memoir, Norcom is renamed Dr. Flint.

†Note the echo in Norcom's claim (as related by Jacobs) of Judge Ruffin's assertion that slavery required "uncontrolled authority over the body." In *Mann,* readers may recall, Ruffin maintained that "the power of the master must be absolute, to render the submission of the slave perfect." See pages 42–43.

I ever catch him lurking around my premises, I will shoot him as soon as I would a dog. . . . I'll teach you a lesson about marriage and free niggers!'"[13]*

Reflecting on this sad episode, Jacobs would express a certain relief that she and her free black suitor had been prevented from marrying. In North Carolina (and indeed in most states that permitted bondage), marriage conferred no legally enforceable protections upon slaves.† It did not keep a slave from being sold away from his or her spouse or separated from his or her children. If Jacobs had "married" her unnamed black admirer, she and any children to whom she might have given birth would have remained the property of her master. In her words:

> Even if [my black lover] could have obtained permission to
> marry me while I was a slave, the marriage would give him no

---

*Dr. Norcom's wife, too, was hostile to the prospect of Harriet marrying:

> My mistress, like many others, seemed to think that slaves had no right to any family ties of their own; that they were created merely to wait upon the family and the mistress. I once heard her abuse a young slave girl, who told her that a colored man wanted to make her his wife. "I will have you peeled and pickled, my lady," said she, "if I ever hear you mention that subject again. Do you suppose that I will have you tending *my* children with the children of that nigger?" The girl to whom she said this had a mulatto child, of course not acknowledged by its father. The poor black man who loved her would have been proud to acknowledge his helpless offspring. [Jacobs, *Incidents,* 1987 ed., 38.]

†According to Thomas R. R. Cobb's pro-slavery treatise, slaves were barred from legally marrying because "to fasten upon a master of a female slave, a vicious, corrupting negro, sowing discord, and dissatisfaction among all his slaves; or else a thief, or a cut-throat, and to provide no relief against such a nuisance, would be to make the holding of slaves a curse to the master" (*An Inquiry into the Law of Negro Slavery in the United States of America* [1858], 246). For an insightful modern discussion, see Margaret A. Burnham, "An Impossible Marriage: Slave Law and Family Law," *Law and Inequality* 5 (1987): 187. The laws of slavery varied by state. A New York statute enacted in 1809, for example, recognized slave marriages, declared the children of such unions to be legitimate, recognized the right of slaves to own and transfer property, and prohibited the separation of spouses. See Edgar J. McManus, *A History of Negro Slavery in New York* (1966), 178.

power to protect me from my master. It would have made him
miserable to witness the insults I should have been subjected to.
And then, if we had children, I knew they must "follow the
condition of the mother." What a terrible blight that would be
on the heart of a free, intelligent father! For *his* sake, I felt that I
ought not to link his fate with my own unhappy destiny.[14]

Jacobs's comments about her thwarted relationship with her black
suitor touch upon another destructive aspect of slavery that continues
to reverberate painfully even today in tensions between black men and
black women.* By declining for the most part to criminalize sexual
coercions of bondswomen, the slave regime not only increased female
slaves' vulnerability to sexual assault but also put enslaved men in a ter-
ible bind. After all, patriarchal expectations ascendant in the nineteenth
century (as today) held that true men must protect their womenfolk
from harm, especially sexual harm.[15] Enslaved men, however, were
largely stripped of the ability to shield their mothers, daughters, sisters,
and lovers from such depredations.

Some slaves did offer militant resistance, challenging or fighting or
even killing those who sexually menaced their loved ones.[16] In one case,
a Mississippi slave murdered his master when he insisted upon sleeping
with the slave's wife. According to the traveler who recounted this incident, the slave confessed his "crime" and said that "he believed he
should be rewarded in heaven for it."[17] Another Mississippi case considered the actions of a slave who killed a white overseer after being
told that the man had raped his wife.† In a case in Virginia, an enslaved
couple killed a master who had demanded that the female partner sub-

---

*According to Orlando Patterson, "It was during the period of slavery . . . that
many of the deep-seated gender attitudes and tensions between Afro-American men
and women . . . were first established" (*Rituals of Blood: Consequences of Slavery in
Two American Centuries* [1998]), 35. More specifically, "in the absence of any
legally recognized marriage rights in his partner, and in the presence of . . . predatory
Euro-American men, who could rape or otherwise sexually manipulate slave women
with impunity . . . the male slave was placed in an impossible situation, one bound
to reduce him to a state of . . . insecurity about women" (ibid.).
†The slave first attempted to poison the overseer, but that effort went terribly awry
when his own wife accidentally ate the food he had poisoned. Now doubly enraged,

mit to sexual intercourse with him. Adding to the horror was the fact that the master was the woman's biological father.[18]

Given the stark, often lethal, punishment meted out for open rebellion, most slaves acceded in varying degrees to the sexual exploitation imposed upon them, their kin, and their loved ones.* "We couldn't do nothing 'bout it," a former slave named Ishrael Massie angrily recalled. "My blood is bilin' now [at the] thoughts of dem times. If dey [slave women] told dey husbands he wuz powerless."[19] "Some poor creatures have been so brutalized by the lash," Harriet Jacobs confided, "that they will sneak out of the way to give their masters free access to their wives and daughters."[20]

One of the most appalling cases in the law of slavery, *State v. Celia,* highlights the triangular tensions created by white men's exploitation of black women.[21] Celia, a black slave, was approximately fourteen years old when she was sold in 1850, in Callaway County, Missouri, to Robert Newsom, a prosperous widowed farmer. Newsom began raping the girl almost immediately after he purchased her. Over the next five years, his sexual assaults gave her two children. In time one of Newsom's other slaves, George, became romantically interested in Celia and

---

the slave stole a gun and shot the man. See *Alfred, a slave v. Mississippi,* 37 Miss. 296 (1859).

*Eugene Genovese maintained that "many black men proved willing to die in defense of their women" (*Roll, Jordan, Roll: The World the Slaves Made* [1974], 422–23). He offered little documentary support for this assertion, however, and my own sense is that the statement was an exaggeration stemming in part from a perceived need to emphasize the slaves' own role in shaping the slave regime and in part from a desire to assuage the wounded pride of black men who, even late in the twentieth century, continued to feel stung by the inability of their forebears to protect their womenfolk from the unwanted sexual attention of white men. More realistic than Genovese's assessment, if also more brutal, is Professor Marli F. Weiner's observation that "given a choice between powerlessness and death, most African American men could only stand by while their women were raped" (*Mistresses and Slaves: Plantation Women in South Carolina, 1830–80* [1998], 140). Actually, the spectrum of alternative courses of action was often broader than this either/or dichotomy, as a number of enslaved men and women succeeded in bargaining for more autonomy and respect than the law provided them. Still, under the slave regime, when white owners of black women were determined to exploit them sexually, there was little that black men could do about it.

began staying with her in her cabin. That, however, proved deterrent to their master, who continued to rape Celia on a regular basis.

Two developments conspired to change this situation in the winter of 1855. First, Celia became pregnant, though she did not know who the father was. Second, George demanded that she somehow put an end to Newsom's sexual incursions. According to Celia's biographer, her pregnancy

> placed an emotional strain upon George that he could not accept. Celia was his lover—he perhaps regarded her as his wife—yet he could not protect her from the sexual advances of the man who owned them both. At this time George faced a dilemma imposed by his own sense of masculinity and his inability to alter the behavior of his master. It was a dilemma common among male slaves. . . . To have confronted Newsom directly at this stage to demand that he cease his sexual exploitation of Celia would been an act that could have cost him his life. . . . So George made a demand of the most vulnerable member of the triangle.[22]

Celia apparently responded by appealing to Newsom's white daughters, one of whom was about her age. The historical record does not reveal whether the younger Newsoms attempted to intervene, but in any case, their father persisted in forcing himself on his slave. She insisted that he stop and threatened to hurt him physically if he failed to comply with her demand. But exercising what he undoubtedly viewed as his rightful prerogative as a master, Newsom continued. One evening when he approached Celia, ignoring her warnings, she killed him by battering his skull with a heavy stick. Afterward, she burned his body.

Ironically, it was George who informed on Celia. Soon after doing so, he escaped. His lover was not so fortunate. During her trial for murder, the judge refused to instruct the jury that a slave could properly be excused for using force to protect herself against a sexual assault by her owner. Celia was subsequently convicted, sentenced to death, and hanged after giving birth to a stillborn child.

Like Celia, Harriet Jacobs tried mightily to resist her master's sexual impositions. Aware of Dr. Norcom's concern for his reputation, she made sure to remain within shouting distance of others whenever she was in his presence. "As a married man, and a professional man," she explained, "he deemed it necessary to save appearances in some degree."[23] Jacobs also forestalled Norcom's lechery by becoming the mistress of another white man, Samuel Tredwell Sawyer, who would sire two children by her before being elected to serve in the United States House of Representatives. Jacobs suggested that she become involved with Sawyer in part to deprive Norcom of a pleasure he apparently coveted: the deflowering of yet another young slave girl. She also hoped that Sawyer might rescue her from Norcom by purchasing her.

Norcom, however, would not agree to sell Jacobs.* In despair, she fled his home, leaving her children behind. After hiding in Edenton for seven years, she finally managed, in 1842, to reach New York City, where, with assistance from abolitionists, she bought her own freedom and that of her children and wrote her autobiography.

Blacks were not the only ones who suffered the baleful consequences of white men's sexual aggressions; white women bore the burden as well. Evidence abounds of white women's intense resentment of the nearby presence of the black women whom their husbands kept as beloved mistresses, convenient concubines, or brutalized sex slaves. As one observer noted:

> [Many southern white women] secretly hated slavery for
> the oldest of human reasons. The southern woman was never
> sure of her husband's fidelity or her sons' morals as long as
> there was a slave woman in the household. The slave woman's

---

* "Sometimes my persecutor would ask me whether I would like to be sold," Jacobs recalled. "I told him I would rather be sold to any body than to lead such a life as I did. On such occasions he would assume the air of a very injured individual, and reproach me for my ingratitude. . . . [He would say,] Have I ever treated you like a negro? . . . And this is the recompense I get, you ungrateful girl." See Jacobs, *Incidents,* 1987 ed., 35.

presence threatened her sovereignty, insulted her womanhood and often humiliated her before her friends. She was confronted with a rival by compulsion, whose helplessness she could not fight. Nor could she hide the mulatto children always underfoot who resembled her own children so strongly that no one could doubt their parentage.[24]

Harriet Jacobs's memoir devotes an entire chapter, "The Jealous Mistress," to the sad fate of those naive northern white women who, beguiled by "romantic notions," married slaveholding southerners. "The young wife soon learns that the husband in whose hands she has placed her happiness pays no regard to his marriage vows," Jacobs declared. "Children of every shade of complexion play with her own fair babies, and too well she knows that they are born [of her husband]. Jealousy and hatred enter the flowery home, and it is ravaged of its loveliness."[25]

Jacobs took a harsher view of southern white women, who, she charged,

often marry a man knowing that he is the father of many little slaves. They do not trouble themselves about it. They regard such children as property, as marketable as the pigs on the plantation; and it is seldom that they do not make them aware of this by passing them into the slavetrader's hands as soon as possible, and thus getting them out of their sight.[26]

She recalled her own experience in informing Dr. Norcom's wife of his sexual extortions. "As I went on with my account," Jacobs wrote, "her color changed frequently, she wept, and sometimes groaned. She spoke in tones so sad, that I was touched by her grief."[27] Mrs. Norcom's suffering did not, however, inspire her to assist the enslaved woman whom her husband had been menacing; instead she thought only of herself. She "felt that her marriage vows were desecrated, her dignity insulted; but she had no compassion for the poor victim of her husband's perfidy. She pitied herself as a martyr; but she was incapable of feeling for the condition of shame and misery in which her unfortunate, helpless slave was placed."[28]* Jacobs was lucky, though, in that Mrs. Norcom's narcissism, ugly though it was, was directed largely inward. In other cases, jealous wives of lecherous slave owners forced the sale of the enslaved women whom their husbands fancied, loved, seduced, or raped.†

More than a few white male perpetrators of sexual crimes also suffered on account of their wrongdoing. This lesson emerges from the oral history of Pauli Murray's ancestors, a tale that Murray carefully researched, established as a written narrative, and published in 1956 as *Proud Shoes: The Story of an American Family*. Murray's great-grandmother Harriet was a slave who was purchased in 1834 by Dr. James Smith of Hillsboro, North Carolina. Smith bought the fifteen-year-old to be his daughter's servant; Harriet was a gift that helped to mark Mary Ruffin Smith's coming out at the age of eighteen. Several years later, the seeds of disaster were sown in the Smith family when Mary's two brothers, Francis and Sidney, graduates of the University of North Carolina, both became sexually attracted to their sister's slave. By this time, Harriet was married to a free Negro with whom she had had a child. Her status as a wife and mother was no obstacle to the Smith brothers; they severely beat her husband, who fled. They then turned on each other. Francis, a doctor, warned his brother, Sidney, a politician, not to force himself on Harriet, but Sidney Smith disregarded his brother's admonition and began regularly to rape the young woman. According to family lore:

---

*Jacobs conceded, however, that Mrs. Norcom's jealous surveillance paid an unexpected dividend in placing some restraint on her despicable husband. At one point, he sought to move Harriet Jacobs into his bedroom, ostensibly to look after one of his children; according to Jacobs, his wife angrily vetoed that idea. See Jacobs, *Incidents* (1987 ed.), 32–33.

†Little has been written about the sexual abuse of slaves by women. For speculation that, as an enslaved child, the great abolitionist Sojourner Truth may have been subjected to such abuse, see Nell Irvin Painter, *Sojourner Truth: A Life, a Symbol* (1996), 14–16.

The more she reviled him the better he seemed to like it. He raped her again and again. . . . Night after night he would force open her cabin door and nail it up again on the inside so that she could not get out. Then he would beat her into submission. She would cry out sharply, moan like a wounded animal and beg for mercy. The other slaves, hearing her cries, trembled in their beds and prayed silently for her deliverance.[29]

Deliverance of a sort came when Francis Smith ambushed his brother as he was leaving Harriet's cabin one evening. Sidney Smith would never fully recover. Although he would later serve a term in the North Carolina state legislature and, remarkably, brag about the daughter he had sired on Harriet through rape, the beating he suffered from Francis took its toll. He began to drink heavily, never married, brooded a great deal, and generally lived what his family considered to be a life far beneath what they had hoped for or expected of him.

Following that bit of sibling warfare, Harriet's defender, Francis, took up with her and fathered four daughters by her. According to Murray, this brother did not rape her great-grandmother. "Perhaps [she] was resigned," Murray speculated. "Or perhaps in her wretched loneliness she was grateful to him and even flattered by his attention."[30] In either case, their arrangement does not seem to have generated much happiness: "Theirs," concluded Murray, "was a distant relationship, barren of all communication, save that of the flesh."[31]

Like his brother, Francis Smith would remain unmarried throughout his life. Mary Ruffin Smith, the person who legally owned Harriet, would never wed, either. It is Murray's contention that the three siblings' marital isolation was no coincidence but instead derived in substantial part from the brothers' relationship with Harriet, and more particularly from Sidney Smith's sexual violence. "Conscience is a ruthless master," Murray noted,

and the Smiths were driven into an enslavement no less wasteful than Harriet's. They were doomed to live with blunted emotions and unnatural restraints, to keep up appearances by acting out a farce which fooled nobody and brought them little comfort. It was a life of baffling contradictions and ambivalences, of snarls and threats and bitter recriminations. Everybody blamed everybody else for what had happened. It was dog eat dog with Sidney and Frank. They quarreled all the time and the family never knew when one of them might murder the other.[32]

Freighted by the triple burden of enslavement, racism, and sexism, most black women in antebellum America endured conditions that are harrowing to contemplate. Annie Young, a former slave, recalled her master letting loose bloodhounds to track down her aunt, who had run away to escape his sexual advances. After he caught her, "he knocked a hole in her head and . . . made her have him."[33] "Bird" Walton related how Ethel Jane, a "yaller gal," was raped by her owner and his son and "couldn't do nothing 'bout it."[34]

In his memoir of life as a slave, Solomon Northrup recounted the tragic story of Patsey, "queen of the field":

Patsey wept oftener, and suffered more, than any of her companions. . . . It had fallen to her lot to be the slave of a licentious master and a jealous mistress. She shrank before the lustful eye of one, and was in danger even of her life at the hands of the other, and between the two she was indeed accursed. . . . Patsey walked under a cloud. If she uttered a word in opposition to her master's will, the lash was resorted to at once to bring her to subjection; if she was not watchful when about her cabin, or when walking in the yard, a billet of wood, or a broken bottle perhaps, hurled from her mistress' hand, would smite her unexpectedly in the face. The enslaved victim of lust and hate, Patsey had no comfort of her life.[35]

Describing her husband's plantation, Fanny Kemble repeated the comments of a young slave woman who had explained to her why she and others had sex with their white overseer. "Oh . . . missis," the slave said, "we do anything to get our poor flesh some rest from de whip; when he made me follow him into de bush, what use me tell him no?

He have strength to make me."[36] In a gloss on the slave's remarks, Kemble noted, "I have written down the woman's words; I wish I could write down the voice and look of abject misery with which they were spoken. Now you will observe that the story was not told to me as a complaint; it was a thing long past and over, of which she spoke only in the natural course of accounting for her children to me."[37]

Though such testimony is moving, what does it really tell us about the incidence of rape under slavery? In a society numbering in the millions, ten, twenty, fifty, or even a hundred anecdotes by themselves can provide little basis for determining whether the events they describe were representative or idiosyncratic. The fact is, no one knows for sure—or can even offer a rigorous quantitative estimate of—the extent to which whites sexually coerced blacks during the slavery era.[38] Some students of the subject have embraced the view that the "peculiar institution" was a depraved environment that not only tolerated but encouraged widespread sexual violence and exploitation; they agree with Professor Sally G. McMillen's assertion that rape "defined most miscegenous relationships."[39] Others, however, argue that rape was far less prevalent than has often been claimed.[40] The reality was complex—probably more complicated than we will ever be able to appreciate satisfactorily. After all, the very meaning of words we use to organize our perceptions—key words such as "rape" change over time and continue to spur and reflect sharp conflicts. Moreover, as previously noted, the evidentiary record has been perhaps irredeemably stunted by the illiteracy of victims and, more decisively, the indifference, if not hostility, of authorities to whom black female suffering was a relatively trivial concern.* There are certain propositions, however, that can be voiced with confidence. Some owners who desired sex with their slaves were prevented from realizing their ambition. Inhibitions included fidelity to their white wives or sweethearts, religious scruples, fear of retaliation, and concern for reputation. At the same time, several features of slavery undercut the influence of these inhibitions. One feature was the remarkable vulnerability of enslaved women. In many places, *all* blacks—free

---

*See pages 44–45.

and enslaved alike—were prohibited from testifying against whites; Celia, for example, was not allowed to tell her story in court. Black women were also burdened by the prevalent belief that they were sexually promiscuous.[41] This belief offered white men a convenient excuse. How could they be condemned, after all, for engaging in sexual relations with women who were, by dint of their race, inherently aggressive and unchaste? How could they be faulted for taking advantage of women whose racial character impelled them to give sex for the asking, without need of persuasion, much less violence? And how could they be blamed for raping a sexually voracious species of human property? These beliefs put down deep and hardy roots. Over seventy years after the abolition of slavery, the white antilynching activist Jessie Daniel Ames would remark on the continuing influence exerted by the mythology of black female lasciviousness: "White men have said over and over . . . that not only was there no such thing as a chaste Negro woman—but that a Negro woman could not be assaulted, that it was never against her will."[42]*

The paucity of antebellum cases featuring black female victims of sex crimes is in itself eloquent testimony to the extreme vulnerability of black women. As historian Sharon Block has observed, "Enslaved women . . . did not have access to legal redress against white men who raped them. [N]o historian has recorded a conviction of a white man for the rape of a slave at any point from 1700 to the Civil War."[43] At the very end of that period, the *black* defendant in an 1859 Mississippi case, *George, a slave v. State,* was convicted of, and sentenced to death for, raping a female slave who was not yet ten years old.[44] The conviction, however, was overturned on appeal. Asserting that slaves had no

---

*Ruling on whether the prior chastity of the victim in a statutory-rape case should be presumed subject to rebuttal, the Florida Supreme Court opined in 1918 that:

> What has been said . . . about an unchaste female being a comprehensively rare exception is no doubt true where the population is composed largely of the Caucasian race, but we would blind ourselves to actual conditions if we adopted this rule where another race that is largely immoral constitutes an appreciable part of the population. [*Dallas v. State,* 76 Fla. 358, 364 (1918).]

rights under the common law, Judge William L. Harris declared that the courts must look to legislation alone to determine what rights they *did* have. Since no statute specifically protected slave girls or women from rape, no law was violated when they were sexually assaulted. The Mississippi legislature subsequently enacted a statute that offered some protection to slave girls, by providing that "the actual or attempted commissions of a rape by a negro or mulatto on a female negro or mulatto, under twelve years of age, is punishable with death or whipping as the jury may decide."[45] The very narrowness of that legislation underscores the sexual oppression visited upon black women. The new law prohibited only the rape of female slaves under the age of twelve, leaving all older slaves unprotected. Moreover, even that scope was further limited, to rapes committed by "negro or mulatto" perpetrators; there was no provision at all for slave rapes—even of children—by whites.* Although the precise extent to which white men used their racial privileges to subject black women to unwanted sex will never be known, it is clear that such abuse cast a chilling shadow that touched most African Americans as an immediate menace. Of all the dreadful cruelties of slavery, among the worst were the widespread sexual violations of black women and the wholesale failure of law and public opinion to redress it.

After the abolition of slavery, two important developments affected the sexual lives of African Americans. First, the black masses were finally

---

*In a few instances, slaves were prosecuted and punished for raping other slaves or free women of color. (See Thomas D. Morris, *Southern Slavery and the Law, 1619–1860* [1996], 306–7; Diane Miller Sommerville, "The Rape Myth Reconsidered: The Intersection of Race, Class, and Gender in the American South, 1800–1877" [Ph.D. diss., Rutgers–New Brunswick, 1995], 143 n. 8.) The rarity of prosecutions involving the latter, however, at once reflected and determined the reality that free blacks were more vulnerable to sexual assault than other unenslaved women. While the law of rape and its administration generally mistreated *all* women, it did not mistreat them equally. The severity of the mistreatment typically followed the society's gender, race, and class hierarchies, with black enslaved women faring worst and free black women just one step above them.

permitted to enter into legally protected matrimonial unions. Second, with the fall of the slave regime, former bondsmen sought to extricate their womenfolk from living and working situations that increased their vulnerability to the sexual overtures or impositions of white men. Nevertheless, African Americans continued to be subjected to racialized sexual abuse.* For one thing, throughout the Reconstruction period, violent white supremacists used rape as a weapon of terror aimed at intimidating or punishing blacks who dared to read, travel, work for themselves, or pursue politics.[46] Although opponents of Reconstruction claimed that talk of racial equality encouraged black men to rape white women, white racists were in fact the principal perpetrators of racially motivated rapes. In the Memphis Riot of 1868, for example, whites angered by the presence of black militiamen attacked the city's black community, murdering, beating, and raping its inhabitants and burning homes and businesses. In subsequent testimony before Congress, black Memphians Frances Thompson and Lucy Smith told of being gang-raped by seven white police officers, and Lucy Tibbs described being raped while pregnant. Later, in congressional hearings aimed at documenting the Ku Klux Klan's terrorist activities, black women from all over the South would testify about being raped by white men enraged by blacks' assertiveness.[47]

The ferocity of the violent reaction against Reconstruction abated somewhat after its fall. Subsequently, however, when Jim Crow pigmentocracy reigned supreme, blacks—and especially black women—continued to be the object of sexual aggressions stemming from the practice and ideology of white supremacy. Black domestic servants working in homes and hotels were perhaps the most vulnerable of all.[48] Isolated from witnesses, stereotyped as sexually lax, and deprived of powerful male protectors, black domestics who were raped or otherwise assaulted by white men stood little chance of receiving redress

---

*Women have historically been more vulnerable to rape in wartime. During the Civil War, this general predicament became a particular affliction for black women, who were targeted by soldiers from both sides. See Susan Brownmiller, *Against Our Will: Men, Women, and Rape* (1975), 127–28; Tera W. Hunter, *To 'Joy My Freedom: Southern Black Women's Lives and Labors after the Civil War* (1997), 20.

from police, prosecutors, juries, or judges. In 1912 a black nurse reported an experience that was all too typical. Dismissed after refusing to permit a white employer to kiss her, she would later recall:

> I didn't know then what has been a burden to my mind and heart ever since; that a colored woman's virtue in [the South] has no protection. When my husband went to the man who had insulted me, the man . . . had him arrested! I . . . testified on oath to the insult offered me. The white man, of course, denied the charge. The old judge looked up and said: "This court will never take the word of a nigger against the word of a white man."[49]

In some southern locales, white lawmakers stymied efforts to enact statutory-rape provisions that would have raised the age of consent, claiming that they would empower Negro girls to threaten white men.[50] "We see at once," Kentucky legislator A. C. Tomkins warned, "what a terrible weapon for evil the elevating of the age of consent would be when placed in the hands of lecherous, sensual negro women!"[51] Moreover, some whites, still clinging to the ways of slavery, perceived black women as being essentially unprotected by law. Thus in 1913 Governor Cole Blease of South Carolina could pardon a white man convicted of raping a black woman because he refused to believe, he said, that the defendant would risk imprisonment for "what he could usually get from prices ranging from 25 cents to one dollar." In pardoning another rapist, Governor Blease candidly averred that he had "very serious doubt as to whether the crime of rape can be committed upon a negro."[52] When white men were convicted of raping black women, they were punished much less severely than black men convicted of raping white women. Between 1908 and 1949, for example, the Commonwealth of Virginia executed not a single white man for rape. During the same period, it put to death forty-five convicted black rapists, all of whose alleged victims were white women. In the eyes of state authorities, deterring and punishing sexual assaults on black women were simply not priorities.[53]

Disabled from calling upon law-enforcement officials with confidence, blacks had to resort to other means of protection and redress. One of these was emigration. According to Professor Darlene Clark Hine, many black women fled the South "to escape both from sexual exploitation . . . and from the rape and threat of rape by white as well as Black males."[54] White men in Indianola, Mississippi, so menaced the black women clerical workers at an insurance company that that firm moved its offices out of state.[55]

Seclusion constituted another means of self-defense. "Negro women of refinement and culture," black educator Robert Russa Morton observed in 1929, "are not often seen in public places, except among their own people. They prefer the protection and shelter of their own homes, for . . . such women are constantly exposed to unwelcome and uninvited attentions of a certain type of white men without any sort of redress or protection in the law."[56] In many instances, the only form of redress available to blacks was publicity—that is, the revelation of the realities of sexual criminality denied by white supremacists. The outstanding practitioner of this mode of resistance was Ida B. Wells-Barnett,[57] a fearless journalist who exposed the failure of state officials to punish seriously those who raped black women. In one case she publicized, a white man in Nashville, Tennessee, was convicted of raping a black girl, went to jail for only six months, and afterward became a detective in that city.[58] Such leniency would, of course, have been unthinkable had the perpetrator been black and the victim white.

The bitter history of white-on-black sexual aggression continues to reverberate in our own time. Illustrative of the powerful emotions it has generated are two episodes from the final quarter of the twentieth century. The first was the Joan Little case; the second was the Tawana Brawley affair.

In 1975 a twenty-one-year-old black woman named Joan Little became a cause célèbre as the defendant in a murder trial. According to the prosecution, Little, an occasional prostitute, lured Clarence Alligood, a sixty-two-year-old jail warden, into her cell by promising to have sex with him. When he ventured in, she killed him in order to escape. The defense's version of events had Alligood repeatedly seeking sex from Little, who constantly rebuffed him. Eventually he entered her cell armed with an ice pick and forced her to perform fellatio on him. At some point during her unwilling ministrations, Little grabbed the ice pick and, in the course of a desperate struggle, mortally stabbed her assailant. What made this case a national news story, of course, was the racial cast of the drama. Keenly aware that white men had for years been raping black women with impunity, various feminist, leftist, and black uplift organizations adopted the defendant as an exemplar of wronged black womanhood. Unlike Celia the slave, Joan Little got to testify at her own trial, a five-week, highly publicized contest decided by a jury composed of six blacks and six whites. And unlike Celia, Joan Little was acquitted.[59]

Twelve years later, on November 28, 1987, in Wappinger Falls, New York, a black teenager named Tawana Brawley curled up in a fetal position in a plastic bag, her body smeared with feces and covered with racist graffiti. She alleged that six white men, including one wearing a policeman's badge, had abducted and raped her.[60] This case, too, became a national cause célèbre. Although the putative victim exhibited a suspicious evasiveness from early on in the evolution of this bizarre saga, a broad cross section of African Americans fervently embraced her and insisted upon her honesty. They did so in part because her alleged ordeal evoked terrible collective memories of white men's sexual brutalizing of black women under the tolerant gaze of white officials. Then, too, they defended Brawley because the controversy over her veracity threatened—or was perceived to threaten—the believability of long-standing and long-neglected complaints regarding the sexual coercion of black women.[61] A grand jury report carefully refuted Brawley's allegations. Among the revealing holes in her story were certain basic and unexplained inconsistencies. She claimed to have been raped by six men, yet no physical evidence—neither genital trauma nor the presence of sperm—corroborated her charge. She claimed to have been held captive in woods for several days, during which time the temperature had dipped to the freezing mark; yet when she was found, her clothes were free of plant materials, and she showed no signs of exposure, dehydration, or malnutrition.*

Some of Brawley's supporters simply refused to disbelieve her, regardless of the facts. Others contended that establishing the facts in this particular instance was less important than putting to effective use the publicity generated by the controversy. Such publicity, it was argued, would advance the propositions that black women have long been the victims of racially motivated sexual violence perpetrated by white men; that these perpetrators have characteristically committed their crimes with impunity; and that their evil deeds have long been obscured by racist notions that render many whites more apt to believe, at any given moment, that a black woman is a whore than that a white man is a rapist.[62] The facts of specific cases, however, *do* matter. They matter even when they inconveniently complicate stories that at first seem starkly simple. Tawana Brawley lied. Her lie attained vitality, even in the glare of exposure, because *real* racially motivated sexual violence has been visited upon black women for centuries without adequate redress or even acknowledgment. For many Americans, especially blacks, the wounds of this history remain unhealed. At the same time, for many other Americans, especially whites, the specter of the white man as racially motivated rapist resides safely in the past and has been superseded by a different, more contemporary, and hence more frightening image: the black man as racially motivated sexual criminal. It is to the problem of the black man as rapist that we will now turn.

---

*The grand jury report also noted that prior to Brawley making her allegations, a black teenage classmate of hers had likewise claimed to have been abducted and raped by white men. Unlike Brawley, this girl later admitted that her story was false. (See Grand Jury of the Supreme Court of New York, County of Dutchess, "Report of the Grand Jury and Related Documents Concerning the Tawana Brawley Investigation" [1988], 56). Eleven years after Brawley made her initial allegations, a New York jury ordered her to pay $185,000 in damages for slandering a man whom she had named as one of her assailants. (See "Judge Orders Brawley to Pay $185,000 for Defamation," *New York Times,* October 10, 1998.)

*White Women, Black Men, and Sexual Coercion, Part 1*

A black man who rapes a white woman does not necessarily do so *because* she is white; nonracial motives undoubtedly animate many interracial rapes.[63] But just as racial beliefs and feelings have prompted some white-on-black rapes, so, too, have they inspired black-on-white ones. Told that they are, by dint of their race, rapacious sexual fiends, some black men have sought to satisfy the negative expectations of frightened strangers. Warned that touching white women could cost them their lives, some black men have insisted upon imposing themselves out of an impulse toward rebellion. Mindful of the sexual crimes that whites have committed against blacks without punishment, some African Americans have viewed the rape of whites as racial payback. On July 13, 1973, near Adel, Georgia, three black men abducted and raped a white woman who had been stranded on a highway by car trouble. During the attack, at least one of the men referred to the woman as a "honky bitch" and a "white bitch."[64] On February 16, 1978, after Lee Beals, a black man, abducted a white female victim in her automobile, he reportedly announced, before raping her, that he "had never had a white bitch before and . . . that she was going to like it."[65] Race was clearly a factor in Nathaniel Reynolds's rape of a thirty-year-old white woman in the early-morning hours of July 7, 1985. According to the victim, when she refused to accept a drink that Reynolds offered her while holding her captive, he put her refusal down to the fact that she was "a white bitch [who didn't] want to drink after no nigger." The victim testified that just prior to raping her, Reynolds said, "Before you die, you're going . . . to know what it feels like to have a nigger cock in you."[66]

In 1992, Ambrose A. Harris and an associate, Gloria Dunn, agreed to steal a car that they would then use in committing another robbery.[67] When Dunn asked what they would do with the people in whatever car they hijacked, Harris reportedly said that he would "tie them up and leave them somewhere" if they were black but kill them if they were white.[68] When Kristin Huggins, a white woman, drove her red Toyota into the parking lot where Harris and Dunn lay in wait, Harris was said to have muttered "I'm going to get that bitch," before raping and murdering her.[69]

In December 1992, near Charleston, South Carolina, four black men assaulted Melissa McLauchlin. Several of the men later confessed that they had made a sort of "New Year's resolution" to abduct, rape, and kill a white woman. Seeking to explain this barbarism, one of the perpetrators maintained that it constituted retaliation for "four hundred years of oppression."[70]

The cases described above all have involved black-on-white, heterosexual, male-on-female rape. But men also rape men. Black-on-white, male-on-male rape occurs often in prison. Again, all manner of motivations spark criminality of this sort; sometimes interracial rapes stem from evil motives or impulses that have nothing to do with race. A substantial proportion of the interracial rape encountered in jails and prisons, however, is attributable at least in part to racial sentiments.[71] In investigating the motivation behind such assaults, researchers have been told by some black perpetrators of sexual violence that "now it is [whites'] turn" to be dominated.[72] Explaining the racial dynamic of rape in the prison in which he was incarcerated, one Negro inmate remarked, "You guys's been cuttin' our b[alls] off ever since we been in this country. Now we're just gettin' even."[73]

"Just Gettin' Even" could well serve as an alternative title for Eldridge Cleaver's *Soul on Ice*, the piece of writing that most vividly articulates the way revenge has seeped into the sexual conduct and fantasies of some black men. Published to great fanfare in 1968, *Soul on Ice* sketches Cleaver's coming of age in prison, offers his reflections on ideas picked up from Norman Mailer, Wilhelm Reich, Frantz Fanon, and Malcom X, and wraps this mix in a hyperbolic rhetoric that for a moment, at least, resonated in influential sectors of American political culture. For our purposes, the most significant aspect of *Soul on Ice* is Cleaver's analysis of his decision to rape white women as a political act. He traced the impulse to a stint in prison in the 1950s for possession of marijuana, during which three events seem to have been pivotal. The first was a confrontation with a prison guard over a photo of a pinup girl. Cleaver recalled that in order to better endure his confinement—"I was in my bull stage and lack of access to females was absolutely a form of torture"—he had pasted the image of a nude girl onto the wall of his prison cell: "Out of the center of *Esquire*," he wrote, "I married a voluptuous bride."[74] That arrangement was unacceptable to a (presumably white) prison guard, who "ripped [Cleaver's] sugar from the wall" and tore her image into pieces.[75] The guard later told Cleaver that he could post a colored pinup girl but not a white one. For Cleaver, this incident marked an awakening: "A terrible feeling of guilt came over me as I realized that I had chosen the picture of the white girl over the available pictures of black girls."[76]

According to Cleaver, the next big step came when he asked a group of fellow blacks about their tastes in women. Most, he noted, indicated a disinclination toward black women. "'I don't want nothin' black but a Cadillac,'" said one. "'If money was black,'" put in another, "'I wouldn't want none of it.'"[77] From that moment on, Cleaver began "to notice how thoroughly . . . a black growing up in America is indoctrinated with the white race's standard of beauty."[78] Instead of being liberating, this knowledge was a burden to him: "It intensified my frustrations," he wrote, "to know that I was indoctrinated to see the white woman as more beautiful and desirable than my own black woman."[79]

The third key event in the evolution of Cleaver's thinking was the highly publicized killing of Emmett Till,* a black youngster from Chicago who was murdered in Mississippi in the summer of 1955 largely for whistling at a white woman. Cleaver recalled:

> One day I saw in a magazine a picture of the white woman with whom Emmett Till was said to have flirted. While looking at the picture, I felt that little tension in the center of my chest I experience when a woman appeals to me. I was disgusted and angry with myself. . . . I looked at the picture again and again, and in spite of everything and against my will and the hate I felt

---

*For more on Emmett Till, see pages 203–5.

for the woman and all that she represented, she appealed to me. I flew into a rage at myself, at America, at white women, at the history that had placed those tensions of lust and desire in my chest.[80]

By the time Cleaver was released from prison, he was ready to embark upon a new career as a politicized rapist of white women. For "practice," he explained, he raped a few black women, crimes about which his memoir says little. When he considered himself "smooth enough," he crossed the racial tracks and began raping white women with a zeal fueled in part by a dialectical attraction and repulsion.*

For a time, Cleaver recalled, he perceived the raping of white women as a justified "insurrectionary act" that permitted him at once to obtain a thrilling revenge, "trampl[e] upon the white man's law," and assuage the aching resentment he felt at white men's historical mistreatment of black women.[81] He claimed, however, that after being reimprisoned on charges of attempted rape, he disavowed his campaign to defile white women and began to be ashamed of what he had done. "For the first time in my life," he averred, "[I] admitted that I was wrong, that I had gone astray—astray not so much from the white man's law as from being human, civilized—for I could not approve the

---

*Cleaver's poem "To a White Girl" reads:

> I love you
> Because you're white,
> Not because you're charming
> Or bright. . . .
>
> I hate you
> Because you're white.
> Your white meat
> Is nightmare food. . . .
>
> Loving you thus
> And hating you so,
> My heart is torn in two.
> Crucified.

[Eldridge Cleaver, *Soul on Ice* (1968), 13–14.]

act of rape."[82] Yet even in the teeth of his disavowal, some ambiguity remained. Most notably he called his rapist yearnings a "revolutionary sickness,"[83] pathological but not altogether bad.

Cleaver was by no means the only African American activist-intellectual of the Black Power era to advance the "militant rapist archetype."[84] Calvin Hernton, for one, posited that due to the distorting impact of oppression upon the psyche of black men, every Negro who had grown up in the Jim Crow South was at heart, if only for a moment in his lifetime, a rapist of white women.[85]* According to Amiri Baraka, whites were right to think of "the black man as potentially raping every white lady in sight," because "the black man should want to rob the white man of everything he has."[86] The writer Cecil Brown similarly asserted that "if [the black man] is to free himself from his own impotent obscurity . . . he must rape the white man's beauty queen."[87]

Eight years after the appearance of *Soul on Ice,* Alice Walker published a novel, *Meridian,* that explores interracial relationships during and after the civil rights revolution. Among its gripping scenes is one featuring a black civil rights worker named Tommy Odds, whose right arm has been amputated because of a wound inflicted on him by white racists. Odds forces himself sexually upon a white colleague named Lynne:

> There was a moment when she knew she could force him from her. But it was a flash. She lay instead thinking of his feel-

---

*Seeking to substantiate his claim, Hernton related a comment made by a friend of his while driving around Nashville, Tennessee. While Hernton did not provide a date for the incident, the overall context suggests that the conversation took place sometime in the late 1950s or early 1960s. As quoted by Hernton, his unidentified friend said:

> Just look at all those proud, white asses shaking like jelly. . . . I hate those white ugly bitches. . . . They think they own the world. And they do. Say, look at that one. What a fine dish! I'd like to rape her with a telegraph pole. . . . No I wouldn't either. I'd use my own penis. Look at them, coming out of those offices, sitting on their fine asses all day, doing nothing. I could screw every one I see. Especially that one over there in the blue skirt. I bet I could make her moan and groan like no white man's ever done, make her *love* me. [*Sex and Racism in America* (1965; reprint, 1981), 66–67.]

ings, his hardships, of the way he was black and belonged to people who lived without hope; she thought about the loss of his arm. She felt her own guilt. And he entered her and she did not any longer resist but tried instead to think of Tommy Odds as he was when he was her friend—and near the end her arms stole around his neck and before he left she told him she forgave him and she kissed his slick rounded stump that was the color of baked liver, and he smiled at her from far away, and she did not know him. "Be seein' you," he said.[88]

The next day, Odds returns, accompanied by three black friends whom he tries to provoke into raping Lynne. When they decline, he taunts them: "'You guys are afraid of her that's all. Shit. Crackers been raping your mamas and sisters for generations and here's your chance to get off on a piece of their goods.'"[89] The narrator of *Meridian* observes that "it was as if Tommy Odds thought Lynne was not a human being, as if her whiteness, the mystique of it, the *danger* of it, the historically *verboten* nature of it, encouraged him to attempt to destroy her without any feelings of guilt."[90] Nonetheless, Lynne refuses to seek from the local, all-white police force either punishment for or protection against Tommy Odds. She is more afraid of the police than she is of him—fearful that they will indiscriminately punish all of the black men in the community, thus intensifying the violence she has been working to end.

Walker has been sternly criticized for the gritty portrayals of Tommy Odds and other, equally unsavory black male characters in her novels.[91] Her detractors argue that such depictions serve only to perpetuate racist stereotypes of black men. Several years after publishing *Meridian*, Walker wrote a story in which she considered what Ida B. Wells, the indefatigable antilynching activist, would have advised her to do with respect to writing about black men raping white women. Walker decided that Wells's advice would have been:

> Write nothing. Nothing at all. It will be used against black men and therefore against all of us. Eldridge Cleaver and LeRoi Jones don't know who they're dealing with. But you remember. You are dealing with people who brought their children to wit-

ness the murder of black human beings, falsely accused of rape. People who handed out, as trophies, black fingers and toes. Deny! Deny! Deny![92]

### The Demonizing of Black Male Sexuality

Throughout much of the antebellum South, states authorized officials to impose harsher penalties on black than on white rapists. Whereas possible prison terms were prescribed for convicted white rapists, castration and death were the potential penalties for black ones. It is still true, however, that in many locales "antebellum white southerners felt less compelled to exact death from a black man accused of sexually violating a white female than did postbellum white southerners."[93] Between 1860 and 1865, for example, Virginia governors (in the midst of the Civil War) commuted the sentences of nearly half of the blacks condemned to death for raping white women. Such intervention stemmed in part from pressures exerted by slave owners who were anxious to avoid losing *their* human chattel to punishments administered by public authorities. And all blacks occasionally benefited from the solicitude of white slave-owning elites that perceived themselves as being sufficiently dominant to be able to afford shows of paternalistic mercy.

All of that changed, however, in the aftermath of the Civil War, when the abolition of slavery and the elevation of blacks to formal racial equality moved whites ferociously to reassert their racial hegemony. During this period, fear and loathing of black advancements ignited an intensified effort to vilify and contain expressions of black "manhood." In an attempt to justify the fervently racist pigmentocracies that arose in the South in the 1890s, white supremacists alleged, among other charges, that the abolition of slavery and the awarding of civil rights to blacks had led to a sharp increase in sexual crimes against white women. "Rape," wrote Claude Bowers in an influential text, "is the foul daughter of Reconstruction."[94]* Defenders of the Jim Crow

---

*See also Myrta Lockett Avary, *Dixie After the War* (1906), 377: "The rapist is the product of the reconstruction period. His chrysalis was a uniform; as a soldier he could force his way into private homes, bullying and insulting white women; he was often commissioned to tasks involving these things. He came into life in the abnor-

regime looked back nostalgically on the slavery era as a time of racial comity, when bondage civilized Negroes and transformed them, despite their latent savagery, into trustworthy, servile beings. One George T. Winston asserted that southern white women "shudder[ed] with nameless horror" when Negroes tamed by slavery passed from the scene, only to be replaced by Negroes spoiled by emancipation. In this new environment, he warned, "the black brute is lurking in the dark, a monstrous beast, crazed with lust. His ferocity is almost demoniacal. A mad bull or a tiger could scarcely be more brutal."[95]* In the post-Reconstruction era, some racists sought to explain "scientifically" the black male's allegedly peculiar sexual power. Writing in the journal *Medicine,* for instance, Dr. William Lee Howard asserted in 1903 that blacks' "attacks on defenseless white women are evidence of racial instincts that are about as amenable to ethical culture as is the inherent odor of the race."[96] The physiological root of the problem, by the doctor's account, was twofold, consisting in "the large size of the Negro's penis" and the fact that blacks lacked "the sensitiveness of the terminal fibers which exists in the Caucasian."[97] As a consequence, Howard intoned, "the African's birthright" was "sexual madness and excess."[98]

Novelists of the day also stigmatized the African American male. The outstanding example was Thomas Dixon Jr., author of *The Leopard's Spots: A Romance of the White Man's Burden, 1865–1900* (1902)

---

mal atmosphere of a time rife with discussions of social equality theories, contentions for coeducation and intermarriage"; Thomas Nelson Page, *The Negro: The Southerner's Problem* (1904), 112: "As the crime of rape of late years had its baleful renascence in the teaching of equality and the placing of power in the ignorant Negroes' hands, so its perpetuation and increase have undoubtedly been due in large part to the same teaching"; W. J. Cash, *The Mind of the South* (1941), 119: What the [white] Southerners felt "was that any assertion of any kind on the part of the Negro constituted . . . an attack on the Southern [white] woman. What they saw, more or less consciously, in the conditions of Reconstruction was a passage toward a condition for her as degrading, in their view, as rape itself."

*Racial liberals of the period assimilated racist stereotypes about the "peculiar" traits of Negroes. Hence, Ray Stannard Baker could write, "Many of the crimes committed by Negroes are marked with almost animal-like ferocity. Once aroused to murderous rage, the Negro does not stop with mere killing; he bruises and batters his victim out of all semblance to humanity" (*Following the Color Line: American Negro Citizenship in the Progressive Era* [1980; reprint, 1964], 180).

and *The Clansman: An Historical Romance of the Ku Klux Klan* (1905). Central to both novels is the rape of white women by black men. An early scene in *The Leopard's Spots* depicts the marriage ceremony of a white couple during the Reconstruction era. The wedding is interrupted by Negro militiamen who beat the groom senseless and abduct the bride-to-be.* Urged on by her father, the white men in attendance shoot at the fleeing militiamen, accidentally killing the bride. Her father comforts the militiamen with the comment that at least they saved her from defilement by the blacks—a fate that, in his view, would have been worse than death.† In that scene, Dixon's readers are at least spared the spectacle of a consummated black-on-white rape. They are not so lucky a few hundred pages later, when an eleven-year-old white girl is raped by a Negro man: the child "lay on the ground with her clothes torn to shreds and stained with blood. . . . It was too plain the

---

*The rhetoric with which Dixon communicated racial dread is worth noting:

> Suddenly a black shadow fell across the doorway. The fiddle ceased, and every eye turned toward the door. The burly figure of a big Negro trooper from a company stationed in the town stood before them. His face was in a broad grin, and his eyes bloodshot with whiskey. He brought his musket down on the floor with a bang. . . .
>
> There was a scuffle, the quick thud of heavy blows and [the groom] fell to the floor senseless. A piercing scream rang from the bride as she was seized in the arms of the Negro. . . . He rapidly bore her toward the door surrounded by the six scoundrels who accompanied him. [Thomas Dixon Jr., *The Leopard's Spots: A Romance of the White Man's Burden, 1865–1900* (1902), 125–26.]

†The imposition of capital punishment for rape is a reflection of the idea that rape can be as evil and destructive as murder. Upholding the legality of capital punishment in such cases, the chief justice of the Georgia Supreme Court asserted that a woman "is entitled to every legal protection of her body, her decency, her purity, and her good name. Anyone so depraved as to rape her deserves the most extreme penalty that the law provides for crime" (*Sims v. Balkcom,* 136 S.E.2d 766, 769 [1964]). The Supreme Court of the United States later invalidated execution as a punishment for most, if not all, rapes (*Coker v. Georgia,* 433 U.S. 584 [1977]). The belief that rape is an evil as bad as or worse than murder remains in force in many parts of the world, often with terrible consequences for women survivors, who are ostracized in the aftermath of their victimization. (See, e.g., Elisabeth Bumiller, "Crisis in the Balkans: Crimes; Deny Rape or Be Hated: Kosovo Victim's Choice," *New York Times,* June 22, 1999.)

terrible crime that had been committed"[99]—a crime too terrible, evidently, even to name. Dixon's novel *The Clansman: An Historical Romance of the Ku Klux Klan* (1905) features another black-on-white rape, this one committed in the presence of the victim's mother. The perpetrator is Gus, a Negro "fiend."*

Afterward, the victim concludes that death would be preferable to living with the shame of having been sexually touched by a Negro, even if by force. Musing resignedly that under the circumstances, death would be sweet, she rejects her mother's suggestion that they move away to a place where people will be unaware of the horror that has befallen them. In the end, they commit suicide together, leaping hand in hand from a cliff.

Imagery of the black man as sexual predator has had far-reaching consequences. Among other things, it helped facilitate the lynchings that claimed between four and five thousand black lives from the 1880s to the 1960s.[100] Of the several defenses that apologists offered for lynching, one of the most popular was the claim that black men's lust for white women was irrepressible or so intense that nothing short of mob violence could control it. White women so aroused black men, according to the southern white writer Philip Alexander Bruce, that the latter were compelled "to gratify their lust at any cost and in spite of every obstacle."[101] Laying the blame for lynching squarely at the feet of Negro sexual outlaws, an apologist for vigilante violence against Negroes wrote in the *Atlantic Monthly* in 1904 that "it [is] with [rape] that lynching begins."[102] In fact, allegations of murder were the most frequent basis for pursuing extralegal revenge; antilynching activists repeatedly proved that rape was not even the most prevalent pretext for mob violence. Yet as Walter White observed, "Despite the evidence . . . showing that only a small percentage of lynched Negroes were even accused of rape, the vast majority of whites in the states where lynchings are most frequently staged really believe that most mob murders are the results of sex crimes."[103] Nevertheless, many violent assaults on black communities did have their beginnings in allegations of black-on-white rape.[104] Per-

---

*The pioneering director D. W. Griffith would later bring Gus to the attention of millions in *Birth of a Nation* (1915), his film adaptation of *The Clansman*.

haps the most consequential of these occurred in 1908 in Springfield, Illinois, in the midst of preparations to honor the centennial of Springfield's favorite son, Abraham Lincoln. Frustrated by its inability to lynch two blacks who had been falsely accused of rape, a white mob instead killed two blacks who were, except by race, wholly unrelated to the suspects. The outrage prompted by these lynchings caused several leading reformers, including W. E. B. DuBois, Mary White Ovington, and John Dewey, to lay the foundations for what would become the National Association for the Advancement of Colored People.[105]

For its first two decades, the NAACP devoted itself primarily to attacking lynching. That proved to be a difficult undertaking. Suffering from what journalist W. J. Cash aptly described as a "rape complex," prominent figures in white southern society maintained that lynching was a necessary evil, a disincentive required to keep the Negro "beast" at bay. "Governor as I am," Benjamin Tillman of South Carolina confessed in 1892, "I would lead a mob to lynch the negro who ravishes a white woman."[106] Five years later, as a United States senator, Tillman would ask on the floor of the Congress, "Shall men cold-bloodedly stand up and demand for [the black man accused of raping a white woman] the right to have a fair trial and be punished in the regular course of justice?" Tillman answered his own question in the negative: "So far as I am concerned, [the Negro *accused* of raping a white woman] has put himself outside the pale of the law, human and divine."[107] In addition to facing the terror of mob violence, black men accused of raping white women were confronted by the specter of "legal lynchings"—sham court proceedings whose principal purpose was to preempt illegal punishments by speedily imposing legal ones. According to Professor George C. Wright, "The decline of lynchings . . . was due in part to the states taking the role of the mob."[108] The shadow that the prospect of lynching sometimes cast on court proceedings is vividly captured in a paradoxical way by a defense attorney's appeal to the jury in a 1907 Louisiana case in which a black man was charged with burglary and intent to rape a white woman:

> Gentlemen of the jury, this man, a nigger, is charged with
> breaking into the house of a white man in the nighttime and

assaulting his wife, with the intent to rape her. Now, don't you know that, if this nigger had committed such a crime, he never would have been brought here and tried; that he would have been lynched, and if I were there I would help pull on the rope.[109]*

The corrosive effects of racial bias and mob pressure have paved the way for the unwarranted convictions of scores of black defendants charged with raping white women. Consider the fate of Ed Johnson, an illiterate Tennessee laborer who was identified by the white victim of a rape with the assistance of a highly suspect police lineup.[110] On the basis of her (mis)identification, Johnson was tried before a judge whose chief object was to kill him "legally" before a mob could do so illegally. Despite the obvious influence of a pervasive prejudgment of the defendant, the trial judge McReynolds denied defense counsel's pleas for a delay or change of venue. During the trial, moreover, McReynolds did nothing to prevent racism and the spirit of the mob from contaminating his courtroom. The gallery cheered the prosecution, jeered the defense, and heckled Johnson throughout his testimony—all without meaningful judicial rebuke. Judge McReynolds did not even intervene when a juror attempted to beat the defendant. Restrained by fellow jurors, the enraged man yelled, "If I could get at him [Johnson], I'd tear his heart out right now."[111] That juror was not removed from the supposedly impartial panel that was to decide Johnson's fate. Racially derogatory comments made by the prosecutor should also have ensured a mistrial, but again the

---

*An episode that took place in 1934 in Desoto County, Mississippi, is similarly revealing. Three black men charged with raping a white teenager were tried in a courthouse ringed with barbed wire, machine guns, and more than three hundred National Guardsmen who faced a mob of several thousand whites. The jury deliberated for only about six minutes before convicting the defendants. The presiding judge immediately condemned the men to death by hanging and then asked jurors, relatives of the victim, and other whites in the courthouse to help disperse the crowd outside. He advised them that a lynching would only help encourage passage of federal antilynching legislation, which would "destroy one of the South's cherished possessions—the supremacy of the white race" (quoted in Neil R. McMillen, *Dark Journey: Black Mississippians in the Age of Jim Crow* [1989], 207).

trial judge permitted the proceedings to degenerate into a spectacle of persecution. Johnson, of course, was convicted and sentenced to die.

After the Tennessee Supreme Court rejected their request for a new trial, Johnson's attorneys appealed to the federal courts for relief. United States Supreme Court Justice John Marshall Harlan ordered local officials to delay Johnson's execution. At this point, however, the thin veneer of legality covering the case gave way entirely, as a mob of white men decided simply to kill Johnson. Well aware of the lynchers' intentions, Sheriff Joseph F. Shipp purposefully abetted their work by leaving a mere skeleton crew of guards on duty at the jail in which Johnson was incarcerated. On the evening of March 19, 1906, with Sheriff Shipp offering only token resistance, a mob seized Johnson and marched him to a nearby bridge, where some years previously another black man had been lynched for allegedly attacking a white woman. Given a final chance to confess, Johnson responded by saying, "God bless you all. I am innocent."[112] He was then hanged, shot, and mutilated. To top it all off, someone pinned a note to his bullet-riddled body, reading: "To Justice Harlan. Come get your nigger now."[113]*

In the infamous case of the Scottsboro Boys, nine black youngsters ranging in age from thirteen to twenty were charged in 1931 with raping two white women aboard a train near Scottsboro, Alabama.[114] The evidence against them consisted principally of the women's allegations. One of the accusers eventually recanted and campaigned for the defendants' release; the other stood by her initial charge but told such implausible and contradictory versions of her story as to make it seem virtually certain that she was lying about the entire episode.

The Scottsboro Boys were subjected to appalling violations of the

---

*In response, the Supreme Court, trying individuals for contempt of court for the first and only time in its history, convicted Sheriff Shipp, a deputy, and four members of the lynch mob and sentenced them to prison terms of sixty to ninety days apiece. When the sheriff returned to Chattanooga after his brief stay in prison, ten thousand people turned up at the train station to greet him. McReynolds remained on the bench until 1921, when he was elected to Congress; he served there for another eighteen years. See Mark Curriden and LeRoy Phillips Jr., *Contempt of Court: The Turn-of-the-Century Lynching That Launched 100 Years of Federalism* (1999).

most rudimentary requirements of fairness. One judge, for example, gave jurors the following instructions on how to interpret evidence relating to allegations of a black-on-white rape:

> Where the woman charged to have been raped, as in this case, is a white woman, there is a very strong presumption under the law that she would not and did not yield voluntarily to intercourse with the defendant, a Negro; and this is true, whatever the station in life the prosecutrix may occupy, whether she be the most despised, ignorant and abandoned woman of the community, or the spotless virgin and daughter of a prominent home of luxury and learning.[115]

Fortunately, sufficient (and sufficiently effective) opposition was marshaled to prevent any of the Scottsboro Boys from being executed. Nonetheless, they collectively served some 104 years in prison for what were almost surely false allegations.*

On occasion, black men have been prosecuted for doing nothing worse than getting too close to white women, or appearing to *think* about being sexually intimate with them, or even just *looking* at them too hard—the infraction known as reckless eyeballing. In 1951 in Yanceyville, North Carolina, for instance, a black man named Mark Ingraham was prosecuted for assault with intent to rape because, from a distance of seventy feet, he had allegedly "undressed" a seventeen-year-old white girl with his eyes and looked at her in a "leering" manner. Thurgood Marshall described the supposed crime as "highway looking and attempting to want."[116] Even more egregious were the ramifications of an utterly innocent exchange that took place in 1958 in Monroe, North Carolina. Two black boys—Fuzzy Simpson, age seven, and Hanover Thompson, age nine—were invited to join a group of five

---

*Two cases stemming from this tragedy led to important decisions by the United States Supreme Court. In *Powell v. Alabama,* 287 U.S. 45 (1932), the Court held that, at least in death-penalty cases, states were obligated to provide defendants with effective legal representation if they could not afford to hire effective legal representation on their own. In *Norris v. Alabama,* 294 U.S. 587 (1935), the Court enforced the Fourteenth Amendment's prohibition against racial discrimination in the selection of jurors.

white children, including two girls. One of the girls remembered that she had played with Hanover when his mother worked as a maid in her family's house. Overjoyed at being reunited with her old friend, she kissed him on the cheek. Later, when she told her mother about it, her mother called the local police, who immediately arrested and jailed the two boys. Within a few weeks, they had been convicted of attempted rape. A Juvenile Court judge sentenced Fuzzy to twelve years in jail and Hanover to fourteen. Commentators around the world pointed to this ridiculous prosecution as an example of the hysteria generated in the white South by the nascent civil rights movement. Although there was no reasonable basis for the incarceration of the two black youngsters, conventional legal appeals submitted to the North Carolina judiciary were rebuffed. What finally saved the boys was a publicity campaign mounted on their behalf by Conrad Lynn, an attorney from New York City who called on Eleanor Roosevelt for assistance. Convinced that a terrible miscarriage of justice had occurred, Mrs. Roosevelt telephoned President Dwight D. Eisenhower, who in turn applied pressure to North Carolina's governor, who ultimately engineered the boys' release.[117]

It would be comforting to think that such tragedies were safely confined to the "bad old days." Such comfort, however, can be enjoyed only at the price of delusion. Many law-enforcement officials persist in viewing blackness, particularly male blackness, as a proxy for an increased risk of certain types of criminality, including rape. There have been substantial changes in racial attitudes over the past half century, but deeply ingrained racist imagery casting the black man as a sexual predator continues to affect perceptions in ways that lead, on occasion, to wrongful prosecutions and convictions. A revealing example is the case of Clarence Brandley, a black man convicted of raping and murdering a white high school student in Conroe, Texas.[118] Brandley sat on death row for six years before being freed, in 1989, by the unearthing of exculpatory evidence, along with evidence of racially discriminatory prosecutorial misconduct.

The demonization of black men has lent itself to all manner of exploitation. Professor Katheryn K. Russell has identified nine instances between 1987 and 1997 of white women fabricating stories of having been raped by black men.[119] In one case, a student at George Washington University reported being raped by two black men, only to admit soon after that she had been lying in an effort to highlight the dangers faced by women on campus. In another instance, a white woman insisted that three black men had kidnapped her at gunpoint from a shopping mall, compelled her to take drugs, and then forced her to have sex with them. Police later concluded that she had made up the story as a cover for having stayed out all night.[120] It is impossible to determine with any certainty why, how, and to what extent race enters into the calculations of those who make such false allegations, but one theory is that in describing their assailants as black, accusers seek to render their fabrications at once more credible, more deserving of sympathy, and more frightening.*

Demonization and its consequences have in turn prompted many blacks to regard allegations of black-on-white crime—particularly sexual crime—with great skepticism; some refuse to condemn black defendants even when their guilt appears patent. This attitude was very much on display in two high-profile cases of the late 1980s and mid-1990s—cases that thereby escalated into major racial controversies. In each instance, the victim was a white woman who had allegedly become the target of black male aggression. The first woman was known only as the Central Park Jogger; the second was Nicole Brown Simpson.

In April 1989 a white woman was supposedly gang-raped in New York City's Central Park by a group of African American and Latino males ranging in age from thirteen to twenty.[121] The incident was highly publicized, the victim widely pitied, and the crime itself harshly condemned. A dissenting perspective was voiced, however, by some who

---

*In 1994 a white woman in Baton Rouge reported that she had been sexually assaulted by a black man who had a tattoo of a serpent on his arm. After police released a sketch of the alleged assailant, twenty-eight other women came forward to say that they had either seen the man or been attacked by him. By the time the initial complainant confessed to having perpetrated a hoax, police had targeted a suspect and were about to arrest him. (See Katheryn K. Russell, *The Color of Crime: Racial Hoaxes, White Fear, Black Protectionism, Police Harassment and Other Macro-aggressions* [1998], 172). That same year, in Virginia, a twelve-year-old-white girl told police that a black man had broken into her family's home and attempted to rape her. She later identified a twenty-one-year-old individual as her assailant. He was convicted of burglary and attempted rape and sentenced to a twelve-year prison term. Fifteen months into his imprisonment, the girl recanted her testimony. In 1995 Virginia's governor pardoned the man, and two years later, the state senate voted to award him $45,000 for his wrongful imprisonment (see ibid., 166–67).

charged that police had slighted the legal rights of the accused—a charge that was subsequently substantiated. Others discerned various forms of racial discrimination in the handling of the case by the police and the news media—noting, for example, that in the same week the attack on the Central Park Jogger made front-page news, twenty-eight other cases of sexual assault were reported in New York, seventeen of them involving the victimization of black women.[122] That none of these other victims was deemed worthy of space on the front pages, or otherwise accorded nearly as much attention as the Central Park Jogger, gave rise to accusations that in the eyes of white arbiters of public opinion, whiteness counted for more than blackness when it came to attracting press and sympathy. Some dissidents ultimately disbelieved the charges against the suspects, in spite of overwhelming evidence of their guilt. In justifying this stance, they repeatedly invoked the memory of past racist miscarriages of justice. Thus it was that "Scottsboro" became a talisman for observers who maintained that the convicted assailants of the Central Park Jogger had themselves been the victims of a racist frame-up.[123]

References to Scottsboro also proliferated following the indictment of black football legend O. J. Simpson for the murder of two whites, one of whom was his former wife. In this case, there were no charges of sexual assault, but Simpson's interracial marriage—and the revelation of affairs he had with numerous other white women—excited many of the social anxieties that commonly surround interracial sex, particularly when relationships between black men and white women turn violent. The Simpson prosecution prompted, among other things, a paroxysm of confession. In the pages of *Mother Jones* magazine, the writer Barbara Grizzuti Harrison was moved to reveal that she both craved and loathed the spark of violence that occasionally lit up her relationship with an unnamed black lover.* And in the pages of the

---

*One especially telling passage went:

> I also admit—at peril to my own psychic balance, to say nothing of my
> reputation—that I am among those women who experience a certain frisson
> when a man threatens to apply physical force to me. (Not any man; the man
> I love.) Oh, there will be the Devil to pay if you leave me, he says, halfway in

*New York Times Magazine,* the journalist Jacqueline Adams admitted that while she hoped the murderer would be caught, the fact of Simpson's marriage to a white woman had its effect on her view of the tragedy. Nicole Brown Simpson, she mused, represented a "wound in the heart of many African Americans: the white wife."[124] More striking still, however, was the racial solicitude afforded to Simpson by many blacks despite his marriage to a white woman, despite his lack of participation in struggles on behalf of black advancement, and despite his evident guilt. Many observers remarked the discrepancy between whites' and blacks' opinions regarding Simpson's culpability, with a majority of whites believing he had been proved guilty and a majority of blacks feeling that the state had failed to prove guilt beyond a reasonable doubt.[125] Perhaps most revealing of the lasting scars left by the racial demonization of the black man was the appreciable number of African Americans who vocally welcomed Simpson's acquittal even as they conceded that his guilt had been proved. "So many black men [have] been hung, lynched, and killed for things they didn't do," one black cabbie reportedly declared, "that it's time for a black man to get off for something he *did* do."[126]

### White Women, Black Men, and Sexual Coercion, Part 2

That some black men (like some men of every racial category) have committed sexual crimes is incontrovertible. Nevertheless, commentators who note and elaborate upon that fact sometimes meet with strenuous objections. Exemplifying this phenomenon is Susan Brownmiller, whose *Against Our Will: Men, Women, and Rape* (1975) is a tour de force of journalism, history, theory, and polemics that, more than any other single book, has made rape a subject of serious and ongoing study, and provided for such study an expanded and engaged audience. One section of *Against Our Will* forcefully challenges the specious

---

the act of love—adding, God help me, to the thrill. Say that again, woman, he says—I have just accused him of treating me like his white whore—and I will break your beautiful face. . . . His words shock me into sobriety; but I would be lying if I didn't say that they nourish my belief—I do wish it weren't so—that he loves me, till death (mine?) do us part. [Barbara Grizzuti Harrison, "Killing Love: A Personal Essay," *Mother Jones,* September 1994.]

notion that *every* black man charged with raping a white woman is necessarily the victim of a trumped-up injustice—or, to put it differently,
that *every* white woman who accuses a black man of rape is necessarily
a liar. This is a matter of considerable consequence in that some defenders of accused black men have deployed derogatory images of white
women for the purpose of neutralizing accusers' allegations. One such
is the stereotype of the white woman who, after consenting to have sex
with a black man, charges him with rape to camouflage from other
whites the reality of her desires—yearnings that would invite contempt
(or worse) if revealed.

That some white women have accused black men of rape in order
to protect their own reputations is also true. In the 1890s Ida B. Wells
wrote about the case of a black man in Ohio who had been imprisoned
for raping a white woman, the wife of a minister. Fifteen years into the
defendant's imprisonment, the woman confessed that she and he had in
fact been lovers, that their intimacies had been wholly consensual, and
that she had testified against him only out of fear.[127]* Similarly, the
black journalist Carl Rowan recalled an incident from his youth in
McMannville, Tennessee, when he happened upon two lovers, a white
girl and a black boy, embracing under the cover of darkness. Startled,
"and with the automatic response of a baby stuck with a pin, the

---

*Ida B. Wells's candor in assailing lynching and its attendant myths put her in con-
siderable danger. In a May 1892 issue of the *Free Speech* newspaper (for which she
was an editor and correspondent), she attacked, in an unsigned editorial, the notion
that black-on-white rape prompted lynchings. Calling that defense an "old thread-
bare lie," she suggested that charges of black-on-white rape stemmed from wrongdoing by white women and warned that "if Southern white men are not careful, they
will over-reach themselves and public sentiment will have a reaction; a conclusion
will then be reached which will be very damaging to the moral reputation of their
women." Wells's stance touched off a violent response. An editorialist for a white
newspaper in Memphis wrote that "the fact that a black scoundrel is allowed to live
and utter such loathsome and repulsive calumnies is a volume of evidence as to the
wonderful patience of southern whites." Another white newspaper urged its readers
to find, brand, and castrate the author of the offending editorial. A mob destroyed
the offices of *Free Speech* and posted a notice promising death to anyone who
attempted to revive the paper. Wells was out of town when the mob did its work;
friends urged her to stay away, and she did—an especially wise choice after her
authorship of the editorial became public knowledge. (See Linda O. McMurry, *To
Keep the Waters Troubled: The Life of Ida B. Wells* [1998], 130–49.)

auburn-haired girl screamed: 'Get up! Stop, you black sonofabitch! Jesus, he's raping me!'"[128] Luckily, no whites were around to hear her scream; otherwise, she might have felt compelled to stick with her fictitious allegation. Instead, the weeping teenager confessed that she had cried rape only to insulate herself against charges of being a nigger lover. While the precise number of black men who have been lynched, executed, or imprisoned on the basis of false claims is difficult—indeed, probably impossible—to determine, the figure, if known, would certainly be appreciable.* It is also the case, however, that the problem of false charges has occasionally been cited to undermine *worthy* prosecutions. Joan Didion reported, for instance, that some defenders of the youngsters accused of raping the Central Park Jogger believed, or at least maintained, that the putative victim was no victim at all but instead had aggressively solicited the sex. Didion quoted a woman who envisioned a very different encounter from the one portrayed by the prosecution: "White slut comes into the park looking for the African man."[129]

Seeking to win a fair hearing for women who allege they have been sexually assaulted, Susan Brownmiller has urged that *all* such claims be accorded proper respect, including rape charges leveled by white women against black men. *Against Our Will* argues that just as derogatory stereotypes of black men have impeded the ability of some observers to distinguish facts from fears, so, too, have derogatory images of white women hampered the ability of others to distinguish facts from fantasy. Emphasizing the need to be attentive to the par-

---

*The threat posed by white women who falsely accuse black men of rape has been explored by more than a few novelists and dramatists. For literary treatments, see, e.g., Harper Lee, *To Kill a Mockingbird* (1962); Ann Petry, *The Narrows* (1953); Chester Himes, *If He Hollers Let Him Go* (1945). See also a film by Paul Snead, *The Affair* (1995), which recounts the hanging of a black soldier on the basis of a false allegation by a white Englishwoman with whom he has been having an affair. Surprised by her husband while in the embrace of her lover, the panicked woman seeks to avoid scandal by claiming to be the victim of assault. For another variation on the theme, see the gripping episode of the televison show *Law and Order,* in which a white woman murders a black man after he tries to end their affair. She subsequently insists that she acted in self-defense when he tried to rape her. In the end, the woman's lie is revealed and she is ultimately imprisoned.

ticulars of any given case, Brownmiller has lamented the tendency of "leftists and liberals with a defense-lawyer mentality" to discount immediately any and every claim by a white woman that she has been raped by a man who happens to be black.[130] Unfortunately, the force of her argument is weakened by her reference to a case that could hardly be more inapposite: the 1955 murder of Emmett Till. On a dare, the black fifteen-year-old went into a store and asked the cashier, a white woman, for a date, then whistled at her. A few days later, the woman's husband, accompanied by his brother-in-law, abducted Till and murdered him. Although their guilt was clear—the defendants themselves scarcely even disputed the allegations—a racist jury acquitted the pair, who subsequently confirmed what interested observers already knew: they had indeed committed the murder. They had initially planned only to beat the youngster but decided to kill him after he failed to show remorse and boasted of sexual intimacies he had enjoyed with white girls back home in Chicago.[131]

The murder of Emmett Till has come to symbolize white supremacist lawlessness and the fate that can befall black men who demonstrate a sexual interest in white women. According to Brownmiller, however, Till's whistle "should not be misconstrued as an innocent flirtation." It was, in her view, "more than a kid's brash prank . . . [;] it was a deliberate insult just short of physical assault, a last reminder to [the cashier] that this black boy, Till, had in mind to possess her." While allowing that "we are rightly aghast that a whistle could be cause for murder," Brownmiller also held that that whistle constituted evidence of a more menacing intention. Recalling that the Till case "became a lesson of instruction to an entire generation of appalled Americans," she added:

> I know how I reacted. At age twenty and for a period of fifteen years after the murder of Emmett Till whenever a black teen-ager whistled at me on a New York street or uttered in passing one of several variations on an invitation to congress, I smiled my nicest smile of comradely equality . . . a largesse I extended with equal sincerity to white construction workers, truck drivers, street-corner cowboys, indeed, to any and all

who let me know from a safe distance their theoretical intent. After all, were not women for flirting? Wasn't a whistle or a murmured "May I fuck you?" an innocent compliment? And did not white women in particular have to bear the white man's burden of making amends for Southern racism? It took fifteen years for me to resolve these questions in my own mind, and to understand the insult implicit in Emmett Till's whistle, the depersonalized challenge of "I can have you" with or without the racial aspect. Today a sexual remark on the street causes within me a fleeting but murderous rage.[132]

The sexual harassment Brownmiller suffered cannot excuse her grossly misguided analysis of of Till's tragic whistle. There is simply no basis in fact for declaring, as she did in *Against Our Will,* that it constituted "a deliberate insult just short of physical assault," or that it was tantamount to murmuring "May I fuck you?" Brownmiller's book rightly chastises those who, when faced with an allegation of black-on-white rape, fall back on the historical oppression of black men to avoid grappling with the facts of the case at hand. Yet in her analysis of the Till case, Brownmiller, too, fell prey to undisciplined extrapolation and specious analogizing. Angered by her own passivity in the face of sexual harassment and her own willingness to be guilt-tripped, Brownmiller vented her long-repressed fury upon a boy killed in cold blood by two men who got away with murder. Of all the possible cases she could have chosen to illustrate her point about the need to deromanticize black men accused of rape, the Till case was perhaps the worst suited to effectuating her aim.* However ill conceived may be Brownmiller's reimagining of Emmett Till's motivations, it is wrong to assert that *Against Our Will* is "pervaded with racist ideas" or that it proposes that "the real danger to women of interracial sexual exploitation in American society is black male rape of white females."[133] Throughout *Against Our Will,* Brownmiller insistently emphasized the centrality of African American oppression to the history of rape in America. She

---

*Brownmiller revisits the controversy over her discussion of the Till case in *In Our Time: Memoir of a Revolution* (1999), but fails to revise her mistaken analysis.

unsparingly documented the sexual victimization of black women and fiercely rebutted those who would obscure or minimize it. True, she erred badly in her discussion of the Till murder, but that is an exception. More characteristic is her apt observation that

> rape is to women as lynching was to blacks. . . . Women have been raped . . . for many of the same reasons that blacks were lynched by gangs of whites: as group punishment for being uppity, for getting out of line, for failing to recognize "one's place," for assuming sexual freedoms, or for behavior no more provocative than walking down the wrong road at night in the wrong part of town and presenting a convenient, isolated target for group hatred and rage.[134]

The decision by Susan Brownmiller, Alice Walker, and others to explore interracial rapes perpetrated by black men was and remains a sound one, for several reasons. Sex and violence, and the interconnectedness of the two, are integral to the story of American race relations. An adequate understanding of that story demands an awareness of *all* of its significant components. That includes, to be sure, familiarity with the demonization of black male sexuality. But it also includes the acknowledgment that some black men have indeed committed rape,* that a disproportionate number of rapes are committed by black men,†

---

*For gripping memoirs that discuss with subtlety the politics of race in the context of black-on-white rape, see Alice Sebold, *Lucky* (1999); Jamie Kalven, *Working with Available Light: A Family's World After Violence* (1999); Susan Estrich, *Real Rape* (1987).

†The United States Justice Department estimates that blacks were responsible in 1999 for nearly 21 percent of rapes and sexual assaults, though blacks comprise only about 13 percent of the population. See *Sourcebook of Criminal Justice Statistics 2000*, p. 204, table 3.30, "Estimated percent distribution of violent victimization by lone offenders by type of crime and perceived race of offender" online at http:www.albany.edu/sourcebook/1995/pdf/t330.pdf; "Overview of Race and Hispanic Origin Census 2000 Brief," p. 8, table 5, "Black or African American Population for the United States 2000" online at http:www.census.gov/prod/2001pubs/c2kbr01-1.pdf.

Justice Department victimization statistics are revealing and helpful but must be handled cautiously. They are estimates based on surveys in which individuals note

and that, as we have seen, racial animus has been part of the ugly mix of sentiments that have driven some black men to inflict sexual violence upon white women.

A desire to avoid legitimating myths that demonize black men has inhibited discussion regarding the plight of black women victimized by black male sexual criminals. Thus, when an African American beauty-pageant contestant named Desiree Washington charged in 1991 that she had been raped by the African American boxing champion Mike Tyson, some blacks responded by reflexively siding with Tyson as a matter of racial defense, regardless of the facts of this particular case. Writing with reference to Washington's situation, Professor Kimberle Crenshaw noted that "Black women who raise claims of rape against Black men are not only disregarded but also sometimes vilified within the African-American community."[135] This is especially true when the man accused is prominent and the case highly publicized, thus bringing to the world's attention criminal conduct of a sort that has often been wrongly and maliciously attributed to black men. According to Crenshaw, "The use of antiracist rhetoric to mobilize support for Tyson represented an ongoing practice of viewing with considerable suspicion rape accusations against Black men and interpreting sexual racism through a male-centered frame. The historical experience of Black men has so completely occupied the dominant conceptions of racism and rape that there is little room to squeeze in the experiences of Black women."[136]

This troublesome reality will remain unchanged so long as excessive anxiety over the image of the black man continues to trigger the suppression of any full and open consideration of rape, a subject over which sentimentality, obfuscation, and innuendo have long held sway.

---

unverified information. Lay versus legal definitions of crime sometimes diverge, and racial attributions are sometimes mistaken. Many women decline to report their victimization. Whether the racial character of a rape substantially affects the likelihood of its being reported has yet to be determined definitively. Some scholarship suggests that while white women underreport their victimization of rape, black women underreport it even more, especially if the assailant is a white man. See Jennifer Wriggins, "Rape, Racism, and the Law," *Harvard Women's Law Journal* 6 (1983), 103, 104 n. 2, 120.

So strong is the impulse toward racial wagon-circling in defense of black masculinity, in fact, that it has pressured some black female victims of black male rapists into forgoing legal redress—a pathetic, regrettable response that is, fortunately, being challenged and revised in black communities across the nation.[137]

Another reason to support Susan Brownmiller, Alice Walker, and others who have been willing to discuss and analyze black male sexual violence is that their work serves as a salutary antidote to a mistaken, albeit influential, line of thought that holds blacks incapable of engaging in "racism." The logic here is that racism is a product of power and racial prejudice, that blacks are devoid of power, and that therefore, by definition, they cannot be racist.[138] This theory is faulty on a variety of grounds, one of which is empirical. Blacks do, in fact, exercise power in American society. Collectively, to be sure, they exercise far less of it than whites, but that is not the same as having no power at all. As politicians, business leaders, personnel directors, admissions officers, judges, police officers, prosecutors, and jurors, blacks clearly exercise substantial discretion that is often unreviewable. But ordinary, even quite lowly, people also have the capacity to wield power in their day-to-day lives. The obscure man who is relatively powerless in many situations can, in a blink, reveal himself to be rather powerful in relation to others whom he is in a position to hurt. For at least a moment, every rapist is powerful in relation to his victim. It is simply untenable to claim, then, that blacks and other discriminated-against people of color have *no* power. And because blacks, like all responsible individuals, have *some* power, their moral hygiene, like everyone else's, warrants close, careful attention.

Nothing better illustrates this point than the prominence of African Americans in positions of authority in the armed services of the United States. In the military, particularly the army, large numbers of blacks are empowered to give orders to large numbers of whites.[139] That such power can be abused was aptly demonstrated by the two most widely publicized of the army sex scandals of 1996 and 1997. One resulted in the courts-martial of soldiers at the Aberdeen Proving Ground, who were charged with committing a broad range of sexual offenses, including rape. The other resulted in the court-martial of the top-ranking enlisted soldier in the army on what amounted to charges of sexual harassment (though the prosecution attempted to press a charge of rape in this case as well). Allegations and insinuations of racial prejudice hovered over these proceedings. At Aberdeen, where some 60 percent of the forty-two drill sergeants were black and an equal percentage of the 2,300 trainees were white, *all* of the court-martialed soldiers were black, while most of their alleged victims were white. The court-martialed sergeant major of the army, Gene C. McKinney, was also black, while again, the majority of his six female accusers were white.

At Aberdeen, the most notorious of the defendants was Delmar Gaither Simpson, a thirty-two-year-old veteran soldier who had escaped small-town poverty in Richburg, South Carolina, by joining the army.[140] A drill sergeant, as were most of the men accused of misconduct, Simpson exercised direct and comprehensive authority over the trainees under his command. He was in charge of conditioning them to embrace a central feature of military life: the habit of following orders. There is no doubt that Sergeant Simpson abused his authority and violated military regulations. He admitted to having sex with eleven trainees, in itself an infraction sufficiently serious to render him vulnerable to a possible prison sentence of thirty-two years. Prosecutors also charged, however, that Simpson had raped six trainees (four whites, one black, and one Latina) on eighteen separate occasions. Simpson categorically denied having forced anyone to have sex with him. He maintained that the sex, though admittedly wrongful, had nonetheless been consensual.

In point of fact, much of the conduct that gave rise to Simpson's conviction for rape seems far removed from what that term typically connotes in the civilian world.* Two rapes, for example, were said to

---

*Much of the case against Simpson with respect to allegations of rape hinged on the contested definition of that crime under military law. Simpson's attorneys argued that most of the rape charges should be dismissed because references to force or threats of force were missing from the trainees' own accounts of the alleged crimes. According to the Uniform Code of Military Justice, a rape conviction requires proof of sexual intercourse "by force and without consent." (See Martha Chamallas, "The New Gender Panic: Reflections on Sex Scandals and the Military," *Minnesota Law Review* 83 [1998]: 305, 344–50.) The presiding judge in Simpson's case ruled, how-

have occurred when Simpson had sex at his off-post apartment with a twenty-one-year-old married trainee. Both of these episodes happened after Simpson had had sex with the same woman on at least six occasions. In both instances, she voluntarily concealed herself in his automobile in order to leave the military base undetected. In both instances, she used keys that Simpson had given her to let herself into his apartment. And in both instances, they spent the evening together at his apartment before he drove her back to the base. On neither of these occasions, nor on others, did she seek help from anyone or attempt to report Sergeant Simpson's actions.* There was, however, other testimony produced at trial that, if believed, indicated that in at least some of the other episodes in question, Simpson had exerted immediate or threatened force to obtain sex from women trainees. One trainee testified that once, after she told Simpson to stop a sexual overture, he had grabbed her hands, forcibly removed her underwear, and, without her consent, penetrated her body. Another testified that the sergeant had put his hand over her mouth to prevent her from protesting.[141] The defense offered reasons to doubt this testimony.[142] One witness had a strong motive for exacting revenge upon Simpson: he had, she believed,

---

ever, that the requisite force need not take the form of immediate or threatened physical violence; in his view, proof of "constructive force" would suffice (ibid., 347). Constructive force consisted of a totality of circumstances that, taken together, constituted duress. The judge ruled that in Simpson's case, a jury might find that such force had been used. Drill sergeants, the judge stressed, "commanded so much authority over trainees—ordering them where to eat and sleep and how to act—that they were like parents" ("Army Judge, in Disputed Ruling, Refuses to Drop Race Charges," New York Times, April 19, 1997). Unsurprisingly, Simpson's attorney strongly objected: "Do we have law that has become so paternalistic that now [women] don't even have to say 'No'?" Frank J. Spinner asked rhetorically. "Are trainees so ignorant that they can't distinguish between a drill sergeant telling them to run up a hill or lie down on a bed?" (Ibid.)

*Another trainee, aged twenty, admitted that she had showered in preparation for having sex with Simpson and then actively participated in sexual intercourse with him. She said that she had not really wanted to have sex with him but had acted as if she did in order to get the intercourse over with as quickly as possible. When defense counsel asked if it was fair to say that Simpson might have believed she *wanted* to have sex with him, the trainee answered in the affirmative (Dana Priest and Jackie Spinner, "For Aberdeen Jury, a Murky Question of Human Relations," *Washington Post*, April 27, 1997, p. A1).

infected her with a sexually transmitted disease and betrayed her by having sex with other trainees. Another purported victim had had sexual relations with two other drill sergeants at Aberdeen and had reportedly bragged about her connection with Simpson. A third witness testified while proceedings were pending against her for being absent without leave. The defense argued that given her own vulnerabilities to criminal prosecution, she was strongly motivated to say whatever the army prosecutors wanted her to say, in order to better her chances of reducing her potential punishment.

Notwithstanding such discrediting efforts on the part of the defense, on May 7, 1997, a jury of two black men, three white men, and one white woman convicted Simpson of a series of offenses, including eleven counts of rape. He was later sentenced to twenty-five years of imprisonment. That constituted the high point of the campaign against sexual crimes at Aberdeen. Over the weeks and months that followed, one officer and scores of other drill sergeants would either plead guilty to the charges against them or be found guilty pursuant to courts-martial. Simpson, though, was unique among them in being convicted of rape, and his trial prompted considerable debate over the propriety of his prosecution and conviction.* One set of critics perceived the trial as but another chapter in the ongoing campaign to repress black men. This view was reinforced when four white women declared at a press conference that army officials had attempted to force them to testify that they had been raped by Simpson even though, in their view, what

---

*Some observers disapproved of what they saw as the gender politics of the prosecution. They argued that what Simpson confronted was not a prosecution aimed at delineating and punishing discrete criminal acts but instead a persecution aimed primarily at providing political cover for high-ranking military officials who wanted to mollify the ire of feminists by showing that they were both willing and able to discipline wayward male soldiers. Critics complained, in short, that Simpson was a scapegoat—an unsavory one, to be sure, but a scapegoat nonetheless.

Other critics charged that the prosecutor's broad definition of rape offered female subordinates an inordinately tempting and powerful weapon to use against male superiors. Still others maintained that the prosecution excessively accentuated women's vulnerability in an integrated armed services. (See, e.g., Hanna Rosin, "Sleeping with the Enemy: How the Army Learned to Love Andrea Dworkin," *New Republic*, June 23, 1997.)

had occurred was consensual sex—a wrong under military rules, but assuredly not the wrong of compelled sexual intercourse.* After Simpson was convicted, the head of a local branch of the NAACP near Aberdeen pronounced the verdict "an attack on the leadership of the African American male."[143]† While the prosecutions at Aberdeen were ongoing, six women charged then–Sergeant Major of the Army Gene C. McKinney with various sexual improprieties.[144] They testified that he had made unwanted propositions, rubbed up against them, attempted to kiss them, and otherwise engaged in sexual harassment of them. One of the women claimed to have been an unwilling participant in sexual intercourse with Sergeant McKinney when she was seven months pregnant.

Described by one journalist as the most notable military trial since Lieutenant William Calley's conviction for murdering Vietnamese civilians, McKinney's court-martial confirmed for some observers that no matter how much success a black man attains, he must always be prepared for racially discriminatory attacks.[145] McKinney himself asserted that racism was largely responsible for the rigor with which he was being prosecuted. Subsequently he downplayed race and emphasized rank, arguing that he was the victim of selective prosecution insofar as officers charged with the type of infractions he had supposedly committed were routinely permitted to retire quietly without forfeiting accumulated benefits and risking imprisonment. In the court-martial itself, however, neither of these claims played much of a role—or at least not openly. The presiding judge ruled that these considerations had no bearing on McKinney's guilt or innocence.

As the case was reported in the press, it initially seemed that the

---

*See Jane Gross, "Veracity of Soldier's Accuser Is Questioned," *New York Times,* February 26, 1998, p. A21.

†Simpson's attorney maintained that "if you're an African-American drill sergeant in the Army, you're an endangered species" ("Sergeant Gets 25-Year Term for 18 Rapes of Recruits," *New York Times,* May 7, 1997, p. A17). See also Leonard Greene, "Is History Repeating Itself in Army Rape Allegations?," *Boston Herald,* March 17, 1997; Julianne Malveaux, "Sex Scandal Shows Racism, Stupidity," *USA Today,* May 9, 1997; Gregory Kane, "Dread of Midnight Interrogators Remains," *Baltimore Sun,* May 21, 1997. For a spirited rejoinder, see E. R. Shipp, "The Army, Power, and Abuse," *New York Daily News,* May 6, 1997.

defendant stood little chance of avoiding conviction; after all, six apparently credible women had independently accused him of harassment. As the proceedings wore on, though, McKinney's aggressive defense opened up large cracks in the prosecution's case. The most potentially damaging of the sergeant major's accusers was described by fellow soldiers as an attention-hungry habitual liar who had earlier leveled false accusations of sexual harassment against another colleague.[146] Several other accusers were revealed to be appearing as witnesses under pressure from army investigators, who had granted them immunity from prosecution for their own purported sexual misdeeds. The woman who claimed to have submitted to sexual intercourse with McKinney despite her advanced pregnancy testified under a grant of immunity for prosecution for adultery; she had brought up the alleged sexual encounter only during her third session with investigators. A major who accused McKinney of having extended two unwelcome sexual invitations to her had herself been given immunity from prosecution for committing adultery with two subordinate officers and fraternizing with an enlisted man. This same officer's name was mentioned in connection with several of the few bits of testimony that made any direct reference to race. Witnesses called by the defense to undermine the major's allegations noted that she had more than once remarked that black men seemed to be particularly interested in her. According to one of these witnesses, she had asked, "Why do you think only black men ask me out? Is it because of my big hips?"[147]

Arrayed against this testimony was an imposing list of character witnesses, a long and distinguished military record, and testimony from McKinney himself. The jury of eight (four officers and four enlisted persons, six whites, one black, and one Latino) acquitted him of all counts stemming from the alleged sexual misconduct.* It did convict him of

---

*The obstruction-of-justice charge was based mainly on a phone call that McKinney had made to one of his accusers, a woman who said he had hounded her for sex for two years. She secretly tape-recorded his call, during which he advised her, "All you have to do is tell them that we talked a lot. You call the office sometimes because you want to talk about career development and that kind of stuff" (Elaine Sciolino, "Top Army Sergeant Was Secretly Taped in Sex Investigation," New York Times, June 28, 1997).

obstructing justice but as punishment merely reprimanded him and reduced his rank by one grade.

Two aspects of the army sex scandals are especially notable. First, the scandals did not give rise to a major racial confrontation. No mainstream politician tried to capitalize on their racial demographics, nor did any major black leaders or organizations press allegations that the prosecutions had been racially selective. For a brief moment, it seemed that Kweisi Mfume, executive director of the NAACP, might be preparing to wage a protest campaign against the prosecutions, but then he rather quickly backed off, distancing himself from the charges of racism voiced by a local NAACP official. Attorneys for several of the defendants asserted that their clients had been the victims of racial selectivity and threatened to elaborate upon these assertions at trial, but in the end, none of the key figures involved in or close to the scandals seems to have believed that there was much to be gained from playing the race card. Second, though all of the defendants undoubtedly suffered substantially during and in the wake of the proceedings against them, the prosecutors as a whole ultimately did not fare well. Even with the advantage of a broad definition of rape, prosecutors at Aberdeen succeeded in securing a rape conviction only against Delmar Simpson. Sergeant McKinney was charged with committing numerous sexual infractions but was acquitted of them all. It is a datum of some note that at the end of the twentieth century, in one of the most highly publicized sex-crime trials in American history, a military jury sided with an African American male against a bevy of tearful white female complainants.*

---

*To the question "What best explains what is [giving rise to the army sex scandals]?" Professor Charles C. Moskos offered the following possible answers:

A) Black men are hitting on white women. B) White women are flirting with black superiors. C) Black women know how to fend off harassment better than white women. D) Cross-racial sexual harassment is more likely to be reported than same-race sexual harassment.

Moskos's preferred answer was "E) All of the above" (Ian Fisher, "Black Soldiers Wrestle with Tangled Notions of Race and Justice in Military," *New York Times,* June 17, 1997).

# FIVE

# The Enforcement of Antimiscegenation Laws

Half an hour after midnight on a chilly evening in 1929, in Sheffield, Alabama, two white police officers barged into a home and found Elijah Fields in the company of Ollie Roden. Fields was a fifty-year-old black man, and Roden a twenty-five-year-old white woman. The police had knocked on the door for about five minutes before entering Fields's house. Once inside, they came across Fields and Roden in an unlit bedroom. Both were fully dressed, except that Roden was wearing no shoes. Asked why he had failed to respond to their knock, Fields said he had been afraid to answer the door. He and Roden were placed under arrest and subsequently indicted under an Alabama law that made it a felony for a black person and a white person to intermarry or cohabit.[1]

At trial, Fields's witnesses—who included Roden's parents—portrayed the episode as one big misunderstanding. The two were not having an affair, they explained; rather, Fields had simply been acting as a good Samaritan. Roden's father, whom he had known for many years, had asked him to transport his daughter from a hospital to a boardinghouse. Fields had been in the process of doing just that when he was intercepted by the police. The defense also stressed Roden's physical infirmities. Some unidentified malady had covered her feet and legs with open sores and ostensibly accounted for her shoelessness at the time of her arrest. Uncontradicted testimony also established that she was incontinent and suffered from unceasing menstruation.

For its part, the prosecution emphasized how presumptively suspicious was the presence of a man and a woman alone together late at night in an unlit bedroom in the man's house. The prosecutor noted, too, that police had previously observed Fields and Roden driving around together in his car, and that on at least one occasion, Fields had allowed Roden to steer, holding his hand on top of hers on the steering wheel—a gesture that in the eyes of the state's attorney, was remarkably and illicitly friendly. In his summation, Assistant Attorney General James L. Screws at one point suggested, "Gentlemen of the jury, suppose it had been your daughter who was treated like this white girl was treated by this negro," and at another told the jurors, even more pointedly, "You should convict . . . in order that similar occurrences may not happen to your daughter."[2] Judge J. Fred Johnson Jr. advised the jury that state law provided that "a white woman and a black man . . . cannot intermarry or live together in adultery or fornication," adding that "it is a felony if they do so." According to the judge, it was not enough for the state to prove that the defendants had engaged in a single act of sexual intercourse, or even occasional sexual acts; rather, it had to show that they had had an ongoing *relationship*—that is, had "live[d] together in fornication" or otherwise been disposed to continue having sex whenever the opportunity arose.[3] Tolerant though it might be of a loveless interracial quickie, or even a commercial transaction, Alabama law was intolerant of interracial romance.[4]

The jury returned a guilty verdict against Fields, whereupon the judge sentenced him to a two-to-three-year prison term. The Alabama Court of Appeals subsequently reversed the conviction, ruling that the jury had lacked an adequate evidentiary foundation for its finding of guilt. "Standing alone," the court concluded, the fact that Fields and Roden had been discovered together in Fields's home at night, "under the circumstances testified to by the arresting officers," was an insufficient basis for conviction. The court also chastised the prosecutor for playing on jurors' racial prejudice, and the trial judge for doing too little to restrain him. "The surrounding atmosphere," according to the appellate court's ruling, "was not conducive to a fair and impartial trial for one of appellant's race accused of such an offense."[5]

Elijah Fields's case illustrates the extent to which, not so very long ago, law-enforcement officials were statutorily empowered to police associations that were perceived to flout conventional codes of racial conduct—particularly those codes which demanded a certain social distance between black men and white women. The officers who initially arrested Fields and Roden probably did believe that the two were in violation of state law. Later, however, after being apprised of Roden's illness and hospitalization and her father's request to Fields, officials must have begun to doubt that they had truly stumbled upon an illegal sexual crossing of the color line. More likely they pressed the case because they wanted to emphasize (perhaps for reasons having to do with electoral politics) that even the *appearance* of sexual intimacy between a black man and a white woman constituted a crime. The transcript suggests that by the time of trial, the prosecutor's real complaint was that Fields and Roden had comported themselves in such a way that onlookers might form the wrong impression of their relationship.

One especially poignant exchange in Fields's trial began with the prosecutor asking the defendant if he "liked" Roden. Clearly afraid that an affirmative response would hurt his case, Fields replied, "I am a negro"—meaning, essentially, that he knew his rightful "place," and that this place precluded him from "liking" a white woman. "I don't especially like [Miss Roden]," he added. "I am very fond of her father and I wanted to help him."[6] A similar disavowal was offered by Ollie Roden. During her testimony, she stated at one point, "I am a white woman and though greatly afflicted . . . have never thought of having sexual intercourse with a negro."

Nothing more vividly reflects American racial pathologies than the tendency of those in authority to use power, especially state power, to discourage interracial intimacies. Fear of interracial partnerships, particularly as they might be institutionalized in marriage, has given rise to "more statutes covering a wider geographical area than any other type of racially restrictive law."[7] At first, in the 1660s, sex was the locus of regulation. In 1662, for example, Virginia doubled fines for those who engaged in interracial as opposed to intraracial fornication.[8]* As the racial regulation of intimacy matured, though, authorities generally chose to police marriage more closely than sex. Indeed, on occasion, the same officials who insisted that interracial marriage posed a dire threat to white civilization resisted attempts to prevent sexual relations across the race line, especially when the trespassing involved white men. In 1895, when delegates to South Carolina's constitutional convention proposed that a prohibition against interracial marriage be added to the state's constitution, Robert Smalls, a black politician, declared that he would support such a provision if it *also* mandated that men convicted of having concubines of a different race be forever barred from holding any political office. Smalls's proposal provoked an uproar. Observers understood that it was aimed at exposing the hypocrisy of white politicians who on the one hand roundly condemned "amalgamation," and on the other frequented black prosti-

---

*Virginia's Act 12 of December 23, 1662, provided that "if any christian shall commit fornication with a negro man or woman, he or she so offending shall pay double the fines [regularly imposed]." Even more consequential was another section of the same act, which stipulated that children fathered by white men and born of black slave women would inherit the legal status of their mothers, thereby becoming slaves for life: "Whereas some doubts have arisen whether children got by any Englishman upon a negro woman should be slave or free, Be it therefore enacted and declared . . . that all children borne in this country shall be held bond or free only according to the condition of the mother" (*Laws of Virginia* [Hening, 1823], 2: 170). For a detailed discussion of the colonial history of Virginia's antimiscegenation provisions, see A. Leon Higginbotham Jr. and Barbara K. Kopytoff, "Racial Purity and Interracial Sex in the Law of Colonial and Antebellum Virginia," *Georgetown Law Journal* 77 (1989): 1967.

Whereas in the Virginia antimiscegenation statute of 1662, legislators distinguished between "Negroes" and "Christians," by the early eighteenth century, "white" was consistently used in contradistinction to "Negro" or "Indian." According to Karen M. Woods, "The conversion of Indians and African slaves may have prompted this redesignation: once people of color became Christian, a new label was needed to separate them from those of European ancestry. . . . The shift from religious language to racial language in miscegenation law reflects the developing ideology of racial inferiority" ("A 'Wicked and Mischievous Connection': The Origins of Indian-White Miscegenation Law," *Legal Studies Forum* 23 [1999]: 37, 54–55).

tutes or kept black concubines. Acting pursuant to that hypocrisy, the convention rejected Smalls's amendment but passed the prohibition against interracial matrimony.[9]

A decade later, in Louisiana, white-supremacist opponents of interracial intimacy endeavored to reinforce that state's prohibition against intermarriage with a proscription against sexual miscegenation. The resistance the measure encountered prompted the editors of the *New Orleans Times-Democrat* to rant:

> The failure to pass a law of this kind is attributable to white degenerates, men who denounced social equality yet practice it, men who are more dangerous to their own race than the most inflammatory Negro orator and social equality preacher, and who have succeeded by some sort of legislative trickery in pigeon-holing or killing the bills intended to protect Louisiana from a possible danger. Such men should be exposed before the people of the state in their true colors.[10]

The newspapermen's frustration was shared by whites in Francisville, Louisiana, who held a mass meeting to denounce what one speaker termed the South's "yellow peril": "Every man familiar with conditions in our midst knows," he averred, "that the enormous increase in persons of mixed blood is due to men of the white race openly keeping Negro women as concubines."[11] In 1908 Louisiana finally enacted a law making "concubinage between a person of the Caucasian race and a person of negro race a felony." Enforcing the law a few years later, police arrested a German-born white man. The indictment against him charged that he had lived with a Negro woman and fathered three children by her. Soon after being indicted, the man died. Although the black woman with whom he had kept company was the named beneficiary of his life-insurance policy, the insurer refused to pay her claim, on the grounds that her lover had committed suicide and that his policy specifically exempted suicide from coverage. In an ensuing lawsuit, a court sided with the insurance company:

The evidence proves with reasonable certainty that the deceased came to his death by his own hands. It is the only reasonable conclusion to adopt. The motive for the act is found in the mortification he would suffer when his family and friends in Europe would learn that he had been arrested, and was to be tried for violating the laws of his adopted country, and in the mortification and ostracism from his friends here when they learned that he claimed he had been married and was living with a negro woman, by whom he had had three children, against the sentiment of almost the entire community, and in violation of the public policy and laws of the State.[12]

The race bar at the altar has a long history in America. In 1664, Maryland severely punished white women who married Negroes or slaves, calling such unions "shameful matches."[13] To prevent "abominable mixture and spurious issue"—meaning mixed-race offspring—the Virginia Assembly decreed that whites who married blacks, mulattoes, or Indians would be banished from the dominion forever.[14] By 1800 ten of the sixteen states then constituting the United States proscribed interracial marriage. By 1913, when Wyoming became the last state to impose a statutory impediment to marital miscegenation, forty-one others had already enacted similar laws, and in so doing armed public authorities and private persons with the means to create and police racial divisions in matters of sex and matrimony.* *Every* state whose black population reached or exceeded 5 percent of the total eventually drafted and enacted antimiscegenation laws.[15] In 1967, when the federal Supreme Court belatedly invalidated antimiscegenation statutes, sixteen states still had laws on the books forbidding interracial marriage.[16]

---

*Alaska, Connecticut, the District of Columbia, Hawaii, Minnesota, New Hampshire, New Jersey, Vermont, and Wisconsin never enacted antimiscegenation laws. See David H. Fowler, *Northern Attitudes Towards Interracial Marriage: Legislation and Public Opinion in the Middle Atlantic and the States of the Old Northwest, 1780–1930* (1987), 336.

From the early eighteenth century onward, *all* antimiscegenation laws in British North America prohibited blacks and whites from marrying one another. Other like prohibitions were imposed upon Native Americans and people of Chinese, Japanese, Filipino, Indian, and Hawaiian ancestry.* Since the founding of the United States, there have been no laws enacted against Christians marrying Jews or against interethnic marriages. In the nineteenth century, many groups that are now classified as ethnic "whites" were thought of as distinct races, among them Jews, Irish, Italians, and Hungarians.[17] Despite the intense social discriminations sometimes practiced against specific ethnic identities—think, for example, of signs reading "No Irish need apply"—state governments never prohibited interethnic marriages among whites. This fact further underscores the unique status of "color" in American life. Although social pressures have been widely brought to bear to discourage interethnic marriage, *state* power was mobilized only when authorities feared that people might marry across the color line.

Antimiscegenation laws varied widely by jurisdiction. Prior to the Civil War, officials in some states punished only whites for crimes of interracial intimacy. This approach was probably rooted in two beliefs: first, that blacks were too irresponsible and too inferior to punish, and second, that it was whites' responsibility to protect the purity of their own bloodlines. This latter belief was closely related to yet another status distinction embedded in antebellum laws regulating intimacy: a

---

*States that singled out other groups besides blacks as being ineligible for marriage to whites included Arizona (Mongolians, Malayans, Hindus, Indians), California (Mongolians, Malayans), Georgia (Japanese, Chinese, Malayans, Asiatic Indians), Mississippi (Mongolians), Montana (Chinese, Japanese), Nebraska (Chinese, Japanese), Nevada (Ethiopians, Malays, Mongolians), and Wyoming (Malayans, Mongolians). See the very useful tabulations of antimiscegenation laws in Fowler, *Northern Attitudes*, 339–439. "Note: Constitutionality of Anti-Miscegenation Statutes," *Yale Law Journal* 58 (1949): 472, 480–83. See also Leti Volpp, "American Mestizo: Filipinos and Antimiscegenation Laws in California," *University of California at Davis Law Review* 33 (2000): 95, 798–801; Lloyd Riley, "Miscegenation Statutes—A Re-evaluation of Their Constitutionality in Light of Changing Social and Political Conditions," *Southern California Law Review* 32 (1958): 28, 29.

gender differential. White women were anointed as the primary gate-keepers of white racial purity, and as such, they became the members of the white community who could, with self-evident justice, be most severely penalized for racial transgressions. Violations included, in ascending order of perceived perfidiousness, having sex across racial lines, marrying across racial lines, and giving birth to a mixed-race baby. Hence, the racial regulation of intimacy has not only pitted white people against colored people; it has also set men against women, both across racial lines and within racial groups.

After the Civil War, to comply with new federal requirements regarding formal racial neutrality, some state authorities felt compelled to mete out to blacks who married interracially the same punishment that was imposed on their white spouses.[18] No less ironic was the fact that in at least some jurisdictions, antimiscegenation laws were likely enforced more stringently *after* the Civil War than before it. The institution of slavery had given the collective ego of whites such a massive boost that many of them were willing to overlook infractions of racial regulations, even to the extent of turning a blind eye on interracial romantic involvements. The abolition of slavery, however, and the assertion of civil and political rights by blacks during Reconstruction, dealt a tremendous blow to the racial self-esteem of southern whites in particular. Many compensated by insisting upon a relentless and exacting observance of both formal and informal rules of racial caste. One hallmark of this period was enhanced criminal enforcement of antimiscegenation laws and every other restriction that reinforced the lesson of white supremacy and black subordination, white purity and black contamination.[19]

Some states, for example, punished those who performed interracial marriages. Mississippi went even further, criminalizing not only interracial marriage but even the *advocacy* of "social equality or of intermarriage between whites and negroes."* Punishments for the vio-

---

*"Any person, firm, or corporation who shall be guilty of printing . . . matter urging or presenting for public acceptance or general information, arguments or suggestions in favor of social equality or of intermarriage between whites and negroes, shall be guilty of a misdemeanor." See Pauli Murray, *States' Laws on Race and Color* (1951, reprint 1997): 247.

lation of antimiscegenation laws included enslavement, exile, whipping, fines, and imprisonment. Such criminal penalties, though, were hardly the only means of enforcing antimiscegenation laws; civil liabilities played an important role as well. Virtually all antimiscegenation laws rendered interracial marriages void—meaning that in the eyes of the state, the parties had never been married. Children of void marriages thus became bastards, with no legal claim to their biological fathers' estates. Neither did the putative "wives" and "husbands" in void marriages have any claim upon their spouses for alimony or child support, death benefits or inheritance. A sibling who initially stood to inherit little or nothing on the death of a married brother or sister could thus significantly improve his or her own lot by proving that the deceased had been of a different race than the bereaved spouse, and that their marriage had therefore violated state law. In that event, property that otherwise would have gone to the spouse went to the sibling instead. Because antimiscegenation laws opened up opportunities for enrichment along these lines, their civil enforcement was often aggressive.

It is impossible to determine precisely what effect antimiscegenation laws had on day-to-day life. Behavior is, after all, shaped by many considerations beyond formal legal sanctions. For black men in certain times and places, for instance, fear of extralegal violence (most notably lynching) was probably a more salient determinant of conduct toward white women than fear of prosecution. It is likewise impossible to calibrate the extent to which antimiscegenation laws were enforced. We do not have comprehensive data on the overall incidence of unlawful miscegenation, or the level of resources allocated to the enforcement of antimiscegenation statutes, or even the total number of criminal or civil suits brought pursuant to those statutes. What we *do* have is the record of hundreds of cases decided by appellate courts—a record that in itself reveals scores of fascinating, poignant, and largely forgotten kinds of problems that judges dealt with in all manner of contradictory ways. While the nature of these cases varied widely, their disposition invariably reflected the difficulties officials encountered in seeking to preserve or to create racial "integrity"—or at least the racial integrity of those defined as "white." At every turn, the impulse to maintain a strict, clean, consistent racial order was confounded by the force and consequences of passion, compassion, and ingenuity. In the end, the antimiscegenation laws were unable to ensure or re-create white racial chastity because desire, humanity, and hypocrisy kept getting in the way.[20]

## Problems of Racial Classification

One difficult task that must be undertaken whenever authorities attempt to effect any sort of racial regulation is the assignment of racial labels to individuals—a task that becomes all the more problematic when those being classified dispute the ascription. Several states adopted the so-called one-drop rule, which defined a person as "Negro" or "colored" if he or she either displayed or was to known to have any trace of (black) African ancestry.[21]* The one-drop rule at once precluded the formal recognition of intermediate racial castes, assuaged anxieties about the perceived loss of racial purity, facilitated racial-group solidarities, and stigmatized any form of white-black amalgamation. It also vividly reflected and animated Negrophobia by suggesting, essentially, that no matter how white a person might appear, even the tiniest dab of Negro ancestry was sufficiently contaminating to make him a "nigger." For all its significance, however, the one-drop rule never monopolized the drawing of race lines. Until 1910, for example, a person could be 24 percent black and still be considered white under Virginia law; from 1910 to 1924, those with 15 percent black ancestry were still classified as white. Only in 1924 did Virginia embrace the one-drop rule.[22] Some

---

*Dramatizing the one-drop rule in her novel *Showboat,* Edna Ferber created Steve, a white man, who marries Julie, a Negro passing for white. Informed that the couple are in violation of a state antimiscegenation statute, a Mississippi sheriff moves to take them into custody. Desperate to avoid arrest, Steve pricks Julie's finger and sucks some of her blood. When the sheriff approaches, Steve says, "You wouldn't call a man a white man that's got negro blood in him, would you?" "No, I wouldn't; not in Mississippi," the sheriff replies. "One drop of nigger blood makes you a nigger in these parts." That formulation allows the pair to remain free. See *Showboat* (1926), 143–45.

Jim Crow states would never demand that degree of racial exclusivity. In the twilight of de jure segregation in Florida, Mississippi, Missouri, and South Carolina, a person could have in his or her genealogy a certain small percentage of African American ancestry but still be white, at least in the eyes of the law.[23]*

Controversies over substantive definitions of what delimited a person's race were further complicated by debate over what would constitute adequate proof of that racial identity. Consider, in this context, the Virginia cases of *McPherson v. Commonwealth* (1877)[24] and *Keith v. Commonwealth* (1935).[25] *McPherson* stemmed from the prosecution of Rowena McPherson and George Stewart, a married couple who were charged with having illicit sexual intercourse with each other. The sex was illicit, the prosecutor argued, because their marriage was void, due to the fact that Stewart was white and McPherson colored. At that time, the commonwealth classified as colored anyone who was more than one quarter black. McPherson insisted that she was insufficiently black to be labeled colored.

At trial, McPherson and Stewart were found guilty by a jury and fined. On appeal, their convictions were overturned. The key to the case, according to the state appellate court, was the uncertain racial identity of one of Rowena McPherson's great-grandmothers. In working its way to a decision, the Virginia Court of Appeals did not ask McPherson how she perceived herself racially; nor did it poll the perceptions of her neighbors or inquire into her personal physical characteristics. Rather, the court focused solely upon the apparent racial character of her lineage.

Fifty-eight years later, the Commonwealth of Virginia prosecuted another couple—Bascomb and Reda Keith—for violating its prohibi-

---

*To add yet another complication, the law of racial classification in some locales varied according to its intended application, with different standards for marriage and attendance in public schools. In Mississippi, for instance, the antimiscegenation law defined a person as black if, in terms of ancestry, he or she was determined to be one eighth or more Negro; by contrast, segregation in public schools relied upon a one-drop rule, holding that *any* Negro ancestry made a child black. See *Moreau v. Grendich*, 114 Miss. 560 (Miss. Sup. Ct., 1917). See also *Tucker v. Blease*, 81 S.E. 668 (S.C. Sup. Ct., 1914).

tion against interracial marriage. That law had been broadened considerably since McPherson and Stewart were tried. At the time of the earlier prosecution, a person with some—but not too much!—Negro ancestry had been able legitimately to marry a white person, but the intervening years had seen the enactment of the one-drop rule.[26] Even so, the prosecution of the Keiths was unsuccessful. Although a jury convicted the couple, the Supreme Court of Appeals of Virginia overturned the verdict. The commonwealth had alleged that the mother of the male defendant, Bascomb Keith, was the daughter of Pat Keith, and that Pat Keith "had negro blood in his veins."[27] The appellate court ruled, however, that regardless of Pat Keith's race, the conviction was improper because the commonwealth had failed to prove beyond a reasonable doubt that Pat Keith was related by blood to Bascomb Keith. This was a decisive lapse because Bascomb Keith denied that Pat Keith was his grandfather. In support of this denial, Bascomb's mother testified that *her* mother had told her that her biological father was one Thomas Belcher, a white man.*

Of course, disputing a state's racial labeling was not always a successful strategy. In York, South Carolina, in 1881 a "white" woman and a "black" man were charged with criminal miscegenation. They defended themselves by declaring that contrary to appearances, the woman was "really" black. At trial, the judge instructed the jury to decide all doubt as to the woman's white ancestry "in her favor"—

---

*An appellate court likewise reversed a miscegenation conviction for want of sufficient evidence in *Knight v. State of Mississippi,* 207 Miss. 564 (1949). In that case, twenty-four-year-old David Knight, an honorably discharged veteran who had always considered himself white, was prosecuted for marrying a white woman because his great-grandmother had allegedly been a Negro. Remarkably, a state assistant attorney general joined Knight's lawyer in calling for the Mississippi Supreme Court to reverse his conviction and its attendant five-year prison term. Looming offstage in this gnarled Faulknerian drama were Newton Knight, a white Mississippian who had fought against the Confederacy in the Civil War, and his companion, Rachel Knight, a former slave. For an excellent exploration of this fascinating case, see Victoria E. Bynum, "Misshapen Identity: Memory, Folklore, and the Legend of Rachel Knight," in Martha A. Hodes, ed., *Sex, Love, Race: Crossing Boundaries in North American History* (1999). See also Victoria E. Bynum, *The Free State of Jones: Mississippi's Longest Civil War* (2001).

whereupon the jurors found her to be white and thus guilty.[28] Nevertheless, the appreciable number of prosecutions stymied by challenges to racial identifications serves to demonstrate that the imposition of racial classifications on individuals was (and remains) more problematic than has commonly been recognized.[29] That point is made even more strikingly by cases in which private parties sought to enforce antimiscegenation laws. In *Bennett v. Bennett,* a civil suit filed in South Carolina in 1940, Virginia Bennett challenged the will of her deceased father, Franklin Capers Bennett.[30] Franklin Bennett's daughter by his first wife, Virginia had gone unmentioned in his will, which instead bequeathed everything to his second wife, Louetta Chassereau Bennett. Virginia Bennett attacked her father's second marriage, and hence his bequest, on two grounds. She asserted that the marriage had been invalid, first because Louetta was Franklin's niece (Louetta's father was Franklin's half brother), and second because Louetta was more than one eighth Negro and thus prohibited by the state's antimiscegenation law from marrying Franklin or, for that matter, *any* white man. Virginia Bennett's motivation seems to have been straightforward enough: under state law, an individual could will no more than one quarter of his or her estate to anyone other than a spouse. If it could be established that the marriage had been invalid, it would follow that only one fourth of Franklin Bennett's estate could go to the woman he had believed to be his wife. The remaining three quarters would then devolve to relatives, with Virginia Bennett presumably standing first in line to benefit.

The Supreme Court of South Carolina rejected Virginia Bennett's arguments. With respect to the claim of incest, the court held that state law made the marriage merely *voidable,* not void. As an expression of its disapproval of uncles marrying nieces, the state permitted parties to such unions to withdraw from them freely, but its disapproval was not so strong as to cause it to declare all such marriages void—that is, devoid of legal legitimacy from the outset, regardless of the wishes of the parties. Since the marriage of Franklin and Louetta Bennett had been not void but only voidable, and since neither party had withdrawn from the marriage prior to Franklin's death, there was no basis for state interference on the ground of incest.

Virginia Bennett's racial attack on the marriage fared no better. While acknowledging that there was "some negro blood in [Louetta Bennett's] veins,"[31] the court nonetheless upheld the validity of the marriage, finding that Virginia Bennett had failed to prove that her stepmother was more than one eighth Negro. In ruling thus, the court affirmatively quoted the factual findings of the trial judge, who had emphasized Louetta's reputation and her participation in activities that were by law or by custom limited exclusively to whites. To the court, it was significant that

> upon the death of [Louetta's] father and mother, she was first taken into the home of white people; then she was placed in a church orphanage for white children; she was confirmed . . . as a communicant of the holy Communion Church of Charleston, a white church; she was taken from the orphanage and placed in a white home as a member of the family; she married a white man, the marriage being solemnized [in] a white church; she votes in the democratic primaries, both City and State, whose rules bar negroes from voting; her children attend the white public schools . . . ; she is generally accepted as a white person.[32]

The court recited these facts without revisiting the rationale that had prompted it to interpret them in a way that favored Louetta Bennett's legal claim. In contrast to the inquiries into racial identity initiated in *McPherson* and *Keith,* the investigation undertaken by the South Carolina Supreme Court did not focus primarily on the nature or extent of the defendant's black ancestry. Rather, it concentrated almost exclusively on whether Louetta had been treated as a white woman by her white neighbors and whether she herself had acted the part.[33]

Precedent also helps to explain the court's approach in this case. As far back as 1835, the South Carolina Supreme Court had weighed factors other than lineage and complexion in the determination of individuals' racial identification. "We cannot say what admixture of negro blood will make a colored person," Judge William Harper declared in a decision handed down that year. "The condition of the individual is not to be determined solely by a distinct and visible mixture of Negro blood, but by reputation, by his reception into society, and [by] his having commonly exercised the privileges of a white man."[34] In addition, two implicit assumptions likely influenced the court in *Bennett v. Bennett*. One was the belief that generally speaking, in any contested case of racial classification, those closest to the subject were probably in the best position to judge. In this instance, Louetta's friends and immediate family deemed her white. The second assumption was that notwithstanding the "taint" in Louetta Bennett's bloodline, it would have been intolerably unfair to revoke her whiteness, insofar as she had been perceived as white, and had genuinely and innocently seen herself that way, all her life. In enumerating the racial checkpoints she had successfully passed over the years—the orphanage, the church, marriage, the voting booth—the court may have been suggesting that Louetta was entitled to whiteness as a matter of adverse possession; in other words, she had enjoyed whiteness for so long that withdrawing that status from her now would be an act of cruelty.[35] Moreover, setting aside considerations as to Louetta Bennett's own fate, the judges may have been moved by concern for the fate of others around her. If the court had reclassified her racially, it would necessarily have rendered her children bastards and embarrassed the many whites with whom she had forged close and strong bonds, including her pastors.

Another factor in the court's decision may well have been a reluctance to excite public anxiety by revoking the racial status of a woman so obviously secure in her whiteness as Louetta Bennett. In the aftermath of a contrary holding, any white South Carolinian might have felt compelled to peer into the mirror with a new intensity and ask nervously, "Where will it end?" Countless surviving jokes about "niggers in woodpiles" bear witness to the truth that black ancestors appear in the genealogies of many families who think of themselves as being exclusively white.

### Knowledge of Racial Identity

Closely related to those cases in which the defendant challenged an alleged racial identity were others, civil or criminal, in which a defendant or plaintiff denied knowledge of his or her partner's true racial affiliation. Three illustrative disputes are *Bell v. State of Texas*,[36] *Locklayer v. Locklayer*,[37] and *Wood v. Commonwealth of Virginia*.[38]

Katie Bell, a white woman, and Calvin Bell, a black man, were wed in 1891, though they had been living together since at least 1880 and had five children. Their relationship evidently attracted little attention until 1893, when they became defendants in a civil lawsuit that had nothing to do with their marriage. In that suit, they testified that they were married; shortly thereafter, officials prosecuted them for violating the state's antimiscegenation law.[39] Calvin was acquitted, but Katie was convicted. She appealed the verdict on the ground that her husband's acquittal should have precluded her own conviction. Her theory seems to have been that logically, in alleged cases of miscegenation, either both defendants must be guilty or both must be innocent. The Texas Court Criminal Appeals disagreed, noting that while "the woman may have known she was white . . . the negro [may] have been ignorant of the fact; one, therefore, may be innocent, and the other guilty."[40] At least in Texas, to be found guilty of miscegenation, a person had to *know* that his or her marriage partner was of a different race.

The turn-of-the-century case of *Locklayer v. Locklayer* arose from a petition by a white woman, Nancy Locklayer, who sought to claim the estate of Jackson Locklayer, her deceased husband. The executor of the estate, J. R. Locklayer, had refused to release it to her, insisting that because Alabama law prohibited interracial marriage, she was not entitled to any of the legal benefits enjoyed by widows. In her suit, Nancy Locklayer asserted that even if her husband had been a Negro, she herself had believed, reasonably and in good faith, that he was white, on the basis of his appearance and his representations to her. She argued that as an innocent victim of Jackson Locklayer's misrepresentations, she should not be penalized by the state's antimiscegenation law.

The Alabama Supreme Court declined to reverse the trial court's judgment in favor of the executor, J. R. Locklayer. Nancy Locklayer had known, after all, that the first wife of her "husband" was, in the court's words, "a negress," and she could hardly have failed to notice that a Negro minister had presided over the ceremony in which she herself was "married."[41] Given the strict segregation of whites and blacks in the Alabama of 1903, such blurrings of the color line would surely have put any reasonable observer on notice that something unusual was going on. No typical white male Alabamian of the day would have consented to be married by a Negro minister! The court seems to have reasoned that under the circumstances, Nancy Locklayer could not plausibly have believed that she was entering into a normal—meaning, intraracial—marriage. Ruling against the plaintiff, the court cleared the way for the deceased man's black relatives to inherit his estate. In this sense, *Locklayer v. Locklayer* was an unusual case, since whites were generally the beneficiaries in private actions brought on the basis of antimiscegenation statutes. J. R. Locklayer proved, however, that black people, too, could make use of the laws prohibiting marriage across the race line.

The intersection of racial classification and marriage was shown in a very different light in *Wood v. Commonwealth,* a case of alleged criminal seduction. In Rockingham County, Virginia, in 1931, Leonard H. Wood was convicted and sentenced to two and a half years in prison for criminally seducing Dorothy Short, "an unmarried female of previously chaste character."[42] Wood's crime consisted of his persuading Short into having sex with him on the basis of his promise of marriage, and then refusing to follow through on that promise. At trial, Wood sought to defend himself by proving that Short was colored. He argued that because she was colored, it would have been unlawful for him to marry her, and that therefore, even if he *had* made such a promise (which he denied), he could not by law have fulfilled it. The trial judge prevented Wood from delving into Short's racial background, but an appellate court reversed his decision and demanded a new trial, holding that the trial court should have permitted the defendant to try to establish whether or not Short was aware that she was colored. According to the appeals court, mere proof that Short was colored did not constitute a sufficient defense for Wood, much as proof that a man was already married would be insufficient to insulate him from a charge of criminal seduction. In both cases, there would exist a legal impediment to the seducer marrying the seduced, but in the court's view, such impediments in themselves, in the absence of the victims' knowledge, would not lessen the victimizers' culpability. However, if it could be shown in either instance that the seduced woman had been aware that marriage was impossible, because her seducer was already married or because he was of a different race than she, the accused would have decisively undercut the main impetus for any seduction prosecution—that is, the protection of the "pure, innocent, and inexperienced woman who may be led astray from the paths of rectitude and virtue by the arts and wiles of the seducer under promise of marriage."[43] If Short had known at the time that she was colored (and, presumably, known as well that she could therefore not lawfully wed Wood), she could not be portrayed as an innocent who had relied to her detriment on her seducer's false promises. If she had been aware of the legal impediment that the "taint" in her blood posed, then she must have been aware, too, that Wood's promise could not be lawfully kept, which necessarily rendered her incapable of being criminally seduced by him. If she had had knowledge of her racial background and had sought to marry Wood in spite of the illegality of that relationship, she would be no less implicated in fraud than he—and surely would be in no position to claim an injury demanding redress by the state's criminal process.

Although the Supreme Court of Appeals of Virginia vacated Wood's conviction, the evidentiary rule it established favored the prosecution upon retrial. That rule placed the burden of persuasion on the defense, requiring Wood to show that Short had been aware she was colored. Wood argued that Short should be presumed to have known her mother's father was a Negro. But the court concluded that "in this case, the natural and human resolve of the mother of the prosecutrix would be to withhold from her the knowledge of what could only humiliate and distress her"—that is, the racial identity of her grandfather—in view of evidence indicating definitively "that she was received and accepted socially by white persons as one of them."[44]

## Conflict of Laws

One dilemma that arose in the enforcement of prohibitions against interracial marriage has resurfaced in recent years in disputes over same-sex unions: Ought a state that prohibits a certain type of marriage recognize such marriages when they have been contracted legally elsewhere? Some states expressly criminalized the knowing evasion of their antimiscegenation statutes,* while a few others that did permit interracial marriage nonetheless voided marriages contracted within their borders by persons seeking solely to evade the marital regulations of their home jurisdictions.† But what treatment should be accorded a couple who had genuinely resided in a permissive jurisdiction, had gotten married there, and then moved to a state that outlawed interracial matrimony?

States answered this question in a wide variety of ways. In South Carolina in 1873, Pink Ross, a black man, married Sarah Spake, a white woman. The couple soon moved to Charlotte, North Carolina, where they lived for three years before being charged with committing fornication. At trial, they cited their lawful marriage in South Carolina as a defense. A trial judge ruled in the couple's favor, as did the state supreme court. While the justices themselves viewed interracial marriage as "immoral" and "revolting,"[45] they noted that theirs was not "the common sentiment of the civilized and Chris-

---

*Virginia was a notable example; see Loving v. Virginia, 383 U.S. 1 (1967).

†Massachusetts and Vermont took this approach. (See "Intermarriage with Negroes—A Survey of State Statutes," 36 Yale Law Journal 858, 865; 1927). By contrast, until 1948, California prohibited interracial marriages from being contracted within the state but freely recognized those performed elsewhere; see Perez v. Lippold, 198 P. 2d 17 (1948). For parallels in same-sex matrimonial law, see generally Andrew Koppelman, "Same Sex Marriage, Choice of Law, and Public Policy," Texas Law Review 76 (1998): 921.

tian world," insofar as in both the United States and Europe, many jurisdictions declined to prohibit miscegenation.[46] Unlike polygamy, they pointed out, interracial marriage was not universally condemned; that being so, a majority on the bench believed that toleration was in order, both to promote interstate comity and to foster uniformity and thus stability in matters touching the all-important area of matrimony. "Upon this question above all others," the majority opinion held, "it is desirable . . . that there should not be one law in Maine and another in Texas, but that the same law shall prevail at least throughout the United States."[47]

Justice Edwin G. Reade strongly disagreed. "If [the interracial marriage] solemnized here between our own people is declared void," he asked, "why should comity require the evil to be imported from another State?"[48] He acknowledged the provision in the federal constitution under which "the citizens of each State shall be entitled to all privileges and immunities of citizens in the several States," but he contended that that provision "does not mean that a citizen of South Carolina removing here [to North Carolina] may bring with him his South Carolina privileges and immunities."[49] All it meant, Justice Reade declared, was that "when he comes here he may have the same privileges and immunities which our citizens have. Nothing more and nothing less."[50] Since North Carolinians had no right to marry across racial lines, it entailed no abridgment of the federal privileges and immunities clause to prevent people from South Carolina from intermarrying. In conclusion, Justice Reade vented his anger: "It is courteous for neighbors to visit and it is handsome to allow the visitor family privileges and even to give him the favorite seat; but if he bring his pet rattlesnake or his pet bear or spitz dog famous for hydrophobia, he must leave them outside the door. And if he bring small pox the door may be shut against him."[51]

Dissentient in North Carolina, Justice Reade's views carried the day in other states. When authorities in Tennessee charged a black man with criminal fornication, he set forth his lawful Mississippi marriage to his white wife as a defense. That argument was rejected by the Tennessee Supreme Court, which maintained that its acceptance would necessarily lead to condoning "the father living with his daughter . . . in lawful wedlock," or the Turk being allowed to "establish his harem at the doors of the capitol"—horrible possibilities both, yet neither "more revolting, more to be avoided, or more unnatural" than interracial marriage.[52]

Virginia likewise declined to tolerate the presence of interracial married couples within its borders, even if they had been married elsewhere legally and with no intention of evading the commonwealth's antimiscegenation statute. In 1877, in Augusta County, Virginia, Andrew Kinney, a black man, was thus indicted, convicted, and fined for lewdly associating and cohabiting with Mahala Miller, a white woman. Kinney asserted as his defense his marriage to Miller in the District of Columbia. The Virginia Court of Appeals concluded, however, that that marriage, though lawful where celebrated, ought not to be recognized in Virginia and therefore could not be invoked as a defense to criminal prosecution for illicit sexual intimacy. "The purity of public morals, the moral and physical development of both races, and the highest advancement of our cherished southern civilization," the court opined, "all require that [blacks and whites] should be kept distinct and separate and that connections and alliances so unnatural that God and nature seem to forbid them should be prohibited by positive law, and subject to no evasion."[53]

A related but distinct issue arose in cases in which relatives charged that one party to an interracial marriage sought to have the union recognized in another, less permissive locale, not out of a desire to live in that jurisdiction but for the purpose of inheriting property. *Miller v. Lucks*[54] posed this problem. In 1923 Pearl Mitchell and Alex Miller were indicted in Hinds County, Mississippi, for unlawful cohabitation. Pearl Mitchell was black, and Alex Miller was white. The district attorney agreed to forgo pressing his case on the condition that Mitchell leave the state. This she did, moving to Chicago, where she was soon joined by Miller. After living together for a number of years, they got married in 1939. Six years later, Pearl Mitchell died. Her relatives believed they were entitled to the property she had owned in Mississippi, and they filed a petition seeking a declaration of ownership. One of their claims was that they, not Alex Miller, should inherit the Mississippi property, since the state prohibited interracial marriage and there-fore, in their view, ought not to recognize for purposes of successorship interracial marriages established in other jurisdictions.

Hoping this might be one of those rare instances when a white-supremacist law would directly benefit blacks, Mitchell's relatives took the position that interracial marriage was so repugnant to the public policy of Mississippi that the state's legal system should decline to legit-imate such unions in any way. Had their argument prevailed, of course, they would have become the sole heirs to Pearl Mitchell's Mississippi estate. But though the Hinds County chancery court ruled in the rela-tives' favor, the state supreme court ruled against them. According to Chief Justice Sydney Smith, the purpose of Mississippi's antimiscegena-tion statute "was to prevent persons of Negro and white blood from living together in [Mississippi] in the relationship of husband and wife."[55] Seen in that light, merely "to permit one of the parties to such a marriage to inherit property . . . from the other does no violence," he held, to the underlying intent of the state's antimiscegenation provi-sions.[56] "What we are requested to do," Justice Smith explained, "is simply to recognize this marriage to the extent only of permitting one of the parties thereto to inherit from the other party in Mississippi, and to that extent it must and will be recognized. This is in accord with the holdings of courts in other states faced with this Negro problem."[57]

### Mistake and Annulment

Because antimiscegenation laws voided unions between those of differ-ent races, they provided disgruntled spouses with a powerful weapon. Theoretically, if a spouse could show that his or her marital partner was of a different race, he or she could leave the marriage free of any obli-gations, since in the eyes of the law, the parties had never been lawfully wed in the first place. Joe R. Kirby, for example, obtained an annulment of his eight-year marriage to Mayellen Kirby by convincing a court that the union violated Arizona's antimiscegenation law, given that he was white and she was "a Negress."[58]* Cyril P. Sunsori advanced a similar

---

*In another Arizona case, a white man was tried for second-degree murder. His "wife," a woman of Native American ancestry, was called as the prosecution's main

argument. Married in May 1935 to Verna Cassagne in St. Bernard Parish, Louisiana, Sunsori petitioned for an annulment only four months later as a counter to his wife's suit for divorce with alimony. Sunsori asserted that the marriage violated the state's antimiscegenation law because he was white and his wife was a person of color, having a traceable amount of Negro blood in her ancestry. Following extensive litigation, including two hearings before the Louisiana Supreme Court, the husband prevailed.[59]

More often, judges displayed a striking solicitude toward women whose white husbands sought separation on such grounds. In many cases, abhorrence of racial mixing in marriage ran up against contempt for cads eager to use any means available to rid themselves of matrimonial and parental responsibilities. Faced with this conundrum, judges frequently viewed the legitimizing of even a racially tainted marriage as the lesser of the evils. Two examples of this judicial preference are *Ferrall v. Ferrall*[60] and *Dillon v. Dillon*.[61] In Georgia, near the end of the 1870s, a Mrs. Dillon sought a divorce and alimony from a Mr. Dillon. Mr. Dillon responded to the suit by denying the legality of Mrs. Dillon's claim that she was really his wife. He charged that she was a Negro, insofar as she had more than one eighth "African" ancestry— the boundary line for whiteness under Georgia law—and had therefore been incapable of lawfully marrying him, a white man. After a jury declared itself unable to decide whether Mrs. Dillon met the state's standard for whiteness, the trial judge decreed that she was indeed the lawful wife of the defendant. The Supreme Court of Georgia affirmed

---

witness against him. He objected to her testimony, claiming spousal privilege. The trial court, affirmed on appeal, rejected the man's argument on the ground that he had never been properly married to his putative "wife" because the state's antimiscegenation law precluded it (*State v. Pass,* 121 P. 2d 882 [Ariz. 1942]).

The same issue arose in California when a Filipino defendant sought to prevent his white wife from testifying against him in a murder trial. The victim was the wife's white lover. A judge ruled that the defendant could not invoke a spousal privilege to prevent the testimony of his "wife" because their marriage violated the state's antimiscegenation statute. See Leti Volpp, "American Mestizo: Filipinos and Antimiscegenation Laws in California," *University of California at Davis Law Review* 33 (2000): 795, 814–16.

that decision, mainly on the ground that in a close case, public policy was best served by courts respecting settled expectations. While conceding that Mrs. Dillon's lineage was "doubtful," the justices nonetheless backed the conclusion reached by the trial judge.[62] For one thing, Mrs. Dillon was not totally black, "but of a complexion approximating that of many white persons of pure blood."[63] In other words, the court noted, this was "not an open, bald case of the intermarriage of an African with a Caucasian."[64] Rather than calculating percentages or charting genealogies, the justices in this case seem to have placed more weight on the fact that both husband and wife at least *appeared* to be white, even if Mrs. Dillon was actually more colored than the law allowed. Since the marriage outwardly conformed to the accepted racial practices of the state, the court was willing to credit its legitimacy, especially in light of certain additional considerations. Perhaps most important of these was that some years earlier (in 1857), Mr. Dillon had successfully petitioned the state legislature to pass a special act granting his wife the rights and privileges of a citizen of Georgia. The justices viewed this act as a good indicator that Mrs. Dillon was sufficiently white as not to be disqualified by Georgia law from marriage to a white man. They also believed it should preclude Mr. Dillon from disputing his wife's racial character. The special statute, the justices held, "does not make [Mrs. Dillon] white, but is conclusive evidence against Mr. Dillon . . . that she is white. He is estopped to controvert it."[65] Having prevailed upon the legislature to bestow on her effective citizenship—a political status that presupposed her status as a white person—Mr. Dillon could not challenge Mrs. Dillon's claim to whiteness. He had made his marital bed, the justices might have said, and he had to lie in it.

Finally, the justices suggested that as a matter of basic fairness, Mr. Dillon should not be permitted to evade his matrimonial and paternal obligations (at least in the context of a marriage to a woman who appeared to be white). In the court's words, "To allow a husband to indulge in scruples about the pedigree of his old wife, when her youth, beauty and strength have all waned, and thus escape responding to her claim for reasonable alimony, would be unwise in policy, unsound in principle."[66]

A similar case was heard by the North Carolina Supreme Court in 1907. Frank S. Ferrall sought to end his marriage to Susie Patterson Ferrall on the grounds that she "was and is of negro descent within the third generation," that he had been ignorant of that fact when they were married, in 1904, and that state law prohibited such marriages.[67]* Mrs. Ferrall denied that she had any Negro ancestors and claimed instead a strain of Indian or Portuguese blood. She maintained that before they were married, she had told her husband that some people said she was part Negro, that those rumors had made her hesitant to marry him, and that it was he who had insisted upon the marriage. The evidence presented at trial disclosed a racial "taint" stemming from Mrs. Ferrall's great-grandfather. The litigation centered on how much of a Negro this forebear had been, and precisely how much of one he would have had to be to render his great-granddaughter ineligible to marry a white man. The trial judge advised the jury that in order to prevail, Mr. Ferrall would have to show that Mrs. Ferrall's great-grandfather had "a real negro," meaning that he "did not have any white blood in him."[68] The jury decided in favor of Mrs. Ferrall, finding that while it was clear that her distant relative had been a Negro, it was unclear whether he had been a "real Negro." The trial judge set aside that verdict, ruling that his own jury instruction had been erro-

---

*Although North Carolina law expressly permitted marriage between whites and other individuals who were not "of negro descent to the third generation inclusive," Mr. Ferrall's attorney pressed for the application of a one-drop standard, arguing that "as long as there remains a touch of negro blood in a [person's] veins, that touch gives the [person her] character and indelibly fixe[s] [the person] with the stamp of inferiority." Even when a person of mixed race appeared to be white, the lawyer announced, his or her "spirit is the spirit of a negro." (See Daniel Jacob Sharstein, "In Search of the Color Line: *Ferrall v. Ferrall* and the Struggle to Define Race in the Turn-of-the-Century American South" [senior thesis, Harvard College, 1994], 21, quoting counsel's brief on behalf of Frank Ferrall.) To enliven his argument, the attorney affirmatively quoted a character in Mark Twain's novel *Pudd'nhead Wilson and Those Extraordinary Twins* (1894; reprint, 1980). Explaining to her son that he is a Negro even though he looks white and has mostly white ancestors, Twain's character Roxy declares, "Thirty-one thirty seconds of you is white and one thirty-second is nigger, and that part of you is your soul."

neous: on further consideration, he had concluded that Mrs. Ferrall *could* properly be deemed colored, and thus disqualified from marrying any white man, even if her great-grandfather had been something less than an undiluted Negro.

The North Carolina Supreme Court reversed the trial judge, reinstated the jury verdict, and ruled that the initial instruction to the jury had been correct. Although the opinion implied that the narrow definition of a "real negro" was mandated by precedent, a more likely explanation for the decision is that the justices could not abide the idea that a man might be permitted freely to dispose of his white-looking wife and children on the grounds that, unbeknownst to anyone, they were "really" Negroes. While this judicial opposition patently stemmed in part from anger at husbands who behaved like heartless cads, it may also have been rooted in a certain empathy for women and children who stood to lose not only the financial benefits of alimony and child support but also, and more fundamentally, the great and manifold privileges of whiteness in a pigmentocracy dominated by whites.

Both of these sentiments were expressed in a concurring opinion in *Ferrall v. Ferrall,* written by Chief Justice Walter Clark. "It would be difficult," he observed, "to find a case so void of merit." Frank Ferrall had

> by earnest solicitation persuaded [Susie Patterson] to become his wife in the days of her youth and beauty. She has borne his children. Now that youth has fled and household drudgery and child-bearing have taken the sparkle from her eyes and deprived her form of its symmetry, he seeks to get rid of her, not only without fault alleged against her, but in a method that will not only deprive her of any support while he lives by alimony, or by dower after his death, but which would consign her to the association of the colored race which he so affects to despise. The law may not permit him thus to bastardize his own innocent children . . . [or to] brand them for all time . . . as negroes— a fate which their white skin will make doubly humiliating to them.[69]

Following the lead of Mr. Ferrall's attorney, Chief Justice Clark likened his client to Tom Driscoll, the villain in Mark Twain's *Pudd'n-head Wilson,* who sells his own mother into slavery to pay off his gambling debts. For Clark, Ferrall—"this husband and father who for the sake of a divorce would make negroes of his wife and children"[70]— deserved nothing but scorn. "He deems it perdition for himself to associate with those possessing the slightest suspicion of negro blood," the chief justice remarked, "but strains of every effort to consign the wife of his bosom and the innocent children of his own loins to poverty and the infamy that he depicts."[71] While Clark endorsed the court's factual holding regarding the racial identity of Mrs. Ferrall, this part of his opinion should not be taken at face value, as it had as its purpose to make more palatable what the court was *really* doing: recognizing a marriage that state law ordinarily would have deemed to be void. In truth, Clark and his colleagues were making an exception, though they did not want to openly acknowledge it as such. Their aim was twofold: first, to prevent a bad man from profiting from his bad conduct, and second, to aid a woman who looked as white as any of them, who was accepted by her neighbors and friends as white, who apparently had been unaware of her Negro ancestry, and who had been embraced as a white woman by her husband over their three years of marriage, during which time she had given birth to two children by him. Unwilling to advertise the real basis of the court's decision, Clark nevertheless obliquely hinted at its motivation when he wrote that "if indeed the plaintiff had discovered any minute strain of colored origin after the youth of his wife had been worn away for his pleasure and in his service, justice and generosity dictated that he keep to himself that of which the public was unaware."[72]

Because Mr. Ferrall had failed to do what "justice and generosity dictated," the court was moved to step into the breach and take up Mrs. Ferrall's cause—by discounting the "strain of colored origin" in her ancestry. Here as elsewhere in the jurisprudence of antimiscegenation law, individual judges injected, on an ad hoc basis, some small measure of decency into a massively indecent regime of racial hierarchy. In *Ferrall,* after all, the chief justice of North Carolina expressly argued that under certain circumstances, "justice and generosity" might permit—even *require*—the evasion of a duly enacted and legitimate statute. Nevertheless, neither the court's principal opinion nor Clark's concurrence offered any general criticism of the state's antimiscegenation law; nor did either denounce in any way the conditions that made identification as a Negro such a humiliating, stigmatizing, and burdensome fate.

### Racial Antimiscegenation Laws in an International Context: Nazism, Apartheid, and Jim Crow

The deployment of racial restrictions on sex and marriage within the United States was hardly an isolated development. Around the world, for centuries, authorities have sought to define, protect, control, and stigmatize communities by imposing constraints on sexual or marital intimacy. In 1366, for example, English officials outlawed English-Irish intimate relations, as manifested in "marriage . . . fostering of children, concubinage or amour, or in any other manner."[73]* For a long period, canon law in Europe proscribed intermarriage between Jews and Christians, with violations punishable by death.[74] In 1644 British authorities in Antigua forbade "Carnall Coppullation between Christian and Heathen."[75] In 1685 the French monarchy enacted a law prohibiting marriage between blacks and whites; the trigger for the legislation was a significant increase in unions between white colonial planters and the black mistresses they brought back with them from Martinique and Guadalupe.[76] King Louis XV became so anxious about interracial matches and the perceived danger they posed that he ordered all Negroes expelled from France.[77] Throughout much of the nineteenth century, "persons of known nobility and known purity of blood" in

---

*This same law forbade Englishmen to wear Irish dress or hairstyles, to speak the Irish language, or to take Irish names. See Woods, "A 'Wicked and Mischievous Connection,'" 37, 43.

Cuba were forced by the Spanish crown to secure official permission before contracting marriages with "negroes, mulattos, and other castes."[78]

In the twentieth century, Nazi Germany and the apartheid regime of South Africa[79] joined many jurisdictions in the United States as governmental practitioners of racial restriction at the marriage altar. The Nazis barred from civil service any person who failed to show that his spouse was "Aryan"; urged doctors and lawyers to oust or exclude from their professional ranks persons married to Jews; organized mobs to stop the wedding ceremonies of mixed couples; banned future marriages between Jews and non-Jews; annulled existing engagements of mixed couples; and eventually prohibited all sexual relations between Jewish and non-Jewish Germans, enforcing the ban in certain cases with capital punishment. The Nazis also created the crime of *Rassenschande*, or "racial shame," a vague infraction for which some Jewish men were prosecuted on the basis of allegations that they had looked lustfully at German women.* The brutality of the Nazis was without peer. In some instances, they tortured to death Jews convicted of *Rassenschande*. In the Netherlands, they exploited their victims' terror by inducing some intermarried Jewish men to undergo sterilization in exchange for certain immunities.

Even the most ruthless dictatorial regimes, however, have found it difficult to administer antimiscegenation laws. When it became clear that the Nazi party planned to outlaw mixed marriages, numbers of mixed couples wed quickly in an effort to establish their marriages before a ban could take effect. And though the Nazis strongly encouraged non-Jewish Germans to divorce their Jewish spouses, relatively few complied. Fearful of provoking adverse public reaction, the Nazis refrained from decreeing the dissolution of preexisting marriages between Jewish and non-Jewish Germans, and generally treated intermarried Jews better than other Jews.[80]

That even after World War II racial legislation within the United States bore a marked similarity to Nazi statutes should serve as a dis-

---

*Recall, here, the American experience with "reckless eyeballing"; see page 196.

turbing antidote to the complacent triumphalism that often infects commentary on American democracy. In 1948 the United Nations Universal Declaration of Human Rights prohibited limitations on the right to marry "due to race."[81]* But it was not until 1967, in *Loving v. Virginia,* that the United States Supreme Court pronounced antimiscegenation laws incompatible with America's fundamental constitutional precepts. The next chapter tells the story of how dissidents eventually erased antimiscegenation laws from American statute books.

---

*It is still the case, though, that authorities in several countries preclude or discourage interracial, interethnic, or interfaith marriage. Saudi Arabia, for example, disqualifies Muslims from interfaith marriages, as do other Muslim nations (see "Malaysia: Forbidden Love: Cross Cultural Romance Sparks Muslim Anger," *Far Eastern Review,* February 1998; "Christians in Exodus from Holy Land," *Toronto Star,* December 24, 1991). In 1996 a Lebanese Christian man was sentenced to a year in jail and thirty-nine lashes for marrying a Muslim woman (see "Christian Gets Jail Term for Marrying Muslim," *The Record,* November 15, 1996).

SIX

# *Fighting Antimiscegenation Laws*

### *The Repeal of Antimiscegenation Laws in Antebellum America: The Massachusetts Example*

In 1839, thirteen hundred Massachusetts women (probably all of them white) submitted a petition to the state legislature urging it to repeal "all laws . . . which make any distinction among [the commonwealth's] inhabitants on account of color."[1] The petition's principal target was a statute enacted in 1705 that prohibited marriage between whites and Negroes or mulattoes. Widely scorned as "politicians in petticoats," the petitioners were subjected to all manner of abuse.[2] The *Boston Morning Post,* for example, suggested that "perhaps some of these ladies despair of having a *white* offer [of marriage], and so are willing to try *de colored race.*"[3] This discrediting strategy was elaborated in a second petition, signed by 193 white men who sarcastically requested that the legislature grant the lady petitioners an exemption from the state's antimiscegenation law. By the men's reckoning, the women should be authorized "to marry, intermarry, or associate with any Negro, Indian, Hottentot, or any other being in human shape, at their will and pleasure."[4] The women petitioners must certainly have been aware that their dissent would draw a sharp rebuke, for they had seen similarly pointed reactions engulf previous attacks on the antimiscegenation law. Eight years earlier, for instance, the outspoken abolitionist William Lloyd Garrison had provoked a firestorm when he condemned the restriction as "an invasion of one of the inalienable rights of every man; namely 'the pursuit of happiness.'"[5] "Of all [Garrison's] acts," one biographer would note, "this was for a time the most unpopular. The press poured upon it unmeasured ridicule and scorn."[6] Some critics denounced him as an "amalgamationist,"[7] while others claimed that his real motivation in decrying the statute was his own wish to take a black wife.

Responding to the women's petition, the legislature's Committee on the Judiciary defended the antimiscegenation law in a report suffused with sexist condescension. The committee began by questioning whether the petition itself was "perfectly consistent with feminine delicacy," given that the "appropriate sphere" of women "has heretofore been in the domestic arch, where there is still space ample enough for the exercise of the gentle charities which make life happy."[8] Then it turned to the substance of the matter, rebuffing the women's plea on the basis of arguments that would be articulated repeatedly over the next century and a half by proponents of antimiscegenation laws. According to the committee, the racial distinctions at issue were race-neutral and therefore fair, since the law placed the same burden on everyone, regardless of race:

> The law declares that the white shall not intermarry with the colored; that the colored shall not be joined to the white. It extends to all citizens without discrimination. Neither by expression nor implication, does it make the slightest superiority in one race or inferiority in another. . . . While the law applies to all colors, to all races, spreading its protection for morality and purity over every member of the community it should not be denounced as unequal.[9]

The committee insisted, moreover, that the state's antimiscegenation law stemmed from God's design, and on that account alone should not be repealed: "[The law] recognizes the distinctions impressed on the families of the human race by that Infinite Wisdom which nothing but the insanity of fanaticism dares to arraign. . . . No statute can annul the law of nature and bleach the skin of the Ethiopian or darken the face of the European."[10]

In addition, the committee maintained that "a law long established should not be repealed except for the purpose of remedying an existing evil, or introducing some probable improvement."[11] In this instance, however, no substantial number of individuals claimed to want to marry across the race line. The women petitioners themselves forswore any such desire, as did, according to the committee, all "intelligent persons of color," some of whom went so far as to "freely declare that they would reject [marriage] with those of the white race with abhorrence."[12] The committee saw no pressing need to act when so many of the law's opponents disavowed any intention of putting a repeal to practical use.

Most of those who attacked the antimiscegenation law did so out of a belief that the state's ban on interracial marriage represented an illicit badge of servitude affixed upon people who, albeit colored, were formally entitled to the equal benefit of the laws. Representative John P. Bigelow, for example, did not wish to condone, much less encourage, interracial unions, which he viewed as "the gratification of a depraved taste";[13] but neither could he tolerate what he perceived to be a state-sponsored vestige of slavery within the free precincts of Massachusetts.

A few opponents, however, declared it a positive good for blacks and whites to marry across racial lines. Writing in 1831, at the beginning of his crusade to remove the Massachusetts antimiscegenation law from the books, William Lloyd Garrison asserted that

> intermarriage is neither unnatural nor repugnant to nature, but obviously proper and salutary; it being designed to unite people of different tribes and nations, and to break down those petty distinctions which are the effect of climate or locality of situation, and which lead to oppression, war, and division among mankind. . . . As civilization and knowledge and republican feelings and Christianity prevail in the world, the wider will matrimonial connexions extend; and finally people of every tribe and kindred and tongue will freely intermarry. By the blissful operation of this divine institution the earth is evidently to become one neighborhood or family.[14]

It is extremely doubtful that, at any point in the nineteenth century (or, for that matter, in the twentieth), amalgamationism commanded the support of more than a tiny group of whites in Massachusetts. But what about blacks? Where did *they* stand with respect to the fight over the commonwealth's antimiscegenation law? Unfortunately, it is difficult to answer that question satisfactorily. Black New Englanders were few in number, and fewer still played prominent roles in the political struggles of the 1830s and 1840s, though more would become active in the 1850s and 1860s. Typically poor, unlettered, and exhausted by the rigors of mere survival in a harsh environment made harsher still by a widespread and debilitating Negrophobia, blacks were largely shunted to the margins of northern "free" society.[15] The lamentably limited information available to us suggests, however, that the majority of blacks deplored the antimiscegenation law insofar as it branded colored people an inferior caste from which whites needed and deserved protection. Nevertheless, most probably declined to invest much effort in assailing the legislation. For one thing, blacks faced other challenges—including fending off slave-catchers, pursuing education, and securing employment—that were widely viewed as being more pressing. Also hindering any significant opposition by blacks to the marriage ban was the fear that such protest might trigger a white reaction that would make it more difficult, if not impossible, for African Americans to achieve ends of greater—or at least more immediate—value than the right to marry across racial lines. Some blacks likely refrained, as well, from overtly attacking the mixed-marriage ban because they were loath to bolster whites' belief that blacks wanted more than anything to *become* white or, barring that, to get as close to whites as possible.*

---

*A striking articulation of this belief is offered by Judge St. George Tucker, a leading eighteenth-century American jurist. Explaining what he perceived to be black men's preference for white women, he maintained that this predilection "may be very naturally ascribed to pride, and ambition to associate with superiors; for . . . there is always a little grain of ambition in love." Quoted in Karen A. Getman, "Sexual Control in the Slaveholding South: The Implications and Maintenance of a Racial Caste System," 7 *Harvard Women's Law Journal* 115, 133 n. 76 (1984).

For other encounters with this attitude and reactions to it, see pages 25 and 109–23.

Then, too, as if the situation were not already complex enough, a small number of blacks in Massachusetts may actually have *defended* the antimiscegenation law. In 1843, after the tide had turned in favor of repeal, a group self-described as consisting of twenty-one colored women submitted a petition supporting the status quo. Its members argued that repeal of the state's antimiscegenation law would "exert a most pernicious influence on the condition of colored women," who would thereby "be deserted by [their] natural protectors and supporters." They predicted that "colored husbands will regret that they married before the change of the law" and consequently would "wish their wives out of the way." Anxious to forestall that outcome, the petitioners implored the legislature not to take an action that would "plunge [blacks] into an abyss of wretchedness, temptation, and ruin."[16] In response, William Lloyd Garrison charged that the colored women's petition had been authored primarily by a white congressman "notorious for his colorphobia," and signed mainly by "the lowest and most disreputable" colored people.[17] Although Garrison's charges may have been accurate, it must be remembered that as we have seen over the course of American history, many black women have objected to the fact or the prospect of black men marrying white women, and in doing so have cited arguments similar to those these petitioners deployed.*

Notwithstanding such obstacles and division, the opponents of the Massachusetts antimiscegenation law slowly succeeded in changing public opinion or, at a minimum, opinion within the state legislature. In 1841 they came within a few votes of repealing the statute; and two years later, they prevailed. Precisely what brought about this transformation in political fortunes is not altogether clear, but to some extent it likely reflected the efforts of reformers to associate the antimiscegenation law with slavery. John Greenleaf Whittier, for example, complained that "so long as Southerners can point to [the antimiscegenation law] . . . the anti-slavery testimony of Massachusetts is shorn of half its strength."[18] Eventually, the relevant committee in the Massachusetts House of Representatives concurred with Whittier's view and

---

*See pages 110–23.

recommended repeal. The statute, it averred, belied "sentiments which we have heretofore expressed to Congress and to the world on the subject of slavery, for by denying to our colored fellow-citizens any of the privileges and immunities of freemen, we virtually assert their inequality, and justify their theory of negro slavery which represents it as a state of necessary tutelage and guardianship."[19] In 1843 Massachusetts became the first state in the United States to repeal an existing antimiscegenation law.*

### Antimiscegenation Laws and Reconstruction

In the aftermath of the Civil War, one vexing and persistent question was whether states would be permitted to retain control over interracial sexual and marital intimacies. Three debates—over the Civil Rights Act of 1866, the Fourteenth Amendment, and the Civil Rights Act of 1875—shed light on the significance of this issue and the ways contending factions dealt with it. The Civil Rights Act of 1866 provided that all persons should have the same rights as whites to make contracts, own property, and testify in court.[20] This law came into being because after slavery was abolished, southern states enacted black codes that subjected African Americans to regulations from which whites were exempt. The leadership of the Republican party (Lincoln's party, the party mainly responsible for crushing the Confederacy, and the party friendliest to the aspirations of blacks in the nineteenth century) feared that the black codes would establish a racial serfdom. To prevent that, the Republicans sought to impose upon states a requirement that, at least with respect to certain fundamental civil rights, they treat colored people the same as whites.

President Andrew Johnson, Lincoln's successor, vetoed the bill because in his view, among other excesses, it posed a threat to the continued viability of state antimiscegenation laws. Some white politicians objected to virtually every measure intended to elevate the Negro, on

---

*It must be noted here, however, that in 1780, prior to the establishment of the United States, Pennsylvania repealed its 1725 antimiscegenation law. See David H. Fowler, *Northern Attitudes Towards Interracial Marriage: Legislation and Public Opinion in the Middle Atlantic and States of the Old Northwest, 1780–1930* (1987), 84–87.

the ground that either directly or indirectly, such reforms must lead inevitably to intermarriage. Commenting on opposition to the extension of suffrage to black men in the District of Columbia, Republican Congressman Glenn W. Scofield observed, "Again, it is said [that this measure] will lead to amalgamation. . . . This is a standing argument with the Opposition and is brought out on all occasions when any legislation is proposed touching the interests of the colored population."[21]

Many Republican proponents of the civil rights bill believed that Johnson, too, was engaging in mere demagoguery when he raised the specter of intermarriage in his veto memorandum. These partisans had, after all, already made explicit their conviction that neither the civil rights bill nor any other legislation demanding equality before the law could reasonably be seen as jeopardizing states' authority to prevent marriage across the race line, so long as the prohibition and any enforcement of it applied equally to every citizen, regardless of his or her race. As Republican Senator Lyman Trumbull remarked, "If the negro is denied the right to marry a white person, [and] the white person is equally denied the right to marry the negro[,] I see no discrimination against either. . . . Make the penalty the same on all classes of people for the same offense, and then no one can complain."[22] In Trumbull's opinion (and probably the opinion of most Republican members of Congress during the Reconstruction era), equality before the law needed to go no further than "symmetrical equality"—meaning blacks and whites being subjected to the same law, even if that law required racial separation.[23]

While President Johnson himself conceded that the Civil Rights Act would not immediately affect state antimiscegenation laws, he nonetheless objected to the bill, arguing that even if it did not abrogate such laws this time around, the assumed authority on which it rested might be invoked at some later date to invalidate state bans on mixed marriages, should Congress wish to reach that far. For "if Congress can abrogate all State laws of discrimination between the two races in the matter of real estate, of suits, and of contracts generally[, why may it not] also repeal the State laws as to the contract of marriage between the two races?"[24] In mentioning interracial marriage in this context, Johnson was doing more than playing the amalgamation card; he was also highlighting, in a vivid way, his broad jurisdictional opposition to any federal civil rights legislation. Simply put, Johnson did not think Congress should have the authority to insist on the states guaranteeing all persons equality before the law, regardless of their race.

A different objection held that because the federal bill was inconsistent with state antimiscegenation laws, it would therefore necessarily invalidate them. This was the position taken by Senator Reverdy Johnson, a distinguished conservative attorney, who maintained that the real issue was whether a "black man has the same right to enter into a contract of marriage with a white woman as a white man has."[25] Senator Johnson asserted that under the Civil Rights Act, "white and black are considered together, put in a mass, and the one is entitled to enter into every contract that the other is entitled to enter into. Of course, therefore, the black man is entitled to enter into the contract of marriage with a white woman."[26] The senator's conception of what the proposed legislation demanded was prescient, anticipating, albeit with a shudder, the individualistic, same-treatment model of civil rights that would succeed toward the end of the twentieth century. In the 1860s, however, few champions of civil rights legislation agreed with Reverdy Johnson. Most instead subscribed to Lyman Trumbull's interpretation, believing that the Civil Rights Act of 1866 would *not* grant colored people a federal right to marry across racial lines. Had the act been more widely perceived as doing what Senator Johnson claimed it did, there is little likelihood that it could have won the votes needed to override President Johnson's veto. But because the legislation was generally seen as mandating only symmetrical equality as opposed to what some termed "perfect equality," its supporters finally carried the day.

When Congress moved to constitutionalize the Civil Rights Act of 1866 through the Fourteenth Amendment, the debate over its effect on state antimiscegenation laws followed a well-rehearsed routine. Opponents charged that amalgamationism lurked behind efforts to raise the Negro to the status of an equal citizen, while outside Congress, some champions of black advancement asserted that the objectives of racial equality would best be symbolized and fostered by the obliteration of *all* racial distinctions embedded in laws. Hence, the great agitator Wendell Phillips proposed the following language for the Fourteenth Amendment: "No state shall make any distinction in civil rights and privileges . . . on account of race, color, or descent."[27] Phillips's suggested wording, however, was overwhelmingly rejected by a Congress seeking a standard that could accommodate the racial distinctions made by race-neutral segregation statutes, including antimiscegenation laws. The historical record strongly indicates that the politicians who framed the Fourteenth Amendment did *not* intend for it to render illegal statutes prohibiting interracial marriage. During debates held prior to congressional passage of the Fourteenth Amendment, its proponents repeatedly denied that it would affect the legality of properly drafted antimiscegenation laws. They argued that the proposed provisions constituted no threat to race-neutral antimiscegenation laws, since such statutes discriminated against no one and no group in particular but rather applied equally to all. Some—perhaps many—of the Amendment's authors did not even mean for it to embrace *political* and *social* as opposed to *civil* rights (e.g., entering into contracts, owning property, and testifying in court).[28] Twenty-nine states retained antimiscegenation laws after the Civil War. The Alabama Supreme Court, for its part, invalidated an antimiscegenation statute pursuant to changes in federal law and the federal constitution,[29] but that notable decision was also idiosyncratic, and it was soon reversed.[30] The near consensus of judicial opinion in the aftermath of the ratification of the Fourteenth Amendment was that neither it nor any of the other reforms of Reconstruction impaired states' authority to prohibit interracial sex or marriage.[31]

The third major debate in Congress over antimiscegenation laws was occasioned by the Civil Rights Act of 1875. This last significant civil rights bill of the Reconstruction period sought, among other benefits, to entitle all persons to "the full and equal enjoyment" of places of public accommodation.[32] Although the legislation nowhere mentioned state antimiscegenation laws, its opponents once again took the opportunity to raise the specter of racial amalgamation. The bill's supporters responded in a variety of ways. A small number openly expressed their hope that its passage would hasten the demise of antimiscegenation laws. Most ignored the issue altogether. And a few others vociferously attacked what they saw as the hypocrisy of those who on the one hand condemned "amalgamation" and on the other tolerated white male sexual aggression. To comment on the nature of the sexual activity between white men and black women in the South, Representative Benjamin F. Butler had the clerk of the House read aloud a letter sent to him by an African American woman from Virginia, who complained that "nothing can ever make us equal with the white race while our daughters are forced to commit adultery by every white man and boy that [chooses] to treat them as dogs."[33]

Black members of Congress pressed this latter point with special vigor.* Representative Alonzo Ransier of South Carolina, for example, noted that while "negro-haters would not open school-houses, hotels . . . or the jury box to the colored people . . . because this contact of the races would, forsooth, 'result injuriously to both,'" they nevertheless "have found agreeable associations with them under other circumstances"—by which "associations" he meant, of course, covert sexual relationships.[34] Representative Joseph H. Rainey, also of South Carolina, was more direct. Observing that amalgamation had already effectively been accomplished, largely through the sexual brutality of those who most loudly condemned the prospect, Representative Rainey asserted that "If the future may be judged from the result of the past, it will require much effort upon the part of the colored race to preserve the purity of their own households from the intrusions of those who have hitherto violated and are now violating with ruthless impunity those precious and inestimable rights which should be the undisturbed heritage of all good society."[35]

Similarly, Representative James T. Rapier of Alabama asked rhetorically, "How can I have respect for the prejudices that prompt a man to turn up his nose at the males of a certain race, while at the same time he has a fondness for the females . . . to the extent of cohabitation?"[36] According to Rapier, this selective aversion to amalgamation—a hankering for illicit sex coexisting with a contempt for honored affection—was by no means a phenomenon limited to the slave past. "Out of four

---

*Between 1869 and 1877, sixteen blacks sat in Congress—fourteen in the House of Representatives and two (both from Mississippi) in the Senate. See Eric Foner, *Reconstruction: America's Unfinished Revolution 1863–1877* (1988), 352.

unfortunate colored women who from poverty were forced to go to the lying-in branch of the Freemen's Hospital here in the District [of Columbia] last year," he remarked, "three gave birth to children whose fathers were white men and I venture to say that if [those men] were members of this body, [they] would vote against the civil rights bill."[37]

During Reconstruction, the color bar at the altar was breached in several places. For a brief period, Alabama's supreme court invalidated that state's antimiscegenation law,[38] and when reformers friendly to Reconstruction overhauled the laws of Arkansas, Mississippi, and South Carolina, they dropped existing antimiscegenation provisions from the statute books.[39] Reconstructionists likewise repealed Louisiana's ban on mixed marriages.[40] In most jurisdictions, the matrimonial color bar remained in force. Still, the reforms of Reconstruction prevented authorities from lawfully excluding blacks altogether from the protections and privileges of matrimony, and that in itself represented a large step forward, inasmuch as exclusion from marriage had been one of the strictures imposed on the great majority of blacks prior to the abolition of slavery. It would nonetheless require almost another century of struggle before state authorities were finally proscribed from mandating racial matching in sex and marriage.

### Limiting Antimiscegenation Laws Between 1890 and 1945

In the aftermath of Reconstruction, racial minorities were subjected to insulting and stultifying restrictions in every sphere of American life, from the ballot box to the factory to the baseball field.[41] A racial bar disqualified foreign-born people of color from eligibility for citizenship. "Nigger" and other, similar slurs were widely and casually employed. Lynchings were prevalent. Five states—Oklahoma, Montana, North Dakota, South Dakota, and Wyoming—enacted for the first time prohibitions against interracial sex or marriage. Having already forbidden intermarriage by statute, other states embedded such bans in their constitutions. In 1901, for example, the Alabama legislature amended the state's constitution to declare that future legislatures "shall never pass any law to authorize or legalize any marriage between any white person and a negro, or a descendant of a negro."[42] No antimiscegenation laws were repealed during this period, nor did any court invalidate prohibitions against interracial intimacy.

This retrogressive climate notwithstanding, after Wyoming promulgated its antimiscegenation law in 1913, no additional states followed suit. Efforts undertaken to enact new antimiscegenation legislation were for the most part rebuffed. Similarly unsuccessful were initiatives by white southern congressmen to win passage of a federal constitutional amendment prohibiting interracial marriage, a federal statute to the same effect, and a law that would at least prevent such unions in the District of Columbia. In sum, between 1890 and 1945, while opposition to racial egalitarianism was ascendant, it was not wholly triumphant. Colored people were pushed to the edges of the American polity but not entirely outside it. Although interracial intimacy continued to be strongly stigmatized, its enemies were unable to outlaw it nationally.

In the second decade of the twentieth century, proponents of antimiscegenation laws campaigned for their passage in the District of Columbia, Wisconsin, Pennsylvania, Ohio, Illinois, New York, New Jersey, Iowa, Kansas, Minnesota, and Washington. There were few surprises in these campaigns. Supporters maintained that antimiscegenation legislation accorded perfectly with the real interests of blacks as well as whites. "I fully believe," declared Ralph R. Downs, a Republican congressman from Pennsylvania, "that the true negro will have that pride in his race and agree . . . that the intermarrying of the races is not for the best of either. . . . Instead of marriage between the two races drawing them closer together and doing away with race prejudice it only adds to [racial bias]."[43] Others appropriated the thinking of eugenicists to argue that humankind as a whole would be better off if race mixing was prevented. Trumpeting its eugenicist origin, the antimiscegenation law proposed for New York contained a provision whereby the parties to an illegal interracial marriage could avoid fines and imprisonment by submitting to sterilization.[44]*

---

*Recall, here, the Nazis' drive to sterilize Jews married to non-Jews in the Netherlands; see page 242.

Remarkably, the effort to extend antimiscegenation laws largely failed. Despite the vogue of eugenicist racial betterment, despite the example provided by the two dozen states that prohibited interracial marriage, despite widespread abhorrence of interracial unions, and despite a political culture that allowed members of Congress to inveigh against "kinky headed blood" and "mongrelization"—despite all of these things and more, few antimiscegenation proposals became law.* This aspect of the segregation era has received little attention from scholars, and indeed, any comprehensive analysis is rendered impossible by the very nature of the historical record. While the relatively few activists on both sides of the issue left useful accounts of their reasoning, we know next to nothing about the thinking of their middle-of-the-road colleagues, whose votes determined the ultimate legislative fate of the proposals. We can thus hazard only an educated guess why the campaigns to extend the reach of antimiscegenation prohibitions did not succeed. Those who sought passage of a constitutional amendment against mixed marriages surely faced the special hurdles that must be overcome by anyone seeking to amend the nation's fundamental charter. For their part, the champions of a national antimiscegenation statute probably encountered resistance from those wary of the federal government becoming involved in matters traditionally dealt with by state law. Partisans of state laws, in turn, were themselves likely met by a certain skepticism with respect to the need for new legislation; after all, informal sanctions already made interracial marriage conspicuously uncommon. But perhaps the most important opposition to antimiscegenation legislation came from vigilant individuals and groups commit-

---

*Note, however, that in 1912 and 1913, Vermont and Massachusetts—jurisdictions that might have been expected to be among the least affected by animus against miscegenation—enacted statutes voiding interracial marriages performed within their borders between persons domiciled in other states that did not permit such unions. This legislation was intended to prevent these two New England states—both of which allowed their own citizens to intermarry—from becoming temporary havens for interracial couples attempting to avoid antimiscegenation laws in their home states. See Byron Curtis Martyn, "Racism in the United States: A History of the Anti-Miscegenation Legislation and Litigation" (Ph.D. diss., University of Southern California, 1979), 909.

ted to protecting African Americans from stigmatizing Negrophobic affronts.

The most significant of the groups actively opposing the spread of antimiscegenation laws was the NAACP. A comprehensive statement of the organization's position was set down in a letter sent to the Wisconsin state legislature on March 8, 1913, when that body was debating a so-called Jack Johnson bill.* Written by Oswald Garrison Villard and W. E. B. DuBois, the letter began by announcing that the NAACP "earnestly protests against the bill forbidding intermarriage between the races."[45] In the next breath, it assured its recipients that the NAACP's opposition was in no sense tantamount to advocacy *in favor of* intermarriage. This is an important point. Rarely did opponents of antimiscegenation laws articulate a desire to facilitate or encourage racial intermarriage, a stance that in most contexts would have been politically suicidal. All too aware that backers of antimiscegenation legislation routinely charged that the real wish of Negroes who sought an end to segregation and disfranchisement was to marry into white society, NAACP leaders were careful to avoid the appearance of advocating intermarriage. Furthermore, as we have seen, substantial numbers of blacks harbored, then as now, a hostile attitude toward interracial unions. The NAACP accordingly took the view that racial intermarriage was in itself neither good nor bad but should be available as an option that individuals were at liberty to reject or choose. The Villard–DuBois letter asserted that beneath the veneer of formal neutrality, antimiscegenation laws amounted to a state-sponsored declaration "that black blood is a physical taint"—a concession that "no self-respecting colored man [or] woman can be asked to [make]."[46]

Superior organization may well have contributed to the NAACP's ability to stymie the spread of antimiscegenation laws. White public opinion as a whole favored such legislation, but in the states in question, the sector of the public that most effectively communicated its wishes to politicians was the sector mobilized by the NAACP. Critical

---

*The name referred, of course, to the famous black prizefighter who married across the color line; see pages 79–85.

to this success were northern black voters. In the South, where racial disfranchisement was the norm, blacks had no means of penalizing politicians who acted against their interests. But in the North, armed with the ballot, they were sometimes able to pressure elected officials or even to win their authentic allegiance.

Struggles on the ideological front were also a factor. Segregationist thinking encountered significant dissent even at the height of the antiblack reaction. Like the American Revolution, Reconstruction let loose egalitarian sentiments that warred against the institutionalization of racism through Jim Crow segregation. The spirit of Reconstruction, as embodied by the NAACP, played a vital role in the successful effort to prevent racists from blanketing the entire nation with antimiscegenation laws.

After Ohio repealed its antimiscegenation laws in 1887, no other state followed its lead until Oregon finally did so in 1951—sixty-four years later. In the sixteen years after *that*, however, more than a dozen states repealed their statutes: Montana (1953), North Dakota (1955), Colorado and South Dakota (1957), California, Nevada, and Idaho (1959), Arizona (1962), Utah and Nebraska (1963), Indiana and Wyoming (1965), and Maryland (1967).[47] To some extent, this legislative trend mirrored a widespread liberalization of personal mores. But then, too, many who would not choose interracial intimacy for themselves became newly reluctant to authorize their government to regulate such delicate private matters. The repeal of antimiscegenation laws further reflected and reinforced developments that attained increasing importance in American life both during and after World War II. One was a growing respect for people of color, especially blacks. Another was the reaction against racial prejudice as practiced by the Nazis. Americans could not help noticing that Hitler, too, had made a point of prohibiting marriage across racial lines. Hence, in 1958, when officials in Nevada tried to prevent the radical union leader Henry Bridges from marrying his Japanese American fiancée, an editorialist for the *San Francisco Chronicle* objected in the following terms:

> Nevada's law interfering with the plans of Harry Bridges
> and Miss Noriko Sawada to marry was dead when invoked,

even though the clerk of the court . . . didn't know it. What killed [the law] was the Twentieth Century's growing recognition that unless a society is to be run on the Hitler concept, race must be no bar to the enjoyment of civil rights.[48]

The reform movement gained momentum as every state that repealed a ban on interracial marriage made it easier for a sister state to do the same. By 1967 the territory covered by antimiscegenation laws had shrunk from thirty states (as of 1930) to sixteen. Whereas such prohibitions had once constituted a widespread phenomenon, by the mid-1960s they were reduced to the status of a regional peculiarity, limited to the South and a few border states. In those jurisdictions, however, they were well entrenched, leaving little chance that regular politics would be able, at least within a foreseeable period, to definitively uproot segregation at the marriage altar. Such eradication would instead require a different sort of politics: the politics of constitutional litigation.

### The Constitutional Attack on Antimiscegenation Laws

Three cases from the post–World War II era—*Perez v. Sharp, Naim v. Naim,* and *Loving v. Virginia*—are key to an understanding of the process by which courts, invoking the federal constitution, eventually rendered unenforceable prohibitions against interracial marriage.

In the 1948 case *Perez v. Sharp,* the California Supreme Court became the first court of the twentieth century to invalidate a state antimiscegenation law on the ground that it violated the federal constitution.[49] Although history has relegated them to the shadows of the United States Supreme Court's ruling in *Loving v. Virginia,* the California justices in fact anticipated their federal brethren by some nineteen years, producing a far more remarkable decision. *Loving* was decided over a decade into the civil rights revolution and thus benefited from the momentum generated by *Brown v. Board of Education,* the march on Washington, the oratory of Martin Luther King Jr., the Civil Rights Act of 1964, and the Voting Rights Act of 1965. *Perez* antedated all of those milestones. When the *Perez* opinion was handed down, Jim Crow segregation was still regarded as constitutionally permissible.

Yet somehow, the California Supreme Court found a way to condemn as constitutionally *im*permissible the Jim Crow bar to interracial marriage.

The controversy began when Andrea D. Perez and Sylvester S. Davis Jr. applied to the clerk of Los Angeles County for a marriage license. On the requisite forms, Perez designated herself as "white," and Davis identified his race as "Negro." The clerk refused to issue them a license, citing a California law that stated that "no license may be issued authorizing the marriage of a white person with a Negro, mulatto, Mongolian or member of the Malay race."[50] California's legislative aversion to interracial marriage dated back to 1850, when the state first enacted a law prohibiting whites from marrying Negroes or mulattoes. In 1880 it extended the ban to unions between whites and Chinese. In 1905 the state rendered "illegal and void" all marriages between whites and Negroes, mulattoes, and "Mongolians," meaning people of Chinese or Japanese ancestry. In 1933 the California Supreme Court ruled that the state's antimiscegenation law, as written, did not prohibit whites from marrying Filipinos,[51] a lapse that the state assembly immediately "cured" by adding "Malays" to the statute.[52]

Complaining that the clerk's refusal to grant them a marriage license was unlawful, Perez and Davis challenged the state antimiscegenation statute, maintaining that it violated the federal constitution. The California Supreme Court agreed, but just barely: the vote was four to three. The principal opinion of the majority was written by Justice Roger J. Traynor, who began by restating the petitioners' main argument: the state's prohibition against interracial marriage violated their First Amendment right to the free exercise of their religion. They averred that since their church—they were both Roman Catholics—did not forbid interracial marriage, they were entitled to receive the sacrament of matrimony notwithstanding the state's antimiscegenation statute. For good reason, Traynor did not expend much effort responding to this weak claim. As Justice John W. Shenk noted in dissent, "The petitioners' alleged right to marry is not a part of their religion in the broad sense that it is a duty enjoined by the church";[53] rather, a marriage between them would simply have been *permitted* under church doctrine. Furthermore, while the Catholic Church did not itself bar interracial marriage, it did counsel priests and parishioners to respect local antimiscegenation laws—a fact that rather sharply undercut the petitioners' charge that the state's prohibition impinged upon their freedom of religious observance. If the church leadership had truly believed that antimiscegenation laws prevented Catholics from freely practicing their religion, it presumably would have objected to such statutes.*

At the heart of Traynor's opinion were two propositions. The first was that marriage was "a fundamental right" that must never be impinged upon "except for an important social objective and by reasonable means."[54] The second was that "race restrictions must be viewed with great suspicion."[55] In Traynor's view, both of these propositions justified subjecting antimiscegenation laws to the most intense form of judicial scrutiny. In dissent, Shenk stressed the presumption of validity conventionally accorded to duly enacted legislation. In response, Traynor maintained that such legislation *lost* its presumptive validity when it impaired the right to marry or when it imposed a color bar. That the law in question imposed a color bar is obvious; less obvious is how, by Traynor's reasoning, it impaired the right to marry. Under the law, both Perez and Davis were free to wed, though Perez was barred from marrying a Negro, mulatto, Mongolian, or Malay, while Davis was barred from marrying any white person. To Traynor, this restriction in and of itself represented a grave infringement on the right to marry, inasmuch as it hampered individuals' freedom to choose their own marriage partners.[56] That was a difficult argument to make in 1948, given that segregation was then still deemed permissible under the federal constitution. According to the U.S. Supreme Court, state-mandated segregation did not wrongfully burden any person's right to enjoy goods or services, so long as those goods or services were equal

---

*Despite its weaknesses, the petitioners' freedom-of-religion argument played an important, perhaps even decisive, role in the outcome of the case. Justice Douglas L. Edmonds, the majority's key fourth vote, embraced that argument exclusively in his concurring opinion. *Perez v. Sharp,* 32 Cal. 2d 711, 740–42 (1948). See also Jack Rowlett Lovell, "Marriage and the Freedom of Religion," *Southern California Law Review* 22 (1948): 27.

to, albeit separate from, those reserved for someone of a different race. The Court assumed that goods and services would be fungible, in the sense that a railway car or school for blacks would possess essentially the same properties as a separate-but-equal whites-only railway car or school. Traynor asserted in *Perez,* however, that the fungibility that was arguably present with respect to some goods and services was absent with respect to marriage. "Since the essence of the right to marry," he wrote, "is freedom to join in marriage with the person of one's choice, a segregation statute for marriage necessarily impairs the right to marry."[57] Human beings, he insisted, would be diminished "by a doctrine that would make them as interchangeable as trains."[58]

Segregationists had long argued that properly drawn antimiscegenation laws were consistent with the federal equal-protection clause because they applied to all persons on the same basis. By this interpretation, Perez, the white woman, was barred from her choice of a spouse on the same terms as Davis, the black man.* Traynor countered with his own, individualistic understanding of the clause: "The decisive question," he suggested, "is not whether different races, each considered as a group, are equally treated. . . . The equal protection clause . . . does not refer to rights of the Negro race, the Caucasian race, or any other race, but to the rights of individuals."[59] Thus, in Traynor's view, restricting the freedom of action of an individual merely because of his race, absent some extraordinary justification, constituted a violation of the equal-protection clause. That people of another race were similarly restricted did not cure the violation. Quoting the U.S. Supreme Court's landmark decision in *Shelley v. Kraemer,* Traynor declared that "equal protection of the laws is not achieved through indiscriminate imposition of inequalities."[60]† Proceeding on the premise that laws restricting

---

*Actually, under the California antimiscegenation law, whites were *more* "burdened"—or some might have said "protected"—than others. While the law foreclosed whites from marrying Negroes, mulattoes, Mongolians, or Malays, it foreclosed Negroes only from marrying whites, leaving them free to wed mulattoes, Mongolians, and Malays.

†In *Shelley v. Kraemer,* the Court held that it was a contravention of the federal constitution for state courts to enforce through equitable relief restrictive covenants stip-

marital freedom or distinguishing among persons purely on a racial basis were presumptively suspect, Traynor subjected the California antimiscegenation law to a withering analysis to determine whether it suitably advanced the purposes enumerated by its defenders. These latter claimed that the statute helped to minimize the number of children produced by interracial unions—a worthy aim, they maintained, because interbreeding degraded the purer racial stock of the parents, resulting in inferior offspring. They also argued that the colored groups designated by the law were themselves physically and mentally inferior to whites and would, if not prevented from engaging in racial mixing, diminish the quality of the population's overall genetic inheritance.

Traynor responded to these arguments along two lines. First, he attacked their empirical basis, contending that the best biological and social scientific knowledge rejected the assertion that racial admixture caused genetic degeneration. Justice Shenk, for his part, maintained that at the very least, there was disagreement on this point, and that it was the province of the legislature to resolve such issues. Traynor, however, disputed the intellectual authority of the sources cited by his colleague. Traynor's rebuttal cited the work of scores of intellectuals who had undermined the foundations of scientific racism during the first half of the twentieth century. While in 1900 the notion that there existed an objective racial hierarchy of intelligence and morality (with whites at the top of the ladder) had been widely accepted among

---

ulating that property was not to be purchased by or sold to persons of a given race (334 U.S. 1 [1948]). This ruling prevented state judges from evicting blacks from homes they had bought. The Court rejected the assertion that racially restrictive covenants were race-neutral insofar as private parties could decide to exclude whites, blacks, Asian Americans, or any other set of individuals. Since anyone might be subject to such proscription, it was argued, depending on the personal biases of private parties, no one race was being singled out by the state; all persons were equally vulnerable to private discrimination. This equal-application theory of equal protection has deep roots; see, for example, *Roberts v. City of Boston,* 59 Mass. 198 (1850); *Pace v. Alabama,* 106 U.S. 583 (1883); *Plessy v. Ferguson,* 163 U.S. 537 (1896). It continues to be voiced from time to time, as in, e.g., *Batson v. Kentucky,* 476 U.S. 79, 134 (1986) (Rehnquist, C. J., dissenting).

(white) educated elites as a fact of nature, by 1948 a pall of skepticism had been drawn over that conviction by such influential thinkers as Franz Boas, Gunnar Myrdal, Ralph Linton, Ruth Benedict, Otto Klineberg, and M. F. Ashley Montagu.[61] Demonstrating the importance of extrajudicial intellectual developments in the judicial determination of "facts," Traynor flatly stated that "modern experts are agreed that the progeny of marriages between persons of different races are not inferior to both races."[62] In a like manner, he dismissed the assertion that there was a real, justifiable, and scientifically verifiable racial hierarchy. "There is no scientific proof," he insisted, "that one race is superior to another in native ability."[63] While it was true that "in the United States catalogues of distinguished people list more Caucasians than members of other races,"[64] the disparity was attributable, Traynor maintained, to factors that were environmental and changeable as opposed to genetic and immutable.

Traynor's opinion did not rest solely upon a rejection of the state's empirical claims. Even supposing, for the sake of argument, that interracial marriage did produce inferior progeny, Traynor noted that he was "unable to find any clear policy in the statute against marriage on that ground."[65] In fact, California law did *not* rigorously attempt to discourage the procreation of mixed-race children. It did not criminalize interracial sex. It did not prohibit whites from marrying Indians. It did not prevent Negroes, mulattoes, Mongolians, and Malays from stepping over racial lines to marry one another. Nor did it withhold recognition of interracial marriages performed in other states where such unions were legal.

With respect to the matter of physical and intellectual inferiority, Traynor acknowledged that the legislature was free to prohibit marriages that were socially dangerous in light of the disabilities of one or both of the parties involved. That, however, was not what the antimiscegenation law did. Rather, it nominated certain races as being "unfit to marry with Caucasians on the premise of a hypothetical racial disability, regardless of the physical qualifications of the individuals concerned."[66]

In regard to the alleged mental inferiority of the colored races,

Traynor remarked on the notable absence of an intelligence test for marriage that was required of or applicable to the population as a whole. He observed, too, that if the state's blanket condemnation of the mental ability of designated races was accepted, there would be no limit to discriminations based upon the supposed inferiority of certain races. It would then be logical to forbid Negroes to marry Negroes, or Mongolians to marry Mongolians, or to decrease a race's numbers by sterilization. Traynor emphasized, in short, the underinclusiveness of the California statute, the laxity of its logic, and the gaping loopholes that prevented it from achieving its purported goals. The absence of a tight fit between the asserted aims of the antimiscegenation legislation and the state's chosen means of realizing those aims permitted the inference, according to Traynor, that the announced goals were not the state's real reasons for enacting and enforcing the challenged legislation, but only a cover for something else, something covert, something unmentionable and constitutionally illicit—namely, state-supported white-supremacist prejudice.*

The contending opinions in *Perez* reflect the extremes of racial sentiment. The contempt for racism that radiates from the majority opinions would attract notice even today; half a century ago, the vehemence of the attack on matrimonial Jim Crow was notable indeed.[67] Thus far, I have focused on Justice Traynor's opinion, but in fact, Justice Jesse W. Carter was equally militant in his denunciation of California's antimiscegenation law. Declining to defer in any way to the statute in question, Carter instead described it as "the product of ignorance, prejudice, and intolerance" and maintained that it had *never* been constitutional—

---

*Another basis on which Traynor voted to strike down the antimiscegenation law was that it was "too vague and uncertain," where "precision is essential in a statute regulating a fundamental right" (*Perez* at 27). In Traynor's view, the statute failed to put Californians on notice as to who was prohibited from marrying whom; then, too, it was silent with respect to the proper racial classification of persons of mixed race. While it did refer to "mulattoes," Traynor complained that this word itself was nowhere defined by the legislature. California law also left uncertain the meanings of "white" persons, "Mongolians," and "members of the Malay race." According to Traynor, it was not at all clear whether, under state law, racial labels were to be applied on the basis of appearance or of ancestry.

that from the outset, even before the Civil War, the antimiscegenation law had been invalid insofar as it "violated the supreme law of the land as found in the Declaration of Independence."[68] After citing the recently promulgated charter of the United Nations as one authority, Justice Carter turned to the Scriptures for inspiration, quoting, "God . . . hath made of one blood all nations of men to dwell on all the face of the earth."[69]

Still, even as the majority of the California Supreme Court articulated its antiracist views through a rhetoric presaging that of the civil rights movement, the judicial minority, as represented by Justice Shenk, unapologetically took as *its* authority the Negrophobic postulates of white supremacists in America and abroad. Shenk approvingly noted, for instance, the Georgia Supreme Court's opinion holding that "the amalgamation of the races is not only unnatural but is always productive of deplorable results."[70]* Thus, in 1948, the same year that the Democratic party showed itself willing to risk the defection of southern Dixiecrats rather than remove the civil rights plank from its political platform—the year, too, that President Harry Truman ordered the desegregation of the armed forces, and Jackie Robinson broke the color barrier in white professional baseball—three justices of the California Supreme Court could still defend the constitutional legitimacy of antimiscegenation laws on the ground that Negroes represented a racial menace to whites.[71]†

The second case that is essential to understanding the constitutional attack upon antimiscegenation laws is *Naim v. Naim,* a dispute in which the Virginia Supreme Court upheld the commonwealth's prohi-

---

*Justice Shenk also recalled that in an address before the Commonwealth Club of California, "Mr. William Gemmil, South African delegate to the International Labor Organization and one well acquainted with social conditions and sociological manifestations in that continent, made the statement that in South Africa, where the European population is greatly outnumbered by the natives, both classes are adamant in opposition to intermarriages, and that the free mixing of all the races could in fact only lower the general level" (*Perez* at 757).

†The state did not appeal *Perez* to the U.S. Supreme Court. Whether then-Governor Earl Warren had anything to do with that decision is unclear; in any event, nineteen years later, Warren himself would face the same issue in a different setting, as the chief justice of the United States Supreme Court.

bition against interracial marriage.[72] In 1955 the Supreme Court of the United States initially indicated that it would review the Virginia courts' handling of the controversy, but then it awkwardly reversed itself, mainly for fear of negative public opinion. *Naim* illustrates the unique status at midcentury of southern antimiscegenation laws, which for many policy-makers, including a majority of the justices of the U.S. Supreme Court, constituted an untouchable third rail of racial politics. *Naim* was also noteworthy in concerning a relationship between a white woman and a man of Chinese ancestry. Although most of the case law generated by antimiscegenation statutes involved blacks and whites, people from all racial backgrounds were directly and adversely affected by these restraints. *

Ham Say Naim was a Chinese sailor who came to the United States in 1942. A decade later, he married Ruby Elaine Lamberth, a white woman. Although they had lived together in Norfolk, Virginia, prior to their marriage, they traveled to North Carolina to wed because they knew that Virginia law forbade whites and people of Asian ancestry from intermarrying. They were married in Elizabeth, North Carolina,

---

*As we have seen, California amended its antimiscegenation law specifically to target people of Chinese, Japanese, and Filipino origin. The federal government, too, sought to discourage interracial intimacy between whites and persons of Asian ancestry. While it never enacted antimiscegenation legislation, it did pass a law that imposed an egregious burden upon female citizens of the United States who wished to wed aliens ineligible for naturalization: pursuant to the Cable Act of 1922, any American woman who wed such an alien was herself immediately stripped of her citizenship. The de facto marriage ban resulted from a racial bar on naturalized citizenship that, for several decades, generally excluded Asians. (See Candice Lewis Bredbenner, *A Nationality of Her Own: Women, Marriage, and the Law of Citizenship* [1998], 16.)

People of color from around the world have been singled out in the United States for formal or informal mistreatment that has egregiously intruded on the most intimate spheres of their lives. This is a matter that warrants closer attention, though it has already benefited from impressive scholarly investigations; see, for example, Rachel F. Moran, *Interracial Intimacy: The Regulation of Race and Romance* (2001), 28–41; Leti Volpp, "American Mestizo: Filipinos and Antimiscegenation Laws in California," *University of California at Davis Law Review* 33 (2000): 795; Megumi Dick Osumi, "Asians and California's Anti-Miscegenation Laws," in Nabuya Tsuchida, ed., *Asian and Pacific American Experience: Women's Perspectives* (1982).

and immediately returned to Norfolk. After only a year, their marriage disintegrated. Ruby Naim filed for an annulment or divorce, claiming that Virginia's Racial Integrity Act rendered their union a nullity from the outset. Her spouse disputed that assertion, arguing that the act itself was a nullity under the federal constitution, and that their marriage was therefore valid.

Nowadays, the decline in anti-Asian prejudice—and indeed, the emergence of the notion of Asian Americans as a "model" minority—make it difficult accurately to reconstruct the contempt, fear, and detestation that Asians and Asian Americans inspired in this country in the first half of the twentieth century.[73] We must, however, recall that aspect of American race relations if we hope to apprehend opposition to intimacy between whites and Asians. Just as racist imagery portrayed black women as immoral and lascivious, so, too, were women of Asian ancestry stigmatized as sexually incontinent. Just as racist stereotyping vilified African American men as sexual fiends, so, too, was the sexuality of Asian American men depicted as fearsome and repulsive. And just as the prospect of blacks and whites joining together for sex, marriage, and the procreation of children sent racists into paroxysms of disapproval, so, too, did the notion of intimacy between European Americans and Asian Americans engender racist rage. Testifying in 1924 before the United States Senate Committee on Immigration, a farmer from Sacramento, California, fumed:

Near my home is an eighty-acre tract of as fine land as there is in California. On that tract lives a Japanese. With that Japanese lives a white woman. In that woman's arms is a baby. What is that baby? It isn't Japanese. It isn't white. I'll tell you what that baby is. It is a germ of the mightiest problem that ever faced this state; a problem that will make the black problem of the South look white.[74]

As we have noted, Ham Say Naim resisted the application of the Racial Integrity Act to his marriage by challenging its validity under the federal constitution. His argument was rejected, first by a trial court and then by the Virginia Supreme Court of Appeals, which handed down an opinion written by Justice Archibald Chapman Buchanan. Buchanan was at pains to distinguish Virginia's antimiscegenation law from the one struck down by the California Supreme Court in *Perez*. Echoing a point made by several law-review commentators, the justice suggested that loopholes in California's antimiscegenation law had called into question its legitimacy. For one thing, that statute (unlike all similar laws in other states) provided no criminal penalties for its violation. Moreover, California recognized interracial marriages contracted elsewhere, even in those cases in which the parties left the state expressly for the purpose of getting married in a jurisdiction where such unions were permitted, all the while intending to return to California. For some observers, the mere existence of these loopholes precluded the state from plausibly claiming that preventing interracial marriage and the proliferation of mixed-race children was an item of major importance on its agenda. Justice Buchanan stressed that the situation was very different in Virginia, where the commonwealth *did* deploy criminal penalties to enforce its prohibition against interracial marriage and specifically forbade parties from knowingly circumventing its antimiscegenation law. Buchanan emphasized, in other words, the tight fit between Virginia's statute and its stated aims. He also reaffirmed certain well-worn arguments in favor of the state's authority to enact a prohibition against interracial marriage. One such justification held that the law was perfectly race-neutral—that is, it applied equally to everyone, and therefore discriminated against no one in particular. Another asserted that while the equal-protection clause of the United States Constitution governed civil and political rights (e.g., jury service, voting, and education), it was not applicable to "social legislation" having to do with family life. That sphere of governmental concern, Justice Buchanan insisted, was instead delegated exclusively to the individual states. Buchanan noted that in *Pace v. Alabama,* the U.S. Supreme Court had upheld a law that imposed a more severe penalty for interracial as opposed to intraracial fornication, and pointed out that quite recently, the Court had declined to review the constitutionality of an antimiscegenation statute.* Buchanan and his colleagues unanimously concluded that there was no provision in the federal constitution "which prohibits the state from enacting legislation to preserve the racial integrity of its citizens, or which denies the power of the state to regulate the marriage relation so that it shall not have a mongrel breed of citizen."[75]

Ham Say Naim appealed to the United States Supreme Court. Although the Court enjoyed great latitude in selecting its docket of cases, in some situations the justices' discretion was superseded by statute. *Naim* was one of those situations. Under the terms of the federal statute governing appeals of state-court decisions to the Supreme Court, the justices were obligated either to determine the validity of the state court's judgment or to declare that the dispute failed to pose a "substantial" federal question. Several of the justices felt torn. Clearly, this case met the latter standard: powerful arguments pointed to the constitutional infirmity of Virginia's Racial Integrity Act, and indeed of all antimiscegenation laws. Yet because it came on the heels of the Court's recent invalidation of de jure segregation in public schooling, the same justices worried that it might be imprudent to consider *Naim,* which might well result in the majority striking down racial segregation at the altar. One unidentified justice reportedly remarked, "One bombshell at a time is enough."[76] That sentiment was seconded by Thurgood Marshall, the chief lawyer for the NAACP, who notably declined to support Ham Say Naim's appeal in the belief that its proximity to *Brown v. Board of Education* was a real detriment.

The problem for the justices was that the statute governing the Court's jurisdiction seemed to preclude evasion, requiring the Court definitively to confirm or reject the Virginia court's judgment. After some prodding by Justice Felix Frankfurter, however, the Court claimed that it could not properly decide the case on the basis of the available

---

*In February and April 1954, the Alabama appellate courts affirmed the criminal conviction of a black woman, Linnie Jackson, who was prosecuted for marrying a white man. See *Jackson v. State,* 72 So. 2d 114 (1954). The United States Supreme Court denied her petition for a review of her conviction (348 U.S. 888 [1954]). For more on *Jackson,* see Peter Wallenstein, "Race, Marriage, and the Law of Freedom: Alabama and Virginia, 1860s–1960s," *Chicago-Kent Law Review* 70 (1994): 371, 414–16.

record. It vacated the ruling of the state judges and remanded the case to the Virginia courts for further proceedings. The Virginia Supreme Court of Appeals subsequently declined the justices' implied invitation to get rid of the matter. It refused to send the case back to the trial judge and instead declared that the record was sufficiently clear to allow the issue in question to be decided. The state court then reaffirmed its original decision.

Newspapers in Virginia lauded the actions of the state supreme court. The headline in the Richmond *Times-Dispatch* was illustrative: "State's High Court Spurns U.S. Order."[77] Ham Say Naim's attorneys sought to capitalize on the lower court's defiance by suggesting that it provided the U.S. Supreme Court with yet another reason to review the Virginia jurists' assessment of the Racial Integrity Act. Others who were closer to the Supreme Court put the matter more bluntly. One of Justice Douglas's law clerks, for example, observed, "It will begin to look obvious if the case is not taken that the [Supreme] Court is trying to run away from its obligation to decide the case."[78] Several of the justices privately agreed, among them Chief Justice Earl Warren. Ultimately, though, Frankfurter's caution carried the day: after Virginia's supreme court reaffirmed its earlier ruling, the federal Supreme Court opted not to review the controversy further, on the ground that the state court's handling of the matter "leaves the case devoid of a properly presented federal question."[79]* Chief Justice Earl Warren prepared a memorandum that would have made public his protest. "Since I regard the order of dismissal as completely impermissible in view of this Court's obligatory jurisdiction," he wrote, "I am constrained to express my dissent. I would NOTE PROBABLE JURISDICTION AND SET THE CASE DOWN FOR ARGUMENT."[80] Warren ultimately reconsidered, however, and decided to hold off on publicizing his dis-

---

*Several distinguished commentators harshly criticized the Court's decision to duck the question posed by *Naim,* which federal law seemed to require it to address. Herbert Wechsler maintained, for example, that the Court's stratagem was "wholly without basis in the law" ("Toward Neutral Principles of Constitutional Law," in *Principles, Politics and Fundamental Law* [1961], 3, 47). See also Gerald Gunther, "The Subtle Vices of the 'Passive Virtues'—A Comment on Principle and Expediency in Judicial Review," *Columbia Law Review* 64 (1964): 1, 10–13.

content. Twelve years later, he would have another chance to express his views on the matter of the Racial Integrity Act. In the most aptly named case in all of American constitutional law, *Loving v. Virginia,* he would write the Supreme Court opinion that invalidated all remaining antimiscegenation statutes.

## Loving v. Virginia

Little suspense attended the announcement of the Court's ruling in *Loving* on June 12, 1967.[81] The decision was practically a foregone conclusion, especially since, in *McLaughlin v. Florida* (1964), the Court had already invalidated a Florida statute that criminalized interracial fornication.[82] That case had arisen from the arrest in Miami Beach, Florida, of Dewey McLaughlin, a black man, and Connie Hoffman (also known as Connie Gonzalez), a white woman. The two were subsequently convicted of violating a Florida statute providing that "any negro man and white woman, or any white man and negro woman, who are not married to each other, who shall habitually live in and occupy in the nighttime the same room shall each be punished by imprisonment not exceeding twelve months, or by fine not exceeding five hundred dollars."[83] Although Florida outlawed lewd cohabitation and fornication in general, without regard to race, convictions for those crimes required proof of intercourse. By contrast, the law proscribing Negroes and Caucasians from occupying "in the nighttime the same room" did not even mention sex; the mere fact of a black and a white of opposite sexes sharing a room after dark satisfied the statute's requirements.

The Florida Supreme Court affirmed McLaughlin and Hoffman's convictions on the strength of *Pace v. Alabama,* the 1882 decision in which the federal Supreme Court had upheld an Alabama statute providing more severe punishment for interracial than for intraracial fornication. In *McLaughlin,* the U.S. Supreme Court overruled *Pace* and reversed the Florida court. The federal justices, however, expressly declined to review that state's ban on interracial marriage, since in their view, the statute had not been called directly into question. Still, observers expected that the Court would soon seize an opportunity to strike down the nation's oldest form of segregation law—an expectation that was met when the Court nullified Virginia's authority to punish Richard Loving and Mildred Jeter for marrying each other.[84]

Loving and Jeter's marriage, in 1958, followed a courtship that had its beginnings in the 1940s, in the rural community of Central Point, in Virginia's Caroline County. Central Point had historically been a locus of a considerable amount of interracial sex among whites, blacks, and Indians. Its population clearly bore the markings of that mixing. Alongside people conventionally perceived as being of one race or another resided substantial numbers of passers. There also seems to have been a tradition of flexibility in race relations within the community, a legacy that contrasted sharply with the rigid customs that characterized Jim Crow segregation elsewhere in Virginia. Thus, for twenty-three years, Richard Loving's father, a white man, did something that would have been thought completely unacceptable in many parts of the South: he worked for a black man, a farmer who also happened to be one of the wealthiest individuals in Central Point. His son, a bricklayer by trade, spent much of his spare time as an adult, moreover, drag-racing a car that he co-owned with two black friends.

Racial flexibility, however, evidently had its limits—limits that, in someone's eyes, were dangerously exceeded when Richard Loving married his young black sweetheart, Mildred Jeter. They traveled to Washington, D.C., to say their vows, apparently believing that was all they needed to do to evade their home state's antimiscegenation law. On returning to Virginia immediately afterward, they moved in with Mildred's parents. Five weeks later, law-enforcement officials rousted them out of bed in the middle of the night on the basis of an anonymous tip. Sheriff R. Garnett Brooks asked them what they were doing in bed together. When the Lovings pointed to the District of Columbia marriage license that hung on their bedroom wall, the sheriff insisted it was invalid in Virginia. He arrested the couple and jailed them; a grand jury subsequently indicted them for violating the state's Racial Integrity Act. The Lovings waived their right to a trial by jury, pleaded guilty, and were sentenced by Judge Leon M. Bazile to a one-year jail term, which was suspended on the condition that they leave Virginia and not return together for a period of twenty-five years. Attempting to justify the commonwealth's policy, Judge Bazile maintained that "Almighty God created the races white, black, yellow, malay and red, and he placed them on separate continents. And but for the interference with his arrangements there would be no cause for [interracial] marriages. The fact that he separated the races shows that he did not intend for the races to mix."[85]

The Lovings moved to the District of Columbia and over the next five years had three children. Unhappy about their exile and hoping to get some relief, Mildred Loving in 1963 wrote a letter explaining her predicament to Attorney General Robert F. Kennedy. The Department of Justice forwarded the letter to the American Civil Liberties Union, which in turn put the Lovings in touch with Bernard S. Cohen and Philip J. Hirschkop, a pair of reform-minded attorneys who agreed to represent them pro bono. After a flurry of action in both federal and state courts, the Lovings' attorneys succeeded in inducing the Supreme Court of Virginia once again to affirm the constitutionality of the Racial Integrity Act. This time around, the U.S. Supreme Court acknowledged its probable jurisdiction, heard oral arguments, and rendered a unanimous decision written by Chief Justice Warren, which reversed the Virginia courts and, after some three hundred years, finally put an end to the enforceability of antimiscegenation laws.

Warren's *Loving* opinion is quite similar in style to the one he wrote in *Brown v. Board of Education*. It is succinct—only ten pages long—and rhetorically restrained. But whereas in *Brown,* Warren had never used the word "racism" (or any similar term), or made reference to any rationale for de jure segregation in schooling, in *Loving,* he made it a point to quote Judge Bazile's ludicrous disquisition on God's intentions and to highlight the justifications offered by the Virginia courts—namely, the preservation of "racial integrity" and the prevention of the birth of "a mongrel breed of citizens," both of which purposes he dismissed as obvious endorsements of "White Supremacy."[86] Nowhere to be found in the opinion, however, is any sustained analysis of the racial ideology that undergirded antimiscegenation laws, or any acknowledgment of the injuries these laws inflicted upon people whose "vice" consisted merely in seeking intimacy with others of the "wrong" race. Still, the opinion accomplished its main aim, which was to extend to the marriage altar the federal constitutional antidiscrimination principle: the state must not invidiously distinguish among persons on a racial basis.

In one aspect of his opinion in *Loving*, Chief Justice Warren followed completely the line of the attorney general of Virginia, who had suggested that given "conflicting views of eminent scientific authorities upon the wisdom or desirability of interracial marriages and the prevention of such alliances," the Court should refrain from taking sides on the issue. "If this Court . . . should undertake such an inquiry," the attorney general had warned, "it would quickly find itself mired in a veritable Serbonian bog of conflicting scientific opinion . . . from the physical, biological, genetic, anthropological, cultural, psychological and sociological point of view."[87] Although the Lovings' brief devoted a few pages to the proposition that "anti-miscegenation laws cause immeasurable social harm,"[88] the Court stayed away from making broad sociological assertions. Perhaps stung by the widespread criticism that his opinion in *Brown v. Board of Education* had relied too heavily on controversial sociological studies, Warren produced in *Loving* a resolutely conventional, legalistic opinion that hardly mentions the debate in academia and other extrajudicial forums over the wisdom of intermarriage or antimiscegenation laws.

In his *Loving* opinion, Warren rejected out of hand the equal-application theory that had long been the first resort of defenders of antimiscegenation statutes. "The fact of equal application," he wrote, "does not immunize the statute from the very heavy burden of justification which the Fourteenth Amendment has traditionally required of state statutes drawn according to race."[89]* Virginia's antimiscegenation law could not sustain this "very heavy burden," he asserted, because it

---

*Here, of course, Warren was creating the very "tradition" upon which his argument was based. If such a tradition had actually existed, there would have been no need for the Supreme Court to strike down segregation at the marriage altar. For more on the Warren Court's invention of traditions, see Randall Kennedy, "The Supreme Court as Teacher: Lessons from the Second Reconstruction," in Bradford P. Wilson and Ken Masugi, eds., *The Supreme Court and American Constitutionalism* (1998).

"patently" could claim "no legitimate overriding purpose independent of invidious racial discrimination."[90] As evidence of its invidiousness, Warren noted that the Racial Integrity Act prohibited only whites from marrying across racial lines; otherwise people of different races were permitted under its terms to freely intermarry among themselves. Thus, while the statute sought to protect the racial integrity of whites, it was indifferent to the racial integrity of nonwhites.* To Warren, it was hence a measure "designed to maintain White Supremacy."[91]

Pressing further, and preempting any effort to salvage the antimiscegenation statutes through their modification, Warren declared that no racial regulation of marriage would survive the Court's scrutiny. "We find the racial classifications in [the act] repugnant," he wrote, "even assuming an even-handed state purpose to protect the 'integrity' of all races."[92] Furthermore, there could be no doubt, he maintained, "that restricting the freedom to marry solely because of racial classifications violates the central meaning of the Equal Protection Clause."[93] Echoing Traynor, Warren also concluded that Virginia's Racial Integrity Act was unconstitutional because it unjustifiably infringed on a fundamental freedom. Describing marriage as "one of the basic civil rights of man," the Chief Justice insisted that "to deny this fundamental freedom

---

*The Racial Integrity Act held that "it shall . . . be unlawful for any white person . . . to marry any save a white person." The act stipulated that persons with "one-sixteenth or less of the blood of the American Indian" could be considered white, provided that they had "no other non-Caucasic blood." This limited grant of whiteness to Virginians with some small fraction of Indian ancestry has often been referred to as the "Pocahontas exception." According to one proponent of the act, the director of the commonwealth's Bureau of Vital Statistics, the aim of the exception was "to recognize as an integral and honored part of the white race the descendants of John Rolfe and Pocahontas and to protect also other white citizens of Virginia who are descendants in part of members of the civilized tribes . . . and who are of no other admixture than white and Indian." (See Walter Wadlington, "The *Loving* Case: Virginia's Anti-Miscegenation Statute in Historical Perspective," *Virginia Law Review* 52 (1966): 1189, 1202 n. 93, quoting [Walter] Plecker, "The New Family and Race Improvement," *Virginia Health Bulletin* 17, extra no. 12 [New Family ser. no. 5, 1925]: 25–26.) Ironically, under the Racial Integrity Act, the marriage of Rolfe and Pocahontas would itself have constituted a felony. For more on the broader meaning of the Pocahontas exception, see pages 483–84.

on so unsupportable a basis as the racial classifications embodied in [the act] . . . is surely to deprive all the State's citizens of liberty without due process of law. . . . Under our Constitution, the freedom to marry, or not marry, a person of another race resides with the individual and cannot be infringed by the State."[94]*

A noteworthy aspect of the *Loving* opinion is the Court's silence on whether the Fourteenth Amendment, as it was originally conceived, was intended to invalidate state antimiscegenation laws. The matter is of some interest because various members of the Supreme Court, as well as a substantial number of interested observers, have historically contended that constitutional provisions should be interpreted largely, if not wholly, by reference to the original intent of the framers of the provisions in question. As we have seen, when the Fourteenth Amendment was drawn up and ratified, the vast majority of its supporters did not envision it as a bar to antimiscegenation laws, so long as they applied equally to all persons.† Indeed, some of the most influential of the Amendment's framers explicitly announced that it would not encroach upon states' authority to impose racially neutral prohibitions on interracial marriage. This history poses a dilemma for thoroughgoing originalists who object to antimiscegenation laws. If they are to stay true to their interpretive philosophy, such originalists must concede that *Loving v. Commonwealth of Virginia* was wrongly decided.‡ This points up the inadequacy and intolerability of rigorous orginalism as a mode of constitutional interpretation. For what some have said about *Brown v. Board of Education* is no less true with respect to *Lov-*

---

*Whereas Traynor had made much of what he saw as the inherent vagueness of antimiscegenation laws, Warren declined to press that argument. "The Lovings," he wrote, "have never disputed . . . that Mrs. Loving is a 'colored person' or that Mr. Loving is a 'white person' within the meanings given those terms by the Virginia statutes" (*Loving v. Commonwealth of Virginia*, 388 U.S. 1, 5 [1967]).

†See pages 249–54.

‡To be sure, as a practical matter, *Loving* is secure. Many originalists who believe that the case was wrongly decided in the first place nonetheless favor letting it stand on the basis of *stare decisis*. Cf. Antonin Scalia, "Originalism: The Lesser Evil," *University of Cincinnati Law Review* 57 (1989): 849.

*ing v. Virginia:* any constitutional theory that cannot support its result is a constitutional theory that should not be supported.[95]*

## *After* Loving

Unlike their counterparts in *Brown v. Board of Education,* opponents of *Loving* were unable to mount anything like a "massive resistance."[96] Whereas officials openly and effectively stymied the enforcement of *Brown* in large areas of the country for decades,† opposition to the implementation of *Loving* was relatively Lilliputian. White antimiscegenationists did not riot, or promulgate congressional manifestoes condemning the Supreme Court, or close down marriage bureaus to prevent the desegregation of matrimony. Initially, of course, a few diehards refused to comply. A federal court in Delaware, for example, had to force local officials to issue a marriage license to a mixed couple.[97] In Miami, Florida, the obstinance of a county judge required the intercession of that state's supreme court, which ordered the judge to grant an interracial marriage license—a ruling in which two justices, including Florida's chief justice, dissented.[98] In 1970 a probate judge near Fort McClellan, Alabama, cited racial grounds in denying a marriage license to a white soldier and his black fiancée. The couple obtained their license only after the United States Justice Department got involved, initiating a suit that would ultimately lead to the judicial invalidation of Alabama's antimiscegenation law.[99] In Jackson, Mississippi, a local judge temporarily enjoined the issuance of a license to yet another mixed couple at the urging of the Southern National party, a white-

---

*It is a delicious irony that the most fervent champion of originalism on the Supreme Court in recent memory is an African American—Justice Clarence Thomas—who was married in Virginia to a white woman named Virginia. See Samuel Marcossan, "Colonizing the Constitution of Originalism: Clarence Thomas at the Rubicon," *Law and Inequality* 16 (1998): 429.

†In a manifestation of resistance to *Brown* that has received too little attention, school officials in some jurisdictions began to assign boys and girls to separate schools when, after a long delay, school districts were finally forced to undertake racial desegregation. See *Moore v. Tangipahoa Parish School Board,* 304 F. Supp. 244 (1969); Robert B. Barnett, "The Constitutionality of Sex Separation in School Desegregation Plans," *University of Chicago Law Review* 37 (1970): 296.

supremacist organization. The delay was cut short when federal courts intervened.[100]

While *Loving v. Virginia* rendered unenforceable the antimiscegenation provisions that remained on the statute books and in the constitutions of several states,* many in those jurisdictions felt it was essential to eradicate those prohibitions entirely, and not allow them to stand as "ghost[s] of a racist past in cold print."[101] Over the course of the next quarter century, that step was taken in one state after another. Virginia repealed its antimiscegenation law in 1968, and West Virginia, Texas, Florida, Oklahoma, and Missouri struck theirs from the books in 1969, as did North Carolina in 1970, Georgia, Louisiana, and Mississippi in 1972, Delaware and Kentucky in 1974, and Tennessee in 1978. South Carolina voters revoked the antimiscegenation provision in that state's constitution in 1998, and in November 2000 Alabama at last removed from its constitution the clause banning the legislature

---

*Loving* also struck a blow for the freedom to marry, a right that extends far beyond the color line to include those discriminated against because of mental retardation, penury, addiction, and other historical bases for exclusion. See the Reverend Robert F. Drinan's prescient article "The *Loving* Decision and the Freedom to Marry," *Ohio State Law Journal* 29 (1968): 358.

Those who seek to uproot exclusions from marriage based on sexual orientation have fervently wielded *Loving* as precedential support for their cause. See, e.g., Mark Strasser, *Legally Wed: Same-Sex Marriage and the Constitution* (1997), 66–67; William N. Eskridge Jr., *The Case for Same-Sex Marriage* (1996), 153–63; Andrew Koppelman, "Same-Sex Marriage and Public Policy: The Miscegenation Precedents," 16 *Quinnipiac Law Review* 105 (1996); James Trosino, "Note: American Wedding: Same-Sex Marriage and the Miscegenation Analogy," *Boston University Law Review* 73 (1993): 93, 107–16.

On the other side, opponents of same-sex marriage strenuously reject the analogy to *Loving*. See, e.g., David Orgon Coolidge, "Playing the *Loving* Card: Same-Sex Marriage and the Politics of Analogy," *Brigham Young University Journal of Public Law* 12 (1998): 201; Lynn D. Wardle, "A Critical Analysis of Constitutional Claims for Same-Sex Marriage," *Brigham Young University Law Review,* 1996, p. 1.

It is my own belief that the struggle to secure the right to marry regardless of the genders of the parties involved will be won in the not so distant future. That achievement, I am convinced, will represent a real step up in the moral elevation of American democracy—a step facilitated, in large part, by previous struggles over race relations.

from authorizing interracial marriage.\* Even at that late date, the outcome was soberingly close, with 40 percent of Alabama's electorate voting to *retain* the prohibition. Still, with that last, long-delayed resolution, formal antimiscegenation provisions were finally erased completely from the American legal system.[102]

---

\*"The Legislature shall never pass any law to authorize or legalize any marriage between any white person and a Negro or descendant of a Negro" (Constitution of Alabama, art. 4, sec. 102 [1901–2000]).

# SEVEN

# Racial Passing

In Massachusetts in the early 1890s, a man named Asa P. Morse proposed marriage to one Anna D. Van Houten. She accepted, only to be informed not long after that he was withdrawing his offer because he had learned that she was of Negro ancestry. She sued him for breach of promise to marry. In his own defense, he charged that she had obtained that promise from him by fraudulently concealing her racial lineage.[1]

At trial, the presiding judge instructed the jury that while, as a matter of law, Van Houten had had a duty to answer truthfully any inquiries Morse made of her, she had been under no obligation to relate to him all the circumstances of her life. Morse apparently conceded that he had never questioned his former fiancée about her racial background. Van Houten won a jury verdict, but her victory was overturned on appeal, on the ground that the trial judge's jury instructions had been faulty. According to the Supreme Judicial Court of Massachusetts, the trial judge had erred by failing to instruct the jury that fraud could also be perpetrated through the assertion of a half-truth. The higher court ruled that "a partial and fragmentary disclosure, accompanied by the willful concealment of material and qualifying facts, would be as much of a fraud as actual misrepresentation."[2] Thus, in this case, if the plaintiff had made favorable statements about her family, she would have been obliged to reveal *everything* material about it. She did not have to say a word about her relatives, but if she *did* talk about them, "she was bound not only to state truly the facts which she narrated, but [to refrain from suppressing or concealing] any facts which were necessary to a correct understanding on the part of the defendant of the facts which she stated."[3]

The Massachusetts justices seem to have suspected Van Houten of painting a portrait of her Charleston, South Carolina, family that had led her fiancé to have a certain impression of it, even as she withheld other facts that would have led him to a very different conclusion. Likely to be established as fact, for instance, was testimony given at trial that the second husband of Anna Van Houten's mother was a colored barber who was also reputed to be Anna's father, and that her mother, too, was about one eighth black. Such omissions, the court asserted, would amount to fraud, which in turn would permit any promises based upon those omissions to be withdrawn without liability. On that ground, the court voided Van Houten's jury verdict and ordered a retrial.

The Supreme Judicial Court of Massachusetts nowhere indicated in *Morse* that it cared much about the character of the relationship between the parties. The case, however, did not involve a breach-of-contract action between two strangers who were, say, buying and selling a carriage; rather, it involved a breach of promise to *marry*. Given that degree of intimacy, it seemed appropriate to expect of both parties greater trust and candor than would ordinarily prevail between contracting partners. It was arguable, in other words, that because she planned to marry him, Van Houten had a fiduciary duty to share with Morse information about herself that she knew or should have known would be important to him, even if doing so might prove detrimental to what she perceived as her own best interests. From this perspective, she erred if (as it appears) she kept silent about aspects of her family that she knew (or should have known) would affect Morse's desire to propose. Her conduct could be said to reflect poorly on her character in that it evinced her willingness to be evasive with respect to a matter that her fiancé would probably consider significant. The argument would run, then, that in the self-denying estate of marriage, all opportunism should be strongly discouraged.

That said, in courtship as in business, it is universally acknowledged that most people will try to put their best foot forward, a strategy that often entails minimizing, if not altogether obscuring, blemishes that, if seen, might alienate an otherwise receptive potential partner. Here it bears recalling Judge Ruffin's observation that "it is not to be expected that [courting] parties will declare their own defects."* Moreover, while marriage should and does impose an added burden of candor between spouses, it should not wholly strip them of defenses that any individual can claim against the world—including a zone of privacy that lies beyond the grasp even of a marital partner. It is at least arguable that certain facts about a person's background fall within this zone, and that in a racist society, racial ancestry may be among those facts.[4] Finally, we may well ask why someone in Van Houten's position should be prompted by law or moral sentiments to propitiate in any way the sorts of racial biases that Morse harbored or to which he was reacting. For law or public morality to require Van Houten to tell Morse of her colored lineage because she knew it would matter to him would perhaps constitute an instance of undue deference to a destructive prejudice.

Given all that, what *is* the proper legal and moral response to this case and others like it? Any attempt to formulate an answer requires familiarity with the phenomenon of passing.

### Passing: A Definition

Passing is a deception that enables a person to adopt specific roles or identities from which he or she would otherwise be barred by prevailing social standards. The classic racial passer in the United States has long been the "white Negro," an individual whose physical appearance allows him to present himself as "white" but whose "black" lineage (typically only a very partial black ancestry) makes him a Negro according to dominant racial rules. There is a difference between the passer and the person who is merely mistaken about his or her racial identity—for example, the man who, having been told all his life that he is white, thinks of himself as white, and holds himself out to be white, though he and everyone else in the locale would change that

---

*See pages 63–65.

identification to "black" were the facts of his ancestry known.* For a time, Gregory Howard Williams lived just such a life.[5]† The son of a white mother and a light-skinned Negro father who pretended to be white, he assumed as a child that he, too, was white.‡ Then, in 1954, when Williams was ten years old, his parents divorced, and he and his brother learned that they were "black" according to the custom by which any known Negro ancestry made a person a Negro. Williams has written vividly of being told of his "new" racial identity:

> I never had heard anything crazier in my life! How could Dad tell us such a mean lie? I glanced [at him as] he sat grim-faced and erect, staring straight ahead. I saw my father as I had never seen him before. The veil dropped from his face and fea-

---

*In a reversal of this scenario, some blacks have unknowingly been perceived as white. St. Clair Drake and Horace R. Cayton, in their book Black Metropolis, recounted the experience of a fair-skinned Negro woman who was initially treated with respect by a white store owner. Unbeknownst to her, the proprietor had taken her to be a white person. The woman learned of the mistake only weeks later, when she returned with her darker-skinned daughter. Seeing the woman in a new light, the storekeeper immediately declined any further contact. (Black Metropolis: A Study of Negro Life in a Northern City [1945; reprint, 1961], 160.) For similar but more recent examples of racial "mistakes," see Toi Derricotte, The Black Notebooks: An Interior Journey (1997); Judy Scales-Trent, Notes of a White Black Woman: Race, Color, Community (1995).

†Williams later became a distinguished legal academic, serving as dean of Ohio State University Law School and president of the American Association of Law Schools.

‡What made Williams's father a "Negro" was simply the ascendant convention that defined as a Negro anyone with a specified fraction of Negro ancestry. As we have seen, lineage has not been the only definer of race; appearance, associations, reputation, and conduct have also been read as signifiers of racial identity (see pages 3–9). But ancestry has always constituted a primary marker.

Williams's father was the son of a Negro woman who worked as a maid in the household of a rich white family in Bowling Green, Kentucky; she was impregnated by a young white man in that household. When her pregnancy began to show, her employer fired her. After the baby was born, whites and blacks alike none too gently suggested that Sallie Williams leave town with her "white nigger" baby. She resisted those demands until her older brother was murdered by unknown assailants; his mutilated body was found lashed to a railroad track. Fearing for her son's safety, Sallie Williams fled to Muncie, Indiana, which became home to Williams's father. (Gregory Howard Williams, Life on the Color Line: The True Story of a White Boy Who Discovered He Was Black [1995], 62.)

tures. Before my eyes he was transformed from a swarthy Italian to his true self—a high-yellow mulatto. My Father was a Negro! We were colored! After ten years in Virginia on the white side of the color line, I knew what that meant.[6]*

In holding himself out as white *before* he learned of his father's secret, Williams was simply mistaken. In occasionally doing so *after* he was informed of his "true" racial identity, however, Williams was passing. As I define the term, in other words, passing requires that a person be consciously engaged in concealment.† Such a person must know about his African American lineage, or black "blood," and either stay quiet about it—in the hope that the combination of silence and a non-black appearance will lead observers to perceive him as white—or expressly assert that he *is* white (knowing all the while that the assertion is false according to ascendant social understandings).[7] Estimates regarding the incidence of passing have varied greatly. In the late 1940s Walter White suggested that each year, "approximately 12,000 white-skinned Negroes disappear[ed]" into white society.[8]‡ During the same

*Trying to prepare his sons for their new lives as blacks, Anthony Williams said, "Life is going to be different from now on. In Virginia you were white boys. In Indiana you're going to be colored boys. I want you to remember that you're the same today that you were yesterday. But people in Indiana will treat you differently" (ibid., 34).

†The line can be thin indeed between concealing a racial identity and neglecting to anticipate and correct possible misconceptions. In the 1950s Raven Wilkinson, a light-skinned African American dancer with the Ballet Russe de Monte Carlo, toured the American South, staying with her white colleagues in whites-only hotels. It could be argued that under those conditions, her silence was tantamount to concealment, and that she was thus passing. It could also be argued, however, that more than mere silence should be required before a person is deemed a passer, lest the definition impose upon anyone in Wilkinson's situation an affirmative duty to disabuse observers of their possible misperception. As it turns out, when pushed to clarify her position, Ms. Wilkinson chose not to pass. When the manager of a Jim Crow hotel asked her directly if she was black, she answered yes and was ordered to leave. See the excellent film *I'll Make Me a World,* aired on PBS (1998); Caryn James, "Black Artists Grappling with Profound Questions of Art and Race," *New York Times,* February 1, 1999.

‡For discussions of Walter White's own encounters with passing and interracial marriage, see pages 287–89.

period, Roi Ottley maintained that there were some five million "white Negroes" in the United States, and that their number was growing by forty to fifty thousand annually.[9]* Professor John H. Burma's figures were considerably lower: in 1946 he posited that some 110,000 blacks lived on the white side of the color line, with between 2,500 and 2,750 more passing every year.[10] The secretive nature of "crossing over" precluded the possibility of obtaining definitive statistics, but it is clear that by the middle of the twentieth century, a great many African Americans at the very least claimed to know others who were engaged in passing.[11]

## Passing Stories

"Blacks" have passed for "white" under a wide range of circumstances.† One extraordinary episode occurred in 1848, when Ellen Craft, the daughter of a master and his slave mistress, escaped from bondage by train, boat, and carriage on a four-day journey from Macon, Georgia, to Philadelphia. Craft presented herself as white, employing her slave husband, William, as part of her disguise: he pretended to be her servant. There was one more twist: Ellen Craft traveled not as a white woman but as a white *man*. In order to obtain freedom for herself and her husband, she thus briefly traversed gender as well as racial lines.‡

---

*Recall that Ottley later became the adoptive father of the little girl at the center of *Green v. City of New Orleans;* see pages 37–38.

†Racial passing has not been all one-way: whites have also, on occasion, passed for black. Howard Griffin and Grace Halsell did so on a temporary basis to gather information about what it was "really" like to be black. Their journalistic exposés, *Black Like Me* (1961) and *Soul Sister* (1969), are the end products of that research. Some white spouses of Negroes have claimed to be black themselves in an effort to deflect the disapproval of individuals and authorities opposed to interracial marriage. See Kathryn Talalay, *Composition in Black and White: The Life of Philippa Schuyler* (1995), 39; Joseph Golden, "Patterns of Negro-White Intermarriage," *American Sociological Review* 19 (1954): 144, 147. See pages 333–38 herein.

‡The Crafts' planning was extraordinary. Because Ellen did not know how to write, she kept her right arm in a sling to forestall any requests to sign documents certifying ownership of William. To dissuade strangers from striking up a conversation with his wife, William applied a poultice to her face.

Even after the Crafts escaped from slavery, they remained vulnerable to recapture, and indeed, slave-catchers from Georgia attempted to arrest them in Boston in 1850. They fled to England, returning to the United States only after the Civil War,

In contrast to the Crafts, who passed for white to journey north and escape slavery, Walter White passed for white to journey south and investigate lynchings.[12] White (introduced earlier in the context of his controversial interracial marriage)* was fair-skinned, blue-eyed, and blond-haired, the son of light-complexioned Negroes who were stalwarts of Atlanta's black middle class. His mother worked at home, and his father was a mail carrier. Due to their coloring, the Whites sometimes found themselves in the middle of racial misunderstandings. When White's mother and sisters boarded segregated streetcars, for example, white men who thought the women were also white often jeered at them as they went to sit in the Negro seats. Much more serious and tragic in its consequences was an incident that took place in 1931, after Walter White's father was struck by an automobile driven by a white physician who practiced at Grady Hospital in Atlanta. At that time, the hospital was divided into two sections. The white section was clean and renovated; the black section, dirty and dilapidated. The physician took the injured man to the white section of the hospital, but before long, a visit by a son-in-law apprised the staff of the "error." In his autobiography, Walter White recounted what happened next: his father "was snatched from the examination table lest he contaminate the 'white' air, and taken hurriedly across the street in a driving downpour . . . to the 'Negro' ward," where he died sixteen days later.[13]

Although Walter White could have passed, he instead decided at an early age to associate himself with the African American community. The crucible in which his sense of communal attachment was formed

---

when slavery had been abolished. See William Craft, *Running a Thousand Miles for Freedom: The Escape of William and Ellen Craft from Slavery* (1860). See also R. J. M. Blackett, "The Odyssey of William and Ellen Craft," in Louisiana University Press's 1999 reissue of Craft, *Running a Thousand Miles for Freedom;* Ellen M. Weinauer, "'A Most Respectable Looking Gentleman': Passing, Possession, and Transgression in *Running a Thousand Miles for Freedom,*" in Elaine K. Ginsberg, ed., *Passing and the Fictions of Identity* (1996).

Slave owners who posted rewards for the return of runaways sometimes warned that their human property—often their own children—might be evading capture by passing for white. See Werner Sollors, *Neither Black nor White yet Both: Thematic Explorations of the Interracial Literature* (1997), 255.

*See page 110.

was the Atlanta riot of 1906.[14] Goaded by false stories about rapes of white women by Negro men, a white mob terrorized blacks in Georgia's capital in an awful explosion of racial hatred. Caught in the city amid marauding whites, young Walter and his father escaped grave injury thanks only to the camouflage provided them by their light complexions. They witnessed terrible crimes being committed against other Negroes:

> We saw a lame Negro bootblack . . . pathetically try to outrun a mob of whites. Less than a hundred yards from us the chase ended. We saw clubs and fists descending to the accompaniment of savage shouting and cursing. Suddenly a voice cried, "There goes another nigger!" Its work done, the mob went after new prey. The body with the withered foot lay dead in a pool of blood in the street.[15]

At one point, a mob menacingly approached the Whites' home, urged on by a participant who yelled, "That's where the nigger mail carrier lives! Let's burn it down! It's too nice for a nigger to live in!" White's father had resolved that he and his son would defend the family homestead with firearms if necessary. He said to Walter "in a voice as quiet as though he were asking me to pass him sugar at the breakfast table . . . 'Son, don't shoot until the first man puts his foot on the lawn and then—don't you miss.'" At that moment, White related,

> there opened up within me a great awareness; I knew who I was. I was a Negro, a human being with an invisible pigmentation which marked me as a person to be hunted, hanged, abused, discriminated against, kept in poverty and ignorance, in order that those whose skin was white would have readily at hand a proof of their superiority. . . . [That way,] no matter how low a white man fell, he could always hold fast to the smug conviction that he was superior to two-thirds of the world's population.[16]

As it happened, the mob never did attack the White house; instead it quickly retreated after being fired upon by the family's black neighbors. Later in life, Walter White would devote much of his attention to defending African Americans against racially motivated violence. His own principal weapon was exposure: on behalf of the NAACP, he gathered facts about lynchings and other atrocities and strategically publicized them in a manner designed to arouse American public opinion. The daring way he went about his mission brought him close to danger. In 1919 he traveled to Phillips County, Arkansas, to investigate the deaths of some 250 blacks who had been murdered in an effort to discourage collective organization by African American cotton farmers. When whites in Phillips County became aware of White's purpose, he was forced to make a hurried escape by train. "You're leaving, mister, just when the fun is going to start," White recalled being told by the conductor. "A damned yellow nigger is down here passing for white and the boys are going to get him." White later observed, "No matter what the distance, I shall never take as long a train ride as that one seemed to be."[17]

Blacks have engaged in temporary passing in many other, less dramatic settings. To advance their professional ambitions, for instance, some have passed as white during the workday, from nine to five, while presenting themselves as African American in their private lives.[18]* Chronicling this phenomenon, "White by Day . . . Negro by Night," a 1952 article in *Ebony* magazine, offered up the following anecdote:

> One girl who passed to get work as a clerk in a Chicago [L]oop department store thought she had lost her job when an oldtime, well-meaning friend of her mother came in and said in happy surprise, "Well, Baby, it sure is good to see this store is finally hiring colored girls." Fortunately she was overheard

---

*Some commentators believe that a few black professional baseball players disguised themselves as whites (or as Indians, Cubans, or Mexicans) and played in the white major leagues prior to Jackie Robinson breaking the color barrier in 1948. At one point, the manager of the Baltimore Orioles attempted to pass off black second baseman Charlie Grant as an American Indian, even going so far as to rename him Chief Tokohama. That effort failed, however, and Grant never played in a regular-season game. See Jules Tygiel, *Baseball's Great Experiment: Jackie Robinson and His Legacy* (1983; reprint, 1984), 25.

only by one other clerk who was a liberal and a good friend of the girl who was passing and the secret did not get out.[19]

Other blacks have passed as white in order to shop, stay, or eat meals at racially exclusive establishments.[20] Writing in the 1940s, sociologists St. Clair Drake and Horace R. Cayton reported interviewing some light-skinned Negroes in Chicago who had gone to such places "just to see what they are like and to get a thrill."[21]

My own mother, Rachel Kennedy, passed as white many times, not visually but aurally. When obliged to speak on the telephone with one authority or another about some important matter—whether to lodge a consumer complaint, deal with the police, or seek employment or educational opportunities—she would adopt an accent that most listeners would associate with a white person. She put on countless stellar performances before an appreciative household audience that viewed these episodes as comic interludes in the American racial tragedy.*

Still other "blacks" have passed for "white" on a long-term or even permanent basis. Several of the children whom Thomas Jefferson sired by Sally Hemings eventually held themselves out as white. Beverly and Harriet Hemings were the first to do so, in the early 1820s, shedding their African American racial identities even as they fled slavery at Monticello. Their sibling Eston Hemings also passed for white; he was emancipated along with his older brother Madison Hemings in 1827 by a provision in his father's will. These brothers remained in Virginia with their mother until her death in 1835, at which point they moved to southern Ohio. By then both had started new families of their own with mixed-race women who, like them, were the offspring of relationships

---

*A young black student at Harvard Law School recently informed me that she and her black friends bargain for expensive items such as automobiles over the telephone or on the Internet, rather than in person; that way, she explained, they could pass for white and thus avoid paying the inflated prices often quoted to black female consumers. See Ian Ayres and Peter Siegelman, "Race and Gender Discrimination in Bargaining for a New Car," *American Economic Review* 85 (1995): 304. See also Debra J. Dickerson, *An American Story* (2000), xi, describing racial passing on the telephone; Jerry Kang, "Cyber-Race," *Harvard Law Review* 113 (2000): 1130, on passing on the Internet.

between masters and slaves. The status, color, and racial background of the Hemings brothers' choice of mates was unlikely to have been accidental. As historians Lucia Stanton and Dianne Swann-White have observed, both men probably sought marriages that would ensure their children of inheriting, in addition to freedom, "a passport to upper-class status within the black community and the probable option to enter the white race."[22]

In Ohio, Madison and Eston Hemings provided modest livings for their families. While the older of the two brothers distinguished himself as a carpenter, the younger made a name for himself as a professional musician. Though Madison was evidently content to restrict his orbit to the small black community in the rural area where they lived, Eston seems to have wanted to cross the race line. That was no simple proposition, however: "Notwithstanding all his accomplishments," one journalist noted, there remained "an impassable gulf" between Eston Hemings and whites—"even the lowest of them."[23] As another journalist later commented, "A nigger was a nigger in those days and that settled it."[24] In fact, the Hemings brothers *were* considered white under Virginia law and arguably under Ohio law as well.* As a matter of social practice, though, anyone with a "visible admixture" of colored blood was deemed by whites to be a Negro. Although Eston Hemings was described as being only "very slightly colored,"[25] for most whites, that was sufficient to stigmatize him. While Madison Hemings stayed in Ohio and became a much respected member of his black community, Eston left. Frustrated by racial exclusion from the jury box, the witness stand, the voting booth, and public schools, he moved his family to Madison, Wisconsin, where he adopted a new name and a new racial identity. He became Eston H. Jefferson, a white man.

---

*For a long time, Virginia classified as "white" any free person who was more than three quarters Caucasian. In Ohio, racial categories were more ambiguous, at least until 1859, when the state decreed that anyone with discernible colored ancestry was to be deemed colored. See Lucia Stanton and Dianne Swann-White, "Bonds of Memory: Identity and the Hemings Family," in Jan Lewis, Peter S. Onuf, and Jane E. Lewis, eds., *Sally Hemings and Thomas Jefferson: History, Memory, and Civic Culture* (1999), 182 n. 5.

The children of Madison and Eston Hemings identified themselves as white. One of Madison's sons, William Beverly Hemings, enlisted in an all-white regiment in the Civil War; another, James Madison Hemings, disappeared and is thought by some in the family to have silently crossed the color line. Neither of these sons married, perhaps for fear that marriage would entail the revelation of the family's closeted racial background.* Eston Hemings's daughter, Anna, lived as a white woman and married a white man. Both of her brothers served as officers in white regiments in the Union Army; Beverly F. Jefferson married a white woman and had a comfortable life as the owner of a prosperous hotel, while John Wayles Jefferson remained single and became a wealthy cotton broker. A few in the Hemings family identified themselves as black. During World War II, one of Madison Hemings's descendants was assigned to a white military unit but refused to join it, demanding instead to be transferred to a black unit. In the 1970s, when Madison Hemings's great-great-great-grandson was but a youngster, he called himself black even when a white neighborhood tough pummeled him repeatedly, screaming, "You're white, I know you're white."[26] These were exceptions, though; to a very large extent, the members of the Hemings family chose to become white.

The children of Michael Morris Healy—a white, Irish-born Georgia planter—and Eliza Clark, one of his slaves, furnishes another remarkable example of permanent passing.[27] Prevented by state law from freeing his slaves, Michael Healy sent his children north, so they could be educated and released from bondage in the event of their father's demise. Several of these children went on to notable careers. James Augustine Healy (1830–1900) was a member of the first graduating class of the College of the Holy Cross in Worcester, Massachusetts. He pursued clerical studies in Canada and France, was ordained in Boston, and served for twenty-five years as the Catholic bishop of Portland, Maine. His brother Alexander Sherwood Healy (1836–75) studied music and canon law in Rome and became rector of

---

*An alternative explanation, of course, is that one or both may have been gay or simply averse to the bonds of matrimony.

the Catholic cathedral in Boston. Michael Augustine Healy (1839–1904) rose to the rank of captain in the Revenue Cutter Service (the precursor to the Coast Guard) and commanded an ice ship off the coast of Alaska. Patrick Francis Healy (1834–1910) graduated from Holy Cross, joined the Society of Jesus, studied at several of Europe's most elite universities, and eventually became the president of Georgetown University.

Benefiting from luck and talent, the Healys were also assisted in pursuing their ambitions by financial wherewithal, the absence of any discernible "taint" of color (except for Alexander Sherwood Healy), and an attitude about their ambiguous racial status that allowed them to separate themselves, with apparent ease, from African Americans. Such detachment was perhaps a sine qua non of their ambitions, for it was the very institution of slavery that provided the capital investment needed to generate the income that fueled the younger Healys' upward mobility. After their father died, his slaves were hired out and then sold for a substantial sum that endowed trust funds for his children.*

For the most part, the Healy children were perceived to be "white." Even the one darker sibling, Alexander Sherwood Healy—whose African heritage, according to one observer, "shew[ed] distinctly in his exterior"[28]—was given a free pass by the Catholic bureaucracy, which seemingly averted its eyes from his "taint." It likewise apparently overlooked the fact that Michael Healy and Eliza Clark had never been properly married. This might have posed an insuperable obstacle to those of the Healys who sought advancement within the Church, since under canon law, special dispensation was required to ordain any candidate for the priesthood who was illegitimate. In the Healys' case, however, the Catholic hierarchy simply looked the other way. The brothers made that easy to do: they revealed as little as possible about

---

*When a slave woman named Margaret sued for her freedom in 1856, agents for the Healy estate contested her claim and prevailed in court, whereupon she was immediately sold, along with three of her children—each of them to a different purchaser. See James M. O'Toole, "Passing: Race, Religion, and the Healy Family, 1820–1920," *Proceedings of the Massachusetts Historical Society* CVIII (1998): 14.

the facts of their origin, distanced themselves from other blacks, and declined to undertake any discernible efforts to improve the lot of African Americans. At base, though, the Healys' noninvolvement in racial matters was no mere tactical decision; rather, it reflected their belief that they were white and no more closely related to blacks than any other white Americans. When James Healy attended Holy Cross, he noted in his diary without objection the comments of classmates regarding "the niggers," and on graduation night he attended, with no apparent sense of irony, a blackface minstrelsy show. He dismissed William Lloyd Garrison as "a fool" and delighted that at a local rally, abolitionists had managed to raise only $1.47 toward the purchase of a slave whom they intended to free. Although a Unionist in the Civil War, James Healy opposed the racial egalitarianism of the Radical Republicans, concerned that they would wrongly subordinate the restoration of sectional harmony to "the protection, the equalization & the super-elevation of the negro."[29] He and his siblings were conservative, religiously devout individualists who thought of themselves as white even if most other Americans, given a full accounting of their lineage, would have classified them otherwise. Yet another ironic aspect of the Healys' saga is that they have been posthumously transformed into blacks by latter-day revisionists who claim them as African American pioneers.[30] In *The Negro Almanac,* for instance, James Augustine Healy is proudly described as "the first Negro Catholic Bishop in the United States," a distinction that he himself would have vehemently disavowed.[31]

Another person who has been championed as a black pioneer, in spite of the fact that she, too, passed for white during much of her lifetime, is Anita Hemings,* whom Vassar College touts as its first black graduate.[32] Born in Boston to a family that identified itself as "black," Hemings evidently shed that identification when she matriculated at Vassar. A suspicious roommate asked her father to investigate the Hemings family, and in the course of doing so, he learned of their negritude and revealed Anita's secret. Although Hemings's fellow students and

---

*No evidence has as yet come to light that Anita Hemings was related to the Hemings family of Virginia.

her teachers felt betrayed by what they viewed as her deceit, college officials permitted her to graduate. Her attempt at passing nevertheless provided tasty fodder for the newspapers. According to a story in *The World* in 1897,

> Society and educational circles . . . are profoundly shocked by the announcement . . . that one of the graduating class of Vassar College this year was a Negro girl, who concealing her race, entered the college, took the four years' course, and finally confessed the truth to a professor. . . . She has been known as one of the most beautiful young women who ever attended the great institution of learning, and even now women who receive her in their homes as their equal do not deny her beauty. . . . Her manners were those of a person of gentle birth, and her intelligence and ability were recognized alike by her classmates and professors.[33]

Hemings's choice of a husband further enmeshed her in passing. She married a "white Negro" physician, Andrew Love, who himself passed for white in order to build a prosperous medical practice catering to the rich on Madison Avenue in New York City. Their daughter, Ellen Love, a 1927 graduate of Vassar, also passed. A professional actress, she tried out for the role of Scarlett O'Hara in *Gone with the Wind,* maintaining subsequently that she had been told the reason she didn't get the part was that her waist was too large.

The most sensational legal case arising from an alleged effort to pass was a lawsuit initiated in 1924 pitting Alice Jones against Leonard "Kip" Rhinelander.[34] Jones was the daughter of a white mother and a black father, a couple of modest means. Rhinelander's parents, by contrast, moved in the highest circles of wealthy white New York society. When they learned that their son had married a colored waitress, they insisted that he end the relationship. Buckling to their demands six weeks into his marriage, Rhinelander sought an annulment, claiming that Jones had deceived him regarding her race. Initially, he alleged that she had tricked him by falsely stating she was white; later, he changed his story, asserting that she had misled him not by outright lying but instead, more subtly, by silently yet knowingly exploiting his mistaken belief that she was Caucasian.

Jones's defense put the legal proceedings on the front pages of the New York dailies for weeks. Her attorney argued that her husband could not have been ignorant as to her racial identity because, in terms of her physiognomy, he knew *everything* there was to know about her. Moreover, the lawyer noted, Rhinelander could not rightly claim to have been hoodwinked, given that he had, so to speak, looked under the hood prior to their marriage. To support this argument, the defense put into evidence two dramatic exhibits. The first was correspondence that clearly indicated the couple had had extensive premarital sexual relations.* The other was Jones herself: her attorney obtained permission for his client to disrobe and show herself, behind closed doors, to the all-male, all-white jury. His purpose in doing so was to demonstrate to the jurors that there were aspects of her physiognomy, including her

---

*One of the letters read, in part:

> My own dearest girl,
>     . . . I took everyone of your notes which I received at General delivery and read them while lying on the bed. Oh! Blessed sweetheart of mine, some of the things you told me brought tears to my blue eyes. . . . When you mentioned the time when we were in bed together at the [Hotel] "Marie Antoinette" something that belonged to me acted the way it usually did whenever I am with you darling, and it just longed for the touch of your passionate little fingers, which have so often made me very, very happy. You know, don't you old Scout, what that "something" is and how it acted when you began being naughty!! Oh, sweetheart, many, many nights when I lay in bed and think about my darling girl it acts the very same way, and longs for your warm body to crawl upon me, take it in your soft, smooth hands, and then work it up very slowly between your open legs!!!! . . .
>
>                                                            Your ever true,
>                                                            loving Len

See Jamie L. Wacks, "Reading Race, Rhetoric and the Female Body: The *Rhinelander* Case and the 1920s American Culture" (senior thesis, Harvard University, 1995). In another letter, Rhinelander asked Jones, "Do you remember, honeybunch, how I used to put my head between your legs and how I used to caress you with my lips and tongue?" (Ibid.)

nipples, that would have put Rhinelander on notice about her race. In his summation to the jury, Jones's attorney stressed that the plaintiff had had "unlimited opportunities to look [at the defendant's body]." He continued:

> I let you gentlemen look at a portion of what he saw. You saw Alice's back above the bust. You saw her breast. You saw a portion of her upper leg. He saw all of her body. And you are going to tell me that he never suspected that she had colored blood! . . . You saw . . . with your own eyes . . . that colored blood was coursing through her veins.[35]*

In his closing argument, Rhinelander's attorney made an all-out plea for the jury to register, through its verdict, its disdain for interracial marriage. "There isn't a father among you," he declared, "who would not rather see his son in his casket than . . . see him wedded to a mulatto woman."[36] The jury nevertheless found in Jones's favor.†

### Judging Passers

Passing has occasioned a broad spectrum of responses, many of them negative. Aggrieved slave owners, for example, regarded as treacherous thieves those runaway slaves who passed for white in their attempt to escape to freedom.[37] Segregationists, for their part, condemned white Negroes as an insidious danger that threatened to infect fatally the American body politic: the passers might, it was feared, "contaminate" white bloodlines by marrying unsuspecting Caucasians. According to historian Joel Williamson, "Southern whites in the early twentieth century became paranoid about invisible blackness."[38] Draping white-supremacist ideology with a mantle of patriotism, Thomas Dixon warned

---

*Jones was never called to testify. One close student of the case suggests that her attorney never put her on the witness stand because she herself sincerely believed that she was white and would have said so if asked, thereby wrecking her legal defense. See Wacks, "Reading Race."

†For another saga of passing in the context of divorce litigation, see William B. Gatewood Jr.'s excellent article "The Perils of Passing: The McCorys of Omaha, Nebraska," *History*, summer 1990, 64.

in his Negrophobic 1902 novel *The Leopard's Spots,* "This Republic can have no future if racial lines are broken and its proud citizenship sinks to the level of a mongrel breed." Dixon believed, with one of his characters, that "a single drop" of Negro blood "kinks the hair, flattens the nose, thickens the lip, puts out the light of intellect, and lights the fires of brutal passions."[39]

The most thoroughgoing effort in American history to prevent and punish passing began in Virginia in the 1920s, with the birth of the Anglo-Saxon Clubs of America.[40] A horror of interracial intimacy and passing prompted club activists to lobby in favor of extending Jim Crow segregation and ferreting out passers, especially those whose children were enrolled in white public schools.* Their racial phobia also inspired them to press the Virginia legislature to narrow the state's definition of precisely who qualified as white, and the regulations governing matrimony. Until 1910 Virginia law classified as white anyone who was no more than one quarter black; after 1910 the allowable fraction was reduced to one sixteenth. In 1924 the Virginia legislature slammed the door shut (almost) all the way, decreeing that "the term 'white person' shall apply only to the person who has no trace whatsoever of any blood other than Caucasian."[41] In deference to the descendants of Pocahontas and John Rolfe, however, the legislature did authorize whites to marry persons "who have one-sixteenth or less of the blood of the American Indian"—a concession that the members of the Anglo-Saxon Clubs bitterly denounced, characterizing it as a loophole through which Negro Indians would be allowed to slip into the bosom of white society. Complaining later of what he viewed as lax enforcement of the Racial Integrity Act, a leader of the Anglo-Saxon Clubs of America complained that "Indians are springing up all over the state as if by

---

*The Anglo-Saxon Clubs also targeted other areas of American life in which they perceived white racial purity to be imperiled. In 1926 they persuaded the Virginia legislature to mandate the racial segregation of audiences for all public performances. This law was aimed specifically at the predominantly black Hampton Institute, which had hosted and sponsored racially mixed audiences and groups of performers, including an all-white glee club directed by a black conductor. See Barbara Bair, "Remapping the Black/White Body: Sexuality, Nationalism, and Biracial Antimiscegenation Activism in 1920s Virginia," in Martha Hodes, ed., *Sex, Love, Race: Crossing Boundaries in North American History* (1999), 401.

spontaneous generation" and demanded that this "breech in the dike be stopped." John Powell declared that "If we are to preserve our civilization, our ideals, the soul of our race, we must call a halt."[42] The Anglo-Saxon Clubs wanted the commonwealth to take additional steps to purify its white population, but that aim was thwarted in the end by opponents who maintained that unless the clubs were restrained, their exacting racialism would lead to a situation in which some of Virginia's leading white families would have to be reclassified as colored—indeed, a situation in which there would be few "real" white Virginians left.[43]*

Although the Anglo-Saxon Clubs barred women from membership, one of their most fervent and interesting champions was female. Louise Burleigh, a well-educated (Radcliffe College), literary-minded person who keenly endorsed the notion of shipping Negroes back to Africa, wrote (but never published) a short story, "Dark Cloud," that vividly captures the sense of dread with which she and some of her peers viewed the possibility of miscegenation between unwitting whites and villainous black passers. In Burleigh's tale, a white New Englander named Alicia Fairchild travels south with her young daughter to attend her mother-in-law's funeral. During the ceremony, Alicia realizes that the deceased woman was black and that therefore her own husband is black as well. Feeling defiled, the victim of a deception that she likens to rape, she destroys her family. She kills her husband, but even more significantly, she kills their daughter, permitting the toddler to be consumed by fire inside a locked church.[44]

White supremacists have not been the only ones to condemn passing; opponents of white supremacy have also objected to the practice. They have done so primarily on two grounds. The first is that passing constitutes a betrayal of African Americans. The second is that its costs outweigh its benefits.

The relationship between passing and racial loyalty was a central issue for Frances Ellen Watkins Harper (1825–1911), an extraordinary black woman who distinguished herself as a journalist, political

---

*For a hilarious parody of racial witch-hunting, a farce based largely on the demands of the Anglo Saxon Clubs, see George S. Schuyler, *Black No More* (1931). See also pages 344–53.

activist, poet, and novelist.[45] Her best-known exploration of this subject is her novel *Iola LeRoy* (1892).[46] Unfolding against the backdrop of the Civil War and Reconstruction, *Iola LeRoy* chronicles the life of a light-skinned Negro woman who refuses to pass. The daughter of a master and a slave whom he freed and married, Iola LeRoy looks white, as did her mother. Indeed, throughout her childhood, Iola believed she *was* white, for her parents shielded her from any knowledge of her black ancestry. Only as a teenager, after her parents die, does Iola learn that she is not only partly black but also a slave. After she is emancipated, Dr. Gresham, a white physician in the Union Army, proposes to Iola, telling her that he knows of her racial background but wants to marry her anyway. "Love, like faith," he observes, "laughs at impossibilities. I can conceive of no barrier too high for my love to surmount."[47] Attracted though she is to him, Iola nonetheless rejects his offer because she is determined "to cast [her] lot with the freed people as a helper, teacher, and friend."[48] In her view, Gresham's proposal presents her with a stark choice: she can marry him, which will ultimately compel her to become white; or she can reject him and stand with her people, a course that will entail remaining black. She opts to do the latter.

To ensure that her readers would understand the decision Iola LeRoy makes is the correct one, Harper emphasized throughout the novel the necessity of choosing racial sides. Thus, some years after Iola first refuses Gresham, she turns him down a second time, explaining, "I don't think that I could best serve my race by forsaking them and marrying you. . . . I must serve the race which needs me most."[49] The novel also introduces other "white Negroes" who heroically eschew passing. At the outset of the Civil War, Iola's brother, Harry, tells the headmaster of his New England preparatory school that he wishes to volunteer for service in the Union Army. When the headmaster points out that his appearance affords him the choice of joining either a black or a white regiment, the narrator informs the reader that "it was as if two paths had suddenly opened before [Harry], and he was forced to choose between them. On one side were strength, courage, enterprise, power of achievement, and memories of a wonderful past. On the other side were weakness, ignorance, poverty, and the proud world's social scorn."[50]

Harry LeRoy, like his sister, chooses the black side. When he volunteers, he expressly asks to be assigned to a colored regiment, a request that puzzles the recruiting officer:

> It was a new experience. He had seen colored men with fair complexions anxious to lose their identity with the colored race and pose as white men, but here was a man in the flush of his early manhood, to whom could come dreams of promotion from a simple private to a successful general, deliberately turning his back upon every gilded hope, and dazzling opportunity, to cast his lot with the despised and hated negro.[51]

Ignoring the officer's scorn ("You are the d——d'st fool I ever saw—a man as white as you are turning his back upon his chances for promotion"),[52] Harry adamantly insists upon being identified as a colored man. "Unless I can be assigned to a colored regiment," he finally declares, "I am not willing to enter the army."[53]*

A third hero who refuses to pass is Dr. Frank Latimer. Although his white ancestry "had effaced all traces of his negro lineage," Latimer,

---

*Another of Harper's characters—the light-skinned Negro Robert Johnson—also rejects a chance at passing:

> "Johnson," said a young officer . . . , "what is the use of your saying you're a colored man, when you are as white as I am, and as brave a man as there is among us. Why not quit this [colored] company, and take your place in the army just the same as a white man? I know your chances of promotion would be better."
> "Captain, you may doubt my word, but today I would rather be a lieutenant in my company than a captain in yours."
> "I don't understand you."
> "Well, Captain, when a man's been colored all his life it comes a little hard for him to get to be white all at once. Were I to try it, I would feel like a cat in a strange garret. Captain, I think my place is where I am most needed. You do not need me in your ranks, and my company does." [Frances Ellen Watkins Harper, *Iola LeRoy*, in William L. Andrews, ed., *The African American Novel in the Age of Reaction: Three Classics* (1992), 34]

like the LeRoys, persists in identifying himself as colored. At one point, he finds himself (and Dr. Gresham) in the company of an outspokenly racist white physician, Dr. Latrobe, who makes all manner of insulting remarks about blacks, unaware that Latimer considers himself a Negro. After listening to Latrobe's tirade and his claims of having a special talent for recognizing even "white niggers," Latimer advises his colleague that despite appearances, he, too, is black:

> "I am one of them," replied Dr. Latimer, proudly raising his head.
> "You!" exclaimed Dr. Latrobe, with an air of profound astonishment and crimsoning face.
> "Yes," interposed Dr. Gresham, laughing merrily at Dr. Latrobe's discomfiture. "He belongs to that negro race both by blood and choice."[54]

At the end of her novel, Harper arranged for Iola LeRoy to marry not Dr. Gresham but Dr. Latimer. Pressing once again her theme of racial duty, she averred that "kindred hopes and tastes had knit their hearts; grand and noble purposes were lighting up their lives; and they esteemed it a blessed privilege to stand on the threshold of a new era and labor for those who had passed from the old oligarchy of slavery into the new commonwealth of freedom."[55]

*Iola LeRoy* is alive with racial ideas that remain influential today. It cautions against individualistic ambition and lionizes blacks who sacrifice self-promotion for what Harper saw as the long-term good of their race as a whole. The novel celebrates black solidarity, champions black racial pride, affirms blacks who recognize their racial obligations, and lauds those blacks who, even if they look white, choose to stand with "their people."

A second rationale against passing holds that the potential benefits are not worth the costs. In the 1990s Ronald E. Hall maintained that "passing for white inflicts psychological trauma on those who try it because it requires them to erect a wall between who they are and could be as persons and who they are or try to be amid white society."[56] In

1950 the Negro actress Janice Kingslow reached much the same conclusion after being offered a lucrative Hollywood contract conditioned on her agreement to change her name and racial identity. In an article entitled "I Refuse to Pass," Kingslow gave her reasons for saying no to the deal: "What good was fame or money if I lost myself? This wasn't just a question of choosing a pleasant-sounding false name to fit on a theatre marquee. [Passing] meant stripping my life clear of everything I was. Everything that had happened to me."[57]

Frank J. Webb had evoked this theme almost a century earlier, in the second novel written by an African American. *The Garies and Their Friends* (1857)[58] is the story of "a family of peculiar construction,"[59] much like Iola LeRoy's family. Mr. Garie is a white slave owner who purchases a woman and then falls in love with, frees, and marries her. Together they produce two children who, according to the novel's narrator, "showed no trace whatever of African origin."[60] The Garies move to Philadelphia to escape the isolation and stultification that are their lot in the slave South, only to find that racism is pervasive in the North as well. Catastrophe soon overtakes them: an evil white man, Mr. Thomas Stevens, having discovered that Mrs. Garie is of African American ancestry, directs a white mob to the family's home. Mr. Garie is murdered, and Mrs. Garie and her newborn die of exposure while attempting to flee. Various family friends help raise the surviving children. Emily Garie, who identifies with blacks, is taken in by blacks; her brother, Clarence, who from an early age has passed for white, goes to live with white friends. Buffeted though she is by the insecurities visited upon all black people in antebellum Philadelphia, Emily nevertheless derives great comfort from her Negro friends and neighbors. When a young black man whom she has known for many years proposes marriage, she happily accepts. This development in turn sets the stage for one of the few occasions on which Emily displays anger. Her response is provoked by a request voiced by her brother: he wants her to break off her engagement, both because he believes she can do better than marry a colored man and because he fears that such a marriage will threaten the secrecy of his own colored lineage. But Emily embraces the choices she has made: "You walk on the side of the oppressor," she tells her brother. "I, thank God, run with the oppressed."[61] She rejects her brother's plea, seeing it as an example of his selfishness and his fundamental miscalculation regarding the ingredients of human happiness. As she tries to explain to Clarence:

> "You ask me to sever, at once and for ever, my connection with a people who, you say, can only degrade me. Yet how much happier am I, sharing their degradation, than you appear to be! . . . I am happy—more happy, I am sure, than you could make me, even by surrounding me with the glittering lights that shine upon your path."[62]

The events that follow verify Emily's assertion. Her wedding is a large, beautiful, loving affair, the beginning of what promises to be a wonderful and lifelong union. Clarence, by contrast, reaps only disappointment.* He proposes marriage to a white woman—a Miss Bates, whom he calls "Little Birdie"—without informing her of his racial background. He realizes there is a good chance that if she knew what he really was, Little Birdie would refuse to marry him. After all, he has already heard her express disapproval regarding an interracial marriage that she read about in a newspaper. When Clarence remarked that the husband and wife must love each other very much, and that further-

---

*After the elder Garies' deaths, when their friends are pondering how best to raise their orphaned children, a debate erupts over the wisdom of allowing Clarence to retain his identity as a white boy, given that the prevailing racial rules of that day and place categorize him as black. One of the black heroes of the novel declares:

> I admit . . . that in our land of liberty it is of incalculable advantage to be white. . . . When I look around me, and see what I have made myself under the circumstances, and think what I might have been with the same heart and brain beneath a fairer skin, I am almost tempted to curse the destiny that made me what I am. . . . Yet, with all I have endured, and yet endure from day to day, I esteem myself happy in comparison with the man, who, mingling in the society of whites, is at the same time aware that he has African blood in his veins, and is liable at any moment to be ignominiously hurled from his position by the discovery of his origin. He is never safe.
> [Frank J. Webb, *The Garies and Their Friends* (1857, reprint 1997), 275]

more, the colored woman in question was "almost white," Little Birdie's reply brought home to him the importance of race to her: "'How could he love her?' asked she wonderingly. 'Love a coloured woman! I cannot conceive it possible,' said she with a look of disgust; 'there is something strange and unnatural about it.'"[63]

In addition to this strong hint as to his fiancée's racial feelings, Clarence also has the benefit of a warning from the white woman who largely raised him after he was orphaned. Arguing that he has a duty to speak up, Miss Bell urges Clarence:

> "Throw away concealment, make a clean breast of it! . . . If you marry her with this secret hanging over you, it will embitter your life, make you reserved, suspicious, and consequently ill-tempered, and destroy all your domestic happiness. . . . [Tell Little Birdie and her parents] ere it be too late. Suppose it reached them through some other source, what would they then think of you?"[64]

At one point, Clarence comes close to telling Birdie the truth. But according to the narrator, when he "looked full in her lovely face, he could not tell her,—the words slunk back into his coward heart unspoken."[65] Thereafter the secret becomes, for Clarence, "a vampire, sucking away, drop by drop, happiness and peace."[66]* Yet still he refuses to defang it by disclosing all to his fiancée. In the end, of course, the worst happens: in a terrible scene, the son of the man who caused the deaths of Clarence's parents recognizes Clarence and reveals his childhood friend's "tainted" family history to Birdie's father, Mr. Bates. Bates then curses his almost-son-in-law as a "contemptible, black-hearted nigger":

---

*Determined to keep his racial identity secret until after his wedding, Clarence confides to his aunt Ada:

> I must shut this secret in my bosom, where it gnaws, gnaws, gnaws, until it has almost eaten my heart away. . . . No escaped galley-slave ever felt more than I do, or lived in more constant fear of detection: and yet I must nourish this tormenting secret, and keep it growing in my breast until it has crowded out every honorable and manly feeling. [Ibid., 235]

"You have acted basely, palming yourself upon us—counterfeit as you were! . . . Had you been unaware of your origin . . . you would have deserved sympathy; but you have been acting a lie, claiming a position in society to which you knew you had no right. . . . Did I treat you as my feelings dictated, you would understand what is meant by the weight of a father's anger; but I do not wish the world to know that my daughter has been wasting her affections upon a worthless nigger; that is all that protects you!"[67]

Thus unmasked as a passer, Clarence loses Little Birdie, who breaks off their engagement, dashing "his greatest hope in life."[68]* He soon finds himself irredeemably isolated: "He was avoided by his former [white] friends and sneered at as a 'nigger,'" and at the same time, "he felt ashamed to seek the society of coloured men now that the whites despised and rejected him."[69] "Oh! Em[ily]," he writes to his sister shortly before he dies of a broken heart, "if my lot had only been cast with yours—had we never been separated—I might have been today as happy as you are."[70]†

Reba Lee's autobiographical account *I Passed for White* (1955) furnishes memorable testimony that passing can be a spurious remedy—a predicament even worse than the one the passer was attempting to

---

*In an interesting twist, Little Birdie is portrayed as a much more attractive figure *after* she is apprised of Clarence's ancestry than she is *before* that event. The novel's narrator suggests that she truly loves Clarence, even after she discovers that he is "really" colored, and calls off their engagement only out of a sense of filial devotion to her father. On learning that Clarence is deathly ill, she insists upon seeing him. Alas, she arrives too late: he dies just moments before she reaches his room. Soon thereafter she, too, dies of a broken heart, joining her lover "where distinctions in race or colour are unknown, and where the prejudices of earth cannot mar . . . happiness" (Frank J. Webb, *The Garies and Their Friends,* ed. Robert Reid-Pharr [1997]).

†Another novel that vividly captures the horror of exposure is Nella Larsen's novel *Passing* (1929). The protagonist, Clare Kendry, is a Negro woman who not only passes for white but marries a white man who despises blacks (or, more precisely, people he *recognizes* as being black). After Clare's husband catches her at a black party, a dreadful scene ensues, during which she jumps (or perhaps is pushed) out a window to her death.

flee.* This fascinating memoir tells the story of a woman whose biological parents were a white man and a light-skinned Negro woman. Lee grew up in Chicago with her mother's family; she never knew her father, a student at the University of Chicago who quickly dropped her mother, a waitress, after she became pregnant. Before Reba was born, her mother married a Negro man who conscientiously raised the child as his own. From an early age, however, Lee resisted being identified as black. She sought out whites as friends, even if they expressed dislike for Negroes, and even when her relationships with them were contingent on her ability to conceal her racial background. Her conduct was shaped in part by the example of her grandmother, who constantly touted the extent to which her relatives had been whitened by miscegenation with slave masters in the antebellum period. "Our family," the grandmother proudly proclaimed, "has some of the best blood of the old South in it."[71]

Lee's behavior was also influenced by her own deep ambivalence toward both blacks and whites. She resented whites for holding themselves out as superior to Negroes; but at the same time, she *herself* felt superior to blacks—or at least to the "niggery" ones:

> I felt bitter when I saw a cheap, flashy white girl walking along as if she owned the earth, but I felt worse when I saw a fat, sloppy Negro girl or a smart-alecky dressed-up one. I was on edge about the Negroes coming up from the South, the ignorant, dirty ones . . . I didn't like them and it gave me a sick, distasteful feeling to have them called "my" race.[72]

Lee finally decided to pass because she yearned to be free of the limitations imposed by her racial identity. She wanted "to work without any colored label" that prejudiced whites against her from the outset and rendered irrelevant her individual talents.

---

*See also Mary Church Terrell, "Why, How, When and Where Black Becomes White," in Lorraine Elena Roses and Ruth Elizabeth Randolph, eds., *Harlem's Glory: Black Women Writing, 1900–1959* (1996); "Why I Never Want to Pass," *Ebony,* June 1959; "I'm Through with Passing," *Ebony,* March 1951.

So Reba Lee reinvented herself. Leaving her relatives a good-bye note that said nothing about where she was going, she fled her home in Chicago, took an airplane to New York City, gave herself a new name, and became a white woman. Now racially privileged, she obtained a clerical job and established social connections that probably would have been denied her in her previous incarnation as a Negro. Through her new friends, she met a rich young white man who asked her to marry him. At first, Lee was happy with her new station—"as thrilled as an actress who sees her name in lights for the first time," she recalled.[73] Over time, however, passing became increasingly onerous. She repeatedly found herself in situations in which whites, thinking she was one of "them," freely damned "the niggers"—a form of verbal aggression that disturbed her, despite her own alienation from blacks. On hearing a man pridefully assert at a dinner party that he wouldn't touch a nigger with a ten-foot pole, Lee told herself, "I'd have to get used to it. It shouldn't be any worse than for my white blood to hear talk against the whites. But it was worse. I had been brought up colored."[74] Even more trying was the difficult task of hiding her past. Having lied to her in-laws about her parents, saying they were dead, Lee showed them letters and gifts she had sent to herself in the name of fictitious friends and relatives. The need to be on guard every moment against making some slip that might unravel her tapestry of lies imposed a burden that she eventually concluded was too heavy to bear. "I had entered the Promised Land," she later mused, "but now that I was there . . . I did not want to go on with it. I was sick to the bone of lying and pretending. I was sick of the fear of being found out."[75]*

---

*The literature on passing makes it clear that the fear of exposure typically constitutes a major onus in passers' lives. The journalist Ray Stannard Baker quoted a black man who succeeded in passing but then decided to cross back and resume his life as a Negro. "No decent man could stand it," the former passer averred. "I preferred to be a Negro and hold up my head rather than to be a sneak" (quoted in *Following the Color Line: American Negro Citizenship in the Progressive Era* [1908; reprint, 1964], 161). Over four decades later, an article in *Ebony* magazine described as pitiable those Negroes who passed for white at work but lived as black at home. They were caught, the writer observed, in "a strange Dr. Jekyll and Mr. Hyde existence—living constantly in fear that their day world will conflict with their night world" ("White by Day . . . Negro by Night," *Ebony*, April 1952). See also Henry

Lee's fear was a realistic one. For all her adeptness at constructing a new identity, she was, inevitably, caught by the sticky web of her past. One evening, she went with her husband and some friends to a jazz club in Greenwich Village, where she was spotted by a black musician who knew her from Chicago. He greeted her familiarly, though she managed to keep him from blowing her cover altogether. Still, the obvious connection between them bothered her husband. Trying to explain it away, Lee told him that she had once briefly attended a multiracial public school back home. The explanation only partly satisfied her husband, who grew even more skeptical following a second incident. Lee got pregnant, a development that terrified her, given the possibility that the baby might have colored skin or kinky hair that would reveal her racial secret. As it turned out, her pregnancy was problematic: she went into labor prematurely and gave birth to a stillborn child. In her anxiety, exhaustion, and agony, she blurted out to a nurse, "Is it black?" That question irreparably poisoned her relationship with her husband, who thereupon began to suspect her of having an affair with the black musician at the jazz club.

Of even greater importance to Lee than the threat of exposure, however, was her discovery that in the end, she did not really like living with whites—or at least with the particular whites with whom she was involved. Far from being a better class of individuals, she realized,

these people were no better, no, not as good, as the colored people I had known. More mannerly, yes, more knowledgeable and cultivated, acquainted with all the good things of life, but for all their background and opportunities they were less genuine, less understanding, less tolerant in their relations to each other. And less happy. The joy of living was not in them. . . . Oh, I liked the charming homes . . . the feeling of privilege. The rich white feeling. I liked what the whites *did* but not what they *were*. . . . I realized now that I had never been truly happy among them.[76]

---

Louis Gates's profile of the passing *New York Times* journalist Anatole Broyard in *Thirteen Ways of Looking at a Black Man* (1990).

So Reba Lee crossed the race line once again. She divorced her husband and went back to her black relatives and friends in Chicago, who, she maintained, accepted her return without recriminations.*

The risk of being exposed, or outed, is just one of many costs that must be considered by those who contemplate passing. Another, ironically, is the loss of status: a well-educated black man who is outstanding in Negro circles, for example, may be only moderately successful or even mediocre in the white world. Presenting the account of a former passer who rejoined the Negro fold, Gunnar Myrdal reported that among the reasons the man gave for his about-face was that while "he [was] 'tops' in the Negro community" for doing a certain job, among whites he was just one of many, and "far from the social ceiling." Moreover, "because his profession was one in which there were few qualified Negro workers, he got his position more easily as a Negro than he would have as a white man."[77]

Similarly ironic is the fact that passers almost always feel compelled to abandon any active participation in struggles on behalf of blacks—activities that are demanding but also gratifying. Such a loss is depicted in James Weldon Johnson's justly lauded *The Autobiography of an Ex-Colored Man* (1912).[78]† The novel chronicles the life of the illegitimate son of a white man and his light-skinned Negro mistress. Although passing long hovers in the background as a possibility for this unnamed

---

*Two circumstances surrounding the writing of this memoir render its reliability even more suspect than is usual for books of its genre. First, "Reba Lee" is a pseudonym. Second, the actual writing was done by Mary Hastings Bradley, to whom "Lee" told her story. Notwithstanding those caveats, I found *I Passed for White* believable and persuasive.

†Johnson (1871–1938) was a lawyer, diplomat, and civil rights leader who served as the first black secretary of the NAACP. He was also a writer who excelled in a variety of genres, producing an autobiography (*Along This Way*, 1933), poetry (*God's Trombones: Seven Negro Sermons in Verse*, 1927), cultural history (*Black Manhattan*, 1930), and, with his brother John Rosamond Johnson, "Lift Every Voice and Sing," often described as the Negro national anthem. Johnson initially published *The Autobiography of an Ex-Colored Man* anonymously; fourteen years later, in 1926, the novel was reissued with his authorship acknowledged. See generally Eugene Levy, *James Weldon Johnson* (1973).

man, he refrains from it until he witnesses the lynching, in the South, of a Negro man accused of "some terrible crime"—most likely the rape of a white woman.[79] This gruesome spectacle evokes in him two contradictory reactions: a closer identification with blacks and, alongside that, a yearning to flee his blackness. Describing the former sentiment, Johnson's protagonist declares that he "could understand why Negroes are led to sympathize with even their worst criminals and to protect them when possible."[80] But as for his impulse to flee any association with the American Negro, he admits that "it was not discouragement or fear or [a] search for . . . opportunity that was driving me out of the Negro race. . . . It was shame, unbearable shame. Shame at being identified with a people that could with impunity be treated worse than animals."[81] The latter impulse predominates; the colored man becomes the *ex*-colored man of the novel's title. He becomes a white man who marries a white woman and gains affluence, thereby attaining "a white man's success."[82] Yet in the end, he feels profoundly dissatisfied with the choice he has made. At a fund-raiser in Carnegie Hall on behalf of the Hampton Institute, he compares himself unfavorably with "that small but gallant band of colored men who are publicly fighting the cause of their race"—men such as Booker T. Washington, who "will be victors even though they should go down in defeat." Next to them, he muses, "I feel small and selfish. I am an ordinarily successful white man who has made a little money. They are men who are making history." Under different circumstances, he notes with a pang of regret, "I too might have taken part in a work so glorious." He concludes that he has chosen the lesser life, and "sold [his] birthright for a mess of pottage."[83]

Another cost of passing is the price of distancing oneself from those who might, even inadvertently, reveal one's racial past. Having told her white husband and in-laws that her parents were dead, Reba Lee had no contact with her biological kin throughout her marriage and pregnancy; she saw her blood relatives again only after she decided to stop passing.[84] In New England in the 1940s, a Negro couple met periodically with black friends in Boston, but only at a safe remove from the New Hampshire town in which they lived as whites.[85] In the 1950s

Buster Williams (Gregory Howard Williams's father) permitted his black mother to stay in his "white" household in Virginia, but solely on the condition that she pretend to be an employee.[86]

Unsurprisingly, a number of writers of fiction have been drawn to this grim theme. In Jessie Redmond Fauset's *Plum Bun: A Novel Without a Moral* (1928), for example, a woman denies knowing her own sibling. In Fauset's novel *Comedy, American Style* (1953), a mother introduces her son as her butler. In Langston Hughes's short story "Passing," a son walks by his mother on the street without acknowledging her.* In Sutton Grigg's *The Hindered Hand* (1895) and Walter White's *Flight* (1926), parents exile children whose dark skin threaten to expose their racial masquerade. In Johnson's *Autobiography of an Ex-Colored Man,* the protagonist treats an old friend like a stranger. In Fannie Hurst's *Imitation of Life* (1933), a passing Negro woman sterilizes herself to guarantee that no dark baby will ever reveal her hidden ancestry to the white husband who believes his wife to be white. In telling these tales, many of the writers (though by no means all of them) point accusatory fingers at the passers. The substance of the charge, typically, is that only someone with a distorted sense of values would subordinate his or her associations with relatives and friends to an ambition of upward mobility realizable solely through deception.

While such moral condemnation is the dominant motif in the fictional and nonfictional literature of racial subterfuge, other perspectives are sometimes expressed. One of Nella Larsen's passers gives voice

---

*Dear Ma,

I felt like a dog, passing you downtown last night and not speaking to you. You were great, though. Didn't give a sign that you even knew me, let alone I was your son. If I hadn't had the girl with me, Ma, we might have talked. . . . Isn't she sweet to look at, all blonde and blue-eyed? We're making plans [to get married]. . . . I will take a box at the Post Office for your mail. . . . I'm glad there's nothing to stop letters from crossing the color-line. Even if we can't meet often, we can write, can't we, Ma?

With love from your son,
Jack

[Langston Hughes, *The Ways of White Folks* (1933, reprint, 1990), 51–55]

to the ambivalence with which many blacks regard the strategy of passing: "We disapprove of it and at the same time condone it. It excites our contempt and yet we rather admire it. We shy away from it with an odd kind of revulsion, but we protect it."[87]* For some observers who grudgingly condone it, racial masquerading may, under certain circumstances, constitute an unpleasant but acceptable adaptation to racist mistreatment. Jessie Redmon Fauset's *Plum Bun* features a Negro character who occasionally passes in order to enjoy restaurants and orchestra seats customarily reserved for whites. She is described tenderly as "employ[ing] her colour very much as she practiced certain winning usages of smile and voice to obtain indulgences which meant much to her and which took nothing from anyone else."[88]† In Fauset's imagining, "It was with no idea of disclaiming her own that [this woman] sat in orchestra seats . . . denied to coloured patrons"; rather, her actions reflected "a mischievous determination to flout a silly and unjust law."[89]

In the nonfiction literature by and about passers, one also finds references to passing as a mode of resistance or subversion. Ray Stannard Baker noted that the act of passing inspired glee among many Negroes because they viewed it as a means of "getting even with the dominant white man."[90] Langston Hughes repeatedly defended such masquerading as a joke on racism.[91] And Gregory Howard Williams reported that when his father lived in Virginia, he derived great psychic satisfaction from defying the rules of segregation by being the husband of a white woman and the president of a (supposedly) lily-white chapter of

---

*In at least one instance in the 1940s, a "white Negro" was urged by other Negroes to pass at work so she would not take up one of the scarce positions allocated to black workers. This woman passed for a decade, quitting only after being assigned the task of typing a business letter expressing her boss's support for Ku Klux Klan activities. She never mailed the letter. See "I'm Through with Passing," *Ebony*, March 1951.

†Of course, some contend that racial passing, like remaining in the homosexual closet, *does* take something from others in that it solidifies the oppressive social conditions that prompt members of oppressed groups to deny identities marked for ostracism. For more on this, see pages 330–32.

the American Legion.* Williams also recalled that his brother got a thrill from romancing white girls who surely would have spurned him had they realized he was a Negro. Relating one such conquest, Mike Williams boasted that after he and the girl finished having sex, he told her gleefully, "You just been fucked by a nigger."[92]

According to the memoirist Shirlee Taylor Haizlip, in Washington, D.C., in the 1930s, one "whites-only" restaurant hired black people as lookouts to identify "white Negroes" who were attempting to pass.[93] In retaliation, a Negro-owned newspaper published the names of the lookouts.† While the editors' motivation may have been only the desire to punish Negroes who aided Jim Crow exclusion, they may also have taken some vicarious pleasure in the knowledge that at least a few Negroes were enjoying facilities that racists had hoped to reserve exclusively for whites. For whatever their own personal motives may be, passers necessarily disrupt policies intended to bar from positions of authority and privilege *all* persons of African ancestry. Narrow though these breaches of the race line may now seem, when opportunities for resistance are few, even the most limited efforts to fool or escape or cheat a repressive social order can be inspiring. This point is made vividly by some descendants of passers who obtained hard-won benefits under difficult circumstances through skillful, albeit deceptive, manipu-

---

*According to Williams:

> The nightly crowds huddled at Grandma's relished Dad's stories about how he tricked the white man. Every time the white man was exposed as a fool, laughter rang out through the shack. The victories were small and inconsequential, but I realized the telling and retelling served the valuable purpose of soothing wounded souls. . . .

[Gregory Howard Williams, *Life on the Color Line,* 63–64]

†As this story about restaurant lookouts indicates, passing provided rampant opportunities for betrayal, extortion, and revenge. The interesting thing about this facet of the passing phenomenon is not that outing occasionally had occurred, but rather that it appears to occur relatively infrequently.

The most horrendous example of outing I have come across involves not lookouts who fingered black passers or exposed gays or lesbians attempting to remain closeted, but Jews who betrayed other Jews seeking to hide in Hitler's Germany; see Peter Wyden, *Stella* (1992). For a searing novel about Jews passing in the shadow of the holocaust, see Louis Begley, *Wartime Lies* (1991).

lation. Professor Cheryl I. Harris, for example, has written admiringly of her grandmother, a Negro woman who passed for white to get a job in a Chicago department store in the 1930s. "Day in and day out," according to Harris, her grandmother "made herself invisible, then visible, for a price too inconsequential to do more than barely sustain her family."[94]* Recounting the experience of a "white Negro" who joined the Washington, D.C., police department in the first decade of the twentieth century, Haizlip noted that "the Negro community knew, celebrated, and kept [the passer's] secret."[95]† Others have responded in much the same way. When Professor Glen Loury realized that some Negroes actually succeeded in pretending to be white, he immediately became intrigued by the phenomenon: "I enjoyed," he has written, "imagining my racial brethren surreptitiously infiltrating the citadels of white exclusivity. It allowed me to believe that, despite appearances and the white man's best efforts to the contrary, we blacks were nevertheless present, if unannounced, *everywhere* in American society."[96]‡

---

*Similarly, Professor Gabriel Chin has memorialized his grandfather, who pretended to be the son of a Chinese emigrant already resident within the United States to avoid being turned away under the Chinese Exclusion Act. For Chin, it was his forebear's "defiance" that made possible his own birth in the United States. See Gabriel J. Chin, "Segregation's Last Stronghold: Race Discrimination and the Constitutional Law of Immigration," *UCLA Law Review* 46 (1998): 1. See also Kitty Calavita, "The Paradoxes of Race, Class, Identity, and 'Passing': Enforcing the Chinese Exclusion Acts, 1882–1910," *Law and Social Inquiry* 25 (2000): 1.

†Ray Stannard Baker wrote of blacks creating a "conspiracy of silence" to protect those of their number who crossed the line to become white; see his *Following the Color Line,* 162.

For a work that dramatizes this theme, see Regina M. Andrews's *The Man Who Passed: A Play in One Act* (Harvard University Press, 1996). At one point in the play, a Negro barber says to a passer who is about to return to Harlem under the cover of darkness, "You know your own people been pretty good to you, Fred! Ain' none of them spotted you out and hunted you down to tell your Boss Fitzgerald that one of the 'Niggers' he hates is working for him, and living right in his own home. It ain't every yellow-faced Negro who can pass for white for fifteen years, hold a white man's job, marry a white woman, and not get caught" (Andrews, *The Man Who Passed,* in Roses and Randolph, eds., *Harlem's Glory,* 48).

‡Professor Judy Scales-Trent has expressed a similar view: "Don't forget, white folks: we see you, we hear you, and we tell our stories. Was that you at a party talking about living in 'Coon City'? Little did you know that one of those 'coons' was at the party and is writing about you even now. . . . We are everywhere, white folks.

In *Lost Boundaries* (1947), W. L. White presented the (true) story of the Johnstons, a family of light-skinned Negroes who passed for white in New Hampshire in the 1930s and 1940s.* The head of the family, Albert Johnston Jr., was a physician. Negro acquaintances were aware of his passing, and some disapproved, but none ever did anything to reveal his secret. One of Johnston's brothers also passed for white. In his case, the elaboration of his new persona included divorcing his Negro wife and marrying a white woman. Even so, his ex-wife declined to out him. As an observer declared, "So strong is the tie between all Negroes, that although they bitterly resent a Negro who has 'gone over,' they will nonetheless guard his secret as though it were their own, and not expose him to a white man."[97]† In other words, paradoxically, Negro solidarity sometimes shielded Negroes who disclaimed their blackness.

---

Beware" (*Notes of a White Black Woman: Race, Color, Community* [1995], 44).

*White's book served as the basis of a film of the same name. One of the most interesting things about the film version of *Lost Boundaries* is that white actors were selected to portray passing blacks. In part, this was because the film's producers believed that white audiences would more easily accept criticism of white racism if it came out of the mouths of other whites—even if those whites were playing characters who were "really" black. For a trenchant analysis of *Lost Boundaries* and other films about passing, see Gayle Wald, *Crossing the Line: Racial Passing in Twentieth-Century U.S. Literature and Culture* (2000).

The paradox of white actors pretending to be Negroes pretending to be whites replicates a similar complication in the film *Gentleman's Agreement* (1947). The hero of that celebrated film is a Christian reporter who exposes and condemns bigotry by posing as a Jew. *Gentleman's Agreement* has been lauded as one of Hollywood's boldest offerings, but ironically, several of the actors who starred in it were themselves passers who changed their names in order to deflect Hollywood's own discriminations against Jewish entertainers. For instance, John Garfield, who played a Jewish veteran in the film, was originally Julius Garfinkle. See Marjorie Garber's incisive essay "Gentility," in her collection *Symptoms of Culture* (1998).

†On seeing a photograph of the Johnstons in a newspaper, I was surprised by their success in passing, because they looked so obviously "black" to me. They were light-skinned, to be sure, but no more so than many other blacks I know. The black author of the newspaper story confirmed my impression, noting that many of his Negro colleagues wondered how the Johnstons could have passed for whites in the first place. Is it possible that Negroes simply have a keener eye for identifying other Negroes, even those who are trying hard to pass? According to Ralph Ellison, "most Negroes can spot a paper thin 'White Negro' every time" (*Shadow and Act* [1953], 124). See also Amy Robinson, "It Takes One to Know One: Passing and Communities of Common Interest," *Critical Inquiry* 20 (1994): 715.

Two of the most important challenges to racial oppression in twentieth-century American constitutional law stemmed from episodes of passing. On May 30, 1942, police in San Leandro, California, questioned a young man who was walking down the street with a date. They suspected him of violating Military Exclusion Order Number 34, which directed all persons of Japanese ancestry in California to report to United States military authorities in preparation for evacuation and internment. When confronted by the police, the man gave his name as Clyde Sarah and said he was of Spanish-Hawaiian ancestry. In fact, he was Fred Totsaburo Korematsu, the son of Japanese parents. In addition to assuming a fake name and altering his draft card, Korematsu had undergone plastic surgery in an attempt to westernize his appearance.[98] In 1944 the United States Supreme Court upheld the constitutionality of the provisions under which Korematsu was punished, in a ruling that has since been widely condemned.[99]

The second case involved a black man, James Hurd, who challenged the constitutionality of a court order that had evicted him from his home. Hurd's white neighbors had sought the order on the ground that he had breached a restrictive covenant providing that the house could neither be sold to nor occupied by a Negro. At trial, Hurd's attorney raised larger legal issues but also pressed a narrow factual objection, asserting that the eviction was improper because his client was actually an American Indian, not a Negro.[100] The counsel for the defense was none other than Charles Hamilton Houston. A great mentor of the African American civil rights bar in the years prior to *Brown v. Board of Education*, Houston was keenly attentive to the ramifications of the tactical choices he made as a litigator. Although he ultimately won on the federal constitutional issue in *Hurd*, he lost on the issue of racial classification. But more important here than the final disposition of the case is the fact that Houston *attempted* to use passing—this time, passing for Native American—as a vehicle for the advancement not only of James Hurd's cause but of the broader cause of racial justice.

Professor Christine B. Hickman has related two stories about black relatives of hers who had bought houses protected by anti-Negro restrictive covenants. Her uncle Clarence Jones was a successful attorney. In Hickman's view, racist stereotyping likely confused Jones's white neighbors, who were evidently unwilling or unable to believe that a hardworking lawyer with three daughters at the University of California at Los Angeles could be black. It was only when one of the daughters got married at the family home that the white neighbors became agitated. "As the various guests arrived," Hickman explained, "the neighbors were forced to see what their social training had not let them see before—the Jones family was undeniably black." Soon after that, the neighbors sued to evict Jones pursuant to the terms of the restrictive covenant on his house. Jones refused to assert that he was anything but a Negro. Although he advanced the same arguments on which James Hurd's attorney would prevail just four years later, he lost his challenge to the constitutionality of the state-backed eviction and was forced to move.[101]

A second uncle of Hickman's—Jack—moved into a (supposedly) all-white neighborhood in Detroit, Michigan, in 1956. When his neighbors learned that he was a Negro (perhaps through the appearance of one of his grandchildren), they demanded that he move. Unlike Clarence Jones, Uncle Jack attempted to pass. He told reporters that he was half Cherokee and half French Canadian, omitting any mention of his African American ancestry. The white neighbors disbelieved his story and increased their pressure, offering to buy the house for two thousand dollars more than he had paid for it and threatening him with mob action if he declined to sell "voluntarily." He soon moved.[102]

While stating that "it would not be fair to find fault with Uncle Jack's denial," Hickman admitted to feeling "a touch of sadness and a twinge of disappointment because Uncle Jack denied who he was."[103]

True, in some—maybe all—cases, passing has served to entrench racial lines of exclusion by reinforcing the norm that certain sectors of society were open only to whites, or at least those who were perceived to be white. It was, moreover, seen as posing such a trivial threat to racist restrictions that some sentries at the color bar permitted racial masquerades to go forward, so long as the passers outwardly obeyed the rules of white supremacy—meaning, notably, so long as they truly pretended to *be* white in exchange for receiving the privileges that white skin conferred.* Such conditional entree, according to Leo Spitzer, made passing

> by and large a personal solution to discrimination and exclu-
> sion. It was an action that, when accomplished successfully,
> generally divorced its individual practitioners from others in
> the subordinated group, and in no way challenged the ideology
> of racism or the system in which it was rooted. Indeed, because
> individuals responding to marginality through . . . passing could
> be viewed as either conscious or unwitting accomplices in their
> own victimization—as persons consenting to the continuing
> maintenance of existing inequalities and exclusionary ideolo-
> gies—it is certainly understandable why they often elicited such
> scathing criticism from their contemporaries.[104]

Passing, however, has always constituted something of a challenge
to racist regimes. That is why such regimes have typically attempted to
prevent it. As a means to escape bondage, passing freed human beings
and helped to belie the canard that slaves were actually content with
their lot. Later on, the successful performance of "white men's work"
by passing Negroes gave the lie to claims that blacks were categorically
incapable of doing such work. As Professor Kevin K. Gaines has noted,
"However imperceptible and individualistic passing was, it also defied
widespread attempts to fix blacks in a socially subordinate 'place.'"[105]
The scope of the subversion was, of course, severely limited by the
practical necessity of keeping the passing secret. But in certain spheres,
a limited subversion was all that could be accomplished in any case.

---

*St. Clair Drake and Horace Cayton found that in Chicago in the 1940s, for exam-
ple, some whites were "willing to overlook a small infusion of Negro blood provided
[that] the person who is passing has no social ties with Negroes" (*Black Metropolis*,
159). Professor James E. DeVries discovered and related the same phenomenon in
his study *Race and Kinship in a Midwestern Town: The Black Experience in Monroe, Michigan, 1900–1915* (1984). According to DeVries, those blacks "who had
the physical attributes to pass and who denied their background were, in effect,
rewarded with the legal appellation 'white.'" Although many whites realized that the
passers "had a 'tainted' lineage, the racist ideology allowed the transition as [the
passers] were moving in the right direction" (Ibid., 152).

Critics have accused passers of complicity in the injustice of the regimes they sought to evade, and in some instances, the charge was undoubtedly true. A few passers even became loud and fervent bigots. Harriet Jacobs, for one, noted that in her hometown, among the most insidious antagonists of slaves, was "a free colored man, who tried to pass himself off for white . . . [and] was always ready to do any mean work for the sake of currying favor with white people. . . . Everybody knew he had the blood of a slave father in his veins; but for the sake of passing himself off for white, he was ready to kiss the slaveholders' feet. How I despised him."[106] But jumping on the racist bandwagon was rarely a necessary entailment of passing, and it is at least plausible that some passers may have tried to challenge racist practices from their newly acquired positions of racial privilege. Successful passing did indeed distance its individual practitioners from others in the subordinated group. The same might be said of various other strategies that have escaped the contempt routinely heaped upon passing. Most notably, the millions of blacks who fled segregationist oppression in the Jim Crow era could be said to have resorted to an "escapist" solution to their plight, in the sense that their strategy, too, distanced them from those they left behind. But few commentators have maligned the participants in the Great Migrations on that account. Foreign immigrants who come to America have often been lionized in the popular culture; not so passers, who nonetheless resemble immigrants in several important respects. The parallel was remarked by a novelist who sympathetically described a passing character as "a naturalized foreigner in the world of wide opportunity."[107] Just as immigrants leave their homelands for what they hope will be better opportunities abroad, sometimes casting away their names and languages in the process, so, too, do passers abandon their racial homeland for what they hope will be a better life on the other side of the color line. But whereas the immigrant is widely hailed for his initiative, the passer is generally cursed as a self-seeking opportunist.

When confronted by oppressive circumstances, people sometimes stand and fight for change. This is often an admirable approach. An alternative strategy is exit, or the conscious decision to leave behind a bad situation and go in search of a better one. Exit, in the words of Professor Albert O. Hirschman, "has been accorded an extraordinarily privileged position in the American tradition." The exhortation "Go west!" is but one of many resonant indicators of the centrality of exit in American history, psychology, and mythology. "The United States owes its very existence and growth," Hirschman wrote, "to millions of decisions favoring exit" over standing and fighting. Nothing is more classically American than the figure of the "successful individual who starts out at a low rung of the social ladder [and] necessarily leaves his own group behind as he rises." This person then "'passes' into, or is 'accepted' by, the next higher group."[108]*

The most sympathetic portrayals of passing are found in the work of Charles W. Chesnutt,† perhaps most notably *The House Behind the Cedars* (1900). Set in the post-Reconstruction era, this novel tells the story of John and Rena Walden, the children of a white man and his mulatto mistress. Determined to break free of the constraints imposed on him by the locals' knowledge of his racially mixed parentage, John leaves his mother's home in North Carolina and moves to South Carolina. There he changes his name to John Warwick, passes for white, marries the widow of a Confederate officer, and establishes a large and prosperous law practice. At first, Rena stays behind with their mother and maintains her association with their colored neighbors, but after a time, at John's urging, she, too, moves to South Carolina and passes for

---

*Hirschman also noted, however, that the successful individual engaged in exit "takes his immediate family along" (Albert O. Hirschman, *Exit, Voice, and Loyalty: Responses to Decline in Firms, Organizations, and States* [1970], 109). One of the things that commentators have found most horrifying and outrageous about passers is that many cut off even their closest relatives. The person who severs familial ties in pursuit of ambition conforms, though, to the template of that most American of obsessions, getting ahead.

†The extraordinarily gifted Chesnutt (1858–1932) was himself a "voluntary Negro"—that is, he could have passed but chose instead to identify himself as black. The first African American writer whose craftsmanship was taken seriously by the white literary establishment, Chesnutt dealt with passing repeatedly in his works. In addition to *House Behind the Cedars*, see his novels *Paul Marchand, F.M.C.* (written in 1921 but published in 1998) and *Mandy Oxendine* (written in 1897 but published in 1997). For more on Chesnutt, see William L. Andrews, *The Literary Career of Charles W. Chesnutt* (1980); Helen M. Chesnutt, *Charles Waddell Chesnutt: Pioneer of the Color Line* (1952).

white. She falls in love with one of her brother's rich white clients and is about to marry him when he accidentally learns of her racial background and, dismayed, withdraws his proposal. John counsels Rena to move to another city and try passing for white once again, but she rejects that idea and instead goes back to the colored community in which they were both raised. Soon after her return, she meets a tragic end while attempting to escape a villainous, sexually threatening black man.

*The House Behind the Cedars* stands as an interesting counterpoint to Frank Webb's *The Garies and Their Friends*. In the latter novel, the sibling who stays black attains happiness, while the sibling who passes reaps only misery. In the former work, by contrast, it is the sibling who returns to the African American fold who suffers; her passing brother seems comparatively blessed in his racial identity as a white man. Unlike many other passers in American fiction, John Warwick evinces no agonized self-doubt regarding his decision to become white. "I've taken a man's chance in life," he tells his mother, "and have tried to make the most of it; and I haven't felt under any obligation to spoil it by raking up old stories that are best forgotten."[109] Still, passing is not without its price for him: it pains him to have to visit his mother's house under the cover of darkness, and he feels acutely the insecurity that menaces all passers. One of the reasons he encourages his sister to pass and to live with or near him is that he longs for the company of at least one person with whom he can be completely open about his racial secret. But in terms of benefits versus costs, there is no question that in John's view, he has made the right choice in passing. "One who had gained so much," he muses, "ought not to complain if he must give a little."[110]

This last remark will doubtless strike some readers as being insulting to blacks, inasmuch as it suggests that John Warwick is (literally) belittling the value of his association with African Americans, referring to it as the one "little" thing he believes he must sacrifice in order to gain "so much"—meaning public recognition as a white man. Some readers will likely condemn this attitude as a manifestation of self-hatred and a form of racial betrayal. But another, perhaps equally valid reading might hold that what makes John "black" is nothing more than racist legislation and custom undeserving of deference. He should have the authority to decide for himself, it may be argued, which racial group, if any, he wishes to be affiliated with. If he chooses to be white, then so be it; he looks white, in any case—it is his appearance, after all, that enables him to pass in the first place. Moreover, it is with whites that he clearly feels most at ease. This is why he can declare that he is giving up "little" by leaving the black community of his childhood and joining the white community of his maturity. If he were giving up what he considered to be "too much," he would presumably decline to pass.

The question of authority over racial affiliation and classification reaches back well into American history, and it remains a vexing issue in our own day. One of the landmarks in the debate was the case of *Plessy v. Ferguson* (1896).[111] That infamous dispute challenged the constitutionality of a state law requiring blacks and whites to be seated apart on trains, in "equal but separate" railway cars. The suit was brought by a shoemaker named Homer Plessy, who was just one eighth black and so light-skinned that he could have passed for white had he so desired.* The case would attain notoriety after the United States Supreme Court rejected Plessy's claim that the law in question branded

---

*Some commentators have maintained, erroneously, that Homer Plessy was trying to pass, and that what he objected to was not racial segregation per se so much as the restrictions binding those who, like him, were "almost white." Plessy's attorney, Albion Tourgee, did complain that the segregation statute unfairly deprived his client of a valuable right—the reputation of belonging to the white race—and one could reasonably infer from that complaint a desire on Plessy's part to be recognized as white. But that particular argument deviated from the overall thrust of Tourgee's brief, which comprehensively attacked racial segregation as a general practice, not merely as it applied to a single individual. It should be noted, moreover, that *Plessy v. Ferguson* was a carefully choreographed test case. The suit was initiated and supported by a group of light-skinned men of color who eschewed and abhorred all racial distinctions. Far from seeking to pass, Plessy had made it known that he was a man of color sitting in a railroad car reserved only for whites. One reason Plessy, a man who was seven eighths white, was chosen to challenge the law was that the example of his persecution highlighted the statute's arbitrariness. See Diana Irene Williams, "New Orleans in the Age of *Plessy v. Ferguson:* Interracial Unions and the Politics of Caste" (senior thesis, Harvard University, 1995); Charles A. Lofgren, *The Plessy Case: A Legal-Historical Interpretation* (1987); Otto H. Olsen, ed., *The Thin Disguise:* Plessy v. Ferguson (1978). See also Amy Robinson, "Forms of Appearance of Value: Homer Plessy and the Politics of Privacy," in Elin Diamond, ed., *Performance and Cultural Politics* (1996).

blacks as inferior. Because the segregation statute applied to whites as well as blacks, the Court ruled that the state was meeting its obligation, under the Fourteenth Amendment, to provide to all persons the equal protection of the law. Less well known was another aspect of Plessy's argument: the contention that the federal Constitution deprived states of the authority to affix racial labels to individuals. In other words, Plessy did not object simply to being relegated to a railroad car that the larger community considered inferior because it had been set aside by law for use by a stigmatized segment of the population; he objected, more fundamentally, to the state's presumption that it could legitimately operate a system of racial matching under which, regardless of their personal wishes, *all* individuals could be assigned racial categories to which they would thenceforth "belong."* Homer Plessy lost this latter argument in 1896. He would lose it again today. While courts have significantly limited the power of states and of the federal government to draw racial lines, they have also permitted such demarcation for purposes they deemed sufficiently compelling.[112] The judiciary has, moreover, upheld governmental authority to assign racial labels to individuals, though labeling undertaken expressly to stigmatize has usually been invalidated. Thus, in 1964, at the urging of black candidates for electoral office, the Supreme Court of the United States struck down a Louisiana statute that required racial designations to be placed above the names of all candidates on state ballots—because, in the Court's

---

*Plessy's brief asserted, in part:

> The act in question . . . proceeds upon the hypothesis that the State has the right to authorize and require the officers of a railway to assort the citizens who engage in passage on its lines. . . . The gist of our case is the unconstitutionality of the assortment. . . . We insist that that the State has no right to compel us to ride in a car "set apart" for a particular race, whether it is as good as another or not. . . . The question is not as to the *equality* of the privileges enjoyed, but *the right of the State to label one citizen as white and another as colored* in the common enjoyment of a common highway. [*Landmark Briefs and Arguments of the Supreme Court of the United States*, vol. 13, edited by Philip B. Kurland and Gerhard Casper (1975), 27, 55–56]

words, the statute marshaled "the power of the State behind a racial classification that induces racial prejudice at the polls."[113] At around the same time, however, the Supreme Court upheld the constitutionality of a Virginia statute requiring that all divorce decrees specify the race of the divorcing parties.[114] The justices offered no explanation for the latter ruling, but their reasoning was likely that this sort of racial designation posed little or no threat of stigmatization and could be helpful in tracking demographic trends. It has been widely assumed, for the same reason, that no constitutional impediments hamper racial identification for purposes of census-taking or the administration of affirmative-action programs.

Among the litany of charges leveled against passing, none has been more prevalent than the complaint that passers are "living a lie." This indictment prompts further investigation into two aspects of passing: first, the complex forms that such deception can take, and second, the nature of those conditions under which deceptiveness may be considered morally and legally permissible.

There are many ways to deceive. At one end of the spectrum is deception through the telling of a clear falsehood—for example, stating that a stoplight was green when one knows in fact it was red. At the other end is deception by omission—as when a person declines to disclose information that might provoke undesirable thoughts or actions on the part of others. This latter strategy has often been the modus operandi of the passer.[115] Intent on obtaining medical training, for instance, Albert Johnston Jr. refrained from informing his white superiors at a hospital that he was a Negro, but neither did he tell them he was white; he simply allowed them to believe what they wanted to believe.*

---

*The United States Navy, however, *did* interrogate him as to his race. During World War II, after Dr. Johnston tried to enlist, a background check suggested that he might not be as white as the navy wanted its officers to be. So a naval intelligence agent came to his office and briefly interrogated him:

Similarly, in passing for white throughout his first years at Colgate College, Adam Clayton Powell Jr. never actually told his classmates that he *was* white; he merely neglected to correct their mistaken assumption to that effect—an assumption based on his appearance.[116]* James Weldon Johnson's character "the ex-colored man," for his part, gives the matter some careful thought and then explains, "I finally made up my mind that I would neither disclaim the black race, nor claim the white race; but that I would change my name, raise a mustache, and let the world take me for what it would; that it was not necessary for me to go about with a label of inferiority pasted across my forehead."[117]

Is this deception? Yes, it is. True, the ex-colored man does not deceive by deploying a positive falsehood; rather, he deceives by purposely leaving unstated certain facts about his situation, an omission that under the circumstances leads most observers to assign him one racial label (white) when, if they knew the facts withheld, they would apply a radically different one (black). The real issue, though, is not whether the passer deceives; as I have defined passing, deception is an

---

"We understand that, even though you are registered as white, you have colored blood in your veins."

"Who knows what blood any of us has in his veins?" said the doctor.

The neat young [intelligence agent], who had been asked to sit down, now got up.

"Thank you very much, Doctor," he said. "That is all we want to know."

Soon after this interview, Johnston received a rejection notice, which said that the navy was "unable to approve [his] application because of [his] inability to meet physical requirements" (quoted in W. L. White, *Lost Boundaries* [1947], 32).

*Once his Negro ancestry had been revealed to the student body, Powell apologized to the few other black students enrolled at the college. According to one biographer, Powell's lineage became common knowledge after some of his white classmates paid a visit to his father's famous Abyssinian Baptist Church in Harlem; see Will Haygood, *King of the Cats: The Life and Times of Adam Clayton Powell, Jr.* (1993), 10–11. Another biographer maintained that his racial background was uncovered by investigators in the employ of an exclusively white fraternity that Powell sought to join; see Charles V. Hamilton, *Adam Clayton Powell, Jr.* (1991), 48–50. Haygood and Hamilton concurred that when Powell's negritude became generally known, his white roommate insisted that he move out, a demand that was supported by the college administration.

essential part of the enterprise. The question is how we should assess the deception. Deceptions are by no means all equal. Some are morally allowable, while others are not. It is one thing to lie to a murderer to protect a prospective victim; it is quite another to lie to a judge to bring down an innocent rival. Many who otherwise condemn passing would readily excuse it as a means to help someone escape death or enslavement—as in the case, for instance, of the Crafts. Similarly, most would agree that while fraud is presumptively bad, there are exceptional situations in which even the most overt deceptiveness—out-and-out lying—may be justified or at least excusable, and that once again, slavery and the threat of lynching both present such situations. But if this proposition is accepted, what precisely defines an "exception"? If deception for the purpose of fleeing slavery is morally permissible, what about deception to evade some of the other oppressions that most blacks have endured? In my own view, passing to avoid these stultifications is morally defensible if it can be accomplished by means that do not impose a morally prohibitive burden on innocent parties. Honesty and candor are surely presumptive virtues, but they are *only* that; when the challenge is to escape immoral oppression, the presumption against dishonesty is overcome.*

The question becomes even more complex when we consider another facet of it. Those who are willing to excuse the deception of racist enemies by a passer may feel quite differently about the deception of others, and particularly of intimates to whom special obligations of trust are owed. In the literature of passing, the dilemma of whether or not to reveal racial secrets to a loved one of another race arises repeatedly. In *The Garies and Their Friends,* for example, Clarence agonizes over his decision to withhold his secret from Little Birdie, and later rues his silence. In *The House Behind the Cedars,* Rena wrestles with whether to tell her white fiancé about her colored background. She is inclined to do so but is talked out of it by her brother. "Why should he know?" John asks. "We haven't asked him for his pedigree; we don't care to know it. If he cares for ours, he should ask for it, and it

---

*For an important analysis of deception by a writer who is generally more intolerant of it than I am, see Sissela Bok, *Lying: Moral Choice in Public and Private Life* (1978).

would then be time enough to raise the question." "I'm afraid he'd be unhappy if he knew," Rena responds, "and it would make me miserable to think him unhappy." Building upon this comment, John asks soothingly, "Do you imagine [George] would be any happier than he is now, or than if he should never know?" The suggestion implicit in this question—that Rena telling George her secret would impose an unwanted burden upon him—helps to convince her to stay quiet. "It had never before occurred to her," interjects the narrator, "to regard silence in the light of self-sacrifice. It had seemed a sort of sin; her brother's argument made of it a virtue. It was not the first time, nor the last, that right and wrong had been a matter of viewpoint."[118]

If Chesnutt raised doubts about imprudent truth-telling, William Dean Howells undertook a frontal attack on it in his novel *An Imperative Duty* (1893). At the center of this drama is a young woman, Miss Aldgate, who is unaware of her racially mixed parentage (white father, colored mother). After being orphaned at an early age, Miss Aldgate is led to believe by her aunt and guardian, Miss Meredith, that she is white.

Howells's characters are repeatedly forced to consider the morality of truth-telling in situations where the truth will predictably wound the person who is told. Thus, prompted by what she takes to be her "imperative duty," Miss Meredith tells Miss Aldgate the truth about her origins, moving the latter to respond: "Why, I must be dreaming. It's as if—as if—you were to come to a perfectly well person, and tell them that they were going to die in half an hour."[119]

Miss Meredith insists, moreover, that Miss Aldgate break the news to her suitors. Himself convinced that under the circumstances, it would be preferable to keep silent, Howells excoriated Miss Meredith in his text, branding her a "duty-ridden" creature "capable of an atrocious cruelty in speaking or acting the truth," a woman who "would consider herself an exemplary person for having done her duty at any cost of suffering to herself and others," a truth-telling absolutist able to declare, at one point, "It is better to die—to kill—than to lie."[120] To accentuate her fanatical "dutiolatry," Howells had Miss Meredith inform the reader that she "would rather see her [niece] perish before

[her] eyes than [be] married to any man who did not know the secret of her."[121]

Race matters a great deal to many of the characters who enliven the fictional literature of passing. George Tryon, for example, breaks off his engagement to Rena when he discovers that she is a Negro. Clarence Garie's plan to marry Little Birdie Bates likewise dissolves after her family is apprised of his racial background. Dr. Olney, the hero of *An Imperative Duty,* eventually marries Miss Aldgate, but he does so *despite* his knowledge of her racial lineage: he proposes to her only because his love for her overwhelms all other considerations. His initial reaction upon learning of her racial "taint" is "a turmoil of emotion for which there is no term but disgust. . . . He found himself personally disliking the notion of her having negro blood in her veins; before he felt pity he felt repulsion . . . a merciless rejection of her beauty, her innocence, her helplessness because of her race."[122] In James Weldon Johnson's novel, the ex-colored man confides his racial secret to the white woman he desires to marry. Over time, she will come to appreciate the individual virtues of her "white Negro" suitor and indeed will ultimately marry him, but when she first learns that he is colored, she, like Dr. Olney, is distressed. As Johnson's protagonist recounts the scene:

> I felt her hand grow cold, and when I looked up, she was gazing at me with a wild, fixed stare as though I was some object she had never seen. . . . Her lips trembled and she attempted to say something to me, but the words stuck in her throat. Then, dropping her head on the piano, she began to weep with great sobs that shook her frail body.[123]*

---

*Revealing his racial secret is a traumatic task for the ex-colored man. He considers keeping quiet about his passing but rejects that alternative as an "indirect deception" that affronts his sense of honor. Still, he dreads telling his beloved the truth about his racial past: "I am sure," he muses, "that I should have found it easier to take the place of a gladiator . . . than to tell that slender girl that I had Negro blood in my veins" (James Weldon Johnson, *The Autobiography of an Ex-Colored Man* [1912], edited and with an introduction by William L. Andrews [1990], 146).

Suppose, though, that Johnson's passer chose instead to withhold the fact of his Negro ancestry. Would that or should that constitute a legal or moral wrong?

## Passing Today

The question posed above is by no means anachronistic in our own day, when passing continues to excite volatile responses.* This is evidenced by the vehemence with which some observers continue to denounce the phenomenon. "Trying to forgive Blacks who pass is difficult," an African American observer notes. "I feel that by passing, they have cursed the memory of every dark skinned person on their family tree."[124] The emotional combustibility of passing and of conduct viewed as being kindred to it is also underscored by the deep resonance of certain sayings—for instance, "Stay black" and "Don't forget where you come from"—that voice, among other things, a fear of racial desertion.[125]†

Racial passing and anxieties about it might be expected to have been rendered marginal by now, given the substantial declines in the intensity and power of antiblack sentiments and practices. Simply being perceived as black no longer bars a person absolutely from most of our

---

*The reader may recall, for example, the heated controversy that surrounded Secretary of State Madeleine Albright several years ago, when journalists reported that she had Jewish ancestors who had perished in the holocaust, and some charged that she, as a practicing Episcopalian, had misleadingly denied knowledge of those facts to maintain distance from her Jewish roots. See Michael Dobbs, *Madeleine Albright: A Twentieth-Century Odyssey* (2000), 377–95; Ann Blackman, *Seasons of Her Life: A Biography of Madeleine Albright* (1998), 272–93. See also Peter Margulies, "The Identity Question, Madeleine Albright's Past and Me: Insights from Jewish and African-American Law and Literature," *Loyola of Los Angeles Entertainment Law Journal* 17 (1997): 595. And, of course, passing with respect to sexual orientation has itself been a central topic of debate in recent struggles for gay and lesbian liberation. Issues here have included disputes over the morality of outing (see, e.g., Larry Gross, *Contested Closets: The Politics and Ethics of Outing* [1993]) and the federal government's "Don't ask, don't tell" policy, which effectively makes passing a requirement of military service for lesbians and gays (see e.g., Janet Halley, *Don't: A Reader's Guide to the Military's Anti-Gay Policy* [1999]).

†Philip Roth's *The Human Stain* (2000) and Danzy Senna's *Caucasia* (1998) demonstrate that literary artists continue to find in passing a powerful vehicle for exploring American culture.

society's attractive opportunities. But for some observers, the spectre of racial disunity, racial disloyalty, and even racial dissolution looms larger now precisely because African Americans have more choice than ever before regarding whom to date, where to live, and what school to attend. With more choices, larger numbers of blacks have more opportunities to distance themselves physically, socially, and psychologically from other blacks.* The prospect of new modes of "passing" by which, regardless of their hue, Negroes become so-called Oreos—black on the outside but white on the inside—has played an important role in prompting some African Americans to pursue a renewed commitment to group solidarity. Some who are stirred by black-nationalist aspirations hope to foster a black communitarianism that would instill in African Americans a heightened sense of racial obligation. Those with this vision—the ideological descendants of Frances Harper—consider it urgent that blacks eschew assimilation into "mainstream" (i.e., "white") society. Many of them also assert unapologetically that blacks ought to prefer one another over nonblack others. A broad array of African Americans, including many who study or work in racially integrated settings, have adopted these premises. They disapprove of blacks marrying whites, oppose interracial adoption of black children, and resist changes in verbal formulations or census classifications that would enable those now deemed "black" to identify themselves differently (e.g., as "multiracial"). For them, all of these are akin to passing, and they condemn as "escapist," "inauthentic," or even "fraudulent" any initiative that might lead to a debilitating "whitening" of what they feel should be an authentically "black" African American community.

Who is "right," then, in the debate over racial passing? Is passing a self-defeating betrayal of the passer's race, or a defensible assertion of

---

*Substantial numbers of people in many (maybe all) minority groups feel torn between, on the one hand, taking full advantages of the opportunities offered by white Anglo Christian America (the "mainstream") and, on the other, maintaining a distinctive community immune from complete assimilation. For recent expressions of and reflections on Jewish anxieties regarding passing, assimilation, and related phenomena, see Alan M. Dershowitz, *The Vanishing Jew* (1997); Elliott Abrams, *Faith or Fear: How Jews Can Survive in a Christian America* (1997); Marjorie Garber, "Gentility," in *Symptoms of Culture* (1998).

individual autonomy? Satisfactory answers cannot be determined in the abstract; they must always depend on the context. In any given instance, we have to ask, what are the consequences of declining to pass? Are there alternative avenues for seeking the same goals? To whom must the passer lie in order to pass? To which groups, if any, does he or she feel a sense of affiliation? To what extent does passing entrench or subvert a particular social order? The answers depend, moreover, on the baseline values of those sitting in judgment.

It should be clear by now that I myself am skeptical of, if not hostile toward, claims of racial kinship, the valorization of racial roots, and politics organized around concepts of racial identity.[126] I am a liberal individualist who yearns for a society in which race has become obsolete as a significant social marker.

I recognize that mobilizations of racial patriotism have prompted useful and inspiring acts of resistance to racism. I applaud, for instance, the magnificent, disciplined rebellion organized in 1954–55 in Montgomery, Alabama, through which blacks, and a few whites, succeeded in desegregating municipal buses. During that famous struggle, Martin Luther King Jr. expressly invoked notions of racial pride to animate Montgomery's blacks, exhorting them to stand together as a people to end Jim Crow seating. Noble though it was in many respects, the boycott—like all movements of collective action—nevertheless relied on coercion to cement the solidarity necessary to defeat the foes of African American advancement. The boycott worked because blacks heeded King's call for them to stay off the buses, but its success was also due in part to implicit and explicit coercion, whereby would-be strikebreakers were made aware that such actions would incur the strikers' wrath. The larger group of Montgomery blacks thus effectively banned individualistic responses by its members to the crisis at hand. Some Negroes who may have wanted to ride the bus were prevented from doing so by fear.[127] That fear, and the coercion from which it sprang, however, were signs not of strength but of weakness. The boycott would have been even more meaningful had there been no blocking of racial exits—that is, had every black in Montgomery felt perfectly free to decide for himself or herself what to do, and then resolved to boycott as a matter of human, not racial but *human*, conscience.

A well-ordered multiracial society ought to allow its members free entry into and exit from racial categories, even if the choices they make clash with traditional understandings of who is "black" and who is "white," and even if, despite making such choices in good faith, individuals mislead observers who rely on conventional racial signaling. Rather than seeking to bind people forever to the racial classifications into which they are born, we should try both to eradicate the deprivations that make some want to pass *and* to protect individuals' racial self-determination, including their ability to revise stated racial identities.

Ironically, some of the bitterest disputes over passing in recent years have involved "whites" charged with posing as "blacks." Consider, for example, the case of Mark L. Stebbins. In 1985 Stebbins faced a recall election that threatened to oust him from his seat on the Stockton, California, city council. A rival claimed that Stebbins had lied to voters in a predominantly Latino and black district, holding himself out as black when he was in fact white. News reports described Stebbins as being both light-skinned and blue-eyed, and on his birth certificate, both of his parents were listed as white. His first wife was also white, but in subsequent marriages, he had twice wed black women, the second of whom he had met at an NAACP meeting. Stebbins himself remembered that his broad nose and curly hair had made him the object of teasing when he was a teenager in rural Washington State, and that classmates had sometimes referred to him as "Niggerhead." He conceded that for the first twenty years of his life, he had thought of himself as white. But he insisted that after moving to Stockton in 1966, in the wake of an engagement with civil rights activism in San Francisco, he had come to the "gradual realization" that he was actually black. Asked in the midst of the recall campaign how he could identify himself as black when his parents were officially classified as white, Stebbins replied that he must be black because he *felt* black. When questioned about Stebbins's racial identity, a black friend remarked that the councilman was "whatever he says his is." He elaborated, "If you say you're black, there is such a curse to it, nobody will argue with you. If you want that loaf of bread, anybody will give it to you."[128] The friend, however, was clearly mistaken in at least one regard: Stebbins's rival, a black politician, *did* argue with him over his purported blackness, and was eventually rewarded by Stebbins's recall.*

Another hotly contested passing dispute concerned claims made by two brothers, Paul and Phillip Malone.[129] Seeking jobs as firefighters in Boston in 1975, they identified themselves on their applications as white. They were rejected. Two years later, they reapplied, but this time they indicated that they were black—a "fact" that undoubtedly improved their chances of being selected, since the fire department was operating under a court-ordered affirmative-action plan intended to remedy a long history of antiblack racial exclusion. The Malones succeeded on their second try. A decade later, when one of the brothers pursued a promotion, someone told fire-department officials that both were racial impostors. In their defense, the Malones insisted they were black, maintaining that after their initial rejection by the fire department, they had discovered that their maternal great-grandmother had been a Negro. The personnel administrator for the Commonwealth of Massachusetts invited the Malones to support their claim that they were black "(1) by visual observation of their features; (2) by appropriate documentary evidence, such as birth certificates, establishing black ancestry; or (3) by evidence that they or their families hold themselves out to be Black and are considered to be Black in the community."[130] The administrator further stipulated that the Malones would be entitled to a favorable ruling "even in the absence of meeting the standard

---

*In the absence of more information than I have at my disposal, it is impossible for me to make an accurate assessment of this outcome. If the voters were convinced on sensible grounds that Stebbins ought to be recalled, there is no cause for concern; representative democracy will have worked as it should. One such sensible ground may have been the belief that the councilman demonstrated unjustified evasiveness in his racial self-presentation. For reasons already explained, I would tend to disagree with this judgment, though it might be a close call in this case. Another possible basis for the recall was the notion that colored people should optimally be represented by colored agents, virtually regardless of those agents' substantive beliefs. This impulse to embrace "our own" on the merits ascribed to appearance and ancestry is venerable but stupid.

[for racial classification], if [it could be demonstrated] that [they] acted in good faith."[131]

An internal hearing gave the Malones an opportunity to make their case. The officer presiding noted that the brothers did not appear to be black and that there existed no convincing documentary evidence linking them to even any remote black ancestry. "White" was the racial designation stamped on the birth certificates of both men, of their parents, and of their parents' parents. As for the maternal great-grandmother whom the Malone brothers described as being black, the hearing officer dismissed their alleged photograph of her as inconclusive. Finally, the officer found no evidence that the Malones had ever identified themselves as black except in their attempt to benefit from the fire department's affirmative-action program.* Against this backdrop, the personnel administrator concluded that the Malones failed to meet an "objective" standard of blackness and, further, that they had not believed in good faith that they were black when they applied for their positions as African Americans. Justice Herbert P. Wilkins of the Massachusetts Supreme Judicial Court subsequently affirmed the administrator's reasoning and ruling.

It would have been helpful for the court to have discussed expressly the relationship between the means used to determine race in the fire department and the purposes of its affirmative-action program.[132] If, for example, the program's goal was to make special opportunities available to those whose apparent blackness had previously caused them to be excluded from eligibility for firefighter positions, it would make sense (in the absence of overwhelming costs detailed below) to limit the class of beneficiaries to those who were apparently black. The same would be true if the aim of the affirmative-action program was to elevate the fire department in the eyes of blacks by demonstrating, in a highly public fashion, that African Americans were now welcomed as firefighters. Both of these scenarios would beg the question of why a person generally perceived to be "white" should be allowed to participate in the program simply because of some idiosyncratic, albeit

---

*In the 1986 census of Milton, Massachusetts, the Malones identified themselves as white. See Bella English, "Color Coordinated," *Boston Globe,* October 12, 1988.

honest, desire to be "black"—the administrator's "good faith" exception.[133]

The strength of the Malone decision, as it was handed down, consists in its implicit, if inarticulate, suggestion that no plausible aim of the affirmative-action plan would have been worth the cost of excluding individuals from racial identifications that they honestly embraced. By insisting that people who might conventionally be described as white could nonetheless be classified as black so long as they truly considered themselves to be black, Justice Wilkins paid appropriate deference to the healthy intuition that a free society ought to permit its members to freely enter and exit racial categories—even for the purpose of gaining access to public entitlement programs—fettered only by the bonds of good faith. Justice Wilkins rightly rejected the baleful notion that state power could or should be used to confine every person to a given racial station, regardless of his or her individual preferences. The merit of this insistence that society must provide ample opportunity for racial self-determination is highlighted by a comparison with the conventional demand that all citizens accept whatever racial category may be impressed upon them at birth by the state. Championing the latter approach, an article written in response to the Malone brothers' case suggests that in order to avoid future instances of racial fraud, governments would do well to revive the practices of noting race on birth certificates and classifying individuals according to the race of their parents. "Those who falsely allege their race," the author of the piece argued, "should be . . . subject to criminal penalties."[134]* The

---

*It bears noting that legislation has been proposed to the United States Congress that would make it a criminal offense for a Native American to pass as a non–Native American for purposes of evading the Indian Child Welfare Act. See the Indian Child Welfare Improvement Act of 1995, S. 764, 104th Cong., 1st Sess. (1995); H.R. 1448, 104th Cong., 1st Sess. (1995); and the Adoption Promotion and Stability Act of 1996, H.R. 3276, 104th Cong., 2d Sess. (1996). These proposals were prompted by a case in which a man seeking to have his children adopted at first disclosed his Indian background on legal documents but then changed his mind after being informed that such information would jeopardize his plans. See In re *Bridget R.*, 49 Cal. Rptr. 2d 507 (1996). For more on this case, see pages 506–11.

In the eyes of many Native Americans, the more pressing problem of passing cuts in the opposite direction with too many whites and others falsely, or at least

motivation behind this call for a racial registration system differs from that behind the racial registries codified by Virginia and other jurisdictions in the Jim Crow era. Here, the driving force is a desire to thwart corruption and the sabotage of programs that have helped many people affiliated with historically oppressed racial groups. Still, whatever the motivation, the prospect of a new wave of racial identification laws is a frightening one. I, for one, believe that it would be better to tolerate some racial fraud, or even a considerable amount of it, under a regime of racial self-identification than to allow affirmative-action programs to be policed via the imposition on individuals of racial identity tests. Indeed, even the abolition of such programs would be preferable to their continuation if intrusive racial policing were to become part of their price.[135] It bears noting, though, that there are remarkably few instances on record in which authorities challenged the participation of individuals in affirmative-action programs on the basis of their not belonging to a given racial category of designated beneficiaries. Criticism *has* been leveled at affirmative-action programs that assist black-owned businesses, on the ground that all too often, such businesses merely pass as "black" when in fact they are really white-run operations.[136] But thus far, there have been few counterparts to the Malone litigation—that is, cases in which the racial bona fides of individuals were challenged.* There is no definitive account of why this is so. My impression is that authorities are rightly loath to investigate or repudiate

---

wrongly, claiming to be Indians. Some Native Americans joke that the largest tribe in the United States will soon be the "wanabi." See Steve Russell, "A Black and White Issue: The Invisibility of American Indians in Racial Policy Discourse," 4 *Georgetown Public Policy Review*, 129, 131 (1999). See also L. Scott Gould, "Mixing Bodies and Beliefs: The Predicament of Tribes," 101 *Columbia Law Review* 702 (2001), and Margo S. Brownell, Note: "Who Is An Indian? Searching for An Answer to the Question at the Core of Federal Indian Law," 34 *University of Michigan Journal of Law Reform* 275 (2000).

*An interesting twist on the Malone episode is the scenario in which a passing "white Negro" passes back, reestablishes a black identity, and secures desirable employment as an African American—sometimes to the consternation of blacks who have never tried to pass and who resent the privileged mobility of those who have. See Doris Black, "How Passing Passed Out," *Sepia*, December 1972: "Now the only passing that is prevalent is from white to black. . . . Being black has become a job asset."

individuals' racial self-identification. It is also my impression, however, that relatively few whites have done what the Malone brothers did. One likely reason that whites who may be tempted to pass for black for purposes of obtaining affirmative-action benefits refrain from doing so is that the perceived risks as a rule outweigh the perceived benefits. One risk, of course, is the reputational harm associated with being revealed as a passer; another is the risk that the masquerade may be all too successful and thus cause the white passer to suffer the racial penalties that "real" blacks continue to face.*

---

*The film *Soul Man* (1986) portrays a spoiled, affluent white student who passes for black in order to win a scholarship earmarked for African Americans. At first, the student is ecstatic: "This is the cushy decade!" he exclaims. "America loves black people." But then, after his skin darkens as a result of a deliberate overdose of tanning pills, he encounters a reality very different from the one he has envisioned. He gets the scholarship money, but he also gets racially harassed by prejudiced police officers, classmates, and a landlord. Reacting to the cue of his darkened skin, strangers see him as a potential rapist, pimp, or mugger instead of what he actually is: a student. In becoming black, the "soul man" thus gets much more than he bargained for. See Clarence Page, "I'm Sold, Man, on the Movie 'Soul Man,'" *Chicago Tribune*, October 29, 1986.

When Mel Ferrer played the part of a passing "white Negro" in *Lost Boundaries,* he and members of his family became targets of antiblack prejudice by people who identified him with the character he portrayed. See Al Weisman, "He Passed as a Negro," *Negro Digest*, October 1951.

# EIGHT

# Passing and the Schuyler Family

Few, if any, families in American history have struggled more articulately with the opportunities and vexations of interracial marriage, transracial parenting, and racial masquerade than George, Josephine, and Philippa Schuyler.* A black journalist who careened ideologically from the left in the 1920s to the far right in the 1960s, George Schuyler married a white woman, praised intermarriage, and authored the novel *Black No More,* a satirical exploration of "passing." Josephine Cogdell, the strong-willed Texan who became his wife, exiled herself to the black side of the race line. Their prodigiously gifted daughter, Philippa, garnered national acclaim for her musical and intellectual achievements as a child before succumbing as an adult to profound unhappiness, racial self-loathing, and a tragic early death.

### The Courtship of George and Josephine Schuyler
George Schuyler was born around 1895 to a father who died when his son was only three and a resourceful, hardworking mother whom he would later describe lovingly as "the apostle of the possible."[1] He grew up in Syracuse, New York, completed high school, and in 1912 enlisted

---

*The only close competition is offered by LeRoi Jones/Imamu Baraka, the author of *The Dutchman;* Hettie Jones, LeRoi Jones's first wife and the author of *How I Became Hettie Jones* (1990); and Lisa Jones, Hettie and LeRoi's daughter, who wrote *Bulletproof Diva: Tales of Race, Sex and Hair* (1994). For more on the Joneses, see pages 112–15.

in the U.S. Army. Like many other African Americans, Schuyler found the military far more inclined than civilian employers to recognize, use, and reward his talents. Still, because the army was thoroughly segregated, Schuyler was permitted to serve his country only alongside other blacks, under the authority of white officers. He nevertheless won promotions, earned a steady paycheck, was able to travel to places he would not otherwise have seen (he especially liked being stationed in Hawaii), and, during a second tour of duty, began to write for publication.

Satisfying though its benefits were, Schuyler's stint in the army did not end well. One day in 1918 Lieutenant Schuyler tried to get his shoes shined at a bootblack stand in the Philadelphia train station, only to be loudly informed by the bootblack, a Greek immigrant, that he would not wait on "a nigger." Schuyler apparently attached great significance to this affront: it prompted him to go absent without leave for three months, a dereliction of duty for which a military court subsequently sentenced him to a five-year prison term. President Woodrow Wilson reduced that sentence to one year, of which Schuyler actually ended up serving only nine months.[2] After that, he spent several frustrating years in New York City trying to find a meaningful niche for himself. During this period, he eked out a meager living washing dishes, working as a stevedore, and being a Sabbath goy. Then, in 1922, he finally got a break. At Harlem meetings of the organization Friends of Negro Freedom, he met A. Philip Randolph, who invited him to help edit and produce *The Messenger,* a journal of socialist, antiracist opinion whose small readership consisted of freethinking, literarily oriented activists and intellectuals. *The Messenger* enabled Schuyler to develop as a writer and provided a forum for a number of others—most notably Countee Cullen, Langston Hughes, Wallace Thurman, Zora Neale Hurston, and Claude McKay—who would go on to be leading figures of the Harlem Renaissance.[3] Schuyler wrote a column for *The Messenger* that he promised would "slur, lampoon, damn, and occasionally praise anybody or anything in the known universe."[4]

George Schuyler met Josephine—"Jody"—Cogdell on July 27, 1927, when, with characteristic boldness, she dropped by the offices of *The Messenger* to introduce herself. She had contributed several poems and articles to the magazine and had admired Schuyler's writings from afar. Now she sought to meet him. Her visit constituted a striking anomaly. She was a twenty-seven-year-old white divorcée from an influential and affluent family that called the West Texas town of Granbury home. Her father was a successful cattle rancher, bank president, and founder of a telephone and electric company who undoubtedly would have hated Schuyler, Randolph, and *The Messenger* on both ideological and racial grounds. Although Jody's father kept a black mistress for over forty years, he managed to remain parochial, ignorant, and intensely racist. His sons, too, were racists, though at least one of them also enjoyed sexual intimacy with a black woman and even sired a child by her. Jody, by contrast, was an open-minded, cosmopolitan, free-spirited "new woman." She ran away from home to marry, quickly got divorced, and then moved for several years to California, where she studied painting, Chinese philosophy, and dance, all the while carefully recording her actions, beliefs, and moods in a series of diaries that she would keep religiously throughout her life.[5]

The evening they met, George Schuyler invited Jody Cogdell out to a restaurant and then took her to a club, where they danced until closing time. After a few more dates, their relationship grew intimate. In her diary entry for August 17, 1927, Jody confided, "George possessed me. My blood is still ringing from it. Somehow, strangely enough, I feel ennobled, I cannot explain why except that a complete satisfaction fills me with wholesomeness and gratitude towards life."[6] Submitting to what she perceived as an altogether unique embrace—"so strong, so virile, so tender," an embrace that was like "a benediction, a purification"—Jody had become George's lover.[7]

Initially, she believed their involvement would be brief. She thoroughly enjoyed his energy, presence, and ministrations. "His lips," she noted, "are softer and more sensuous than white lips."[8] Nor was that his only advantage: "The prowess of the fellow is classic," she observed. "He is subtle, masterful, bold, tender, seductive, imaginative. I come from his arms as from a religious experience. . . . No wonder the white man fears the negro—yes, he is a menace to their civilization."[9] Cogdell's delight in Schuyler as a lover—"Never was there such a man! He is Herculean"—served only to point up the deficits of her prospective white suitors: "They are all spoiled, smug or affected and I don't like the pasty white of their skins. . . . They all somehow appear to me as useless, superfluous, anemic, emasculated poor specimens beside the virile, fresh-looking blacks and suave-tongued mysterious-eyed mulattoes."[10]

Notwithstanding that preference, Cogdell felt certain that society's disapproval of interracial romance would be impossible for her to overcome. Her fears were confirmed repeatedly by her family and friends, not least the white man with whom she had lived in California before coming east. John Garth, a painter, paid her a visit in New York in an effort to win back her affection. When she advised him that he should feel free to go out with other women, he assumed that she was seeing another white man. Upon learning that it was Schuyler who was "the other man," Garth referred to him as a "nigger" and exclaimed, "What will your father say? What will [your sister] say? Your brothers ought to come up here and kill you both! And they will when they find out!"[11] Later, during another phase of the same argument, he screamed, "I hope you are pregnant and have a black baby!" When she replied that she hoped so, too, he retorted ominously (and with tragic prescience), "You'll probably end by committing suicide!"[12]

Over the course of a few days, Cogdell and Garth continued to fight over her new relationship with Schuyler. At one point, Garth made the terrible mistake of asking about the details of her nascent affair:

How long have you been Schuyler's mistress?
*Oh, six weeks or so. . . .*
Schuyler's the lucky chap, eh? You and a nigger? I always thought you'd do something like this. You've always had a Negro complex. You were probably an easy mark for him.
*He's not that kind at all.*
Oh, he's not sexual?
*Yes, he is ultrasexual. . . . If some of you superior Nordics knew half of what he knows about love you would not have to be so afraid of black competition. He is a marvelous lover and possesses the most gigantic anatomy.*

I thought you described him as a short man.
*Only in height. He is a person of surprising contrasts.*[13]

Jody Cogdell was reminded of just how deviant her intimacy with
Schuyler would cause her to appear to most white Americans when her
sister, Lena, came to visit. She recalled that Lena "broke up a dinner
party because one of the guests, a very blond and Nordic [looking]
movie star, expressed a regret that 'owing to American prejudice she
could not do a picture opposite a certain Negro actor,' who, she said,
was the handsomest man she had ever seen."[14] The uninformed bigotry
of Lena's husband, Ben, only amplified Cogdell's misgivings. She
remarked in her diary that on one occasion, a newspaper account of an
interracial marriage greatly distressed her brother-in-law: "'Aren't there
some states which permit intermarriage?' I asked casually from the bedroom. 'Certainly not!' he answered. 'Maybe Mexico does, but no *civilized* country permits such unnatural unions . . . !'"[15] A brief encounter
with a Catholic priest also drove home the point. Time was, the priest
told Jody, when "a decent white woman wouldn't go with a Jew." But
now, he complained, "they're crazy for the Jews . . . and Chinese, too!
Everything's changing like that. Pretty soon it'll be the niggers."[16]

Jody Cogdell understood what it would mean for her to marry a
black man. She knew how much many whites detested such matches;
her own family had given her a vivid tutorial on the subject. She also
knew that in the eyes of many whites, her status as the wife of a
black man would almost literally blacken her. Her attraction to George
Schuyler, however, overrode her fears. Describing swooningly his
"African profile, brooding and proud," she wrote in her diary:

> It draws me, undoes me, makes me long to sacrifice for
> it. . . . I want to say "Devour me, Negro, devour me." Aloud I
> say, "I should like you to kill me, Schuyler. . . ." "Sweet Heart,"
> he exclaims, looking shocked. Then a mischievous smile lights
> up his countenance, he leans over me with his long hands ges-
> turing diabolically. He takes my white throat in his hands and
> the pretense leaves his face and a sensuous look of cruelty

enters it as he sinks his fingers into my flesh. My lips meet his and I feel like a white rabbit caught in the coils of a glistening black snake. . . . Then I know that I love him. Oh God, how I love him as I've never loved before.[17]

Jody Cogdell and George Schuyler were wed on January 6, 1928, in New York City. Determined to keep her family in the dark about the relationship, she used her married name from her first brief union on the marriage certificate. To forestall any other difficulties, she also characterized herself as "colored."[18]

## Black No More

The culture of passing captivated George Schuyler. His most lasting contribution to American letters is a satirical exploration of the phenomenon, entitled *Black No More: Being an Account of the Strange and Wonderful Workings of Science in the Land of the Free*, A.D. *1933–1940* (1931).[19] A work of science fiction, it mocks what Schuyler perceived to be the silly racial myths of the day—myths that in the novel inspire all manner of mischief, from murder, to obsessive efforts to alter skin and hair, to the automatic rejection of suitors who, if given a chance, would prove loving, loyal, and pleasurable partners.

*Black No More* is premised on the discovery of a process that is able to make black people white. Max Disher, the protagonist, is "tall, dapper and smooth coffee-brown. His negroid features had a slightly satanic cast and there was an insolent nonchalance about his carriage."[20] When we meet him on New Year's Eve, 1933, he is in a sour mood because he has just broken up with his "high 'yallah'" girlfriend.* At the Honky Tonk Club, an after-hours joint in Harlem, Max's spirits rise when he spies a white woman "who ha[s] seemingly stepped from heaven or the front cover of a magazine."[21] Despite a

---

*According to the narrator, Max and his best friend "had a common weakness rather prevalent among Aframerican blacks: They preferred yellow women. Both swore there were three things essential to the happiness of a colored gentleman: yellow money, yellow women and yellow taxis" (George Schuyler, *Black No More* [1931; reprint, 1987], 19).

friend's warnings, Max asks the woman to dance. She turns him down, declaring, "I never dance with niggers!,"[22] but her rejection only reinforces Max's resolve to woo her. A means of doing so presents itself to him when he learns that one Dr. Junius Crookman, a black scientist, has found a way to transform Negroes into Caucasians. Max decides to subject himself to Crookman's treatment because "the statuesque and haughty blonde was ever in his thoughts. He was head over heels in love with her and realized there was no hope for him to ever win her as long as he was brown."[23] Max is among the first to sign up at Black-No-More, Incorporated, an enterprise dedicated to whitening Negroes through a regimen that calls for the subject to ingest "revolting concoctions" while strapped into something resembling "a cross between a dentist's chair and an electric chair."[24] In Max's view, however, the potential rewards will more than justify the relatively brief discomfort he must suffer. When he looks into the mirror after his treatment, he is

> startled, overjoyed. White at last! Gone was the smooth, brown complexion. Gone were the slightly full lips and Ethiopian nose. Gone was the nappy hair that he had straightened so meticulously ever since the kink-no-more lotions first wrenched Aframericans from the tyranny and torture of the comb. There would be no more expenditures for skin whiteners; no more discrimination; no more obstacles in his path. He was free! The world was his oyster and he had the open sesame of a pork-colored skin![25]*

Adopting a new name to go with his new persona, Max Disher becomes Mathew Fisher, moves to Atlanta, and begins casting about

---

*Max continues to luxuriate in his triumphant reformation: "It thrilled him to feel that he was now indistinguishable from nine-tenths of the people of the United States; one of the great majority. Ah, it was good not to be a Negro any longer!" A little later, the narrator observes, "[Max] had strolled through the Times Square district before but never with such a feeling of absolute freedom and sureness. No one looked at him curiously because he was with a white girl, as they had when he came down here with Minnie, his former octoroon lady friend. Gee, it was great!" (*Black No More*, 36, 39).

for a way to make lots of money. He attaches himself to a corrupt white minister, the Reverend Henry Givens, who is the demagogic head of the Knights of Nordica, a fictionalized replica of the Ku Klux Klan. Givens wants to revitalize the organization so he can more profitably embezzle its membership dues. Fisher becomes Given's partner and devises a strategy to exploit impoverished whites: Fisher begins spreading the word that Dr. Crookman's Black-No-More is creating a veritable army of "white Negroes" who will, through fraudulent marriages, irrevocably contaminate white bloodlines. The scheme is successful beyond its author's expectations: poor whites join the Knights in record numbers, to the financial enrichment of both Givens and Fisher.

In addition to a fortune, Fisher eventually acquires a wife. Givens's daughter Helen, it turns out, is none other than the viciously racist ("I don't dance with niggers!") beauty who once rejected Max/Mathew in Harlem; no longer burdened by blackness, Fisher is now seen by her as suitable marriage material. Having achieved that goal, Fisher seeks to accomplish more: he mounts a campaign to install his father-in-law in the White House as the presidential candidate of the Democratic party. The effort seems set to succeed until a pair of obstacles arise. The first is that Helen is pregnant and due to give birth just *before* the election—a blessed event that, depending upon the baby's coloration, threatens to reveal Fisher's true racial identity. The second is that the Anglo-Saxon Association, a group devoted to the protection of white racial purity, has begun to expose the colored ancestry of all sorts of influential "white" figures. On the eve of the balloting, these two developments overlap. Helen has the baby, who is indeed dark. But before anyone thinks to point a finger at Mathew Fisher, the Anglo-Saxon Association reveals to the press that the Reverend Givens himself is of Negro descent. Helen tearfully apologizes to her husband and begs him not to abandon her: "If I'd only known," she says, "I would have spared you this disgrace. . . . Oh, Mathew, honey, please forgive me. I love you, my husband. . . . Please don't leave me!"[26] While Mathew could with impunity reject her, simply by spewing back at her the racist dogma that she and her father have voiced throughout their lives, he takes a more honorable tack. He comes out of his own racial closet and tells his wife the truth about his background, at which revelation Helen experiences

a wave of relief. . . . There was no feeling of revulsion at the thought that her husband was a Negro. There once would have been but that was seemingly centuries ago when she had been unaware of her remote Negro ancestry. She felt proud of her Mathew. She loved him more than ever. They had money and a beautiful, brown baby. What more did they need? To hell with society! Compared to what she possessed, thought Helen, all talk of race and color was damned foolishness.[27]

Nor is Helen alone in feeling chastened by the knowledge of her own family's racial history and grateful for Mathew's love and honesty: the Reverend Givens is also moved. "I guess," he concludes, "we're all niggers now."[28]

Schuyler sardonically "dedicated" *Black No More* to "all Caucasians in the great republic who can trace their ancestry back ten generations and confidently assert that there are no Black leaves, twigs, limbs, or branches on their family trees."[29] In his estimation, this group had a membership of precisely none—or at least no one honest or sensible, since in Schuyler's view, white Americans of the twentieth century could not reasonably claim, or suppose themselves, heirs to a pure white bloodline. In *Black No More,* he dramatized his detestation of such claims through the person and plight of Mr. Arthur Snobbcraft, the scion of one of the First Families of Virginia, the president of the Anglo-Saxon Association, and the vice presidential candidate of the Democratic party:

[Snobbcraft] had devoted his entire life to fighting for two things: white racial integrity and Anglo-Saxon supremacy. . . . He had been the genius that thought up the numerous racial integrity laws adopted in Virginia and many of the other Southern states. He was strong for sterilization of the unfit: meaning Negroes, aliens, Jews, and other riff-raff, and had an abiding hatred of democracy. . . . Snobbcraft's pet scheme . . . was to get a genealogical law passed disfranchising all people of Negro or unknown ancestry.[30]

To advance this latter scheme and obtain information that would embarrass his political opponents, Snobbcraft finances a secret genealogical investigation that ends up backfiring in the most galling fashion. The research indicates that a large percentage of whites have black ancestors, many of whom were "white Negroes" who deviously insinuated themselves into the Caucasian population. More to the point, however, is that Snobbcraft himself is among those "contaminated." The chief researcher, Dr. Samuel Buggerie, informs Snobbcraft that one of his forebears was the offspring of "an English serving maid and a black slave."[31] This fact is more than a mere blow to Snobbcraft's ego; when revealed to the public, it becomes a threat to his political and even his physical existence. Trounced at the polls, he tries to flee the country by plane with Buggerie (who is likewise of "tainted" ancestry) after realizing that his disillusioned followers are bent on exacting revenge. When the plane runs out of fuel, they are forced to land in Happy Hill, Mississippi, where they engage in a desperate ploy of reverse passing. Guessing that it will be safer for them to pose as rare, dark-skinned Negroes than to acknowledge their real identities, the two men blacken themselves with shoe polish. The problem is, they have guessed incorrectly: Happy Hill is an insular community of intensely religious white Christians, all of whom are quite prepared to murder any dark-skinned person they can get their hands on. Over the town's general store and post office hangs a sign bearing the following message: NIGER REDE & RUN. IF U CAN'T REDE, RUN ENEYHOWE.[32] Snobbcraft and Buggerie, in blackface, are given an appropriate welcome, but just as they are about to be burned at the stake, they persuade their tormentors to look under their clothes at portions of their bodies that are not covered with shoe polish. At the sight of their prisoners' pale white skins, the mob, though disappointed, relents—but only temporarily. No sooner have Snobbcraft and Buggerie begun to relax and to enjoy once again the pleasure of racial privilege than the Happy Hill

mob learns of their flight and of the allegation that they are "white
Negroes." They are recaptured and tormented anew, and this time, the
mob shows no mercy. In a gory episode that gives Schuyler ample
opportunity to condemn the all too familiar brutality of the Jim Crow
South, Snobbcraft and Buggerie are castrated, shot, and burned.
Among the crowd that witnesses the atrocity are "two or three
whitened Negroes, who, remembering what their race had suffered in
the past, would fain have gone to the assistance of the two men."[33]
They are too afraid, however, to do anything but watch—yet even their
inactivity puts them in jeopardy, causing them to be "looked at rather
sharply by some of the Christ Lovers because they did not appear to be
enjoying the spectacle as thoroughly as the rest."[34] Taking the hint,
"the whitened Negroes began to yell and prod the burning bodies with
sticks and cast stones at them. This exhibition restored them to favor
and banished any suspicion that they might not be one-hundred-
percent Americans."[35] Being considered authentically white thus comes,
for these onlookers at least, at an exorbitant price, requiring them to
express delight in the torture and murder of fellow human beings.

The most striking feature of George Schuyler's fictional treatment
of African American culture is his suggestion that given the chance,
Negroes would desert black churches, sororities and fraternities, political organizations, and colleges en masse in favor of being white. He
imagined that "in straining every nerve to get the Black-No-More treatment, the colored folk forgot all loyalties, affiliations and responsibilities. No longer did they flock to the churches on Sundays or pay dues in
their numerous fraternal organizations. They stopped giving anything
to the Anti-Lynching campaign."[36] This envisioned exodus from blackness is embraced by Negroes of all sorts in Black No More. Max
Disher/Mathew Fisher, for example, is emblematic of middle-class,
northern, young urban black men of the 1930s; a veteran of World
War I who soldiered in France, he is working, when the novel opens, as
an agent for the Aframerican Fire Insurance Company. Although he is
politically aware, he has nevertheless distanced himself from any committed political activism on behalf of the black community. But the
lacerating sharpness of Schuyler's satire penetrates beyond Max's rela-

tively bourgeois world and the Negro rank and file; it also skewers the Negro leadership. At first, black leaders oppose Black-No-More, Incorporated. Forming a Committee for the Preservation of Negro Racial Integrity, they call upon their followers to evince black solidarity and racial pride by forgoing Crookman's whitening process. When their exhortations are ignored, they appeal to the attorney general of the United States to take legal action. When that approach also fails, they join the legion of blacks seeking "chromatic emancipation."[37]

Two real-life figures bore the brunt of Schuyler's lampooning in *Black No More*. One was W. E. B. DuBois, cast in the novel as Dr. Shakespeare Agamemnon Beard. A founder of the NAACP, the editor of its publication *The Crisis*, and the author of scores of important books, including *The Souls of Black Folk*, DuBois became, in Schuyler's fiction, a founder of the League for Social Equality, a man who writes "scholarly and biting editorials in *The Dilemma* denouncing the Caucasians whom he secretly admired and lauding the greatness of the Negroes whom he alternately pitied and despised."[38] Even as Beard deifies black women in print, he hires only "comely yellow stenographers with weak resistance."[39] Stymied in his efforts to stem the popularity of Black-No-More, Beard himself takes the treatment, becomes a "new white," and eventually lands a job as a genealogical researcher for the Anglo-Saxon Association.

Schuyler's other major target was Marcus Garvey, the black-nationalist founder of the Universal Negro Improvement Association. *Black No More*'s Garvey stand-in, Santop Licorice, is portrayed as "very profitably" advocating the emigration of all American Negroes to Africa, even though "he [has] not gone himself and [has] no intention of doing so."[40] In a ferocious dig at Garvey's pomposity, Licorice is exalted as the "Provisional President of Africa, Admiral of the African Navy, Field Marshall of the African Army and Knight Commander of the Nile."[41] Garvey's notorious inability to cooperate with other black leaders is meanwhile portrayed by Licorice's attempts "to save the Negroes by vigorously attacking all of the other Negro organizations."[42] And finally, Garvey's alliance with white-racist proponents of antimiscegenation laws finds a parallel in Licorice joining with the Reverend Givens and the Knights of Nordica to condemn Black-No-More, Incorporated. When he fails to win popular support, however, Licorice himself capitulates and resorts to Dr. Crookman's whitening treatment.

The narrator of *Black No More* explains that Dr. Crookman "was what was known in Negro society as a Race Man," meaning that he "prided himself above all on being a great lover of his race."[43] Paradoxically, though, as the best means of improving the position of Negroes, Crookman advocates the eradication of blackness: "He was so interested in the continued progress of the American Negroes that he wanted to remove all obstacles in their path by depriving them of their racial characteristics."[44] He reasons that "if there were no Negroes there could be no Negro problem. Without a Negro problem, Americans could concentrate their attention on something constructive."[45]

This method of "solving" the race problem was no mere figment of George Schuyler's imagination. Many people have actively sought to discover ways of whitening blacks, and many more have mused longingly about the prospect of such an invention. In 1929 the *Pittsburgh Courier* heralded Dr. Yusaburo Noguchi's announcement that he had found a means of whitening Negroes by the use of sunlight, ultraviolet rays, special diets, and glandular treatments.[46] In a 1949 article entitled "Can Science Conquer the Color Line?," Walter White suggested, rather hopefully, that the results of recent dermatological experiments held some promise for turning into reality the "dream" of making black skin white.[47] That White in particular should have viewed the prospect of large-scale passing by blacks in a positive light is intriguing, given that he himself, as we have seen, declined to pass.* His rationale explained the apparent contradiction: in his view, "The whole progress of civilization has been a constant enlargement of human freedom— in other words, of human *choice*," and a workable method of race-changing could open up "a new avenue for enlarging the range of

*See page 287–89.

human free choice."[48]* Half a century later, echoing White's enthusiasm over the idea of a biotechnological subversion of the race line, Orlando Patterson posited that "more and more in the coming decades, Americans will gain the means to genetically manipulate human appearance," as "science is likely to create dramatic new methods of changing hair texture and skin color."[49] While anticipating that "many African Americans [will] chose straight-haired whiteness for themselves or their progeny," he nonetheless predicted that others would opt for "varying degrees of hybridity."[50]

In America and elsewhere, some colored people have taken a different, less scientific approach to genetic engineering. A number of African Americans, for instance, have carefully chosen mates lighter than themselves in the aim of producing still lighter children, who are in turn expected to marry even lighter spouses—a trend that effectively amounts to a strategy of "long-range eugenic planning."[51] In Brazil, many intellectuals and politicians have looked to the process of "whitening" as the best way to mitigate their country's racial conflict. "There is no danger . . . that the Negro problem will arise in Brazil," wrote a notable Brazilian literary critic in 1899. "Before it could arise it was already resolved by love. Miscegenation has robbed the Negro element of its numerical importance, thinning it down into the white population. . . . Race mixture is facilitating the prevalence of the superior element. Sooner or later it will perforce eliminate the Negro race here."[52] The conclusion of Schuyler's novel suggests that in America, however, even wholesale whitening would not cure the national obsession with color. Dr. Crookman, the father of race-changing, becomes the surgeon general of the United States and publishes a monograph on the differences in skin pigmentation between "real whites" and those made white by the Black-No-More treatment: the "new Caucasians," he points out, are several shades whiter than the "real" Caucasians. It is here that Schuyler's satirical wit fixes the larger culture in its sights:

---

*At another point, White asserted that a chemical race-changing agent would enable dark-skinned Negroes "to break the barriers that hem them in, let them live like other Americans and be judged on their own merits" ("Can Science Conquer the Color Line?," *Look*, August 30, 1949).

To a society that had been taught to venerate whiteness for over three hundred years, [Crookman's] announcement was rather staggering. What was the world coming to, if the blacks were whiter than the whites? . . . If it were true that extreme whiteness was evidence of the possession of Negro blood, of having once been a member of the pariah class, then surely it were not well to be so white![53]

The ramifications of Dr. Crookman's report run in several directions. Some of the "real whites" develop a prejudice against the exceedingly pale "new whites." Pseudoscientists declare that the pale whites are mentally inferior, and a few states begin to consider legislating the segregation of pale-white children.* Some "real whites" start "to look around for ways to get darker. It became the fashion for them to spend hours at the seashore basking naked in the sunshine and then to dash back, heavily bronzed, to their homes, and, preening[,] . . . lord it over their paler, and thus less fortunate[,] associates."[54] A group of "new Caucasians" found the Down-with-White-Prejudice League, which distributes pamphlets asserting "that those of exceedingly pale skin [are] just as good as anybody else and should not, therefore, be oppressed."[55] Other "new Caucasians" conceive a new form of passing: armed with cosmetic concoctions such as Blandine's Egyptienne Stain, they impart a long-lasting light-brown tinge to their pale skin. White faces grow "startlingly rare," Americans are ever more "enthusiastically mulatto-minded," and it becomes increasingly common "to see a sweet young miss stop before a shop window and dab her face with charcoal."[56]

---

*Professor Handen Moutthe announces "that as a result of his long research amongst the palest citizens, he [is] convinced they [are] mentally inferior and that their children should be segregated from the others in school." Obviously intending to associate Moutthe with real-life "scientific" racists who lent widespread legitimacy to notions of black inferiority, Schuyler cast the professor as an "eminent anthropologist" well known for his popular work *The Sex Life of Left-Handed Morons Among the Ainus*. "[Moutthe's] findings were considered authoritative," the narrator notes archly, "because he had spent three entire weeks of hard work assembling his data" (*Black No More*, 220).

## George Schuyler's Politics

In certain ways, Schuyler's career was marked by strong continuities. Throughout his life, he would remain a vocal champion of interracial marriage, perennially rebutting the notions that there existed some instinctive aversion between blacks and whites, that only people of the lowest standing intermarried, and that interracial marriages were by their very nature doomed to unhappiness.[57] In his view, in fact, miscegenation offered the "ultimate solution" to American racial conflict, in that "amalgamation of the two so-called races [would] form a new one, more handsome, more healthy, more cultured, more secure, more civilized than either the present day whites or blacks."[58]

In other ways, Schuyler's politics shifted dramatically. Like John Dos Passos and Max Eastman, Schuyler began his career as a man of the left and finished it as a man of the right.[59] Early on—in the 1920s, 1930s, and 1940s—the cruelty, stupidity, hypocrisy, and destructiveness of white racism supplied him with his principal target. In a 1927 article entitled "Our White Folks," he repeatedly compared whites unfavorably to blacks, "a people who confront a continuous barrage of insult and calumny and discrimination from the cradle to the grave."[60] The African American, he wrote,

> being more tolerant than the Caucasian, is ready to admit that all white people are not the same, and it is not unusual to read or hear a warning from a Negro orator or editor against condemning all crackers as prejudiced asses, although agreeing that such a description fits the majority of them. The Ethiop is given to pointing to individual pinks who are exceptionally honorable, tolerant and unprejudiced. In this respect, I venture to say, he rises several notches higher than the generality of ofays, to whom, even in this day and time, all coons look alike.[61]*

---

*Moreover, according to Schuyler, blacks

> laugh to themselves when they hear white folks refer to them as ugly and black. Thanks to the whites who are always talking about racial purity, the

In "Traveling Jim Crow," written in 1930, Schuyler related with controlled fury the indignities visited on blacks wishing to get from point A to point B, through segregation and other forms of discrimination practiced on trains, in taxis, and elsewhere. "Next to being strictly honest," he quipped with characteristic bite, "there is no more trying state in this humdrum Republic than being simultaneously a negro and a traveler." (Even the "troubles of Job seem trivial," he added, "in comparison with those that bedevil the poor Aframerican who ventures forth to see his country.")[62] An essay published in 1944 is a third exemplar of Schuyler's sustained attack on white racism. Anticipating a theme that would become popular two decades later, he insisted that the racial difficulties that were so often ascribed to "the Negro problem" actually arose from "the Caucasian problem." He elaborated, "The only sense in which there is or has been a Negro problem is in the colored folk's natural human aversion and opposition to conquest, enslavement, exploitation and debasement during the long and bloody period of Caucasian military ascendancy."[63]

Schuyler did not spare his fellow blacks if and when he felt they were deserving of criticism. He harshly denounced the black government of Liberia for condoning the virtual enslavement of many of its citizens.[64] He dismissed as mere "hokum" the claims of those who asserted the existence of a uniquely black aesthetic.[65] And he chided black Americans for failing to resist more vigorously their racial subordination, noting, "The unsentimental behaviorist must regretfully conclude that in the main [the African American] is inured to and satisfied with his pariahdom."[66] But Schuyler's central message remained consistent: for him, it was imperative above all else to challenge white racism. As an isolationist in the thirties and forties, opposing American belligerency toward the Axis powers, Schuyler insisted that for Negroes, defeating Jim Crow should be more important than defeating Hitler.

---

Negroes possess within their group the most handsome people in the United States, with the greatest variety of color, hair and features. Here is the real melting-pot, and a glorious sight it is to see. Ugly people there are, certainly, but the percentage of beautiful folk is unquestionably larger than among the ofay brethren. [George Schuyler, "Our White Folks," *American Mercury*, December 1927]

While conceding that the Nazis, the Fascists, and the Japanese imperialists were doing terrible things abroad, he continued to demand, "What about democracy for Negroes at home?"[67] He grieved for the Jews suffering under Hitler and for the kulaks under Stalin, but he grieved even more for the Negroes being lynched in Mississippi.

After World War II, Schuyler adopted a dramatically more accommodationist tone in his writings about race relations. He came to believe that white racism in the United States was so powerful and so dangerous that Negroes would risk committing collective suicide if they proceeded in such a way as to furnish Negrophobes with a plausible pretext for large-scale, violent repression. In 1966 he observed:

> Not having any illusions about white people *per se,* I have long been fearful that this increasing racial animosity . . . might lead to actual civil war which would certainly lead to genocide. Nobody who knows history can discount this. . . . I have not forgotten that an American administration put more than 100,000 Japanese-Americans in concentration camps . . . or that the Turks massacred 800,000 Armenians . . . nor is the fate of the Amerindians of the eastern United States to be forgotten.[68]

Somewhat inconsistently, Schuyler also concluded that even at their worst, the evils of American racism paled in comparison with the evils perpetrated by Communist regimes behind the Iron Curtain.

Many black opinion and organizational leaders eschewed communism during the Cold War;[69] the NAACP, for example, excluded Communists from membership. But no other prominent black even approached Schuyler in terms of the vehemence with which he advanced his anti-Communist views. By the 1950s communism had replaced white supremacy as his primary target. He unstintingly supported the most notorious anti-Communist demagogue of the era, Senator Joseph R. McCarthy—championed him so wholeheartedly, in fact, that he quit the anti-Communist American Committee for Cultural Freedom (ACCF) after it deigned to question the senator's reckless methods. Decrying what he characterized as the ACCF's "intellectual mob action, i.e., a lynching," Schuyler praised McCarthy for "dutifully investigating the Communist menace."[70]

Schuyler's break with those whom he perceived to be insufficiently anti-Communist propelled him toward the right wing of American politics. By the 1960s he was supporting Barry Goldwater for president and had joined the John Birch Society. In his writings, anger toward reformers had come to eclipse anger over the inequities they sought to reform, a trend that included a cranky, bitter, unequivocal condemnation of the civil rights movement. Schuyler's objection to the choice of Martin Luther King Jr. as the winner of the 1964 Nobel Peace Prize offered the most vivid and consequential illustration of his about-face. In William Loeb's infamously reactionary *Manchester Union Leader,* Schuyler wrote:

> Neither directly or indirectly has Dr. King made any contribution to world (or even domestic) peace. Methinks the Lenin Prize would have been more appropriate. . . . Dr. King's principal contribution to world peace has been to roam the country like some sable Typhoid Mary, infecting the mentally disturbed with perversion of Christian doctrine, and grabbing fat lecture fees from the shallow-pated.[71]

Similarly representative of Schuyler's far-right phase is his 1973 article "Malcolm X: Better to Memorialize Benedict Arnold," published in *American Opinion,* the journal of the John Birch Society. Branding Malcom X "a pixilated criminal," Schuyler complained that the murdered black nationalist

> is now being eulogized as a great Negro leader. If this were true it would be a serious indictment of the colored people of this country. Malcom was a bold, outspoken, ignorant man of no occupation after he gave up pimping, gambling and dope-selling to follow Mr. Muhammad. Like most of the loud-mouthed black leaders, he had but a tiny following.

From there, Schuyler broadened his attack, charging that most of the organizations that billed themselves as being devoted to the advancement of black people were in fact

insignificant groups of hustlers and braggarts organized to bulldoze white people into handing out charity or to snatch a little transient graft. . . . During the past generation the black "leaders" afflicting the nation have been mediocrities, criminals, plotters, and poseurs like Malcom X. Go down the list and you have to search hard to find even a few that are worthy of even an invitation to tea.

And perhaps not even that many, in his opinion: Schuyler declined to name a single black protest leader whom he found acceptable.[72]

The most unfortunate aspect of these and other, equally ill-considered screeds is not that they ended Schuyler's ability to be taken seriously as a commentator by all but devotees of the far right—by the mid-1960s his best thinking and writing were things of the past in any case—but rather that for many younger intellectuals and activists, these were all there *was* of him. Schuyler's antics near the end of his career so besmirched his reputation that many who might have profited from reading his earlier writings never did so, because they believed, erroneously, that he had never been anything other than an embittered preacher of reactionary dogma.

### Philippa Schuyler

George and Josephine Schuyler's most remarkable creation was their daughter, Philippa, who was born on August 2, 1931. From the outset, her parents put her in the public eye. Every black newspaper in New York announced her birth. At three, she was the subject of an admiring profile in the *New York Herald Tribune,* and at four, she received a mention in *Time* magazine. When she was eight, her photograph appeared in *Look,* above a caption that dubbed her "the Shirley Temple of the Negroes." The object of all this publicity was, in truth, an extraordinary child: by five, she was typing up stories and poems, composing musical scores, and, blessed with perfect pitch and an uncanny ability to concentrate, spending hours at a stretch at the piano, perfecting performances that would win her the distinction of being the youngest person ever awarded a place on the honor roll maintained by the National Piano Teachers Guild.[73]

Something beyond normal parental pride lay behind the Schuylers' push for public recognition of their child's achievements. They saw such publicity as a healthy corrective to the popular denigration of Negroes, and a useful rebuttal to fears regarding the progeny of interracial couples. Offering an explanation of why she subjected her daughter to the pressures of numerous contests and recitals, Jody noted in one of her scrapbooks that it was "as much for the education of America as for the education of Philippa."[74]

For a while, Philippa Schuyler seemed to ascend from triumph to triumph. When she was just eight years old, she was selected (by the Women's Service League of Brooklyn) as one of thirteen "colored women" to be recognized at the World's Fair for distinguished service to their race and sex. A year later, officials at the World's Fair named a day after her, and on Philippa Duke Schuyler Day—June 19, 1940—the diminutive nine-year-old gave two concerts, performing works by Bach, Schumann, and Rimsky-Korsakov. She also played several compositions of her own, including "The Goldfish," "The Jolly Pig," and "The Cockroach Ballet." During an interview afterward, a reporter decided to test her parents' claim that Philippa loved reading newspapers. Asked for her opinion on the war in Europe, the prodigy ventured, "I hate to say it, but I think the allies are cooked."[75]

In 1946, after Philippa performed for an audience of twelve thousand at the Lewisohn Stadium in New York City, a correspondent for the *New York Times* reported that she had "revealed herself as a pianist, without regard to age, of extraordinary natural talent . . . and . . . disclosed imagination to be found only in artists of a high level."[76] A year later, having heard the teenager play her own "Fairy Tale Symphony," the celebrated composer and critic Virgil Thomson compared her to the young Mozart. Under the halo of such plaudits, Philippa Schuyler became a role model for numerous youngsters, especially black children, many of whom were undoubtedly told by their ambitious parents that if they practiced diligently on the piano (or whatever instrument), they, too, might one day be a credit to their race.

There was, however, another, less heady side to Philippa's world. Jody Schuyler loved her daughter, but she also smothered her. Philippa was deprived of the pleasure of playmates her own age. Her musical coaches, who might otherwise have provided some comforting companionship, never lasted very long under the pressures of Jody's impatience, capriciousness, and jealousy. George Schuyler, while superficially affectionate toward Philippa, proved to be a rather distant father, frequently away pursuing his journalistic projects. His parents were dead, and his siblings seem to have played no role in their niece's life. Jody's parents and siblings, for their part, refused even to acknowledge her daughter's existence. To top it all off, Philippa's prodigious musical accomplishment itself became a snare. As her skill and fame grew, so, too, did her capacity to make money—a capacity that her mother rigorously exploited, to the extent that the child became a mainstay of the family economy. Philippa, in short, was a juvenile celebrity endowed with many enviable qualities. Happiness, however, was nowhere on that list.

Sadly, Philippa's situation did not improve as she got older. Her acclaimed talent did not win her entree into prized venues that were closed to her on account of racism. Moreover, she always felt that her race—or, more precisely, the *perception* that she was colored—distorted people's assessment of her music, leading either to excessive praise due to lowered expectations or to niggardly plaudits wrung from an unwillingness to concede that any colored person could perform so ably. Most depressing of all, it seems, were the just appraisals of her performances, for by all accounts, while she was excellent, she was not truly great— and greatness was what she strove for above all. She suffered severe disappointment at her inability to climb to the very highest circles of musicianship.

Something of a literary prodigy as well as a musical one, Philippa wrote several books reflecting her wide travels, attraction to Roman Catholicism, interest in politics (she was as fervently anti-Communist as her father), and intellectual restlessness. Published when its author was still in her teens, *Adventures in White and Black* (1950) was an amalgam of autobiography and fiction. Her next effort was *Who Killed the Congo?* (1962), an analysis of the country's troubled birth that pleased conservatives (who doubted black Africans' capacity for self-government) and outraged militant anticolonialists (among them Kwame Nkrumah, who wrote Philippa a castigating letter). Finally, the travelogue *Jungle Saints: Africa's Heroic Catholic Missionaries* (1963) recorded the good works of nuns and priests she had encountered on her extensive tours. Mired in unhappiness as she was, alas, these accomplishments pleased her no more than the others.

In January 1959, nearing the end of a global performing tour, Philippa visited the colony of Ruanda-Urundi (now the nations of Rwanda and Burundi). She confided in a letter to her mother that on her certificate of entry into the colony, she had identified herself as "white"—"just to see if I could get away with it"—and also in order to be eligible for residence in one of the colony's best lodgings, a whites-only hotel in which she succeeded in getting a room.[77] A short time later, Philippa again described herself as white, this time on a form that she had to complete before entering South Africa, where, according to her biographer, she "quickly became the darling of a white society of music lovers."[78] On her return to the United States, with her mother's support, she embarked upon a comprehensive campaign to remake herself, applying for a new passport under a new name (Felipa Monterro y Schuyler), changing her birth date, and avoiding all mention of anything that could tie her to her previous identity. "Remember," she wrote to her mother, "NOTHING in my Congo book must refer to any racial ancestry connected with me. No photos either."[79] Later, in another letter to Jody, she insisted that "NOWHERE in my forthcoming book [*Jungle Saints*] do I want the word *negro* or *colored* mentioned in connection with me, NOWHERE."[80] During this same period, her father made the "mistake," in Philippa's eyes, of writing about her in a book he was working on, tentatively titled "The Negro in America." Upon learning of her inclusion in the manuscript, she fired off a furious note to her mother:

> I was shocked by your news that George put me in that book despite my express instructions to the contrary. Apparently he wishes to handicap me. . . . Get me OUT of that book. Everyone here [in Europe] thinks of me as a Latin, and that's the way I want it. Anyone who has any paternal sentiments would want a child to escape suffering. I look like any other of the Sicilians, Greeks, Spaniards, or Portuguese here in Rome. I am not a Negro, and won't stand for being called one in a book that will circulate in countries where that taint has not been applied to me. It makes all future effort on my part to forge a worthwhile niche for myself in society where I will be accepted as a person not as a strange curiosity useless. I had thirty miserable years in the USA because of having the taint of being a "strange curiosity" applied to me, and I sure don't want to bring that taint along with me to a foreign country and thus have thirty more miserable years.[81]

One cannot help wondering what the author of *Black No More* said to his passing daughter, and how he felt about her reinvention of herself. Schuyler himself said nothing about the matter in his autobiography, but Philippa's biographer has pointed to a convincing clue that Jody Schuyler did relay their daughter's sentiments to her husband, and that he acceded to her wishes: in the nearly fifteen-hundred-page manuscript of "The Negro in America" that resides in the Schomburg Collection (the book was never published), there are five pages that were supposed to contain a biographical entry on Philippa. Pasted over those pages, rendering invisible the print below, are three layers of blank paper.

Keeping Philippa's two identities straight posed real difficulties for both mother and daughter. On one occasion, Philippa wired Jody asking for money. Jody wired back: Under what name she should send the funds? Philippa could not answer the question, having forgotten what name she had registered under at the hotel! In 1963 she applied as "Felipa Monterro" for a job as a lecturer with the John Birch Society. Jody was just about to seek the same position on her daughter's behalf when she received by express mail a note from Philippa which read, in part, "DON'T contact [the John Birch Society speakers' bureau]! They have just written FELIPA MONTERRO . . . that they want *her* on a tour. . . . They're just as eager to have FELIPA MONTERRO, as they were to have Philippa Schuyler. AND IT'S MUCH BETTER THIS WAY."[82]

When Philippa finished her book *Jungle Saints,* her mother suggested that she publish it under her own well-known name and add an introduction by "F. Monterro." Philippa disagreed: "*No* the book will *not* be by Philippa Schuyler—that dreadful name with which I certainly am not going to burden myself more than necessary. . . . Not *one* person takes me for a (Negro!) And nobody in my whole life ever has unless it was written up in my publicity."[83]

Philippa clearly believed that she could pass for white abroad and perhaps even within the United States, despite the considerable publicity she had received as the "Negro Shirley Temple." She felt encouraged by the fact that a number of blacks whom she had met before her transformation seemed not to recognize her under the influence of her new name. And she took heart in knowing that so many of her previous concerts in the United States had been before segregated audiences comprised overwhelmingly of Negroes. Now she hoped to perform before predominantly *white* audiences. She was prepared to wear hairpieces and other accouterments to disguise herself, and if she got in a pinch and found herself facing a situation in which members of an audience were sure to recall her past, she would simply decline to perform: "IF, IF, IF someone should recognize me, I could always say that Miss Monterro developed laryngitis, or leprosy or bubonic plague or something and couldn't come at the last minute."[84]

Another unhappy feature of Philippa's life that warrants close scrutiny was her inability to form a sustained and pleasurable romantic attachment to anyone. Here, as elsewhere, race loomed large in her mind. Among the eleven requirements she once listed for a suitor, the first was "He must be white."[85] (Her loneliness becomes perhaps a little more understandable when we note that among her requirements, love is listed next to last.) Of the men with whom she was sexually intimate, only one—Georges Apedo-Amah, a Ghanaian diplomat—was black, and he got her pregnant. Appalled by the idea of giving birth to a child fathered by a black man—and scared, too, that her pregnancy by Georges might ruin her chances of marrying another man with whom she was seriously involved—Philippa had an abortion.

The lover she came closest to marrying was a white Frenchman named Maurice Raymond. Reporting to her mother on the progress of the romance, Philippa wrote excitedly, "I have a chance to put my roots down in an important European country with a white husband who wants to boost my career."[86] Envisioning the family she and Raymond would create, she mused, "Imagine if we had a child, it would be perfect: Have his eyesight; his green eyes; his health and stamina; his Aryan appearance; my talents; AND NO NEGRITUDE."[87]

She and Raymond in fact went so far as to seek a marriage license in France. But on being told that they would have to wait for a few days and that he would have to fill out a routine questionnaire about his background, Raymond insisted that they would be better off traveling to Scotland, where he thought they could get married more quickly. He was mistaken: Scotland, too, required couples to wait out a "cooling off" period. Alarmed by Raymond's peculiar urgency, Jody Schuyler persuaded Philippa to hold off on marrying him, at least for a while. This enraged Raymond, who proceeded to send the Schuylers a postcard on which he wrote derogatory remarks about her pregnancy and abortion and affixed a photograph of a woman, probably Philippa, engaged in sex. This ugly gesture ended their relationship.*

The final scene of the Philippa Schuyler drama was ruthlessly brief. In 1966 United States Ambassador Henry Cabot Lodge invited her to South Vietnam to perform a piano concert for wounded soldiers. She accepted the invitation, but she went to Vietnam as more than a per-

---

*In 1965 French authorities prosecuted Raymond. On his conviction, they destroyed the negatives of the offending photographs and sentenced him to forty days in prison. See Kathryn Talalay, *Composition in Black and White* (1995), 258.

former; she also went under the auspices of William Loeb, who had asked her to write about the war for the *Manchester Union Leader*. Rabidly anti-Communist, like her father, Philippa championed the American war effort. She was aware, however, that it was no simple matter of good versus evil. "This is the funniest mixed up war I ever saw," she wrote to her mother from Saigon. "Everyone around here must have done something wrong in their last reincarnation and is getting punished for it now. . . . The Vietcong are AWFUL CRUEL; the Americans are AWFUL CRUDE; and the South Vietnamese are AWFUL CORRUPT. Take your choice."[88]

She also became aware that African American soldiers, sent halfway around the world to fight for democratic values, were themselves being subjected to racial discrimination by their own government. As we have seen, Philippa typically sought to avoid any association with blacks. In Vietnam, moreover, as in most places she visited, her amorous desires gravitated toward white men, not black. At the same time, she appears to have felt some sympathy for colored people, particularly blacks, and some anger about white American racism—both emotions unprecedented in her life. Condemnation of white racial chauvinism became a central theme in her last letters to her mother. When her clothes were stolen, she asked rhetorically, "Do you know . . . who showed sympathy? NO WHITE AMERICAN. A Vietnamese girl gave me a dress. An American Negro gave me a dress. A European Catholic gave me a dress. BUT NO WHITE AMERICAN even gave me a button to put on a dress."[89] In another letter, she asserted that "the American white man *resents* a colored person being in any role but servant or entertainer."[90]

Around the same time that her father was ridiculing the civil rights movement, Philippa was beginning to voice feelings that were very much in tune with it. What seems to have prompted this new attitude was a steady barrage of racial affronts that she suffered herself or saw other blacks or Vietnamese suffer. "Half of my encounters with THE WHITE AMERICANS," she wrote in her last letter home, "are abortive, negative, or unpleasant. They are the worst advertisements for America's supposed democracy I ever saw."[91]

Three days later, on May 9, 1966, near Da Nang, Vietnam, Philippa Schuyler died, the victim of a freakish helicopter crash. As if that were not tragic enough, Philippa's death mortally wounded her mother psychologically. A week before the second anniversary of her daughter's death, Josephine Cogdell Schuyler hanged herself while her husband slept just steps away.

George Schuyler lived on. But the loss of his wife and daughter cast a terrible pall over his final, lonely years. He died in New York on August 31, 1977.

# NINE

# Racial Conflict and the Parenting of Children: A Survey of Competing Approaches

Racial conflicts have intersected occasionally with disputes over parental custody of children. How have such cases been resolved and how *should* they be handled? These are the principal questions addressed in this chapter and the chapters that follow. They bring us back to our point of departure—the fight over the adoption of Jacqueline Henley—and prompt consideration of other episodes in which social pressures prevented children from being parented by people of the "wrong" race. No issue discussed in these pages is more troubling. The perception of interracial parenting as a "problem" in need of fixing has led to some horrific solutions, including the *killing* of children whose very existence provided evidence of interracial sex. According to Harriet Jacobs and other chroniclers of the slave regime, this was sometimes the fate that awaited babies born to white women impregnated by enslaved black lovers.[1] Another baleful "solution" has been the custom or policy of race matching, which assigns children a permanent racial identity and requires that they be raised by adults of the same race. In the slavery era, authorities designated as both colored and enslaved the offspring of free white men and enslaved black women. By so labeling the children and mandating that they be reared within the black slave community, authorities sought to buttress racial boundaries that had already been crossed in the children's procreation. By treating as unambiguously "black" the human products of interracial sexual unions, authorities strove—usually successfully—to thwart any inclination toward interracial parenting.*

After emancipation, race matching remained the norm. The white southern writer Lillian Smith recalled that when she was growing up in Jasper, Florida, in the first decade of the 1900s, "a little white girl was found in the colored section of our town, living with a Negro family in a broken down shack."[2]† After a brief investigation, the authorities came to the conclusion that the child must have been kidnapped. They took her into protective custody and placed her in the Smiths' home, where she and Lillian became friends. After a while, a colored orphanage called the Smiths to inform them that though the girl *looked* white, she was actually colored. On learning this, the family and their friends readily decided that it would not be proper for the child to remain within a white household. So she was sent back to "Colored Town," presumably to be raised by the very people from whom she had earlier been "rescued."

In 1949 a baby boy was born to Ann Armstrong, a married white woman living in Jackson, Mississippi.[3] The child's father was an African American who frequented the café owned by Armstrong and her (white) husband. Perceiving immediately that the baby's biological father must be a Negro, a hospital nurse urged Armstrong to put him up for adoption and tell her husband that he had been stillborn. Armstrong refused and instead pretended that her husband was indeed the father. She made sure that the baby was designated as white on his birth certificate, named him Larry Michael Armstrong, and repeatedly reminded her spouse that her grandmother had had dark hair and eyes. To deflect her neighbors' suspicions, she did everything she could to

---

*Masters often sold the children they sired by slave women to spare themselves (and their white wives) the embarrassment of seeing their biological offspring raised as slaves. The auction block, then, was another of the many venues in which race matching flourished.

†Smith (1897–1966) was a social rebel who openly attacked segregation before the civil rights revolution. One of her novels, *Strange Fruit* (1944), focuses on a clandestine interracial love affair; it caused tremendous controversy on publication. For more on Smith, see Anne C. Loveland, *Lillian Smith: A Southerner Confronting the South* (1986).

turn Larry into the mirror image of his older brother—a child who, it seems, really *had* been sired by Fred Armstrong. She tried, for example, "to close the skin-color gap between the brothers" by dressing them like twins, in identical cowboy outfits or Budweiser uniforms, with their names embroidered above the shirt pockets.[4] For two years, the whites in town looked the other way as Ann Armstrong sought to perfect her ruse. But then her carefully constructed deception began to fall apart. For one thing, no matter how much his mother combed Larry's hair, the kinks stayed in it.* As the Negro strain in Larry's lineage became increasingly evident, the Armstrongs' fellow whites became increasingly intolerant. On one occasion,

> when Ann took Larry for his booster shots, she entered the main door of the doctor's office and gave her name to the nurse. The woman frowned at the child and pointed Ann to the colored waiting room. . . . "You'll have to wait in there," she said.
>
> Ann raised her chin, ready to protest. There was plenty of room here on the couch, where she had waited for the doctor in the past. She opened her mouth to speak, but the nurse crossed her arms in front of her and prepared to hold her ground. Ann guided Larry into the next room. And watched him as he examined the keyhole and knob. Like the sky before an October rain, he seemed to blacken before her eyes.

Eventually, Ann Armstrong's neighbors stopped speaking to her. A cross was burned on her lawn. Neighborhood children refused to play with Larry and contemptuously referred to him as a "nigger"; the authorities made it clear that he would not be permitted to attend "white" public schools. The owner of a truck that Fred Armstrong drove to make deliveries, who had formerly allowed him to bring Larry

---

*Hair texture, as we have seen (p. 13) has long been an important racial signal. Attempting to determine the race and, by extension, the status—slave or free—of a party in a lawsuit, Judge St. George Tucker maintained that hair texture was a more reliable guide than skin color. Dark skin disappeared relatively quickly, he asserted, through miscegenation, but a "wooly head of hair. . . disappears the last of all" (*Hudgins v. Wright,* 11 Va. [1 Hen & M.] 134 [1806]).

and his brother along for the ride, now took him aside and said, essentially, "You've got to do something about the nigger. . . . Your little boy can still ride in the truck, but the nigger got to go."[5]

Stung, Armstrong sought a black home for Larry and ultimately found him one with a childless couple in Los Angeles. Helen and Johnny Spain adopted Larry Armstrong and renamed him Johnny Larry Spain. The Spains attempted to inject some normalcy into their new charge's life, but their best efforts could not overcome the deep unhappiness that continued to shadow him. Ironically, he encountered racial animosities in California that mirrored those he had faced in Mississippi: taunted down south for being too dark, he was teased out west for being too light. In time, he won the acceptance of his black peers, but that brought a new set of problems. As a teenager, Johnny fell in with a group of hoodlums. His delinquency reached a horrifying climax in 1966, when he murdered a man during the course of a robbery. Remarkably, after many dangerous and tumultuous years of incarceration,* he was released from prison and sought a reconciliation with his white relatives.

A third instance of blocked interracial parenting is powerfully portrayed in an autobiographical documentary film entitled *Secret Daughter* (Public Broadcasting System, 1966), produced by June Cross. Cross was the product of a relationship between a white woman, Norma Greve, and a black man, James Arthur Cross, respectively an aspiring actress and a vaudeville comic.[6] They lived together as a family for only a short while, until James Cross's drunken, violent abusiveness forced Greve to flee with their infant child in tow.† When June was four, her

---

*During his imprisonment for murder, Johnny Spain became a member of the Black Panther party. In 1971 he participated in an attempted prison breakout during which three guards and two prisoners were killed. One of the slain prisoners was the prominent Black Panther George Jackson. For his involvement in this incident, Spain was again convicted of murder. In 1988 he was released from prison, thanks in part to his lawyer's argument that officials had violated his rights by shackling him in front of a jury. See *Spain v. Rushen,* 883 F. 2d 712 (9th Cir. 1989).

†James Cross appears to have been a thoroughly irresponsible character. He also sired a daughter by another white woman, with whom he had only a fleeting relationship; this child, too, was given up for adoption by her mother. See June Cross, *Secret Daughter* (PBS, 1996).

mother asked her friends Paul and Peggy Bush, a childless black couple, if they would help her out by raising her daughter. They agreed to do so and thus became June's de facto parents. Greve handed her child over to the Bushes for several reasons. One motivation was her concern for June: economically insecure, nursing stifled career ambitions, linked romantically with a string of men, and living among racist whites, Greve doubted that she would ever be able to provide her daughter with a wholesome home environment. But a noxious combination of cowardice and selfishness also played a role. Fearing the disapproval of her racist peers, Greve wanted to be rid of all evidence that she had once consorted sexually with a black man.

In the early 1960s Greve married the white actor Larry Storch and moved to Los Angeles. June visited them every summer but was always presented in public as the Storches' adoptee, an abused little girl whom they had "saved." June eventually tired of this ruse and at one point demanded that her mother simply stop introducing her to people to whom the truth of her parentage could not be revealed. Yet even as an adult, she declined to condemn her mother: "If you're going to get angry," she remarked in one interview, "get angry at the society that put [my mother] in a position where she had to [act the way she did]."[7]*

June Cross, Johnny Spain, and Lillian Smith's anonymous friend were all displaced from their homes as children because certain adults could not abide the prospect of interracial parenting. Each case was

---

*Of course, June Cross's mother was not forced to delegate to friends the burden of parenthood, nor was she compelled to misportray her daughter; those were *choices* that Norma Greve made. According to June, Norma stated on one occasion that if things had been a little different, she would have raised the child herself instead of sending her to live with the Bushes. In one of the most painful moments in *Secret Daughter,* June Cross recounts that

> Once when I was about seven or eight I was visiting my mother, and we were taking a bubble bath. She looked at me and said that if I had not gotten darker as I grew older, I could have stayed with her. That moment is frozen in time: my mother's bamboo-colored skin, my toffee-colored hand; her straight auburn hair, my tight black curls . . . the white bubbles falling in my eyes.

handled informally, outside the courtroom. But what has been the outcome when disputes over interracial parenting have been litigated?

### Race, Divorce, and Custody Battles

Custody battles in divorce proceedings are notoriously ferocious. It should come as no surprise, then, that upon the collapse of some interracial marriages, husbands and wives have attempted to manipulate the racial beliefs of courts in a desperate effort to secure preferred custody placements.*

For many years, judges believed—and, in some instances, openly stated—that custody should be granted to the parent whom society deemed to be the most similar racially to the child. In 1950, when James Ward, a black man, petitioned for a divorce from his white wife, Maralynn, on grounds of infidelity and drunkenness, he sought custody of their two daughters. Largely affirming the decision of a trial judge, the state supreme court of Washington ruled that the children should be placed in the custody of James Ward's mother. There was a sound basis on which to predicate this judgment—testimony suggested that Maralynn Ward had indeed neglected her children—but the court was not content to decide the case on that basis alone. The justices felt moved also to comment on the interracial character of the dispute, describing the Ward children as "unfortunate girls" who were the "victims" of a mixed marriage.† The justices asserted that because the girls were "colored," they would "have a much better opportunity to take their rightful place in society if they [were] brought up among their

---

*In recent years, groups of lawyers have sought to establish guidelines for gay and lesbian parties who are dissolving relationships, guidelines aimed at dissuading them from exploiting antigay prejudices as weapons of litigation in child custody and other disputes. See William B. Rubenstein, "Divided We Propagate: An Introduction to 'Protecting Families: Standards for Child Custody in Same-Sex Relationships,'" *UCLA Women's Law Journal* 10 (1999): 143; Gay and Lesbian Advocates and Defenders, "Protecting Families: Standards for Child Custody in Same-Sex Relationships," *UCLA Women's Law Journal* 10 (1999): 151. I know of no similar efforts that have been undertaken with regard to interracial relationships.

†Although interracial marriages were legal in the state of Washington, the justices clearly viewed such matches as a form of social pathology. The justices' abhorrence

own people"—meaning, of course, *black* people. Applying the one-drop rule without discussion of legal authority, the Washington State justices simply decided that the children were "colored," even though one of their parents was "white."[8] Having presumed to affix a racial label to the girls, the court then presumed to know the place they should and would occupy in society, and the means by which they should be socialized to their station.[9]

In 1981, in Amityville, New York, Linda Farmer (a white woman) divorced Billie Farmer (a black man), citing physical abuse and infidelity.[10] Billie sought custody of the couple's six-year-old daughter, Bethany, arguing, in part, that because she had the physical characteristics of an African American and would be generally perceived as such, he, as an African American, would be better able than his Euro-American wife to offer a home in which the child's interests would be well served. Although three "experts" testified in favor of paternal custody (voicing concerns about racial identity and cultural competency that we shall explore in a later chapter),* Justice Eli Wagner awarded custody to the mother. He did so because her history with the child indicated that she was more likely than her former husband to provide a stable and loving home environment. In his ruling, Justice Wagner maintained that

---

of mixed marriage received no challenge from the lawyers involved in the case. In their brief, Mrs. Ward's attorneys insisted, revealingly, that "you cannot put a white sow and a black boar into the same pen and get white pigs." They went on to depict their client as a naive white woman who had been debauched by a callous, scheming, older black man. "Under the facts," they wrote in their brief, "this colored man took this girl, who never knew what iniquity was before the marriage, then took her to all the colored clubs and introduced her to liquor and then he, after bringing about this tragedy, and ruining her life, walk[ed] away, chuckling to himself that he ha[d] ruined one young, white girl." (Brief of Appellant, *Ward v. Ward,* in the Supreme Court of the State of Washington. This brief can be found in the Interracial Intimacies Collection, Harvard Law School Library.) The attorney for James Ward countered by describing in detail Maralynn's fondness for liquor and her sexual interest in one of her husband's friends. "Color apparently is not a detriment to happiness as she sees it," he wrote. "Her second choice is another man of color" (Brief of Respondent, *Ward v. Ward,* in the Supreme Court of the State of Washington. This brief, too, can be found in the Interracial Intimacies Collection, Harvard Law School Library).
*See pages 437–46.

"as between two natural parents of different races who have opted to have a child, neither gains priority for custody by reason of race alone."[11] The judge did not wholly negate a preference for race matching in making the custody decision; in fact, he expressly noted that he had assessed "the race of the parties and the child, along with a host of other relevant considerations."[12] What distinguished Justice Wagner from the trial judge in *Ward* was that in Wagner's view, race was not "a dominant, a controlling, or crucial factor" but merely something "to be weighed along with all other material elements of the lives" of those involved in the custody hearing.[13]

In 1990 an appellate court in Illinois ruled that race should presumptively play *no* role in determining custody arrangements for a child in the aftermath of a divorce.[14] Soon after Alice and Victor Burton divorced, in 1987, they jointly stipulated that Alice would have temporary custody of their one-year-old son. At a later hearing, she sought sole custody, while her ex-husband requested joint custody. At that hearing, Victor Burton's attorney stated that his client should *not* be granted sole custody. Yet sole custody was precisely what the judge awarded him, despite the fact that the child had lived with his mother since birth, despite evidence that the mother had issued two emergency protective orders against the father after he made violent threats against her, and despite the father's admitted inability to care for the child financially. An intermediate appellate court reversed the trial judge. "It is apparent," the court observed, "that the trial judge's custody determination is contrary to the manifest weight of the evidence and constitutes an abuse of discretion."[15] What had prompted such a misjudgment? In the view of the appellate court, the trial judge "must have considered the race of the parties when [he] made [his] custody determination"[16]— nothing else could explain such an unfounded decision. Alice Burton was white, while her ex-husband, Victor, was black. Perhaps the judge's racially discriminatory order had been aimed at punishing Mrs. Burton for a perceived breach of racial etiquette. Or perhaps the judge had believed, like the justices in *Ward,* that colored children belonged with "their own people." In any event, the appellate court concluded that the trial judge had erred in even considering the races of the parties involved.

The decision of the Illinois appellate court in *Burton* reflects the strong tendency since the mid-twentieth century, in both federal and state law, toward making racial discrimination presumptively illicit. That presumption can be overcome. But by and large, American constitutional and statutory law discourages people, and particularly officials, from drawing racial distinctions. Even in contexts in which an antidiscrimination norm has been held to apply, however, it is often difficult for appellate courts to ensure that trial judges will refrain from using illicit racial criteria in making custody determinations.* After all, appellate courts generally grant considerable deference to trial judges, especially in domestic-relations disputes, and most trial judges will demonstrate greater subtlety than the one who presided over the Burtons' case. If a trial judge refrains from mentioning that racial considerations influenced his or her custody decision, and instead offers plausible, nonobjectionable, nonracial explanations for that decision, it is unlikely that the judgment will be reversed by higher courts.† A chilling example is what occurred in Tennessee in the mid-1990s when a white couple named Teri and Richard Parker divorced and fought over custody of their child.[17] Richard Parker alleged that his wife had been carrying on a sexual affair with an African American physician for whom she worked as a nurse. Evidence gathered by a private investigator supported this claim, though Mrs. Parker herself steadfastly denied it. While conceding that both of the Parkers were fit parents, Allen W. Wallace of the Tennessee Chancery Court awarded custody of the child to Richard Parker on the ground that Teri Parker's "primary concern" was for her paramour. She appealed, charging that Chancellor Wallace's disapproval of her supposed interracial sexual relationship had had an illicit impact on the custody determination.

---

*The same point obtains regarding the relationship of trial judges to administrative officers such as child-welfare bureaucrats, who can typically expect broad deference. It is within the gap left open by such deference that illicit discriminatory conduct can hide.

†For cases in which appellate courts affirmed trial courts that seem, despite assertions to the contrary, to have taken race into account in custody decisions, see *Schexnayder v. Schexnayder*, 371 So. 2d 769 (La. Sup. Ct. 1979) and *Murphy v. Murphy*, 124 A. 2d 891 (Conn. Sup. Ct. 1956).

Chancellor Wallace denied this, and appellate courts upheld his custody decision.

Close study of this case reveals that the chancellor's actual handling of the dispute belied his denial. He permitted a nurse practitioner to testify as an expert witness about the "adverse consequences" that the child would suffer if his custodial parent was known to be engaged in an intimate interracial relationship. After one witness—Mrs. Parker's mother—made a negative comment about such relationships, the chancellor remarked that he and she were of "the same school," even though "society today feels differently than the way we were brought up."[18] Moreover, without prompting from any party, and though there had been no hint that the black physician had harmed the Parkers' child in any manner, Chancellor Wallace stipulated as a condition of the mother's visitation rights that the child could have no contact with her alleged paramour. A panel of the Court of Appeals of Tennessee later pronounced itself "troubled" by the chancellor's ruling, noting (with reference to a federal Supreme Court decision to which we shall soon turn)* that Wallace had erred by allowing testimony to the effect that the mother's involvement in an interracial relationship might harm the child. According to the appellate panel, the chancellor had compounded his error by holding that the child could have no contact with his mother's employer and alleged paramour, an aspect of the ruling for which there was absolutely no support in the record. Remarkably, however, the court of appeals accepted the trial judge's statement that race had played no part in his decision making. The Supreme Court of Tennessee then affirmed that ruling. That appellate courts would acquiesce to such judicial deception or, at best, innacuracy is reprehensible. This example serves, however, as a useful reminder of why, in the long run, the transformation of public opinion is even more important than the transformation of legal formalities. The judicial system, by itself, will never satisfactorily police the conduct of decision makers whose personal aims and sentiments are in opposition to the law. More decisive

---

*See pages 380–86.

than the establishment of legal doctrines pointing in the right direction is the inculcation of a public opinion that will manifest itself in the actions of judges and other decision makers prompted by their own intuition to move in that direction.

### "Saving" White Children from Multiracial Households

The racial regulation of child-custody determinations has another flash point in cases where a party objects to arrangements that would make a child part of a new, multiracial household after death or divorce has disrupted his or her initial, monoracial family. Such objections are typically raised by someone who at least *knows* the child, though in some instances, strangers have taken it upon themselves to "rescue" white children from the "taint" of association with racially mixed families. In 1909, for example, in Albermarle County, Virginia, W. J. Maybee filed a complaint with H. Gibbs, a justice of the peace, urging that two children be removed from the custody of their mother and stepfather and placed under the control of the Children's Home Society, a state-run institution for white juveniles in need of adult supervision.[19] A state law provided that justices of the peace could remove from parental custody "any child under the age of fourteen years [who was found to be] growing up without education or salutary control, and in circumstances exposing such child to a dissolute and vicious life."[20] Maybee contended that Lucy Moon should be stripped of her children because, after the death of her first husband (the father of her children), she had remarried and maintained a household with John Moon, the son of a white man and a woman who was one eighth black. In Maybee's view, the racially mixed character of the Moon household was sure to adversely affect the social standing of Lucy's children. The justice of the peace agreed and ordered a sheriff to seize the children and remand them to the custody of the Children's Home Society. A judge affirmed this order on the grounds that Lucy Moon "had married a person with colored blood, who was only recognized as a colored man, and that the associations of [the children], who were of pure blood and gentle ancestors, would be with persons of mixed blood, and that they would be deterred from association with gentle people of white blood."[21] Legally,

John Moon was *not* a Negro; at that time, according to state racial classifications, he was "white." But despite Moon's official legal status, many of his white neighbors regarded him as something less than a "real" white person—a situation that would, in the judge's opinion, irremediably injure the "pure" white children living in his household. John Moon's racial smudge, the judge feared, would rub off on the children, make them subject to ostracism, and thus preclude them from taking their rightful place in their community.

On appeal, Lucy Moon did not dispute that her husband was partly colored. "It is to be regretted," she wrote, "that the husband of your petitioner has a taint of colored blood in his veins."[22] But she insisted that *legally* he was white, that he provided her and her children with "a comfortable and happy home," and that neither he nor she was guilty of any crime, drunkenness, or other vice. Lucy Moon argued, moreover, that she and her husband were culturally competent to raise "pure white" children. Toward that end, she noted, she and John Moon did not "associate with negroes" but instead were active members of a circle of friends, in-laws, and relatives who were either legally white (albeit "tainted" with some colored blood) or "pure white"—a group within the county that constituted "a little coterie to themselves."[23] Assuming this statement was true, we may speculate that the Moons' avoidance of Negroes was a purely defensive measure made necessary by Mr. Moon's "taint." Or perhaps the Moons—like most, if not all, of their white neighbors—believed that white adults fraternizing with Negroes was indicative of a dangerous social deviancy. Whatever the motivation, the fact that Lucy Moon pointed to her and her husband's ostracism of Negroes as a sign of their healthy normalcy vividly illustrates the extent to which blacks were viewed as a separate and inferior racial caste in the Jim Crow South.

The Moons eventually prevailed. On November 16, 1911, the Supreme Court of Appeals of Virginia reversed the lower courts and restored Madeline and Ruby to the custody of their mother. Observing that the children "were comfortably cared and provided for by their mother and their step-father," the justices held that state law "furnishes no authority for depriving a mother of the care and custody of her children merely because she has married into a family lower in the social scale than that in which she was reared, even though her husband has negro blood in his veins."[24] So long as the quantum of "negro blood" was sufficiently small to qualify the man as white, and thus render the couple eligible for marriage, the court saw no warrant for state interference.

In yet another scenario giving rise to litigation aimed at "saving" white children from subsumption into multiracial households, white men have sought to recover custody of their offspring from white ex-wives or ex-girlfriends who remarried or became involved with black men.* As a rule, most jurisdictions impose a heavy burden of persuasion on those seeking to obtain custody modifications, in part out of a desire to foster stability in the lives of children and in part to discourage the relitigation of issues presumably settled by the initial custody determination. Not infrequently, however, exceptions have been made for white women who marry black men. Women in this situation have thus come to fear child-custody modifications, despite the legal system's bias against such changes.†

---

*For an excellent cinematic exploration of this problem, see Larry Peerce's *One Potato, Two Potato* (1966).

For a real-life example, consider the case of Poppy Cannon. In 1949, after Cannon married Walter White, her former husband, Charles Claudius Phillippe, a white man, demanded full custody of their daughter, even though he had earlier agreed that the child should live with her mother. Walter White's race had made Phillippe rethink his concession. In a letter to Cannon, he explained that when he first accepted that arrangement, he had "never had the slightest hint that [she] would marry a negro and that [their daughter would] live in a household with a negro stepfather." He asked his ex-wife to set aside "any personal feelings or selfish considerations" and send their child to live with him "before irreparable damage is done to her." He further expressed his astonishment that Cannon "would thrust this terrible onus" on one so young. Cannon refused his request, and their daughter continued to live with her and her new husband. See Poppy Cannon, *A Gentle Knight: My Husband, Walter White* (1956).

†An interesting variation was a case in which a white father sought to reclaim custody of his mixed-race adopted children from his white ex-wife. He argued that she was insensitive to their black identity, while he—having made black friends and become a vice president of the local chapter of the NAACP—was attuned to their blackness and able to nurture it. The supreme court of Iowa upheld the trial court's

Parties seeking custody modifications usually articulate (and are probably actually moved by) altruistic motives. They maintain that they wish to rescue the children in question from the confusion, ostracism, and hostility that must inevitably attend being raised in an interracial household. Or they claim that they want to protect the children from losing the heritage and privileges of whiteness.[25] In many cases, additional motivations are likely present. One of these may be revenge: there are few more hurtful ways to punish a woman than to take away her children. Another is deterrence: one of the most effective means of dissuading a woman from pursuing (or even contemplating) certain sorts of romance is to let her know that it might well cost her the custody of her children.

The most significant custody-revocation case is *Palmore v. Sidoti*.[26] In May 1980, in Tampa, Florida, Judge Morison Buck certified the divorce of Linda and Anthony Sidoti and awarded Linda Sidoti custody of their three-year-old daughter, Melanie. Sixteen months later, Anthony Sidoti asked Judge Buck to modify the custody arrangement, charging that his ex-wife had failed to provide Melanie "with an environment conducive to the rearing of a child of such tender age, and certainly has not acted in the best interest and welfare of said minor child."[27] Sidoti listed a number of complaints, among them that on at least two occasions, Melanie had suffered from head lice; that she had been sent to day care in dirty and mildewed clothes; and that her mother was inadequately attentive to the child's hygiene and did not consistently pick her up from day care in a timely fashion. Sidoti's chief grievance, however—and the issue that turned the dispute into an important constitutional case—was that his former wife had had "a black male living with her for some period of time, a fact that she did not try to conceal from [Melanie,] and [that], in fact, [she had] even permitted the child to be in the same bed with them on different occasions."[28]

Judge Buck responded to the petition by withdrawing custody from Linda Sidoti, who had by that time married Clarence Palmore, the

---

denial of his petition. See In re *The Marriage of Gay Mikelson and Thomas Lee Mikelson*, 299 N.W. 2d 670 (1980).

black male referred to by Anthony Sidoti. Buck granted custody to her ex-husband, who had also remarried (though that marriage was apparently intraracial). The judge stipulated that Linda Palmore should be allowed reasonable visitation privileges, and that neither she nor her former husband should take Melanie out of the immediate area without the court's prior approval. Judge Buck did not rule that Linda Palmore was an unfit mother; indeed, he expressly noted that both parents were devoted to their daughter. But he did fault Linda for cohabiting premaritally with Clarence Palmore. "It is of some significance," the judge concluded, "that the mother did see fit to bring a man into her home and carry on a sexual relationship with him without being married to him. Such action tended to place gratification of her own desires ahead of her concern for the child's future welfare."[29] For Judge Buck, however, the decisive factor was not the extramarital sex itself but rather the racial identity of the mother's sexual partner. This was the issue to which he devoted most of the explanation of his decision. By his own account, the custody-modification order was not a gesture of solidarity meant to signal support for Anthony Sidoti's sense of racial aggrievement: "The father's evident resentment of the mother's choice of a black partner," he averred, "is not sufficient to wrest custody from the mother."[30] Rather, he insisted, his decision rested solely on his consideration of Melanie's best interests. He ruled against Linda Palmore—who he conceded was a fit mother—because he believed that opponents of interracial intimacy would make life difficult for her daughter. Judge Buck expressed no sympathy for those opponents; indeed, he distanced himself from them. But he suggested that it would be wrong to disregard their influence when it stood a good chance of negatively affecting Melanie's social standing. "Despite the strides that have been made in bettering relations between the races," he observed, "it is inevitable that Melanie will, if allowed to remain [in the custody of her mother] . . . suffer from the social stigmatization that is sure to come."[31]

Judge Buck believed that he was acting within his authority in rescuing Melanie Sidoti from the ostracism that would result if she remained with her mother in a multiracial household. The United States Supreme Court came to a different conclusion, ruling in a unanimous opinion authored by Chief Justice Warren Burger. Burger maintained that the case possessed three salient features. First, it concerned the relationship of a mother to her biological child. Second, it involved the relationship between the state and a child—a relationship in which the state's duty to protect the child's interest must be of "the highest order."[32] Third, its disposition constituted an act of judicial racial discrimination, since clearly "the outcome would have been different had [the mother] married a Caucasian male of similar respectability [to the black man whom she in fact married]."[33]

The stated motive of Judge Buck's custody-modification order was neither malevolent nor irrational; the trial judge had asserted that he wanted only to advance the best interests of the child. The Supreme Court recognized this as a weighty concern, acknowledging that "the goal of granting custody based on the best interests of the child is indisputably a substantial governmental interest."[34] The justices also allowed that there was reason to believe, with Judge Buck, that an interracial household might impose certain burdens upon Melanie that would be absent if she were to live with her white biological father: "There is a risk," the Court affirmed, "that a child living with a stepparent of a different race may be subject to a variety of pressures and stresses not present if the child were living with parents of the same racial or ethnic origin."[35]

The real question, as the Court saw it, was "whether the reality of private biases and the possible injury they might inflict are permissible considerations for removal of an infant child from the custody of its natural mother."[36] The Court's answer was no: "The Constitution cannot control such prejudices, but neither can it tolerate them. Private biases may be outside the reach of the law, but the law cannot, directly or indirectly, give them effect."[37] In other words, at least in this case, the Court would not permit the opponents of interracial intimacy to exercise a heckler's veto: "The effects of racial prejudice, however real, cannot justify a racial classification removing an infant child from the custody of its natural mother found to be an appropriate person to have such custody."[38]

On several previous occasions, the Court had ruled that judges ought not to trim federal constitutional rights in an effort to placate prejudice or avoid hostility. In 1917, for example, the Supreme Court invalidated a Kentucky law that limited, on a racial basis, the buying and selling of houses. The state argued that the law was justified as a means of promoting the public peace by preventing racial conflict. In response, the Court declared that "important as is the preservation of the public peace, this aim cannot be accomplished by laws or ordinances which deny rights created or protected by the Federal Constitution."[39] Similarly, in 1958, when school officials in Little Rock, Arkansas, requested recision of an already underway desegregation program to quiet the violent protests of white segregationists, the Court rebuffed their request, avowing, "Law and order are not . . . to be preserved by depriving the Negro children of their Constitutional rights."[40] And in 1963 the Court ruled against city officials in Memphis, Tennessee, who sought temporarily to extend the racial segregation of parks in order to "prevent interracial disturbances, violence, riots, and community confusion and turmoil." Denying their petition, the Court declared that "constitutional rights may not be denied simply because of hostility to their assertion or exercise."[41]

Notwithstanding these precedents, there are at least two problems with the Court's absolutistic rhetoric and reasoning in *Palmore*. First, they do not realistically reflect the Court's own actions over time: regardless of the language cited above, the Supreme Court *does* in fact take into account public reaction in designing the scope of constitutional rights and remedies. It may do so only implicitly or covertly, but it does so nonetheless. The most famous example of this is *Brown v. Board of Education*. Initially, the Court invalidated the segregation of public schools. Subsequently, however, it qualified its holding to permit the continuation of segregated schooling, provided that local authorities began to signal their willingness to desegregate their facilities at some future date. The Court concocted an alternative rationale for authorizing this delay, but the *actual* reason was its desire to accommodate and pacify white segregationists.[42]

The second problem with *Palmore* is that at every level, jurists unquestioningly accepted the notion that prejudice against a multiracial household should count only as a negative factor. The possibility was nowhere raised that standing firm against communal bigotry might actually set a desirable example or otherwise be a positive good *for the children involved.* This idea did surface, however, in a custody-modification battle involving antilesbian social prejudice. In that case, a judge remarked that when subjected to bigotry, children

> may sometimes have to bear themselves with greater than ordinary fortitude. But this does not necessarily portend that their moral welfare or safety will be jeopardized. It is just as reasonable to expect that they will emerge better equipped to search out their own standards of right and wrong, better able to perceive that the majority is not always correct in its moral judgments, and better able to understand the importance of conforming their beliefs to the requirements of reason and tested knowledge, not to the constraints of currently popular sentiment or prejudice.
>
> Taking the children from [the parent with whom they have been satisfactorily living] can be done only at the price of sacrificing those very qualities they will find most sustaining in meeting the challenges inevitably ahead. Instead of forbearance and feelings of protectiveness, it will foster in them a sense of shame for their mother. Instead of courage and the precept that people of integrity do not shrink from bigots, it counsels the easy option of shirking difficult problems and following the course of expedience. Lastly, it diminishes their regard for the rule of human behavior . . . that we do not forsake those to whom we are indebted for love and nurture merely because they are held in low esteem by others.[43]

In assessing *Palmore,* we would also do well to remember that there often exists a gap between formal rights declared on paper and the actual enjoyment of those rights. This gap was vividly illustrated by the frustration faced by Linda Sidoti Palmore after her victory. Even though the Supreme Court itself had ruled in her favor, she did not regain custody of her daughter. During the pendency of the case, Anthony Sidoti had moved Melanie and his new wife to a new home in Texas. After losing in the federal Supreme Court, he appealed for help to various state courts, which responded affirmatively. First, a Texas judge issued a restraining order that barred Linda Palmore from taking custody of Melanie. Then Judge Buck, in Florida, granted Anthony Sidoti's request to transfer the case to judicial authorities in Texas. Linda Palmore appealed that ruling, but to no avail. A Florida intermediate appellate court found that Judge Buck had acted within allowable bounds of discretion when he ruled that a judge in Texas would be in a better position than he to exercise continuing jurisdiction over the case.[44] Although the Florida court noted that Anthony Sidoti had violated the terms of the modified custody order by taking his daughter to Texas without prior judicial approval, it declined to construe his action as an instance of outright abduction. It was willing to accept Sidoti's claim that he had moved to Texas for valid business reasons and not to evade Florida's judicial process. The Florida court also rejected the argument that allowing Sidoti to retain custody of his child amounted to defiance of the Supreme Court's ruling. The Supreme Court, it noted, had not expressly ordered that custody of Melanie be awarded to Mrs. Palmore or that the Florida courts refrain from transferring jurisdiction to Texas courts.

As we have seen, *Palmore* stands for the proposition that federal constitutional law prohibits state judges from modifying postdivorce child-custody arrangements to forestall feared community hostility stemming from a mother's interracial romantic association. Nevertheless, some judges will order such modifications anyway, citing pretextual reasons for their decisions. With that said, *Palmore* does appear to have made a difference in the resolution of some litigated disputes. In Fulton County, Georgia, for instance, the marriage of a white couple, Sheila Mae and Orville Joseph Boleman, dissolved in divorce. They agreed that he would have custody of their child and that she would have visitation rights away from her ex-husband's residence, on the condition that the child would at no time be in the presence of "any" African American male—a stipulation aimed at Mrs. Boleman's black lover. After she married that lover, her former husband refused to permit her to visit with her son outside of his residence. Incredibly, a trial judge upheld the validity of this arrangement. Rather quickly, however, an appellate court, citing *Palmore*, invalidated it. The state, the court declared, "cannot sanction such blatant racial prejudice, especially where it also interferes with the rights of a child in the parent/child relationship."[45]

*Palmore* does not merely prohibit racial discriminations based on bad motives, such as a husband's resentment over the racial identity of his ex-wife's new lover; it also prohibits racial discrimination based on *good* motives, such as the desire to protect a child from the ostracism that he or she might be subjected to as a member of a multiracial household. In 1978 Danny Holt and his wife were divorced, and she was granted custody of their daughter. Six years later, after she remarried, this time to a black man, her former husband sought to modify their custody arrangement. His motivation appears to have been legitimate concern regarding the taunts that his ten-year-old child had to endure at school in the aftermath of her mother's remarriage. Whereas in *Palmore,* the white father had justified his request for a custody modification on the ground that his daughter ran the *risk* of being taunted by other children because her mother had married an African American, in *Holt,* risk was superseded by certainty. Dawn Holt was in fact teased viciously by certain classmates about the race of her mother's second husband. The teasing got even worse after her mother's new pregnancy became apparent. In response, Dawn at first voiced a desire to escape her predicament by joining her father, then underscored that desire by walking to his workplace and begging him to take custody of her. Although a judge granted Danny Holt custody, the Supreme Court of Kentucky reversed, relying heavily upon *Palmore.*[46]*

## Adoption

Under what circumstances, if any, should racial differences be weighed in arranging adoptions? This question does not have a long history.

---

*Although the Kentucky Supreme Court disapproved of the trial court's initial handling of the case, it left open the possibility of modifying the custody arrangement, in deference to Dawn Holt's objection to her mother's new domestic arrangement. Whatever the cause, the court ruled, "the child's emotional reaction to her mother's marital circumstances may enter into deciding what is in [her] best interest" (*Holt v. Chenault,* 722 S.W. 897, 898 [Ky. Sup. Ct. 1987]).

Before the 1950s it was hardly ever posed, simply because the very idea of interracial adoption was virtually inconceivable.* Now, however, controversies over interracial adoptions abound. They have inspired novels, films, large bodies of literature in various academic disciplines, numerous court cases, and a score of state and federal statutes. Several different viewpoints have significantly shaped the debate. One wholly rejects the propriety of interracial adoptions. Another objects specifically to interracial adoption involving Native American children, a topic to which a subsequent chapter of this book is devoted.† Many observers would permit decision makers to take race into account, but only alongside other considerations deemed relevant to the determination of which candidate might be best suited to raise a particular child. This view sees nothing wrong in authorities preferring to match children of a given race with adoptive parents of the same race, so long as such matches can be made relatively promptly. Another position urges the application in the context of adoption of the same antidiscrimination rules that generally prevail in American social life. Proponents of this approach believe that it is presumptively ill conceived for officials to give race any weight at all in matching prospective adoptees with prospective adopters. Yet another outlook would seek to prohibit not only officials but also private adopters from being racially selective in matching or choosing adoptive children.

Let's examine these positions and variations on them more closely.

*Jim Crow Statutory Bans on All Black-White Interracial Adoptions*
While most jurisdictions prior to the 1960s took for granted the

---

*It is worth noting here, for example, that the subject of interracial adoption is nowhere considered in such comprehensive works as St. Clair Drake and Horace R. Cayton, *Black Metropolis: A Study of Negro Life in a Northern City* (1945); Gunnar Myrdal, *An American Dilemma: The Negro Problem and Modern Democracy* (1944); and Charles S. Mangum Jr., *The Legal Status of the Negro* (1940). See also Jacqueline Macaulay and Steward Macaulay, "Adoption for Black Children: A Case Study of Expert Discretion," *Research in Law and Sociology* 1 (1978): 265, 266: "Transracial adoption was first regarded as unthinkable."
†See pages 480–518.

inadvisability of black-white interracial adoptions, only Texas and Louisiana actually went to the trouble of forbidding them by statute.* The Louisiana law stated the prohibition indirectly, stipulating that "a single person over the age of twenty-one years, or a married couple jointly, may petition to adopt any child of his or their race."[47] The Texas law was blunter: "No white child can be adopted by a negro person nor can a negro child be adopted by a white person."[48] These statutes were invalidated, along with countless other segregationist laws, during the civil rights revolution of the 1960s and 1970s.

First to come under attack was the Texas statute. Walter Strawn Jr., a soldier in the United States Army who was stationed in El Paso, petitioned to adopt his wife's two illegitimate daughters, both of whom lived with the couple. A state court denied his petition, citing the statutory prohibition on interracial adoption and the fact that Strawn was "a member of the negro race" while the girls were "members of the white race."[49] On appeal, however, in In re *Gomez,* a Texas state court became (in 1967) the first in the nation to strike down on federal (as well as state) constitutional grounds a law banning interracial adoption. The Texas court inferred from a long list of decisions, including *Loving v. Virginia,* that there no longer existed any legal basis on which the state could prohibit, solely by reason of their race, whole classes of adults from adopting whole classes of children, regardless of individual needs and capacities. The court also noted that apart from legal doctrine, the state's policy was terribly punitive with regard to the children in the case at bar. After all, the petitioner's adoption of the children would both legitimize them and enable them to receive benefits as dependents of a member of the United States armed forces.

---

*Kentucky passed a law specifying that if "within a five-year period after an adoption is finalized a child reveals traits of ethnological ancestry different from those of the adoptive parents and of which the adoptive parents had no knowledge or information prior to the adoption, the adoption can be canceled." Missouri enacted a similar provision: "An adoption may be set aside within five years when a person shall prove to be a member of a race, the members of which are prohibited by the laws of this state from marriage with members of the race to which the parents by adoption belong." Pearl Buck mentions these laws in her neglected, informative, and wise *Children for Adoption* (1964), 138–39.

The Louisiana statute requiring segregation in adoption was challenged in 1970 by two couples. Guillermo and Caroline Compos, a white couple, wrote to an adoption agency licensed by the state to inquire into the possibility of adopting a black child. The agency responded that it could not even consider the couple's request in light of the state's adoption law. A second couple, Edmond and Gerda Norman, a black man and white woman, were told that as a mixed couple, they would be ineligible to adopt *any* child of *any* race, given the law's racial requirements. The state argued that its adoption statute did not manifest any invidious or arbitrary racial discrimination but instead promoted the best interests of children by mandating their placement in homes where they could be raised "naturally." It was patently "unnatural," the state maintained, for white parents to beget a black child, or black parents to beget a white one. A three-judge federal court, taking account of what it perceived to be "the realities of American society," acknowledged that "an interracial home in Louisiana presents difficulties for a child, including the possible refusal by a community to accept the child."[50] For that reason, the judges declared, "we regard the difficulties inherent in interracial adoption as justifying consideration of race as a relevant factor in adoption."[51] The Louisiana statute went too far, however; according to the court, its fatal flaw was that it made race matter too much. Instead of counting race merely as one relevant variable, the statute codified race as "the determinative factor," worthy of crowding out and overwhelming all other considerations.*

The *Gomez* and *Compos* decisions marked the end of Jim Crow statutory prohibitions against interracial adoption.

*Policies Barring Blacks from Adopting White Children*    Although most of the extant commentary on interracial adoption has focused on white adults' adoption of black children, the prospect of black adults adopting white children deserves more than a footnote. From 1910 to 1981 South Carolina carried on its books a statute that read, in part:

---

*The author of this decision was Judge Fred J. Cassibry. Seventeen years earlier, it was to Cassibry that the Greens initially turned in their efforts to adopt Jacqueline Henley. See page 6.

It shall be unlawful for any parent, relative or other white person in this State, having control or custody of any white child . . . to dispose of, give or surrender such white child permanently into the custody, control, maintenance or support of a Negro. Any person violating the provisions of this section shall be guilty of a misdemeanor.[52]

This provision reflected the assumption that while it might sometimes make sense to allow whites to adopt blacks, it *never* made sense to allow the reverse. At the heart of this assumption lay the belief that blacks were inferior, the certainty that they could never have anything to offer a white child that would be equal (much less superior) to the minimum available from whites, and the fear that permitting a white child to be adopted by blacks would be tantamount to turning him or her *into* a Negro—a tragic declension, in contrast to the transformation of a Negro child into a white person, which would constitute (so the argument ran) a hopeful ascent.

The prospect of a black adult adopting a white child occasioned an important decision in 1955.[53] In Washington, D.C., the white mother of an illegitimate child sired by a white man married a black man who subsequently sought to adopt her son. The black man was a taxi driver and law-school student; his white wife was a homemaker. From the time of their marriage, the couple had supported the boy and raised him as their own, alongside the two other children they had together. Asked to sign off on the recommendation of child-welfare officials that the husband be permitted to adopt his wife's child, United States District Court Judge Alexander Holtzhoff noted that "ordinarily such an adoption . . . should be not only approved but encouraged."[54] But this was no ordinary case, Judge Holtzhoff continued. It was an anomaly sure to beget a difficult social problem, in that "the boy when he grows up might lose the social status of a white man by reason of the fact that by record his father will be a negro if this adoption is approved."[55] The judge therefore refused to approve the adoption, for fear that it would strip the child of his potentially valuable racial standing. In a decision reminiscent of that handed down in *Green,* Judge Holtzhoff ruled, in essence, that it would be better for the boy to remain illegitimate but white than to become legitimate but black—or, more precisely, to become the legal son of a black man.

The logic of Judge Holtzhoff's ruling would have effectively barred the adoption of *any* white child by *any* black adult, since in every such instance it could be said that the youngster would be compelled to forfeit his or her social standing as a white person if the adoption were approved. Holtzhoff's ruling, however, was short-lived, reversed by the United States Court of Appeals in a unanimous and influential opinion authored by Judge David Bazelon. "There may be reasons why a difference in race, or religion, may have relevance in adoption proceedings," Bazelon wrote on behalf of the three-judge panel. "But that factor alone cannot be decisive in determining a child's welfare."[56] In this instance, the appellate court concluded, the trial judge had erred in relying exclusively on racial considerations when other factors should have been accorded "controlling weight":[57]

> The child is living in the happy home of its natural mother and stepfather, receiving the same loving care they give to the two children born of their marriage. That it is in the best interests of the child to live in the home with the natural mother is obvious. It is equally plain that the child will continue to live there no matter what disposition is made of this case. Hence denial of adoption could only serve the harsh and unjust end of depriving the child of a legitimated status in that home.[58]*

---

*For a critical commentary on this case written from a segregationist perspective, see William F. Pope, "Interracial Adoption," *South Carolina Law Quarterly* 9 (1957): 630. Asserting that it was "extremely doubtful" that other jurisdictions would follow Judge Bazelon's lead, Pope insisted that

> in view of the grave psychological and social problems involved, the racial similarity between the adopting parents and child should be a condition precedent to considering other aspects of the child's welfare. Before granting a petition that for all legal purposes changes the race of an individual it would seem that a better means of insuring the welfare of the child would be to postpone determination until the child is old enough to make the decision for himself. [Ibid., 632]

We may note here that Judge Bazelon did not invalidate the policy of routinely taking race into account in determining the propriety of adoptions. He simply ruled that race *alone* could not be determinative, and that in this particular case, other considerations overwhelmingly militated in favor of allowing the adoption to proceed.*

Anxieties continue to erupt even today when blacks seek to adopt whites. In Detroit, Michigan, in the late 1990s, for example, a woman named Regina Bush tried to adopt a nine-year-old girl named Stacey.[59] Stacey had then been living with Bush for over a year as a foster child, and Bush had already adopted Stacey's half sister. Local child-welfare officials nevertheless attempted to block the second adoption, objecting to it on racial grounds, because by their criteria, Bush was black and Stacey was white. Stacey and her sister shared the same white biological mother, but Stacey's biological father was white, while her sister's father was black. That made for a difference in how they were treated by the various agencies involved. The welfare bureaucracy seemed to chafe at the prospect of allowing Bush, a black woman, to adopt a youngster who was pure white as opposed to just partly white. The authorities maintained that Stacey would be better served by being moved to foster care in a white household than by being adopted by Bush—despite the bonding that had already occurred, despite Bush's positive record as an adoptive parent, and despite the typical preference for raising siblings in the same household. The child-welfare authorities acquiesced to the adoption only after Bush turned in desperation to an attorney, who sued on her behalf.

---

*The political commitments of the couple added another wrinkle to the case. In the midst of the anti-Communist red scare of the 1950s, they refused to sign a declaration stipulating that they did not belong to any subversive organization named in a list maintained by the attorney general. Judge Holtzhoff cited this as an alternative ground for denying the husband's petition to adopt. The appellate court reversed him on this point as well, holding that at least in the context of a petition to adopt, refusal to sign a loyalty declaration could not be counted as an adverse reflection upon the petitioner's character (In re *Adoption of a Minor*, 288 F. 2d 446, 447–48 [D.C. Cir. 1955]).

*Preferences for Same-Race Adoption of Black Children*   Although several of the cases discussed above involved white children whom blacks sought to adopt, by far the greater part of the debate over race in adoption has concentrated on black adoptees. Many people believe that a special effort should be made to match black children with black adults. Some object categorically to interracial adoption or are willing to permit it only as a last-ditch alternative to long-term foster or institutional care. These are the champions of strong race matching. Other advocates of race matching are less rigid. While they concede that interracial adoption is typically preferable to prolonged stays in foster homes or orphanages, they urge the programmatic facilitation of same-race adoptions. They favor a policy of moderate race matching.*

*Strong Race Matching*   With regard to African American children, the most influential endorsement of strong race matching in the post-segregation era has come from the National Association of Black Social Workers (NABSW). In 1972 this group condemned the interracial adoption of black children, declaring that

> Black children should be placed only with Black families whether in foster care or for adoption. Black children belong, physically, psychologically and culturally, in Black families in order that they receive the total sense of themselves and develop a sound projection of their future. . . . Black children in white homes are cut off from the healthy development of themselves as Black people.[60]

The NABSW maintained that its position was based on "the necessity of self-determination from birth to death, of all Black people, the need of our young ones to begin at birth to identify with all Black people in a Black community," and "the philosophy that we need our own to build

---

*A later chapter considers the special treatment accorded Native American children through the Indian Child Welfare Act (ICWA). See pages 480–518.

a strong nation."[61] The authors of this position paper committed themselves to returning to their communities and putting an end to interracial adoption, which they characterized as a "particular form of genocide."[62]

The reference to genocide in this document was neither a careless word choice nor an isolated occurrence; it was, instead, indicative of a considered ideology elaborated over a period of years by many representatives and allies of the NABSW. Audrey Russell, a pioneer of the organization's campaign, described transracial adoption as a "diabolical trick" that amounted to a "lethal incursion on the black family."[63] Thirteen years later, testifying before the United States Senate, the NABSW president declared, "We view the placement of Black children in white homes as a hostile act against our community. It is a blatant form of race and cultural genocide."[64] More recently, NABSW officials have toned down their rhetoric and even gone so far as to suggest that the group would support some interracial adoptions under exceptional circumstances.* This softening of stance and language, however, is mainly tactical, part of a public-relations strategy aimed at improving the NABSW's public image.† For the NABSW rank and file, it remains an article of faith that the interracial adoption of black children constitutes cultural genocide.

---

*In its 1994 position paper, for example, the NABSW outlined one acceptable scenario: "Transracial adoption of an African-American child should only be considered after documented evidence of unsuccessful same-race placements [has] been reviewed and supported by appropriate representatives of the African-American community." Quoted in Amanda T. Perez, "Note: Transracial Adoption and the Federal Adoption Subsidy," *Yale Law and Policy Review* 17 (1998): 201, 210. It bears noting that no guidance is given here on how long the search for a same-race placement should be pursued before the transracial alternative may be resorted to, or how "appropriate representatives" of the African American community are to be identified.

†The predicate for this statement is my own personal experience with representatives of the NABSW in various public and private settings. Convinced that I, as a black man, could not possibly be wholly antagonistic to their point of view, several NABSW activists and supporters have explicitly told me that while they continue to believe that the interracial adoption of black children is "cultural genocide," they realize that such talk is off-putting and that it is politic to repackage their message in a less provocative wrapping.

   The proponents of strong race matching articulate arguments that can usefully be divided into two categories: those that focus on what is best for blacks as a group, and those that focus on what is best for an individual black child. The key claim of the former arguments is that strict race matching is necessary to advance the collective interest of blacks, because without it, the African American community will "lose" an appreciable number of black children—children who, the reasoning goes, will be taken away by whites and acculturated in ways that will erode their ability to participate in struggles on behalf of their fellow blacks. The suspicion is that interracial adoption will create a host of "Oreos," or Negroes who are black on the outside but white on the inside.* The fear is that because of their upbringing in white house-holds, these children (and *their* children in turn) will lack any deep, urgent, or educated sense of affiliation with their black forebears and contemporaries—the bone-deep sense of identification that enables many African Americans to say, without ambivalence, that black people are "*my* people." The contention is that they will miss the numberless experiences that facilitate the ease of communication and empathy that allow even blacks who are strangers to come together quickly for pur-poses of giving and receiving collective aid. They will miss the essential lessons to be learned in the 'hood (for example, the facts of life regard-ing prevalent police attitudes toward young black men), miss identity-forging events (for example, having the opportunity to represent black organizations in competitions against white organizations), miss the cultural immersion that most African Americans take for granted (for example, sharing certain forms of dance, playing the dozens, becoming familiar with distinctive modes of religious observance). Some might push the point even further and assert that blacks adopted by whites represent not only a loss to the African American community but a danger as well—a sort of Negro Trojan horse. Unaware that Negro adoptees have been raised by whites, other blacks might repose in them

---

*For a discussion of the concept of "apples"—Native Americans who are red on the outside but white on the inside—see pages 500–503. And for commentary on "bananas"—Asian Americans who are purportedly yellow on the outside but white on the inside—see Eric Lin, *The Accidental Asian: Notes of a Native Speaker* (1998).

a mistaken confidence. Blacks raised by whites might be trusted as soul brothers and soul sisters, even though they lack the emotional and cultural upbringing that would make such presumptive trust sound. Raised by white adults, African American adoptees, in short, will look black but identify white.

With respect to the interests of individual children, proponents of strong race matching contend that white adoptive parents will be unable to inculcate in black youngsters the "coping skills" they will need to survive and flourish in a racist society. They also argue that white adoptive parents will be incapable of instilling in black children a healthy sense of self-love and self-acceptance. Of course, these qualities are difficult enough for black parents to nurture in their black biological children, given our society's pervasive celebration of whiteness and denigration of blackness. But proponents of strong race matching maintain that this difficulty must lapse into impossibility when the parents of black youngsters are white. For one thing, the proper cultural and spiritual development of a child requires relatives, friends, neighbors, religious institutions, clubs, schools—the proverbial village. The reality of racial separation means, however, that the great majority of whites live in distinctly *white* villages, communities in which black youngsters, deprived of black role models, are likely to feel lonely, alien, misunderstood, and always and unavoidably DIFFERENT—unpromising soil indeed for the cultivation of happy, relaxed, confident, well-adjusted adults.

Although the NABSW position condemning virtually all transracial adoptions has never been formally embraced by any jurisdiction in the post–Jim Crow United States, it has been and remains influential.[65] The late 1960s witnessed a small but significant upturn in the number of whites adopting blacks. In 1968 733 black children were placed in white homes nationwide; just a year later, the figure had risen to 1,447. In 1970 the number went up again, to 2,284. Then the NABSW announced its opposition and mobilized resistance. It got results, and almost immediately: in 1973 the number of black children adopted by whites declined, to 1,091. In 1974 the total fell to 747.[66]

By the 1990s the NABSW's grip on adoption practice had been somewhat loosened. Academics criticized the organization's position with a new aggressiveness.[67] So, too, did ordinary American citizens, who responded through organizing, publicity, and litigation.* In 1994 Congress enacted legislation that imposed limits on race matching by agencies receiving federal funds.[68] Two years later, it tightened those strictures.[69] As a consequence of these and other developments, race matching is now on the defensive, and interracial adoption is on the rise. In 1998, of 36,000 adoptions of foster children in the United States, about 15 percent were transracial, most involving black children and white adults.[70] Still, as I shall show in more detail below, opposition to interracial adoptions remains very much alive.[71] And in any publicized dispute concerning such adoptions, the NABSW can be expected to play a role.

One way the NABSW succeeded in chilling black-white interracial adoption was by persuading or otherwise compelling influential agencies in the child-care system to toe the line it laid down. That it was so effective in these efforts seems all the more remarkable because, for all the significance it attaches to interracial adoption, the NABSW itself has never produced or sponsored anything that can responsibly be described as "research." In attacking interracial adoption, it has variously put the onus of persuasion on the defenders of transracial placements; posited unsubstantiated assertions; or—again, without any hint of corroborative evidence—claimed that damage caused by interracial adoptions must surely become manifest at a later date. Yet despite its indifference and even its contempt for rigorous sociological investigation, the NABSW is an organization to which important actors in the provision of child-welfare services often defer. The history of the Child Welfare League of America (CWL) is illustrative in this regard. The CWL is the oldest and largest nonprofit organization in the United States devoted to promoting the interests of children, particularly those who are most vulnerable. Initially, CWL adhered to race matching, but in 1968 it revised its approach: "Racial background in itself," the league proposed, "should not determine the selection of the home for

---

*Organizations that mirror this phenomenon include the National Council for Adoption and the National Committee to End Racism in America's Child Care System. Their efforts deserve a careful study.

a child. . . . It should not be assumed . . . that difficulties will necessarily arise if adoptive parents and children are of different racial origin."[72] In 1973, however—clearly in reaction to the NABSW's pronouncements and agitation—the CWL flip-flopped and once again embraced race matching. "It is preferable," it now declared, "to place children in families of their own racial background."[73] Since its acquiescence to the NABSW, the CWL has consistently favored a program of race matching.[74]

The pall that opponents of interracial adoption have been able to cast over the idea of interracial placements represents, among other things, effective mau-mauing. On numerous occasions during the course of my research, I encountered child-welfare caseworkers who spoke with me about their work only on the condition that they remain anonymous. Their primary fear, they said, was reprisal from colleagues who would regard their disagreement on the issue of strong race matching as evidence of either racism (if the caseworker was white) or Uncle Tomism (if the caseworker was black).

By putting a black face on vocal opposition to transracial adoption, the NABSW opened up a new line of attack against this form of interracial intimacy. Skilled though they may be in dealing with white skeptics or antagonists, defenders of transracial adoption have often been unnerved by black opponents. Fear of ostracism, feelings of guilt, and a sense of self-doubt are among the emotions that inhibit a wide array of people—especially whites—from forcefully responding to black critics of interracial adoption.*

*Moderate Race Matching* Proponents of moderate race matching, like champions of strong race matching, insist that officials ought to give preference to black adults as adopters of black children. The difference between the two factions is that the "strong" advocates are willing to go further to impose race matching. They are willing to wait indefinitely, if need be, to ensure that a black child is raised by a black adult.

---

*For more on the self-doubt experienced by some whites who adopt interracially, see pages 453–68.

The "moderates," by contrast, are willing to turn to transracial adoption after substantial efforts to find same-race placements have failed. The ethos of moderate race matching was codified in several states that enacted legislation ordering child-welfare authorities to privilege same-race adoptions. California, for example, used to direct its child-welfare bureaucracy to search exclusively for same-race adoptive care for ninety days after a child became eligible for adoption. California also prohibited its officials from arranging transracial adoptions after the ninety-day period "unless it [could] be documented that a diligent search" for a same-race family had been undertaken.[75]*

In 1993 the *New York Times* editorial page also endorsed moderate race matching. While eschewing the NABSW's categorical rejection of interracial adoption, the *Times* proclaimed that "clearly matching adoptive parents with children of the same race is a good idea."[76] Moderate race matching also prevailed in the Multiethnic Placement Act of 1994 (MEPA), the first federal statute specifically concerned with matters of race in adoption.[77] Sponsored by Senator Howard Metzenbaum, this legislation prohibited any agency that received federal funds from categorically denying interracial adoptions, but it expressly *permitted* the use of race as *a* factor along with others in the determination of foster care and adoption placements.† MEPA reflected the confusion that often attends adoption policy. In introducing his bill, Senator Metzenbaum maintained that it "reaffirms the fundamental principle that our child welfare system should judge people by the content of their character and not by the color of their skin." That sounded very much like a repudiation of race matching. But then later in the same speech,

---

*Several other states enacted similar provisions, though all of them have now been repealed, invalidated, or superseded by federal statutory law. See Rita J. Simon and Howard Altstein, "The Relevance of Race in Adoption and Social Practice," *Notre Dame Journal of Law, Ethics, and Public Policy* 11 (1997): 171, 173–75; Elizabeth Bartholet, "Where Do Black Children Belong? The Politics of Race Matching in Transracial Adoption," 139 *University of Pennsylvania Law Review* 1163, 1189 (1991).

†"An agency . . . may consider the cultural, ethnic, or racial background of the child and the capacity of the prospective foster or adoptive parents to meet the needs of a child of this background as one of a number of factors used to determine the best interests of a child" (42 U.S.C. 5115a. [a][2]).

Metzenbaum voiced his belief that "every child who is eligible for adoption has the right to be adopted by parents of the same race if that is possible"—a statement that suddenly elevated moderate race matching from a mere policy preference to a "right."[78]*

*Against Race Matching/For Loving Parenting Regardless of Race*
Although race matching remains a powerful force, it now faces substantial opposition in legislatures, courts, and other arenas of public opinion. Americans have come increasingly to question the notion that, all other things being equal, adults of a given race are "of course" best equipped to raise children of the same race. The society is moving toward approving an antidiscrimination norm in foster care and adoption. An important landmark in this development was the 1996 Inter-Ethnic Adoption Amendment (IAA) to MEPA.[79] As we have seen, MEPA expressly permitted agencies to take race into account in determining where to place a child—provided that it was not relied upon as the *sole* reason for delaying or denying a placement for foster care or adoption. The IAA, by contrast, rescinds authorization to consider race as a factor *at all*. It stipulates that any organization receiving funds from the federal government may not delay or deny the placement of a child for foster care or adoption on the basis of race, color, or national origin.†

The IAA, however, has yet to halt entirely the practice of race matching. Many pertinent officials, including judges, are still guided by the premises of race matching, and many ordinary citizens deem its moderate form eminently reasonable. Even many adopters and adoptees

---

*To his credit, Senator Metzenbaum rather quickly repudiated his own legislation and supported important amendments to it. See "Statement of the Honorable Howard Metzenbaum, a Former Senator from the State of Ohio," Hearings Before the Subcommittee on Human Resources of the Committee on Ways and Means, House of Representatives, 150th Congress, Second Session, September 15, 1998, pp. 34–38.

†It should be noted that several states, including Pennsylvania, Wisconsin, and Texas, have also passed antidiscrimination legislation aimed at race matching. See Rita Simon and Howard Altstein, "The Relevance of Race in Adoption Law and Social Practice," *Notre Dame Journal of Law, Ethics & Public Policy* 11 (1997): 171, 173.

who have together created loving multiracial families nonetheless believe that, all other things being equal, same-race adoption is preferable to interracial adoption. They are wrong. While less misdirected than strong race matching, moderate race matching is still grievously mistaken. Elaborating that point is the aim of the next chapter.

# TEN

# The Tragedy of Race Matching in Black and White

Race matching is a destructive practice in *all* its various guises, from moderate to extreme. It ought to be replaced by a system under which children in need of homes may be assigned to the care of foster or adoptive parents as quickly as reasonably possible, *regardless* of perceived racial differences. Such a policy would greatly benefit vulnerable children. It would also benefit American race relations.[1]

First, consider the fact that at any given moment, hundreds of thousands of dependent children are bereft of parental protection, guidance, nurturance, and love. In the mid-1990s, more than half a million children lived in foster homes or institutions.[2] This pool of parentless children is a tragic consequence of the personal catastrophes and social failures that kill parents, or maim them, or otherwise render them unfit to carry out their parental responsibilities. Among the gravest threats in this regard are disease, murder, child abuse, abandonment, drug addiction, imprisonment, and poverty. A disproportionately large percentage of parentless children are black. This is not a statistical accident; rather, it stems from a long and bitter history of slavery, segregation, and racially selective neglect and mistreatment. Disproportionately large numbers of blacks among the ranks of parentless children also reflect racial selectivity in the private preferences of those seeking to become foster or adoptive parents, the great majority of whom have a preference for children of the same race as themselves. This is especially so with respect to adoption. Because white adults dominate adoption markets both in numbers and in financial resources, their racial preferences have elevated the relative value of white children, who are, generally speaking, in higher demand than black children.

It is important to note that black adults do *not* lag in their willingness to adopt; indeed, relative to their share of the population, they are more likely to adopt than whites.[3] In many locales, however, the pool of black parentless children overwhelms the available number of black prospective adoptive parents. In New York City in 1993, 75 percent of the children waiting for adoptive homes were African American, while blacks constituted only 21 percent of the city's population.[4] In the mid-1990s, African American youngsters constituted 88 percent of the 40,000 children in the custody of the Cook County child-welfare authority, while only one third of the county's residents were African American.[5] In such circumstances, even if their numbers increased considerably, black adopters alone would be unable to provide homes for all of the black children in need of parents.

Some students of the subject assert that there is no real need for interracial adoption, as sufficient numbers of black adults would offer foster and adoptive homes to black children if only wrongful impediments could be removed. Even if black prospective foster and adoptive parents were being treated unfairly, the proper remedy would be to challenge the mistreatment directly, *not* to hold parentless children hostage in an attempt to force authorities to stop mistreating black prospective parents.* Invidious discriminations against black prospective adoptive parents have certainly been carried out historically.[6] But now that problem, though perhaps still active in certain places, is greatly diminished overall. Moreover, in many locales authorities make special efforts to recruit black foster and adoptive parents, even to the point of lowering or waiving general requirements.†

---

*The same point pertains to mistreatment of black social workers. See pages 415–16.
†My comment is no brief in favor of "general requirements" per se. Over the years authorities have wrongly imposed many general requirements for eligibility to become a foster or adoptive parent—proof of infertility, a residence sufficiently large to house a child in his own separate room, being married. The requirement that a prospective adoptive parent be of the "correct" race—namely, the same race as the child—is yet another of these mistaken general requirements.

Finally, even if there were a sufficient supply of prospective black foster and adoptive parents to accommodate all needy black youngsters, the question would remain: Is race matching a sound practice? For me, the answer is no. But before we consider the most difficult hypothetical case, let's return to the gritty reality of large numbers of children, disproportionately children of color, languishing in foster care or institutions as opposed to preferable adoptive settings. Race matching likely contributes to this problem.[7] Anecdotal evidence suggests that in order to place children with adults deemed racially correct, social workers who strongly champion race matching will (at least temporarily) either decline to make a child eligible for adoption until a suitable black household can be found, or list only blacks on the roster of possible adoptive placements for the child. This strategy of racially aligning children and adults imposes a burden of delay, pushing back the moment at which a child becomes the primary responsibility of an adult who is willing to become his or her permanent parent. A delay of this kind is a cost in and of itself. In addition, it carries collateral consequences, insofar as it diminishes the chances that the child will *ever* be adopted. That is because for many adults, children become less attractive as potential adoptees as they age. What seems at first to be merely a brief wait may thus prevent certain youngsters from being adopted at all.

Race matching also hurts black potential adoptees by thinning the ranks of those who might adopt them. Whites who might otherwise have been happy to adopt regardless of racial differences may feel intimidated or stigmatized by race-matching policies and rhetoric.[8] Any degree of race matching is a signal that authorities consider interracial adoption inferior to same-race adoption as a solution to a child's predicament. By treating interracial adoption as an unusually risky, deviant, or troubling endeavor, officials often signal that for them, it is at best only "better than nothing."

By chasing away a substantial number of prospective adoptive parents, race-matching policies necessarily condemn some children to a childhood without any permanent parents whatsoever, or to a longer wait for adoption than they otherwise would have had to endure. A full understanding of the destructiveness of this unnecessary burden requires an assessment of institutional care and foster homes.[9] Institutional care as it is currently configured typically offers parentless children a bleak existence. It is possible to imagine institutional settings in which stable, long-term, nurturing adult supervision could be provided to children in need. But in the United States, no such alternative is presently available. Instead, we have institutional settings in which no single adult is cloaked with even the temporary mantle of "parent," and in which children are thus deprived of every benefit of having in their corner an adult whose primary responsibility, twenty-four hours a day, is the well-being of his or her charges. Many institutional homes are, moreover, beset by a wide array of interrelated difficulties: insufficient pay for staff, poorly trained and unmotivated employees, and high turnover of personnel.

Good foster care offers children an essential refuge from the catastrophe of parentlessness. "Many foster parents qualify for sainthood," Professor Elizabeth Bartholet rightly notes. "They nurture children not 'their own' without any expectation of the long-run benefits of permanent parenthood."[10] But even at its best, foster care is laced with insecurity insofar as a foster home is a *temporary* home. Because foster care is by definition transitional, it poses inherent impediments to the creation of nurturing relationships. In some places, foster parents are actually discouraged from attempting to elevate the status of their wardship from foster care to adoption. Under such circumstances, many foster children and foster parents will refrain from investing themselves fully in one another. Why fall in love only to face the heartbreak of being pulled apart?

Then, too, behind the rhetoric of parenting that attends any discussion of foster care is the hard reality of economics. Adults who act as foster parents provide a service for which they are paid: foster parenting is a *job*. That it is a paid service does not, of course, preclude the possibility that genuine paternal and maternal sentiments may evolve. But for some (probably many) foster-care providers, the job is just that, and they bring to the task the cold-blooded rationality of employment. This means that in order to derive a maximum financial benefit, some foster parents can be expected to minimize their labor and keep to a minimum outlays for which they receive no reimbursement or compensation. It is not difficult to imagine how excruciating must be the moral and psychological tensions that lurk within the political economy of foster care.

Above and beyond this structural problem are troubling contingencies. The foster-care population has skyrocketed even as the population of foster parents recruited by traditional means has plummeted. At the same time, political pressures have mounted to recruit more black adults to serve as foster (and adoptive) parents. Largely in response to these two overlapping trends, local governments have been reaching out to marginal or even high-risk families to care for juvenile wards, whose number has burgeoned. "As compared to the typical pool of prospective adoptive parents, the foster parent pool is much worse off in socioeconomic terms. Many have incomes at or below the poverty level and live in neighborhoods characterized by [widespread illicit drug use], violence, and poor schools."[11] As a consequence, with troubling frequency, child-welfare bureaucracies have been hurting the very youngsters they are attempting to help, by placing them in foster homes that are little better and sometimes *worse* than their homes of origin.[12]

The strongest argument against race matching, then, is that it inhibits or even prevents the progress of parentless children toward adoption—the alternative that would give them their best chance of a long-term, secure family attachment.* But other arguments can also be made against the practice. First off, insofar as race matching is a form of racial discrimination, it bears a burden of justification that cannot be sustained. Proponents of race matching have frequently been able to shift onto their antagonists the burden of persuasion, but this is precisely the opposite of what should be its proper allocation. Those who wish to engage in racial selectivity should be called upon to justify *their* position, given that racial discrimination is presumptively wrong. Federal and state statutory and constitutional law generally either forbids such discrimination absolutely or allows it only exceptionally, when

---

*For discussion about the realities of interracial adoption from the perspective of adopters and adoptees, see pages 447–79.

those who seek to discriminate can offer a compelling justification. In the interracial-adoption controversy, the onus of persuasion has illogically fallen on those who desire to *remove* racial considerations as a routine factor in child-placement decision making. By rights, proponents of race matching should have to defend the racial discrimination they embrace. And before they can be permitted to differentiate racially among prospective adoptive parents, supporters of race matching should have to make a case—a strong case—for their approach. It is the race matcher, in other words, who should bear the burden—the heavy burden—of justifying what American law presumptively prohibits: judging people, even if only in part, on the basis of their apparent racial background.

As we have noted, one oft-cited rationale for favoring same-race placements for black children is that African American parents can typically better equip African American youngsters with the tools they will need if they are to survive and prosper in a racist society dominated by whites. As Judge Theodore Newman of the District of Columbia Court of Appeals wrote:

> The black child must learn to develop certain survival skills. Regardless of how she is identified by herself or her family, she will be identified as a black person by society and will inevitably experience racism. Black and other minorities develop survival skills for coping with such racism, which they can pass to their children expressly, or, more importantly, by unconscious example. . . . Parents of interracial families may attempt to learn these lessons and then teach them, but most authorities recognize that this is an inferior substitute for learning directly from minority role models. . . . Few white parents even claim they can teach such skills.[13]

Those who confidently assert, with Judge Newman, that black adults are better able than whites to parent black children rely on the hunch that as inevitable victims of antiblack racism themselves, black adults will be more capable of teaching their charges how to face and overcome that racism. This is not, however, a proper basis for racial selectivity. Judge Newman's assertion, after all, rested only on a hunch. There is no definitive evidence that black foster or adoptive parents are better on average at raising black children than are white foster or adoptive parents. Many people simply take this on faith, as a matter of "common sense." But common sense is often tainted by baleful habits of thought and can be highly resistant to unexpected realities.

Those who propound the "survival skills" justification typically slight any possibility that white parents may have valuable knowledge of their own to impart to black youngsters on the subject of prejudice, racial and otherwise. As Professor Kim Forde-Mazrui has pointed out,

> white people, as individuals, have not been spared maltreatment from others, and white parents routinely teach their children how to cope with insults from others. . . . [A white person] called "commie" for protesting [against the Vietnam war] or a woman referred to as "girl" by her boss has some experience from which to empathize with her Black child who is called "nigger" at school. A person who stutters, limps, or cannot hear well also gains analogous experience that could benefit a Black child.[14]

Some might argue that racism is more pervasive and debilitating than the types of prejudice alluded to by Forde-Mazrui. Even if that is so, however, why should we not assume that here, as in other areas, parents will endeavor to familiarize themselves with and master the challenges faced by their children? We presume that parents who are initially ignorant as to deafness or genius will educate themselves if they have a deaf or intellectually advanced child. Similarly, we should presume that parents who know nothing of the realities of being black in America will learn what they can about antiblack racism and related challenges.

Whites, moreover, might be able to bring to bear on behalf of their black children advantages generally denied to blacks. They might be able to share knowledge gleaned from their experience on the white side of the racial divide. As for forestalling the crippling psychological complexes that racism often insidiously fosters within the minds of

African Americans, Professor Forde-Mazrui has shrewdly remarked that a message of racial equality voiced by a white parent may, to a child, have greater credibility than the same message offered up by a black parent, inasmuch as the black parent could be perceived as having a more self-interested stake in refuting claims of white superiority. In Forde-Mazrui's words, "A white parent's denial of Black inferiority may be more believable because it is less self-serving."[15]

Another weakness of the race matchers' "survival skills" justification derives from their romanticization of the heuristic value of simply being a victim. Victimization *may* teach a person valuable lessons that he or she will be able to pass on to others, or it may not. People of all kinds frequently fail to learn from or impart to others the available lessons embedded in various experiences. The experience of victimization is only a *potential* asset; a person must do something with it before it can become an *actual* asset.[16] Moreover, if victimization can be a source of useful knowledge, it can also be a source of destructive myopia. It is certainly true that many African Americans have passed down to their progeny wise counsel proofed in the crucible of racial injustice.[17] But the champions of race matching typically suggest that the burdens imposed on black adults by white racism are *invariably* met by responses that are both self-protective and socially beneficial— the sort of responses, that is, that *should* be held up for emulation. Unfortunately, the truth is that racism can also cripple its victims and, worse, result in the development of adaptive behaviors that may lead those victims to hobble their own children. Cruelly frustrated by racial bars that have now been lowered, some blacks discourage their offspring from pursuing certain educational or occupational ambitions though such aims are now attainable.[18] Some African Americans have so internalized Negrophobic attitudes that they themselves harbor antiblack racial prejudices.[19]* Much of the energy of the civil rights and Black Power movements was aimed at undoing the cycles of self-limitation, self-contempt, and self-destruction set in motion by a cruelly oppressive social order dominated by white racism. Despite the best

---

*See Randall Kennedy, *Nigger: The Strange Career of a Troublesome Word* (2002).

efforts of those movements, however, black self-destructiveness persists and must be taken into account in any serious assessment of the internal racial dynamics of black communities. In sum, African American victims of racial oppression take away from their experiences all kinds of lessons. Some victims acquire and pass on commendable beliefs. Others assimilate and perpetuate pernicious notions such as the idea that "Niggers ain't shit."[20]

Mention of social pathology in black communities often triggers yet another spate of attacks on interracial adoption.[21] One charge is that such adoptions denigrate African American communities by implying that blacks are unable to care for "their own." Another complaint is that some defenses of interracial adoption are predicated on the belief that black adults have little of worth to offer black children. In response, three points are important to voice. First, it is probably true that some defenders of interracial adoption embrace racist stereotypes about blacks, including the derogatory notion that African Americans are generally incompetent when it comes to building strong families. The mere existence of such attitudes, however, in no way invalidates the conclusion that interracial adoptions should be freely permitted. People do sometimes favor good policies for bad reasons. Racism, after all, animated a substantial number of anti-slavery whites who opposed Negro bondage precisely because it entailed the presence of blacks.[22]

Second, responsibility for addressing the plight of parentless children in America should not be allocated along racial lines, with African American adoptees being designated as the special province of blacks, Euro-American adoptees as that of whites, and so on.* The plight of African American children should be deemed an *American* problem, to be dealt with by the whole of American society. Concomitantly, the unmet needs of these children should be seen as reflecting badly not on any discrete racial group—blacks—but on American society in its entirety. That there exist so many parentless children in terrible circum-

---

*For a discussion of the special case of Native Americans, see pages 480–518.

stances, a disproportionate number of whom are black, is not an Afro-American disgrace but an American disgrace.

Third, there are things more important that the perceived image problems arising from transracial adoption. Expeditiously placing children in secure homes should be a higher priority than assuaging hurt racial pride.*

America's terrible experience with racial oppression has made racial discrimination the paradigmatic *disfavored* method of sorting people. Racial discrimination is frowned upon precisely because it has so often been used for bad ends, with disastrous consequences: obvious examples include Negro slavery, segregation, and disenfranchisement; the bar against Chinese immigration; the internment of people of Japanese ancestry; and police profiling of Latinos and people of apparent Arab ancestry. Against this historical backdrop, we should distrust all who would draw racial lines, even (or perhaps *especially*) when they insist that they are doing so for good reasons.† We should resist authorizing the government to use race in any way as an index of relative worthiness. When the government does so, it deviates from the principle that individuals should be judged by their own particular conduct and not on the basis—not even *partly* on the basis—of racial ascriptions, which are so often permeated by ignorance and bias. Race-dependent decision making erodes a habit that we ought to encourage—the difficult-to-

---

*Some nations have discouraged adoptions of "their" children by foreigners because of wounded national vanity and related sentiments. See Rita J. Simon and Howard Altstein, *Adoption Across Borders: Serving the Children in Transracial and Inter-country Adoptions* (2000), 7–9, 18. See also Alessandra Stanley, "Hands Off Our Babies, A Georgian Tells America," *New York Times,* June 29, 1997.

†Does anyone *ever* admit to pursuing a policy for evil reasons? Slaveholders, for instance, maintained that bondage was *good* for Negroes (see Erik L. McKitrick, ed., *Slavery Defended: The Views of the Old South* [1963]). Likewise, segregation was justified on the grounds of convenience and respect for all—colored people as well as whites (*Plessy v. Ferguson,* 163 U.S. 537 [1896], upholding equal but separate accommodations in intrastate railway travel).

maintain practice of individualizing persons—and strengthens a reflex that we should seek to overcome: the impulse to lump people together according to gross (in this case, racial) classifications, which tend to cloud rather than clarify our perception of the human virtues and vices in which we should be most interested.

A striking feature of the interracial-adoption debate is the willingness of race matching's proponents to defend it by reference to racial generalizations. Previously I called into question whether these generalizations are sound; now, for the sake of argument, I will stipulate to their soundness. Let us assume, for example, that for the most part, black adoptive parents *are* better able to raise black children than white adoptive parents. Even if we could somehow determine that this assumption is accurate, would it justify racial selectivity in adoption proceedings? No, it would not. Consider other contexts in which racial discrimination is (or should be) rejected regardless of the accuracy of the generalizations upon which it is said to rest. As a constitutional and statutory matter, employers are prohibited from preferring white over black applicants for jobs—even jobs for which, in general, the whites are better qualified than the blacks. Allowing employers to credentialize whiteness—that is, to view it as a proxy for an increased probability of superior merit—would often make sense in terms of market rationality. Under certain conditions, preferring whites on a racial basis would maximize profits by efficiently lowering search costs for labor.[23] But law and public opinion rightly condemn such discrimination, even where it might be effectuated without racial animus. There are many reasons for our condemnation. One is that we rightly believe it is unfair for a black job applicant to have his or her particular assets obscured by stereotypical characteristics that may accurately describe African American applicants in general but inaccurately describe the individual candidate in question. Even if it were true that ninety-nine out of a hundred black applicants were less well qualified than their white competitors, law and public opinion would still insist—correctly—that the one hundredth black candidate should suffer no negative prejudgment by a prospective employer on account of the performance of the other blacks. Rigorous adherence to this antidiscrimination regime is an essential requirement for ridding society of the pernicious habit of submerging individuals in the racial group to which they are said to belong.

To drive the point home, let's look at another context in which racial discrimination is rife. Police routinely factor in race when making judgment calls about which citizens they will scrutinize more closely than others. This is commonly referred to as racial profiling. Pursuant to this practice, police habitually treat blacks differently—that is, with greater suspicion—than they do similarly situated whites. When pressed to justify their racially discriminatory conduct, police often echo the proponents of race matching in offering a probabilistic rationale: they maintain that they are simply playing the odds when they register blackness, along with other considerations, as a slight but discernible cautionary factor. Opponents of racial profiling rightly criticize this racially discriminatory practice because it necessarily stigmatizes individual blacks, even if that is not the intent of the police, and even if some reasonable factual predicate exists for the profiling scheme. Opponents of racial profiling object, in short, to the imposition of a special racial burden on law-abiding blacks because of lawbreaking by other blacks. These critics argue that even for the purposes of law enforcement, there should be no exception to the strong disapprobation of racial line-drawing, and that racial generalizations should not be permitted to short-circuit the process whereby officials judge individuals without regard to their race.[24] The same arguments should apply to race matching, which is in essence just another form of racial profiling. Unfortunately, many who object to the police use of blackness as a marker for caution for purposes of law enforcement nevertheless tolerate or even support social workers' use of whiteness as a similar marker in assessing prospective adoptive parents for African American children.*

---

*The interests of adopters should be subordinate to the interests of adoptees, but that is *not* to say that adopters should have no legal protection. Their emotional investment in the adoption process is almost certain to be considerable, and it warrants care. Moreover, agencies' failure to show decent solicitude to white adopters will likely dissuade some observant and interested parties from pursuing adoption in this country, which will in turn hurt the entire class of American children eligible for adoption. See Erika Lynn Kleiman, "Caring for Our Own: Why American Adoption

Nor do the generalizations end with prospective parents. Proponents of race matching assert that not only are the white adults who seek to adopt black children likely to come up short, but so are their relatives, neighbors, and friends—the "village" that, for good or ill, participates in the raising of children.[25] Proponents of race matching counsel against exposing black youngsters to supposedly high risks of rejection in predominantly white communities. They contend that it is wrong to draft children to serve as soldiers in an ideological crusade. This argument is at heart a reprise of the opinion handed down by the state judge in *Palmore v. Sidoti,* who modified custody arrangements for a white child after her mother decided to marry a black man. The judge expressed his desire to shield the child from the stigma that he feared would be attached to her if she lived in a multiracial household.* Like the *Palmore* judge, race matchers insist that they are simply trying to be "realistic." They are, however, conspicuously inattentive to certain concrete realities, including the actual, as opposed to merely the imagined, conduct of whites who adopt black children.† Moreover, if the racial demographics of residence and similar issues are of such pressing concern, why not raise them in *every* case, for black as well as white prospective parents? Surely *some* black prospective adoptive parents also live in "white and prejudiced" communities, yet the race matchers seem to have no intention of holding *their* choice of residence against them. Furthermore, why be concerned only with the risks posed by white racism? Why not consider equally the risks that disproportionately burden black communities? Yet race matchers would undoubtedly (and rightly) object to any selection process that screened out black adopters because of high rates of drug abuse, violence, lead poisoning, and AIDS in black neighborhoods.

Some champions of race matching have charged defenders of interracial adoption with enlisting children as crusaders on behalf of "integration." There are at least two answers to this charge. The first is that

Law and Policy Must Change," *Columbia Journal of Law and Social Problems* 30 (1997), 327.
*See pages 380–86.
†See pages 447–68.

many proponents of race matching are themselves only too happy to draft parentless children into their own campaign for black solidarity. The second is that society as a whole does—and should—"use" children as the front line in certain sorts of battles. Notable among these is the push for universal literacy, in pursuit of which society insists that children be educated, regardless of their own desires or those of their parents or guardians. Society demands that youngsters receive a specific minimal amount of education, in the belief that such a requirement is good for society as a whole as well as for those who will one day inherit it. Similarly, governments should demand that agencies place parentless children in loving homes without regard to race, as quickly as possible, because such placements will benefit both society as a whole and, even more, the children themselves. Society as a whole can only profit from the erosion of racial superstition, which forms the bedrock of race matching. And parentless children can only profit from obtaining as soon as possible the security and nurture provided by decent parents, regardless of race.

Thus far I have primarily focused upon the openly acknowledged ideological motivation behind the race-matching campaign spearheaded by the NABSW. It bears mentioning, however, that there have been other, more material and self-interested motivations in play as well. It is not coincidental that the regime of racial regulation that the NABSW prefers would nicely serve the professional, organizational, and economic interests of the NABSW and its membership. After all, if public policy makes racial sorting in adoption and foster care essential, then surely there will be a greater need for the "racial expertise" of social workers—especially *black* social workers—who understand and insist that race should matter, must matter, in this area. Society, however, ought not permit the most vulnerable of our children to become fodder for professional or organizational aggrandizement. Of course, black social workers (like black prospective adoptive parents and black children in need of foster or adoptive care) have encountered racial exclusion, neglect, and discrimination by white-dominated bureaucracies.

The defensive racial mobilization of black social workers in the 1960s and 1970s did not spring up arbitrarily. It arose from frustration with and anger at people, agencies, organizations, and governments that had, often for racist reasons, disregarded black social workers and pushed them to the margins of their profession. But the proper response to the mistreatment or underutilization of black social workers is not to hold children hostage while adult plaintiffs seek relief. The proper response is to address wrongs directly while simultaneously facilitating the adoption of parentless children as quickly as possible—which means, among other things, a process that is free of the delays and complications entailed by race matching.

Under the standard I espouse, race would not be allowed to play any part in the selection of adoptive families, unless there was some compelling justification substantiated by specific evidence directly relevant to the case at hand. Race could be taken into account, for example, if a prospective adoptive parent indicated that she was interested only in adopting a child of a given race; or if an older child insisted that he or she wanted to be adopted only by adults of a particular race.* Note, however, that in neither of these cases is the state, by its own initiative, permitted to privilege the creation of monoracial families over that of multiracial families, or to credentialize race by making it a proxy for either desirable or undesirable traits.

---

*What should happen if a parent who is surrendering a child for adoption indicates that it is her wish to have the child adopted only (or prefereably) by a person or persons of a given race? This question poses a number of difficult problems that I will have to address all too summarily. One feels a tug toward crafting a policy that enables this parent to help guide her child's future. The notion that a parent should be allowed to play a role in determining who raises a child after her parental rights have been terminated finds expression in a variety of ways including state statutes that expressly provide that the surrendering parent's religious preferences should be accommodated if possible (on religious protection laws, see pages 438–46). I believe, however, that the government ought not to bend a nondiscrimination policy to effectuate the racial preferences of surrendering parents. Doing so goes a step beyond accommodating the racial preferences of prospective adoptive parents—an accommodation to which I urge acquiescence (see pages 434–37). There is, I realize, a tension between these two positions. As I noted at the outset, the question poses difficult problems to which I respond tentatively rather than confidently.

The government ought to welcome the prospect of multiracial adoptive families just as enthusiastically as it does that of monoracial adoptive families. Even in a situation in which two equally attractive candidates—one black couple and one white couple—are simultaneously petitioning to adopt a youngster, agencies should not use race matching to break the tie. Nor should they prefer to place the child *within* as opposed to *across* racial lines. Officials should not assume that, all other things being equal, a same-race adoption is preferable to a transracial adoption. Nor should they favor same-race conventionality over interracial heterodoxy. Officials should simply accord identical decent treatment to monoracial and multiracial families.

Although I have made a point of distinguishing between "strong" and "moderate" race matching, in real life, the distinction is blurred. What begins on paper as "moderate" race matching typically degenerates in practice into the "strong" version, largely because keeping the two separate is beyond the capabilities of child-welfare bureaucracies and the courts that oversee them.* This is so for a variety of reasons, including the propensity to exaggerate the significance of race, the prevalence and intensity of strong race-matching tendencies within social-worker bureaucracies, and the difficulty of ferreting out the covert racial considerations buried in decentralized, low-visibility, open-ended, highly discretionary child-placement decisions. Therefore, not only principles of equality but also more pragmatic considerations counsel in favor of the institution and enforcment of a *strict* antidiscrimination norm in

---

*We should learn more quickly from past mistakes. In the context of jury selection, efforts to distinguish between trial-related and wholesale racial discrimination in the deployment of peremptory challenges failed. See Kennedy, *Race, Crime, and the Law* (1997), 193–230. The Supreme Court belatedly jettisoned the distinction by prohibiting *all* racially discriminatory peremptory challenges. See *Batson v. Kentucky*, 476 U.S. 79 (1986); *Georgia v. McCollum*, 505 U.S. 42 (1992). Efforts to distinguish between reasonable and unreasonable racial profiling have also been unsuccessful. See Kennedy, *Race, Crime, and the Law*, 136–67.

adoption. Nothing less will break the deeply entrenched habit of race matching that remains rife throughout this country. This lesson has been demonstrated by scores of decisions, including that handed down in the most hard-fought, most brightly illuminated interracial-adoption struggle in the case law, a protracted immersion into heartbreak entitled *Drummond v. Fulton County Department of Family and Children's Services.*[26]

At the center of this case was a boy named Timothy Lee Hill, who was born in Georgia on November 17, 1973, to a white woman from whom he was soon taken by the state on account of alleged parental unfitness. When Timothy was one month old, local officials placed him for foster care with Robert George Drummond, a worker in an automobile assembly plant, and Mildred Pauline Drummond, a housewife and gospel singer. Like Timothy's birth mother, the Drummonds were white. The appropriate racial designation for Timothy himself was unclear. His mother did not know the identity of his biological father, who may have been one of her apparently numerous sexual partners or one of the several men who allegedly raped her. Although she could not specifically identify him, she believed that Timothy's father was most likely an African American, which supposition was embraced by all of the major actors who determined the course of the boy's early life.

The Drummonds fell in love with Timothy while he was in their care, and after about six months, they expressed their wish to adopt him if and when he became legally eligible for adoption. Several agency officials responded by questioning the wisdom of a white couple adopting a putatively colored child. The Drummonds later recalled assuring the officials that they "would teach Timmy to appreciate his black heritage" and would "seek guidance from other parents of children of different racial backgrounds."[27] The officials maintained, however, that the child would "make a better adjustment and have a better life with a black couple in a black community."[28]

Over the course of the next few months, the stated desire of the Drummonds to adopt Timothy waxed and waned. They would apparently acquiesce when agency staffers insisted that the boy would be better off with a black adoptive family, but then, after thinking about the matter a bit more, they would reaffirm their wish to adopt him. After the parental rights of Timothy's birth mother were terminated, the Drummonds filed an adoption petition. At the same time (and without notifying the Drummonds), the agency began to look for a black adoptive home in which to place the child. On November 21, 1975, nearly twenty staff members of the Fulton County Department of Family and Children's Services met to decide whether or not to approve the Drummonds' petition. The Drummonds' caseworker, who was in favor of permitting them to adopt their foster son, was excluded from the meeting, ostensibly on the ground that it did not concern her, as it focused on an adoption matter and she was a foster-care social worker.

At the meeting's end, the agency staff decided to reject the Drummonds' petition, having concluded that the boy would be better off in an appropriate black adoptive home. A few days later, however, when officials notified the Drummonds, they mentioned for the first time some additional factors supposedly involved in the decision. These included the Drummonds' respective ages (Mrs. Drummond was fifty-one and Mr. Drummond thirty-nine), their relative lack of education (neither had attended college), and their place of residence (a rural, predominantly white neighborhood). Faced with the prospect of losing Timothy, the couple filed a lawsuit claiming that the agency's use of race in assessing their petition was a violation of federal constitutional law.

The Drummonds lost the first round of their judicial fight. United States District Court Judge Charles Moye Jr. dismissed their equal-protection challenge, ruling that it was not unconstitutional for state child-welfare officials to take race into account in assessing the proposed adoption of a colored child by a white family, provided that their decision-making process was directed at securing the placement that would be, in their expert opinion, in the best interest of the child. Judge Moye conceded that an across-the-board, automatic prohibition of interracial adoption without regard to the specifics of an individual case would have been invalid, but in his view, nothing of the sort was at work here. As he saw it, the state authorities were willing, under some circumstances, to place children transracially, though in general, they preferred same-race adoptions. In this case, the experts simply did not believe that the interest of this purportedly mixed-race child would be best served by permitting him to be adopted by this particular white couple. In testimony before the judge, the agency officials asserted that while they would be open to placing a colored child with the *right* white family, the Drummonds were not that family, at least not for Timmy. To back up this assertion, they listed several other cases in which their department had approved the adoption of colored children by white families.

Throughout the proceedings, Judge Moye repeatedly averred that he would not substitute his own opinion of what was best for Timmy for the presumably expert advice of the Fulton County Department of Family and Children's Services. His duty, he emphasized, was merely to make sure that in exercising its discretion, the department had stayed within the broad boundaries marked off by federal law. After hearing the testimony of both sides in the case, the judge decided that the agency had done just that. He concluded that department officials could, without violating federal constitutional restrictions, take race into account in assessing an adoption petition, so long as race was not *all* they took into account—in other words, so long as the issue of race did not wholly eclipse every other factor in the decision. Convinced that the authorities were not unalterably opposed to transracial adoption in every case, no matter what the circumstances, and persuaded that some attention had been paid to nonracial aspects of Timmy's situation, Judge Moye ruled in favor of the state.

Had the Drummonds been fighting this battle on their own, Judge Moye's ruling would have ended the matter. But with the assistance of the Georgia chapter of the American Civil Liberties Union, the couple was able to appeal and then to win round two of the fight over Timmy. A panel of the United States Court of Appeals reversed Judge Moye, on various grounds, including its belief that a fuller hearing was needed to determine whether the Drummonds' petition had been denied "solely on account of race."[29]

Paul H. Roney, one of the three judges on the appellate panel, strongly dissented. Noting that the trial judge had found as a matter of fact that race was not the only basis for the department's decision, he argued that this finding should be deferred to inasmuch as it was not "clearly erroneous." He also remarked that at oral argument, counsel for the Drummonds had "conceded that the record would not support a finding that the agency decision was based solely on race."[30] There was, then, in his view, no need for further fact finding. All that was needed, he averred, was an answer to the following question: May a state agency "not acting under the imperative of any law or unyielding automatic rule, but rather in the exercise of its own discretionary concepts of successful child placement, [lawfully] take into consideration as an important factor the race of the child and the prospective parents[?]"[31] He responded in the affirmative.

Although Judge Roney was unable to sway his colleagues on the three-judge panel that initially heard the Drummonds' case, he later managed to persuade a majority of the judges of the entire appellate court to reverse the panel's decision. His opinion thus became the ruling opinion that governed the federal constitutional law of a large section of the United States (Texas, Louisiana, Mississippi, Alabama, Georgia, and Florida). Writing on behalf of the court as a whole, Judge Roney maintained that "'the difficulties inherent in interracial adoption' justify the consideration of race as a relevant factor in adoption."[32] He did not articulate precisely how much weight state authorities could give to the race factor, but the logic of his opinion and the factual backdrop of the dispute out of which it arose suggest that in the view of Roney and a majority of his colleagues, race could properly figure significantly in agencies' decision making. According to Roney, federal constitutional law did not inhibit child-welfare officials from engaging in race matching, provided that race was not in and of itself automatically determinative, and provided that the officials, in exercising their professional judgment, were seeking to advance the interests of the wards under their care. Adoption agencies, Judge Roney pointed out,

> frequently try to place a child where he can most easily become a normal family member. The duplication of his natural biological environment is a part of that program. Such factors as age, hair color, eye color, and facial features of parents and child are considered in reaching a decision. This flows from the belief that a child and adoptive parents can best adjust to a normal family relationship if the child is placed with adoptive parents

who could have actually parented him. To permit consideration of physical characteristics necessarily carries with it permission to consider racial characteristics. This Court does not have the professional expertise to assess the wisdom of that type of inquiry, but it is our province to conclude . . . that the use of race as one of those factors is not unconstitutional.[33]

*Drummond* offers a sobering portrait of the judicial oversight of "moderate" race matching. Most egregious is Judge Roney's misrepresentation of the character of the administrative process to which the Drummonds were subjected. It was a process marred by several failings, the worst of which was a pattern of deceitfulness that should have been obvious to all concerned with the case. From the moment the agency officials resolved to reject the Drummonds' petition, they began to fabricate a record that would enable them to minimize the actual extent to which racial considerations had dominated their deliberations. That was why, with the first indications of resistance from the Drummonds, staff members began to mention factors—such as age—that had previously played no part in the department's assessment of the couple. This strategy continued even as the officials gave sworn testimony in court. One department supervisor testified, for example, that after rejecting the Drummonds, she and her colleagues had not ruled out placing Timothy in another white adoptive home; they had simply thought it more likely, she said, that he would end up in a black home. This assertion was contradicted by the same official's previous deposition testimony, by the minutes of the meeting at which the Drummonds' petition had been denied, and by the statements of several other department staffers who had earlier insisted that Timmy needed to be placed with a black adoptive family—not any particular family, not the "right" family, but simply *some* black adoptive family that the agency would find.*

---

*According to the minutes, "A vote was taken and it was a group decision that it would not be in Timmy's best interest to leave him in the Drummond home, and that we would begin immediately to look for an appropriate black adoptive home" (Deposition of Kay P. Dallinger, *Drummond v. Fulton County Dept. of Family and*

Despite these discrepancies, a majority of the appellate-court judges expressed admiration for the department's agents. Judge John R. Brown, for instance, enthused in a concurring opinion that "the record shows that those charged with the awesome responsibility of Timmy's best interest were concerned, sensitive and sincere professionals."[34] As substantiation for this proposition, he noted that in describing their deliberations, department officials had explained that "the discussion lasted approximately three hours and the group consensus not to allow the Drummonds to adopt Timmy was carefully thought out and personally painful for all those present."[35] The opposing legal claim, however, was not that the officials were necessarily mean-spirited but rather that they simply acted in a manner violative of the federal Constitution. Warm, hospitable, nice, compassionate people can nonetheless conduct themselves in ways that fall afoul of federal constitutional requirements. No doubt the Fulton County authorities really *were* "concerned, sensitive and sincere professionals"—but *sincere* proponents of bad ideas are often the worst kind of fanatics. Where the insincere ones can easily be bought off or discouraged, the true believers are as a rule irrepressible and likely to fight for what they genuinely feel is right, even if it entails engaging in deception. As for the chief judge's reliance on the officials' self-characterization as evidence in support of their conduct, one can only register astonishment and wonder how an experienced jurist could possibly credit so self-serving a statement. Of *course* these decision makers would believe and assert that their conclusion was "carefully thought out"! The court portrayed the decisive meeting of the department's agents as a considered deliberation suffused with "expertise," but in fact, that was hardly the case. Nearly twenty staff members met to discuss the Drummonds' petition; of that number, only one had had any direct, sustained contact with the Drummonds or seen them interact with Timmy. This person urged that the couple's petition be approved.* Her recommendation was overridden

---

*Children's Services,* Appendix at 173, on file at the Harvard Law School Library, in the Interracial Intimacies Collection).

*This social worker, too, preferred race matching as a general policy, but in this case, her intuitive presumption against interracial adoption was overcome by her direct

by nothing more than the notion—the mere hunch, really—that a racially mixed child would be better off in a black adoptive home. And not even a *specific* black adoptive home, but merely a generic one. Furthermore, neither in the minutes of the meeting nor in testimony recounting it was any mention made of the downside of moving Timmy. In other words, prior to the onset of litigation when the department began, under the influence of counsel, to rationalize its conduct in anticipation of judicial oversight, none of the agency social workers appears to have given much thought to the trauma the boy would likely suffer upon being taken from the only home and the only parents he had ever known.

After crediting unduly the conduct of the officials whose actions were being challenged by the Drummonds, the court went on to heap further undue praise on the "expertise" with which that conduct had

---

observation of the care and commitment that the Drummonds lavished upon Timmy. While her memorandum to the department urging approval of the Drummonds' petition shows that she ultimately reached the right conclusion, it also reflects vividly the casualness and utter subjectivity that characterized the Fulton County social workers' approach to their task. Assessing the Drummonds' treatment of their foster son, she wrote after one visit to their home, "It turns me off a little to see them getting him to 'perform or do tricks'" (*Drummond v. Fulton County Dept. of Family and Children's Services,* 547 F.2d 835, 845 (5th Cir. 1977). What constituted the "performance" referred to here? The social worker did not explain. Maybe any reasonable observer would have been "turned off" by the performance, whatever it was—or maybe not. Maybe what this social worker objected to was nothing more than the Drummonds showing off some trick or talent of Timmy's in which they took delight—the sort of activity that "natural" parents engage in all the time without prompting a second thought. The social worker added that conversations with her colleagues had made it clear that "there definitely is a fear [that Timmy] could be pampered, spoiled and over protected by [the Drummonds]" (Ibid.). Perhaps this observation homed in on a genuine overprotectiveness on the couple's part, or perhaps it reflected an admirable prudence on their part and an *under*protectiveness on the part of the social workers who privately chastised them. None of this would matter much in the regular course of things; criticism of the ways people raise their children is a staple of neighborhood gossip. In this case, however, each little complaint supplied a nonracial justification for the rejection of the Drummonds' adoption position—justifications that the department could later point to as proof that race, though actually decisive, had not been the only factor it had considered in reaching its conclusion.

been based. "Constitutional strictures against racial discrimination," Judge Roney maintained, "are not mandates to ignore the accumulated experience of unbiased professionals." But what was the nature of this "accumulated experience"? In his first *Drummond* opinion, Roney had cited a few articles from "the social service world" that presumably displayed the sort of wisdom he would later exalt. The articles in question, however, are hardly models of scholarship. One, entitled "On Transracial Adoption of Black Children," was published in the journal *Child Welfare*.[36] It was written by Edmond D. Jones, then the assistant director of Family and Children's Services in Baltimore, Maryland. This "unbiased professional" asserted that parentless black childen should be placed *only* in black adoptive homes. If the need for such homes outstripped the supply despite comprehensive recruitment efforts, he recommended putting black youngsters in "permanent foster care and small group care within the black community."[37] But why would a supposed champion of the fortunes of black children consign them to a future with no family at all rather than allow their adoption by any white family? Because, wrote Jones, "I question the ability of white parents—no matter how deeply imbued with good will—to grasp the totality of the problem of being black in this society. I question their ability to create what I believe is crucial in these youngsters—a black identity."[38]* To his credit, Jones proceeded in the very next breath to admit that "creation of a black identity is a problem for many black parents also."[39] To his profound *dis*credit, he in no sense connected this concession to his earlier critique of whites. Nor did he ever explain why he urged the exclusion only of whites as prospective adoptive parents if indeed "many" black parents were likewise deficient when it came to fostering the (unspecified) black identity he perceived as so crucial.

Eschewing any pretense of intellectual rigor, Jones scornfully condemned the adoption of a black child by a white couple but failed to review the alternatives facing the youngster. Of the family's subsequent

---

*One has to wonder whether any *black* person (or person of any race) can be said to have "grasp[ed] the totality of the problem of being black" in America. Did W. E. B. DuBois? Malcolm X? Martin Luther King Jr.? Edmond Jones?

move to Georgia, Jones remarked (in an aside that hauntingly presaged the Drummond tragedy), "I suppose the city doesn't matter, but something about black kids in white families in Atlanta still turns me off."[40]

In fairness to Jones, it must be noted that he did not put himself forward as a learned professional in matters related to adoption. To the contrary, he declared, "I am not by status, background or temperament, a child welfare expert." He had been "designated a child welfare person," he averred, solely "through expansion of the scope of my duties."[41] It was a United States Court of Appeals that improperly elevated Jones to an intellectual status that was wholly unwarranted.

In *Drummond,* a legal bureaucracy's strong aversion to interracial adoption meant that the petition of two white foster parents in Georgia was doomed to rejection from the moment they first voiced their desire to adopt the black child under their care. By prohibiting only an expressly stated or total bar against interracial adoption, *Drummond* made it virtually impossible for anyone bound by that ruling to overturn on federal constitutional grounds racially discriminatory rejection of an adoption petition. The appellate-court ruling maintained that race matching of the sort at issue in *Drummond* did not violate the Constitution, since public officials considered race in a "nondiscriminatory fashion" and inflicted no racial slur or stigma by exercising some degree of racial selectivity in arranging adoptions. It is not altogether clear what the court meant by "nondiscriminatory" consideration of race. Perhaps it referred to the fact that the department's race matching applied to all races, not merely to one racial group. Just as the agency preferred to place black children in black adoptive homes, so, too, did it prefer to place white children in white adoptive homes. As for the reference to stigma, perhaps the court was asserting that racial distinctions that might plausibly insult certain racial groups should be viewed differently than racial distinctions that are clearly not intended to inflict such harms. Since *Drummond,* the Supreme Court has handed down several decisions that are at variance with the doctrines applied by the Fifth Circuit Court of Appeals. Most significantly, the Supreme Court has insisted on several occasions that *all* racial discriminations are presumptively invalid. In the course of barring the racially discriminatory peremptory challenge, for example, the Court rejected the argument that this device should be given constitutional latitude because lawyers could use it to exclude potential jurors of *all* races—white as well as black, red as well as yellow.[42] Moreover, in the process of striking down various sorts of affirmative-action programs, the Court rejected arguments that racial discriminations aimed at assisting racial minorities should be held to a more relaxed standard than racial distinctions aimed at containing racial minorities.[43] The Supreme Court seems to believe, at least for the time being, that racial discrimination, whatever its asserted purpose, is always suspect and can be upheld only under exceptional circumstances and on the basis of compelling justifications.* The current landscape of federal constitutional doctrine, therefore, is very different from that which served as a backdrop for *Drummond*. It is a landscape inhospitable to Judge Roney's language and reasoning.

Some champions of racial affirmative action avoid criticizing race matching because they believe that such criticism will strengthen the forces amassed against affirmative action. They fear that any wider commitment to antidiscrimination norms could jeopardize discriminations aimed at helping racial minorities. They swallow race matching quietly to protect affirmative action. Their anxiety is readily understandable. Some of the rhetoric directed against race matching does indeed echo that employed against affirmative action, and some individuals and organizations that have been hostile to affirmative action have been likewise antagonistic to race matching. At the same time, there are a

---

*Two notes of caution, however, must be sounded here. First, the Supreme Court is closely divided over the proper interpretation of constitutional equality; even small changes in Court personnel could be consequential in this area. Second, in the area of voting rights, the Court has legitimated the use of race in redistricting, provided that the race factor is not predominant (*Miller v. Johnson,* 515 U.S. 900 [1995]). That opaque formula sounds very much like the one articulated in *Drummond* and other decisions that have sanctioned moderate race matching.

number of prominent critics of race matching who are also proponents of affirmative action.* They attack the former practice on the ground that in that context, there is insufficient justification for the deployment of racial criteria; they defend the latter on the ground that in that context, there is a sufficiently compelling rationale—righting past wrongs, preempting current bias against blacks, the dissemination of knowledge through "diversity," gaining the benefit of an appearance of fair inclusion—to justify the use of racial criteria. One can, in other words, sensibly support certain forms of affirmative action while simultaneously decrying race matching; one may embrace the one and renounce the other. There is no getting around the fact, however, that the antidiscrimination rhetoric, ethos, and organizational support that infuse much of the attack on race matching also nourish opposition to affirmative action. As a political versus a narrowly logical matter, therefore, there does exist a dilemma for those—and I am one—who tend to be tolerant of affirmative action but intolerant of race matching. I am ambivalent about the continuation of racial affirmative-action programs. They have performed a great service and manifest features of American political culture in which everyone, including their opponents, can justly take pride. But they do draw racial lines, a toxic activity that should be avoided absent compelling arguments to the contrary. There *are* such arguments in favor of maintaining at least certain affirmative-action programs. But there are also, as we have seen, imperative reasons to obliterate race matching. If dismantling affirmative action must be part of the price of effectively doing away with race matching, it is no more than I, for one, am willing to pay.

### The Reaction Against Race Matching

The years following *Drummond* saw a steady accumulation of cases in which race-matching policies played a major role in preventing or

---

*Among those opposed to both affirmative action and race matching are Clint Bolick and Charles Fried. Supporters of affirmative action who are against race matching include Laurence Tribe and Elizabeth Bartholet. See Steven A. Holmes, "Bitter Racial Dispute Rages over Adoption," *New York Times,* April 13, 1995; "Law Professor's Letter to United States Senate," 140 *Congressional Record,* S 14195 (October 5, 1994).

delaying adoptions, often in situations in which prospective adopters and adoptees had already bonded.[44]

In Washington, D.C., the city's Department of Human Resources placed an ailing four-month-old black baby girl in the custody of white foster parents after her biological mother, an unwed teenager, relinquished her parental rights to the child. After several months during which they nursed the baby to good health, the foster parents sought to adopt the child. They already had several children, three biological and one—a black boy—adopted. Initially, the department approved the foster parents' petition to adopt their new charge. But before proceeding further, the foster mother insisted that the department notify the child's biological father, a teenager who, until this point, had had nothing to do with the baby. Once notified, he objected. At that point, his mother and stepfather petitioned to adopt the baby. The department then revoked its earlier recommendation and instead recommended approval of the new petition for adoption. After hearing, a judge determined that the white foster parents were "a stable, middle-income, affectionate family" whose members "clearly love the child in question."[45] He also acknowledged that "sudden changes of the family setting or other vital parts of one's environment can cause uncertainty, emotional distress, and a sense of insecurity," and that, more specifically, "another change in the life of this child will cause some degree of injury or harm to her."[46] The judge found the matter to be a close call, but ultimately ruled in favor of the stepfather and grandmother. Although one might have thought that the issue of a blood tie might predominate in the disposition of the case, race constituted the factor that appeared decisive in the judge's mind. "The question of race is important," he declared. "Notwithstanding love and affection," he said, "severe questions of identity" would later arise if the child were raised by white adoptive parents.[47] So the court chose what it thought to be the better alternative.*

---

*Eventually, the foster parents prevailed. The District of Columbia Court of Appeals vacated the trial judge's ruling. See *In the Matter of the Petition of R.M.G. and E.M.G.*, 454 A. 2d 776 (D.C. App. 1982). Subsequently, the stepfather and grandmother withdrew their petition in favor of a new petition submitted by the foster

In Philadelphia, Pennsylvania, a five-month-old baby named Raymond Bullard was placed under the care of John and Marilyn McLaughlin on an emergency basis because his birth mother was unable to care for him. Although Raymond was supposed to stay with the McLaughlins for only ninety days, he stayed with them for two years before he was suddenly removed, over their objections, by the Philadelphia Department of Human Services. He was removed pursuant to the department's race-matching policy: inasmuch as Raymond was black, the department thought it best for him to be placed in a black foster home. By all credible accounts,* the McLaughlins had provided Raymond with attentive, nurturing, loving care. The problem, in the eyes of the department, was that Raymond was black and the McLaughlins were white.

After Raymond was removed from the care of the McLaughlins, to whom he had grown greatly attached, he fell into a severe depression. Fortunately, after expensive and grueling litigation initiated by the McLaughlins, they and Raymond were reunited.[48]

In Washington County, Maryland, a black, drug-addicted six-month-old baby named Tiffany R. was placed for foster care in the home of a white couple, Michael and Sylvia Mauk. Tiffany had suffered neglect at the hands of her birth mother, a drug addict, and had also been abused sexually. The Washington County Department of

---

parents. (The denouement of the lawsuit was reported to me a number of years ago by several of the parties and attorneys involved.) Still, the lawsuit delayed the adoption. It also likely contributed to the accurate perception that, in many locales, attempting to effectuate a transracial adoption entails making oneself vulnerable to heightened risk of emotional trauma—a perception that dissuades some people from even attempting such an adoption.

*After the onset of litigation, department officials attempted to concoct nonracial justifications for removing Raymond. In this instance, however, the race-matching bureaucrats encountered less credulous judges than those who prevailed in *Drummond*. Sweeping aside the department's fabrications, and recognizing that adherence to race matching was the only real basis for the removal, United States District Judge John B. Hannum dismissed officials' criticism of the McLaughlins as "part of an attempt to explain prior culpable conduct" (*McLaughlin v. Pernsely*, 693 F. Supp. 318, 321 [E.D. Pa. 1988]). At a prior administrative proceeding, the presiding official declared that it would be "an understatement to say that the testimony provided by the [department's] representatives was less than credible" (Ibid.). The out-and-out deception engaged in by officials even while under oath in court proceedings is a notable—and ongoing—feature of the continuing struggle over transracial adoption.

Social Services sent Tiffany to the Mauks because they were known for their nurturance of drug-addicted infants. It also bears noting that, prior to taking in Tiffany, the Mauks had adopted two children to whom they had previously afforded foster care—children a judge described as "a four-year-old African American female, and . . . a four-year-old biracial boy."[49]

It was undisputed that when Tiffany first arrived at the Mauks' home, her development was far below average for a child her age and that after a year under their care, she improved dramatically, reaching a normal range of development. The deep mutual attachment that quickly joined Tiffany and the Mauks was also undisputed; soon after she was placed with them, the Mauks began to inquire into the possibility of adopting her. Nonetheless, pursuant to its embrace of race matching, the department decided to remove Tiffany from the Mauks and to place her instead with a black foster family. In the midst of this wrangling, Tiffany accidentally fell into a swimming pool and lapsed temporarily into unconsciousness. Physicians treating Tiffany recommended that, in light of this trauma, the department refrain from changing custody arrangements, at least for a while. Rejecting this suggestion, the department removed Tiffany from the Mauks' home two days after the accident. Four months later, Tiffany continued to refer to the Mauks as "Mommy and Daddy" on those occasions when they were permitted to visit her at her new home. In this case, as in *Drummond* and *McLaughlin,* child-welfare officials lied in order to ensure a racially matched outcome. They asserted that a desire to reunite Tiffany with her biological siblings was the principal reason for removing her from the Mauks. In truth, as a judge found, the department's main aim was to effectuate a same-race placement.*Although a judge found that the department violated federal constitutional standards, preferred explanations for its actions that were not credible, and inflicted "grave

---

*In addition to offering deceptive testimony about their own aims, county officials in this case charged without any substantiating evidence that the father of the man seeking to adopt Tiffany had exhibited racial prejudice against an African American girl whom his son had already adopted. The Maryland Court of Appeals described the officials' charges as a "fabrication" (In re *Adoption No. 2633*, 646 A. 2d 1036, 1048 [Md. App. 1994]).

injustices" upon the Mauks, he also decided to leave undisturbed the same-race adoption that the department had facilitated after denying the Mauks' petition to adopt.

Cases such as these established the predicate for a reaction from people who were directly hurt by race matching, onlookers outraged by what they perceived as bureaucratic stupidity and arrogance, citizens angered by what they saw as callous disregard for the futures of vulnerable children, activists affronted by an unjustifiable deviation from racial antidiscrimination standards, and individuals of all sorts who discerned that behind the most ardent defenses of race matching resided ugly sentiments, including antiwhite resentments, that ought not be allowed to guide public policy. Journalistic accounts and commentary put race matching in a bad light.* Scholars in various disciplines attacked the theoretical underpinnings and practical consequences of race matching.† And committed reformers with organizational backing and political savvy succeeded in capturing the attention of powerful lawmakers. All of these forces combined to generate changes at every level of government. The most important reflection of and contribution to this new hostility to race matching was congressional action in the 1990s. After a false start with the Multi Ethnic Placement Act (MEPA) in 1994, Congress in 1996 finally prohibited race matching by agencies receiving federal funds with the InterEthnic Adoption Amendment (IAA) in 1996.

There is little doubt that the IAA will push norms and practices away from the race-matching paradigm.[50] There is good reason to sus-

---

*A vivid journalistic exposé that played a large role in attracting my attention to this subject was Kathie Dobie's excruciating account, "Black Kids, White Homes," *Village Voice,* August 8, 1989. See also Cynthia Tucker, "A Loving Home Matters More than Ethnic Origin," *The Atlanta Journal and Constitution,* November 28, 1993; Mona Charen, "The New Racism in Adoptions," *Newsday,* January 8, 1992; Beth Brophy, "The Unhappy Politics of Interracial Adoption," *U.S. News & World Report,* November 13, 1989.

†The empirical studies of interracial adoption by Rita J. Simon and Howard Altstein were highly influential. See, for example, *Adoption, Race, and Identity* (1992). Another important scholarly intervention was Elizabeth Bartholet's "Where Do Black Children Belong? The Politics of Race Matching in Adoption," 139 *University of Pennsylvania Law Review* 1163 (1991).

pect, however, that this statutory prohibition will not by itself quickly or comprehensively eradicate the deeply rooted custom of race matching. The law extends only to agencies receiving federal funds; those that proceed without such funding are free to engage in race matching (absent some other legal impediment).* No large government or private bureaucracy is currently devoting the resources necessary to monitor and ensure compliance with the IAA nationwide. The Department of Health and Human Services is the federal agency principally charged with enforcing the legislation, but well-entrenched officials within the department were opposed to the law in the first place and, absent strong prodding, will take no aggressive steps to advance its implementation. The same is true of many local and state administrative and judicial authorities; some courts even take the position that while the legislation applies to child-welfare agencies, it does not apply to judges.[51] Furthermore, even when efforts are made to effect the statute, enforcement will always be difficult given the ease with which racially discriminatory decisions can be camouflaged by pretext,† the willingness of antagonists to lie, the disinclination of many judges to look

---

*I favor extending the IAA nondiscrimination standard to cover all adoption agencies, including those that receive no federal funding and are therefore currently outside the reach of the IAA. See Elizabeth Bartholet, "Correspondence: Private Racial Preferences in Family Formation," *Yale Law Journal* 107 (1998): 2351, 2356.

†In *In the Matter of the Welfare of D.L.*, 486 N.W. 2d 375 (Minn. 1992), officials approved the adoption of a child by her paternal grandparents, even though they had previously had no contact with her. An adoption petition filed by the foster parents who had nurtured the child since she was four days old was rejected. The child and the grandparents were black; the foster parents were white. The court justified the adoption decision on the ground that Minnesota law presumes that adoptive placement with family members is in the best interests of a child. Substantial evidence suggests, however, that a commitment to race matching was the real motivation for both the welfare officials and the trial judge who ratified their judgment.

In the case In re *T.J., M.D., & C.J.*, 666 A. 2d 1 (D.C. App. 1995), officials removed a child from the care of his foster mother after she petitioned to adopt him and the boy's great-aunt sought custody. The boy and the great-aunt were black; the foster mother was white and a lesbian. A trial court ruled in favor of the foster mother but was reversed on appeal, on the ground that it had failed to show sufficient deference to the preferences of the child's biological mother. Again, there is reason to believe that race-matching bias played a tacit part in the decision; more speculative is the possibility that antigay sentiment was a factor.

beyond the explanations proffered by child-welfare agents, and the understandable reluctance of officials to injure innocent parties by cutting off federal funding to a jurisdiction, even if its officials are failing to comply with federal requirements. The only thing that will decisively end the practice of race matching is a persistent and vocal campaign to educate and transform public opinion.

### Should We Prohibit All Racial Selectivity?

I have argued thus far that governments should bar the use of race as a proxy for preferred or disfavored traits, and that therefore they should also, except in narrowly defined circumstances, prohibit officials from making racially selective placement decisions for foster care or adoption. I have argued, too, that with very few exceptions, governments should not be permitted to set or implement racially based cultural-competency standards. I have maintained that officials charged with selecting adoptive parents in America's racially diverse society should be guided by a clear and rigorous antidiscrimination regime. That leaves open the question, however, of racial selectivity on the part of prospective adoptive parents. How should society respond to *their* expressed racial preferences? Professor R. Richard Banks has insistently placed that question on the agenda and staked out a provocative response to it.[52]

Banks has convincingly suggested that the racial preferences of prospective parents constitute an important subject whose significance has been neglected in the relevant literature. He has noted that "[prospective] adoptive parents, most of whom are white, prefer white children to black children."[53] Because whites outnumber blacks in America, this means that white children typically have a larger group of potential parents interested in them, a statistic that probably contributes significantly to better chances of being adopted and of being adopted more quickly than their black counterparts. In Banks's view, white parents' "racial preferences produce inequality just as surely as race matching, even if they produce it differently. Adoptive parents' racial preferences deny to black children access to a pool of potential adoptive parents comparable to that available to white children."

To rectify this unjustified differential in access, Banks has proposed a policy of "strict nonaccommodation" whereby adoption agencies would decline to accommodate adopters' racial preferences. Agencies, he has suggested, should not only be directed to cease listing children in color-coded directories for the benefit of racially selective prospective parents; they should also "make clear to prospective adoptive parents that their racial preferences are to play no role in the parents' selection of a child to adopt." Under Banks's scheme,

> Prospective adoptive parents . . . would be informed at the outset that the adoption process is not one in which racial discrimination is allowed. Parents would be encouraged to withdraw from the process if they did not think that they could abide by that rule, and adoption officials would have the authority to remove parents from the process if they determined that the parents in fact were discriminating on the basis of race. Parents could even be asked to sign a nondiscrimination agreement just as do other parties who do business with or enter into a relationship with the government.

I agree with Banks that the racial selectivity of prospective adoptive parents can impose burdens on children, particularly children who belong to racial minorities. I also agree with his belief that child-welfare officials should be prohibited from taking any initiative to encourage racial selectivity on the part of prospective adoptive parents. It should be illegal for such officials either to ask those seeking to adopt to state a racial preference in a child or to offer to prospective parents racially coded lists or directories of children eligible for adoption. I disagree with Banks, however, on the notion of prohibiting racial selectivity on the part of prospective parents. Here he pushes a good idea—racial nondiscrimination—past its rightful and prudent boundaries. First, it is essential that people be allowed an ambit of privacy within which they may form intimate relationships, even if those relationships are based on considerations that are properly thought to be silly or even pernicious.[54] Choosing a child to adopt, like choosing a mate to marry, should be located within that ambit, safely insulated from the sort of intrusion that Banks has advocated. Racial selectivity in dating, friendship, and marriage also imposes disadvantages on those associated with disfavored racial groups in society. But Banks has nowhere recommended prohibiting racial selectivity in *those* contexts—and for good reason. Such a prohibition would be a grotesque incursion on personal privacy, and it would require endowing officials with a frightening amount of power. Similarly grotesque is the idea of tossing a person or a couple out of the adoption market on the ground that racial considerations played a part in his/her/their decision regarding which child to adopt. In other venues in which antidiscrimination norms have been imposed—for example, employment, housing, and public accommodations—lawmakers have been careful to leave some breathing room for *private* racial discrimination. They have thus avoided authoritarian comprehensiveness.[55] In deference to personal privacy and with a well-considered hesitance to avoid unduly empowering officials, lawmakers should show similar restraint with respect to foster care and adoption.

There are other reasons to object to Banks's proposal. If implemented, it would likely pressure some number of prospective adoptive parents to conceal their racial feelings in order to remain eligible to adopt at all using the resources of an approved agency. It serves no one's interest, however, to place a child with adults who would actually prefer a youngster of a different race. Indeed, to do so would seem merely to invite disaster for all concerned. If implemented, Banks's proposal would also likely dissuade a substantial number of people from entering the adoption market, or at least those portions of it subject to the regulations that he envisions. This is a heavy cost that Professor Banks has not adequately taken into account. As Professor Bartholet has noted, "Our public adoption system already drives away many prospective adopters, black and white, by virtue of its negative, restrictive, bureaucratic nature. . . . We should be drawing prospective parents into our public adoption system, not driving them away."[56]

### Should Black Children Be Deemed to "Belong" to Black America?
Thus far I have argued that race matching is bad for children in need of adoptive or foster homes. But what about the claim that regardless of

the consequences for individual children, race matching is good for blacks as a group, as a people, as a separate and distinct political entity, because it represents the will of the black community and thus reflects and encourages communal self-determination? Those who support race matching on these grounds see it as a jurisdictional matter that defines communal identity and power. They want the black community to be like recognized Indian tribes in having acknowledged authority over members and relations with other political entities.[57] I realize that the yearning for some sort of separate American commonwealth is an ambition of long lineage.[58] I prefer, however, a competing ambition— one that seeks to create in fact as well as in theory a multiracial united polity in which all persons are treated equally and decently as *individuals* and not as agents of racial groups to which they are said to "belong."

### Religious Matching and Race Matching: A Comparison

In the law governing child-placement decisions—as in many areas of American life—racial conflicts reflect and exacerbate more general problems. Race matching mirrors and enlarges related tragedies, including the stigma that still enshrouds adoption, the infectiousness of parochialism, and society's failure to construct a secure safety net for parentless children. Here it is useful to recall one of Judge Roney's defenses of race matching, his observation in *Drummond* that child welfare officials have often insisted upon matching regimes of all sorts.* Some devotees of matching have been motivated by a desire to conceal telltale signs that a parent-child relationship has been created "artificially" by law rather than "naturally" by biology. Seeking to mimic nature as closely as possible, officials were once known to take into account such factors as hair color, eye color, and facial features in arranging or preventing adoptions. Others have been motivated by a desire to keep children within the group to which they are said to "belong" by nature or imputation. Hence scores of states enacted laws that decreed, whenever possible, juvenile adoptees should be placed

---

*See page 421.

with adopters of the same religion as the child.[59] Ways in which religious matching has been similar to and different from race matching illuminate both.

Substantial numbers of states have enacted so-called religious protection laws designed to promote adoptive matching on the basis of religion.* The religious protection laws typically paid more attention to defining religious boundaries than did race-matching laws or customs pay attention to defining racial boundaries. While the latter casually assumed that any discernible African American ancestry was sufficient to label a child as "black" (or Negro or colored),[60] the religious protection statutes recognized that determining the religious identity of a child too immature to have received religious training or internalized religious beliefs might pose real problems. Some states responded by making the boundary line the religion of the biological parents, others by making the boundary line the religion of either biological parent, still others by delegating to agencies or courts the task of affixing a religious identity unto the child.[61]

Religious protection laws have typically been written in ways that give flexibility to administrative and judicial officers, providing that "if possible," courts should place a child under the care and control of persons having the same religious identity as the child.† What "if possible" can actually mean in operation is, of course, quite variable. Some judges have applied religious protection laws loosely, displaying a ready

---

*Although relatively few states now express a statutory preference for religious matching (beyond attempting to defer to the wishes of biological parents when they give children up for adoption), several states continue to carry on their books the traditional religious protection laws. See, for example, Connecticut (Conn. Gen. Stat. § 46b-129 j [2001]); Delaware (10 Del. C. § 1009 [b][9] 2001); Illinois (Ill. Comp. Stat. Ann. §20 505/7 [2001]); Maryland (Md. Fam. Code. Ann §5-520 [2001]); New York (N.Y. CLS Soc. Serv. § 373 [2002]).

†Maine's law was notably more demanding than most. It used to require religious matching in every case "where a suitable family of such faith could be found," and allowed for temporary placement across lines of religion only until "a suitable family" could be found (Me. Rev. Stat. Ann. Tit. 22, § 3795 [1965]). This provision was repealed in 1967. Ellen S. George and Stephen M. Snyder, "A Reconsideration of the Religious Element in Adoption" (56 *Cornell Law Review* 780, 791–92 [1971]).

willingness to permit a cross-religious adoption in circumstances where the alternative was delay. Others have applied religious protection laws rigidly.

In 1954 in Massachusetts, a couple petitioned to adopt twin children, a boy and a girl. At that time, a statute provided that "In making orders for adoption, the judge when practicable must give custody only to persons of the same religious faith as that of the child."\* The petitioners, the Goldmans, had raised the twins for about three years, ever since they were two weeks old. The Goldmans, then, were the only parents that the children had ever known. Though no objection was raised regarding the care that the Goldmans had bestowed upon the children, a judge denied their petitions for adoption, noting that while the biological parents of the twins were Catholics, the Goldmans were Jews.† The judge noted that the biological mother of the twins had consented in writing to the Goldmans' petition and to their plans to raise the children as Jews. He also acknowledged that no other adults had come forward seeking to adopt the twins. That fact could easily have been used to provide the predicate for a determination that, at least in this case, practicability compelled permitting the requested adoption. The judge

---

\*The law went on to stipulate that "In the event that there is a dispute as to the religion of the said child, its religion shall be deemed to be that of its mother. If the court, with due regard for the religion of the child, shall nevertheless grant the petition for adoption of a child proferred by a person or persons of a religious faith or persuasion other than that of the child, the court shall state the facts which impelled it to make such a disposition. See Petitions of Goldman, 121 N.E. 2d 843, 844 (Mass. 1954).

This law was repealed in 1970 and replaced with a provision which mandates that "If, at the time of surrender of the child for adoptive custody, the parent or parents . . . requested a religious designation for the child, the court may grant a petition for adoption of the child only to a person or persons of the religious designation so requested, unless a placement for adoptive custody based on such request would not have been in the best interest of the child." (Mass. Ann. Laws ch. 210 § 5B.)

†In its ruling upholding the denial of the adoption petition, the Supreme Judicial Court of Massachusetts also noted that while the petitioners have "dark complexions and dark hair," the twins are "blond, with large blue eyes and flaxen hair" (Petitions of Goldman, 121 N.E. 2d 843, 844 [Mass. 1954]).

assigned to the case, however, was clearly a strongly committed proponent of the religious-protection statute who wanted to keep its exceptions exceedingly narrow. Judge John V. Phelan determined that there
were "many Catholic couples of fine family life and excellent reputation who have filed applications with the Catholic Charities Bureau for
the purpose of adopting Catholic children of the type of the twins, and
are able to provide the twins with a material status equivalent to or better than that of the petitioners, and with whom the twins could be
placed immediately."[62] This allusion to an immediate placement with a
Catholic family was pure supposition; in fact, no one other than the
Goldmans had come forward to offer the children an adoptive home.
Remarkably, moreover, neither the trial judge nor the appellate judges
appear to have much considered the traumatic consequences to the
Goldmans and the twins of undoing a de facto parent-child relationship
several years in the making. On this point, the Supreme Judicial Court
of Massachusetts offered only silence. Thus, at around the same time
that courts in Louisiana were precluding the adoption of Jacqueline
Henley pursuant to a racial protection statute, courts in Massachusetts
were precluding the adoption of the Goldmans' wards pursuant to a
religious protection law.

New York state has been, and continues to be, committed to religious protection in adoption proceeding. Its constitution (supported by
a bevy of supplementary statutes) provides that a child shall be placed
"when practicable, in an institution or agency governed by persons, or
in the custody of a person, of the same religious persuasion as the
child."[63] The reference to institutions or agencies is important. The
state made them equivalent to available adoptive individuals for purposes of religious protection, thus making it all the harder to justify
interreligious adoptions. Commenting on New York's approach, a state
legislator observed (at some point in the 1960s) that while the law

> does not mandate that agencies keep children in foster homes
> for their entire childhood on the ground that no adoptive home
> of the same religion is available, this is what happens. It is
> known to happen even if the mother of the child might wish
> the child to have the advantage of being reared in an adoptive

home though it be of a different religion. Children are thus deprived of a home of their own simply because no qualified persons of the alleged religion of the child are available.[64]*

Subsequently, court rulings and public sentiment have substantially moderated religious matching regimes, even in those jurisdictions in which it was most deeply entrenched. In a 1970 case, for example, the distinguished judge Nanette Dembitz ruled that New York's racial protection law could be maintained only if it was construed to require religious matching in circumstances where attempting to effectuate some placements would neither preclude nor substantially delay alternatives—even if they were cross-religious. Judge Dembitz held that this narrowing of the state's policy on religious conformity was necessary because otherwise the policy would unconstitutionally deny certain children an equal chance to obtain the benefits of adoption.[65] The judge recognized that in religious matching, as in race matching, those most subject to unjustifiable hurt are typically, though unsurprisingly, those most vulnerable—youngsters in need of new parents.

A final feature of religious protection regimes that is relevant to ongoing debates over race matching are efforts by officials or even private parties to police the thinking and beliefs of prospective adopters. In 1965 the Burkes, a couple in New Jersey, sought to adopt. Their

---

*Another feature of New York's support for religious protection has had a profoundly racial consequence. The state has delegated to private agencies the task of caring for many of the state's parentless children and nourished such agencies with general tax revenues. Many of these private agencies are sectarian, primarily Catholic or Jewish. Often the publicly funded religious child-welfare agencies were better than their frequently impoverished secular counterparts. Funded in part by state subsidies, the religious agencies preferred "their own" children, which meant that non-Catholic or non-Jewish parentless children tended to be pushed into the poorer, less desirable nonreligious institutions. The preferences for Catholic and Jewish youngsters had the effect of burdening needy black youngsters disproportionately, since most of them were Protestants. For a sobering journalistic account of the hardships and inequities associated with New York's child-welfare system and efforts to reform it through litigation, see Nina Bernstein, *The Lost Children of Wilder: The Epic Struggle to Change Foster Care* (2001). See also *Wilder v. Sugarman*, 385 F. Supp 1013 (S.D. N.Y. 1974); *Wilder v. Bernstein*, 645 F. Supp. 1292 (S.D. N.Y. 1986); *Wilder v. Bernstein*, 848 F. 2d 1338 (2nd Cir. 1988).

effort was temporarily stymied when the state Bureau of Children's Services refused to consider them because of their lack of religious affiliation. When they sued, the state changed its requirement that adopters provide a reference from a cleric, and in 1967 the Burkes finally succeeded in adopting a baby boy. Two years later, the couple sought to adopt again. Although a local child-welfare agency found them to be fit, a judge denied their petition. He found them to be unfit because they did not believe in the existence of a supreme being. Ironically, the judge based his ruling on the ground of religious liberty. According to him, the child in question "should have the freedom to worship as she sees fit and not be influenced by parents or exposed to the views of prospective parents who do not believe in a Supreme Being."[66] The first prong of that reasoning is laughable. If parental influence alone is seen as a denial of a child's freedom to worship as she will see fit, then logically, *any* prospective parent should be disqualified. After all, under the judge's reasoning, the influence of religious parents would presumably deny the child's freedom to be an atheist. The second prong of the judge's reasoning was itself an affront to freedom of religion by constructively making subscription to some religion a litmus test for fitness as an adoptive parent.

The New Jersey Supreme Court reversed the judge and granted the adoption, holding that neither disbelief in God nor nonaffiliation with a religion was alone sufficient to deem the Burkes unfit adoptive parents. But displaying the same penchant for unprincipled compromise we have seen in the race-matching case law, the state appellate court expressly declared that religious belief could properly be considered as a factor (though not the decisive factor) in evaluating parental fitness and that a judge could properly "probe into the religious background and convictions of prospective adopting parents in the same way as it and the investigating agencies may probe into all aspects of their lives to determine fitness."[67] The New Jersey court permitted in a religious context, in other words, what is disturbingly prevalent in proceedings relating to interracial adoption: probes designed to ensure that prospective adopters have beliefs that are "appropriate" or "acceptable." Although many would-be adopters will acquiesce to religious competency testing, such investigations are hostile to what should be fundamental precepts of political and religious liberty.* Their baselines of assessment are either insidiously hidden, concealing the orthodoxy that the investigators seek to impose; or dangerously vague, empowering investigators with excessive discretion. Concurring with the New Jersey Supreme Court's grant of the adoption petition, but disagreeing with its allowance of probes into the religious convictions of prospective adoptive parents, Chief Justice Joseph Weintraub ably focused upon the baseline problem:

> I can think of nothing more unmanageable than an inquiry into a man's religious, spiritual and ethical creed. There is no catalogue of tolerable beliefs. Nor would the nature of man permit one, for man is inherently intolerant as to matters unknowable, and the intensity of his tolerance is twin with the intensity of his views. I assume the [court] would never deny adoption "solely" because of a belief in that area, but if the belief may be considered . . . then how much may be charged against an applicant who is a Jehovah's Witness and therefore opposed to blood transfusions [?] . . . And since a man's religious, spiritual and ethical views may be more evident in his position on specific subjects than in his abstract statement of his faith, will it be all right to inquire of his attitude toward . . . capital punishment, or divorce, or abortion [?] . . . No matter how it is phrased or explained, an inquiry into religious, spiritual and ethical views can mean no more than this, that a man or a woman is unfit or

---

*Even worse are cases in which a court has made it a condition of adoption that a child be brought up in a particular religion. New York even allowed courts to abrogate adoptions pursuant to evidence that could be presented by anyone that adoptive parents were seeking to change the religion of an adopted child. Rightly objecting to such measures, Leo Pfeffer remarked that such measures should be "repugnant to a free democratic people that the internal life of a family should be subject to state control and state supervision. A free family in a free society should not be required to adopt a state-appointed Big Brother." "Religion in the Upbringing of Children," 35 *Boston University Law Review* 333, 359 (1955).

a bit unfit, to be a parent, natural or adoptive, if his or her thoughts exceed the tolerance of the mortal who happens to judge in a placement bureau or in the judiciary.[68]

A very similar problem presents itself in the racial context insofar as many people—including those who are relatively tolerant of transracial adoptions—assume that it is proper to investigate whether prospective adoptive parents have sufficient "cultural competency" to raise a black child and to require adoptive parents to receive "assistance" from those who have the supposed authority to teach them about racially appropriate modes of parenting.[69] California provides by statute that authorities "may consider the cultural, ethnic, or racial background of the child and the capacity of the prospective adoptive parent to meet the needs of a child of this background as one of a number of factors used to determine the best interest of the child."[70] In a case in Chicago, a ruling in a bitter custody dispute over a black child was based in part on a judge's belief that expert witnesses had paid insufficient attention to whether the white couple seeking to adopt the black boy for whom they had served as foster parents could address adequately the child's purported racial/cultural needs.[71] In a case in Rhode Island, the fitness of a white couple to adopt a black youngster for whom they had cared as foster parents was challenged, in part, because they knew little or nothing about Kwanza and had no plans to celebrate it.[72]

Although proponents of cultural competency screening and training maintain that assessment and "assistance" is all about "culture" and not "race" per se, the speciousness of that claim is revealed upon noting that when the adoption of children of color is in question, it is only *white* prospective adopters who are examined. Black prospective adopters somehow escape being quizzed about the racial demographics of their circle of friends, congregations, and neighborhoods; they are somehow exempted from tests concerning African American history and society; they are somehow spared intrusive queries about their perception of the prevalence of white racism and effective means for overcoming it. If cultural competency rather than racial protection were the real concern, then presumably black prospective adoptive parents would also require testing.

Proponents of cultural competency screening often portray it as an uncontroversial matter of mere common sense—a simple way to ensure that nonblack adoptive parents of black children know certain racial fundamentals that virtually all black adults already know by virtue of their experience as blacks in a society dominated by whites. This portrayal, however, misleadingly suggests that the "black community" is characterized by a homogeneity in perspective, practice, and aspiration that is refuted by reality. The baseline problem that bedevils religious testing also bedevils racial cultural competency testing. Is a good sense of blackness evidenced by a youngster's listening to rap music and attending Morehouse College? What about preferring Mozart and attending Princeton? What about preferring gospel music and attending The Citadel? Do we really want the government to declare any of these preferences as more or less black or more or less good? By what criterion would such judgments be made? The opinions of Marian Wright Edelman?[73] Margaret A. Wright?[74] Darlene and Derek S. Hopson?[75] Jawanza Kunjufu?[76] Alvin Poussaint and James Comer?[77] Benjamin Spock?[78] A diverse society that aspires to be appropriately pluralistic, democratic, and attentive to individual autonomy and liberty ought not allow officials to make adoption or foster care placement decisions according to considerations such as these.

Those who champion cultural competency screening and monitoring often invoke two scenarios as sure-fire examples of why cultural competency policing is essential. One involves the grooming of black children's hair, particularly the styling that is said to be right for black girls. The complaint is that all too often whites are simply unaware of how to fashion correctly black people's hair. The other involves the appropriate advice to offer to a black child who has been called "nigger." The complaint here is that all too often whites are simply at a loss as to how to counsel a black child usefully in the face of racist taunting. Although those who invoke these scenarios seem to believe that there exists a narrow band of correct and distinctively "black" responses, there is, in reality, a wide array of intelligent, responsible ways in which African Americans handle these matters. Some black parents straighten their daughters' hair, while others braid it, while others let it grow out with minimal tending.[79] Some black parents instruct their children to physically attack people who call them nigger—that was my (black) father's advice. Others instruct their children to ignore such taunts—that was my (black) mother's advice.[80] Respect for the variety that characterizes black parents' responses should be mirrored by respect for the variety that characterizes white parents' responses—reactions that are often helpfully nourished by advice from black friends. Assistance, however, should not be imposed. If white parents of black children want to elicit and use advice from blacks, that is fine, indeed, wise. On the other hand, if white parents decide that they want to pursue their own independent course, they should be allowed to do so without ideological oversight from the government. Opposition that would challenge efforts to dictate the ideological choices that black parents make (or would want to make) in raising their children should be mirrored by opposition to efforts to dictate the ideological choices that white parents make (or would want to make) in raising *their* children—regardless of whether these children are connected to the parents by biology or adoption.

Plainly there is no proper authoritative criterion for grading the racial appropriateness of parenting—only the very real specter of an imposition of orthodoxies that come innocuously packaged as "cultural competency." The chilling effect that religious or cultural or racial competency examinations create,* the prejudices they elicit, and the tendency toward bullying that they encourage make them sources of unfairness and oppression that should be erased.†

---

*The groveling posture that some candidates for adoptive parenthood assume in order to win approval from child-welfare officials whom they perceive to be skeptical of their ability to raise children of a different race or religion or culture from their own is a heartrending spectacle. In the case of the Burkes in New Jersey, the trial judge openly expressed his surprise at their unapologetic expression of their views. He claimed to have been favorably impressed by their articulate honesty. In view of his ruling, however, one is entitled to conjecture that their very forthrightness may have added to his determination to stymie their attempt to adopt. See In re *Adoption of "E"*, 279 A. 2d 785, 788 (N.J. 1971); Note, "In re *Adoption of E:* First Amendment Rights and Religious Inquiry in Adoption Proceedings," 24 *Maine Law Review* 149 (1972).

†Unfortunately, cultural, religious, and racial competency testing remains prevalent. In Montana, authorities may "gather and use, in an appropriate, non-arbitrary manner, information concerning the . . . religious beliefs of a prospective adoptive parent" (Mont. Code. Ann. § 42-4-201 [2001]). Pennsylvania directs that preplacement reports on prospective adoptive parents include "an investigation of [their] religious background" (23 Pa. C. S. § 2530 [2002]).

# ELEVEN

# White Parents and Black Children in Adoptive Families

Whites who seek to adopt black children are widely regarded with suspicion. Are they ideologues, more interested in making a political point than in actually being parents? Are they people so desperate to be parents that they will accept a black child even though they would really prefer a white one? Are they dangerously naive about the realities of racism? Are they racial missionaries intent on "saving" black children from blackness? Are they trying to obtain juvenile slaves? These and similar questions lurk behind the intense scrutiny focused on white adults who adopt black children. As Professor Joyce Ladner has written, "The most perplexing and controversial aspect of transracial adoption is parental motivation. Members of all groups in the society, whether hostile or sympathetic observers, are equally anxious to know from these parents, 'Why did you adopt *this* kind of child[?]'"[1]

Like whites who marry across racial lines, whites who adopt interracially are often presumed to be either neurotic or foolish. Moreover, like other ostracized minorities, white adoptive parents of black children are prone to internalize the prejudices against them. Many believe the myths that portray them as merely "better-than-nothing" parents, whom society can grudgingly resort to when no same-race option is available for a black child. Reforming this state of affairs will require first refuting myths of white parental inferiority, not only in the minds of the wider public but also in the minds of white adoptive parents themselves.

Most adults who seek to adopt would prefer a child of their own race.[2] That largely explains why, relative to parentless black children, parentless white ones are more in demand, face a shorter wait before being adopted, and earn higher fees for the intermediaries who facilitate private adoptive transactions.[3]* In the 1980s a federal-government investigation found that a healthy black infant typically waited about four times as long for placement as a healthy white infant.[4] By the 1990s, the disparity had renamed the same or widened. One study demonstrated that a black infant was less likely to be adopted than a white child aged three to five—a revealing statistic, given the strongly negative effect that older age has on children's prospects of adoption.[5] These trends do not stem exclusively from the racial preferences of would-be adopters, the large majority of whom are white; also significant are race-matching policies and their alienation of prospective parents who might otherwise have pursued white-black interracial adoptions. But other factors notwithstanding, the racial preference for white children remains a decisive and pervasive influence within the adoption system,† dictating, among other things, the way children are

---

*Racial and color preferences affect adoption markets outside as well as inside the United States. Noting that both domestic and international adoption markets are calibrated by "the human equivalent of the gold standard: the healthy white infant," Carol Lloyd and Hank Pellissier recounted in "Interracial Adoption: One Couple's Story" (Salon.com, August 1997) that when they "cruised the World Wide Web for data on international orphans," they discovered children listed with

> photos, biographies, and price tags attached—like used automobiles, except that the cost variation is largely based on color. A paraplegic Bulgarian tot with a cleft palate costs $30,000, whereas a mobile and dentally normal Chinese or Guatemalan urchin runs only $15,000. And black children? Absolutely nothing. The Caribbean islands of Martinique, Grenada, and Barbados offer free black children to anyone who wants to fly there and pick them up.

See also Mike Lindblom, "Reverend Criticizes Adoption Fees Based on Race," Seattletimes.com, March 1, 2002; "'Buying and Selling' Preacher Calls Adoption Fees Discriminatory," abcnews.com, March 12, 2002; Jim DeFeder, "How Much for a White Baby?," *Talk*, December 1999–January 2000.

†This central but neglected point was made by Professor Richard Banks in his important and provocative article "The Color of Desire: Fulfilling Adoptive Parents'

labeled. Nothing more succinctly evinces the broadly disfavored status of black children on the adoption market than the fact that they are conventionally described as juveniles with "special needs," or pegged as "hard to place"—labels created for and routinely attached to children with physical or mental disabilities.[6]

According to certain measures, neither the prevalence nor the intensity of racial preference is as great as some might suppose. In a 1999 study conducted by the National Center for Health Statistics, 51 percent of white women who were planning to adopt stated that they would prefer to adopt a white child; 73 percent indicated that they would accept a black child.[7] Among black women planning to adopt, though 52 percent expressed a preference for a black child, fully 86 to 89 percent said they would be willing to adopt a white or other non-black child.[8] It is entirely possible, of course, that a substantial number of these respondents were either fooling themselves or giving what they guessed was the "correct" answer rather than being candid. Moreover, apart from personal preferences, there often are external influences that militate in favor of same-race adoptions. The experience of Ann Kimble Loux and her husband is illustrative here. This white couple already had three biological children of their own when they decided, in the 1970s, to adopt another child or two. They were not indifferent on the matter of race: they wanted a "cross-racial" child.* But Ann Loux's

---

Racial Preferences Through Discriminatory State Action," *Yale Law Journal* 107 (1998): 864.

*In writing about this episode, Loux neglected to explain precisely what she meant by "cross-racial." I take the term as used by her to mean a child who was partly white and partly black, or "mixed." For the full account, see Ann Kimble Loux, *The Limits of Hope: An Adoptive Mother's Story* (1997).

Loux's expressed preference for a "cross-racial" as opposed to a black child hints at a color hierarchy that still figures in American life—particularly in the adoption market, where lighter-skinned colored children have long been favored over darker-skinned ones. The prevalence of biracial children among "black" children adopted by whites is a striking feature that has been largely ignored in the debate over interracial adoption. For an exception to this general omission, see Julie C. Lythcott-Haims, "Where Do Mixed Babies Belong? Racial Classification in America and Its Implications for Transracial Adoption," *Civil Rights–Civil Liberties Law Review* 29 (1994): 531. In an early-1970s study of 204 white couples in the Midwest who adopted interracially, Rita Simon and Howard Altstein found that "most of the

father objected and informed her that if she and her spouse did adopt transracially, she would not be allowed to bring the youngster to visit him. "At first I refused to be threatened," she later recalled, "but the more I considered it, the sillier it seemed to leave one family behind to get another."⁹ The couple ended up adopting two white girls.

Transracial parenting has a surprisingly long history, albeit one that began essentially by accident: some of the first white-black adoptions were undertaken by whites who adopted black children by *mistake,* later learned of their error, and kept the children anyway.* To "protect" those who made such mistakes, the Kentucky and Missouri legislatures enacted laws specifying that any adoption could be annulled within five years of its finalization if the child in question proved to be of a different race than his or her adoptive parent(s), provided that the parent(s) had not known this fact beforehand.¹⁰ One of the first documented instances of formal, intentional interracial adoption was a placement made in Minneapolis, Minnesota, in 1948. The child was a black infant who had been bounced around so many times in foster care that the black social worker assigned to his case, Laura Gaskins, simply refused "to place [him] in yet another foster home."¹¹ Gaskins tried but failed to recruit black adoptive parents for him—a failure due, she believed, to the paucity of blacks then living in the area. When no black adoptive home could be found, Gaskins decided to place the baby in a white one.

Around the same time, the Nobel Prize–winning author Pearl Buck was starting up Welcome House, one of the first private agencies in the country to encourage black-white as well as other forms of interracial, interethnic, and international adoptions.¹² Buck herself adopted several

---

families wanted a racially mixed child" (*Transracial Adoption* [1977], 81). See also Joyce Ladner, *Mixed Families: Adopting Across Racial Boundaries* (1977), 49; Pearl S. Buck, "Should White Parents Adopt Brown Babies?," *Ebony,* June 1958, p. 27: "Even the Negro, it seems, prefers to be light-colored, or to adopt a light-colored child, rather than dark."

*Some white parents knowingly adopted light-skinned children of colored parentage and passed them off as white. See Jacqueline Macaulay and Stewart Macaulay, "Adoption for Black Children: A Case Study of Expert Discretion," *Research in Law and Sociology* 1 (1978): 265, 279.

children who had been fathered by black American servicemen stationed in Germany and Japan. Focusing in particular on the plight of abandoned children in Asia, she predicted that "there will be enough homes for the half-white children but not for those who are half-Negro. And, alas, [because of Asian racism] the half-Negro children will have the most difficult time in the land of their birth."[13] From there, Buck elaborated on her own situation:

> One of my own beloved adopted children happens . . . to be the child of an American Negro soldier and a German [white] mother. She came to us as a little refugee child from Germany, and she has stayed because we love her too well to let her go. She is our living answer to prejudice. . . . She is our treasure. To all criticism I have but one reply. She is happy with us and we are happy with her. That is all that is required to make a good family.[14]

Throughout the 1960s, an increasing number of groups began to publicize the desperate situation of parentless black children and to press public and private agencies to permit their adoption by white adults. One coalition of Minnesota social workers let it be known that they would consider all who applied to adopt black children, regardless of the applicants' race; they also worked cooperatively with a pioneering civic organization named Parents to Adopt Minority Youngsters (PAMY). By 1965 this program had facilitated the transracial adoption of twenty Negro children—a modest total, to be sure, but a significant beginning nonetheless, given the initiative's departure from accepted practice.[15] The Minnesota experiment was beset by skeptics who worried about the motives of white adoptive parents, the discrimination that black adopted youngsters would face in predominantly white neighborhoods, and the loneliness that could be their lot, especially in adolescence, if the parents of their white playmates became more exclusionary for fear that interracial friendship might lead to interracial sex and marriage.[16]   Some of the group's fellow social workers, the great majority of whom were white, fervently opposed the transracial adoptions. But the program continued anyway, thanks mainly to pressure from local activists buoyed by the ascendant optimism of the civil rights revolution. After all, what could better embody Dr. King's dream of interracial brotherhood and sisterhood than the creation of interracial families through adoption?*

By the end of the decade, according to Professors Jacqueline and Stewart Macaulay, "transracial adoption seemed to be the 'in' thing for progressive [adoption] agencies."[17] The Child Welfare League of America (CWL) reversed itself and began urging authorities *not* to presume that crippling difficulties were the inevitable concomitant of transracial placements. Indeed, the CWL noted, "in most communities there are families that have the capacity to adopt a child whose racial background is different from their own. Such couples should be encouraged to consider such a child."[18] Likewise indicative of changing mores were the favorable articles published in such venues as *Ebony, Look, Parents Magazine,* and the *New York Times Magazine.* These developments reflected and in turn inspired a striking increase in the rate of black-white interracial adoptions. In 1968, of 3,122 black children placed for adoption nationally, 733—or 23 percent—were placed in white homes; in 1971 the figure was 2,574 out of 7,420, or nearly 35 percent.[19]†

In 1972, however, the National Association of Black Social Workers (NABSW), adding a new and influential weight to the forces that had traditionally resisted interracial adoption, asserted that such arrangements constituted a form of "cultural genocide."‡ With that condemnation, the number of white-black adoptions quickly plummeted; in 1973 there were only half as many as there had been just two years earlier.[20] Keenly aware of their new vulnerability, many of those

---

*During one civil rights protest demonstration in Boston in the 1960s, white mothers marched with black children, and black mothers with white children, to bring to life a vision of multiracial justice and harmony (J. Anthony Lukas, *Common Ground* [1985], 18). For some parents, adopting transracially is an ongoing way of supporting that vision. See Janice Gilmore, "Interracial Adoption Furthers King's Cause," *Omaha World-Herald,* January 12, 2001.

†That same year, forty to eighty thousand black youngsters were adoptable. See Macaulay and Macaulay, "Adoption for Black Children," 284. Here as elsewhere, statistics on adoption must be taken as rough approximations, since information gathering in this area is characteristically inconsistent and incomplete.

‡See pages 393–95.

wishing to effectuate interracial adoptions—prospective adoptive parents, sympathetic social workers, interested agencies—curtailed their open proselytizing and instead proceeded quietly and cautiously. They are still doing that today, and for good reason. For while much has changed—any determined adopter is in a much better position now than ever before—opposition to black-white interracial adoption remains widespread.

Who are the whites who cross the black-white racial frontier to adopt? Where do they live? What do they think? How do they pursue their parenting responsibilities? No comprehensive, up-to-date survey exists.[21] From the fragmentary record we do have, it is clear that they vary considerably in terms of their residence, socioeconomic standing, politics, religious observance, and other characteristics. Some are glaringly well off financially (among this group are Oscar de la Renta and Steven Spielberg), but are merely solidly middle class. Studies conducted in the 1970s indicated that a notable percentage of adoptive white parents had higher than average levels of education and professional training.[22] Many would prefer to adopt white children but, confronted by prohibitively long waits, willingly adopt black children, for whom the wait is shorter. Others, however, want black children from the start. Many live in urban areas outside the South, on the East and West coasts. But some live in places that observers might find surprising: Utah, Wyoming, Iowa, Tennessee, New Hampshire, Indiana. Some harbor political views that put them on the leftish end of the political spectrum; others are decidedly on the right.[23]

Over the past decade, a few white adoptive parents of black youngsters have written revealing memoirs about their experiences. Three are particularly noteworthy: J. Douglas Bates's *Gift Children: A Story of Race, Family, and Adoption in a Divided America* (1993); Jana Wolff's *Secret Thoughts of an Adoptive Mother* (1997); and Sharon E. Rush's *Loving Across the Color Line: A White Adoptive Mother Learns About Race* (2000).[24]

In 1970 Bates and his wife, Gloria, decided to adopt a child. They already had two biological children, both boys; Gloria Bates wished to add a daughter. Her husband did not want her to have another baby, but he was amenable to the idea of adopting an older girl. Encouraged by friends who were also contemplating adoption—and were willing to adopt regardless of the child's race—the Bateses contacted the Oregon Children's Services Division. Douglas Bates would later recall telling agency officials that while the child's age mattered to him and his wife, her race did not. From that point on, things moved quickly. "Within four months," Bates would write, the agency "brought us a [four-year-old] daughter who turned out to be healthy, beautiful and black."[25]

The little girl, Lynn, had been born to a white mother and a black father, both of whom were serving prison sentences for possession of illicit drugs (heroin). On their release from prison, they neglected to claim their child, who was then sent to a white couple for foster care while the state began the process of terminating her biological parents' parental rights.

Douglas and Gloria Bates met Lynn by prearrangement at a mall, where they found her and a social worker playing with some rabbits and kittens at a pet store. As Bates remembered it, on entering the store,

> we gaped at the little girl. She looked just as she did in the photographs, wearing the same red and white plaid dress and white stockings and shiny shoes that the kindly social worker had purchased for her. . . .
>
> Gloria was standing stiffly at my side, and I could sense she was highly upset. . . .
>
> I whispered, "We can turn around and walk right out the door."
>
> Gloria took my hand and squeezed it a little. "No we can't," she said.
>
> Then she led me firmly, as she would so many times in the years ahead, toward our destiny—back to the rear of the store, back to the kittens and rabbits and the little girl who had waited so terribly long to meet her mom and dad.[26]

Two years later, the Bateses adopted another child, the product of a relationship between a black man and a fourteen-year-old white girl. The neglected and abused baby had initially been adopted by a different white couple, who had returned her after realizing that they could not bear up under the opprobrium heaped on them by their disapproving white neighbors. Gloria and Douglas Bates met the little girl and proceeded to adopt her, changing her name to Liska.

From the outset, the Bateses faced the considerable task of protecting their new children from racism, prejudice against adoptees, and kindred menaces. "What you . . . have now is like a clear, pristine mountain stream," Douglas Bates's uncle declared with reference to his newphew's biological children. "Why would you want to spoil something so pure by mixing it with polluted, muddy water?"[27] Neighborhood children in the Bateses' white, working-class community routinely referred to Lynn and Liska as "niggers." This prompted the Bateses to move their family to a more affluent neighborhood that they thought would be more enlightened. And it probably was, but that did not prevent the sons and daughters of doctors and lawyers from also taunting the Bates girls with racial slurs. Although both girls encountered prejudice at school, Lynn seems to have endured the crueler mistreatment. During a rehearsal for a play, for example, a group of elementary school boys insisted that Lynn hold their sleeves rather than their hands. At first, Douglas and Gloria Bates tried to minimize the incident, suggesting that perhaps it had had nothing to do with race, that maybe the boys were simply being naughty. But Lynn quickly disabused them of that comforting hypothesis: the boys, she told them, had "said that they didn't want to get African cooties."[28] Some of the white girls were just as mean. In the fourth grade, a group of them threatened to beat Lynn if, in the bathroom, she used anything other than the one toilet with a black, as opposed to a white, seat. Lynn recalled that even after she complied with their commands, "these girls would crawl up on the adjacent stalls and look down at me and start laughing and making fun of the black girl on the 'black' toilet."[29] This behavior stopped only after Gloria Bates barged into the school to police the situation.

Neither Lynn nor Liska distinguished herself academically—but then neither did either of the Bates boys. When they got older, unfortunately, the girls repeatedly made disastrous romantic decisions, which mired them in destructive relationships and left them with babies whom they were ill prepared to raise. Soon after graduating from high school, Lynn got pregnant by a man to whom she stayed married for only a brief period. Her stated reasons for having a baby at such a young age were achingly poignant: "I wanted to feel like I belonged to someone, genetically, and that they belonged to me—having the same blood running down their backbone and sharing the same facial features. . . . When I gave birth . . . I felt that physical bond for the first time in my life."[30]* Liska, too, became pregnant shortly after she finished high school. Not only did she have the baby without benefit of marriage to the father, but she moved to Los Angeles to live with another man. This new lover, Bernard Lee, promised to marry her and adopt her baby, but he failed to follow through on either pledge. That failure should not have been difficult to anticipate: according to Bates, Lee was an unemployed, drug-abusing, and violent ex-convict who had fathered a child named Stink by a drug-addicted prostitute.

After Liska eventually walked out on him, Lee threatened to kill her family. In one of several messages he left on the Bateses' telephone answering machine, he reportedly said, "Go ahead, Liska. Care about them white motherfuckers up there. Care about them when you go to their funeral. 'Cause like I said, I'm for real. Okay? I'm for real. And I know where you're at."[31] In another message, he ranted, "Liska you think your ass gonna hide behind one of those white motherfuckers? Call a white man daddy? What kind of motherfuckin' shit is that? Suppose to be my bitch, callin' this white motherfucker daddy. He ain't your daddy. He don't give a fuck about you."[32] Douglas Bates sought police protection, and he also engaged in self-help, purchasing a twelve-gauge shotgun. Lee never did pay his threatened visit to the Bates house, but had he done so, Bates was by his own account prepared to use deadly force to protect his family.

In certain respects, Douglas Bates's book bolsters the case *for* race matching. He and his wife at times seem to have been appallingly ignorant about white racism, and their daughters undoubtedly paid a price

---

*In the view of Ann Kimble Loux, "It makes perfect sense that so many adopted children yearn to procreate and are often successful in their teens. These young people know nothing of their own roots; naturally, they want to create blood kin and a history of their own" (*The Limits of Hope*, 128).

for their racial isolation in schools and neighborhoods. *Gift Children* convincingly argues, moreover, that one contributing cause of Liska's blind attraction to Bernard Lee was the parochialism of her upbringing: "In our community of one hundred thousand," Bates wrote, "with barely a sprinkling of people of color, Liska had never met anyone quite like [him]."[33] Bereft of the sort of practical instruction that might have immunized her against Lee's infectious influence, Liska had little resistance and caught a bad case of infatuation.

The author recognized that he and his wife had been slow to seek assistance and unsophisticated in their methodology. He confessed, too, that he sometimes questioned the wisdom of the commitment they had made that long-ago day in the pet shop:

> Why, I wondered, did our daughters—long after their teenage years—continue so desperately to turn toward men for their sense of identity and self-esteem? Was it born of their formative years prior to adoption? Were they subconsciously searching for the love they felt was missing in their lives? Were they acting out personality traits that Gloria and I had destructively and unwittingly instilled in them through clumsy parenting? Or was it all a reaction to the roiling forces of race, gender, and biology in the transracial adoption they had experienced?[34]

*Gift Children* also presents, however, compelling testimony that should inspire the defenders of interracial adoption. When Liska and Lynn needed significant outlays of parental love, engagement, counsel, protection, forgiveness, or money, Douglas and Gloria Bates appear to have given unstintingly. Indeed, they seem to have devoted more energy and resources to their adopted than to their biological children and, in doing so, demonstrated a measure of generosity even beyond that required by the obligations of parenthood.

Finally, Douglas Bates's memoir offers the voice of a white adoptive parent of black children who is unembarrassed and unafraid to declare that ultimately, in matters of parenting, racial knowledge is less important than personal commitment; that the interracial aspect of such an adoption may be a source of strength and benefits, not solely one of discord and difficulty; and that what parentless children need most of all is not someone who looks like them but someone who *loves* them. Bates refrained from claiming that transracial adoptions were preferable to same-race adoptions, but neither did he concede—as so many white adoptive parents of colored children have done—that same-race placements should be privileged over interracial ones. Reflecting on his own family's experience, Bates wrote:

> Through the adoption of Lynn and Liska, we moved beyond [integration] and achieved assimilation—and not the . . . unilateral kind affecting only blacks. For us the process cut both ways with whites changing, too. Over twenty-three years, two African American girls grew up with a special under-standing of both races, black and white, and with a valuable ability to function in both worlds, bridging two cultures. At the same time, their lives touched those [of their white adoptive kin] who "grew up" along with Lynn and Liska. In our family, relationships have transcended race.[35]

Generalizing from his particular history, Bates asserted that interracial adoptions "are an acceptable alternative and should not be outlawed or even restricted."[36]

Some readers will, of course, blame the Bates girls' problems largely on their interracial upbringing. But those who would embrace that position should acknowledge that many black adoptive and biological parents have also found themselves impotently witnessing the self-destruction of their troubled children. And before confidently pinning the blame for black adoptees' later difficulties on their adoption by white parents, readers should also consider other possibilities, including preadoption traumas, the endemic social seductions that entice young people from all sorts of family backgrounds, and the pressures brought to bear or magnified by external disapproval of interracial households.

Sobering though Douglas Bates's memoir may be, it is hardly an account of unrelieved failure. In closing, it offers glimpses of redemption and renewal, as it shows both Liska and Lynn pursuing education and job training and establishing new relationships with men who appear to be solid and respectful. "My spouse and I have no illusions about tidy, fairy-tale endings," concluded Bates,

> and life continues to mix our blessings with setbacks. . . . But we have a surprising store of resilience, and we still have plenty of determination and hope. Granted, like the country as a whole, we've realized that some of our dreams for our children have not come true. So we're making new dreams. And rather than wallowing in our disappointments, we're choosing instead to look ahead with optimism, rejoicing in how far we've come as a family.[37]

Jana Wolff, the author of *Secret Thoughts of an Adoptive Mother*, is a married white Jewish woman who found, after multiple technology-assisted attempts, that she and her white Jewish spouse were unable to conceive a child. They pursued adoption and were immediately confronted by racial choices they had never before considered. In Wolff's words:

> The intrusively thorough application forms presented options like they were menu items—healthy, or other than healthy; white, or other than white; newborn, or other than newborn—but we knew that our responses would dictate our options. If we chose "white, healthy, newborn," our wait would be years; if we chose "other than white, less than healthy, other than newborn," we could have a baby within weeks.[38]

Wolff and her husband indicated that while they wanted a healthy infant, they "didn't feel a strong need to be matched by race or features."[39]* Their willingness, she wrote,

---

*Wolff's memoir does not make clear whether, apart from what they communicated to others, she and her husband had any personal racial preference. This seems a notable ambiguity, given the attentiveness to racial matters evinced in other parts of the book.

to parent a child of a different race had more to do with naïveté than with altruism. . . . . We didn't understand that we might be taking on a job even bigger than parenting . . . that of transmitting a culture that was not ours. We simply knew that we wanted a baby, we believed that we would be good parents, and we presumed we could love any color. Naïveté served us well in expediting our application and expanding our adoption options.[40]

An attorney contacted by the Wolffs soon put them in touch with a pregnant teenager, who wanted to meet with them before deciding whether she would allow them to adopt her unborn baby. The girl was Mexican American; the "biracial" boy who had impregnated her but now wanted nothing to do with their child was a senior in high school, the star of the football team, and the class valedictorian. As the Wolffs understood it, the baby was expected to be "half Hispanic, a quarter African American, and a quarter Caucasian."[41]* They flew to Los Angeles from Hawaii to meet the pregnant teenager. This display of their seriousness (and their affluence) perhaps paid off, for the girl chose them to adopt her child. A couple of months later, they returned to California to be with the teenager through her labor and delivery. A few days after the birth, when the legal formalities had been taken care of, the Wolffs took their baby son home.

The third of the memoirists, Sharon Rush, produced an account that is quite dissimilar from Wolff's in a number of respects. Unlike Wolff, Rush has remained silent about the origins of her adopted child. Also unlike Wolff, she has declined to reveal what lay behind her desire to adopt. And Rush, again unlike Wolff, is a single parent. In other ways, however, the two women seem strikingly similar. Both have stressed that interracial adoption opened their eyes to a world of

---

*The designation of "Hispanics" as a distinct "race" is of relatively recent vintage and continues to be attended by controversy. After all, there are many who view themselves as African American Hispanics or Caucasian Hispanics. See Peter Skerry, *Counting on the Census: Race, Group Identity, and the Evasion of Politics* (2000), 37–40; Orlando Patterson, "Race by the Numbers," *New York Times,* May 8, 2001.

antiblack racism about which they had previously been utterly ignorant. "I've evolved," Wolff has declared, "from an unenlightened white
woman who thought that all people should be treated equally, to an
enlightened one, who knows they are not."[42] Echoing that sentiment,
Rush has related that in her "predaughter days," she "did not realize
that [her] White liberal views on race and race relations were inadequate to comprehend how profound and pervasive racial inequality is
in our society."[43] Douglas Bates likewise emphasized what appears to
be an almost universal phenomenon for white adoptive parents of
black children, noting the extraordinary extent to which he suddenly
found himself face-to-face with prejudices to which he had until then
been oblivious. Wolff and Rush, however, have expended more effort
than Bates on documenting the prejudices they and their children
encountered.

Perhaps unsurprisingly, it is Rush, a law professor at the University
of Florida, who has offered the most detailed and most far-reaching
indictment of the three. Some of her harshest criticism is reserved for
those who ostensibly "mean well":

> Almost without exception, when I tell a White person that
> [my daughter] is African American, the person responds, "Oh,
> but she doesn't look it," or "But you'd never know." Moreover,
> if the person is a woman, she inevitably grabs my arms as she
> makes her remarks, a typical behavior among women signify-
> ing sympathy (as in, "Oh, I'm so sorry to hear that").[44]

For Rush, such remarks "are deeply offensive because they imply that
being African American is something to be ashamed of and that if
people knew the truth about my daughter, she would no longer be
beautiful and people also would think less of her." It is her belief, moreover, that racial prejudice exacerbated the case of bureaucratic inertia
that temporarily kept her daughter out of a public school program for
gifted children. According to Rush, she never would have been admitted without aggressive parental intervention, and even then, after her
belated acceptance made her the only black child in the program, she
continued to face invidious racial discrimination. Upon visiting the

school, Rush discovered, for example, that her child had been shoved to the back of the classroom, virtually out of sight. As she described the scene, "The only Black child in the class was stuck off in the corner, behind a desk she could not see over and no one could see . . . behind."[45] In this and other instances (for example, when her daughter was erroneously accused of theft at an airport), Rush inferred a racial bias from circumstantial evidence. But sometimes the racial—indeed, the *racist*—basis of hurtful actions or words was explicit, as on one occasion when, in Rush's own home, a family friend of her father's bemoaned the presence of "niggers" in his neighborhood.[46]

As portrayed in their memoirs, Bates, Wolff, and Rush do what we wish all parents would do: protect, nurture, and teach their young. They offer their children a guiding, steadying, comforting hand, rebuke those who say hurtful things to them, and fight to make sure they are never shortchanged for any reason at all, much less because of racism. They acquaint their children with other people and with institutions, books, and rituals, in the hope that these resources will impart learning, happiness, and a decent sense of self-regard. As long as Douglas Bates, Jana Wolff, and Sharon Rush draw breath, their children will likely enjoy the great privilege of having access to someone who will love them no matter what.

The apparent parental virtues of these memoirists, however, do not in themselves guarantee the merit of either their interpretations of events or their policy prescriptions. For one thing, like many black parents of black children, Wolff and Rush (as far as we can judge from their books) suffer from a surfeit of suspicion that causes them to rely overmuch on racism as an explanation for every insult and injury. For them, virtually anything bad or disappointing that happens to their children, if whites are in any way involved, must be related to race. "Loving my son as I do," Wolff has written,

> I have become an acute barometer of bias: I notice where race makes a difference, and I can't find a place where it doesn't. Attuned to the slightest suggestion of discrimination and prejudice, in even the most innocent and mundane places, my antennae are always up. I've seen racism on playgrounds, in

swimming pools, in glances, in books, on applications, and at the doctor's office.[47]

Wolff's anxious vigilance is understandable, given the significant presence of antiblack prejudice within American society. Still, certain of her charges seem overwrought. Among the examples of "friendly racism" listed in her memoir, for instance, is a question put to her son by other children, who ask how he can be black when his mother is white. To be sure, that query must have became a bore for the Wolffs, and it is one that can, under some circumstances, be posed in a denigrating fashion. But it can also be posed innocently, with no hint of conscious or unconscious animus, a question arising out of simple curiosity—after all, it *is* quite unusual to see a white mother with a black son. The latter interpretation is surely plausible, especially if the questioner is a young child. Yet Wolff seemingly dismissed this possibility out of hand, asserting instead that "racism . . . is never innocuous, no matter how slight or unintentional"—as if it were self-evident that the very question itself constituted a species of "racism" in the first place.[48] Rush, for her part, took a slightly more sophisticated approach in her accounting, at least signaling her awareness of competing explanations for ambiguous events. Here, too, however, racism invariably emerges as *the* explanation of choice for the problems faced by her child. For Rush, racism is as ubiquitous as the wind: "I approach each day," she has asserted, "genuinely hoping [that] it will be a good one for [my daughter] and that however the day's racism decides to evidence itself will be only 'mildly' hurtful. Some days are better than others on the racism barometer."[49]

In both Wolff and Rush, one can discern a curious combination of hubris and self-doubt. Both obviously felt sufficiently confident of their perceptions to write books presumably intended to contribute to the emotional and contentious debate over interracial adoption; and both have applauded their own self-measured progress from naïveté to wisdom. At the same time, and much more disturbingly, both have engaged in vigorous self-denigration by essentially assimilating large portions of the myth of race matching. One chapter in Wolff's memoir, for example, is entitled "Whites Raising Blacks: Good Intentions, Bad

Qualifications."[50] White parents, for Wolff, are limited by an "inherent inadequacy . . . to teach their children of color about [black culture]."[51] Bemoaning what seemed to her the inevitable absence of authenticity in whatever she and her husband did to inculcate in their son a good sense of racial identity, Wolff averred, "We can read about Langston Hughes and march in the Martin Luther King Jr. parade. We can visit the First Baptist Church for the Kwanza celebration, role-play the story of Amazing Grace, and talk about prejudice; but it is not enough. It is not enough because it is not the real thing. . . . We are ultimately inadequate dispensers of racial wisdom."[52]* Rush has managed to be even more self-deprecating in her account. Beyond echoing Wolff's claims about the inherent inadequacy of white parents, Rush has insisted that whites—*all* whites, herself included—are racist. "I am racist," she has maintained, "because I am part of the institution of white privilege."[53]† Rush has also unequivocally embraced race matching.[54] It is "undoubtedly true," according to her, that "a Black child will have a greater understanding of his or her racial identity if he or she is raised by Black parents."[55] Similarly, in her opinion, "Black parents can affirm and provide security about a Black child's identity in ways that a White parent cannot."[56] She has thus concluded that "transracial adoptions should be last resorts."[57] For Rush, the placement of her daughter in her care—in the care of *any* white adult—was defensible only in the absence of a better option, in the form of a readily available black adoptive parent.

Nothing more poignantly reflects the continuing grip of racialist superstition on American society than the myopia of Sharon Rush, Jana Wolff, and others who, despite their own fruitful experiences with interracial parenting, have conceded and continue to concede—

---

*Despite having trumpeted her sense of inadequacy, Wolff has hesitated to assign herself mere "better than nothing" status. "I love [my son] too much to believe," she has written, "that he'd have been better off with other parents." Still, in her words, "I can understand such an unthinkable thought" (*Secret Thoughts of an Adoptive Mother* [1997], 138).
†That all whites are racist is a popular idea in certain precincts. See, e.g., Gail Steinberg and Beth Hall, *Inside Transracial Adoption* (2000), 291: "There are only two kinds of white people: racists and racists in recovery."

wrongly—that opponents of the practice are correct in claiming that whites, because of their race, are *necessarily* either inadequate as caretakers of black children or inferior to black parents. A large part of the problem is the vulnerability of people such as Wolff and Rush to destructive mau-mauing. Rush in particular has evinced a pathetic inability to criticize any idea emanating from anyone whom she perceives to be authentically black. In her book, there are no bad black people, no unsound decisions made by blacks, and no questionable policies advanced by black groups. By her accounting, whites are the only ones whose behavior is in need of improvement. A long list of episodes is recited in which whites said ugly things to her or her daughter, but not one instance of a black person doing so is described. Perhaps Rush's memoir is an accurate depiction of what she and her child experienced; if so, it seems to me that they were lucky. Many interracial adoptive households have suffered all manner of ostracism at the hands of disapproving blacks—from placards of protest in the yards of neighbors to raucous picketing, from harsh words to reproachful silence.[58] This attendant feature of interracial adoption is all too common and well known, yet there is no mention of it in Rush's account.

By any logic, any white adoptive parent of a black child who writes a memoir about the experience would seem duty-bound to confront the NABSW. Yet the closest Rush has come to doing so is to suggest—not directly but merely by implication—that race matching, if taken too far, might impose excessive costs upon parentless black children. For Rush, "Both sides in the [interracial adoption] debate have meritorious arguments."[59] Such fearful equivocation is painful to read. Rush has written movingly of her love for her daughter and the potential of interracial relationships to generate knowledge and emotions that are socially beneficial. She has taken a forthright stand against white racism. Yet in the face of black contempt for interracial loving, she has been virtually mute. Both Rush and Wolff have so internalized the myths of white parental inferiority that they have felt compelled repeatedly to minimize their own contribution and potential. In reviewing the effects of the adoption on her own existence, Wolff has cited two consequences, one negative and one positive. The negative is that the interracial aspect of her family has made her life more difficult; the positive is that it has made her life richer. In discussing how the situation has affected her son, however, she has noted only the negative, evidently unwilling even to consider the possibility that for him, too, being raised in the unconventional environment of an interracial household might offer added benefits alongside those added costs.[60]

For her part, Rush has asserted that her child "would benefit from having a Black parent in her life. . . . A Black parent would be able to understand her pain of racism in ways that I still cannot articulate. Perhaps this deeper connectedness would empower my own daughter in ways I do not understand."[61] Given her confession of ignorance on such matters, it seems curious that Rush should state so confidently what a black parent would know and do. After all, on what basis could she possibly claim such certainty? But more to the point is the context of this troubling assessment. Rush has here subordinated her own knowledge and abilities not to a specific individual with known qualities but to an abstract, unnamed generality—"a Black parent"—who, as particularized in any of many millions of personas, might be wholly lacking in useful knowledge about "the pain of racism," or the best ways of productively managing it, or, most important of all, the art of parenting.

It should by now be clear to readers that I strongly disagree with Wolff and Rush on crucial questions of culture, law, politics, and parenting. Nevertheless, I support their right to adopt children regardless of their race. Moreover, I support their right to adopt interracially without first having to convince child-welfare authorities that they will raise their children in a manner that is "racially appropriate." This is, as I noted previously, a critical issue.* Some opponents of interracial adoption have begun to use "cultural competency" as a new and ostensibly nonracial justification for precluding, delaying, or otherwise disfavoring such placements. Now, instead of objecting to white adoptive parents on account of their race, these opponents are simply pronouncing them culturally incompetent to raise black children—or in any case, less competent than blacks. Even some stalwart defenders of interracial

---

*See pages 441–46.

adoption are so anxious about this supposed cultural deficit that they insist that white prospective parents of black children must demonstrate some minimal appreciation of the importance of race in modern American life. To meet cultural-competency requirements, many whites who wish to adopt black children are moving to racially integrated neighborhoods, cultivating friendships with black colleagues, worshiping at predominantly black churches, and eliciting instruction from "experts" on blackness and interraciality.

Some of the activity sparked by the new concern over cultural competency is positive in that it encourages at least some whites to learn useful things or think about important issues that they might otherwise have overlooked. One major problem here, however, is that the concern is racially parochial inasmuch as it is typically triggered only in the context of a white person's efforts to adopt a black child. If cultural competency is so essential, why not require it of *all* adoptive parents, black as well as white? The presumption is, of course, that as a matter of racial grace, black adults necessarily know what should be communicated to black children. But many blacks are, like many whites, woefully ill informed about black history, naive regarding the social inequities blacks face, and ignorant with respect to matters that some experts consider essential. Yet the proponents of cultural-competency standards never broach the idea of subjecting black adoptive parents of black children to such testing. Their selectivity is by no means accidental: the application of cultural-competency standards to blacks as well as whites would raise to the level of political controversy such knotty questions as precisely what should be tested, what should constitute an acceptable answer, and how to demarcate passing and failing. (Imagine what would happen if more whites than blacks passed a cultural-competency test for parenting black children!) Until and unless such testing can be rendered transparent and fair, the suspicion will (and should) persist that cultural competency is not the real object of concern but is instead a proxy for continuing anxiety over the prospect of whites parenting black children.

———

The reader comes away from their memoirs with the impression that J. Douglas Bates, Jana Wolff, and Sharon Rush are good, generous, intelligent people who have succeeded in doing something that warrants high praise: affording parentless youngsters a better chance in life than they otherwise would have had. That these white people crossed racial lines to adopt redoubles the praise they are due. But much needed now are people who not only will cross racial lines but will do so unapologetically, adamantly refusing to espouse the racial myth of white parental inferiority. One such defiant soul is Albert J. Reynolds. In a letter to the editor published in the *Des Moines Register,* Reynolds wrote, "I am a white man with a white wife, and thirty-three years ago we adopted a five-day-old black baby girl. She grew up with six siblings, all white. Today she is a vice president with Morgan Stanley Dean Witter. . . . Tell me this marvelous young woman is somehow handicapped and I'll laugh in your face and throw you off my porch."[62] If interracial adoption is to flourish, more participants and supporters must follow Reynolds's example. They will have to do more than merely defend such placements as a second-rate alternative to same-race adoptions; they will have to attest to the still-neglected potential of multiracial adoptive families—a potential for love and triumph that is no less compelling than the seed of possibility nurtured by any other sort of family.

The voices of the adoptees themselves have rarely been heard in the debate over white-black interracial adoption. This is largely because only recently have an appreciable number reached the age at which they can articulate for themselves—with some adult perspective—their thoughts and feelings about not only their upbringing but also public policy in this area. The contending sides are now vying for their support. The proponents of race matching like nothing better than to cite a black adoptee raised by white parents who maintains that same-race adoptions are preferable. Similarly, opponents of race matching are thrilled when they can quote "graduates" of transracial adoptions who express satisfaction with their upbringing and decry racial discrimination in the placement of parentless children. Some adoptees raised in interracial settings promote the notion that their background has made them authorities on the subject. One declares, for example, that transracial adoptees "*are* the experts, just from our experience."[63] Another labels the remarks of adoptees "the most authentic testimony of all."[64] And some observers will be tempted to defer to these witnesses because they bear a supposed "authority of experience." One difficulty, however, lies in determining which of them to defer to, since adoptees' opinions conflict. An even more fundamental challenge consists in deciphering, evaluating, and making use of the asset that is deemed to endow adoptees with their special wisdom—namely, their experience. In reading memoirs and other accounts by adoptees, one encounters not the raw experience of interracial adoption but rather an interpretation of it. The interpretation may be limited by ignorance—much about their childhood and upbringing, after all, remains unknown to children—or distorted by any of the many contingencies that can influence us all, including the desire to offend or to refrain from offending, the wish to buttress or undercut a given policy, and the ability or inability to break free of learned responses to certain stimuli.

Taken together, memoirs, oral interviews, journalistic accounts, and sociological investigations suggest that few adoptees feel interracial adoptions ought to be categorically prohibited. A substantial number, however, do believe that same-race placements are preferable and that special measures should be taken to facilitate such placements, even if it means delaying some adoptions. In this context, we may consider the argument of Asher D. Isaacs, who was born to a white mother and a black father.[65] When he was eighteen months old, Isaacs was adopted by "a white Jewish family" who lived in a largely white suburb of Buffalo. "My adoptive parents," Isaacs has written, "believed that the world should be color blind, so they raised me in the same way as they did their three biological children."[66] According to Isaacs, "My family never addressed the fact that my skin was brown or my hair curly. Nor did they discuss with me social and political issues relating to the African-American community. My parents did not see a need to expose me to Black culture, history, or role models."[67] In Isaacs's view, his upbringing caused him profound injury. In high school, he recalled, "I simply denied my African-American heritage. I longed to be fully white . . . and I silently cursed my nose, lips, hair and skin color."[68] Isaacs excelled in ways that made him an attractive candidate to colleges. He maintained an A average and was senior-class president and first clarinetist in the all-county band. Part of that success, though, was purchased at the price of condoning racism. White friends would make bigoted antiblack remarks in his presence and then turn to him and tell him they did not think of *him* as being black. That gesture was sufficient mollification, for Isaacs, by his own admission, "took pride in not being considered black."[69]

Isaacs went on to attend Colgate University, where his college years were characterized by alienation ("I developed an intense feeling of not fitting in with either Blacks or whites"), embarrassment ("I made every effort to disassociate myself from [the Black] community because I did not want to be identified as Black"), and anguish. "I cannot fully describe," he has written, "the feelings of loneliness and shame that I felt while sitting in a room of white students with whom I felt I identified and enduring the silence that follow[ed] when someone used the term 'nigger' before realizing that I was present."[70] Because of such incidents, he began to avoid the white students, but at the same time, he felt isolated from his fellow blacks.

Not only did this sense of marginality preclude the possibility of any deep and lasting sense of happiness for Isaacs; it also adversely affected his collegiate activities. In his words:

> Instead of believing in myself . . . I became withdrawn. I did not readily participate in class or take part in extra-curricular activities because of my insecurity and confusion about my racial identity. Although I learned that we simply do not live in a "color blind" world, I felt that I had no one to turn to in order to help me understand what it meant to be an African American man in our society.[71]

To Isaacs's mind, this unease was a legacy of his upbringing: "Being raised by a family that did not appreciate the significance of racial differences and the importance of developing a positive racial identity in a black child left me unprepared to face the complexities of being an African-American male." He has credited his salvation to meeting "someone who shared my biracial heritage and who helped me begin developing a positive racial identity." With this person's assistance, he explained, "I developed friendships with other Blacks. I also began to read African-American history and literature—something to which I had never been exposed." Through these friendships and his belated immersion in black culture, Isaacs "learned to appreciate the sense of community that exists among African-Americans and . . . realized that I am a welcome and needed member of the community."

Moved to action by his own experience, and armed with a legal education obtained at the UCLA School of Law, Isaacs penned a detailed account of one interracial adoption—his own—then prescribed what, for him, would constitute proper racial regulation of such placements. "All Black children," according to him, "need to develop a positive racial identity in order to value themselves and their identity rather than succumb to racism and prejudice which may lead them to feel inadequate or inferior regardless of their individual accomplishments."[72] To meet this need, Isaacs proposed a model statute pursuant to which preference for adoption would be given in the following order:

> (a) relatives, (b) families of the same race or ethnicity as the child, (c) families of a different racial or ethnic heritage that demonstrate awareness, understanding, and appreciation of [the] child's racial heritage and a willingness to promote positive racial or ethnic identity in the child, and finally (d) families willing to develop such awareness, understanding, and appreciation through counseling[,] including training in how to promote the child's racial or ethnic identity.[73]

To prevent excessive delays in moving children from institutional or foster care to adoption, Isaacs advocated the imposition of a twelve-month time limit for authorities to arrange either an adoption by relatives or a same-race placement.

While Isaacs has disclaimed "contend[ing] that any family, Black or white, is more or less able to love and care for any child,"[74] his argument seems to be precisely that black adults are better able than whites to care for black children. In any case, for him, the central point is that "love is not enough": black children have special needs in our race-conscious world, he has asserted, and *all* of those needs must be addressed, not just some of them. Thus, in Isaacs's opinion, if black families are available to adopt black children, they should be given preference in adoption—in the interest of the black child.[75]*

Isaacs's criticism of his upbringing and his embrace of moderate race matching are by no means unusual among that small cadre who identify themselves as African American or biracial veterans of interracial adoption. A number of them are represented in *In Their Own Voices* (2000), a compilation of first-person accounts organized and transcribed by Rita J. Simon and Rhonda M. Roorda.[76] *In Their Own Voices* features interviews conducted from 1996 to 1998 with twenty-four adoptees, most of whom were then between the ages of twenty-two and thirty-one. Like Isaacs, several of the interviewees recounted excruciating episodes of racism or racial isolation. In the Chicago suburb to which Donna Francis was taken as an infant in 1971, for example, neighbors expressed their disapproval of her adoptive parents' racial unorthodoxy by sending them hate mail and burning a cross on their lawn. Kimberly Stapert related a painful memory from her child-

---

*Echoing Isaacs, Rachel Noerdlinger, an African American raised by Euro Americans, has charged that she "should have been better prepared [by her parents] for the real world." Insisting that interracial adoption ought to be only "a last resort," Noerdlinger has held that while "love should be enough, love does not prepare an African American child for the society we live in. And love does not replace the importance of knowing your own ethnicity and culture" ("A Look at . . . Interracial Adoption: A Last Resort; The Identity My White Parents Couldn't Give Me," *Washington Post*, June 30, 1996). See also Sue Anne Pressley, "Texas Interracial Adoption Case Reflects National Debate; Family Waged a Legal Fight for 2 Black Youngsters," January 2, 1997, *New York Times* (quoting biracial social worker raised by adoptive white family: "It's a bad idea to put a black child in a white home. . . . It's impossible for someone of one culture to teach another culture. . . . You have to live it in order to absorb it").

hood in Grand Rapids, Michigan, in the late 1970s: "I was playing with some neighborhood kids who were white. There was dog poop on the ground and they said I was the color of poop, that black people are the color of poop. That was really, really hurtful. I remember feeling small and ashamed."[77]

Several of the interviewed adoptees, again like Isaacs, articulated a deep sense of regret. One remarked that she always felt "half-baked. There's never a feeling of accomplishment or achievement or that it's all coming together for me. The piece that seems to be missing is my blackness."[78]

Some of the adoptees quoted in *In Their Own Voices* echoed Isaacs's strong support for race matching and cultural-competency requirements. Among them was Donna Francis, whose adoptive white parents were targeted by the cross burnings mentioned above. On a personal level, Francis voiced nothing but fondness for the couple who took her in: "Never within my family," in her words, "have I ever felt uncomfortable or out of place or not fully their daughter."[79] Yet in the larger context, she favored race matching. "I believe," she avowed, "that a black child should, if possible, be placed with a black family or a black single mother or a black single father as long as it is a stable household."[80] She conceded that if "there are no black adults willing or able to adopt then I would rather have that child with a family who loves the child rather than in foster care," but insisted that "if a black child is placed with a white family, the family needs to go through more than the typical steps in the adoption process. . . . White parents need to understand that they cannot treat a black child like a white child. They need to expose the child to his or her culture. These families need extra training." She had reached this conclusion after seeing "a lot of kids who have been transracially adopted, and [who] are very confused. These kids do not like being black. . . . They would rather be white."

Also coming down on this side of the debate was Jessica Pelton, who grew up in a multiracial international family in West Rupert, Vermont. One brother was the biological child of Pelton's white adoptive parents, another brother was an adopted Korean American, and an adopted sister was biracial (meaning, evidently, half white and half black). Much though she loved her parents—indeed, her entire family—Pelton was unable to "look fondly upon white people adopting non-white children."[81] This attitude reflected her sense that despite the valiant efforts of her parents, she had paid dearly for growing up in a white household: the price was confusion, isolation, and low self-esteem. Asked what associations she had with the phrase "transracial adoption," Pelton replied, "Difference. Self-identity. Frustration. Anger. Loneliness."[82]

Nicolle Yates was another interviewee who simultaneously lauded her white adoptive parents and advocated race matching. Yates grew up in York, Pennsylvania, as one of fifteen youngsters parented by a couple who had been active supporters of the civil rights movement. Three were the couple's biological children; the other twelve were adopted. "I believe," Yates declared, "that love transcends all racial barriers." She cited her own family, moreover, as proof that "race does not have to be a negative issue."[83] Still, she held that "Black kids need to learn coping skills to maneuver successfully in a racist world. Who better to teach them than adults who faced it themselves[?]"[84] Poignantly grappling with the facts of her own upbringing, Yates concluded, "If I didn't know my parents and love them, I'd choose a black family."[85] Why?

> Primarily because of all the time I spent obsessing about my identity and where I fit in. Also, in dealing with racist issues, my adoptive parents couldn't give me a clear perspective from their experiences of how I was to understand what I was feeling. My parents could sympathize with me over what I endured because of my race, but they couldn't empathize with me.

Like some of her fellow interviewees, Yates nonetheless rejected the notion of barring interracial adoptions categorically: "I'd rather someone ended up confused but had the opportunity to grow up in a loving family regardless of race, than for that child to remain in foster care all his or her childhood."[86] Interracial adoption, in her view, should be an available option, but the ideal would always be a black family for a black child.[87]

How should opponents of race matching respond to such testimony? The first point to stress is that opinion is divided. Of the twenty-four interviewees in *In Their Own Voices,* not one was unequivocally opposed to interracial adoption under any circumstances. Thirteen were in favor of what I have described as moderate race matching—namely, a policy of preferring same-race adoptions so long as they can be arranged without excessive delay. At least one other seemed altogether conflicted on the issue. When the interviewers solicited his thoughts on transracial adoption, a man identified only as Ned at first responded, "A big part of me says it's fantastic. I know for a fact that my parents love me and raised me to the best of their ability and that I had fabulous opportunities. I love my parents and get along well with them. I also feel confident that this same kind of situation could happen for countless others."[88] Yet later, when asked, "Do you support the [NABSW's] view that transracial adoption is not in the best interest of the black child, that indeed it is cultural genocide?," he answered, "A part of me affiliates strongly with that. I understand that argument and even agree with it."[89]

Eight of the interview subjects contended (with varying degrees of clarity) that race matching was bad policy.[90] One of the eight, Laurie Goff, felt that "people should stop being so stressed about the issue. Kids need to be adopted. There's a six-year waiting list for white children. If you want to adopt a black child or a Hispanic child or any child of color, these kids are ready to be adopted. Because many social workers and others in the community have a problem with transracial adoption, these kids lose out."[91] Unlike those other adoptees who complained about the interracial aspect of their upbringing, Goff declared, "My experiences having been adopted into a white family have been fabulous. . . . I was incredibly lucky to have been adopted into a family that adores me. That's the bottom line. It doesn't matter what the color of your skin is. What matters is whether the people who adopt you are willing to sacrifice their lives for you."[92] Asserting that "no family is perfect," Goff urged others in similar situations to "be happy with what they have and not let other people depress them by saying it's hard to be adopted by white people. Saying that is evil and wrong."

Likewise upbeat about interracial adoption was Rhonda Roorda, the coeditor of *In Their Own Voices* and herself such an adoptee. Born to African Americans, Roorda was initially placed in an African American foster home, where she remained for two years. She was subsequently adopted by a white couple who reared her in the predominantly white Maryland and Virginia suburbs of Washington, D.C. To the question "Are you glad that you were transracially adopted?" Roorda's answer was an emphatic yes: "I'm very thankful I was adopted transracially. I was given a permanent loving home and a solid foundation. It's so easy to harp on the difficulties and hold on to the negative experiences. But I believe that because I was transracially adopted, I had to confront issues of race and identity head on. I didn't have the option of being complacent."[93]*

Beyond the pages of *In Their Own Voices* are other people of color raised by white parents who defend—indeed, champion—interracial adoption. Kristen Albrecht has been one of the most energetic and outspoken of them. The director of the Transracial Adoption Group, Albrecht has credited cross-racial adoption with being "the most successful affirmative action program of the 1970's, putting a large number of black and biracial children into middle-class families."[94] Refusing to consign it to the status of a mere "second best alternative," Albrecht has instead praised interracial adoption as "an inherently good thing."

In addition to noting the plurality of views that people of color hold on this issue, proponents of interracial adoption must challenge the "authority of experience" that is all too often automatically conceded to those transracial adoptees who, as adults, support race matching.

---

*At another point in her interview, Roorda was asked whether she would have preferred to be adopted by black parents. She answered no but then almost immediately expressed her gratitude at having an African American godfamily (Rita J. Simon and Rhonda M. Roorda, eds., *In Their Own Voices: Transracial Adoptees Tell Their Stories* [2000], 213).

Far from lending persuasive force to their arguments, such veterans' autobiographical polemics exemplify the tendency of people to imagine, without due investigation, that the pastures of others must be greener than their own. Suffusing Asher Isaacs's account of his experiences as a transracial adoptee, for example, is a fanciful glorification of black families. By his reckoning, "Black homes . . . are best equipped to combat racism and help the Black child develop a positive racial identity. . . . [A] Black family, having personally experienced racism and prejudice, can help the child to cope with any negative experiences and can positively affirm the child's pride in her racial identity."[95]

It is true, of course, that there exist numerous exemplary black parents who do the wonderful things envisioned by Isaacs. But unfortunately, even assuming that all of the blacks who seek to adopt would make equally worthy parents, there are simply too few of them to accommodate the dismayingly large numbers of parentless black children in need of homes. Even if every unwarranted impediment to adoption were removed, there would still be a yawning gap between the supply of black adult adopters and the demand of black juvenile adoptees. And in any case, to be realistic, we must revise our overly rosy assumptions about the character of black parents, biological *and* adoptive. Many are truly praiseworthy, but an appreciable percentage—like a substantial percentage of white parents—leave much to be desired, if they are not entirely unfit. Isaacs's sunny, uncomplicated vision of black parents ignores certain negative features of black family life that have been repeatedly illuminated by an ideologically and methodologically diverse group of witnesses and participants.* Among these features are racial self-hatred, other dysfunctional responses to

---

*See, e.g., Orlando Patterson, *Rituals of Blood: Consequences of Slavery in Two American Centuries* (1998); Marguerite A. Wright, *I'm Chocolate, You're Vanilla: Raising Healthy Black and Biracial Children in a Race-Conscious World* (1998); M. Belinda Tucker and Claudia Mitchell-Kernan, eds., *The Decline in Marriage Among African Americans* (1995); Cornel West, *Race Matters* (1993); Michelle Wallace, *Black Macho and the Myth of the Superwoman* (1979); Daniel Patrick Moynihan, "The Case for National Action," in Lee Rainwater and W. L. Rainwater, eds., *The Moynihan Report and the Politics of Controversy* (1967); E. Franklin Frazier, *The Negro Family in the United States* (1939).

oppression, virulent forms of sexism and homophobia, and the perpetuation of self-defeating habits and customs. An observation made by
Professor Lee Rainwater in a classic 1966 article remains distressingly
apposite in 2002: "The caste-facilitated infliction of suffering by
Negroes on other Negroes and on themselves appears most poignantly
within the confines of the family. . . . The victimization process as it
operates in families prepares and toughens its members to function in
the ghetto world, at the same time that it seriously interferes with their
ability to operate in any other world."[96] Absent from the reasoning of
Isaacs and other interracial adoptees who embrace race matching is any
inkling that, largely as a consequence of racist oppression and other
burdens, a significant number of black parents may in fact be ill
equipped to pass on the values, skills, and experiences that many expect
of them as a matter of course. Isaacs has invoked a happy idyll in which
black "social support" groups spin a wholesome cocoon that will
swaddle the adoptive black child as he or she matures; the realities of
drug abuse, gangs, criminality, predatory sexual mores, and destructive
peer pressure are nowhere to be seen in this fantasy. Like many other
interracial adoptees who champion race matching, Isaacs has "exposed" the isolation, frustration, and anxiety he felt while growing up
in a white family—as if these and related difficulties did not confront all
sorts of children raised by all sorts of parents, not excluding black children brought up by black parents. Isaacs's argument posits that it was
the (purported) racial myopia of his white adoptive parents that caused
him the greatest emotional harm, particularly in terms of his racial self-
identity. But even granting the accuracy of his accusations, how could
he sensibly insist that he would have fared better emotionally with
black adoptive parents? He might well have fared worse. There is no
way of knowing.

The emergence of "rainbow families" formed by adoptions is a fascinating, poignant, encouraging landmark in the maturation of American
race relations. It is the story of adults of all backgrounds who have
decided to share their lives with vulnerable children. It is the story of

adults willing to do so even at the cost of having to cross racial lines that all too many still perceive as impassable frontiers. It is the story of progressive reform. Recall that not so long ago, officials in many parts of the United States openly and unapologetically denied adoptions across racial lines. Remember the plight of Jacqueline, the parentless child we met at the beginning of this book. Fortunately, to a large extent, the ideology and practice of both the old and the new styles of racial segregation in adoption have been formally repudiated and placed on the road to extinction. Unfortunately, resentments and myths akin to those that have primarily ensnared black children in race-matching regimes also ensnare Indian children. Worse, while race matching is generally on the defensive, it remains a large, potent, and *legitimate* presence with respect to Native Americans. The flawed premises on which the federal government continues to encourage, indeed require, race matching for Native American children are the subject of the next chapter.

## TWELVE

# Race, Children, and Custody Battles:
# The Special Status of Native Americans

In the United States, Indian children in need of foster care or adoptive homes fall under a different legal regime than prevails for all other children. The federal Indian Child Welfare Act (ICWA) not only permits but *requires* officials to attempt to match Native American children with Native American adults.[1] The act goes beyond merely recognizing the authority of Indian tribes to arranging adoptions or foster care on behalf of their juvenile members—an authority that rests upon the unique semisovereign status of federally registered tribes*—and actually *imposes* a matching requirement on states as a matter of federal law. ICWA's matching policy and several of the rationales used to justify it are ill conceived and counterproductive. The policy and its purported justifications decrease the likelihood that needy children will find adoptive homes, popularize hurtful superstitions, and reinforce claims that unfairly stigmatize substantial numbers of non-Indian adoptive parents. To correct these problems, Congress would do well to reform ICWA.[2]

---

*Nothing more vividly illustrates the tenuousness of Native American political authority than the fact that a tribe's legal status under federal law is determined by the United States government. Following a tradition established by European powers, the United States has constantly exercised its mastery over Native American political entities by arrogating to itself the power to name them, define them, and even construct their membership and leadership. See Felix Cohen, *Handbook of Federal Indian Law* (1982 ed.), 3–46; L. Scott Gould, "Mixing Bodies and Beliefs: The Predicament of Tribes," *Columbia Law Review* 101 (2001): 702, 718–26.

Indian tribes that are recognized by the United States occupy a singular place in the American legal system. Their relationship to the federal government and the states is complex, controversial, and ever changing. In general, though, recognized Indian tribes are regarded by United States courts as being "domestic dependent nations,"[3] ultimately subservient to the federal government but independent from state control (in the absence of federal law to the contrary) and endowed with a semisovereign status pursuant to which they may exercise governmental powers over their own members. The tribes are distinct political communities that, in the words of the Supreme Court, "have power to make their own substantive law in internal matters . . . and to enforce that law in their own forums."[4] Tribal law governs members of tribes in Indian country, except where it has been superseded by federal law. The Indians who constitute recognized tribes therefore possess a collective character that has no parallel in American life, as their territorial base, court systems, and political standing set them apart.[5]

Widely viewed by whites as an inferior colored race—"the Red man"—Native Americans have repeatedly been subjected to all manner of oppression, from massacres and forced migrations—what might now be termed "ethnic cleansing"—to exploitation, fraud on a massive scale, and degrading discriminations.[6*] The consequences have been devastating. By any number of revealing indices, Indians, especially those on reservations, typically fare poorly in comparison with non-Indians, particularly whites. In 1989 the average median income for Americans of all races was $30,056; the corresponding average for reservation Indians was $12,459. The average unemployment rate for Amer-

---

*The multiracial character of American history means, among other things, that whites are not the only ones who have engaged in racial oppression. Blacks have also participated in the subordination of other nonwhite peoples, including the subjugation of Indian tribes. See, e.g., Gail Buckley, *American Patriots: The Story of Blacks in the Military from the Revolution to Desert Storm* (2001), 110–62 (describing the black "Buffalo Soldiers" who helped the United States to conquer Indian nations). Blacks and Indians have also long been involved in cooperative, indeed loving, relationships. See *The Indian-Black Experience in North America,* James F. Brooks, ed. (2002). The conflicts and intimacies experienced by blacks and Indians is a subject warranting further study, publicity, and synthesis.

icans of all races was 6.3 percent; for reservation Indians, 25.6 percent. The average child poverty rate for Americans of all races was 13.1 percent; for reservation Indians, 50.7 percent. Among Americans of all races, 75.2 percent had graduated from high school; among reservation Indians, it was 53.8 percent. Among Americans of all races, a little over 5 percent lacked a telephone where they lived. Among reservation Indians, the figure was nearly 29 percent. Though the situation for Indians living outside of reservations is usually less distressing, it is clear that they, too, as a general matter, lag markedly in socioeconomic terms. As Professor David E. Wilkins writes, "The most reliable statistics we have paint a portrait of a Native America that remains largely mired in oppressive levels of poverty."[7]

Indian communal life consists of more than mere survival. Native Americans produce art, knowledge, and communities to which people of varied backgrounds turn for pleasure and enlightenment.[8] It cannot sensibly be denied, however, that destructive social vices, exacerbated by impoverishment and stigmatization, have taken a terrible toll: among Indians, suicide, alcoholism, child abuse, and the like are dismayingly prevalent.[9]

A peculiar duality characterizes the image of the Indian. Often cruelly stereotyped as "savages," Indians have also been romanticized as emblems of independence, free-spiritedness, and martial glory (in contrast to the widespread association of blacks with dependence, servility, and cowardice).[10] Yet paradoxically, even this relative privileging of Indians in the American pigmentocracy has resulted in injury. It encouraged efforts to assimilate them coercively, the single feature of their oppression that many Indians most abhor. One constant menace has been the effort to "save" Native Americans by stripping them of their "primitive" customs and forcing them to adopt the ways of white folk. In the late nineteenth century, for instance, Congress enacted legislation—the infamous Dawes Act—that unilaterally abolished many Indian tribal governments and broke up Indian reservations. The express purpose of the act was to demolish Indian communalism and thereby force Indians to become individualistic farmers, just like the white neighbors to whom they were compelled to sell their "surplus" land. Although the act was justified on humanitarian grounds, by people who sincerely believed that the Indians' tradition of collective landholding posed an impediment to their "progress;" and in practice the legislation robbed Indians and benefited whites. In 1887 Indian tribes collectively owned some 138 million acres; by 1934 they owned only about 48 million.[11]

The attack on Indian communal landholding was accompanied by other coercive strategies. On official documents in some locales, authorities substituted English names for Indian ones that were deemed to be too difficult for whites to pronounce.[12] In order to provide Indian children with a "proper" education, officials often removed them from what was perceived to be the "contamination" of their parents, native languages, and tribal customs. In many schools funded and managed by the federal government, instruction was limited to English, and harsh regulations explicitly forbade the use of any Indian tongue. Voicing a widely shared sentiment among whites, one commissioner of Indian Affairs declared in 1887 that "The first step to be taken toward civilization, toward teaching the Indians the mischief and folly of continuing in their barbarous practices, is to teach them the English language."[13]

In addition to coercive assimilationism, Native Americans have also had to battle a deep current of anti-Indian animus and contempt that has been manifested in actions and laws designed to *isolate* Native Americans. For example, the Virginia antimiscegenation law of 1691 that sought to prevent "abominable mixture and spurious issue" prohibited whites from marrying not only "negroes" or "mulattoes" but also Indians. Seven states would eventually proscribe marriage between whites and Indians.[14] Apart from formal ostracism, moreover, many informal stigmas have been affixed to Indians, an ugly fact of American life that is displayed in the use of such derogatory terms as "red nigger" and "timber nigger," which retain currency today as abusive epithets.[15]

Still, for all the smears they have had to endure, Native Americans as a group have also been credited with positive traits often denied to the Negro, including intelligence, bravery, nobility, and capacity for improvement. This explains in part why the marriage of Pocahontas and John Rolfe has remained a celebrated memory even for many who have been otherwise obsessed with protecting white racial purity; why several of America's most distinguished white statesmen (most notably Thomas Jefferson) championed the idea of amalgamation between Indians and whites;* and why there is a certain fashionableness, even glamour, in laying claim to Indian ancestry.

The racial reputation of Indians, particularly the perception that they are preferable to blacks, also accounts, in part, for the striking demographic differences that attend whites' association with both groups through marriage and adoption: Euro Americans have been much more likely to marry or adopt Native Americans than to marry or adopt African Americans.[16] Writing about white-Indian transracial adoption in 1960, a researcher noted that American Indian children possessed "special sources of appeal to prospective adoptive parents not available to children of other racial minorities." He observed that many whites regarded Indians with "unabashed admiration as truly 'the first Americans' or the only 'real' Americans."[17] The straight hair and light complexions of many Indian children also enhanced their value in the eyes of at least some white prospective adopters who wanted their charges to be able to pass as white. Asked whether he and his wife would consider adopting an Indian child, one participant in the Indian Adoption Project remarked: "[We] decided that it would be okay as long as the child would be light-skinned. . . . We did not want the child to be taken for part-Negro."[18]† In any event, a substantial

---

*To encourage white-Indian intermarriage in colonial Virginia, Patrick Henry proposed legislation that would have offered bounties for such matches and free public education for the progeny. Jefferson urged his fellow whites "to let our settlements and theirs meet and blend together, to intermix, and become one people." See Gary B. Nash, *Forbidden Love: The Secret History of Mixed-Race America* (1999), 9. Often greed played a role in this receptiveness to interracial intimacy with Indians, with marriage serving as yet another method for whites to appropriate Indian property. In 1908, in Tennessee, in the segregationist *Taylor-Trotwood Magazine*, a writer urging white men to proceed westward encouraged them to be on the lookout for marriageable Indian women. "She is a thing of beauty and a joy forever, and she and each of her sisters has a great big farm." Brian W. Dippie, *The Vanishing American: White Attitudes and U.S. Indian Policy* (1982), 248.

†Another participant expressed his appreciation that an agency had been able to assure him and his wife that they would be able to obtain for adoption a child who "would not be too dark or have any Negroid feature." The adopter declared that he and his wife had no prejudice against dark children but that in their community "it

number of white adults who never would have adopted a black child did prove willing to adopt an Indian one.

Over time, the opponents of such adoptions succeeded in garnering sufficient support in Congress to ensure the passage of ICWA in 1978—six years after the NABSW's initial attack on black-white interracial adoption. According to its congressional sponsors, ICWA was intended to address a crisis that both reflected and generated three great harms.* The first of these was the unwarranted separation of Indian children from their families by state agencies. The U.S. House of Representatives report that explained and justified ICWA maintained that "the wholesale separation of Indian children from their families is perhaps the most tragic and destructive aspect of American Indian life today."[19] Surveys of states with large Indian populations indicated that approximately 25 to 35 percent of all Indian children were removed from their families and placed in foster homes, adoptive homes, or institutions. According to the House

---

would be difficult to get such a child accepted." Quoted in David Fanshel, *Far From the Reservation: The Transracial Adoption of American Indian Children* (1972), 92.

Other participants expressed alternative perspectives. One woman, for example, commented that, "When the agency worker told us about Indian children, we became interested and pursued it. One of the biggest appeals to us was the fact that these were children who other people did not want as easily, whereas we never really cared what children looked like because we just wanted children." Ibid at 84. Similarly a woman stated that "Above all [she and her husband] wanted a child who might not have as wide a chance for adoption as the traditional blond, blue-eyed baby. We wanted a child who needed a home." Ibid at 90. A man remarked that he and his wife "were not going to be choosy—if we had our own child, we could not be choosy." He also commented that he had always felt that the Indians had had "a tough break" and that he sympathized with them. "[E]ven as a boy I would root for the Indians rather than the cowboys." Ibid at 83–84.

*ICWA states:

The Congress hereby declares that it is the policy of this Nation to protect the best interests of Indian children and to promote the stability and security of Indian tribes and families by the establishment of minimum federal standards for the removal of Indian children from their families and the placement of such children in foster or adoptive homes which will reflect the unique values of Indian culture, and by providing for assistance to Indian tribes in the operation of child and family services. [Indian Child Welfare Act of 1978, Public Law 95-608; November 8, 1978; 25 U.S.C. §1902 (2001).]

report, "The disparity in placement rates for Indians and non-Indians [was] shocking." In Minnesota, Indian children were placed in foster care or adoptive homes at a per capita rate five times greater than that for non-Indian children; in Montana, at a rate thirteen times greater; and in South Dakota, at a rate sixteen times greater. In Wisconsin, the report noted, "the risk run by Indian children of being separated from their parents is nearly 1,600 percent greater than it is for non-Indian children."[20]

According to ICWA's proponents, the second great harm addressed by the legislation was the placement of Indian children with non-Indian foster or adoptive families. "In addition to the trauma of separation from their families," the House report declared, "most Indian children in placement or in institutions have to cope with the problems of adjusting to a social and cultural environment much different [from] their own."[21] A 1969 survey conducted in sixteen states had found that approximately 85 percent of all Indian children in foster care were living in non-Indian homes.[22] The problem with that, in the view of the act's proponents, was that placing Indian children in non-Indian foster care or adoptive homes cut those children off from their roots and deprived them of environments that reflected and nourished the unique values of Indian culture.

The third harm cited by champions of ICWA was related not to the substance of child-placement decisions but rather to the question of who had the rightful authority to make such decisions. Supporters of the legislation charged that state officials routinely infringed upon tribal sovereignty. They insisted that a new statute was needed to reinforce the doctrine that Indian tribes were sovereign entities, outside the jurisdiction of the states except where otherwise specified by federal law. Such legislation, they believed, would be a necessary precursor to, and sign of, a renaissance in tribal self-determination.

Congress responded by drafting a law that would govern child-custody proceedings concerning Indian children.* At the heart of the statute are two key provisions. First, it provides that if a child resides

---

*A child-custody proceeding is defined as a hearing to determine either parental rights (that is, to decide whether parental rights should be terminated) or the placement of a child for foster care or adoption (25 U.S.C. §1903 [1]). ICWA has no

on an Indian reservation or has been made the ward of a tribal court, the tribal court has exclusive jurisdiction. If an Indian child resides off the reservation, the state and tribal courts have *concurrent* jurisdiction. In such cases, however, the tribal court enjoys a presumptive prefer- ence, for ICWA stipulates that on the petition of either the child's par- ents or the tribe, proceedings in the state court shall be transferred to the tribal court, except in cases of "good cause," where an objection is made by either parent, or when the tribe declines jurisdiction.[23] Second, ICWA directs that "In any adoptive placement of any Indian child under State law, a preference shall be given, in the absence of good cause to the contrary, to a placement with (1) a member of the child's extended family; (2) other members of the Indian child's tribe; or (3) other Indian families."[24]* The law contains two qualifications. A judge may deviate from the statutory preferences for "good cause" or if the child's tribe establishes a different set of preferences.

There are good and bad elements in ICWA, and elements that are a mixture of both. On the positive side, the legislation reflects and pro- motes a renewed assertiveness on the part of Indian tribal authorities. As Professor Joane Nagel has observed, since the 1960s "there has been a steady and growing effort on the part of many, perhaps most, Native American communities to preserve, protect, recover, and revitalize cul- tural traditions, religious and ceremonial practices, sacred or tradi- tional roles, kinship structures, languages, and the normative bases of community cohesion."[25] Communities long mired in despair and apathy have become politically engaged, directing their energies both inward, toward self-improvement, and outward, toward protest. According to Nagel, this renewal has manifested itself in an "explosive growth in the number of Indian organizations and associations, news- papers, tribal colleges, and American Indian Studies programs . . . as

---

bearing on child-custody decisions stemming from divorce, juvenile delinquency hearings, or state interventions not involving the removal of a child.

The act defines an "Indian child" as an unmarried person under eighteen who either is a member of an Indian tribe or is eligible for such membership as the biolog- ical child of a member (25 U.S.C. §1903 [3]). For more on the controversy surround- ing the definition of an Indian child, see pages 504–11.

*ICWA imposes a similar hierarchy for foster care. See 25 U.S.C. §1915 (b).

well as lobbying, litigation, and activism."[26] Affronted by the insinuation that Indian cultures had nothing worthwhile to offer the world, Indian leaders and their non-Indian allies supported the enaction of ICWA as a way of proclaiming that Native American culture was valuable and that Native American children who were separated from it stood to lose resources of incalculable worth. ICWA also served as a repository for the genuine desire of many non-Indian politicians to repudiate historical anti-Indian prejudice.

Notwithstanding those benefits, ICWA evinces deep flaws germane to the principal concerns of this book. First, although congressional backers of the act portrayed the Indian child-care crisis as being overwhelmingly the fault of racially discriminatory officials who robbed Indian families of their children (often to satisfy the wants of childless non-Indians), I will argue that there is good reason to question the accuracy of this scenario. Second, I challenge the supposed "expertise" upon which substantial portions of ICWA are said to be based. ICWA's congressional supporters credited the testimony of "experts" who claimed that Indian children typically suffered psychological damage when adopted by non-Indians. In the quarter century since ICWA's passage, these claims have been further enshrined and disseminated as fact by judges and scholars. I contest the validity of this proposition and show that the oft-cited study that purports to justify it is representative of the worst kind of junk social science. Third, ICWA invites, indeed facilitates, bad decisions by judges who are charged with enforcing the statute.

Fortunately, in a substantial number of cases, judges have come up with creative ways to avoid the social wreckage to which robust or even neutral application of ICWA would lead. However, when one finds oneself praying that judges will interpret a statute narrowly, emphasize its exceptions, and discern limitations that are otherwise absent, one is surely in the presence of a statute in need of reform. ICWA is such a law. It requires state officials to pursue affirmatively a dubious mission of racialist communalism. It does this, moreover, purporting to help Indian children. It would be one thing for the United States to justify ICWA simply in terms of enlarging the jurisdiction of Indian tribes and encouraging pan-Indian solidarity (regardless of the consequences to affected children). It is another (and worse!) thing for the United States to support ICWA largely in terms of serving the best interest of the children involved. As applied, the statute not only fails too often to fulfill that aim; ICWA also diverts attention away from the most menacing threats that face the vulnerable children caught up in the politics of Native American identity.

### Congress's Diagnosis of the Indian Child-Welfare Crisis

Although Congress's interpretation of the Indian child-welfare crisis has been widely accepted and endlessly reiterated,[27] its foundations are of questionable soundness. The 1978 House report identified state child-welfare agencies and courts as virtually the exclusive culprits.* According to the report, these instruments of state power and their personnel were generally uninformed about Indian culture, blinded by ethnocentrism, nowhere restrained by clear rules, and prone to mistreat Indians. An extended quotation from the House report provides a characteristic sampling of its rhetoric, presentation of evidence, and reasoning:

> Very few Indian children are removed from their families on the grounds of physical abuse. One study of a North Dakota reservation showed that these grounds were advanced in only 1 percent of the cases. Another study of a tribe in the Northwest showed the same incidence. The remaining 99 percent of the cases were argued on such vague grounds as "neglect" or "social deprivation" and on allegations of the emotional damage the children were subjected to by living with their parents.
>
> Indian communities are often shocked to learn that parents they regard as excellent caregivers have been judged unfit by non-Indian social workers.

---

*I have relied primarily on the House report because the bill proposed by the House of Representatives was the one that was ultimately enacted. See *U.S. Code Congressional and Administrative News,* 95th Congress, 2d Sess. 1978, 7530.

In judging the fitness of a particular family, many social workers, ignorant of Indian cultural values and social norms, make decisions that are wholly inappropriate in the context of Indian family life and so they frequently discover neglect and abandonment where none exists. . . . One of the grounds most frequently advanced for taking Indian children from their parents is the abuse of alcohol. However, this standard is applied unequally. In areas where rates of problem drinking among Indians and non-Indians are the same, it is rarely applied against non-Indian parents.[28]

According to the House report, "The abusive actions of social workers would largely be nullified if more judges were themselves knowledgeable about Indian life and required a sharper definition of the standards of child abuse and neglect."[29] The report's authors concluded, however, that state judges were little more conscientious in this regard than the social workers whose decisions they reviewed.

To justify assigning priority to state officials as the primary malefactors, the act's architects seeded ICWA's legislative history with allusions to tragic tales of state authorities unwarrantedly intruding on Indian families, separating children from their relatives and tribes, and then placing them with non-Indian families for foster care or adoption, all out of ignorance of or disrespect for Indian culture.[30] Consider, for example, the following representative testimony, elicited by Senator James G. Abourezk (Dem. South Dakota) from Goldie Denny, then the director of Social Services for the Quinault Nation:

> CHAIRMAN ABOUREZK: Ms. Denny, I think you ought to tell a couple of horror stories while the administration witnesses are here.
>
> Ms. DENNY: I will tell my own.
> When I was approximately four years old, I was one of five children. Our mother was deceased. We lived with our father. My grandmother came in to help take care of us.

My sister and I were removed by the welfare department because we were caught out in the street barefoot, wading in mud puddles. I don't see anything wrong with being barefoot, wading in mud puddles. I had a good time. I might have been a little dirty, but dirt washes off. But what's up in the head does not wash off.

There was no reason for that type of removal. I was returned home, but that is one instance.

CHAIRMAN ABOUREZK: For the record, is that the kind of thing that goes on around the country, around Indian reservations, when the non-Indian social welfare agencies decide that they know what is best for Indian kids?

MS. DENNY: Absolutely.[31]

There is much that should be troubling about this exchange. First, no corroborating evidence was sought by the committee chair or offered by the witness, even though the accuracy of recall by an adult remembering an incident that occurred in early childhood might well be questioned. Perhaps Ms. Denny's story *was* accurate. But it might have been mere lore that was presented to her as truth by her father or other adult guardians when she was young in order to insulate her from ugly realities. Ironically, by adopting such a credulous stance toward the accounts of Ms. Denny and the other witnesses with whom they sympathized, Senator Abourezk and his colleagues deprived the witnesses of the opportunity to provide more persuasive testimony.

A second problem is that though this episode was explicitly labeled a "horror story" by the senator, Ms. Denny was, by her own admission, returned to her family. If in fact she was returned quickly, with an acknowledgment of error by the child-welfare officials involved, then the case would begin to look very different from her portrayal of it. Unfortunately, her testimony failed to specify how long she was in the custody of the officials or under what circumstances they restored her to her family. And finally, while Ms. Denny unhesitatingly asserted that experiences like the one she recalled happened all over the country, nothing in her testimony offered any sound basis for believing that she had knowledge on which to predicate such an opinion.

Given the supposed pervasiveness and regularity of unwarranted removals, it would seem reasonable to expect that the legislative record would offer at least a few detailed, substantiated examples. Instead, one finds only conclusory characterizations based solely upon the allegations of a parent or a representative of a parent, or Indian parents in general. Altogether missing are the evenhanded descriptions of cases that might allow a careful reader to have some confidence in the accuracy of the accusations being made. Helpful sources of such confidence would be investigations by disinterested third parties, or analyses discussing with some modicum of seriousness alternative interpretations to those advanced by ICWA's partisans. Such sources, however, are nowhere to be found in the House and Senate reports.

Over the past twenty-five years, scores of judges and scholars have recounted the legislative history of ICWA. Most of them, however, either have failed to notice or have overlooked the shoddiness of the congressional analysis behind the legislation. An exception was Garry Wamser, who noted that "it is impossible to determine from the Congressional reports whether the indictment of state intervention into Indian family life is justified. The reports clearly evidence a bias which far exceeds [their] statistical and testimonial base."[32]

Perhaps the weakness of ICWA's legislative history is a commonplace flaw. Perhaps it reflects nothing more than complacency on the part of congressional staffers who, lulled into indifference by the near consensus, felt less obliged than they otherwise might have been to be thorough in gathering evidence and substantiating conclusions. Findings, moreover, may be correct even if they are poorly supported. In this instance, though, various considerations cast a pall over ICWA's factual predicate. One is the noticeable dearth of commentary about purported "child stealing" offered by observers who have shown a keen attentiveness to other types of wrongs inflicted upon Indian peoples. Vine Deloria's writings chronicle the mistreatment of Native Americans. Yet Deloria has made only passing reference to ICWA and said virtually nothing about the official misdeeds that were supposed to have prompted the legislation. William Byler, one of ICWA's most influential champions, insisted in 1974 that "the wholesale separation of Indian children from their families is perhaps the most tragic and destructive aspect of American Indian life today" (a statement that would be repeated in the Senate report accompanying ICWA).[33] In that same year, Deloria published a book, *Behind the Trail of Broken Treaties: An Indian Declaration of Independence,* that did not even touch on the issue.*

Professor Francis Paul Prucha devoted several pages to the historical background of ICWA in his magisterial treatise *The Great Father: The United States and the American Indians* (1984).[34] His account tracks that provided in the congressional reports, but it is regrettably lacking in independent documentation. Prucha replied principally on the congressional hearings and findings, as well as on several law-review articles—which in turn cite only the same congressional sources. One other source used by Prucha was a volume entitled *The Destruction of American Indian Families* (1977). Published by the Association on American Indian Affairs, this book offers useful information on that organization's self-perception of its involvement in child-welfare policy. Steven Unger, the editor of the volume, declared that

> in the past decade the Association on American Indian Affairs (AAIA) has reunited scores of Indian families whose children were taken from them by federal and state agencies without just cause and without due process of law. During the course of this work, the AAIA realized the crying need of concerned professionals and lay people for a regular source of information that would collect and expose the isolated experiences of different tribes and demonstrate the national scope of the Indian child-welfare crisis. In 1974 the Association began publishing

---

*In an afterword to a reissue of the book in 1985, Deloria mentioned the passage of ICWA, but with no suggestion that it had addressed a massive tragedy: "1978 also saw the pass[age] of the Indian Child Welfare Act, which changed some forms of procedure in child adoption and placement and provided for the disposition of Indian children who were tribal members" (*Behind the Trail of Broken Treaties: An Indian Declaration of Independence* [1974; rev. ed., 1985], 282).

*Indian Family Defense,* a newsletter exclusively concerned with Indian child-welfare issues. To respond to the need for a more comprehensive source of information than a newsletter could provide, publication of this volume was undertaken.[35]

One might think that such a volume would provide substantiation for the claims made by the proponents of ICWA. But *The Destruction of American Indian Families* yields up no more factual specificity or analytical rigor than the congressional reports. Here again are allusions to "shocking" racial disparities in child removals and adoptions without investigation of alternative theories of causation.* Here again are broad assertions poorly supported by allusive accounts in which the parties involved are never named or the disputes in question are described only tendentiously.[36] And here again, too, are sweeping empirical claims with no evident basis in credible empirical research.[37]†

---

*William Byler discussed "some causative factors" behind the crisis. While acknowledging that "the reasons appear very complex" and conceding that he and his colleagues were still "very far from perceiving [these reasons] clearly or in their entirety," he nevertheless proceeded to assert definitively that bias by state officials was the main culprit and that poverty, joblessness, poor health, substandard housing, and low educational attainment were lesser factors. *The Destruction of American Indian Families,* ed., Steven Unger (1997), 2–7.

†With similar vagueness, some commentators have maintained that the Church of Jesus Christ of Latter-Day Saints has aggressively wrested Indian children away from their parents and tribal communities for the purposes of "civilizing" them and converting them to Mormonism. Patrice Kunesh-Hartman has charged, for example, that the "Latter-Day Saints Placement Program removed as many as two thousand Hopi and Navajo children every year from their reservations, placing them in Mormon homes throughout the country" ("The Indian Child Welfare Act of 1978: Protecting Essential Tribal Interests," *University of Colorado Law Review* 60 [1989]: 131, 135–36). Citing Kunesh-Hartman, Donna J. Goldsmith made the same claim, adding that the Mormons "often employ[ed] fraudulent means to obtain consents to adoption from the Indian parents" ("Individuals vs. Collective Rights: The Indian Child Welfare Act," *Harvard Women's Law Journal* 13 [1990]: 1, 5 n. 19). In congressional testimony, certain witnesses also condemned Mormons' handling of Indian children (testimony before the Senate Select Committee on Indian Affairs by Don and Barbara Reeves, August 7, 1977). While these accusations may in fact be true, they should be handled with extreme caution because their substantiation is so inadequate. Kunesh-Hartman's and Goldsmith's articles both cite as an authority Rex Weyler's *Blood of the Land: The Government and Corporate War Against the*

*The Destruction of American Indian Families* also offers up lawyers, lobbyists, social workers, and academics who, in presenting their arguments, seem to have simply ignored relevant but inconvenient facts and analyses. Professor David Fanshel's book *Far from the Reservation: The Transracial Adoption of American Indian Children* (1972) was conspicuously germane to any discussion of adoption policies geared to Native Americans. It was the best description available of the acculturation of Indian children taken in by non-Indian families. Yet nowhere is it mentioned in either *The Destruction of American Indian Families* or the House report that constitutes the primary congressional explanation of ICWA.

*Far from the Reservation* had its origins in the Indian Adoption Project, a program underwritten from 1957 through 1968 by the federal Bureau of Indian Affairs and the Child Welfare League of America. According to Fanshel,

> The purpose of the Indian Adoption Project was to stimulate the adoption of American Indian children on a nation-wide basis. From 1940 to the early 1950's there had been many programs designed to promote the adoption of all children—the handicapped child, the child in the older age group, and children of other racial groups both within the United States and from foreign lands. But the Indian child requiring adoption services remained the "forgotten child," left inadequately cared for on the reservation, without a permanent home or parents he could call his own. The results of a 1957 nation-wide survey showed that there were approximately 1000 Indian children legally free for adoption who were forced to live in foster homes and institutions because adoptive resources had not been found for them.[38]

---

*American Indian Movement* (1982). Yet Weyler's discussion of this issue is, like most of his book, extremely biased. It depends wholly on the accounts of witnesses whose observations and opinions the author apparently took on faith, and offers no corroborating information. For a favorable view of the Mormons' interaction with Native American children, see the testimony of George Lee, an Indian Mormon (Senate Select Committee on Indian Affairs, August 4, 1977).

With the assistance of certain Indian tribes, state child-welfare authorities, and private adoption agencies, the Indian Adoption Project sought to recruit adoptive families for these parentless children. Under the project's auspices, 395 Indian children were placed in adoptive homes, most if not all of which were non-Indian.

Fanshel's depiction of the Indian child-welfare situation contradicts the congressional portrayal. Whereas Congress identified state child-welfare officials' widespread and unwarranted removal of Indian children from their homes of origin as the central vice, and the placement of Indian children with non-Indian caregivers as a major problem, Fanshel decried the *passivity* of social workers and the *paucity* of non-Indian placements for Indian children. And whereas Congress concluded that adoption by non-Indians posed a considerable threat to the well-being of Indian children, especially as they matured, Fanshel came to a very different conclusion: commenting on the children whose adoptions he had followed for four to five years, he noted that in his view they were "doing remarkably well as a group."[39] More specifically, he remarked that "the children appear to be well imbedded within their adoptive families" and that their adoptive familial relationships "appear to be as close and devoted as one would find in other kinds of adoptive families or in biological family units."[40] Impressionistic observations such as these are, of course, prone to betray the observer's bias. But one detail that makes Fanshel's commentary on this point particularly credible is that he strongly favored tribal authority over child-custody matters in Indian country and ardently preferred placing Indian children with Indian adults.*

---

*According to Fanshel:

The fate of most Indian children is tied to the struggle of Indian people in the United States for survival and social justice. Their ultimate salvation rests upon the success of that struggle. Whether adoption by white parents of the children who are in the most extreme jeopardy in the current period—such as the subjects of our study—can be tolerated by Indian organizations is a moot question. It is my belief that only the Indian people have the right to determine whether their children can be placed in white homes.

*Far from the Reservation: The Transracial Adoption of American Indian Children* (1972), 341. Elsewhere, Fanshel states that Indian children should have the opportu-

Congress asserted that ICWA was a response to the Indian child-welfare crisis. No crisis, however, can be self-defining; rather, *people* must define it. Among the actors who defend the Indian child-welfare crisis were tribal leaders with incentives to broaden their jurisdiction and burnish the image of communal life in Indian country. Also involved were proponents of Red Power, men and women committed to fostering a sense of pan-Indian nationalism. In other words, ideological, emotional, financial, and organizational imperatives similar to those that have animated other group protection schemes contributed to the mobilization on behalf of ICWA.

Another set of important figures in this drama were members of Congress who sympathized with those whom they perceived to be Indian leaders and friends of the Indian. Genuinely disturbed by what they saw as the unfair treatment of Indians by state officials, compounded by indifference on the part of federal authorities, a cadre of aroused congressmen decided to enact some sort of responsive legislation. These politicians' commitment, however, was always qualified: they were willing to act but only so long as they did not encroach upon well-protected legislative turf or generate expensive draws on the federal treasury. This helps to explain the limited nature of Congress's framing of the Indian child-welfare crisis. In *Far from the Reservation*, Professor Fanshel portrayed a large, complex social disaster that reflected and generated poverty, anomie, drug dependency, child neglect, and wanton violence. The authors of ICWA, by contrast, depicted a rather simple problem that could be laid almost entirely on the doorstep of bigoted or ignorant state officials. Addressing Fanshel's version of the crisis would have required attacking poverty and its kindred curses, a notoriously difficult and costly undertaking. But Congress's version could be solved merely by the passage of a new law that would curtail the power of state officials.

Chief Calvin Isaacs of the Mississippi Band of Choctaw Indians pressed this point in his testimony before Congress. A supporter of

---

nity "for a good life within their own family, or at least within a family of their own tribal heritage. This is by far the most preferred plan for caring for deprived Indian children" (ibid., 49).

ICWA, he nevertheless observed that it focused upon only "a small part of the problem compared to the challenge of combating poverty, substandard [and] overcrowded housing, child abuse, alcoholism, and mental illness on the reservation. These are the forces which destroy our families."[41] Eighteen years later, in the *Indian Child Welfare Act Handbook* (1975), B. J. Jones would echo that assertion. Jones, like Chief Isaacs, supported ICWA. But in the end, he argued, it was "a procedural statute for a substantive problem. The underlying problems that lead to the breakup of many Indian families [are] not, in many instances, the by-products of faulty state institutions but [are] instead . . . the results of social ills in the family." Those social ills, he complained, "receive little, if any, attention in ICWA."[42]

ICWA's architects stressed the disparity between the numbers of non-Indian versus Indian children who were removed from the care of their biological parents and placed in adoptive homes. This disparity has been commonly cited as if its meaning were a self-evident signal that state authorities were discriminating against Indian parents.* Before any such proposition can properly be asserted with confidence, however, plausible contending explanations must be addressed. Unfortunately, ICWA's framers did not verify that the non-Indian and Indian families being compared were otherwise similarly situated. In other words, they did not negate the counterhypothesis that much of the purportedly "racial" disparity was actually attributable not to invidious discriminations by state officials but to some other cause—perhaps to

---

*An egregious example may be found in the congressional testimony of Reena Uviller, who was then the director of the Juvenile Rights Project of the American Civil Liberties Union:

> The untoward number of extra-tribal placements results . . . from a failure to provide poor Indian families with the means to raise their children, and from too great a willingness by state officials to meet the growing adoption demands [for Indian] children as [non-Indian] couples . . . find the number of white children available for adoption dramatically reduced. The effect has been the destruction of Indian family life [, which] has been aptly characterized as a form of genocide (testimony before the Senate Select Committee on Indian Affairs, August 4, 1977).

the disproportionate impact of disease, unemployment, violence, and familial dysfunction on Native Americans. In the aftermath of ICWA, Indian children still run a far greater risk than other children of being involuntarily removed from the care of their biological parents.[43] This may be due in part to ineffective enforcement of ICWA, but it is more likely attributable to corrosive socioeconomic conditions that lie beyond ICWA's remedial scope.*

### The Alleged Inferiority of Non-Indian Parenting: The Perils of Junk Social Science

A constant (and familiar) refrain among proponents of ICWA is that Indian adoptive parents are better able than their non-Indian counterparts to give Indian children a proper upbringing. In the opinion of Esther Mays, of the Native American Child Protection Council, for instance,

> the Indian home is better equipped to handle and service the needs of Indian children. The Indian home nurtures the traditions and the way of life for the Indian world. This type of environment would allow the child to remain aware of his cultural heritage and identity. The Indian home is more prepared and

---

*As Professor Joan H. Hollinger notes:

> The rate of off-reservation placement for Indian children remains high. A decade after the enactment of the ICWA, Indian children are still being placed out of their original families at a rate nearly five times greater than that for all children in the United States. . . . In addition to the high rates of placement of children away from their parents, there are nearly as many other signs of disintegration of family life on many Indian reservations as there were twenty years ago. [See "Native American Children" in *Adoption Law and Practice*, Joan H. Hollinger et al., eds., vol 2 (2001): 15–83.]

See also Russel L. Barsh, "The Indian Child Welfare Act of 1978: A Critical Analysis," *Hastings Law Journal* 31 (1980): 1334: "The Indian Child Welfare Act does little to alter the conditions that Congress held responsible for the unwarranted breakup of Indian families. . . . The Act's emphasis is on removal and placement, not prevention."

better suited to understand and provide the emotional feeling of well-being that the child requires and needs.[44]

A related charge is that Indian children raised by non-Indians (typically whites) will almost invariably be damaged as a result of their adoptive parents' cultural shortfall.[45] A revealing iteration of this argument was offered up in the congressional testimony of Dr. Joseph Westermeyer of the University of Minnesota, who subsequently published his remarks in an article that has been cited by such authorities as the Supreme Court of the United States.[46] In "The Apple Syndrome in Minnesota: A Complication of Racial-Ethnic Discontinuity," Westermeyer described what he viewed as a pathological condition that he dubbed the "apple syndrome." The term "apple," Westermeyer wrote, "refers to racially Indian people with ethnic preferences of the majority society, i.e., 'Red' or Indian on the outside and 'White' on the inside."[47] It was undesirable for children to become apples, Westermeyer claimed, because this identity ill prepared them to occupy their rightful place in American society, and that lack of preparedness in turn rendered them vulnerable to psychiatric and social difficulties. According to Westermeyer,

Early placement of Indian children in non-Indian homes did not immediately precipitate problems bringing them to clinical recognizance. Problems developed during adolescence when, as racially Indian teenagers, they tried to assert their White ethnic identity. While earlier their families had accepted their White ethnic affiliation, now society refused to permit the racially Indian/ethnically White person to assume White ethnic affiliation. The White parents—who had not undergone similar experiences—were unable to anticipate the child's rejection experiences [or to] provide a racial-ethnic model appropriate to the adolescent's dilemma. . . . Repeated rejections by the very ethnic group with whom [these teenagers] shared values, attitudes, and behaviors led initially to anger, followed by attempts to reject White ethnicity. This resulted in anger and rejection of self, since White ethnicity had become an inextricable part of their self concept.[48]

But even worse than early placements of Indian children in white households were later placements, Westermeyer explained, because

placements in the homes of their traditional White enemy further exacerbated adolescent identity issues. . . . Imposition of White foster parents at that point was a social message to these young people that (1) Indian people cannot take care of their own children, and (2) White people are the competent ones who can meet such problems.[49]

Describing the methodology behind his study, Westermeyer wrote:

Among some 100 American Indian patients seen by the author during 1968–78, approximately one-fourth were reared for part or all of their childhood in non-Indian foster homes, adoptive homes, and group homes. The "apple syndrome" was manifest in 17 people of this group reared away from Indian homes and communities; it was not encountered among those reared in Indian homes and communities.

During the same period several people were encountered socially who were racially Indian and had been reared in predominantly non-Indian settings, but who did not manifest the "apple syndrome." Since they had not experienced problems requiring psychiatric care, they were assessed for factors that might have served to protect them against this syndrome.[50]

Although Westermeyer's musings have been repeatedly cited as intellectual authority by legislators, judges, advocates, and scholars,*

---

*According to B. J. Jones, director of the Northern Plains Tribal Judicial Institute, "One of the most convincing studies relied upon by Congress in enacting the placement preference provisions of the act was completed by Dr. Joseph Westermeyer" (B. J. Jones, "The Indian Child Welfare Act: In Search of a Federal Forum to Vindi-

they are in fact an egregious example of junk social science. The principal pool of subjects Westermeyer relied upon as the basis for his far-reaching assertions comprised only "some 100 American Indian patients" he had seen in a single state over the course of a decade. These people had been referred to him for psychiatric therapy. Their diagnoses ranged from schizophrenia to affective psychosis to alcoholism; four had attempted suicide, and one was a rapist. The ostensible control group to which Westermeyer compared his patients consisted merely of "several people . . . encountered socially." The small size of this "study," its limited geographic scope, the way in which its subjects were drafted, and its population by individuals who were by definition overcome by psychiatric problems all served to negate any general claim that might have been made on behalf of Westermeyer's observations. The same limitations should likewise restrain any claims of causality linking adoption with negative outcomes. It would seem reasonable to expect that anyone citing Westermeyer as an authority would confront the problematic features of his study. These gaping deficiencies, however, have been overlooked or ignored. Those who have affirmatively cited Westermeyer appear never to have noted the rather obvious objection that no reliable generalizations could possibly be made about Indians raised in non-Indian households on the basis of a small sample of psychiatrically troubled patients.

Westermeyer blamed on white parental inadequacy the unsuccessful efforts of Native American teenagers to cope with the racial prejudices of their white peers and their adoptive parents. White caretakers were unable, he charged, to anticipate adoptees' experiences or to provide models appropriate to their adolescent dilemmas.[51] But Westermeyer offered no substantiation whatsoever for this charge: nothing in

---

cate the Rights of Indian Tribes and Children Against the Vagaries of State Courts," 73 *North Dakota Law Review* 395, 457 n. 46 [1997]). For another example of uncritical reliance upon Westermeyer's study, see Madelyn Freundlich, "The Role of Race, Culture, and National Origin," in *Adoption* 72 (2000). Worst of all, given the influence of the Supreme Court, was Justice William J. Brennan's legitimizing citation to Westermeyer's work in his opinion for the Court in *Mississippi Band of Choctaw Indians v. Holyfield*, 490 U.S. 30, 33 n. 1 (1989).

his article suggests that he actually spoke with the caretakers or took any other steps to obtain reliable information about their caretaking skills or methods. Nor did he show that the problems he purported to isolate were attributable to the race of the caretakers as opposed to some other cause, such as *pre*adoption trauma or prejudice against interracial adoption.[52]*

Westermeyer has portrayed apple syndrome as a sociopsychological malady. But why should a child's innocent pursuit of happiness in a multiracial household be viewed as pathological just because he or she was reviled by bigoted neighbors? And so what if an Indian child embraced the cultural preferences of the non-Indian majority? Must *every* Indian child evince only those preferences that Westermeyer has judged appropriate for an Indian to harbor? Was it wrong for an Indian child to behave in ways that contradicted conventional—often lowered—expectations as to the ways Indians were supposed to act? Was it inappropriate for Indian children to abandon what some have deemed to be their "place" or to conduct themselves in a fashion that some might regard as "acting white"?

Dr. Westermeyer clearly determined in his own mind how Indians should act and what their self-perceptions should be. His utterly subjective musings, however, should not be confused with rigorous social science.

---

*Westermeyer's article also includes a section on yet another sampling of Indians who were raised in non-Indian adopted homes but did not become "apples." It is based on Westermeyer's observations of three people whom he "encountered socially." At least one of these three was a man who might well have been characterized as an "apple" by another observer: of three eighths Indian ancestry, he was married to a white woman and, by his own admission, viewed the plight of Indians from a self-determined position as "a concerned 'outsider,' or White person." Confusion over who is or is not an "apple" by Westermeyer's definition casts a pall over the term's usefulness as a device for generating social-scientific data and conclusions. Problematic, too, is that Westermeyer's article offers no theory to account for those Indians adopted by non-Indians who escape apple syndrome (Joseph Westermeyer, "The Apple Syndrome in Minnesota: A Complication of Racial-Ethnic Discontinuity," *Journal of Operational Psychiatry* 10 [1979]: 134, 137–38).

*Limiting the Reach of ICWA: The Existing Indian Family Doctrine*
ICWA brings into sharp relief a problem that we have encountered before: the difficulty of labeling individuals with group identities. ICWA defines an "Indian child" as an unmarried person under eighteen who is either a member of a federally recognized Indian tribe *or* the biological child of a member of an Indian tribe *and* himself or herself eligible for membership in that tribe.[53] At first blush, this standard may seem straightforward and unobjectionable. In practice, though, ICWA fails to take into account the complexities of American life, including the prevalence of mixed marriage or cohabitation between Indians and non-Indians, the frequency of breakups and attendant disputes over childrearing decisions, and subtleties regarding the individual embrace and societal attribution of racial, ethnic, cultural, and tribal identities. Professor Joan Hollinger has pointed out, for example, that ICWA's definition of an Indian child "excludes some children who have been raised as Indians, while including some who have had no prior contact with Indian society."[54] Elaborating, she has explained that

> children whose Indian parents are not themselves eligible for a particular tribe's membership because they do not have that tribe's requisite quantum of Indian blood are not covered by the Act even though they may have been brought up on a reservation or in an Indian community. Children whose mother belongs to one tribe and whose father belongs to another may not be eligible for membership in either parent's tribe because they do not meet the blood quantum requirements of either tribe, and would themselves be outside the scope of the Act. By contrast, children of Indian parents who have never resided in or near an Indian community, are covered by the Act if the quantum of their Indian blood qualifies them for membership in a particular tribe.[55]

Case law highlights some of the difficulties encountered in seeking to identify precisely *which* children ICWA should cover. Consider *In re Baby Boy Doe,*[56] a case concerning a child born in Idaho in 1989. The biological mother was a non-Indian, and the biological father an enrolled member of a federally recognized tribe. The father and mother were unmarried and had no contact with each other for most of the mother's pregnancy and for a substantial length of time following the birth of their son. Shortly after the child was born, the mother asked an agency to arrange for him to be adopted. She chose as adoptive parents a non-Indian married couple. When the biological mother and the prospective adoptive parents together sought to have the parental rights of the biological parents formally terminated, a problem arose: because the birth mother indicated that the baby's biological father was a member of an Indian tribe, notice of the termination proceeding had to be sent to the tribe and to the father. At a hearing, a proxy for the father and the tribe announced that the father wanted custody of his son, that he had applied to enroll the baby in the tribe, and that the tribe itself wished to intervene and have the entire matter transferred to the tribal court. In a subsequent hearing, the same representative advocated placing the boy with the child's paternal aunt and uncle, who lived on the tribe's reservation.

A literal reading would have made the terms of ICWA applicable to the child, inasmuch as he was the biological offspring of a member of a federally recognized tribe and was himself eligible for tribal membership. In the judge's view, however, the intent of the statute was to protect *existing* Indian families—kin groups that perceived themselves families in some fashion, that considered themselves Indians, and that had already established real affiliation with a recognized tribe. He concluded that in this case there *was* no Indian family—or at least no Indian family of the sort that ICWA was meant to preserve. After all, the custodial parent was a non-Indian who claimed no membership in any Indian tribe. The child, moreover, had never had appreciable contact with any Indian community. The judge's rationale—that ICWA applied only to children within Indian families that had significant cultural, social, or political ties to a tribe—is known as the "existing Indian family doctrine."[57] Supporters of this doctrine fear that without it, ICWA will be extended to situations outside of the law's intended or otherwise appropriate scope, touching children and custodial parents with little or no familiarity or affiliation with an Indian tribe. Opponents fear, in contrast, that it will be used to usurp tribes' rightful authority and, in the process, remove from Indian communities the youth on which their long-term survival will depend.

In *Baby Boy Doe,* the state supreme court of Idaho reversed the trial judge, rejected the existing Indian family doctrine, and ordered that the trial court adjudicate the dispute pursuant to the dictates of ICWA.* While several courts have agreed with that decision, others have dissented and embraced the trial judge's approach.[58]

One example of the latter was *In re Bridget R.*[59] The case involved Bridget and Lucy, twins born on November 9, 1993, in Los Angeles County, California. Their parents, Richard and Cindy, were an unmarried couple who lived together in the city of Whittier, with their two older sons, one and two years old. Impoverished and consigned to a public shelter for housing, Cindy and Richard felt unable to care for the expected twins and decided before they were born to give them up for adoption. For assistance with the arrangements, they turned to an attorney. Richard initially told the attorney that he was one quarter American Indian, but after being informed that the disclosure of his Indian ancestry would delay or maybe even preclude the babies' adoption, he changed his self-presentation, omitting from the relevant legal forms any mention of his Indian heritage. In a word, he passed. Cindy, too, was part Indian by lineage, with ancestral ties to the Yaqui tribe in Mexico. But it was Richard's American Indian ancestry that concerned the attorney and would become a central issue in the dispute that was to engulf the twins. In the ninth month of Cindy's pregnancy, she and Richard met with social workers who provided them with counseling and other services required

---

*The existing Indian family doctrine was first coined in *In re Baby Boy L.,* 643 P. 2d 168 (Kan. 1982), a case involving a child born in Wichita, Kansas, on January 29, 1981, to an unmarried, non-Indian woman who soon thereafter gave him up for adoption to a white couple. The baby's biological father, an enrolled member of the Kiowa Indian tribe, resided at the Kansas State Industrial Reformatory. In order to effectuate the adoption, the state moved to terminate the biological father's parental rights. The father, with the assistance of his tribe, countered by invoking ICWA and requesting, pursuant to the statute's hierarchy of preferences, that his son be placed with a member of his extended family, with other members of the Kiowa tribe, or with some other Indian family. Over his mother's objections, the tribe enrolled Baby Boy L. as a member and petitioned to transfer the dispute to a tribal court.

by state law. Two weeks after Cindy gave birth, she and Richard signed documents turning the newborns over to a social-service agency, on the understanding that they would be placed for adoption with the Rosts, an Ohio couple who had paid Richard's attorney approximately fourteen thousand dollars to cover expenses associated with Cindy's pregnancy (and, of course, the attorney's fees).

A few days after Cindy and Richard relinquished their parental rights, the Rosts took the twins back to Ohio. Several months later, they filed a petition there to adopt Bridget and Lucy.

Just when the Rosts finally allowed themselves to believe that they had crossed the most difficult terrain they would face in the adoption process, a problem was developing that would put at risk their tender hopes. About a month after the girls' birth, Richard told his mother, Karen, about the adoption. Without his knowledge, she contacted a representative of her tribe, who in turn got in touch with Richard's attorney and officials of the Los Angeles County Children's Court. Asserting that the twins were potential members of his tribe, the representative announced his intention of intervening in any proceedings concerning them. At the same time, Richard's mother submitted tribal enrollment applications for herself, her son, and her two grandsons. A short while later, another representative of the tribe wrote to the social-service agency that had arranged the adoption, declaring that the twins were of Indian descent and that their paternal grandmother wanted them to be placed within her extended Indian family.

Even as Richard's mother was prodding him to help her regain custody of the twins, his relationship with Cindy was markedly deteriorating. On numerous occasions, she claimed, he hit and kicked her, broke furniture, and abused their young sons by picking them up by the neck, shaking them, poking them in the face, or hitting them in the head. On April 27, 1994, Cindy obtained a restraining order that required Richard to remain no less than one hundred yards from her and their two boys at all times. The previous week, Richard had sent child-welfare officials a letter rescinding his relinquishment of parental rights over the twins. Bowing to his mother's wishes, he now sought to retrieve the girls from their adoptive family in Ohio and place them with his sister.

Applying ICWA, a trial court ruled in Richard's favor.* An appellate court reversed. While insisting that it had "no quarrel with the proposition that preserving American Indian culture is a legitimate, even compelling, governmental interest,"[60] the court asserted that this interest would not be vindicated by the application of ICWA "to children whose biological parents do not have a significant social, cultural, or political relationship with an Indian community."[61] The court maintained that "it is almost too obvious to require articulation that the 'unique values of Indian culture' will not be preserved in the homes of parents who have become fully assimilated into non-Indian culture."[62] Essentially, the court's reasoning was that while ICWA was justifiably applicable to authentic Indian families, it did *not* cover those who labeled or otherwise self-identified themselves as Indians only opportunistically, for purposes of litigation. In the case at hand, Lucy and Bridget's father had had no relationship with any federally recognized Indian tribe prior to his attempt to belatedly invoke ICWA. Indeed, Richard had expressly *disclaimed* any Indian identity and had never enrolled himself in his mother's tribe; it was his mother who had enrolled him. Under these circumstances, the court ruled, the twins and their biological parents should not be considered an Indian family for purposes of enforcing ICWA.

The appeals court further declared that there was a federal constitutional basis for engrafting the existing Indian family doctrine limitation onto ICWA. A basic tenet of statutory interpretation is that judges should interpret statutes in such a way as to protect them from constitutional invalidation if at all possible. Here the California court of appeals ruled that at least in this instance, the only way to rescue ICWA was to read it as not pertaining to Bridget and Lucy. According to Jus-

---

*ICWA stipulates that certain requirements must be met before parental rights to an Indian child can be voluntarily terminated. Any consent obtained in the absence of these criteria is invalid and may be so declared at any time subsequently. Because these requirements were not met prior to the twins' adoption, the trial court invalidated the voluntary relinquishment of parental rights, ordered the removal of Bridget and Lucy from their adoptive home, and directed that they be placed in the custody of the extended family of their biological father (*In re Bridget R.*, 49 Cal. Rptr. 2d 507, 514–15 [1996], 117 Sup. Ct. 693 [1997]).

tice H. Walter Croskey, the court's reading of the statute was decisively shaped by several different constitutional imperatives, two of which are directly relevant to our concerns. The first of this pair is what the court described as children's constitutionally protected "liberty interest in the continuity and stability of their homes."[63] The strongest single note sounded by Justice Croskey in his opinion was that under the Due Process Clause of the federal constitution, "the rights of children in their family relationships are at least as fundamental and compelling as those of their parents."[64] Indeed, the court maintained that

> if anything, children's familial rights are more compelling than adults', because children's interests in family relationships comprise more than the emotional and social interests which adults have in family life; children's interests also include the elementary and wholly practical needs of the small and helpless to be protected from harm and to have stable and permanent homes in which each child's mind and character can grow unhampered by uncertainty and fear of what the next day or week or court appearance may bring.[65]

The interest in continuity arose in this case because the twins would be subjected to instability if they were removed from the care of the Rosts, the only parents they had ever known, and turned over to strangers—strangers with whom they shared a blood tie, true, but strangers nonetheless.

The second imperative that the California court of appeals cited was the Equal Protection Clause of the federal Constitution. A full appreciation of the court's argument here requires an awareness that unique standards govern federal constitutional law as it applies to Native Americans. In employment, for example, the government cannot prefer candidates on a racial basis absent a showing of compelling justification, a standard that is difficult to meet.[66] By contrast, affirmative action for members of recognized Indian tribes *is* permitted, so long as the government can show that its policy is reasonable—something that is relatively easy to do. The federal Supreme Court's rationale for treating "racial" regulations differently from regulations governing members of recognized Indian tribes is that the latter designation constitutes a "political" and not a "racial" category.[67] Indian tribes, so the argument runs, are discrete political entities under the jurisdiction and protection of the federal government. Thus, when ICWA imposes special rules regarding "Indian children," it is promoting not *racial* regulation (which is disallowed absent a compelling justification that can survive strict judicial scrutiny) but some form of political regulation unique to Indian tribes (in which the federal courts broadly defer to the legislative and executive branches).

This racial status/political status distinction and its maintenance presuppose the drawing of some credible dividing line. That line is the idea that a person's status as a member of an Indian tribe depends on something more than just "race"—that "something" being a discernible, voluntary relationship to the tribe. In the opinion of the California Court of Appeals, that existing Indian family doctrine acted as an essential brake to keep ICWA from slipping into mere racial regulation. In other words, ICWA was constitutionally valid, according to the court, so long as it was applied in contexts in which there existed some actual, voluntary living relationship between tribes and their members. Where such a relationship was absent, ICWA should not obtain.[68]

The existing Indian family doctrine is susceptible to a variety of criticisms. It is a judicial revision of Congress's handiwork. The doctrine appears nowhere in the legislation and during ICWA's journey toward enactment Congress explicitly rejected the inclusion of a provision with the same aim.[69] It is not altogether clear that the doctrine is required to save ICWA from constitutional invalidation; in contrast to Justice Croskey, some learned students of the field maintain that ICWA's requirement of tribal membership is properly viewed as a political rather than a racial classification.[70] Critics of the existing Indian family doctrine complain, moreover, that it invites state court judges to determine the contours of Indian identity. They maintain that state officials should not be the ones to determine who is Indian enough to reap the benefits that ICWA confers.[71]

There is considerable force to these objections. In my view, however, the existing Indian family doctrine is good policy. If it is not already a proper element of ICWA, it should be made so by amendment.* The existing Indian family doctrine (or some such device) is good because it impedes a party in a child-custody dispute from opportunistically deploying some nominal link with a Native American tribe to create a fictive identity for the sake of litigation. To permit the foisting of a tribal identity upon a child even against the wishes of custodial parents (or a custodial parent) who had theretofore had no significant contacts with the tribe is to facilitate a communal authoritarianism that ought not be tolerated.

The matter is different if the custodial parents are actual members of a tribe. In 1985 a couple who were enrolled members of the Mississippi Band of Choctaw Indians and resided on a reservation in Neshoba County, Mississippi, deliberately left the reservation and traveled some two hundred miles away to give birth to twins whom they subsequently transferred with the blessings of the state to a non-Indian couple for purposes of adoption. The tribe objected and moved to vacate the adoption on the ground that under the circumstances, ICWA vested exclusive jurisdiction in the tribal court. Ultimately, the Supreme Court agreed with the tribe.[72] As a strictly jurisdictional matter, the Court's ruling is unobjectionable. By living on and returning to the reservation, the biological parents clearly affiliated themselves with the tribe and can properly be deemed to have chosen to abide by the tribe's norms. Just as domiciliaries of a state can rightly be made to submit to that state's jurisdiction, so, too, can domiciliaries of a reservation (or other bona fide members of a tribe) be rightly made to submit to the tribe's jurisdiction. People who have not chosen to affiliate themselves with a tribe, however, should not all of a sudden and mysteriously find themselves or the children they are raising put under tribal jurisdiction.†

---

*Over the years members of Congress have proposed without success several bills that would have codified the existing Indian family doctrine. See, for example, H.R. 3275, 104th Cong. (1996).

†It should be stressed here that at issue in the situations under discussion is which government—state or tribal—has the authority to determine the placement of children. The outcome of the jurisdictional struggle does not automatically dictate the substance of the placement decision. After the Supreme Court's ruling in favor of the Choctaw tribe, for example, the tribal court decided that the white woman who had

*ICWA, Matching, and the Ideology of Cultural Preservation*

The United States Supreme Court has identified as ICWA's "most important substantive requirement"[73] the provision requiring that absent the exercise of tribal jurisdiction and "good cause" to the contrary, state officials must place any child covered by the legislation with, first, members of his or her extended family; second, other members of the same tribe; or third, other Indian families. This provision establishes a moderate matching regime. Although it plainly disfavors the adoption of Indian children by non-Indians, it does not explicitly bar such adoptions. Indeed, under its terms, the first preference for adoption may be a non-Indian branch of a child's extended family—an increasingly likely possibility, given the high incidence of intermarriage between Indians and non-Indians. Yet clearly

> the drafters of ICWA frowned upon adoptions of Indian children by non-Indian families . . . because of the potential effect that the removal of the Indian child from his or her culture has on both the child and the tribe. Congress, after long hours of testimony and investigation, concluded that in the overwhelming majority of cases . . . it would be in the child's best interest to be adopted by a family that would preserve the child's unique Indian culture and heritage.[74]

Congress's conclusion was faulty. First, with respect to the matter of the individual child, we have seen the fatuousness of the "expert" opinions upon which Congress apparently relied when it codified fears of the sort expressed by Dr. Westermeyer. Assertions regarding the pre-

---

sought to adopt the children (her husband had died during the pendency of the litigation) should be granted permanent custody, insofar as she constituted the only surviving parent the twins had ever known. See Marcia Coyle, "After the Gavel Comes Down: It's Never Over When It's Over, Parties Before the Supreme Court Find Out," *National Law Journal*, February 25, 1991. In other cases, too, tribal courts have left Indian children with non-Indian families with whom they have bonded. See Christine Metteer, "Hard Cases Make Bad Law: The Need for Revision of the Indian Child-Welfare Act," 38 *Santa Clara Law Review* 419, 422 n. 24 (1998).

sumptive superiority of Indian over non-Indian parenting for Native American children should be rebuffed on the same grounds as claims for the greater merit of black over nonblack child rearing for African American children.*

The second argument in favor of ICWA's placement hierarchy is that it will help preserve Indian communities whose cultural distinctiveness and corporate identities are being washed away through assimilation. One major difference between African American and Native American communities is sheer numbers. The African American population is sufficiently large that its communal structures will likely be unaffected by any adoption policy. By contrast, the Native American population is so meager in some locales that even relatively small demographic shifts may be significant.[75]

Asserted fears of cultural "extinction," however, are overblown—a rhetorical bogeyman. What is called "extinction" is actually the transformation of cultures through interaction with others—a benefit (and bane) that is virtually unavoidable in the absence of strong (and decidedly unpleasant efforts) to distance groups from the assimilative forces of the modern world. I see little virtue in burdening the living, particularly youngsters who have no choice in the matter, for the sake of preserving—freezing—group identities as they are presently constituted.

The matching provision of ICWA has survived in part because those most directly burdened by it, parentless Indian children, have no effective political voice; their purported champions primarily represent the governing cadres of Indian advocacy groups and tribes. Indians marrying non-Indians undoubtedly pose a greater assimilative "threat" than non-Indians adopting Indian children. Yet imagine the fate of a proposed federal Indian Cultural Preservation Act that would discourage such marriages, perhaps by requiring mixed couples to wait longer than others to secure marriage licenses. Adults—Indian and non-Indian alike—would not stand for it!

ICWA's matching provision has also survived because, in an appreciable number of cases, officials, including judges, have disregarded or

---

*See pages 407–11.

maneuvered around ICWA's hierarchy of preferences by invoking the statute's "good cause"* exception.[76] By finding good cause to deviate from the placement preferences mandated by ICWA, officials have alleviated pressures on the statute that might otherwise have overwhelmed it politically, as happened where popular revulsion catalyzed congressional action against race matching outside the context of adoptions involving Native American children. The matching provision of ICWA has thus been reshaped on an ad hoc basis through litigation. The problem with this mode of legal change, however, is that it tends to be uneven. While some judges have manipulated ICWA to avoid results that would (and should) have discredited the statute, others have applied it straightforwardly, even when their doing so was patently destined to have terrible human consequences. One vivid example of this latter type of application is *In re S.E.G.*, a decision by the state supreme court of Minnesota.[76] In 1994 the court was called upon to adjudicate a case involving three Native American siblings born between 1984 and 1987. The mother was a member of the Chippewa tribe; the father was a white man. The mother voluntarily placed the children in foster care, where between 1988 and 1991, two of the children were moved six times and the other five. In August 1991 all three were reunited in the foster home of E.C. and C.C., a non-Indian couple. The youngsters remained there for several months before being moved again, this time to a Native American preadoptive home. That placement, however, lasted only nine days, after which the children were returned to E.C. and C.C. A few months after that, they were again moved, to a Native American foster home; when that placement, too, fell apart (within two months), they were placed with yet one more Native American foster family.

---

*Congress left "good cause" undefined in ICWA. 19 U.S.C. §1915(a). Bureau of Indians Affairs Guidelines offer as considerations for determining good cause the preferences of biological parents or the child when the child is of sufficient age, the extraordinary physical or emotional needs of a given child, and the unavailability of suitable families for placement after a diligent search has been made for families meeting the statutory preference criteria. Bureau of Indian Affairs Guidelines, 44 Fed. Reg. 67,583 (1979). These guidelines are not regulations and have been granted varying degrees of deference by courts.

The non-Indian couple, E.C. and C.C., petitioned to adopt the children. Their petition was opposed by the Leech Lake Band of Chippewa, who insisted that since there was no "good cause" for deviating from the placement preferences designated by ICWA, the three should remain in the custody of their latest Indian foster home.

The Chippewa presented to the court "expert" witnesses who, echoing Dr. Westermeyer, testified that "Native American children who grow up in non-Native homes suffer from intense identity crises in adolescence."[77] In addition, three social workers, each of whom was qualified by the court as an "Indian expert," posited that, all things considered, it would be best to attempt to "stabilize" the children in the foster home. An official with the Minnesota Chippewa Tribe Human Services Division declared that he was in the process of recruiting an Indian adoptive home for them.

The trial court held that there was good cause to deviate, in this instance, from ICWA's preferences for placement. Although a court of appeals affirmed, the Minnesota Supreme Court disagreed and reversed. The trial court had cited as its ground for deviating from the ICWA preference hierarchy the fact that the children in question had "extraordinary physical and emotional needs"—one of the valid "good cause" grounds set forth by the Bureau of Indian Affairs—but the state supreme court ruled that that conclusion had been founded on insufficient "expert" testimony. The trial judge had held that given the availability of an adoptive home, an otherwise adequate foster home failed to meet the children's need for permanence. But the Minnesota Supreme Court rejected that conclusion, charging that it had been "based on the improper assumption that the need for permanence could only be met through adoption."[78] Satisfied that there in fact existed no "good cause" to deviate from ICWA's terms, and that the foster home acceptably addressed the children's need for stability, the Minnesota Supreme Court decreed that the adoption petition of E.C. and C.C. must be denied.[79]

That *In re S.E.G.* constitutes a plausible interpretation of ICWA's preferencing scheme should cast a heavy pall over it. After all, based upon this scheme, a state supreme court mandated that three hard-to-place children be denied an immediate opportunity to be adopted by two competent adults (their fitness was never questioned) in favor of being kept on in a foster home. Even after over a year of searching, state officials had been unable, by the time of the supreme court's decision, to find an adequate Indian adoptive home. By the court's logic, however, further delay did not much matter, for the terms of ICWA would preclude the children's placement with non-Indian adoptive parents even if it could be known for certain that an Indian adoptive family would *never* be found for them. That was because, according to the court's reading of ICWA, their continued placement in the Indian foster home was fine—indeed, required—so long as that home was deemed "adequate."

If *In re S.E.G.* was an isolated ruling, it could be written off as a sport—a disaster for the particular children at issue, yes, but a mere juridical oddity. But it was (and is) *not* alone. In the case of S.E.G. and her siblings, numerous amici curiae, including the Minnesota commissioner of Human Services, representatives from several Indian tribes, and various Indian advocacy groups, urged the result reached. Such support suggests that absent legislative intervention, the *S.E.G.* decision will not be the last in which a state court, acting pursuant to federal law, issues an order that channels a child toward the plainly inferior of the available placement options.*

If they are to address systematically the predicament faced by parentless Indian children, policymakers need to do several things. First and foremost, Congress should take the necessary steps to neutralize those influences, especially poverty, which most likely contribute to the disproportionate presence of Native Americans among those in need of foster and adoptive care. ICWA suggests that socioeconomic deprivation is not the main cause of the child-welfare crisis, that much more significant is the problem of state officials' ethnocentrism. I have proposed several reasons to doubt that assessment. In light of these doubts, Congress ought to revisit this subject. Yes, dominant groups have sometimes coercively adopted the children of subordinated ones.[80] Yes, some

---

*For similarly bad, perhaps even worse, judgments, see *In re C.H.*, 997 P. 2d 776 (Mont. 2000); *In the Adoption of Riffle*, 922 P. 2d 510 (Mont. 1996).

people who regard themselves as "child savers" have wrested children from their homes of origin out of a misguided desire to "free" them from an environment perceived to be contaminated.[81] Yes, racism of various sorts constitutes a large presence in the history of adoption in America.[82] Yes, ambiguous legal criteria have facilitated undue and unwanted interventions by officious child-welfare bureaucrats.[83] Yes, there is plenty in American history that makes plausible the conventional story that Indian families were ransacked by racist officials who in effect stole their children and thereby perpetrated a massive and horrible moral crime.

Congress failed, however, to document responsibly its version of that story, and, as I have shown, there is reason to believe that Congress's version is substantially exaggerated. Given the continuing influence of its historical findings, Congress is obligated to reconsider them. This is no mere academic matter. Based on its understanding of the pertinent history, for example, Congress toughened the procedural standard that state authorities must meet before removing a child from an Indian family covered by the legislation. Whereas typically a child may be removed from his or her home on a showing of clear and convincing evidence of neglect or abuse, under ICWA, state authorities must adduce evidence that proves beyond a reasonable doubt that an Indian child is being seriously abused or neglected.[84] Intended to assist Indian children, this provision on balance harms them by making it too difficult to remove them from the hellish conditions that confront all too many youngsters who languish helplessly behind the closed doors of their homes.[85] There is reason to be cautious when it comes to permitting state officials to intrude into the delicate, hard-to-fathom precincts of the home.[86] But influenced by its own hyperbole, Congress in ICWA went too far.

Second, to avoid or at least minimize racialist opportunism in the context of child-custody disputes, the federal government should codify some form of existing Indian family doctrine.* ICWA should not be

---

*Congress has both declined to enact legislation that would have codified the existing Indian family doctrine (see, for example, the Adoption Promotion and Stability

permitted to become a snare with which tribes or disgruntled litigants capture children with no previously established tribal association.

Third, Congress should certainly abolish part—maybe all—of the matching regime that ICWA mandates. Though there is a "political" dimension to Indian tribes that distinguishes them from other subgroups in American society that have been labeled as "races," the racial element of ICWA becomes glaringly plain when one revisits its hierarchy of adoptive placement.[87] The statute directs that, in the absence of good cause to the contrary, preference for adoption should first be given to a member of the child's extended family—a kinship bias. The statute then directs that preference be given to other members of the child's tribe—a tribal/political bias. Then ICWA mandates that preference should be given to "other Indian families"—a purely racial bias. When the United States Supreme Court upheld a system of preferences in federal employment for members of recognized tribes, it concluded that the distinction in question was political rather than racial. It noted that the preference operated to exclude many individuals who were racially classified as "Indians."* By contrast, the third of ICWA's preferences refers not to tribal affiliation but mere Indianness as the desired characteristic. To that extent, ICWA probably represents the last stand of open race matching in America. The United States should prohibit *all* governments under its aegis—federal, state, and tribal—from engaging in race matching. This means, at a minimum, that the third prong of the ICWA placement hierarchy ought to be repealed or invalidated and that the remainder of the scheme ought to be searchingly reconsidered.

---

Act of 1996, H.R. 3286, 104th Cong. [1996]) and legislation that would have barred the use of the doctrine (see S. 1976, 100th Cong., 133 Cong. Rec. S18, 533 (Daily ed. Dec. 19, 1987).

*Morton v. Mancari*, 417 U.S. 535, 553 (1973). For instructive commentary on controversies related to classifying Native Americans in racial or political terms see David E. Wilkins, *American Indian Politics and the American Political System* (2002), especially "Indian Peoples are Nations, Not Minorities" 41–62; Carole Goldberg, "Americans Indians and 'Preferential' Treatment," *UCLA Law Review* 49 (2002), 943; L. Scott Gould, "Mixing Bodies and Beliefs;" David Williams, "The Borders of the Equal Protection Clause: Indians as Peoples," *UCLA Law Review* 38 (1991): 759.

# Afterword

Commentary on race relations in the United States can be usefully divided into two broad traditions. One is a pessimistic tradition that doubts either the wisdom or the possibility of achieving racial harmony on the basis of racial equality. Thomas Jefferson was a racial pessimist, claiming with certainty that "the two races, equally free, cannot live in the same government" because "nature, habit, [and] opinion [have] drawn indelible lines of distinction between them."[1] Similar assertions have been made with respect to Native Americans, Asian Americans, Latino Americans, and others who have been perceived as inferior outsiders to Euro American communities. Running counter to this current is an optimistic tradition that affirms both the wisdom and the possibility of bringing into being a racially egalitarian society in which individuals may enjoy their freedoms without racial constraint. Champions of this tradition have included Frederick Douglass, Lydia Maria Child, Wendell Phillips, and Martin Luther King Jr. Although both of these traditions figure prominently in the stories I have told in the previous pages, it should be clear by now that I myself am firmly in the latter camp.

There are realistic grounds for believing that in terms of race relations, better days lie ahead, when the beneficent transformations wrought by the civil rights revolution will be reinforced and deepened by new variations on familiar influences (e.g., immigration), technological innovations (e.g., the Internet), novel conceptions of personal and communal identity (e.g., enlarged possibilities for racial self-classification), and daily decisions made by ordinary people driven by the perennial human yearning for companionship and love—decisions that are manifest in ever increasing rates of interracial dating, marriage, and adoption. I am aware of the baleful extent to which America remains a pigmentocracy, to which white-supremacist notions, though coded, retain their influence, and to which some reactions against white racism have generated new cycles of destructive resentments, paranoias, and prejudices carried on by people of color. But I am aware, too, that the United States is a far different place from—a considerably *better* place than—the country into which Jacqueline Henley was born.

It is important, of course, to recognize the failure of our society to live up to its aspirations. Racial injustice, in addition to other social iniquities, remains a central feature of the American scene that affects practically every sphere of life. The toxins loosed by conquest, slavery, and segregation have continued to poison the body politic, in large part because of our inadequate resolve to right past wrongs. One manifestation of that sickness is the massive extent to which racial alienation continues to govern our intimate associations. Still, it is also important to recognize that through intelligent, militant, persistent effort, our democracy's condition can be improved. A keen appreciation of this fact and a willingness to build upon it can be effective antidotes to the enervating sense of impotency that sometimes grips all too many Americans and dissuades them from acting decisively to change what needs changing.

To improve race relations in the sphere of intimate association, we need to attend to three tasks. While the first of these does not relate to intimate association specifically, it nevertheless will condition decisively the choices that people make when it comes to selecting friends, partners, and spouses. That task is to raise the shamefully low standard of living in which far too many Americans, a disproportionate number of whom are colored, now find themselves mired. The extent to which racial minorities are conspicuously encumbered by poverty, unemployment, lesser educational opportunities, and like deprivations is the *minimum* extent to which they will continue to be marginalized in the common market for companionship. Second, Americans should permit neither states nor the federal government to engage in routine race matching. In the eyes of the law, race should play no role in ranking families; multiracial ones must be deemed the equals of their mono-racial counterparts. Third, individuals can greatly assist in improving matters by refusing to embrace unthinkingly inherited habits and by daring to put into action humane ideals.

# Notes

## Introduction

1. *Green v. City of New Orleans*, 88 So.2d 76, 78 (La. Ct. App. 1956), (quoting trial testimony of Mrs. McBride).

2. The story of Jacqueline Henley/Lynn Ware as recounted here is based primarily on a reported court decision as well as the briefs, record, and trial-court decision in her case. See *Green*, 88 So.2d 76; *Green v. City of New Orleans*, No. 337–854, slip op. (La. Dist. Ct. Aug. 22, 1955); Brief on Behalf of Jacqueline Ann Henley, *Green* (No. 20,696); Record, *Green*, No. 337–854 (hereafter, "Record"). These materials are on file at the Harvard Law School Library, in the Interracial Intimacies Collection.

   My narrative also relies in part on interviews with Lynn Ware, Burton Klein, Lillie Mae Green, and Catherine Oberholtzer, all conducted by me in June 1998.

   See also Virginia R. Dominguez, *White by Definition: Social Classification in Creole Louisiana* (1986), 87–89; "The Dixie Orphan Whites Won't Have, Negroes Can't Adopt," *Jet*, February 7, 1957 (hereafter "Dixie Orphan"); James O'Byrne, "Invented Concepts Distort Our Lives," *New Orleans Times-Picayune*, August 15, 1993.

3. See Record of June 17, 1955, at 5.

4. See Record of July 12, 1955, at 3, 7.

5. See Record of June 17, 1955, at 6.

6. See "Dixie Orphan."

7. See Record of June 17, 1955, at 3.

8. According to Catherine Oberholtzer, the white social worker in charge of the Greens' case, African American caseworkers in New

Orleans in the 1950s constructed color charts to assist Negro prospective adoptive parents, who often noted on their applications that they were specifically looking for a child of a given color (usually light-skinned) and with a given hair texture (usually "good hair," meaning straight or slightly curly but definitely *not* kinky). Interview with the author, New Orleans, L.A., June 1998.

On color differentiations among blacks, see Kathy Russell, Midge Wilson, and Ronald Hall, *The Color Complex: The Politics of Skin Color Among African-Americans* (1992) and Trina Jones, "Shades of Brown: The Law of Skin Color," 49 *Duke Law Journal* 1487 (2000).

9. See *Green v. City of New Orleans,* 88 So.2d at 76, 78.

10. See Petition for Writ of Mandamus at 1; *Green v. City of New Orleans,* No. 337–854.

11. For a comprehensive listing of Louisiana's segregation statutes, see Pauli Murray, ed., *States' Laws on Race and Color* (1951; rev. ed., 1997). For a history of the struggle that erased those statutes, see Adam Fairclough, *Race and Democracy: The Civil Rights Struggle in Louisiana, 1915–1972* (1995).

12. See Calvin Trillin, "American Chronicles Black or White," *New Yorker,* February 24, 1986.

13. See *Green,* No. 337–854.

14. Record of July 12, 1955, at 31–32.

15. Ibid. at 32.

16. Record of June 17, 1955, at 21.

17. *Green,* 88 So.2d at 76, 78 (quoting letter).

18. Record of June 17, 1955, at 22, 25.

19. Ibid. at 32–33.

20. Author's interview with Burton Klein, June 1998.

21. Record of June 17, 1955, at 21, 22.

22. *Green,* 88 So.2d at 80.

23. Ibid. at 80–81 (quoting *Treadway v. Louisiana,* 56 So.2d 735, 739 [La. Ct. App. 1952]).

24. Ibid. at 81. Compare Cheryl Harris, "Whiteness as Property," *Harvard Law Review* 106 (1993): 1709.

25. *Green,* 88 So.2d at 80.

26. *Green,* No. 337–854.

27. See *Green,* 88 So.2d at 81.

28. See ibid. (Janvier, J., dissenting).

29. Ibid. at 82.

30. Ibid.

31. For useful commentary on the idea of "race," particularly the impact of "scientific" fallacies on the evolution of that idea, see Thomas F. Gossett, *Race: The History of an Idea in America* (new ed., 1997); Ivan Hannaford, *Race: The History of an Idea in the West* (1996); Luca Cavalli-Sforza, Paolo Menozzi, and Alberto Piazza, *The History and Geography of Human Genes* (1994); James C. King, *The Biology of Race* (1981); Ashley Montagu, *Man's Most Dangerous Myth: The Fallacy of Race* (4th ed., 1964).

32. Brief on Behalf of Jacqueline Ann Henley at 10, *Green*, 88 So.2d 76 (No. 20,696).

33. An interesting article discussing *Green* may indicate that the case is finally making its way into the canon of race-relations jurisprudence. See Robert Westley, "First-Time Encounters: 'Passing' Revisited and Demystification as a Critical Practice," *Yale Law & Policy Review* 18 (2000): 297; see also Randall Kennedy, "Race Relations Law in the Canon of Legal Academia," in Jack Balkin and Sanford Levinson, eds., *Legal Canons* (2000).

34. Sander Gilman, *Difference and Pathology: Stereotypes of Sexuality, Race, and Madness* (1985), 81.

35. A miscellany of instructive texts that either analyze or manifest obsession with the sexual dimension of racial conflict includes Daniel M. Friedman, *A Mind of Its Own: A Cultural History of the Penis* (2001); Stanley Crouch, *Don't the Moon Look Lonesome* (2000); Chris Rock, *Roll with the New* (1997); Harry Steropoulos & Michael Uebel, eds., *Race and the Subject of Masculinization* (1997); Jan Nederveen Peterese, *White on Black: Images of Africa and Blacks in Western Popular Culture* (1992); bell hooks, "Selling Hot Pussy," in *Black Looks: Race and Representation* (1992); Anonymous, *Leda in Black on White* (1991); Richard Pryor, *That Nigger's Crazy* (1987); Lattie Gosett, "Is it true what they say about colored pussy?," in Carole S. Vance, ed., *Pleasure and Danger: Exploring Female Sexuality* (1984); Gordon Parks Jr., *Superfly* (1972); Melvin van Peebles, *Sweet Sweetback's Baadasss Song* (1971); Cecil Brown, *The Life and Loves of Mr. Jiveass Nigger* (1969); Eldridge Cleaver, *Soul on Ice* (1969); Iceberg Slim, *Pimp* (1969); Winthrop Jordan, *White over Black: American Attitudes Towards the Negro 1550–1812* (1968); Calvin Hernton, *Sex and Racism in America* (1965); Norman Mailer, "The White Negro," in *Advertisements for Myself* (1959).

36. See Gayl Jones, *Corregidor* (1975); Alice Walker, *Meridian* (1976); James Baldwin, *Another Country* (1962) and *Tell Me How Long the*

*Train's Been Gone* (1968); Richard Wright, *Native Son* (1940) and *Uncle Tom's Children* (1938); William Faulkner, *Absalom, Absalom!* (1936), *Go Down Moses* (1942), and *Light in August* (1932); Jean Toomer, *Cane* (1923). See also Werner Sollors, *Neither Black Nor White Yet Both: Thematic Explorations of Interracial Literature* (1997); James Kinney, *Amalgamation! Race, Sex, and Rhetoric in the Nineteenth-Century American Novel* (1985).

37. See Tyler Gray, "Look for Plenty of Power Plays on 'Jeopardy,'" *Orlando Sentinel,* November 17, 1997.

38. Daryl Cumber Dance, *Shuckin' and Jivin': Folklore from Contemporary Black Americans* (1978), 193.

39. Thomas Jefferson, *Notes on the State of Virginia,* ed. William Peden (1955), 139.

40. Winthrop D. Jordan, *White over Black: American Attitudes Toward the Negro, 1550–1812* (1968), 151. Professor Jordan makes this statement facetiously, of course, condemning the attitude it mirrors.

41. See Donald Bole, *Toms, Coons, Mulattoes, Mammies, and Bucks: An Interpretive History of Blacks in American Films* (1989); Thomas Cripps, *Slow Fade to Black: The Negro in American Film, 1900–1942* (1977).

42. Ntozake Shange, "Fore/Play," in Miriam DeCosta-Willis, Reginald Martin, Roseann P. Bell, eds., *Erotique Noire/Black Erotica* (1992), xix.

43. See Alexis de Tocqueville, "The Present and Probable Future Condition of the Three Races That Inhabit the Territory of the United States," in *Democracy in America* (Phillips Bradley, ed., Vintage Books 1990 [1835]); see also Randall Kennedy, "Tocqueville and Racial Conflict in America: A Comment," *Harvard BlackLetter Law Journal* 11 (1994): 145.

44. *Kinney v. Commonwealth,* 71 Va. (30 Gratt.) 858, 869 (1878).

45. *Pace v. State,* 69 Ala. 231, 232 (1881), aff'd, *Pace v. Alabama,* 106 U.S. 583 (1883).

46. *Loving v. Virginia,* 388 U.S. 1, 3 (1967), (quoting the opinion of the trial court that convicted the Lovings).

47. 60 U.S. 393 (1857).

48. Ibid. at 393, 409.

49. Abraham Lincoln, *Speeches and Writings, 1832–1858* (Library of America, 1989), 397–98.

50. Sidney Kaplan, "The Miscegenation Issue in the Election of 1864," in *American Studies in Black and White: Selected Essays 1949–1989,* ed. Allan D. Austin (1991), 48–49. See generally Forrest G. Wood,

*Black Scare: The Racist Response to Emancipation and Reconstruction* (1968).

51. Alfred Avins, "Anti-Miscegenation Laws and the Fourteenth Amendment: The Original Intent," *Virginia Law Review* 52 (1966): 1224.

52. See Alexander M. Bickel, "The Original Understanding and the Segregation Decision," *Harvard Law Review* 69 (1955): 1, 58; R. Carter Pittman, "The Fourteenth Amendment: Its Intended Effect on Anti-Miscegenation Laws," *North Carolina Law Review* 43 (1964): 92, 108; Avins, "Anti-Miscegenation Laws," 1253; Samuel Marcosson, "Colorizing the Constitution of Originalism: Clarence Thomas at the Rubicon," *Law and Inequality* 16 (1998): 429, 451. But see Steven A. Bank, "Anti-Miscegenation Laws and the Dilemma of Symmetry: The Understanding of Equality in the Civil Rights Act of 1875," *University of Chicago Law School Roundtable* 2 (1995): 303.

53. Quoted in Leslie H. Harris, "From Abolitionist Amalgamators to 'Rulers of the Five Points': The Discourse of Interracial Sex and Reform in Antebellum New York City," in Martha Hodes, ed., *Sex, Love, Race: Crossing Boundaries in North American History* (1999), 198.

54. Quoted in David H. Fowler, *Northern Attitudes Towards Interracial Marriage: Legislation and Public Opinion in the Middle Atlantic States and the States of the Old Northwest, 1780–1930* (1987), 157.

55. *Plessy v. Ferguson,* 163 U.S. 537, 557 (1896), (Harlan, J., dissenting). See Otto H. Olsen, ed., *The Thin Disguise: Turning Point in Negro History:* Plessy v. Ferguson, *A Documentary Presentation, 1864–1896* (1967), 53.

56. W. W. Wright, "Amalgamation," *DeBow's Review* 29 (July 1860): 13, quoted in Peter W. Bardaglio, *Reconstructing the Household: Families, Sex, & the Law in the Nineteenth Century South* (1995), 49.

57. Gunnar Myrdal, *An American Dilemma: The Negro Problem and Modern Democracy* (1944; twentieth-anniversary edition, 1962), 1:57.

58. Ibid., 1:54–55.

59. Tom P. Brady, *Black Monday* (1955), 65. See also John Bartlow Martin, *The Deep South Says "Never"* (1957), 16; James Graham Cook, *The Segregationists* (1962), 14, 16.

60. See, e.g., George S. Schuyler, "Do Negroes Want to Be White?," *American Mercury,* June 1956, p. 55; Lawrence Otis Graham, *Member of the Club: Reflections on Life in a Racially Polarized World* (1995), 35. See also Myrdal, *American Dilemma,* 1:62.

61. See Rick Hertzberg, "Bad News for Bigots," *New Yorker,* March 12, 2000. See Frank Bruni with Nicholas D. Kristof, "The 2000 Campaign: The Texas Governor: Bush Rues Failure to Attack Bigotry in Visit to Campus," *New York Times,* February 28, 2000; Lizette Alvarez, "The 2000 Campaign: The Religion Issue: Democrats in Congress Introduce Resolution Attacking Bob Jones U. as Intolerant," *New York Times,* March 1, 2000; Gustav Niebuhr, "The 2000 Campaign: The Religion Issue: Interracial Dating Ban to End," *New York Times,* March 4, 2000.

62. Personals Advertising Questionnaire Materials 1-3 (on file with Harvard Law School Library in Interracial Intimacies Collection) [hereinafter Personals Material]; *Boston Magazine,* February 2000, 186–87; *New York,* February 21, 2000, 151, 153; *Philadelphia,* February 2000, 180–81, 183.

63. Alexander Bickel, *The Morality of Consent* (1975), 133.

64. William van Alstyne, "Rites of Passage: Race, the Supreme Court, and the Constitution," *University of Chicago Law Review* 46 (1979): 775.

65. All three ads from *Interrace,* no. 45 (1999).

66. Personals Material.

67. Ibid.

68. Ibid.

69. Exceptional writings that do grapple with the racial ethics of private decision making in intimate contexts include Rachel Moran, *Interracial Intimacy: The Regulation of Race and Romance* (2001); Jerry Kang, "Cyber-Race," *Harvard Law Review* 113 (2000): 1131; R. Richard Banks, "The Color of Desire: Fulfilling Adoptive Parents' Racial Preferences Through Discriminatory State Action," *Yale Law Journal* 107 (1998): 975; Lisa Peets, "Racial Steering in the Romantic Marketplace," *Harvard Law Review* 107 (1994): 877; Larry Alexander, "What Makes Wrongful Discrimination Wrong? Biases, Preferences, Stereotypes, and Proxies," *University of Pennsylvania Law Review* 141 (1992): 149.

70. See Lawrence Blum, "Moral Asymmetries in Racism," in Susan E. Babitt and Sue Campbell, eds., *Racism and Philosophy* (1999).

71. On the national outcry against Bob Jones University's policy banning interracial dating, see David S. Broder, "South Carolina's Shame," *Washington Post,* March 29, 2000.

72. Frederick Douglass, "The Present and Future of the Colored Race in America: An Address Delivered in Brooklyn, New York, on 15 May

1863," in *The Frederick Douglass Papers,* vol. 3, *1855–63,* ed. John W. Blassingame (1985), 576.

73. Author's interview with Lynn Ware, June 1998.

74. Author's interview with Lillie Mae Green, June 1998.

75. Author's interview with Burton Klein, June 1998.

76. See *Compos v. McKeithen,* 341 F. Supp. 264 (E.D. La. 1972).

## Chapter One:
### In the Age of Slavery

1. On slavery in North America, see Ira Berlin, *Many Thousands Gone: The First Two Centuries of Slavery in North America* (1998); Thomas D. Morris, *Southern Slavery and the Law, 1619–1860* (1996); Peter Kolchin, *Unfree Labor: American Slavery and Russian Serfdom* (1987); John W. Blassingame, *The Slave Community: Plantation Life in the Antebellum South* (rev. and enl. ed., 1979); Paul D. Escott, *Slavery Remembered: A Record of Twentieth-Century Slave Narratives* (1979); Eugene Genovese, *Roll, Jordan, Roll: The World the Slaves Made* (1974); Edgar J. McManus, *Black Bondage in the North* (1973); Winthrop Jordan, *White over Black: American Attitudes Toward the Negro, 1550–1812* (1968); Kenneth M. Stampp, *The Peculiar Institution: Slavery in the Ante-Bellum South* (1956); Ulrich B. Phillips, *American Negro Slavery: A Survey of the Supply, Employment and Control of Negro Labor as Determined by the Plantation Regime* (1918); T. R. R. Cobb, *An Inquiry into the Law of Negro Slavery in the United States: To Which Is Prefixed, An Historical Sketch of Slavery* (1858); William Goodell, *The American Slave Code in Theory and Practice: Its Distinctive Features Shown by Its Statutes, Judicial Decisions, and Illustrative Facts* (1853).

2. Excellent scholarship on interracial sex during the slavery era is constantly being published. Among the works that I consulted were the following: Peter W. Bardaglio, *Reconstructing the Household: Families, Sex, and the Law in the Nineteenth-Century South* (1995); Victoria Bynum, *Uniquely Women: The Politics of Social and Sexual Control in the Old South* (1992); John D'Emilio and Estelle B. Freedman, *Intimate Matters: A History of Sexuality in America* (1988); Elizabeth Fox-Genovese, *Within the Plantation Household: Black and White Women of the Old South* (1988); Herbert G. Gutman, *The Black Family in Slavery and Freedom, 1550–1925* (1976); Martha Hodes, *White Women, Black Men: Illicit Sex in the Nineteenth-*

*Century South* (1997); Ann Patton Malone, *Sweet Chariot: Slave Family and Household Structure in Nineteenth-Century Louisiana* (1992); Melton A. McLaurin, *Celia: A Slave* (1991); Dorothy Sterling, ed., *We Are Your Sisters: Black Women in the Nineteenth Century* (1984); Brenda E. Stevenson, *Life in Black & White: Family and Community in the Slave South* (1996); Merli F. Weiner, *Mistresses and Slaves: Plantation Women in South Carolina, 1830–1860* (1998); Catherine Clinton, "Caught in the Web of the Big House: Women and Slavery," in Walter J. Fraser Jr. et al., eds., *The Web of Southern Social Relations: Women, Family and Education* (1985), and " 'Southern Dishonor': Flesh, Blood, Race and Bondage," in Carol Bleser, ed., *In Joy and in Sorrow: Women, Family, and Marriage in the Victorian South, 1830–1900* (1991); Karen A. Getman, "Sexual Control in the Slaveholding South: The Implications and Maintenance of a Racial Caste System," *Harvard Women's Law Journal* 7 (1984): 115, Thelma Jennings, " 'Us Colored Women Had to Go Through Plenty': Sexual Exploitation of African American Slave Women, *Journal of Women's History* 1 (1990): 45; Nell Irvin Painter, "Of *Lily,* Linda Brent and Freud: A Non-Exceptionalist Approach to Race, Class, and Gender in the Slave South," *Georgia Historical Quarterly* 76 (1992): 241; Joshua D. Rothman, " 'Notorious in the Neighborhood': An Interracial Family in Early National and Antebellum Virginia," 67 *Journal of Southern History* 273 (2001); Joshua D. Rothman, "To Be Freed from That Curse and Let at Liberty: Interracial Adultery and Divorce in Antebellum Virginia," 106 *The Virginia Magazine of History and Biography* 443 (1998).

3. Angela Davis, *Women, Race, and Class* (1981), 25–26. See also Saidiya V. Hartman, *Scenes of Subjection: Terror, Slavery, and Self-Making in Nineteenth-Century America* (1997): "The extremity of power and the absolute submission of the slave render suspect or meaningless concepts of consent and will. . . . In the case of slave women, the law's circumscribed recognition of consent and will occurred only in order to intensify and secure the subordination of the enslaved . . . and deny injury, for it asserted that the captive female was both will-less and always willing" (page 81). This argument is buttressed by a notion embraced by certain feminists, who hold that under conditions of patriarchy, most, if not all, heterosexual sex amounts to coerced sex. See, e.g., Andrea Dworkin, *Intercourse* (1987).

4. *State v. Mann,* 13 N.C. (2 Dev.) 263 (1829).

5. Ibid. at 266.

6. Ibid. at 267.

7. Ibid. at 266.

8. Ibid.

9. Harriet Jacobs, *Incidents in the Life of a Slave Girl, written by Herself* (1861, edited and with an introduction by Jean Fagan Yellin, 1987), 55.

10. Valerie Smith, introduction to Jacobs, *Incidents in the Life of a Slave Girl,* xxxiii.

11. Annette Gordon-Reed, *Thomas Jefferson and Sally Hemings: An American Controversy* (paperback ed., 1998), 168. See also Patricia Hill Collins, *Black Feminist Thought* (second edition, 2000) at 162–63: "To characterize interracial sex [even under slavery] purely in terms of the victimization of Black women would be a distortion, because such depictions strip Black women of agency. . . . Even within these power differentials, genuine affection characterized some sexual relationships between Black women and White men."

12. See Agnes C. Baro, "Spheres of Consent: An Analysis of the Sexual Abuse and Sexual Exploitation of Women Incarcerated in the State of Hawaii," *Women & Criminal Justice* 8 (1997): 61; "Cruel and Unusual: A Special Report on Women and the Prison System," *Women's Review of Books,"* July 1997; Human Rights Watch Women's Rights Project, *All Too Familiar: Sexual Abuse of Women in U.S. State Prisons* (1996).

13. Stephen Shulhofer, *Unwanted Sex: The Culture of Intimidation and the Failure of Law* (1998), 137.

14. See Randall Kennedy, *Race, Crime, and the Law* (1997), 37–38.

15. Ibid., 34–36.

16. Drew Gilpin Faust, *James Henry Hammond and the Old South: A Design for Mastery* (1982), 87.

17. See Kent Anderson Leslie, *Woman of Color, Daughter of Privilege: Amanda America Dickson, 1849–1893* (1995), 1.

18. See D'Emilio and Freedman, *Intimate Matters* (1988), 103: "When white men emancipated their mistresses and mulatto children in their wills they implied that more than mere physical exploitation characterized these relationships."

19. Thomas E. Buckley, S.J., "Unfixing Race: Class, Power, and Identity in an Interracial Family," in Martha Hodes, ed., *Sex, Love, Race: Crossing Boundaries in North American History* (1999).

20. Ibid., 167.

21. See Adrienne D. Davis, "The Private Law of Race and Sex: An Antebellum Perspective," *Stanford Law Review* 51 (1999): 221.

22. See Judith Kelleher Schafer, *Slavery, the Civil Law, and the Supreme Court of Louisiana* (1994), 180, 184.

23. See *Lenora f.w.c. v. Scott*, 10 La. Ann. 651 (1855).

24. See *Reed v. Crocker*, 12 La. Ann. 436 (1857).

25. See *Audat v. Gilly*, 12 Rob. 323 (La. 1845); Schaefer, "'Open and Notorious Concubinage,'" 193–94.

26. See *Adams v. Routh*, 8 La. Ann. 121 (1853).

27. *Marie v. Avart*, 6 Mart. (O.S.) (La. 1819). See also Schaefer, "'Open and Notorious Concubinage,'" 197–98.

28. The outstanding contribution to this topic is Annette Gordon-Reed's *Thomas Jefferson and Sally Hemings: An American Controversy*. See also Thomas Jefferson Foundation, *Report of the Research Committee on Thomas Jefferson and Sally Hemings* (2000), (www.monticello.org); Jan Lewis, Peter S. Onuf, and Jane E. Lewis, eds., *Thomas Jefferson: History, Memory, and Civic Culture* (1999); Stephanie L. Phillips, "Claiming Our Forefathers: The Legend of Sally Hemings and the Tasks of Black Feminist Theory," *Hastings Women's Law Journal* 8 (1997): 401; Scot A. French and Edward L. Ayers, "The Strange Career of Thomas Jefferson: Race and Slavery in American Memory, 1943–1993," in Peter S. Onuf, ed., *Jeffersonian Legacies* (1993); Virginius Dabney, *The Jefferson Scandals: A Rebuttal* (1981); Fawn Brodie, *Thomas Jefferson: An Intimate History* (1974).

29. Thomas Jefferson Foundation, *Report of the Research Committee*, part 6.

30. Madison Hemings's memoir is reprinted in Gordon-Reed, *Thomas Jefferson and Sally Hemings*, 245.

31. Ibid. at 259.

32. Jan Lewis, "The White Jeffersons," in Lewis, Onuf, and Lewis, eds., *Thomas Jefferson*, 142.

33. Douglas L. Wilson, "Thomas Jefferson and the Character Issue," *Atlantic Monthly*, November 1992, pp. 56, 62.

34. Dumas Malone, *Jefferson and His Time* (1948–1981), 214. See also John C. Miller, *The Wolf by the Ears: Thomas Jefferson and Slavery* (1997); Andrew Burstein, *The Inner Jefferson: Portrait of a Grieving Optimist* (1995); Dabney, *Jefferson Scandals*.

35. See French and Ayers, "Strange Career," 429–34.

36. Ibid., 444.

37. Wilson, "Character Issue," 62.

38. Gordon-Reed, *Thomas Jefferson and Sally Hemings*, 116.

39. See, e.g., Dabney, *Jefferson Scandals*, 123; Miller, *Wolf by the Ears*, 207.

40. Letter from Thomas Jefferson to Edward Coles (Aug. 25, 1814) in Merrill D. Peterson, ed., *Thomas Jefferson: Writings* (1984), 1343. See also Thomas Jefferson, *Notes on the State of Virginia* (Frank Shuffelton, ed., 1999), 151.

41. See Jefferson, *Notes on the State of Virginia*, 145–46.

42. Dabney, *Jefferson Scandals*, at 123–24.

43. Douglass Adair, "The Jefferson Scandals" in Trevor Colburn, ed., *Fame and the Founding Fathers* (1974), 182.

44. Cf. *Lolita* (1955).

45. See Irving Brant, *James Madison* 2 (1941–1961): 283; Gordon-Reed, *Thomas Jefferson and Sally Hemings*, 112.

46. Gordon-Reed, *Thomas Jefferson and Sally Hemings*, 187.

47. Quoted ibid., 61.

48. For scholarly support for this proposition, see Phillips, "Claiming Our Forefathers"; Gordon-Reed, *Thomas Jefferson and Sally Hemings*. For a cinematic version of this view, see *Sally Hemings: An American Scandal* (2000). And for an important novel that advances this argument, see Barbara Chase-Riboud, *Sally Hemings* (1979).

49. Chase-Riboud, *Sally Hemings*, 298–99.

50. An outstanding contribution to this subject is Hodes, *White Women, Black Men;* see especially pages 19–38.

51. Ibid.

52. See Joshua D. Rothman, "'To Be Freed from That Curse and Let at Liberty': Interracial Adultery and Divorce in Antebellum Virginia," *Virginia Magazine of History and Biography* 106 (1998): 443; Hodes, *White Women, Black Men*, 68–95.

53. Hodes, *White Women, Black Men*, 74.

54. Ibid.

55. Ibid., 69.

56. Ibid., 70.

57. Ibid.

58. Ibid.

59. Ibid., 457.

60. Ibid., 448.

61. See Michael S. Hindus and Lynne E. Withy, *The Law of Husband and Wife in Nineteenth-Century America: Changing Views of Divorce*, ed. D. Kelly Weisberg (1982); Roderick Phillips, *Putting Asunder: A History of Divorce in Western Society* (1988); Glenda Riley, *Divorce: An American Tradition* (1991).

62. Rothman, "'To Be Freed from That Curse,'" 445–46. Professor Rothman generously shared with me additional data that slightly

changes the numbers he included in his article. The changes do not affect his overall conclusions. The new data will be published in his book *Notorious in the Neighborhood: Sex and Families Across the Color Line in Virginia, 1787–1861* (2003).

63. Ibid., 477.

64. *Scroggins v. Scroggins*, 14 N.C. (3 Dev.) 535 (1832).

65. Ibid. at 545–46.

66. Ibid. at 541–42.

67. Ibid. at 542.

68. Ibid.

69. Ibid. at 544.

70. Ibid. at 544–45.

71. Ibid. at 545.

72. *Barden v. Barden*, 14 N.C. (3 Dev.) 548 (1832).

73. See Gary B. Mills, "Miscegenation and the Free Negro in Antebellum 'Anglo' Alabama: A Reexamination of Southern Race Relations," *Journal of American History* 68 (1981): 16, 23.

74. See Buckley, "Unfixing Race," 164.

75. Ibid., 170. All of the legal documents drafted after Robert Wright's death referred to him as "coloured," "black," or "negro." For more on Robert Wrights's identity, see ibid., 174: "For many if not most important purposes, class and economic condition, rather than race, constructed [Wright's] identity." However, race did cast a pall over Wright's basic status as a freeman. Hence, "When he traveled outside Virginia, he was careful to carry on his person a certified copy of his emancipation papers" (ibid.).

76. Ibid., 171.

77. Ibid., 174.

78. Ibid., 182.

79. There is some literature on interracial intimacy in the North. See, e.g., Leslie M. Harris, "From Abolitionist Amalgamators to 'Rulers of the Five Points': The Discourse of Interracial Sex and Reform in Antebellum New York City," in Hodes, ed., *Sex, Love, Race*; Graham Hodges, "'Desirable Companions and Lovers': Irish and African Americans in the Sixth Ward, 1830–1870," in Ronald H. Bayor and Timothy J. Meagher, eds., *The New York Irish* (1996). Much more work, however, remains to be done on the subject.

80. Mills, "Miscegenation."

81. Leonard L. Richards, *"Gentlemen of Property and Standing": Anti-Abolition Mobs in Jacksonian Democracy* 43 (1970).

Chapter Two:
From Reconstruction
to Guess Who's Coming to Dinner?

1. See Eric Foner, *Reconstruction: America's Unfinished Revolution, 1863–1877* (1988), 85–86: "Beginning in 1865, and for years thereafter, whites throughout the South complained of the difficulty of obtaining female field laborers. . . . All blacks resented the sexual exploitation that had been a regular feature of slave life, and shared the determination that the women no longer labor under the direct supervision of white men." See also Williamson (1980, 1995), 90 ("Simple freedom for Negro people resulted in a large measure of physical separation between the races. . . . The relatively plentiful opportunities for bodily contact between the master class and the slaves afforded by the peculiar institution diminished drastically in freedom"); Leon F. Litwack, *Been in the Storm So Long: The Aftermath of Slavery* (1980), 266 ("The abolition of slavery tended to diminish [sexual interracial contacts] by freeing black women from the whims and lusts of their masters").

2. George Brown Tindall, *South Carolina Negroes, 1877–1900* (1952), 296–97.

3. Martha Hodes, *White Women, Black Men: Illicit Sex in the Nineteenth-Century South* (1997), 150–51.

4. See A. T. Morgan, *Yazoo; or On the Picket Line of Freedom in the South, a Personal Narrative* (1968).

5. See Tindall, *South Carolina Negroes,* 296–97.

6. W. E. B. DuBois, *The Philadelphia Negro: A Social Study* (1899), 366.

7. See Benjamin Quarles, *Frederick Douglass* (1948); Waldo E. Martin Jr., *The Mind of Frederick Douglass* (1984); William S. McFeely, *Frederick Douglass* (1991); Nathan Irvin Huggins, *Slave and Citizen: The Life of Frederick Douglass* (1980).

8. Martin, *Mind of Frederick Douglass,* 99, quoting the *Franklin Gazette* (Va.), February 1, 1884.

9. See McFeely, *Frederick Douglass,* 320.

10. Quoted in Waldo E. Martin Jr., *The Mind of Frederick Douglass* (1984), 95.

11. Booker T. Washington, *Frederick Douglass* (1906; reprint, 1969), 306.

12. Quoted in McFeely, *Frederick Douglass,* 320.

13. See Maria Diedrich, *Love Across the Color Line: Ottilie Assing and Frederick Douglas* (1999).

14. Quarles, *Frederick Douglass,* 298, quoting the *Washington Post,* May 30, 1897.

15. Martin, *Mind of Frederick Douglass,* 100, quoting the *Oswego Record,* February 2, 1884.

16. Booker T. Washington, *Frederick Douglass,* 307, quoting an 1893 address by Douglass.

17. Martin, *Mind of Frederick Douglass,* 99, quoting letter from Douglass to Elizabeth Cady Stanton, May 30, 1884.

18. See Charles S. Johnson, *Backgrounds to Patterns of Negro Segregation* (1943); Leon F. Litwack, *Trouble in Mind: Black Southerners in the Age of Jim Crow* (1998); C. Vann Woodward, *The Strange Career of Jim Crow* (3d rev. ed., 1974); Richard Wright, *Black Boy: A Record of Childhood and Youth* (1945).

19. See Ray Stannard Baker, *Following the Color Line: American Negro Citizenship in the Progressive Era* (1908; reprint, 1964), 165.

20. See Allison Davis et al., *Deep South: A Social and Anthropological Study of Caste and Class* (1941; reprint, 1988), 31.

21. John Dollard, *Caste and Class in a Southern Town* (1937; 3d. ed., 1957), 147–48.

22. Allison Davis et al., *Deep South,* 33–34.

23. See *Dees v. Metts,* 17 So.2d 137 (Ala. 1944).

24. Ibid. at 141.

25. Ibid. at 140–41.

26. Ibid. at 144 (Bouldin, J., dissenting).

27. Ibid. at 139.

28. Ibid. at 141.

29. Ibid. at 142.

30. On the controversies generated by Jack Johnson and his interracial sexual adventures, see Kevin J. Mumford, *Interzones: Black/White Sex Districts in Chicago and New York in the Early Twentieth Century* (1997); Randy Roberts, *Papa Jack: Jack Johnson and the Era of White Hopes* (1983); Al-Tony Gilmore, *Bad Nigger!: The National Impact of Jack Johnson* (1975); Finnis Farr, *Black Champion: The Life and Times of Jack Johnson* (1965).

31. Quoted in Randy Roberts, *Papa Jack,* 74–75.

32. Ibid.

33. Quoted ibid., 141.

34. Mumford, *Interzones,* 4.

35. Randy Roberts, *Papa Jack,* 141–42, quoting the *Omaha Evening World-Herald,* September 13, 1912, p. 12.

36. Randy Roberts, *Papa Jack,* 173.

37. Ibid., 146.
38. Ibid., 146–47.
39. Ibid., 146.
40. Ibid.
41. Ibid., 158.
42. Ibid.
43. Ibid.
44. *Congressional Record* 49 (1912): 502.
45. Ibid.
46. Ibid.
47. Ibid.
48. Ibid.
49. Ibid.
50. Ibid., 504.
51. Ibid., 503–4.
52. Myrdal, *American Dilemma,* 1:57.
53. See Robin D. G. Kelly, *Hammer and Hoe: Alabama Communists During the Great Depression* (1999) and *Race Rebels: Culture, Politics and the Black Working Class* (1994), 103–60; Gerald Horne, *Black Liberation/Red Scare: Ben Davis and the Communist Party* (1994); Mark Naison, *Communists in Harlem During the Depression* (1983); Wilson Record, *The Negro and the Communist Party in Conflict* (1964). For informed analyses that stress the lingering biases, resentments, and discomforts that soured interracial relations within the Communist movement, see Paul Lyons, *Philadelphia Communists, 1936–1946* (1982); George A. Charney, *A Long Journey* (1968).
54. See Richard Iton, *Solidarity Blues: Race, Culture and the American Left* (2000), 118.
55. See, e.g., Irving Howe and Lewis Coser, *The American Communist Party: A Critical History* (1962); Nathan Glazer, *The Social Basis of American Communism* (1961).
56. Glazer, *Social Basis of American Communism,* 171.
57. Naison, *Communists in Harlem,* 136.
58. See Horne, *Black Liberation/Red Scare*; Naison, *Communists in Harlem.* See also Harry Haywood, *Black Bolshevik: Autobiography of an Afro-American Communist* (1978); Yelena Khanga with Susan Jacoby, *Soul to Soul: A Black Russian-American Family, 1865–1992* (1992).
59. Naison, *Communists in Harlem,* 137.
60. See Dale Russakoff, "Lani Guinier Is Still Alive and Talking," *Washington Post Magazine,* December 12, 1993.

61. Rowley, *Richard Wright* (2001), 307.
62. Conrad Lynn, *There Is a Fountain: The Autobiography of Conrad Lynn* (1993), 82, 113.
63. See Renée Christine Romano, "Crossing the Race Line: Black-White Interracial Marriage in the United States, 1945–1990" (Ph.D. diss., Stanford University, 1996), 24.
64. Myrdal, *American Dilemma*, 1:58.
65. Ibid., 60.
66. Paul R. Spickard, *Mixed Blood: Intermarriage and Ethnic Identity in Twentieth-Century America* (1989), 288.
67. Romano, "Crossing the Line," 27.
68. Ibid., 27 (emphasis omitted).
69. See Joseph Golden, "Social Control of Negro-White Intermarriage," *Social Forces* 36 (1958): 267, 268. See also Joseph R. Washington Jr., *Marriage in Black and White* (1970), 193: "While there is no way of accounting statistically for the number of potential black-white marriages broken up by parental pressure, the number is no doubt considerable."
70. Robert Edward Thomas Roberts, "Negro-White Intermarriage: A Study of Social Control" (master's thesis, University of Chicago, 1940), 72.
71. Ibid., 68.
72. See Hettie Jones, *How I Became Hettie Jones* (1990), 62–64.
73. See James McBride, *The Color of Water: A Black Man's Tribute to His White Mother* (1997), 1–2; Robert E. T. Roberts, "Negro-White Intermarriage," 71.
74. See "The Case Against Mixed Marriage," *Ebony,* November 1950, pp. 50, 52; "Where Mixed Couples Live," *Ebony,* May 1955, p. 61.
75. "The Case Against Mixed Marriage," *Ebony,* November 1950, p. 54.
76. Quoted ibid.
77. See Elaine Neil, "Persecution in New York," in Cloyte M. Larsson, ed., *Marriage Across the Color Line* (1965).
78. See Romano, "Crossing the Line," 249.
79. Melba Pattillo Beals, *White Is a State of Mind: A Memoir* (1999), 267.
80. Quoted ibid.
81. Quoted ibid., 268.
82. See Tilden G. Edelstein, "Othello in America: The Drama of Racial Intermarriage," in J. Morgan Kousser and James M. McPherson, eds., *Region, Race, and Reconstruction: Essays in Honor of C. Vann Woodward* (1982), 179, 182.

83. See ibid., 183–84.

84. Ibid., 186.

85. Ibid.

86. Quoted in Martin Duberman, *Paul Robeson: A Biography* (1988), 263.

87. Lynn, *There Is a Fountain,* 104.

88. See Charlene Regester, "Black Films, White Censors: Oscar Michaux Confronts Censorship in New York, Virginia, and Chicago," in Francis G. Couvares, ed., *Movie Censorship and American Culture* (1996), 171.

89. Ibid., 178.

90. See Gerard Gardner, *The Censorship Papers: Movie Censorship Letters from the Hays Office, 1934 to 1968* (1987), 213. See also Thomas Cripps, *Slow Fade to Black: The Negro in American Film, 1900–1942* (1977); Nickieann Fleener, "The Worst Case of Racial Equality He Ever Saw: The Supreme Court, Motion Picture Censorship, and the Color Line," in Thomas L. Tedford et al., eds., *Perspectives on Freedom of Speech: Selected Essays from the Journals of the Speech Communication Association* (1987).

91. See Thomas Cripps, *Making Movies Black: The Hollywood Message Movie from World War II to the Civil Rights Era* (1993), 265.

92. Brian Ward, *Just My Soul Responding: Rhythm and Blues, Black Consciousness, and Race Relations* (1998), 103, quoting *The Southerner,* March 1956, p. 5.

93. Ibid., 104. See also L. Martin and K. Seagrave, *Anti-Rock: The Opposition to Rock 'n' Roll* (1988).

94. Ward, *Just My Soul Responding,* 105–6.

95. Ibid., 103, quoting *The Southerner,* August 1956, p. 16.

96. Ibid., 107.

97. Ibid.

98. See David Allyn, *Make Love Not War: The Sexual Revolution, An Unfettered History* (2000); John D'Emilio and Estelle B. Freedman, *Intimate Matters: A History of Sexuality in America* (1988, 1997 2nd ed.).

99. See Ernest Porterfield, *Black and White Mixed Marriages* (1978), 27. See also Robert B. McNamara, Maria Tempenis, and Beth Walton, *Crossing the Race Line: Interracial Couples in the South* (1999). John H. Burma, "Interethnic Marriage in Los Angeles, 1948–1959," *Social Forces* 42 (1963): 156; David M. Heer, "Negro-White Marriages in the United States," *Journal of Marriage and the Family* 27 (1966): 262.

100. On Lena Horne, see James Haskins and Kathleen Benson, *Lena: A Personal and Professional Biography of Lena Horne* (1984); Lena Horne and Richard Schickel, *Lena* (1965). On Dorothy Dandridge, see Donald Broyle, *Dorothy Dandridge: A Biography* (1997). On Eartha Kitt, see Eartha Kitt, *Alone with Me: A New Autobiography* (1976) and *(I'm Still Here) Confessions of a Sex Kitten* (1991). On Pearl Bailey, see Pearl Bailey, *Between You and Me: A Heartfelt Memoir on Learning, Loving and Living* (1989); *Talking to Myself* (1971); *The Raw Pearl* (1968).

101. See "Chubby Checker and Dutch Beauty Queen Catherine Lodders," *Jet*, November 17, 1960.

102. See Sammy Davis Jr., Jane Boyar, and Burt Boyar, *Why Me?: The Sammy Davis, Jr., Story* (1989), 116–20. Sammy Davis Jr. was reputed to have had sexual relations with scores of white women before and after his marriage to Britt. See *The Sammy Davis Jr. Reader*, Gerald Early ed. (2001).

103. Ibid., 129. See also Victor Lasky, *J.F.K.: The Man and the Myth* (1963), 113.

104. Sammy Davis Jr., et al., *Why Me?*, 124.

105. Sammy Davis Jr., Boyar, and Boyar, *Yes I Can* (1965), 184.

106. Claudia Feldman, "Marian Wright Edelman, Remembering the Past, Changing the Future," *Houston Chronicle*, April 30, 1999; Joanna Bigger, "The Protector," *Washington Post*, May 18, 1986.

107. See David Bradley, "Novelist Alice Walker: Telling the Black Woman's Story," *New York Times*, January 8, 1984. For Walker's thinly veiled, fictionalized account of her relationship with Leventhal, see Alice Walker, *The Way Forward Is with a Broken Heart* (2000).

108. "We Fell in Love," *Newsweek,* September 16, 1963.

109. "Where Integration Led to Intermarriage," *U.S. News & World Report*, September 16, 1963.

110. Charlayne Hunter-Gault, *In My Place* (1992; reprint, 1993), 252.

111. See Doug McAdam, *Freedom Summer* (1988), 93–95, 144–45; Sara M. Evans, *Personal Politics: The Roots of Women's Liberation in the Civil Rights Movement and the New Left* (1979, reprint, 1980), 78–82; Alvin F. Poussaint, "The Stresses of the White Female Worker in the Civil Rights Movement in the South," *American Journal of Psychiatry* 123 (1966): 401.

112. Doug McAdam, *Freedom Summer* (1988), 93.

113. Ibid.

114. David Harris, *Dreams Die Hard* (1982), 67.

115. Evans, *Personal Politics,* 80.
116. Quoted in Albert C. Persons, *The True Selma Story* (1965), 29.
117. Quoted ibid., 7.
118. Ibid., 146.
119. Mary Stanton, *From Selma to Sorrow: The Life and Death of Viola Liuzzo* (1998), 147.
120. Ibid., 57–59.
121. Compare Marjorie Hunter, "Rusk Was Ready to Quit Cabinet," *New York Times,* September 22, 1967, p. 35, to Dean Rusk with Richard Rusk, *As I Saw It* (1990), 581.
122. "A Marriage of Enlightenment," *Time,* September. 29, 1967, p. 28.
123. For useful discussions of *Guess Who's Coming to Dinner?,* see Thomas E. Wartenberg, "'But Would You Want Your Daughter to Marry One?': The Representation of Race and Racism in *Guess Who's Coming to Dinner?*", *Journal of Social Philosophy* 25 (1994): 99; Donald Spoto, *Stanley Kramer: Film Maker* (1978), 273–81; Donald Bogle, *Toms, Coons, Mulattoes, Mammies, & Bucks: An Interpretive History of Blacks in America Films* (1973, 1989 expanded edition), 215–19.
124. Joseph Morgenstern, *Newsweek,* December 25, 1967.
125. *Time,* December 15, 1967, p. 108.
126. Andrew M. Greeley, "Black and White Minstrels," *The Reporter,* March 21, 1968.
127. Morgenstern, *Newsweek,* December 25, 1967.
128. See Spoto, *Stanley Kramer,* 275–76.
129. See, e.g., Stanley Kramer with Thomas M. Coffey, *A Mad, Mad, Mad, Mad World: A Life in Hollywood* (1997), 218: "As far as I know, *Guess Who's Coming to Dinner?* was the first picture ever on this subject."

### Chapter Three:
### From Black-Power Backlash to the New Amalgamationisnism

1. See, e.g., Orlando Patterson, *Rituals of Blood: Consequences of Slavery in Two American Centuries* (1998), 165, and *The Ordeal of Integration: Progress and Resentment in America's "Racial" Crisis* (1997); Randall Kennedy, "How Are We Doing with *Loving:* Race, Law, and Intermarriage," *Boston University Law Review* 77 (1997): 815; Joseph R. Washington Jr., *Marriage in Black and White* (1972).
2. Cornel West, *Race Matters* (1993; reprint, 1994), 122.

3. See Leslie M. Harris, "From Abolitionist Amalgamators to 'Rulers of the Five Points': The Discourse of Interracial Sex and Reform in Antebellum New York City," in Martha Hodes, ed., *Sex, Love, Race: Crossing Boundaries in North American History* (1999), 195, quoting from *Freedom's Journal,* August 17, 1827.

4. Charles H. King Jr., "I Don't Want to Marry Your Daughter," in Cloyte M. Larsson, ed., *Marriage Across the Race Line* (1965), 35.

5. Two articles in particular do an excellent job of bringing together and clarifying black objections to interracial marriage: Anita L. Allen, "Interracial Marriage: Folk Ethics in Contemporary Philosophy," in Naomi Zack, ed., *Women of Color and Philosophy* (2000); Charles W. Mills, "Do Black Men Have a Moral Duty to Marry Black Women?," *Journal of Social Philosophy* 25 (1994): 131.

6. See Franklin Fosdick, "Is Intermarriage Wrecking the NAACP?," *Negro Digest,* June 1950, p. 52. See also Walter White, *A Man Called White: The Autobiography of Walter White* (1948). On White's marriage to Poppy Cannon, see Poppy Cannon, *A Gentle Knight: My Husband, Walter White* (1956).

7. Nick Kotz and Mary Lynn Kotz, *A Passion for Equality: George A. Wiley and the Movement* (1977), 293.

8. See Malcom X and James Farmer, "Separation or Integration: A Debate," in August Meier and Francis L. Broderick, eds., *Black Protest Thought in the Twentieth Century* (2d ed., 1971).

9. Renée Christine Romano, "Crossing the Line: Black-White Interracial Marriage in the United States, 1945–1990" (Ph.D. diss., Stanford University, 1996), 203–4.

10. See Margarete Henson, letter to the editor, *Ebony,* November 1970.

11. Romano, "Crossing the Line," 196.

12. Ibid.

13. See Hettie Jones, *How I Became Hettie Jones* (1990); Amiri Baraka, *The Autobiography of LeRoi Jones* (1984); Werner Sollors, *Amiri Baraka/LeRoi Jones: The Quest for a "Populist Modernism"* (1978); Amiri Baraka, *The LeRoi Jones/Amiri Baraka Reader,* ed. William J. Harris (1991).

14. Baraka, *Jones/Baraka Reader,* 94.

15. Ibid., 96–97.

16. Baraka, *Autobiography,* 193.

17. Ibid., 169.

18. Stanley Kauffmann, "LeRoi Jones and the Tradition of the Fake," *Dissent* 12 (1965): 207.

19. Joyce Black, letter to the editor, *Village Voice,* September 12, 1968.

20. Lula Miles, letter to the editor, *Ebony*, August 1969, p. 19.

21. Miraonda J. Stevens, letter to the editor, *Ebony*, September 1969, at 22.

22. Quoted in Paul Spickard, *Mixed Blood: Intermarriage and Ethnic Identity in Twentieth-Century America* (1989), 302.

23. Katrina Williams, letter to the editor, *Ebony*, July 1974, pp. 16–17.

24. Mary A. Dowdell, letter to the editor, *Ebony*, November 1969, pp. 22–24.

25. See *Jungle Fever* (1991). For commentary on the film, see Nelson George, *Blackface: Reflections on African-Americans and the Movies* (1994) 114–17; Stanley Kauffmann, *"Jungle Fever,"* New Republic, July 29, 1991; Jack Kroll, "Spiking a Fever," *Newsweek*, June 10, 1991.

26. Lawrence Otis Graham, *Member of the Club: Reflections on Life in a Racially Polarized World* (1995), 27–67.

27. Ibid., 29.

28. Bebe Moore Campbell, "Black Men, White Women: A Sister Relinquishes Her Anger," in Marita Golden, ed., *Wild Women Don't Wear No Blues: Black Women Writers on Love, Men and Sex* (1993), 120–21.

29. Graham, *Member of the Club*, 57.

30. Ibid., 41.

31. See Robert Suro, "Mixed Doubles," *American Demographics,* November 1999.

32. See Daniel Lichter et al., "Race and the Retreat from Marriage: A Shortage of Marriageable Men?," *American Sociological Review* 57 (1992): 781, 797.

33. See Yanick St. Jean and Robert E. Parker, "Disapproval of Interracial Unions: The Case of Black Families" in Cerdell K. Jacobson, ed., *American Families: Issues in Race and Ethnicity* (1995).

34. Campbell, "Black Men, White Women," 117.

35. Graham, *Member of the Club,* 42.

36. Ibid., 45.

37. Ibid., 66.

38. Ibid.

39. Ibid., 29–30.

40. See Derryl Feers and Claudia Deane, "Biracial Couples Report Tolerance; Survey Finds Most Are Accepted by Families," *Washington Post,* July 5, 2001; "Poll Underscores a Change in Attitude," *USA Today,* November 3, 1997; Susan Christian, "Young Don't Feel as Bound by Racial Lines," *Los Angeles Times,* September 12, 1994.

41. On Thomas and his confirmation hearings, see Douglas Scott Gerber, *First Principles: The Jurisprudence of Clarence Thomas* (1999); Anita Fay Hill and Emma Coleman Jordan, eds., *Race, Gender, and Power in America: The Legacy of the Hill-Thomas Hearing* (1995); Jane Mayer and Jill Abramson, *Strange Justice: The Selling of Clarence Thomas* (1994); Toni Morrison, ed., *Race-ing Justice, En-gendering Power: Essays on Anita Hill, Clarence Thomas, and the Construction of Social Reality* (1992).

42. Laura Blumenfeld, "The Nominee's Soul Mate: Clarence Thomas's Wife Shares His Ideas. She's No Stranger to Controversy. And She's Adding to His," *Washington Post,* September 10, 1991.

43. See U.S. Bureau of the Census, "MS-3 Interracial Married Couples: 1960 to Present," January 7, 1999.

44. See Douglas J. Besharov and Timothy S. Robinson, "One Flesh," *The New Democrat,* July/August 1996.

45. Nathan Glazer, "Black and White After Thirty Years," *The Public Interest,* September 1995. See also Michael Lind, "The Beige and the Black," *New York Times Magazine,* August 16, 1998.

46. Kevin Merida, "In Defense of Love Beyond Race," *Washington Post,* December 14, 1997.

47. See David Owen, "The Straddler," *The New Yorker,* January 30, 1995.

48. Julia Malone, "Facing the Racial Question: More Categories in the Census?," *The Atlanta Journal and Constitution,* October 15, 1997.

49. See Stuart Elliott, "The Media Business: Advertising," *New York Times,* April 19, 1996.

50. See Nichelle Nichols, *Beyond Uhura* (1994), 194–97; William Shatner with Chris Kreski, *"Star Trek" Memories* (1993); Mary Murchison-Edwords, *Interrace,* March/April 1992, p. 40.

51. See David Nicholson, "'True Colors': Fox's 'Blended Family' Sitcom," *Washington Post,* July 28, 1991; "The Last Taboo? Does Wave of Interracial Movies Signal a Real Change?," *Ebony,* September 1991.

52. See Ed Siegel, "On Film, Stage and TV, Love Is Becoming Colorblind," *Boston Globe,* June 25, 2000; Greg Braxton, "TV Finds Drama in Interracial Dating," *Los Angeles Times,* March 22, 2000; Ed Siegel, "Of TV, Race, and Romance," *Boston Globe,* November 17, 1991; Nikki Finke, "It's Not Just Another Sitcom: Robert Guillaume Says New Show's Interracial Romance 'No Big Deal,'" *Los Angeles Times,* April 5, 1989. See Greg Braxton, "Colorblind or Just Plain Blind?," *Los Angeles Times,* February 9, 1999; Donna Britt,

"Hard to Be Colorblind about Love," *Washington Post,* June 11, 1999; Donna Britt, "Even on 'ER,' Race and Love a Touchy Mix," *Washington Post,* April 9, 1999.

53. For commentary on *An American Love Story,* see Teresa Wiltz, "'Love Story': Overstaying Its Welcome," *Washington Post,* September 11, 1999; Paula Span, "Modern Family Life in Black and White: PBS Documentary Chronicles an Interracial Marriage," *Washington Post,* September 9, 1999; Caryn James, "In a Family Portrait, the Future," *New York Times,* September 5, 1999.

54. See especially Charles Taylor's fine article "Black and Taboo All Over," Salon.com, February 14, 2000.

55. See generally Werner Sollors, *Neither Black nor White yet Both: Thematic Explorations of Interracial Literature* (1997); Marcia Press, "The Black Man–White Woman Thing: Images of an American Taboo" (Ph.D. diss., Indiana University, 1989); Jonathan David Little, "Definition Through Difference: The Tradition of Black-White Miscegenation in American Fiction" (Ph.D. diss., University of Wisconsin–Madison, 1988); James Kinney, *Amalgamation! Race, Sex, and Rhetoric in the Nineteenth-Century American Novel* (1985); Judith R. Berzon, *Neither White nor Black: The Mulatto Character in American Fiction* (1978).

56. See Elise Virginia Lemire, "Making Miscegenation: Discourses of Interracial Sex and Marriage in the United States, 1790–1865" (Ph.D. diss., Rutgers, the State University of New Jersey–New Brunswick, 1996), 69–106.

57. John Oliver Killens, *'Sippi* (1967), 342.

58. Cecil Brown, *The Life and Loves of Mr. Jiveass Nigger* (1969), 205.

59. Ibid., p. 54.

60. Frank Hercules, *I Want a Black Doll* (1967), 22.

61. James Kinney, *Amalgamation! Race, Sex, and Rhetoric in the Nineteenth-Century American Novel* (1985), 192.

62. Frank Yerby, *Speak Now* (1969), 96.

63. Ibid., 226.

64. Ann Allen Shockley, *Loving Her* (1974; reprint, 1997), 84.

65. Ibid., 187.

66. See, e.g., LeRoi Jones, *Home: Social Essays* (1966); Frances Cress Welsing, *The Isis Papers* (1991); Nathan and Julia Hare, *The Endangered Black Family: Coping with the Unisexualization and Coming Extinction of the Black Race* (1984). For criticism of antigay and antilesbian beliefs among African Americans, see Devon W. Corbado, "Black Rights, Gay Rights, Civil Rights," *UCLA Law Review*

47 (2000): 1467, 1473–78; Keith Boykin, *One More River to Cross: Black and Gay in America* (1996), 155–211; Phillip Brian Harper, *Are We Not Men? Masculine Anxiety and the Problem of African-American Identity* (1996), 3–39; Kobena Mercer and Isaac Julien, "Race, Sexual Politics and Black Masculinity: A Dossier," in Rowena Chapman and Jonathan Rutherford, eds., *Male Order: Unwrapping Masculinity* (1988), 138–40; Cheryl Clarke, "The Failure to Transform: Homophobia in the Black Community," in Barbara Smith, ed., *Home Girls: A Black Feminist Anthology* (1983).

67. Shockley, *Loving Her,* 84–85.

68. See, e.g., Claudine Chiawei O'Hearn, ed., *Half and Half: Writers on Growing Up Biracial and Bicultural* (1998); Naomi Zack, ed., *American Mixed Race: The Culture of Macrodiversity* (1995); Lise Funderburg, *Black, White, Other: Biracial Americans Talk About Race and Identity* (1994); Maria P. P. Root, ed., *Racially Mixed People in America* (1992).

69. Carlos A. Fernandez, "United We Stand!," *Interrace* 59, November/December 1989.

70. See, e.g., Susan R. Graham, "Grassroots Advocacy," in Zack, ed., *American Mixed Race*; Deborah A. Ramirez, "Multiracial Identity in a Color-Conscious World," in Maria P. P. Root, ed., *The Multiracial Experience: Racial Borders as the New Frontier* (1996).

71. S. Graham, "Grassroots Advocacy," p. 186.

72. See the commentary at www.projecttrace.com.

73. See, e.g., George F. Will, "Dropping the 'One Drop' Rule," *Newsweek,* March 25, 2002 (championing the California Racial Privacy Initiative); Yehudi O. Webster, "Twenty-one Arguments for Abolishing Racial Classification," *The Abolitionist Examiner,* June/July 2000 (www.multiracial.com).

74. For criticism, see Jon Michael Spence, *The New Colored People: The Mixed-Race Movement in America* (1997); Tanya Kateri Hernandez, "'Multiracial' Discourse: Racial Classifications in an Era of Color-Blind Jurisprudence," *Maryland Law Review* 57 (1998): 97; Christine B. Hickman, "The Devil and the One Drop Rule: Racial Categories, African Americans and the U.S. Census," *Michigan Law Review* 95 (1997): 1161; Lisa Jones, *Bulletproof Diva: Tales of Race, Sex and Hair* (1994), 53–66.

75. See Maria P. P. Root, A Bill of Rights for Racially Mixed People, in Root, ed., *The Multiracial Experience: Racial Borders as the New Frontier* (1996), 7.

76. See Brenda-Jean Winchester, "More Than a Pretty Face," *Interrace*, April/May 1995, p. 36.

77. O'Hearn, *Half and Half*, xiv.

78. Funderberg, *Black, White, Other*, 10.

79. See Kathy Russell, Midge Wilson, and Robert Hall, *The Color Complex: The Politics of Skin Color Among African Americans* (1992).

80. Ibid., 319–44.

81. Matt Kelley, "Exposure," *Mavin*, spring 2000, p. 7.

82. *Interrace*, November/December 1989.

83. Funderburg, *Black, White, Other*, 323.

84. *Interrace*, April 1994.

85. Ibid.

86. Ibid.

87. See Winchester, "More Than Just a Pretty Face"; Candy Mills, "A Star Is Reborn," *Interrace*, November 1993, p. 38 (on Peggy Lipton); Ed Bradley, "Eartha Kitt," *Interrace*, September/October 1990, p. 10.

88. Charlene McGrady, "Success Story #1," *Interrace*, spring/summer 1993.

89. Ibid.

90. See Mary China, "Success Story #2," *Interrace*, September/October 1993, p. 31.

91. Maurice Smith, "Success Story #7," *Interrace*, August/September 1994, p. 5.

92. See Tia L. Daniel, "An Overview of Historical Amalgamationists and the Modern Amalgamationist Impulse" (third-year paper, Harvard Law School, 1998), 40 (on file at the Harvard Law School Library, Interracial Intimacies Collection).

93. See Candy Mills, "Messengers of Truth," *Interrace*, December 1993, p. 28.

94. Nicholas Anderson, "Success Story #8," *Interrace*, October/November 1994. See also Candy Mills, "The Christians," *Interrace*, May/June 1992, p. 11; Tracy Albright-Creque, "Success Story #9," *Interrace*, December/January 1995, p. 39; Candy Mills, "Goodnight Aunt Pearl, We'll Miss You," *Interrace*, September/October 1990, p. 23.

95. Nicole Bouchet, "On the Contrary," *Interrace*, vol. 9, no. 43 (1998), p. 10.

96. Sarah Farmer, "Why Being Called 'Nigger Lover' Doesn't Offend Me," *Interrace*, July/August 1991, p. 10.

97. Ibid.

98. *Interrace,* November/December 1992, p. 16.

99. Ibid.

100. Ibid.

101. Ibid.

102. Ibid., 17.

103. Ibid. See also Lloyd H. Carter, "The Other Cheek," *Interrace,* March/April 1991, p. 7.

104. Sandy Carillo, "If You Don't Stand for Something, You Will Fall for Anything," *Interrace,* July/August 1992, p. 34.

105. Maureen T. Reddy, *Crossing the Color Line: Race, Parenting, and Culture* (1994), 10.

106. Ibid., 6.

107. Ibid., 7.

108. Ibid., 17.

109. Mathabane, *Love in Black and White: The Triumph of Love over Prejudice and Taboo* (1992), 32.

110. Ibid., 35.

111. Ibid., 50.

112. Ibid.

113. Ibid., 194.

114. Ibid., 216.

115. Ibid., 260.

116. See Anthony Wallace, *Jefferson and the Indians: The Tragic Fate of the First Americans* (1999); Brian W. Dippie, *The Vanishing American: White Attitudes and U.S. Indian Policy* (1982).

117. Franz Boas, "The Problem of the American Negro," *Yale Review* 10 (1921): 394–95.

118. Norman Podhoretz, "My Negro Problem—and Ours," in *Doings and Undoings: The Fifties and After in American Writing* (1964), 370.

119. See Michael Lind, *The Next American Nation: The New Nationalism and the Fourth American Revolution* (1995).

120. Ibid., 290.

121. See Orlando Patterson, *The Ordeal of Integration: Progress and Resentment in America's "Racial" Crisis* (1997), 193–98.

122. Patterson, *Rituals,* 155.

123. Patterson, *Ordeal,* 197.

124. Patterson, *Rituals,* 165–66.

125. Ibid., 165.

126. Calvin C. Hernton, *Sex and Racism in America* (1981), 192.

127. Patterson, *Ordeal,* 198.
128. See Anthony W. Marx, *Making Race and Nation: A Comparison of South Africa, the United States, and Brazil* (1998), 68.


## Chapter Four:
### Race, Racism, and Sexual Coercion

1. Audrey Edwards, "Sleeping with the Enemy," in Marita Golden, ed., *Wild Women Don't Wear No Blues* (1993), 97, 102.
2. For nonfiction, see, e.g., Dorothy Roberts, *Killing the Black Body: Race, Reproduction, and the Meaning of Liberty* (1997); Darlene Clark Hine, "Rape and the Inner Lives of Black Women in the Middle West: Preliminary Thoughts on the Culture of Disemblance," *Signs* 14 (1989): 912; Angela Y. Davis, *Women, Race and Class* (1981). For fiction see, e.g., Benilde Little, *Good Hair: A Novel* (1996); Toni Morrison, *Beloved* (1987); Sherley Ann Williams, *Desa Rose* (1986); Octavia Butler, *Kindred* (1979); Gayl Jones, *Corregidor* (1975); Pauline Elizabeth Hopkins, *Contending Forces* (1900). See also Catherine Clinton, "Rape, Memory, and African-American Women," in Genevieve Fabre and Robert O'Meally, eds., *History and Memory in African-American Culture* (1994).
3. "Frederick Douglass Discusses Slavery, 1850," in Herbert Aptheker, ed., *A Documentary History of the Negro People in the United States* (2d ed., 1969), 1:309, 313. For condemnation of sexual abuse by other black abolitionists, see Henry Highland Garnet, introduction to letter from Harriet A. Jacobs to Horace Greeley, June 19, 1853, in C. Peter Ripley, ed., *The Black Abolitionist Papers,* vol. 4 (1991), 164, wherein Garnet asserts that slave women lived "unprotected from the lust of tyrants"; "Speech by Sarah P. Redmond, Delivered at the Red Lion Hotel, Warrington, England, 2 February 1859," *Warrington Times,* February 5, 1859, reprinted in Ripley, ed., *The Black Abolitionist Papers,* (1985), 435, 438, claiming that 800,000 mulattoes in the United States were the product of rape.
4. Herbert G. Gutman, *The Black Family in Slavery and Freedom, 1550–1925* (1976), 400, quoting James L. White.
5. W. E. B. DuBois, *Darkwater: Voices from Within the Veil* (1920), 172.
6. *The Collected Poems of Sterling A. Brown,* selected by Michael S. Harper (1980), 56. From the poem "Strong Men."
7. Malcolm X with Alex Haley, *The Autobiography of Malcolm X* (1964), 3.

8. Patricia Hill Collins, *Black Feminist Thought: Knowledge, Consciousness, and the Politics of Empowerment* 162 (2d ed., 2000).

9. Harriet A. Jacobs, *Incidents in the Life of a Slave Girl, Written by Herself* (1861; edited and with an introduction by Jean Fagan Yellin, 1987).

10. See also Hélène Lecaudey, "Behind the Mask: Ex-Slave Women and Interracial Sexual Relations," in Patricia Morton, ed., *Discovering the Women in Slavery: Emancipating Perspectives on the American Past* (1996); Brenda E. Stevenson, *Life in Black and White: Family and Community in the Slave South* (1996); Neal Kumar Katyal, "Men Who Own Women: A Thirteenth Amendment Critique of Forced Prostitution," *Yale Law Journal* 103 (1993): 796–803; Catherine Clinton, "'Southern Dishonor': Flesh, Blood, Race, and Bondage," in Carl Bleser, ed., *In Joy and in Sorrow: Women, Family, and Marriage in the Victorian South, 1830–1900* (1991); idem, "Caught in the Web of the Big House: Women and Slavery," in Walter J. Fraser et al., eds., *The Web of Southern Social Relations: Women, Family and Education* (1985), 19; Thelma Jennings, "'Us Colored Women Had to Go Through a Plenty': Sexual Exploitation of African-American Slave Women," *Journal of Women's History* 1 (winter 1990): 45; Hine, "Rape and the Inner Lives of Black Women."

11. Harriet Jacobs, *Incidents,* 1987 ed., 27.

12. Ibid., 18.

13. Ibid., 40.

14. Ibid., 42.

15. See Marli F. Weiner, *Mistresses and Slaves: Plantation Women in South Carolina, 1830–80* (1998), 135; Bertram Wyatt-Brown, *Southern Honor: Ethics and Behavior in the Old South* (1982).

16. See, e.g., *State v. Tackett,* 8 N.C. (1 Hawks) 210 (1820); *Alfred, a slave v. Mississippi,* 37 Miss. 296 (1859).

17. Susan Brownmiller, *Against Our Will: Men, Women, and Rape* (1975), 161; see also Leon F. Litwack, *Been in the Storm So Long: The Aftermath of Slavery* (1979; paperback ed., 1980), 239, describing an episode in which a slave killed his master for sexually assaulting his wife.

18. See James Hugo Johnston, *Race Relations in Virginia and Miscegenation in the South, 1776–1860* (1937; reprint, 1970), 307–9.

19. Weiner, *Mistresses and Slaves,* 140.

20. Jacobs, *Incidents,* 1987 ed., 44.

21. See Melton A. McLaurin, *Celia: A Slave* (1991).

22. Ibid., 25.

23. See Jacobs, *Incidents,* 1987 ed., 33.

24. Pauli Murray, *Proud Shoes: The Story of an American Family* (1956; reprint, 1999), 37. For fictional portrayals of white women's jealousy, see William Wells Brown, *Clotel; or, The President's Daughter* (1853); Charles W. Chestnutt, *The Marrow of Tradition* (1901).

25. Jacobs, *Incidents,* 1987 ed., 36.

26. Ibid.

27. Ibid., 33.

28. Ibid.

29. Murray, *Proud Shoes,* 43.

30. Ibid., 46.

31. Ibid., 47.

32. Ibid.

33. Elizabeth Fox-Genovese, *Within the Plantation Household: Black and White Women of the Old South* (1988), 326.

34. Stevenson, *Life in Black and White,* 138.

35. Solomon Northrup, *Twelve Years a Slave* (1853), 189.

36. Fanny Kemble, *Fanny Kemble's Journals,* ed. Catherine Clinton (2000), 158, 159.

37. Ibid., 159. See also Catherine Clinton, *Fanny Kemble's Civil Wars* (2000).

38. Compare, e.g., Robert W. Fogel and Stanley Engerman, *Time on the Cross: The Economics of Negro Slavery* (1974), with Herbert Gutman and Richard Sutch, "Victories All? The Sexual Mores and Conduct of Slaves and Their Masters," in Paul A. David, Herbert G. Gutman, et al., *Reckoning with Slavery: A Critical Study in the Quantitative History of American Negro Slavery* (1976); see also Barbara J. Stufflebeem, "A Skeptical Note on Sexual Exploitation, Slavery, and Cliometry," in Robert W. Fogel, Ralph A. Galantine, and Richard C. Manning, eds., *Without Consent or Contract: The Rise and Fall of American Slavery: Evidence and Methods* (1989), 3: 597: "The haunting image of the southern white male as sexual predator cannot be laid to rest by cliometric arguments that coerced sex with one's slaves would interfere unduly with the rational management of a plantation or that it would have conflicted with Victorian sexual mores." See also Peter Kolchin, *Unfree Labor: American Slavery and Russian Serfdom* (1987), 112.

39. Sally G. McMillen, *Southern Women Black and White in the Old South* (1992), 23. See also Ronald G. Walters, "The Erotic South: Civilization and Sexuality in American Abolitionism," *American Quarterly* 25 (1973): 177.

40. See, e.g., Ulrich B. Phillips, *American Negro Slavery: A Survey of the Supply, Employment and Control of Negro Labor as Determined by the Plantation Regime* (1918); Fogel and Engerman, *Time on the Cross.*

41. See Roberts, *Killing the Black Body,* 10–12; Winthrop D. Jordan, *White over Black: American Attitudes Toward the Negro, 1550–1812,* (1968; paperback ed., 1969), 151.

42. Quoted in Jacquelyn Dowd Hall, *Revolt Against Chivalry: Jessie Daniel Ames and the Women's Campaign Against Lynching* (1976; rev. ed., 1993), 331.

43. See Sharon Block, "Lines of Color, Sex, and Service: Comparative Sexual Coercion in Early America," in Martha Hodes, ed., *Sex, Love, Race: Crossing Boundaries in North American History* (1999), 142. See also Diane Miller Sommerville, "The Rape Myth Reconsidered: The Intersection of Race, Class and Gender in the American South, 1800–1877" (Ph.D. diss., Rutgers–New Brunswick, 1995); idem, "The Rape Myth of the Old South Reconsidered," *Journal of Southern History* 61 (1995), 481.

44. *George, a slave v. State,* 37 Miss. 316 (1859).

45. Ibid. at 320.

46. See Tera W. Hunter, *To 'Joy My Freedom: Southern Black Women's Lives and Labors After the Civil War* (1997), 33–35; Catherine Clinton, "Bloody Terrain: Freedwomen, Sexuality and Violence During Reconstruction," *Georgia Historical Quarterly,* summer 1992.

47. See Hunter, *To 'Joy My Freedom,* 126–31; Litwack, *Been in the Storm So Long,* 280; Gerda Lerner, ed., *Black Women in White America: A Documentary History* (1972), 180–88.

48. See David Katzman, *Seven Days a Week: Women and Domestic Service in Industrializing America* (1978), 216–17; John Dollard, *Caste and Class in a Southern Town* (3d ed., 1937, 1957), 147; Leon F. Litwack, *Trouble in Mind: Black Southerners in the Age of Jim Crow* (1998), 36–37; Hunter, *To 'Joy My Freedom,* 106. For a glimpse of this reality through the prism of a novel, see Walter White, *Flight* (1926).

49. See Lerner, ed., *Black Women in White America,* 155–56.

50. See Leslie K. Dunlap, "The Reform of Rape Law and the Problem of White Men: Age-of-Consent Campaigns in the South, 1885–1910," in Hodes, ed., *Sex, Love, Race,* 360.

51. Ibid.

52. Quoted in Litwack, *Trouble in Mind,* 269.

53. See Eric W. Rise, *The Martinville Seven: Race, Rape, and Capital Punishment* (1995); Randall Kennedy, *Race, Crime, and the Law* (1997).

54. Hine, "Rape and the Inner Lives of Black Women," 914.
55. Neil R. McMillan, *Dark Journey: Black Mississippians in the Age of Jim Crow* (1990), 18.
56. Robert Russa Morton, *What the Negro Thinks* (1929), 34–35. See also Dollard, *Caste and Class,* 3d ed., 146.
57. See Linda O. McMurray, *To Keep the Waters Troubled: The Life of Ida B. Wells* (1998).
58. See Ida B. Wells-Barnett, "Southern Horrors: Lynch Law in All Its Phases" (1892), in *On Lynchings* (1990).
59. See James Reston Jr., *The Innocence of Joan Little: A Southern Mystery* (1977); Fred Harwell, *A True Deliverance* (1979).
60. See "Grand Jury of the Supreme Court, State of New York, County of Dutchess, Report of the Grand Jury and Related Documents Concerning the Tawana Brawley Investigation" (1988); Robert D. McFadden et al., *Outrage: The Story Behind the Tawana Brawley Hoax* (1990); Mike Taibbi and Anna Sims-Phillips, *Unholy Alliances: Working the Tawana Brawley Story* (1989).
61. See Patricia J. Williams, *The Alchemy of Race and Rights* (1991), 174. See also "The Victims of the Brawley Case," *New York Times,* September 28, 1988, p. A22; Pete Hamill, "Black Media Should Tell the Truth," *New York Post,* September 29, 1988, p. 5.
62. See, e.g., Barbara Omolade, *The Rising Song of African American Women* (1994), 186; William Kunstler interview with Jon Kalish, *New York Newsday,* June 23, 1988.
63. For discussions of motivations behind rape, see Linda Brookover Bourque, *Defining Rape* (1989); Brownmiller, *Against Our Will;* Leo Ellis, *Theories of Rape: Inquiries into the Causes of Sexual Aggression* (1989); Randy Thornhill and Craig T. Palmer, *A Natural History of Rape: Biological Bases of Sexual Coercion* (2000).
64. See *Eberheart v. State,* 206 S.E. 2d 12, 14 (Ga. 1974), *vacated,* 433 U.S. 917 (1977).
65. *State v. McCreuiston,* 608 S.W. 2d 460, 464 (Mo. Ct. App. 1980).
66. *Reynolds v. Commonwealth,* 367 S.E. 2d 176, 178 (Va. Ct. App. 1988); see also Brief for Appellant, *Reynolds v. Commonwealth,* 367 S.E. 2d 176 (Va. Ct. App. 1988, No. 0517-86-1), at 7.
67. See *State v. Harris,* 716 A.2d 458 (N.J. 1998).
68. Ibid. at 465.
69. Ibid.
70. G. J. Krupey, "Black-on-White Crime," in Peter Collier and David Horowitz, eds., *The Race Card: White Guilt, Black Resentment, and the Assault on Truth and Justice* (1997), 196, 207. See also Chris

Sosnowski, "Death Penalty to Be Sought for Garner," *Post and Courier,* April 14, 1995; Richard Green Jr., "Trials Are Judge's Swan Song," *Post and Courier,* March 2, 1998.

71. See James E. Robertson, "Cruel and Unusual Punishment in United States Prisons: Sexual Harassment Among Male Inmates," *American Criminal Law Review* 36 (1999): 1, 17–18; Daniel Lockwood, *Prison Sexual Violence* (1980), 29; Anthony M. Scacco Jr., *Rape in Prison* (1975), 47–65; Richard Tewksbury, "Fear of Sexual Assault in Prison Inmates," *Prison Journal* 60 (1989): 62, 63; Leo Carroll, *Hacks, Blacks, and Cons: Race Relations in a Maximum Security Prison* (1974), 184–85. See also James B. Jacobs, *New Perspectives on Prisons and Imprisonment* (1983), 72–74; *Stroman v. Griffin,* 331 F. Supp. 226, 228 (S.D. Ga. 1971); Donald Goines, *White Man's Justice, Black Man's Grief* (1973), 49–74. But see Nobhuhle R. Chonco, "Sexual Assaults Among Male Inmates: A Descriptive Study," *Prison Journal* 60 (1989): 72, 73 for the argument that height and weight are more significant variables than race in explaining patterns of prison rape.

72. Scacco, *Rape in Prison,* 48.

73. Carroll, *Hacks, Blacks, and Cons,* 184–85.

74. See Eldridge Cleaver, *Soul on Ice* (1968), 7.

75. Ibid.

76. Ibid., 8.

77. Ibid., 9.

78. Ibid., 10.

79. Ibid.

80. Ibid., 11.

81. Ibid., 14.

82. Ibid., 15.

83. Ibid., 16.

84. Marcia Press, "That Black Man–White Woman Thing: Images of an American Taboo" (Ph.D. diss., Indiana University, 1989).

85. See Calvin C. Hernton, *Sex and Racism in America* (1965; reprint, 1981), 66.

86. LeRoi Jones, *Home: Social Essays* (1965), 227.

87. Cecil M. Brown, "Of Rape and Choice," *Village Voice,* October 17, 1968, p. 4.

88. Alice Walker, *Meridian* (1976), 159.

89. Ibid., 161.

90. Ibid., 162.

91. See Ishmael Reed, *Airing Dirty Laundry* (1993), 13, 56. See also Mel Watkins, "Sexism, Racism, and Black Women Writers," *New York Times,* June 15, 1986, p. 1.

92. Alice Walker, "Advancing Luna—and Ida B. Wells," in *You Can't Keep a Good Woman Down* (1981), 85, 94.

93. Sommerville, "Rape Myth of the Old South," 485. See also Martha Hodes, *White Women, Black Men: Illicit Sex in the Nineteenth-Century South* (1997); Joel Williamson, *New People: Miscegenation and Mulattoes in the United States* (1980); A. E. Keir Nash, "Fairness and Formalism in the Trials of Blacks in the State Supreme Courts of the Old South," *Virginia Law Review* 56 (1970): 64; idem, "A More Equitable Past? Southern Supreme Courts and the Protection of the Antebellum Negro," *North Carolina Law Review* 48 (1970): 197, 199–200.

94. Claude G. Bowers, *The Tragic Era: The Revolution After Lincoln* (1929), 308.

95. See George M. Frederickson, *The Black Image in the White Mind: The Debate on Afro-American Character and Destiny, 1817–1914* (1971), 298.

96. Ibid., 279.

97. Ibid.

98. Ibid., 279. See also Henry McHattan, "The Sexual Status of the Negro—Past and Present," *American Journal of Dermatology and Genito-urinary Disease* 10 (January 1906): 8; Hunter McGuire and G. Frank Lydston, "Sexual Crimes Among the Southern Negroes Scientifically Considered: An Open Correspondence," *Virginia Medical Monthly* 20 (May 1893): 105.

99. Thomas Dixon Jr., *The Leopard's Spots: A Romance of the White Man's Burden, 1865–1900* (1902), 375.

100. See Stewart E. Tolney and E. M. Beck, *A Festival of Violence: An Analysis of Southern Lynchings, 1882–1930* (1995); W. Fitzhugh Brundage, *Lynching in the New South: Georgia and Virginia, 1880–1930* (1993); George C. Wright, *Racial Violence in Kentucky, 1865–1940: Lynchings, Mob Rule, and "Legal Lynchings"* (1990); Stephen J. Whitfield, *A Death in the Delta: The Story of Emmett Till* (1988); Wells-Barnett, *On Lynchings*; Robert L. Zangrando, *The NAACP Crusade Against Lynching, 1909–1950* (1980); Walter White, *Rape and Faggot: A Biography of Judge Lynch* (1962).

101. Philip Alexander Bruce, *The Plantation Negro as a Freeman* (1889), 83–84.

102. Clarence H. Poe, "Lynching: A Southern View," *Atlantic Monthly,* February 1904.

103. White, *Rape and Faggot,* 56–57. See also Ida B. Wells-Barnett, "A Red Record: Tabulated Statistics and Alleged Causes of Lynchings in the United States, 1892–1893–1894," in *On Lynchings*; Brundage, *Lynching in the New South.*

104. See David C. Cecelski and Timothy B. Tyson, eds., *Democracy Betrayed: The Wilmington Race Riot of 1898 and Its Legacy* (1998); Litwack, *Trouble in Mind,* 315–19; Michael D'Orso, *Like Judgment Day: The Ruin and Redemption of a Town Called Rosewood* (1996); Scott Ellsworth, *Death in a Promised Land: The Tulsa Race Riot of 1921* (1982); Charles Crowe, "Racial Massacre in Atlanta, September 22, 1906," *Journal of Negro History* 54 (1969): 150; idem, "Racial Violence and Social Reform—Origins of the Atlanta Riot of 1906," *Journal of Negro History* 53 (1968): 234.

105. See James L. Crouthamel, "Springfield Race Riot of 1908," *Journal of Negro History* 45 (1960): 164, 180.

106. See Whitfield, *Death in the Delta,* 3.

107. Ibid., 4.

108. See Wright, *Racial Violence in Kentucky,* 223. See also Steven F. Lawson, David R. Colburn, and Darryl Paulson, "Groveland: Florida's Little Scottsboro," *Florida Historical Quarterly* 64 (1986): 1.

109. Kennedy, *Race, Crime, and the Law,* 88–89.

110. See Mark Curriden and Leroy Phillips Jr., *Contempt of Court: The Turn-of-the-Century Lynching That Launched 100 Years of Federalism* (1999).

111. Ibid., 109.

112. Ibid., 213.

113. Ibid., 214.

114. See James Goodman, *Stories of Scottsboro* (1994); Dan T. Carter, *Scottsboro: A Tragedy of the American South* (1969; rev. ed., 1979).

115. Kennedy, *Race, Crime, and the Law,* 101.

116. Quoted in Jack Greenberg, *Crusaders in the Courts* (1994), 101. See also *McQuirter v. State,* 63 So. 2d 388 (Ala. Ct. App. 1953).

117. See Conrad J. Lynn, *There Is a Fountain: The Autobiography of Conrad Lynn* (1979 2d ed., 1993), 141–57.

118. See Nick Davies, *White Lies: Rape, Murder, and Justice Texas Style* (1991); *Ex parte Brandley,* 781 S.W. 2d 886 (Tex. Crim. App. 1989).

119. Katheryn K. Russell, *The Color of Crime: Racial Hoaxes, White Fear, Black Protectionism, Police Harassment, and Other Macroagressions* (1998), 157–73.

120. Ibid., 165.

121. See Timothy Sullivan, *Unequal Verdicts: The Central Park Jogger Trials* (1992); Joan Didion, *After Henry* (1992), 253–319; special section, "The Central Park Rape," *Village Voice,* May 8, 1989, p. 25; Susan Saulny, "Convictions and Charges Voided in '89 Central Park Jogger Attack," *New York Times,* December 20, 2002.

122. See Kimberle Crenshaw, "Mapping the Margins: Intersectionality, Identity Politics, and Violence Against Women of Color," *Standard Law Review* 43 (1991), 1266–69.

123. See, e.g., Al Sharpton with Anthony Walton, *Go and Tell Pharoah: The Autobiography of the Reverend Al Sharpton* (1996).

124. Jacqueline Adams, "The White Wife," *New York Times Magazine,* September 18, 1994.

125. See, e.g., Jerelyn Eddings, "Black and White in America," *U.S. News & World Report,* October 16, 1995; Betsy Streisand et al., "The Verdict's Aftermath," ibid.; Nathan Glazer, "Black and White After Thirty Years," *The Public Interest,* September 1995.

126. Nick Charles, "The O.J. Papers: Nobility Savaged," *Village Voice,* November 1, 1994, p. 23.

127. Jacqueline Jones Royster, ed., *Southern Horrors and Other Writings: The Anti-Lynching Campaign of Ida B. Wells, 1892–1900* (1997), 54–55.

128. Carl Rowan, *South of Freedom* (1952; reprint, 1997), 33.

129. Didion, *After Henry,* 297.

130. Brownmiller, *Against Our Will,* 254.

131. See Whitfield, *Death in the Delta,* 20–21.

132. Brownmiller, *Against Our Will,* 273.

133. Davis, *Women, Race and Class,* 178; bell hooks, *Ain't I a Woman* (1981), 53. See also Paula Giddings, *When and Where I Enter: The Impact of Black Women on Race and Sex in America* (1984), 310.

134. Brownmiller, *Against Our Will,* 281.

135. Crenshaw, "Mapping the Margins," 1273.

136. Ibid.

137. See, e.g., Charlotte Pierce-Baker, *Surviving the Silence: Black Women's Stories of Rape* (1998); Lori Robinson, "I Was Raped," *Emerge,* May 1997, p. 42.

138. See, e.g., Paula S. Rothenberg, "Defining 'Racism' and 'Sexism,'" in Paula S. Rothenberg, ed., *Racism and Sexism: An Integrated Study* (1988), 5–6. "Racism involves the subordination of people of color by white people. Blacks can be prejudiced, but racism means, at least, prejudice plus power."

139. See, generally Charles C. Moskos and John Sibley Butler, *All That We Can Be: Black Leadership and Racial Integration the Army Way* (1996). Several conversations with Professor Moskos significantly enriched my understanding of this subject.

140. On the trial of Delmar Simpson, see Gregory L. Vistica, "Rape in the Ranks," *Newsweek,* November 25, 1996; Peter T. Kilborn, "An Army Accused—A Special Report: Sex Abuse Cases Sting Pentagon, but the Problem Has Deep Roots," *New York Times,* February 10, 1997; Dana Priest and Jackie Spinner, "Close Look at Army Cases Urged: Black Caucus Weighs In on Aberdeen Sex Scandal," *Washington Post,* March 13, 1997; Jackie Spinner and Dana Priest, "Consensual Sex Was Rampant at Army Base: Inquiry Finds Breakdown of Discipline at Aberdeen," *Washington Post,* March 30, 1997; Elaine Sciolino, "Army Trial Raises Questions of Sex, Power and Discipline," *New York Times,* April 12, 1997; Scott Wilson, "APG Sergeant Called Predator: As Rape Trial Begins, Simpson Is Accused of Abusing His Power," *Baltimore Sun,* April 12, 1997; Elaine Sciolino, "Rape Witnesses Tell of Base out of Control," *New York Times,* April 15, 1997; Scott Wilson, "Recruits Testify Sex Was Forced: Two Witnesses Recount Circumstances of Alleged Rape at APG," *Baltimore Sun,* April 15, 1997; Elaine Sciolino, "Military Women Are Vulnerable to Abuse, Psychiatrist Says," *New York Times,* April 16, 1997; Neil A. Lewis, "Sergeant's Lawyers Start Case by Accusing Two of His Accusers," *New York Times,* April 22, 1997; Elaine Sciolino, "Closing Arguments Heard in Army Sex Case," *New York Times,* April 25, 1997; Jackie Spinner, "Aberdeen Case Now in Hands of Army Jury; Legal Experts Say Outcome Could Affect Other Trials," *Washington Post,* April 25, 1997; Dana Priest, "For Aberdeen Jury, a Murky Question of Human Relations," *Washington Post,* April 27, 1997; Elaine Sciolino, "Sergeant Convicted of 18 Counts of Raping Female Subordinates," *New York Times,* April 30, 1997; Jackie Spinner, "Aberdeen Sergeant Convicted of Rape," *Washington Post,* April 30, 1997; Scott Wilson, "Aberdeen Sergeant Convicted: Court-Martial Finds Simpson Guilty of 18 Counts of Rape; Could Go to Prison for Life; Case Is Only Part of Army-Wide Scandal of Sexual Misconduct," *Baltimore Sun,* April 30, 1997; Elaine Sciolino, "The Army's Problem with Sex and Power," May 4, 1997; Scott Wilson, "Aberdeen Sergeant Gets 25 Years; Jury's Decision Fails to End Debate on Race, Sex, Power in Military; This Should Be a Flare," *Baltimore Sun,* May 7, 1997; "Sergeant Gets 25-Year Term for 18 Rapes of Recruits," *New York Times,* May 7, 1997.

141. See Elaine Sciolino, "Closing Arguments Heard in Army Sex Case," *New York Times,* April 25, 1997, p. A12. According to Sciolino, "A parade of witnesses testified that [Simpson] pushed them, grabbed their arms, pinned them down . . . and threatened them if they reported what had occurred. One of the alleged victims said he put his hand over her mouth to prevent her from protesting" (ibid.).

142. See Brief on Behalf of Appellant, United States Army Court of Criminal Appeals, *United States v. Delmar G. Simpson,* Case No. Army 5700775. Mr. Frank J. Spinner, Simpson's civilian counsel, graciously forwarded a copy of the brief to me.

143. Sciolino, "Sergeant Convicted of 18 Counts."

144. On the trial of Gene C. McKinney, see Eric Schmitt, "Top Enlisted Man in Army Stands Accused of Sex Assault," *New York Times,* February 4, 1997; idem, "Sex Harassment Case Polarizes Soldiers," *New York Times,* February 16, 1997; Elaine Sciolino, "In Limbo: A Soldier's Soldier Reviews His Rise and Fall," *New York Times,* June 16, 1997; idem, "Sexual Harassment Hearing for Top Enlisted Man," *New York Times,* June 26, 1997; Dana Priest, "Sergeant Major Asked Accuser to Mislead Probe; Recorded Phone Call Is Played at Hearing," *Washington Post,* June 28, 1997; Elaine Sciolino, "Top Army Sergeant Was Secretly Taped in Sex Investigation," *New York Times,* June 28, 1997; idem, "Harassment Charge Detailed in Hearings," *New York Times,* July 26, 1997; Philip Shenon, "Hearings Against Sergeant Major Conclude," *New York Times,* August 26, 1997; Neil A. Lewis, "Sergeant Major Says Army Investigators Induced Accusers to Lie," *New York Times,* August 28, 1997; Jane Gross, "Soldier's Court-Martial Provides Look at Leniency for Top Officers," *New York Times,* February 4, 1998; idem, "Veracity of Soldier's Accusers Is Questioned," *New York Times,* February 26, 1998; idem, "Court-Martial Ends with Talk of Character," *New York Times,* March 11, 1998; idem, "Former Top Sergeant of Army Is Acquitted of All Sex Charges," *New York Times,* March 14, 1998; Bill McAllister, "McKinney Not Guilty of Sexual Misconduct; Sergeant Major Convicted of Obstruction," *Washington Post,* March 14, 1998; Jane Gross, "When Character Counts," *New York Times,* March 15, 1998; Dana Priest, "McKinney Accusers Tell of Hardships; Army Blamed for Failing to Protect Witnesses' Reputations," *Washington Post,* March 16, 1998; Glen Skoler, "The Half Told Story of Sgt. Maj. McKinney," *Washington Post,* March 22, 1998.

145. See Jane Gross, "Graphic Narrative About Sex and Tales of Revenge Begin a Court-Martial," *New York Times,* February 10, 1998, p. A10.

Another journalist called the sex scandals the cultural equivalent of My Lai.

146. Jane Gross, "Focus Is Put on Soldier's Accuser," *New York Times,* March 3, 1998.

147. Ibid.

## Chapter Five:
### The Enforcement of Antimiscegenation Laws

1. My description is based upon an opinion rendered by the Court of Appeals of Alabama, *Fields v. State,* 132 So. 605 (1931), and the record of the case (hereafter, Record), on file at the Harvard Law School Library, Interracial Intimacies Collection. The Record contains the indictment, the judge's jury instructions, objections made by defense counsel, and the testimony offered at trial.

2. Record, 5.

3. Ibid., 1–2.

4. See *Gilbert v. State,* 23 So. 2d 22 (Ala. Ct. App. 1945); *State v. Brown,* 108 So. 2d 233, 235 (La. 1959). See also Andrew Koppelman, "Same Sex Marriage, Choice of Law, and Public Policy," *Texas Law Review* 75 (1998): 921, 950.

5. *Fields v. State,* at 606.

6. Trial record of *Fields v. State,* 132 So. 605 (1931) at pages 19–20, on file at Harvard Law School Library, Interracial Intimacies Collection.

7. Jack Greenberg, *Race Relations and American Law* (1959), 353.

8. *Laws of Virginia* (Hening, 1823), 2:170.

9. See Joel Williamson, *After Slavery: The Negro in South Carolina During Reconstruction, 1861–1877* (1965).

10. Ray Stannard Baker, *Following the Color Line: American Negro Citizenship in the Progressive Era* (1908; reprint, 1964), 166, citing *New Orleans Times-Democrat,* February 15, 1906).

11. Ibid., 167–68.

12. *Von Buelow v. Life Insurance Co.,* 9 New Orleans App. (La.) 143, 145–46 (1912).

13. Quoted in Kevin Mumford, "After Hugh: Statutory Race Segregation in Colonial America, 1630–1725." *American Journal of Legal History* 43 (1999): 280, 285. This is an exceptionally searching article that has received too little attention.

14. See A. Leon Higginbotham Jr. and Barbara K. Kopytoff, "Racial Purity and Interracial Sex in the Law of Colonial and Antebellum Virginia," *Georgetown Law Journal* 77 (1989): 1967. See also Walter

Wadlington, "The *Loving* Case: Virginia's Anti-miscegenation Statute in Historical Perspective," *Virginia Law Review,* 52 (1966): 189.

15. See Joseph Golden, "Patterns of Negro-White Intermarriage," *American Sociological Review* 19 (1954): 144.

16. On the evolution of antimiscegenation laws, see Martyn, "Racism in the United States." Martyn's three-volume dissertation is a great resource; that it has never been published is unfortunate. See also Harvey M. Applebaum, "Miscegenation Statutes: A Constitutional and Social Problem," *Georgetown Law Journal* 53 (1964): 49; Andrew Weinberger, "A Reappraisal of the Constitutionality of Miscegenation Statutes," *Cornell Law Quarterly* 42 (1957): 208; Peter Wallenstein, "Race, Marriage and the Law of Freedom: Alabama and Virginia, 1860–1960s," *Chicago-Kent Law Review* 70 (1994): 371; Walter Wadlington, "The *Loving* Case."

17. See *Saint Francis College v. Majid Ghardan All-Khazraji,* 481 U.S. 604 (1987); *Shaare Tefila Congregation v. Cobb,* 481 U.S. 615 (1987). See also Matthew Frye Jacobson, *Whiteness of a Different Color: European Immigrants and the Alchemy of Race* (1998).

18. See *Ex parte Francois,* 9 Cas. 5047 (C.C.W.D. Tex. 1879); Charles S. Mangum Jr., *The Legal Status of the Negro* (1940), 241.

19. See Martha Hodes, *White Women, Black Men: Illicit Sex in the Nineteenth-Century South* (1997); Gary B. Mills, "Miscegenation and the Free Negro in Antebellum 'Anglo' Alabama: A Re-examination of Southern Race Relations," *Journal of American History* 68 (1981): 16. Diane Miller Sommerville has shown that the same held true for responses to rape—that is, black men charged with raping white women generally fared better in the antebellum South than in the South of the Jim Crow era. See her article "The Rape Myth in the Old South Reconsidered," *Journal of Southern History* 61 (1995): 481. See also Pauli Murray, ed., *States' Laws on Race and Color* (1951; reprint, 1997), 247.

20. See George M. Fredrickson, *White Supremacy: A Comparative Study in American and South African History* (1981), 94.

21. See Mangum, *Legal Status of the Negro,* 6. See also F. James Davis, *Who Is Black: One Nation's Definition* (1991), 5.

22. See Richard B. Sherman, "The Last Stand: The Fight for Racial Integrity in Virginia in the 1920s," *Journal of Southern History* 56 (1988): 69.

23. See "Note: Who Is a Negro," *University of Florida Law Review* 11 (1958): 235.

24. 69 Va. (28 Gratt.) 939 (1877).

25. 165 Va. 705, 181 S.E. 283 (1935).

26. *Keith v. Commonwealth,* at 706. On changes in Virginia statutory scheme of racial classification, see Wadlington, "The *Loving* Case."

27. *Keith v. Commonwealth,* 707.

28. See George B. Tindall, *South Carolina Negroes, 1877–1900* (1952; reprint, 1966), 298.

29. For discussion of contemporary problems involving racial classifications, see Christopher A. Ford, "Administering Identity: The Determination of 'Race' in Race-Conscious Law," *California Law Review* 182 (1994): 1231; Christine B. Hickman, "The Devil and the One Drop Rule: Racial Categories, African Americans, and the U.S. Census," *Michigan Law Review* 95 (1997): 1161; Leonard Brynes, "Who Is Black Enough for You? The Analysis of Northwestern University Law School's Struggle over Minority Faculty Hiring," *Michigan Journal of Race and Law* 2 (1997): 205; Luther Wright Jr., "Who's Black, Who's White and Who Cares: Reconceptualizing the United States' Definition of Race and Racial Classifications," *Vanderbilt Law Review* 48 (1995): 513.

30. 10 S.E. 2d 23 (S.C. 1940).

31. Ibid. at 25.

32. Ibid. at 33.

33. On various methods used by judges to determine a person's race, see Ariela Gross, "Litigating Whiteness: Trials of Racial Determination in the Nineteenth-Century South," *Yale Law Journal* 108 (1998): 109.

34. *State v. Cantey,* 20 S.C.L. 614 (1835).

35. Cf. Cheryl I. Harris, "Whiteness as Property," *Harvard Law Review* 106 (1993): 1707.

36. 25 S.W. 769 (Tex. Crim. App. 1894).

37. 139 Ala. 354 (1903).

38. 159 Va. 963 (1932).

39. See Charles Frank Robinson II, "The Antimiscegenation Conversation: Love's Legislated Limits, 1866–1967" (Ph.D. diss., University of Houston, 1998), 43–44.

40. *Bell v. State of Texas,* at 769.

41. *Locklayer v. Locklayer,* at 358.

42. *Wood v. Commonwealth,* at 964.

43. *Commonwealth v. Wright,* 27 S.W. 815 (Ky. 1894). For useful discussions of seduction, see Jane E. Larson, "'Women Understand So Little, They Call My Good Nature "Deceit"': A Feminist Rethinking of Seduction," *Columbia Law Review* 93 (1993): 374; Mary Frances

Berry, "Judging Morality: Sexual Behavior and Legal Consequences in the Late-Nineteenth-Century South," *Journal of American History* 78 (1991): 848–53.

44. *Wood v. Commonwealth*, at 966–67.
45. *State v. Ross*, 76 N.C. 242, 244, 246 (1877).
46. Ibid. at 246.
47. Ibid. at 247.
48. Ibid. at 249.
49. Ibid. at 250.
50. Ibid.
51. Ibid.
52. *State v. Bell*, 66 Tenn. (7 Baxter) 9, 11 (1872).
53. *Kinney v. Commonwealth*, 71 Va. (30 Gratt.) 858 (1878).
54. 203 Miss. 824 (1948).
55. Ibid. at 832.
56. Ibid.
57. Ibid.
58. *Kirby v. Kirby*, 24 Ariz. 9 (Sup. Ct. 1922).
59. See *Sunseri v. Cassagne*, 191 La. 209 (1938); 195 La. 19 (1940).
60. 153 N.C. 174 (Sup. Ct. 1910).
61. 60 Ga. 204 (Sup. Ct. 1878).
62. Ibid. at 207.
63. Ibid.
64. Ibid.
65. Ibid. at 208.
66. Ibid. at 207–8.
67. *Ferrall v. Ferrall*, at 174.
68. Ibid. at 175.
69. Ibid. at 180.
70. Ibid. at 181.
71. Ibid.
72. Ibid. at 180.
73. Karen M. Woods, "A 'Wicked and Mischievous Connection': The Origins of Indian-White Miscegenation Laws," *Legal Studies Forum* 23 (1999), 43.
74. See James A. Brundage, *Sex, Law and Marriage in the Middle Ages* (1993), 28.
75. See Fernando Henriques, *Children of Caliban: Miscegenation* (1974), 93.
76. Ibid., 153.

77. Ibid.

78. See Verena Martinez-Alier, *Marriage, Class and Colour in Nineteenth-Century Cuba: A Study of Racial Attitudes and Sexual Values in a Slave Society* (1974).

79. See John Dugard, *Human Rights and the South African Legal Order* (1978); Gwendolen M. Carter, *The Politics of Inequality: South Africa Since 1948* (1958, 1977).

80. See Nathan Stoltzfus, *Resistance of the Heart: Intermarriage and the Rosenstrasse Protest in Nazi Germany* (1996); Inga Müller, *Hitler's Justice: The Courts of the Third Reich* (1991), 90–119. See also the brief but powerful treatment of this subject in Raul Hillberg, *Perpetrators, Victims, Bystanders: The Jewish Catastrophe, 1933–1945* (1992), 131–38.

81. See Article 16 of the Universal Declaration of Human Rights: "Men and women of full age, without limitation due to race, nationality or religion, have the right to marry and found a family" (Henry J. Steiner and Philip Alston, *International Human Rights in Context: Law, Politics, Morals* [1996; 2d ed., 2000]), 1378.

## Chapter Six:
### Fighting Antimiscegenation Laws

1. See Louis Ruchames, "Race, Marriage, and Abolition in Massachusetts," orig. pub. in *Journal of Negro History* 40 (1955): 250, repr. in Paul Finkelman, ed., *Race, Law, and American History 1700–1990—Race and Law Before Emancipation* (1992), 448.

2. Ibid., 455.

3. Ibid.

4. Ibid.

5. Ibid., 448–49.

6. Ibid., 449.

7. Ibid.

8. Ibid., 457–58.

9. "Committee on the Judiciary Report Respecting Distinctions of Color, House of Representatives, February 25, 1839," reprinted in the *Liberator*, March 15, 1839.

10. Ibid.

11. Ibid.

12. Ibid.

13. Ruchames, "Race, Marriage, and Abolition," 451.

14. Ibid., 451–52.

15. See James Oliver Horton and Lois E. Horton, *In Hope of Liberty: Culture, Commentary and Protest Among Northern Free Blacks, 1700–1860* (1997); Leon F. Litwack, *North of Slavery: The Negro in the Free States, 1790–1860* (1961).

16. Ruchames, "Race, Marriage, and Abolition," 470.

17. Ibid.

18. John Greenleaf Whittier, "Equal Laws—The Lynn Petition," *The Liberator*, vol. 9, p. 30, col. 1, February 22, 1839.

19. Massachusetts House of Representatives, House Report nos. 46 (March 6, 1840) and 7 (January 19, 1841). See also Litwack, *North of Slavery*, 105–6.

20. Civil Rights Act of 1866, 14 Stat. 27 (1866).

21. See Alfred Avins, "Anti-Miscegenation Laws and the Fourteenth Amendment: The Original Intent," *Virginia Law Review* 52 (1966): 1230.

22. Ibid., 1232.

23. For a different view, see Steven A. Bank, "Anti-Miscegenation Laws and the Dilemma of Symmetry: The Understanding of Equality in the Civil Rights Act of 1875," *University of Chicago Roundtable* 2 (1995).

24. Andrew Johnson, "To the Senate of the United States," March 27, 1866, in *A Compilation of the Messages and Papers of the Presidents, 1789–1897*, vol. 6, ed. James D. Richardson (1899), 407.

25. Bank, "Anti-Miscegenation Laws and the Dilemma of Symmetry," 320.

26. Ibid.

27. See Andrew Kull, *The Color-Blind Constitution* (1992), 62.

28. See Samuel Marcosson, "Colorizing the Constitution of Originalism: Clarence Thomas at the Rubicon," *Law and Inequality* 16 (1998): 429; Bank, "Anti-Miscegenation Laws and the Dilemma of Symmetry," 303; Avins, "Anti-Miscegenation Laws and the Fourteenth Amendment," 1224; R. Carter Pittman, "The Fourteenth Amendment: Its Intended Effect on Anti-Miscegenation Laws," *North Carolina Law Review* 43 (1964): 92; Alexander M. Bickel, "The Original Understanding and the Segregation Decision," *Harvard Law Review* 69 (1955): 1.

29. See *Burns v. State*, 48 Ala. 195 (1872).

30. See *Green v. State*, 58 Ala. 190 (1877).

31. See, e.g., *Pace v. Alabama*, 106 U.S. 583 (1883); In re *Hobbs*, 12 F. Cas. 262 (N.D. Ga. 1871), (No. 6,550); *State v. Hairston*, 63 N.C. 451 (1869); *Lonas v. State*, 50 Tenn. (3 Heisk) 287 (1871); *Fresher v. State*, 3 Tex. Ct. App. 263 (1877).

32. See Bank, "Anti-Miscegenation Laws and the Dilemma of Symmetry," 323–35.

33. Ibid., 332.

34. Ibid.

35. Ibid.

36. Ibid., 333.

37. Ibid.

38. *Burns v. State,* 48 Ala. 195 (1872), *rev'd by Green v. State,* 58 Ala. 190 (1877).

39. See David H. Fowler, *Northern Attitudes Towards Interracial Marriage: Legislation and Public Opinion in the Middle Atlantic States and the States of the Old Northwest, 1780–1930* (1987), 346, 391, 418. See also Charles S. Mangum Jr., *The Legal Status of the Negro* (1940), 241–42.

40. Fowler, *Northern Attitudes,* 377; Mangum, *Legal Status of the Negro,* 241.

41. See generally Rayford Logan, *The Betrayal of the Negro from Rutherford B. Hayes to Woodrow Wilson* (1970); C. Vann Woodward, *The Strange Career of Jim Crow* (1955); Charles S. Johnson, *Patterns of Negro Segregation* (1943).

42. See Gilbert Stephenson, *Race Distinctions in American Law* (1910), 80.

43. See Byron Curtis Martyn, "Racism in the United States: A History of the Anti-Miscegenation Legislation and Litigation" (Ph.D. diss., University of Southern California, 1979), 922.

44. Ibid.

45. Ibid., 919–20.

46. Ibid., 920.

47. Brief of the NAACP as Amicus Curiae in *Loving v. Commonwealth of Virginia* in *Landmark Briefs and Arguments in the Supreme Court of the United States: Constitutional Law,* vol. 64, eds. Philip B. Kualand and Gerhard Casper (1975), 892.

48. *San Francisco Chronicle,* December 13, 1958.

49. *Perez v. Sharp,* 32 Cal. 2d 711 (1948).

50. Ibid. at 712.

51. See *Roldan v. Los Angeles County,* 18 P. 2d 706 (1933).

52. *Perez* at 747 (Shenk, J., dissenting). See generally Leti Volpp, "American Mestizo: Filipinos and Antimiscegenation Laws in California," *University of California at Davis Law Review* 33 (2000): 795.

53. *Perez,* 744.

54. Ibid., 714.

55. Ibid., 719.

56. Ibid., 717.

57. Ibid.

58. Ibid., 725.

59. Ibid., 716.

60. Ibid., 717.

61. See Elazar Barkan, *The Retreat of Scientific Racism: Changing Concepts of Race in Britain and the United States Between the World Wars* (1992); Stephen J. Gould, *The Mismeasure of Man* (1982); Daniel J. Kevles, *In the Name of Eugenics: Genetics and the Uses of Human Heredity* (1985).

62. *Perez* at 720.

63. Ibid., 723.

64. Ibid.

65. Ibid., 721.

66. Ibid., 723.

67. *Perez* occasioned a proliferation of commentary in law reviews. For opinion strongly applauding the decision, see "Constitutionality of Anti-Miscegenation Statutes," *Yale Law Journal* 58 (1949): 472; "Constitutional Law—Miscegenation Statute Violates Due Process and Equal Protection Clauses of the United States Constitution," *University of Pennsylvania Law Review* 97 (1949): 438; Ida Gobelet Turner, "Constitutional Law—Miscegenation Law Questioned," *University of Kansas City Law Review* 17 (1949): 146; "Statutory Ban on Interracial Marriage Invalidated by Fourteenth Amendment," *Stanford Law Review* 1 (1949): 289; Louis F. DiGiovanni, "Constitutional Law—Miscegenation Statute," *Notre Dame Lawyer* 24 (1949): 410; Theophile J. Weber, "Statutory Prohibitions Against Interracial Marriages," *Wyoming Law Review* 3 (1949): 159; "Constitutionality of State Anti-Miscegenation Statutes," *Illinois Law Review* 43 (1949): 866; "Constitutional Law: Equal Protection of the Laws: California Anti-Miscegenation Laws Declared Unconstitutional," *California Law Review* 37 (1949):122.

    For critical commentary, see "Constitutional Law—Validity of Statutory Prohibitions of Interracial Marriages," *Tennessee Law Review* 20 (1949): 675; Phillip D. Anderson, "Constitutional Law: Validity of Anti-Miscegenation Statutes Under the Fourteenth Amendment," *University of Florida Law Review* 2 (1949): 283; "Constitutional Law—Miscegenation Statutes—Statutory Prohibitions Against Inter-Racial Marriages Held Unconstitutional," *Vanderbilt Law*

*Review* 2 (1949): 307; Charles B. Henley, "Constitutional Law—California Miscegenation Statutes Void Because Violation of Equal Protection of Laws Clause of United States Constitution," *Mississippi Law Journal* 20 (1949): 378.

68. *Perez*, 732, 736.

69. Ibid., 733, quoting the apostle Paul, Acts, 17:26.

70. *Perez*, 750.

71. For a useful analysis of "scientific" arguments favoring antimiscegenation laws, see Keith E. Sealing, "Blood Will Tell: Scientific Racism and the Legal Prohibitions Against Miscegenation," *Michigan Journal of Race and Law* 5 (2000): 559.

72. 197 Va. 80 (1955), *remanded,* 350 U.S. 891, *aff'd,* 197 Va. 734, *appeal dismissed,* 350 U.S. 985 (1956). For a comprehensive analysis of this case, see Gregory Michael Dorr, "Principled Expediency: Eugenics, *Naim v. Naim,* and the Supreme Court," *The American Journal of Legal History* 42 (1998): 119.

73. See Ronald Takaki, *Strangers from a Different Shore: A History of Asian Americans* (1989). See also Charles J. McClain, *In Search of Equality: The Chinese Struggle Against Discrimination in Nineteenth-Century America* (1994); Dan Caldwell, "The Negroization of the Chinese Stereotype in California," *Southern California Quarterly* 53 (1971): 123.

74. *Japanese Immigration Legislation: Hearings on S. 2576 Before the Senate Committee on Immigration, 68th Cong., 1st Sess.* (1924), 5, statement of Mr. V. S. McClatchy.

75. *Naim,* 197 Va., 89.

76. See Walter Murphy, *Elements of Judicial Strategy* (1964), 193.

77. Dorr, "Principled Expediency," 156 n. 159.

78. Ibid.

79. *Naim,* 350 U.S. 985 (1956).

80. See Dennis J. Hutchinson, "Unanimity and Desegregation: Decision-making in the Supreme Court 1948–1958," *Georgetown University Law Journal* 68 (1979): 62–67.

81. *Loving v. Commonwealth of Virginia,* 388 U.S. 1 (1967). On the decision as a foregone conclusion, see Avins, "Anti-Miscegenation Laws and the Fourteenth Amendment," 1224. See also David E. Seidelson, "Miscegenation Statutes and the Supreme Court: A Brief Prediction of What the Court Will Do and Why," *Catholic University Law Review* 15 (1966): 156; "The Supreme Court: Strict Caution in Miscegenation," *Time,* December 18, 1964. "The Supreme Court: The Bedroom Issues," *Newsweek,* December 21, 1964.

82. *McLaughlin v. Florida,* 379 U.S. 184 (1964).

83. Ibid. at 186.

84. See Robert A. Pratt, "Crossing the Color Line: A Historical Assessment and Personal Narrative of *Loving v. Virginia,*" *Howard Law Journal* 41 (1998): 229.

85. *Loving* at 3.

86. Ibid. at 7.

87. *Landmark Briefs and Arguments of the Supreme Court of the United States: Constitutional Law,* ed. Philip Kurland, vol. 64 (1975), 834.

88. Ibid., 772.

89. *Loving* at 9.

90. Ibid. at 11.

91. Ibid.

92. Ibid. at 11–12 n. 11.

93. Ibid. at 11.

94. Ibid. at 12.

95. See Michael W. McConnell, "Original Intent and the Desegregation Decisions," *Virginia Law Review* 81 (1995): 947, 952–53.

96. See Derrick Bell, *Race, Racism, and American Law* (1972), 283; Robert J. Sickels, *Race, Marriage and the Law* (1972), 111–16.

97. *Davis v. Gately,* 269 F. Supp. 996 (D.C. Del. 1967).

98. See *Van Hook v. Blanton,* 12 Race Rel. L. Rep. 2079 (1968).

99. *United States v. Brittain,* 319 F. Supp. 1058 (N.D. Ala. 1970).

100. Sickels, *Race, Marriage and the Law,* 116. See also *Davis v. Ashford,* 2 Race Rel. L. Rep. 152 (S.D. Miss. 1970).

101. See Andrew Marshall, "Dragging Alabama to the Altar: Old Habits—And Laws, Such as on Interracial Marriage—Die Hard in This Deep South State," *The Independent* (London), June 27, 1999.

102. "The 2000 Elections, State by State: South," *New York Times,* November 9, 2000.

## Chapter Seven:
### Racial Passing

1. See *Van Houten v. Morse,* 162 Mass. 415 (1894).

2. Ibid., 418.

3. Ibid., 417.

4. See Anita Allen, "Lying to Protect Privacy," *Villanova Law Review* 44 (1999): 161.

5. Gregory Howard Williams, *Life on the Color Line* (1995).

6. Ibid., 34.

7. Among the works I have consulted are Adam Lively, *Masks: Blackness, Race, and the Imagination* (2000); Gayle Wald, *Crossing the Line: Racial Passing in Twentieth-Century U.S. Literature and Culture* (2000); Marjorie Garber, *Symptoms of Culture* (1998), 141–152; Susan Gubar, *White Skin, Black Face in American Culture* (1997); Werner Sollors, *Neither Black nor White: Thematic Explorations of Interracial Literature* (1997), 246–84; Elaine K. Ginsberg, ed., *Passing and the Fictions of Identity* (1996); Everett V. Stonequist, *The Marginal Man: A Study in Personality and Culture* (1937); Louis Fremont Baldwin, *From Negro to Caucasian, or How the Ethiopian Is Changing His Skin* (1929); Robert Westley, "First-Time Encounters: 'Passing' Revisited and Demystification as a Critical Practice," *Yale Law & Policy Review* 18 (2000): 297; Kenji Yoshino, "Assimilationist Bias in Equal Protection: The Visibility Perception and the Case of 'Don't Ask, Don't Tell,'" *Yale Law Journal* 108 (1998): 485, 528; G. Reginald Daniel, "Passers and Pluralists: Subverting the Racial Divide," in Maria P. P. Roots, ed., *Racially Mixed People in America* (1992).

8. See Walter White, "Why I Remain a Negro," *Saturday Evening Post,* October 11, 1947.

9. See Roi Ottley, "5 Million U.S. White Negroes," *Ebony,* March 1948.

10. See John H. Burma, "The Measurement of Negro 'Passing,'" *American Journal of Sociology* 52 (1946): 1822. See also William M. Kephart, "The 'Passing' Question," *Phylon* 9 (1948): 336.

11. See Gunnar Myrdal, *An American Dilemma: The Negro Problem and Modern Democracy,* vol. 2 (1944, reprint, 1962), 687; St. Clair Drake and Horace R. Cayton, *Black Metropolis: A Study of Negro Life in a Northern City* (1945; reprint, 1961), 159: "'Passing' is one of the most prevalent practices that has arisen out of the American pattern of race relations." See also Lawrence Otis Graham, *Our Kind of People: Inside America's Black Upper Class* (1999), 376–93.

12. See Walter White, *A Man Called White: The Autobiography of Walter White* (1948).

13. Ibid., 136.

14. See Charles Crowe, "Racial Violence and Social Reform—Origins of the Atlanta Riot of 1906: Racial Massacre in Atlanta, September 22, 1906," in Paul Finkelman, ed., *Lynching, Racial Violence, and Law* (1992), 9.

15. Walter White, *A Man Called White,* 9.

16. Ibid., 11.

17. Ibid., 51.

18. See Drake and Cayton, *Black Metropolis*, at 162–63.

19. "White by Day ... Negro by Night," *Ebony*, April 1952.

20. Drake and Cayton, *Black Metropolis*, 162.

21. Ibid., 162. See also Adele Logan Alexander, *Homeland and Waterways: The American Journey of the Bond Family, 1846–1926* (1999), 454–55; Constance McLaughlin Green, *The Secret City: A History of Race Relations in the Nation's Capital* (1967), 207.

22. Lucia Stanton and Dianne Swann-White, "Bonds of Memory: Identity and the Hemings Family," in Jan Lewis, Peter S. Onuf, and Jane E. Lewis, ed., *Sally Hemings and Thomas Jefferson: History, Memory, and Civic Culture* (1999), 163.

23. Ibid.

24. Ibid.

25. Ibid., 164.

26. Ibid., 172.

27. See James M. O'Toole, "Passing: Race, Religion, and the Healy Family, 1820–1920," *Proceedings of the Massachusetts Historical Society*, 1998, p. 1.

28. Ibid., 19.

29. Ibid., 15.

30. See, e.g., Harry A. Ploski and Roscoe C. Brown Jr., *The Negro Almanac* (1967), 804, describing James Augustine Healy as "the first Negro Catholic Bishop in the United States." See also Mabel Smythe, ed., *The Black American Reference Book* (1976), 454.

31. Harry A. Ploski and Roscoe C. Brown, Jr., *The Negro Almanac* (1967), 804.

32. See Jillian A. Sim, "Fading to White," *American Heritage*, March 1999.

33. Ibid.

34. An illuminating discussion of this case may be found in the excellent college senior thesis by Jamie L. Wacks, "Reading Race, Rhetoric, and the Female Body: The *Rhinelander* Case and 1920s American Culture" (Harvard College, 1995). An abbreviated but more accessible version of the paper is included in Werner Sollors, ed., *Interracialism: Black-White Intermarriage in American History, Literature, and Law* (2000). Useful discussions of the Rhinelander case can also be found in Earl Lewis and Heidi Ardizzone, *Love on Trial: The American Scandal in Black and White* (2001); Elizabeth Marie Smith, "'Passing' and the Anxious Decade: The *Rhinelander* Case and the 1920s," (Ph.D. dissertation, Rutgers University, 2001).

35. Wacks, "Reading Race."

36. "Reading Race" in Sollors, ed., p. 171.

37. See the *Maryland Journal* and the *Baltimore Advertiser,* July 13, 1787, in *Runaway Slave Advertisements: A Documentary History from the 1730s to 1790,* vol. 2, *Maryland,* ed. Lathan A. Windley (1983), 366. See also Sollors, *Neither Black Nor White,* 225; John Hope Franklin and Loren Schweninger, *Runaway Slaves: Rebels on the Plantation* (1999).

38. Joel Williamson, *New People: Miscegenation and Mulattoes in the United States* (1980; reprint, 1995), 103.

39. See Thomas Dixon, *The Leopard's Spots: A Romance of the White Man's Burden, 1865–1900* (1902), 101, 124; reprinted in *Thomas Dixon: The Reconstruction Trilogy* (1994).

40. See Barbara Bair, "Remapping the Black/White Body: Sexuality, Nationalism, and Biracial Antimiscegenation Activism in 1920s Virginia," in Martha Hodes, ed., *Sex, Love, Race: Crossing Boundaries in North American History* (1999); Paul A. Lombardo, "Miscegenation, Eugenics, and Racism: Historical Footnotes to *Loving v. Virginia,*" *U.C. Davis Law Review* 21 (1988): 421; Richard B. Sherman, "'The Last Stand': The Fight for Racial Integrity in Virginia in the 1920s," *Journal of Southern History* 49 (1988): 69.

41. See Walter Wadlington, "The *Loving* Case: Virginia's Antimiscegenation Statute in Historical Perspective," *Virginia Law Review* 52 (1966): 1189, 1202.

42. Quoted in Sherman, "'The Last Stand,'" 81.

43. See Bair, "Remapping the Black/White Body," 402.

44. Ibid., 412–13.

45. See Melba Joyce Boyd, *Discarded Legacy: Politics and Poetics in the Life of Frances E. W. Harper, 1825–1911* (1994); Frances Smith Foster, ed., *A Brighter Day Coming: A Frances Ellen Watkins Harper Reader* (1990).

46. Frances E. W. Harper, *Iola LeRoy* (1892). There are several excellent editions of this novel. The one I have used and refer to here is included in William L. Andrews, ed., *The African American Novel in the Age of Reaction: Three Classics* (1992).

47. Harper, *Iola LeRoy,* in Andrews, ed., *Three Classics,* 86.

48. Ibid., 88.

49. Ibid., 177–78.

50. Ibid., 96.

51. Ibid., 97.

52. Ibid.

53. Ibid.

54. Ibid., 179.

55. Ibid., 204.
56. Ronald E. Hall, "Blacks Who Pass," in Herb Boyd and Robert L. Allen, eds., *Brotherman: The Odyssey of Black Men in America—An Anthology* (1995), 474.
57. Janice Kingslow, "I Refuse to Pass," *Negro Digest*, May 1950.
58. See Frank J. Webb, *The Garies and Their Friends* (1857; paperback edition, ed. Robert Reid-Pharr, 1997).
59. Ibid. (1997 ed.), 1.
60. Ibid., 2.
61. Ibid., 336.
62. Ibid., 335–36.
63. Ibid., 331.
64. Ibid., 326.
65. Ibid., 331.
66. Ibid., 345.
67. Ibid., 354.
68. Ibid., 380.
69. Ibid., 380–81.
70. Ibid., 381.
71. Reba Lee, *I Passed for White* (1955), 2.
72. Ibid., 76.
73. Ibid., 157.
74. Ibid., 180.
75. Ibid., 259.
76. Ibid., 260.
77. Myrdal, *An American Dilemma*, 686.
78. James Weldon Johnson, *The Autobiography of an Ex-Colored Man* (1912; reissue edited and with an introduction by William L. Andrews, 1990).
79. Ibid. (1990 ed.), 135.
80. Ibid., 137.
81. Ibid., 139.
82. Ibid., 141.
83. Ibid., 154.
84. Lee, *I Passed for White*, p. 270.
85. W. L. White, *Lost Boundaries* 24 (1947).
86. Gregory Howard Williams, *Life on the Color Line*, 32–33.
87. Nella Larsen, *Passing* (1929; reprint edited and with an introduction by Deborah E. McDowell, 1986), 185–86.
88. Jessie Redmond Fauset, *Plum Bun: A Novel Without a Moral* (1928; reprint, 1990), 15.

89. Ibid.

90. Ray Stannard Baker, *Following the Color Line: American Negro Citizenship in the Progressive Era* (1908; reprint, 1964), 162–63.

91. See, e.g., "Jokes on Our White Folks," in *Langston Hughes and the Chicago Defender: Essays on Race, Politics, and Culture, 1942–62,* ed. Christopher C. DeSantis (1995); "Fooling Our White Folks," *Negro Digest,* April 1950; "Why Not Fool Our White Folks," *Chicago Defender,* January 5, 1958.

92. Gregory Howard Williams, *Life on the Color Line,* 174.

93. Shirlee Taylor Haizlip, *The Sweeter the Juice* (1994), 64. See also Green, *The Secret City,* 207.

94. Cheryl I. Harris, "Whiteness as Property," *Harvard Law Review* 106 (1993): 1707, 1711.

95. Haizlip, *The Sweeter the Juice,* 63.

96. Glenn C. Loury, *One by One from the Inside Out: Essays and Reviews on Race and Responsibility in America* (1995), 2.

97. W. L. White, *Lost Boundaries,* 60.

98. See Peter Irons, "Justice at War: The Story of the Japanese American Internment Cases" (1983), 93–94.

99. 323 U.S. 214 (1944).

100. See Clement Vose, *Caucasians All: The Supreme Court, the NAACP, and the Restrictive Covenant Cases* (1959), 85–86; *Hurd v. Hodge,* 334 U.S. 24, 27 n. 2 (1948).

101. See *Stone v. Jones,* 152 P.2d 19 (Cal. Ct. App. 1944).

102. See "Buyer Beware," *Time,* April 16, 1956, p. 24.

103. See Christine B. Hickman, "The Devil and the One Drop Rule: Racial Categories, African Americans, and the U.S. Census," *Michigan Law Review* 95 (1997): 1161–69.

104. Leo Spitzer, *Lives in Between: The Experience of Marginality in a Century of Emancipation* (1999), 180.

105. See Kevin K. Gaines, *Uplifting the Race: Black Leadership, Politics, and Culture in the Twentieth Century* (1996), 229.

106. Harriet Jacobs, *Incidents in the Life of a Slave Girl Written by Herself* (1861; reprint, edited by Jean Fagan Yellin, 1987), 119.

107. See Charles W. Chesnutt, *The House Behind the Cedars* (1900), 45.

108. Albert O. Hirschman, *Exit, Voice, and Loyalty: Responses to Decline in Firms, Organizations, and States* (1970), 108–9.

109. Chesnutt, *House Behind the Cedars,* 12.

110. Ibid., 20.

111. 163 U.S. 537 (1896).

112. See, e.g., *Korematus v. United States,* 323 U.S. 214 (1944); *Regents of the Univ. of California v. Bakke,* 438 U.S. 265 (1978).

113. *Anderson v. Martin,* 375 U.S. 399, 402 (1964), *rev'g* 206 F. Supp. 700 (D. La. 1962). For useful commentary on *Anderson,* see Andrew J. Kull, *The Color-Blind Constitution* (1992), 164–67.

114. *Hamm v. Virginia,* 230 F. Supp. 156 (E.D. Va.), *aff'd mem.* 379 U.S. 19 (1964).

115. W. L. White, *Lost Boundaries,* 19.

116. See Will Haygood, *King of the Cats: The Life and Times of Adam Clayton Powell, Jr.* (1993), 9–13; Charles V. Hamilton, *Adam Clayton Powell, Jr.* (1991), 48–50.

117. Johnson, *Autobiography of an Ex-Colored Man,* 139.

118. Chesnutt, *House Behind the Cedars,* 56.

119. William Dean Howells, *An Imperative Duty* (1893), 75.

120. Ibid., 34.

121. Ibid., 54.

122. Ibid., 44.

123. Johnson, *Autobiography,* 149.

124. Hall, "Blacks Who Pass," 475.

125. See Bill E. Lawson, "Uplifting the Race: Middle-Class Blacks and the Truly Disadvantaged" in Bill E. Lawson, ed., *The Underclass Question* (1992); Alvin Poussaint, "The Price of Success: Remembering Their Roots Burdens Many Blacks to Mainstream with Feelings of Either Guilt or Denial," *Ebony,* March 1988. See also Bebe Moore Campbell, "Staying in the Community," *Essence,* December 1989.

126. See Randall Kennedy, "My Race Problem—And Ours," *Atlantic Monthly,* May 1997.

127. See Randall Kennedy, "Martin Luther King's Constitution: A Legal History of the Montgomery Bus Boycott," *Yale Law Journal* 98 (1989): 999.

128. Jay Mathews, "Hue and Cry: Blue-Eyed Official Ran as Black, Faces Recall," *Washington Post,* May 6, 1984.

129. *Malone v. Haley,* Supreme Judicial Court for Suffolk County No. 88-339, July 25, 1989, Associate Justice Herbert P. Wilkins presiding. Unfortunately, this decision has never been published. It may be found in the Interracial Intimacies Collection at the Harvard Law School Library. For commentary on this case, see Christopher A. Ford, "Administering Identity: The Determination of 'Race' in Race-Conscious Law," *California Law Review* 82 (1994): 1231; Luther Wright Jr., "Note: Who's Black, Who's White, and Who Cares:

Reconceptualizing the United States' Definition of Race and Racial Classifications," *Vanderbilt Law Review* 48 (1995): 513.

130. *Malone v. Haley* at 16.

131. Ibid. at 16 n. 7.

132. See Ford, "Administering Identity," 1281.

133. Compare Paul Brest and Miranda Oshinge, "Affirmative Action for Whom?," *Stanford Law Review* 27 (1995): 855.

134. Wright, "Note, Who's Black, Who's White, and Who Cares," 513.

135. Cf Boris Bittker, *The Case for Black Reparations* (1973), 127, suggesting that the dangers attending the need to police claimants may outweigh the value of offering reparations to victims of antiblack racial oppression in the United States.

136. See Michael Oreskes, "The Set-Aside Scam: Corruption and Quotas in the Construction Industry," *New Republic,* December 24, 1984; Vernon C. Thompson, "Minority Firms vs. Minority Fronts," *Washington Post,* June 12, 1979.

### Chapter Eight:
#### Passing and the Schuyler Family

1. For more on George Schuyler, see Jeffrey Brown Ferguson, "The Newest Negro: George Schuyler's Intellectual Quest in the Nineteen Twenties and Beyond" (Ph.D. diss., Harvard University, 1998); Harry McKinley Williams Jr., "When Black Is Right: The Life and Writings of George S. Schuyler" (Ph.D. diss., Brown University, 1988); George S. Schuyler, *Black and Conservative: The Autobiography of George S. Schuyler* (1966).

2. Kathryn Talalay revealed this previously unknown chapter of Schuyler's life in *Composition in Black and White: The Life of Philippa Schuyler* (1995). Talalay has noted that Schuyler omitted any mention of the episode in his autobiography and his oral reminiscences for the Columbia University Oral History Project.

3. See Sandra Kathryn Wilson, ed., *The* Messenger *Reader: Stories, Poetry, and Essays from the* Messenger *Magazine* (2000).

4. Williams, "When Black Is Right," 53.

5. For biographical information on Josephine Cogdell, see Talalay, *Composition in Black and White.* For an airbrushed published version of her courtship with and marriage to George Schuyler, see Cogdell's memoir "An Interracial Marriage," *American Mercury,* March 1946. For alternative renderings, see Talalay's account and

Cogdell's private diaries, which are available for study in the Manuscripts, Archives and Rare Books Division of the Schomburg Center for Research in Black Culture, New York City.

6. Talalay, *Composition in Black and White*, 19.

7. Ibid., 20.

8. Ibid., 18.

9. See Josephine Cogdell diary for 1927, Schomburg Center for Research in Black Culture.

10. Ibid.

11. Talalay, *Composition in Black and White*, 22, quoting Cogdell diary.

12. Ibid., 29.

13. Ibid., 23–24.

14. Ibid., 30.

15. Ibid.

16. Ibid., 25.

17. Ibid., 29.

18. Ibid., 39.

19. The most useful current reissue of *Black No More* is the Northeastern University Press edition (1987), which offers an insightful introduction by James A. Miller. My own citations to *Black No More* refer to this edition. Also of interest is the Modern Library edition (1999), with an introduction by Ishmael Reed. Instructive interpretive analyses of *Black No More* may be found in J. Martin Favor, *Authentic Blackness: The Folk in the New Negro Renaissance* (1999); Michael Peplow, *George S. Schuyler* (1980); John M. Reilly, "The Black Anti-Utopian," *Black American Literature Forum*, fall 1978; James A. Miller, introduction to 1987 edition; Williams, "When Black Is Right"; Ferguson, "The Newest Negro."

20. George S. Schuyler, *Black No More*, 1987 ed., 17.

21. Ibid., 20.

22. Ibid., 23.

23. Ibid., 30.

24. Ibid., 34–35.

25. Ibid., 35.

26. Ibid., 191–92.

27. Ibid., 192–93.

28. Ibid., 193.

29. Ibid., dedication page.

30. Ibid., 153–54.

31. Ibid., 179.

32. Ibid., 204.

33. Ibid., 217–18.

34. Ibid., 218.

35. Ibid.

36. Ibid., 85–86.

37. Ibid., 87.

38. Ibid., 90.

39. Ibid.

40. Ibid., 101–2.

41. Ibid., 102.

42. Ibid., 103.

43. Ibid., 55.

44. Ibid.

45. Ibid.

46. See "Racial Metamorphosis Claimed by Scientist," *Pittsburgh Courier,* November 2, 1929. Cited in Williams, "When Black Is Right," 192.

47. Walter White, "Can Science Conquer the Color Line?," *Look,* August 30, 1949.

48. Ibid.

49. Orlando Patterson, "Race Over," *New Republic,* January 10, 2000.

50. Ibid.

51. Leo Spitzer, *Lives in Between: The Experience of Marginality in a Century of Emancipation* (1999), 179.

52. See Thomas E. Skidmore, *Black into White: Race and Nationality in Brazilian Thought* (1993), 73, quoting José Veríssimo.

53. Schuyler, *Black No More,* 1987 ed., 219.

54. Ibid., 221.

55. Ibid., 220.

56. Ibid., 222.

57. See George S. Schuyler, *Racial Intermarriage in the United States: One of the Most Interesting Phenomena in Our National Life* (1929); idem, "When Black Weds White," *Modern Monthly,* February 1934; idem, *Black and Conservative,* 163–64.

58. George S. Schuyler, "Views and Reviews," *Pittsburgh Courier,* March 15, 1935: "I believe miscegenation is the way—perhaps the only way—the race problem is going to be solved in these United States."

59. See John P. Diggins, *Up from Communism: Conservative Odysseys in American Intellectual History* (1977).

60. George S. Schuyler, "Our White Folks," *American Mercury,* December 1927.

61. Ibid.

62. George S. Schuyler, "Traveling Jim Crow," *American Mercury*, August 1930.

63. George S. Schuyler, "The Caucasian Problem," in Rayford Logan, ed., *What the Negro Wants* (1944, reprint, 2001), 282.

64. See George S. Schuyler, *Slaves Today: A Story of Liberia* (1931; reprint, 1969).

65. See George S. Schuyler, "The Negro-Art Hokum," *The Nation,* June 16, 1926.

66. George S. Schuyler, "Do We Really Want Equality?," *The Crisis,* April 1937.

67. George S. Schuyler, "Views and Reviews," *Pittsburgh Courier,* October 12, 1940.

68. Schuyler, *Black and Conservative,* 344–45.

69. See Wilson Record, *The Negro and the Communist Party* (1951); Wilson Record, *Race and Radicalism: The NAACP and the Communist Party in Conflict* (1964).

70. See Williams, "When Black Is Right," 348, quoting letter from George S. Schuyler to Sol Stein, November 1, 1954.

71. George S. Schuyler, "King No Help to Peace," *Manchester* (New Hampshire) *Union Leader,* November 10, 1964.

72. George S. Schuyler, "Malcolm X: Better to Memorialize Benedict Arnold," *American Opinion,* February 1973.

73. See Talalay, *Composition in Black and White,* 45–61.

74. Ibid., 53.

75. Ibid., 81.

76. Ibid., 106–7.

77. Ibid., 223.

78. Ibid.

79. Ibid., 224.

80. Ibid.

81. Ibid.

82. Ibid., 226.

83. Ibid., 229.

84. Ibid., 226.

85. The manuscript is now in the Manuscripts Archives and Rare Books Division of the Schomburg Center for Research in Black Culture, New York City, Schomburg Collection.

86. Talalay, *Composition in Black and White,* 235.

87. Ibid., 234.

88. Ibid., 267.

89. Ibid., 274.
90. Ibid.
91. Ibid.


*Chapter Nine:*
*Racial Conflict and the Parenting of Children:*
*A Survey of Competing Approaches*

1. See Harriet A. Jacobs, *Incidents in the Life of a Slave Girl, Written by Herself* (1861), edited and with an introduction by Jean Fagan Yellin (1987).
2. Lillian Smith, *Killers of the Dream* (1949; reprint, 1994).
3. See Lori Andrews, *Black Power, White Blood: The Life and Times of Johnny Spain* (1996, 1999). See also Chip Brown, "The Transformation of Johnny Spain," *Esquire,* January 1988.
4. Andrews, *Black Power, White Blood,* 14.
5. Ibid., 15.
6. June Cross, *Secret Daughter* (Public Broadcasting System, 1996). See also Les Payne, "Using a Cannon to Open a Door," *Newsday,* December 1, 1996; Sheryl McCarthy, "A Grown Child Tries to Untangle Her Roots," *Newsday,* November 28, 1996; Frederic M. Biddle, "When Color Lines Are Drawn Within a Family," *Boston Globe,* November 26, 1996.
7. Michael A. Lipton and Stephen Sawicki, "White Lie: June Cross Exposes the Skeleton in Her Mother's Closet—Herself," *People,* December 2, 1996.
8. My description of *Ward v. Ward* is based on the decision rendered by the Washington Supreme Court (216 P. 2d 755 [1950]) and the briefs filed by the parties in the case, all in the Interracial Intimacies Collection at the Harvard Law School Library. For useful commentary on the issues raised by *Ward,* see Renée Christine Romano, "Crossing the Race Line: Black-White Interracial Marriage in the United States 1945–1990" (Ph.D. diss., Stanford University, 1996); Gayle Pollack, "The Role of Race in Child Custody Decisions between Natural Parents over Biracial Children," *Review of Law and Social Change* 32 (1997): 630; "Note: Custody Disputes Following the Dissolution of Interracial Marriages: Best Interest of the Child or Judicial Racism?," *Journal of Family Law* 19 (1980): 97.
9. The Washington State appellate court would subsequently criticize *Ward;* see *Tucker v. Tucker,* 542 P. 2d 789 (1975).

10. *Farmer v. Farmer,* 109 Misc. 2d 137 (N.Y. Sup. Ct. 1981).

11. Ibid. at 147.

12. Ibid.

13. Ibid.

14. In re *Marriage of Alice E. Burton and Victor D. Burton,* 1990 Ill. Ap. Lexis 191 (Ill. App. 5th Dist. February 15, 1990).

15. Ibid.

16. Ibid.

17. *Parker v. Parker,* 986 S. W. 2d 557 (S. Ct. Tenn. Middle Section 1999).

18. Ibid. at 560.

19. See *Moon v. Children's Home Society,* 112 Va. 737 (1911).

20. Ibid. at 738.

21. Ibid. at 741.

22. See brief for Lucy Moon at p. 4, on file in Interracial Intimacies material at the Harvard Law School Library.

23. Ibid.

24. *Moon v. Children's Home Society,* 112 Va. at 741–42.

25. See, e.g., *Commonwealth of Pennsylvania ex rel. Fred H. Myers v. Pandora Myers,* 360 A. 2d 587 (Pa. Sup. Ct. 1976); *Wambles v. Coppage,* 333 So. 2d 829 (Ala. Civ. App. 1976).

26. *Palmore v. Sidoti,* 466 U.S. 429 (1984). For salient commentary on *Palmore,* see Robert T. Carter and Ellen Gesmer, "Applying Racial Identity Theory to the Legal System: The Case of Family Law," in Chalmer E. Thompson and Robert T. Carter, eds., *Racial Identity Theory* (1997); Eileen M. Blackwood, "Note: Race as a Factor in Custody and Adoption Disputes," *Cornell Law Review* 71 (1985): 209; Lisa Jonas and Marshall Silverberg, "Comment: Race, Custody and the Constitution: *Palmore v. Sidoti,*" *Howard Law Journal* 27 (1984): 1549; Robert B. Weinstock, "Note: *Palmore v. Sidoti:* Color-Blind Custody," *American University Law Review* 34 (1984): 245.

27. Petition for Modification of Final Judgment in re the Marriage of Anthony J. Sidoti and Linda A. Sidoti, September 30, 1981. Joint Appendix of Petitioner and Respondent at page 11 in *Palmore v. Sidoti,* No. 82–1734, Supreme Court of the United States.

28. Ibid., 11–12.

29. Memo of Judge Morison Buck, February 4, 1982. Joint Appendix of Petitioner and Responent at pages 21–22 in *Palmore v. Sidoti,* No. 82–1734, Supreme Court of the United States.

30. Ibid., 21.

31. Ibid., 32.

32. *Palmore v. Sidoti,* 466 U.S. at 433.

33. Ibid., 432.

34. Ibid., 433.

35. Ibid.

36. Ibid.

37. Ibid.

38. Ibid., 434.

39. *Buchanan v. Warley,* 245 U.S. 60, 86 (1917).

40. *Cooper v. Aaron,* 358 U.S. 1, 16 (1958).

41. *Watson v. Memphis,* 373 U.S. 526, 535 (1963).

42. Paul Gewirtz, "Remedies and Resistance," *Yale Law Journal* 585 (1983): 92; Dennis J. Hutchinson, "Unanimity and Desegregation: Decisionmaking in the Supreme Court, 1948–1958," *Georgetown Law Journal* 1 (1979): 68.

43. *M.P. v. S.P.,* 404 A. 2d 1256 (N.J. Super. Ct. 1979).

44. See *Palmore v. Sidoti,* 472 So. 2d 843 (Ct. App. Fla. 1985).

45. See *Turman v. Boleman,* 510 S.E. 2d 532, 534 (Ct. App. Ga. 1998). See also *Isom v. Isom,* 538 N.E. 2d 261 (1989); In re *Marriage of Ann M. Brown,* 480 N.E. 2d 246 (Ct. App. Ind. 1985).

46. *Holt v. Chenault,* 722 S.W. 2d 897 (Ky. 1987).

47. See *Compos v. McKeithen,* 341 F. Supp. 264 (E.D. La. 1972)

48. See In re *Gomez,* 424 S.W. 2d 656 (Tex. Cir. App. 1967).

49. Ibid. at 657.

50. *Compos v. McKeithen,* 341 F. Supp. at 266.

51. Ibid.

52. South Carolina Code 10-2587.9 et seq. (Supp. 1972). This statute was repealed by 1981 Act No. 71-3, eff. May 19, 1981.

53. See In re *Adoption of a Minor,* 228 F. 2d 446 (D.C. Cir. 1955).

54. Ibid. at 447.

55. Ibid.

56. Ibid.

57. Ibid. at 448.

58. Ibid.

59. See Jack Kresnak, "Interracial Adoption Fight Ends; Black Woman, White Child Finally Together," *Houston Chronicle,* April 18, 1998. See also the statement of Patrick T. Murphy, Cook County public guardian, Hearing Before the Subcommittee on Human Resources of the United States House of Representatives Committee on Ways and Means, 150th Congress, Second Session, September 15, 1998, at 116–125.

60. Position paper issued by the National Association of Black Social Workers, April 1972, reprinted in Rita J. Simon and Howard Alstein, *Transracial Adoption* (1977), 50.

61. Ibid.

62. Ibid., 52.

63. G. C. Fraser, "Disease Programs Scored by Blacks," *New York Times,* April 9, 1972, p. 29, quoting Audrey Russell.

64. See "Barriers to Adoption 1985": Hearings on S.999-288 Before the Senate Committee on Labor and Human Resources, 99th Cong., 1st Sess. (1985), 217–18, for the testimony of William Merritt, president of the National Association of Black Social Workers.

65. See Elizabeth Bartholet, "Where Do Black Children Belong? The Politics of Race Matching in Adoption," *University of Pennsylvania Law Review* 139 (1991): 1163, 1179–81; Jacqueline Macaulay and Stewart Macaulay, "Adoption for Black Children: A Case Study of Expert Discretion," *Research in Law and Sociology* 1 (1978): 265, 286: "The counter-revolution was sparked by the National Association of Black Social Workers." On the international influence of the NABSW, see Peter Hayes, "The Ideological Attack on Transracial Adoption in the USA and Britain," *International Journal of Law and the Family* 9 (1995): 1.

66. See Macaulay and Macaulay, "Adoption for Black Children," 285.

67. See, e.g., Bartholet, "Where Do Black Children Belong?"

68. Multiethnic Placement Act of 1994, Pub. L. No. 103-382, 102 Stat. 3518 (1994).

69. Interethnic Adoption Amendment, Pub. L. No. 104-188, § 1808(a)(3) (1996).

70. See Courtenay Edelhart, "Adoption Backers Address Concerns Expressed by Foes," *Indianapolis Star,* September 3, 2000. See also Clark Kaufman, "Transracial Adoptions Encounter Opposition," *Des Moines Register,* November 13, 2000.

71. See, e.g., Elizabeth Bartholet, *Nobody's Children: Abuse, Neglect, Foster Drift, and the Adoption Alternative* (1999), 113–40; Hayes, "Ideological Attack," 1.

72. Quoted in Macaulay and Macaulay, "Adoption for Black Children," p. 283.

73. Ibid.

74. See, e.g., Joseph Crumbley, *Transracial Adoption and Foster Care: Practice Issues for Professionals* (1999).

75. See Cal. Civ. Cod §§ 276, 276(2) (West Supp. 1991), amended by Cal. Civ. Code §§ 222.35, 222.37 (West Supp. 1991).

76. "Black Children, White Parents," *New York Times,* November 27, 1993.

77. See Multiethnic Placement Act of 1994. See also Howard M. Metzenbaum, "S.1224—In Support of the Multiethnic Placement Act of 1993," *Duke Journal of Gender Law and Policy* 2 (1995): 165; Randall Kennedy, "Orphans of Separatism: The Painful Politics of Transracial Adoption," *American Prospect,* spring 1994.

78. See *Congressional Record* 139: S. 8712, statement by Mr. Metzenbaum (for himself and Ms. Mosely-Braun). See also Senator Howard M. Metzenbaum, "S-1224 C, In Support of the Multiethnic Placement Act of 1993," *Duke Journal of Gender Law and Policy* 2 (1995): 165.

79. Pub. L. No. 104-188 § 1808(a)(3) (1996).

### Chapter Ten:
### *The Tragedy of Race Matching in Black and White*

1. Writings propounding race matching include Ruth-Arlene Howe, "Transracial Adoption (TRA): Old Prejudices and Discrimination Float Under a New Halo," *Boston University Public Interest Law Journal* 6 (1997): 409; Cynthia P. Mabry, "Love Alone in Transracial Adoption—Scrutinizing Recent Statutes, Agency Policies, and Prospective Adoptive Parents," *Wayne Law Review* 42 (1996): 1347; Ruth-Arlene Howe, "Redefining the Transracial Adoption Controversy," *Duke Law Journal of Gender Law and Policy* 2 (1995): 131; Twila L. Perry, "The Transracial Adoption Controversy: An Analysis of Discourse and Subordination," *New York University Review of Law and Social Change* 21 (1993–94): 33; James S. Bowen, "Cultural Convergences and Divergences: The Nexus Between Putative Afro-American Family Values and the Best Interests of the Child," *Journal of Family Law* 26 (1987–88): 487; Amuzie Chimezie, "Transracial Adoption of Black Children," *Social Work* 20 (1985): 296.

   Notable among the works arguing against race matching are Rita Simon and Howard Altstein, *Transracial Adoption* (1977); Rita Simon and Howard Altstein, *Transracial Adoption: A Follow-up* (1981); Rita Simon and Howard Altstein, *Transracial Adoptees and Their Families* (1987); Elizabeth Bartholet, "Where Do Black Children Belong? The Politics of Race Matching in Adoption," *University of Pennsylvania Law Review* 139 (1991): 1163; Kim Forde-Mazrui, "Black Identity and Child Placement: The Best Interests of Black and Biracial Children," *Michigan Law Review* 92 (1994): 925; Shari

O'Brien, "Race in Adoption Proceedings: The Pernicious Factor," *Tulsa Law Journal* 21 (1986): 485; Peter Hayes, "The Ideological Attack on Transracial Adoption in the USA and Britain," *International Journal of Law and the Family* 9 (1995): 1; Amanda T. Perez, "Transracial Adoption and the Federal Adoption Subsidy," *Yale Law and Policy Review* 17 (1998): 201; Rebecca Varan, "Desegregating the Adoptive Family: In Support of the Adoption Anti-Discrimination Act of 1995," *John Marshall Law Journal* 30 (1997): 593.

2. Elizabeth Bartholet, *Nobody's Children: Abuse and Neglect, Foster Drift, and the Adoption Alternative* (1999), 81.

3. See Rita J. Simon and Howard Altstein, "The Relevance of Race in Adoption Law and Practice," *Notre Dame Journal of Law, Ethics and Public Policy* 11 (1997): 171: "Black families have always adopted at a higher rate than white families."

4. See Erika Lynn Kleiman, "Caring for Our Own: Why American Adoption Law and Policy Must Change," *Columbia Journal of Law and Social Problems* 30 (1997): 327, 334; Statistical Abstract of the United States 1975, p. 25, table no. 25: Cities with 100,000 Inhabitants or More in 1970—Population, 1950 to 1973, and Area, 1970.

5. Patrick T. Murphy, *Wasted: The Plight of America's Unwanted Children* (1997), 155.

6. See Andrew Billingsley and Jeanne M. Giovannoni, *Children of the Storm: Black Children and American Child Welfare* (1972).

7. Perez, "Transracial Adoption and the Federal Adoption Subsidy."

8. David S. Rosettenstein, "Trans-Racial Adoption and the Statutory Preference Schemes: Before the 'Best Interests' and After the 'Melting Pot,'" *St. John's Law Review* 68 (1994): 137, 142.

9. There exists no comprehensive and up-to-date survey of juvenile foster or institutional care. For impressionistic accounts portraying the harrowing conditions faced by too many parentless children, see Nina Bernstein, *The Lost Children of Wilder: The Epic Struggle to Change Foster Care* (2001); Patrick T. Murphy, *Wasted: The Plight of America's Unwanted Children* (1997); Ronald B. Taylor, *The Kid Business* (1981); Kenneth Wooden, *Weeping in the Playtime of Others* (1976). See also Bartholet, *Nobody's Children*, 59–97; Thomas P. McDonald et al., *Assessing the Long-Term Effects of Foster Care: A Research Synthesis* (1993); Deborah A. Frank, Perri E. Klass, Fenton Earls, and Leon Eisenberg, "Infants and Young Children in Orphanages: One View from Pediatrics and Child Psychiatry," *Pediatrics* 97 (1996): 569.

10. Bartholet, *Nobody's Children*, 86.

11. Ibid.

12. See Nina Bernstein, "New Report Cites Concerns over City Foster Care," *New York Times,* May 2, 2001; Bob Herbert, "In America; An Unending Tragedy," *New York Times,* February 26, 1998; David Armstrong, "DSS Lets Criminals Give Care: 115 Offenders Cleared to be Foster Parents," *Boston Globe,* April 28, 1996; Doris Sue Wang, "Tighter Rules Set for Foster Parents," *Boston Globe,* September 27, 1998.

13. See 435 A. 2d 776, 802–3.

14. Forde-Mazrui, "Black Identity and Child Placement," 925, 954.

15. Ibid., 954.

16. See Randall Kennedy, "Racial Critiques of Legal Academia," *Harvard Law Review* 102 (1989): 1745.

17. Perry, "The Transracial Adoption Controversy," 65: "It is . . . probably true that not all Black parents successfully teach their children how to cope effectively with racism in American society."

18. See, for example, Signithia Fordham and John Ogbu, "Black Students' School Success: Coping with the Burden of 'Acting White,'" *Urban Review,* 1986, p. 176. But see Philip J. Cook and Jens Ludwig, "The Burden of 'Acting White': Do Black Adolescents Disparage Academic Achievement?," in Christopher Jencks and Meredith Phillips, eds., *The Black-White Test Score Gap* (1998).

19. See Trina Jones, "Shades of Brown: The Law of Skin Color," *Duke Law Journal* 49 (2000): 1487; Taunya Lovell Banks, "Colorism: A Darker Shade of Pale," *UCLA Law Review* 47 (2000): 1705; Richard Seltzer and Robert L. Smith, "Color Differences in the Afro-American Community and the Differences They Make," *Journal of Black Studies* 21 (1991): 279; Michael Hughes and Bradley R. Hertel, "The Significance of Color Remains: A Study of Life Chances, Mate Selection, and Ethnic Consciousness Among Black Americans," *Social Forces* 69 (1990): 1105. See also *Castanada v. Partida,* 430 U.S. 482, 504 (1977) (Marshall, J., dissenting); Darryl Cumber Dance, *Shuckin' and Jivin': Folklore from Contemporary Black America* (1978), 77; E. Franklin Frazier, *Black Bourgeoisie* (1957); Gordon Allport, *The Nature of Prejudice* (1953); J. Saunders Redding, *Stranger and Alone* (1950); Chris Rock, *Rock This!* (1997), 17: "Who's more racist: black people or white people? Black people. You know why? Because black people hate black people, too."

20. See Dance, *Shuckin' and Jivin'*; Randall Kennedy, *Nigger: The Strange Career of a Troublesome Word* (2002).

21. See Perry, "The Transracial Adoption Controversy," 94–95.

22. See Eric Foner, *Free Soil, Free Labor, Free Men: The Ideology of the Republican Party Before the Civil War* (1970).

23. See Richard A. Epstein, *Forbidden Grounds: The Case Against Employment Discrimination Laws* (1992); Cass Sunstein, "Why Markets Don't Stop Discrimination," in Ellen F. Paul, Fred D. Miller Jr., and Jeffrey Paul, eds., *Reassessing Civil Rights* (1991); David A. Strauss, "The Law and Economics of Racial Discrimination in Employment: The Case for Numerical Standards," *Georgetown Law Journal* 79 (1991): 1619.

24. See Randall Kennedy, *Race, Crime, and the Law* (1997), p. 136–67.

25. Chimezie, *Transracial Adoption of Black Children,* 299–300.

26. See *Drummond v. Fulton County Dept. of Family and Children's Services,* 408 F. Supp. 382 (N.D. Ga. 1976), rev'd, 547 F. 2d 835 (5th Cir. 1977), 563 F. 2d 1200 (5th Cir. 1977) (district court affirmed by banc court of appeals), cert. denied, 437 U.S. 910 (1978).

27. Drummonds' Affidavit Appendix at 6, on file at the Harvard Law School Library, in the Interracial Intimacies Collection.

28. Brief of Appellants at 6, on file at the Harvard Law School Library, in the Interracial Intimacies Collection.

29. *Drummond,* 547 F. 2d at 857.

30. Ibid. at 857–58 n. 2.

31. Ibid. at 858.

32. *Drummond,* 563 F. 2d, 1205.

33. Ibid., 1205–6.

34. Ibid., 1211.

35. Ibid.

36. Edmond D. Jones, "On Transracial Adoption of Black Children," *Child Welfare* 51 (1972): 156.

37. Ibid.

38. Ibid.

39. Ibid.

40. Ibid.

41. Ibid.

42. *Batson v. Kentucky,* 476 U.S. 79 (1986).

43. See *Adarand Constructors, Inc. v. Pena,* 515 U.S. 200 (1995); *City of Richmond v. J. A. Croson Co.,* 488 U.S. 469 (1989).

44. For a particularly vivid journalistic account, see Kathy Dobie, "Black Kids, White Homes," *Village Voice,* August 8, 1989. See also Beth Brophy, "The Unhappy Politics of Interracial Adoption," *U.S. News & World Report,* November 13, 1989.

45. *In the Matter of the Petition of R.M.G. and E.M.G.* 454 A. 2d 776, 781 (D.C. App 1982).

46. Ibid., 781.

47. Ibid., 782.

48. See *McLaughlin v. Pernsley,* 654 F. Supp. 1567 (E.D. Pa 1987); *McLaughlin v. Pernsley,* 693 F. Supp 318 (E.D. Pa. 1988), aff'd 876 F. 2d 303 (CA 3 1989).

49. In re *Adoption No. 2633,* 646 A. 2d 1036, 1039 (Md. App. 1994).

50. See, e.g., *In the Interest of Malik S.,* 1999 WL 3111 77 (Conn. Sup. Ct. 1999).

51. See, e.g., *Adoption of Vito,* 418 N.E. 2d 1188 (Mass. App. Ct. 1999).

52. See R. Richard Banks, "The Color of Desire: Fulfilling Adoptive Parents' Racial Preferences Through Discriminatory State Action," *Yale Law Journal* 107 (1998): 875.

53. This and the following quote, ibid., 888, 894.

54. Ibid., 943.

55. The Federal Civil Rights Act of 1964, which prohibits racial discrimination in privately owned places of public accommodation, exempts private clubs. Federal laws that prohibit discrimination in employment and housing exempt certain small employees and small owner-occupied residences. Similar exemptions can be found in state antidiscrimination laws. See generally Derrick Bell, *Race, Racism, and American Law* (4th ed., 2000); Amy Gutman, ed., *Freedom of Association* (1998).

56. See Elizabeth Bartholet, "Private Racial Preferences in Family Formation," *Yale Law Journal* 107 (1998): 2351, 2353: "I do place some value on autonomy, and do not think the state should get in the business of limiting choice in marriage, procreation, or adoptive relationships."

57. See, for instance, Cynthia G. Hawkins-Leon, "The Indian Child Welfare Act and the African American Tribe: Facing the Adoption Crisis," *Brandeis Journal of Family Law* 36 (1998): 201.

58. See, e.g., Eddie S. Glande Jr., ed., *Is It Nation Time?: Contemporary Essays on Black Power and Black Nationalism* (2002); Dean E. Robinson, *Black Nationalism in American Politics and Thought* (2001); Wilson Jeremiah Moses, *Classical Black Nationalism: From the American Revolution to Marcus Garvey* (1996); John H. Bracey Jr., August Meir, and Elliot Rudrick, eds., *Black Nationalism in America* (1970).

59. See Homer H. Clark Jr., *The Law of Domestic Relations in the United States* (2d ed., 1988): 912–19; Donald L. Beschle, "God Bless the Child?: The Use of Religion as a Factor in Child Custody and Adoption Proceedings," *Fordham Law Review* 58 (1989): 383; Note, "Religious Matching Statute and Adoption," *New York University Law Review* 51 (1976): 262; Ellen S. George and Stephen M. Snyder, "A Reconsideration of the Religious Element in Adoption," *Cornell Law Review* 56 (1971): 780; Lawrence List, "A Child and a Wall: A Study of 'Religious Protection Laws'," *Buffalo Law Review* 13 (1963): 9.

60. See Julie C. Lythcot-Hains, Note: "Where Do Mixed Babies Belong? Racial Classification in America and Its Implications for Transracial Adoption," *Harvard Civil Rights—Civil Liberties Law Review* 29 (1994): 531.

61. George and Snyder, "A Reconsideration of the Religious Element in Adoption," at 783–84.

62. Petitions of Goldman at 845.

63. New York Constitution art. 6, § 32. See also *Wilder v. Bernstein,* 848 F. 2d 1338, 1341 (2d Cir. 1988).

64. Quoted in George and Snyder, *A Reconsideration of the Religious Element in Adoption,* at 788 n. 38.

65. See *In the Matter of Efraim C.,* 314 N.Y.S. 2d 255 (N.Y. Family Ct. 1970).

66. *In re Adoption of "E,"* 271 A. 2d 27, 30 (Essex County Ct., Probate Div. 1970).

67. *In re Adoption of "E,"* 279 A. 2d 785, 792 (N.J. 1971).

68. Ibid.

69. See e.g., Joseph Crumbley, *Transracial Adoption and Foster Care: Practice Issues for Professionals* (1999); Asher D. Isaacs, "Interracial Adoption: Permanent Placement and Racial Identity—An Adoptee's Perspective," *National Bar Journal* 14 (1995): 126, 154–55.

70. Cal. Fam. Code § 8709 (2001).

71. See Dirk Johnson, "Former Cocaine User Regains Child in Racial Custody Case," *New York Times,* March 19, 1999. Later, because of changed circumstances, the judge awarded permanent custody to the white couple. See Frank Main, "Burkes Named Baby T's Guardians," *Chicago Sun-Times,* January 4, 2002.

72. See Stacey A. Teicher, "Fight Over Mixed Race Adoptions," *Christian Science Monitor,* April 14, 1999. I was put forward as an expert witness in this case by the white couple that ultimately prevailed.

73. Marian Wright Edelman, *The Measure of Our Success: A Letter to My Children and Yours* (1992).

74. Marguerite A. Wright, *I'm Chocolate, You're Vanilla: Raising Healthy Black Children and Biracial Children in a Race-Conscious World* (1998).

75. Darlene Powell Hopson and Derek S. Hopson, *Different and Wonderful: Raising Black Children in a Race-Conscious Society* (1990).

76. Jawanza Kunjufu, *Critical Issues in Educating African American Youth: A Talk with Jawanza* (1997); idem., *Countering the Conspiracy to Destroy Black Boys* (1990); *Developing Positive Self Images and Discipline in Black Children* (1984).

77. Alvin F. Poussaint and James Comer, *Raising Black Children* (1992).

78. Benjamin Spock, *Dr. Spock on Parenting* (1988).

79. See, e.g., Ingrid Banks, *Hair Matters: Beauty, Power, and Black Women's Consciousness* (2000).

80. See Randall Kennedy, *Nigger: The Strange Career of a Troublesome Word* (2002, reprint 2003).

## Chapter Eleven:
### White Parents and Black Children
### in Adoptive Families

1. Joyce Ladner, *Mixed Families: Adopting Across Racial Boundaries* (1977), 39. See also Elizabeth Shepherd, "Adopting Negro Children: White Families Find It Can Be Done," *New Republic,* June 20, 1964: many social workers "found it difficult to understand why any white couple would take such a risk"—i.e., of adopting a colored child.

2. Students of adoption who disagree sharply on other matters concur on this point. Compare Madelyn Freundlich, *Adoption and Ethics: The Role of Race, Culture and National Origin in Adoption* (2000), 21–22, with Elizabeth Bartholet, *Family Bonds: Adoption and the Politics of Parenting* (1993), 113.

3. See Freundlich, *Adoption and Ethics,* 19–20; R. Richard Banks, "The Color of Desire: Fulfilling Adoptive Parents' Racial Preferences Through Discriminatory State Action," *Yale Law Journal* 107 (1998): 875, 880–81; Myriam Zrecny, "Race-Conscious Child Placement: Deviating from a Policy Against Racial Classification," *Chicago-Kent Law Review* 69 (1994): 1121, 1125.

4. See Office of Analysis and Inspection, Office of the Inspector General, *Minority Adoption* (1988), 7–8.

5. Richard P. Barth, "Effects of Age on the Odds of Adoption versus Remaining in Long-Term Out-of-Home Care," *Child Welfare* (1997): 285, 296.

6. See, for example, Rosemary J. Avery, ed., *Adoption Policy and Special Needs Children* (1997).

7. Eight-nine percent stated that they would accept a nonblack child of a different race.

8. See Anjani Chandra et al., "Adoption, Adoption Seeking, and Relinquishment for Adoption in the United States, Advance Data," reprinted in National Council for Adoption, *Adoption Factbook* (1999): 86.

9. Ann Kimble Loux, *The Limits of Hope: An Adoptive Mother's Story* (1997), 2.

10. See Ky. Rev. Stat. § 199. 540(1)(1971); Mo. Stat. Ann. § 543.130 (1952). The Missouri law was repealed in 1982. The Kentucky law remains on the statute books.

11. Ladner, *Mixed Families,* 60.

12. See Pearl S. Buck, *Children of Adoption* (1964); Peter Conn, *Pearl S. Buck: A Cultural Biography* (1996), 312–14.

13. Pearl S. Buck, "Should White Parents Adopt Brown Babies?," *Ebony,* June 1958, p. 27.

14. Ibid., 28.

15. See Harriet Fricke, "Interracial Adoption: The Little Revolution," *Social Work* 10 (July 1965): 92; Shepherd, "Adopting Negro Children."

16. Shepherd, "Adopting Negro Children."

17. Jacqueline Macaulay and Stewart Macaulay, "Adoption for Black Children: A Case Study of Expert Discretion," *Research Law and Sociology* 1 (1978): 283.

18. Ibid., 284.

19. Ibid., 285.

20. Ibid.

21. Useful research on the history of white adoptive parenting may be found in Ladner, *Mixed Families;* Rita Simon and Howard Altstein, *Transracial Adoption* (1977); Lucille Grow and Deborah Shapiro, *Black Children, White Parents: A Study of Transracial Adoption* (1974).

22. Simon and Altstein, *Transracial Adoption,* 75–77.

23. See Kaufman, "Transracial Adoptions Encounter Opposition"; Courtney Edelhart, "Adoption Backers Address Concerns Expressed by Foes," *Indianapolis Star,* September 3, 2000; Rodger L. Hardy,

"TLC: Utah Adoption Agency Finds Homes for Black Babies," *Deseret News* (Salt Lake City, Utah), August 23, 2000; David Crary, "We Are Family—Some Adoption Issues Are Clearly Black and White," *Commercial Appeal* (Memphis, Tennessee), July 30, 2000; Lucie May and Marie McCain, "Case Tests Bonds of Love and Race; Lawsuit Could Break New Ground on Interracial Adoption Policies," *Cincinnati Enquirer,* July 9, 2000.

24. See also Becky Thompson, *Mothering Without a Compass: White Mother's Love, Black Son's Courage* (2000).

25. J. Douglas Bates, *Gift Children: A Study of Race, Family, and Adoption in a Divided America* (1993), 29.

26. Ibid., 48–49.

27. Ibid., 65.

28. Ibid., 118.

29. Ibid., 119.

30. Ibid., 215.

31. Ibid., 4.

32. Ibid., 5.

33. Ibid., 3.

34. Ibid., 238–39.

35. Ibid., 268.

36. Ibid.

37. Ibid., 269–70.

38. Jana Wolff, *Secret Thoughts of an Adoptive Mother* (1997), 36–37.

39. Ibid., 38.

40. Ibid., 38–39.

41. Ibid., 25.

42. Ibid., 128.

43. Sharon E. Rush, *Loving Across the Color Line: A White Adoptive Mother Learns About Race* (2000), 5.

44. This and the following quote, ibid., 24.

45. Ibid., 66.

46. Ibid., 89.

47. Wolff, *Secret Thoughts of an Adoptive Mother,* 131.

48. Ibid.

49. Rush, *Loving Across the Color Line,* 77.

50. Wolff, *Secret Thoughts of an Adoptive Mother,* 135.

51. Ibid., 127.

52. Ibid., 137.

53. Ibid., 12.

54. In her memoir, Wolff never squarely states her position on whether authorities should prefer same-race over interracial adoptions, but the tenor of her remarks suggests that she, too, subscribes to what I have termed moderate race matching.

55. Rush, *Loving Across the Color Line,* 92.

56. Ibid.

57. Ibid., 93.

58. See Gail Steinberg and Beth Hall, *Inside Transracial Adoption* (2000); Rita J. Simon and Rhonda M. Roorda, eds., *In Their Own Voices: Transracial Adoptees Tell Their Stories* (2000), p. 122, 131, 169; Bates, *Gift Children,* p. 107–9; Bonnie Miller Rubin, "Transracial Adoption Fight Ain't Just Skin Deep; Kids Are Caught Between Two Worlds, Two Viewpoints," *Chicago Tribune,* July 19, 1998.

59. Rush, *Loving Across the Color Line,* 138.

60. Wolff, *Secret Thoughts of an Adoptive Mother,* 138.

61. Rush, *Loving Across the Color Line,* 183.

62. Albert J. Reynolds, Letter to the Editor, "Proof That Transracial Adoption Can Work," *Des Moines Register,* December 4, 2000.

63. See Simon and Roorda, eds., *In Their Own Voices,* 100.

64. Rachel Noerdlinger, "A Look at . . . Interracial Adoption: A Last Resort; The Identity My White Parents Couldn't Give Me," *Washington Post,* June 30, 1996.

65. See Asher D. Isaacs, "Interracial Adoption: Permanent Placement and Racial Identity—An Adoptee's Perspective," *National Black Law Journal* 14 (1996): 126.

66. Ibid.

67. Ibid.

68. Ibid., 127.

69. Ibid., 126.

70. Ibid., 127.

71. All quotes this paragraph, ibid., 128.

72. Ibid.

73. Ibid., 154.

74. Ibid., 131.

75. Ibid.

76. See also Sandra Patton, *Birthmarks: Transracial Adoption in Contemporary America* (2000), 62–98.

77. Simon and Roorda, eds., *In Their Own Voices,* 91.

78. Ibid., 62.

79. Ibid., 37.

80. This and following quotes by Donna Francis, ibid., 38.
81. Ibid., 70.
82. Ibid., 71.
83. Ibid., 143.
84. Ibid., 149.
85. This and the following quote by Nicolle Yates, ibid., 148.
86. Ibid., 152.
87. See also Noerdlinger, "A Look at . . . Interracial Adoption"; Sue Anne Pressley, "Texas Interracial Adoption Case Reflects National Debate; Family Waged a Legal Fight for Two Black Youngsters," *Washington Post,* January 2, 1997.
88. Simon and Roorda, eds., *In Their Own Voices,* 325.
89. Ibid., 326.
90. Ibid., 133, 135, 173, 192, 212, 226, 245, 274.
91. Ibid., 124.
92. This and the following quote by Laurie Goff, ibid., 133.
93. Ibid., 211.
94. This and the following quote by Kristen Albrecht, from Tamar Lewin, "Two Views of Growing Up When the Faces Don't Match," *New York Times,* October 27, 1998.
95. Isaacs, "Interracial Adoption: Permanent Placement and Racial Identity," 140.
96. Lee Rainwater, "Crucible of Identity in the Lower-Class Family," *Daedelus* 95 (1966); 172.

## Chapter Twelve:
### Race, Children, and Custody Battles:
### The Special Status of Native Americans

1. See 25 U.S.C. §§ 1901–1963 (1994). Some states have passed analogous legislation. See, for example, the Minnesota Indian Family Preservation Act, Minn. Stat. 260.751–260.835 (2000).
2. For work that is in opposition to the positions I advance, see Christine Metteer, "Pigs in Heaven: A Parable of Native American Adoption Under the Indian Child Welfare Act," *Arizona State Law Journal* 28 (1996): 489; idem, "Hard Cases Making Bad Law: The Need for Revision of the Indian Child Welfare Act," *Santa Clara Law Review* 38 (1998): 419; idem, "The Existing Indian Family Doctrine: An Impediment to the Trust Responsibility to Preserve Tribal Existence and Culture as Manifested in the Indian Child Welfare Act," *Loyola of Los Angeles Law Review* 30 (1997): 647; Lorie M. Graham,

"'The Past Never Vanishes': A Contextual Critique of the Existing Indian Family Doctrine," *American Indian Law Review* 23 (1998): 1; Jeanne Louise Carriere, "Representing the Native American: Culture, Jurisdiction, and the Indian Child Welfare Act," *Iowa Law Review* 79 (1994): 585.

For work that is broadly consonant with my approach, see Christine D. Bakeis, "The Indian Child Welfare Act of 1978: Violating Personal Rights for the Sake of the Tribe," *Notre Dame Journal of Law, Ethics, and Public Policy* 10 (1996): 543; Michele K. Bennett, "Native American Children: Caught in the Web of the Indian Child Welfare Act," *Hamline Law Review* 16 (1993): 953. An excellent synthesis from which I greatly benefited is Barbara Ann Atwood's "Fleshpaints Under the Indian Child-Welfare Act: Toward a New Understanding of State Court Resistance," *Emory Law Journal* 51 (2002): 587.

3. *Cherokee Nation v. Georgia,* 30 U.S. 1, 17 (1831). For useful introductions to the labyrinthine legal doctrine regarding the relationship between tribes, states, and the United States, see Felix Cohen, *Handbook of Federal Indian Law* (1982 ed.); L. Scott Gould, "The Consent Paradigm: Tribal Sovereignty at the Millennium," *Columbia Law Review* 96 (1996): 809.

4. *Santa Clara Pueblo v. Martinez,* 436 U.S. 49, 55–56 (1978).

5. On the status of Indian tribes in the American polity and the way that unique status bears on jurisdiction over child-placement decisions, see Christine M. Metteer, "A Law unto Itself: The Indian Child Welfare Act as Inapplicable and Inappropriate to the Transracial/Race-Matching Adoption Controversy," *Brandeis Law Journal* 38 (1999–2000): 47, 52–57; Barbara Ann Atwood, "Fighting over Indian Children: The Uses and Abuses of Jurisdictional Ambiguity," *UCLA Law Review* 36 (1989): 1051.

6. See generally Francis Paul Prucha, *The Great Father: The United States Government and the American Indians* (1984); Angie Debo, *A History of the Indians of the United States* (1970); Rennard Strickland, "Genocide-at-Law: An Historic and Contemporary View of the Native American Experience," *University of Kansas Law Review* 34 (1986): 713.

7. See David E. Wilkins, *American Indian Politics and the American Political System* (2002), 158.

8. Ibid. at 157.

9. See, e.g., Wilkins, *American Indian Indian Politics,* 157–60; Larry Echohawk, "Child Sexual Abuse in Indian Country: Is the Guardian

Keeping in Mind the Seventh Generation," *New York University Journal of Legislation & Public Policy* 5 (2001): 83.

10. See Brian W. Dippie, *The Vanishing American: White Attitudes and U.S. Indian Policy* (1982); Robert F. Berkhofer Jr., *The White Man's Indian: Images of the American Indian from Columbus to the Present* (1978).

11. See Cohen, *Handbook of Federal Indian Law,* 138.

12. See Daniel F. Littlefield Jr. and Lonnie E. Underhill, "Renaming the American Indian 1890–1913," *American Studies* 12 (1971): 33.

13. Quoted in Francis Paul Prucha, *The Great Father: The United States Government and the American Indians* (1984), 690.

14. See Paul R. Spickard, *Mixed Blood: Intermarriage and Ethnic Identity in Twentieth-Century America* (1989), 374–75; Robert J. Sickels, *Race, Marriage, and the Law* (1972), 64.

15. See, e.g., *Lac Du Flambeau Band of Lake Superior Chippewa Indians v. Stop Treaty Abuse—Wisconsin Inc.,* 41 F. 3d 1190, 1192–93 (7th Cir. 1994).

16. See Karl Eschbach, "The Enduring and Vanishing American Indian: American Indian Population Growth and Intermarriage in 1990," *Ethnic and Racial Studies* 18 (1995): 89, 95; Gary Dan Sandefer and Trudy McKinnell, "American Indian Intermarriage," *Social Science Research* 15 (1986): 347.

17. David Fanshel, *Far from the Reservation: The Transracial Adoption of American Indian Children* (1972), 21.

18. Ibid., 84.

19. *U.S. Code Congressional and Administrative News,* 95th Cong., 2d Sess. 1978 [hereafter *U.S. Code Cong. & Admin. News*], pp. 7530, 7531.

20. Ibid., 7531.

21. Ibid.

22. Ibid.

23. See 25 U.S.C. § 1911.

24. 25 U.S.C. § 1915 (a). ICWA further stipulates, however, that a placement made pursuant to a tribal preference is only permissible so long as the placement "is the least restrictive setting appropriate to the particular needs of the child." 25 U.S.C. § 1915 (c).

25. Joane Nagel, *American Indian Ethnic Renewal: Red Power and the Resurgence of Identity and Culture* (1996), 6. See also Stephen Cornell, *The Return of the Native: American Indian Political Resurgence* (1988).

26. Nagel, *American Indian Ethnic Renewal,* 6.

27. See, for example, *Mississippi Band of Choctaw Indians v. Holyfield,* 490 U.S. 30, 32 (1989): "Senate oversight hearings in 1974 yielded numerous examples, statistical data, and expert testimony documenting what one witness called 'the wholesale removal of Indian children from their homes . . . the most tragic aspect of Indian life today'"; *In the matter of Custody of S.E.G.,* 521 N.W. 2d 357, 358 (Minn. 1994): "Testimony before Congress indicated there were widespread abuses in the placement of Indian children by courts and welfare agencies in states with Indian populations"; Jose Mansiveis, "A Glimmer of Hope: A Proposal to Keep the Indian Child-Welfare Act of 1978 Intact," *American Indian Law Review* 22 (1997): 22; Jeanne Louise Cerriere, "Representing the Native American: Culture, Jurisdiction, and the Indian Child Welfare Act," *Iowa Law Review* 79 (1994): 585; Russel Lawrence Barsh, "The Indian Child Welfare Act of 1978: A Critical Analysis," *Hastings Law Journal* 31 (1980): 1287.

28. *U.S. Code Cong. & Admin. News,* 7532.

29. Ibid., 7533.

30. See hearings before the House Committee on Interracial Insular Affairs, February 9 and March 9, 1978; hearings before the Select Committee on Indian Affairs, United States Senate, August 4, 1977; hearings before the Subcommittee on Indian Affairs of the Committee on Interior and Insular Affairs, United States Senate, April 8 and 9, 1974.

31. Testimony of Goldie Denny, director of Social Services, Quinault Nation, before the Senate Select Committee on Indian Affairs, August 4, 1977.

32. Garry Wamser, "Child Welfare Under the Indian Child Welfare Act of 1978: A New Mexico Focus," *New Mexico Law Review* 10 (1980): 412.

33. Testimony of William Byler before the Senate Subcommittee on Indian Affairs, April 9, 1974.

34. Prucha, *The Great Father,* 1153–57.

35. Steven Unger, ed., *The Destruction of American Indian Families* (1977), iii.

36. See ibid., 3–6.

37. See ibid., 63.

38. Fanshel, *Far from the Reservation,* 35.

39. Ibid., 323.

40. Ibid.

41. Testimony of Calvin J. Isaacs, tribal chief, Mississippi Band of Choctaw Indians, representing the National Tribal Chairmen's Asso-

ciation, before the Senate Select Committee on Indian Affairs, August 4, 1977.

42. B. J. Jones, *The Indian Child Welfare Act Handbook* (1995), 111. See also Russel Lawrence Barsh, "The Indian Child Welfare Act of 1978: A Critical Analysis," *Hastings Law Journal* 31 (1980): 1334.

43. See Madelyn Freundlich, *Adoption and Ethics: The Role of Race, Culture, and National Origin in Adoption* (2000), 82–83; McEachron, N., S. Gustowsson, S. Cross, and A. Lewis, "The Effectiveness of the Indian Child Welfare Act of 1978," *Social Service Review* 70 (1996): 451; Margaret C. Plantz, Ruth Hubbell, Barbara J. Barrett, and Antonia Dobree, "Indian Child Welfare, A Status Report: Final Report of the Survey of Indian Child Welfare and Implementation of the Indian Child Welfare Act and Section 482 of the Adoption Assistance and Child Welfare Act of 1980" (1988).

44. Testimony of Esther Mays before the Senate Subcommittee on Indian Affairs, April 9, 1974.

45. See, for example, Robert Bergman, "The Human Cost of Removing Indian Children from Their Families," in Unger, ed., *The Destruction of American Indian Families,* 35; Carl Mindell and Alan Gurwitt, "The Placement of American Indian Children—The Need for Change," in ibid., 63.

46. See the testimony of Dr. Joseph Westermeyer, Department of Psychiatry, University of Minnesota, before the Senate Subcommittee on Interior and Insular Affairs, April 9, 1974; Joseph Westermeyer, "The Apple Syndrome in Minnesota: A Complication of Racial-Ethnic Discontinuity," *Journal of Operational Psychiatry* 10 (1979): 134; *Mississippi Band of Choctaw Indians v. Holyfield,* 490 U.S. 30, 33 n. 1 (1989).

47. Westermeyer, "The Apple Syndrome," 134.

48. Ibid., 138.

49. Ibid.

50. Ibid., 134.

51. Ibid., 138.

52. See Margaret Howard, "Transracial Adoption: Analysis of the Best-Interest Standard," *Notre Dame Law Review* 59 (1984): 503, 537: "if a transracially placed child is experiencing problems related to his or her racial identity, we cannot know whether these problems were caused by the transracial placement or whether the child would experience them anyway."

53. 25 U.S.C. §1903(4).

54. Hollinger, "Native American Children," 15-12.

55. Ibid.

56. *In re Baby Boy Doe*, 849 P. 2d 925 (Idaho 1993).

57. The existing Indian family doctrine has attracted considerable comment. See Hollinger, "Native American Children," 11-16, 39–59; Metteer, "The Existing Indian Family Doctrine," 647. See also Graham, "'The Past Never Vanishes,'" 1; Toni Hahn Davis, "The Existing Indian Family Exception to the Indian Child Welfare Act," *North Dakota Law Review* 69 (1993): 465.

58. Decisions adopting the existing Indian family doctrine include *In re Bridget R.*, 49 Cal. Rptr. 2d 507 (Ct. App. 1996), cert denied, 519 U.S. 1060 (1997); *In re D.S.*, 577 N. E. 2d 572 (Ind. 1991); *Rye v. Weasel*, 943 S.W. 2d 257 (Ky. 1996); *Hampton v. J. A. L.*, 658 So. 2d 331 (La. 1995).

    Decisions rejecting the doctrine include *A.B.M. v. M.H.* 651 P. 2d 1170.(Alaska 1982); *Michael J. V. Michael J.*, 7 OP. 3 3d 960 (Ariz. Ct. App. 2000); In re *Adoption of a Child of Indian Heritage*, 543 A. 2d 925 (N.J. 1988).

59. *In re Bridget R.*, 49 Cal. Rptr. 2d 507 (1996), *review denied*, Sup. Ct., May 15, 1996; *cert. denied, Cindy R. v. James R.*, 117 Sup. Ct. 693 (1997).

60. *In re Bridget R.* at 526.

61. Ibid.

62. Ibid.

63. Ibid.

64. Ibid. at 524.

65. Ibid.

66. See, for example, *Adarand Constructors, Inc. v. Pena*, 515 U.S. 200 (1995).

67. See *Morton v. Mancari*, 417 U.S. 535, 553–54 (1994). See generally Carole Goldberg, "American Indians and 'Preferential' Treatment," *UCLA Law Review* 49 (2002): 943.

68. The federal Supreme Court has not yet resolved the legal status of the existing Indian family doctrine. The courts that have addressed the issue are split. Court rulings rejecting the existing Indian family doctrine include *Baby Boy Doe* at 925, 931–32; *In re D.S.*, 597 N.E. 2d 572, 573–74 (Ind. 1991); *In re Child of Indian Heritage*, 543 A. 2d 925, 932 (N.J. 1988); *In re Adoption of Riffle*, 922 P. 2d 510, 513 (Mont. 1996); *Quinn v. Walters*, 881 P. 2d 795, 808–9 (Or. 1994).

    Decisions embracing the existing Indian family doctrine include

*In re S.C.,* 833 P. 2d 1249 (Okla. 1992); *In re Adoption of Infant Boy Crews,* 825 P. 2d 305 (Wash. 1992); *Hampton v. JAL,* 658 So. 2d 331 (La. Ct. App. 1995), *aff'd* 662 S. 2d 478 (La. 1995).

69. See Metteer, "The Existing Indian Family Exception" at 660.

70. See Atwood, "Fleshpaints Under the Indian Child Welfare Act" at 630.

71. Ibid. at 633.

72. *Mississippi Band of Choctaw Indians v. Holyfield,* 490 U.S. 30 (1989).

73. See *Holyfield* at 36.

74. Jones, *The Indian Child Welfare Act Handbook,* 92.

75. See, for example, *C.L. v. P.C.S.,* 17 P. 3d 769 (Alaska 2001); *People ex rel. A.N.W.,* 976 P. 2d 365 (Colo. Ct. App. 1979).

76. *In re S.E.G.,* 521 N.W. 2d 357 (Minn. 1994).

77. Ibid. at 360.

78. Ibid. at 364.

79. For criticism of *S.E.G.,* see Hassan Saffouri, "Comment—The Good Cause Exception to the Indian Child Welfare Act's Placement Preferences: The Minnesota Supreme Court Sets a Difficult (Impossible?) Standard," *William Mitchell Law Review* 21 (1995), 1191. Joseph G. Twomey, "Note: Considering a Native American Child's Need for Permanent Placement Under the Indian Child Welfare Act: *In re S.E.G., A.L.W., and V.M.G.,* 521 N.W. 2d 357 (Minn. 1994)," *Hamline Law* Review 18 (1995): 281. For commentary supporting the decision, see Erik W. Aamot-Snapp, "Note: When Judicial Flexibility Becomes Abuse of Discretion: Eliminating the 'Good Cause' Exception in Indian Child Welfare Adoptive Placements," *Minnesota Law Review* 79 (1995): 1167.

80. See, for example, "Bringing Them Home: Report of the National Inquiry into the Separation of Aboriginal and Torres Strait Islander Children from Their Families" (1997), available on the World Wide Web at http://www.austlii.edu.au/au/special/rsproject/rsjlibrary/hreoc/stolen/. See also Laura Oren, "Righting Child Custody Wrongs: The Children of the 'Disappeared' in Argentina," *Harvard Human Rights Journal* 14 (2001): 123.

81. See Stephen O'Connor, *Orphan Trains: The Story of Charles Loring Brace and the Children He Saved and Failed* (2001); Miriam Z. Langsam, *Children West: A History of the Placing-Out System of the New York Children's Aid Society, 1853–1890* (1964).

82. See, for example, Linda Gordon, *The Great Arizona Orphan Abduction* (1999).

83. See Michael Wald, "State Intervention on Behalf of 'Neglected' Children: Standards for Removal of Children from Their Homes, Monitoring the Status of Children in Foster Care, and Termination of Parental Rights," *Stanford Law Review* 28 (1976): 623.

84. 25 U.S.C. § 1912.

85. For a searing indictment of indifference to child abuse and neglect, see Elizabeth Bartholet, *Nobody's Children: Abuse, Neglect, Foster Drift, and the Adoption Alternative* (1999).

86. See Michael Wald, "State Intervention on Behalf of 'Neglected' Children: A Search for Realistic Standards," *Stanford Law Review* 27 (1975): 985; "State Intervention on Behalf of 'Neglected' Children: Standards for Removal of Children from Their Homes, Monitoring the Status of Children in Foster Care, and Termination of Parental Rights," *Stanford Law Review* 28 (1976): 623.

87. 25 U.S.C. § 1915 (a).

### Afterword

1. Letter from Thomas Jefferson to Edward Coles, in *Thomas Jefferson: Writings,* Merrill D. Peterson, ed., 1984, p. 44.

# Bibliography

## Books

Alexander, Adele Logan. *Homelands and Waterways: The American Journey of the Bond Family, 1846–1926* (1999)

Andrews, Lori B. *Black Power, White Blood: The Life and Times of Johnny Spain* (1999)

Azoulay, Gibel. *Black, Jewish, and Interracial* (1997)

Bardaglio, Peter. *Reconstructing the Household: Families, Sex, and the Law in the Nineteenth Century South* (1995)

Barron, Milton L., ed. *The Blending American: Patterns of Intermarriage* (1972)

Bartholet, Elizabeth. *Family Bonds: Adoption and the Politics of Parenting* (1993)

———. *Nobody's Children: Abuse, Neglect, Foster Drift, and the Adoption Alternative* (1999)

Bates, J. Douglas. *Gift Children: A Study of Race, Family, and Adoption in a Divided America* (1993)

Bell, Derrick. *Race, Racism, and American Law* (1972, 2000)

Bennett, Lerone, Jr. *Before the Mayflower: A History of Black America* (1962, 1982)

Berlin, Ira. *Many Thousands Gone: The First Two Centuries of Slavery in North America* (1998)

---

This bibliography includes a selection of work from which I have benefited. It does not include every item credited in my footnotes and endnotes. It does include items that have been broadly useful in preparing this volume and items that may be particularly interesting to students of interracial intimacy who might want to press their inquiry beyond the pages of this book.

Berry, Brewton. *Almost White* (1963)

Berzon, Judith R. *Neither White Nor Black: The Mulatto Character in American Fiction* (1978)

Bleser, Carol, ed. *In Joy and in Sorrow: Women, Family, and Marriage in the Victorian South, 1830–1900* (1991)

Blumberg, Rhoda Goldstein and Wendell James Roye. *Interracial Bonds* (1979)

Brown, Cecil. *The Life and Loves of Mr. Jiveass Nigger* (1969)

Brown, William Wells. *Clotel, or The President's Daughter* (1853)

Brownmiller, Susan. *Against Our Will: Men Women, and Rape* (1975)

Buck, Pearl. *Children for Adoption* (1964)

Bynum, Victoria. *The Free State of Jones: Mississippi's Longest Civil War* (2001)

———. *Uniquely Women: The Politics of Social and Sexual Control in the Old South* (1992)

Camper, Carol., ed. *Miscegenation Blues: Voices of Mixed Race Women* (1994)

Cannon, Poppy. *A Gentle Knight: My Husband, Walter White* (1956)

Carter, Dan T. *Scottsboro: A Tragedy of the American South* (1969, rev. ed. 1979)

Cash, W. J. *The Mind of the South* (1941)

Chase-Riboud, Barbara. *Sally Hemings* ( 1979)

Chesnutt, Charles W. *Essays and Speeches,* ed. Joseph R. McElrath Jr., Robert C. Leitz III, and Jesse S. Crisler (1999)

———. *House Behind the Cedars* (1900)

———. *The Marrow of Tradition* (1901)

———. *Mandy Oxendine* (written in 1897 but published in 1997)

———. *Paul Marchand, F.M.C.* (written in 1921 but published in 1998)

Cleaver, Eldridge. *Soul on Ice* (1969)

Clinton, Catherine. *Fanny Kemble's Civil Wars* (2000)

———. *The Plantation Mistress: Women's World in the Old South* (1982)

Clinton, Catherine and Michele Gillespie, eds. *The Devil's Line: Sex and Race in the Early South* (1997)

Cobb, Thomas R. R. *An Inquiry into the Law of Negro Slavery in the United States of America* (1858)

Collins, Patricia Hill. *Black Feminist Thought: Knowledge, Consciousness, and the Politics of Empowerment* (second edition, 2000)

Conn, Peter. *Pearl S. Buck: A Cultural Biography* (1996)

Cott, Nancy F. *Public Vows: A History of Marriage and the Nation* (2000)

Craft, William. *Running a Thousand Miles for Freedom: The Escape of William and Ellen Craft from Slavery* (1860)

Cripps, Thomas. *Slow Fade to Black: The Negro in American Film, 1900–1942* (1977)

Crouch, Stanley. *Don't the Moon Look Lonesome* (2000)

Davis, F. James. *Who Is Black? One Nation's Definition* (1991, 2001)

DeCosta-Willis, Miriam, Reginald Martin, and Roseann P. Bell, eds. *Erotique Noire/Black Erotic* (1992)

D'Emilio, John, and Estelle B. Freeman. *Intimate Matters: A History of Sexuality in America* (1988)

Derricotte, Toi. *The Black Notebooks: An Interior Journey* (1997)

Dippie, Brian W. *The Vanishing American: White Attitudes and U.S. Indian Policy* (1982)

Dixon, Thomas, Jr. *The Leopard's Spots: A Romance of the White Man's Burden 1865–1900* (1903)

———. *The Clansmen: An Historical Romance of the Ku Klux Klan* (1905)

Dollard, John. *Caste and Class in a Southern Town* (Doubleday, 3d ed., 1937, 1957), p. 147–48

Dominguez, Virginia R. *White by Definition: Social Classification in Creole Louisiana* (1986)

Drake, St. Clair, and Horace R. Cayton. *Black Metropolis: A Study of Negro Life in a Northern City* (1945, 1961)

Fabi, M. Giulia. *Passing and the Rise of the African American Novel* (2001)

Fanon, Frantz. *Black Skin, White Masks* (1967)

Faulkner, William. *Absalom, Absalom!* (1936)

———. *Go Down, Moses* (1942)

———. *Light in August (1932)*

Fauset, Jessie Redmon. *Plum Bun: A Novel Without a Moral* (1990, 1928)

———. *There Is Confusion* (1924)

Ferber, Edna. *Show Boat* (1926)

Fogg-Davis, Hawley. *The Ethics of Transracial Adoption* (2002)

Foner, Eric. *Reconstruction: America's Unfinished Revolution, 1863–1877* (1988)

Fowler, David H. *Northern Attitudes Towards Interracial Marriage: Legislation and Public Opinion in the Middle Atlantic States of the Old Northwest, 1780–1930* (1987)

Fox-Genovese, Elizabeth. *Within the Plantation Household: Black and White Women of the Old South* (1988)

Franklin, John Hope. *From Slavery to Freedom* (1947, 2000)

Frederickson, George M. *The Black Image in The White Mind: The Debate on Afro-American Character and Destiny, 1817–1914* (1971)

———. *White Supremacy: A Comparative Study in American and South African History* (1981)

Freundlich, Madelyn. *Adoption and Ethics: The Role of Race, Culture and National Origin in Adoption* (2000)

Funderburg, Lise. *Black, White, Other: Biracial Americans Talk About Race and Identity* (1994)

Gatewood, William B. *Aristocrats of Color: The Black Elite, 1880–1920* (1990)

Genovese, Eugene. *Roll, Jordan, Roll: The World the Slaves Made* (1974)

Giddings, Paula. *When and Where I Enter: The Impact of Black Women on Race and Sex in America* (1984)

Ginsberg, Elaine K., ed. *Passing and the Fictions of Identity* (1996)

Golden, Marita, ed. *Wild Women Don't Wear No Blues: Black Women Writers on Love, Men and Sex* (1993)

Goodell, William. *The American Slave Code* (1856)

Gordon, Milton M. *Assimilation in American Life: The Role of Race, Religion, and National Origins* (1964)

Gordon-Reed, Annette. *Thomas Jefferson and Sally Hemings: An American Controversy* (1998)

Graham, Lawrence Otis. *Member of the Club: Reflections on Life in a Racially Polarized World* (1995)

Grow, Lucille, and Deborah Shapiro. *Black Children, White Parents: A Study of Transracial Adoption* (1974)

Gubar, Susan. *White Skin, Black Face in American Culture* (1997)

Gutman, Herbert G. *The Black Family in Slavery and Freedom, 1550–1925* (1976)

Haizlip, Shirlee Taylor. *The Sweeter the Juice* (1994)

Hartman, Saidiya V. *Scenes of Subjection: Terror, Slavery, and Self-Making in Nineteenth-Century America* (1997)

Hernton, Calvin C. *Sex and Racism in America* (1965, 1981)

———. *Coming Together: Black Power, White Hatred, and Sexual Hangups* (1971)

Himes, Chester. *If He Hollers Let Him Go* (1943)

———. *Lonely Crusade* (1947)

———. *Pinktoes* (1961)

———. *The Third Generation* (1954)

Hodes, Martha, ed. *Sex, Love, Race: Crossing Boundaries in North-American History* (1999)

———. *White Women, Black Men: Illicit Sex in the 19th-Century South* (1997)

Hollinger, David A. *Postethnic America: Beyond Multiculturalism* (1995)

Howells, William Dean. *An Imperative Duty* (1893)

Hunter, Tera. W. *To 'Joy My Freedom: Southern Black Women's Lives and Labors After the Civil War* (1997)

Jacobs, Harriet A. *Incidents in the Life of a Slave Girl, Written by Herself* (1861, 1987)

Johnston, James Hugo. *Race Relations in Virginia and Miscegenation in the South, 1776–1860* (1937, 1970)

Jones, Gayl. *Corregidor* (1975)

Jones, Hettie. *How I Became Hettie Jones* (1990)

Jones, Lisa. *Bulletproof Diva: Tales of Race, Sex and Hair* (1994)

Jordan, Winthrop D. *White over Black: American Attitudes Toward the Negro, 1550–1818* (1968)

Killens, John Oliver. *'Sippi* (1967)

Kinney, James. *Amalgamation! Race, Sex, and Rhetoric in the Nineteenth-Century American Novel* (1985)

Ladner, Joyce. *Mixed Families: Adopting Across Racial Boundaries* (1977)

Larsen, Nella. *Passing* (1929)

Lazarre, Jane. *Beyond the Whiteness of Whiteness: Memoir of a White Mother of Black Sons* (1997)

Lee, Reba. *I Pass for White* (1955)

Lerner, Gerda, ed. *Black Women in White America: A Documentary History* (1972)

Leslie, Kent Anderson. *Woman of Color, Daughter of Privilege: Amanda America Dickson, 1849–1893* (1995)

Lewis, Jan, Peter S. Onuf, and Jane E. Lewis, eds. *Sally Hemings and Thomas Jefferson: History, Memory, and Civic Culture* (1999)

Lind, Michael. *The Next American Nation: The New Nationalism and the Fourth American Revolution* (1995)

Malcomson, Scott L. *One Drop of Blood: The American Misadventure of Race* (2000)

Malone, Ann Patton. *Sweet Chariot: Slave Family and Household Structure in Nineteenth-Century Louisiana* (1992)

Martinez-Alier, Verena. *Marriage, Class, and Colour in Nineteenth-Century Cuba: A Study of Racial Attitudes and Sexual Values in a Slave Society* (1974)

Mathabene, Mark, and Gail Mathabene. *Love in Black and White: The Triumph of Love Over Prejudice and Taboo* (1992)

McBride, James. *The Color of Water: A Black Man's Tribute to His White Mother* (1997)

McLaurin, Melton A. *Celia: A Slave* (1991)

McMillen, Sally G. *Southern Women Black and White in the Old South* (1992)

McNamara, Robert B., Maria Tempenis, and Beth Walton. *Crossing the Race Line: Interracial Couples in the South* (1999)

Moran, Rachel F. *Interracial Intimacy: The Regulation of Race and Romance* (2001)

Morris, Thomas D. *Southern Slavery and the Law 1619–1860* (1996)

Mumford, Kevin J. *Interzones: Black/White Sex Districts in Chicago and New York in the Early Twentieth Century* (1997)

Murray, Pauli. *Proud Shoes: The Story of an American Family* (1956, 1999)

Murray, Pauli, ed., *States' Laws on Race and Color* (1951, 1997)

Myrdal, Gunnar. *An American Dilemma: The Negro Problem and Modern Democracy* (1944, 1962)

Naison, Mark. *Communists in Harlem During the Depression* (1983)

Nash, Gary B. *Forbidden Love: The Secret History of Mixed-Race America* (1999)

O'Hearn, Claudine Chiawei, ed. *Half and Half: Writers on Growing Up Biracial and Bicultural* (1998)

Painter, Nell Irvin. *Southern History Across the Color Line* (2002)

Patterson, Orlando. *The Ordeal of Integration: Progress and Resentment in America's "Racial" Crisis* (1997)

———. *Rituals of Blood Consequences of Slavery in Two American Centuries* (1998)

Patton, Sandra. *Birthmarks: Transracial Adoption in Contemporary America* (2000)

Peplow, Michael W. *George S. Schuyler* (1980)

Petry, Ann. *The Narrows* (1953)

Porterfield, Ernest. *Black and White Mixed Marriages* (1978)

Reddy, Maureen T. *Crossing the Color Line: Race, Parenting, and Culture* (1994)

Roberts, Dorothy. *Killing the Black Body: Race, Reproduction, and the Meaning of Liberty* (1997)

Roberts, Randy. *Papa Jack: Jack Johnson and the Era of White Hopes* (1983)

Rogers, J. A. *Sex and Race: Negro-Caucasian Mixing in All Ages and in All Lands* (1942, 1967)

Romano, Renée. *Erosion of a Taboo: Black-White Marriage in the United States from World War II to the Present* (2003)

Root, Maria P. P. *Love's Revolution: Interracial Marriage* (2001)

———. *The Multiracial Experience: Racial Borders as the New Frontier* (1996)

———. *Racially Mixed People in America* (1992)

Rothman, Joshua D. *Notorious in the Neighborhood: Sex and Families Across the Color Line in Virginia, 1787–1861* (2003)

Russell, Kathy, Midge Wilson, and Ronald Hall. *The Color Complex: The Politics of Skin Color Among African Americans* (1992)

Rush, Sharon E. *Loving Across the Color Line: A White Adoptive Mother Learns About Race* (2000)

Schuyler, George S. *Black No More: Being an Account of the Strange and Wonderful Workings of Science in the Land of the Free,* A.D. *1933–1940* (1931, 1987)

———. *Racial Intermarriage in the United States: One of the Most Interesting Phenomena in Our National Life* (1929)

Senna, Danzy. *Caucasia* (1998)

Shockley, Ann Allen. *Loving Her* (1997, 1974)

Sickles, Robert J. *Race, Marriage, and the Law* (1972)

Simon, Rita, and Howard S. Alstein. *Transracial Adoption* (1977)

Simon, Rita J., and Rhonda M. Roorda, eds. *In Their Own Voices: Transracial Adoptees Tell Their Stories* (2000)

Skidmore, Thomas E. *Black Into White: Race and Nationality in Brazilian Thought* (1993)

Smith, Lillian. *Strange Fruit* (1944)

Sollors, Werner, ed. *Interracialism: Black-White Intermarriage in American History, Literature, and Law* (2000)

Sollors, Werner. *Neither Black Nor White Yet Both: Thematic Explorations of Interracial Literature* (1997)

Spencer, Jon Michael. *The New Colored People: The Mixed-Race Movement in America* (1997)

Spickard, Paul R. *Mixed Blood: Intermarriage and Ethnic Identity in Twentieth-Century America* (1989)

Spitzer, Leo. *Lives in Between: The Experience of Marginality in a Century of Emancipation* (1999)

*State's Laws on Race and Color* (1951, 1997)

Steinberg, Gail, and Beth Hall. *Inside Transracial Adoption* (2000)

Stember, Charles Herbert. *Sexual Racism: The Emotional Barrier to an Integrated Society* (1976)

Stephenson, Gilbert Thomas. *Race Distinction in American Law* (1910)

Sterling, Dorothy, ed. *We Are Your Sisters: Black Women in the Nineteenth Century* (1997)

Stevenson, Brenda E. *Life in Black & White: Family and Community in the Slave South* (1996)

Stoltzfus, Nathan. *Resistance of the Heart: Intermarriage and the Rosenstrasse Protest in Nazi Germany* (1996)

Stuart, Irvin, and Lawrence Abt, eds. *Interracial Marriage: Expectations and Realities* (1973)

Talalay, Kathryn. *Composition in Black and White: The Life of Philippa Schuyler* (1995)

Tenzer, Lawrence E. *A Completely New Look at Interracial Sexuality: Public Opinion and Select Commentaries* (1990)

Thompson, Becky. *Mothering Without a Compass: White Mother's Love, Black Son's Courage* (2000)

Thurman, Wallace. *Infants of the Spring* (1932)

Toomer, Jean. *Cane* (1923)

Tucker, M. Belinda, and Claudia Mitchell-Kernan, eds. *The Decline in Marriage Among African Americans* (1995)

Twain, Mark. *Pudd'nhead Wilson and Those Extraordinary Twins* (1894)

Walker, Alice. *Meridian* (1976)

Wallace, Anthony. *Jefferson and the Indians: The Tragic Fate of the First Americans* (1999)

Wallace, Michelle. *Black Macho and the Myth of the Superwoman* (1979)

Weiner, Merli F. *Mistresses and Slaves: Plantation Women in South Carolina, 1830–1860* (1998)

White, W. L. *Lost Boundaries* (1947)

Wilkinson, Doris, ed. *Black Male/White Female: The Sociology of Interracial Marriage and Courtship* (1975)

Williams, Gregory Howard. *Life on the Color Line: The True Story of a White Boy Who Discovered He Was Black* (1995)

Williamson, Joel. *New People: Miscegenation and Mulattoes in the United States* (1980, 1995)

Wolff, Jana. *Secret Thoughts of an Adoptive Mother* (1997)

Wright, Marguerite A. *I'm Chocolate, You're Vanilla: Raising Healthy Black and Biracial Children in a Race-Conscious World* (1998)

Yerby, Frank. *Speak Now* (1969)

Zack, Naomi, ed. *American Mixed Race: The Culture of Microdiversity* (1995)

Zack, Naomi. *Race and Mixed Race* (1993)

## Articles in Academic or Professional Journals

Alexander, Larry. "What Makes Wrongful Discrimination Wrong? Biases, Preferences, Stereotypes, and Proxies," 141 *University of Pennsylvania Journal* 149 (1992)

Allen, Anita. "Lying to Protect Privacy," 44 *Villanova Law Review* 161 (1999)

Annella, Sister M. "Some Aspects of Interracial Marriage in Washington, D.C., 1940–1947," *Journal of Negro Education* 25 (fall 1967): 380–91

Applebaum, Harvey. "Miscegenation Statutes: A Constitutional and Social Problem," *Georgetown Law Journal* 53 (fall 1964): 49–91

Atwood, Barbara Ann. "Fleshpaints under the Indian Child Welfare Act: Toward a New Understanding of State Court Resistance," 51 *Emory Law Journal* 587 (2002)

Avins, Alfred. "Anti-Miscegenation Laws and the Fourteenth Amendment: The Original Intent," 52 *Virginia Law Review* 1224 (1966)

Bahl, Anjana. "Color-Coordinated Families: Race Matching in Adoption in the United States and Britain," 28 *Loyola University of Chicago Law Journal* 41 (1996)

Bakeis, Christine D. "The Indian Child Welfare Act of 1978: Violating Personal Rights for the Sake of the Tribe," 10 *Notre Dame Journal of Law, Ethics, and Public Policy* 543 (1996)

Bank, Steven A. "Anti-Miscegenation Laws and the Dilemma of Symmetry: The Understanding of Equality in the Civil Rights Act of 1875," 2 *University of Chicago Law School Roundtable* 303 (1995)

Banks, R. Richard. "The Color of Desire: Fulfilling Adoptive Parents' Racial Preferences Through Discriminatory State Action," 107 *Yale Law Journal* 975 (1998)

Banks, Taunya Lovell. "Colorism: A Darker Shade of Pale," 47 *UCLA Law Review* 1705 (2000)

Barnett, Larry. "Students' Anticipations of Persons and Arguments Opposing Interracial Dating," *Marriage and Family Living* 25 (August 1963): 355–57

Barnett, Robert B. "The Constitutionality of Sex Separation in School Desegregation Plans," 37 *University of Chicago Law Review* 296 (1970)

Barron, Milton. "Research to Intermarriage: A Survey of Accomplishments and Prospects," *American Journal of Sociology* 57 (November 1951): 249–55

Barth, Richard P. "Effects of Age on the Odds of Adoption Versus Remaining in Long-Term Out-of-Home Care," 76 *Child Welfare* 285, 296 (1997)

Bartholet, Elizabeth. "Transracial Adoption and Race Separatism in the Family: More on the Transracial Adoption Debate," 2 *Duke Journal of Gender Law and Policy* 99 (1995)

———. "Where Do Black Children Belong? The Politics of Race Matching in Transracial Adoption," 139 *University of Pennsylvania Law Review* 1163 (1991)

Beigel, Hugo. "Problems and Motives in Interracial Relationships," *Journal of Sex Research* 2 (November 1966): 185–205

Berry, Mary Frances. "Judging Morality: Sexual Behavior and Legal Consequences in the Late-Nineteenth-Century South," 78 *Journal of American History* 854 (1991)

Blackwood, Eileen. "Race as a Factor in Custody and Adoption Disputes: *Palmore v. Sidoti*," *Cornell Law Review* 71 (November 1985): 209–26

Bloomfield, Maxwell. "Dixon's *The Leopard's Spots*: A Study in Popular Racism," *American Quarterly* 16.3 (fall 1964): 387–401

Bond, Horace Mann. "Two Racial Islands in Alabama," *American Journal of Sociology* 36 (January 1931): 552–67

Bowen, James. "Cultural Convergences and Divergences: The Nexus Between Putative Afro-American Family Values and the Best Interests of the Child," 26 *Journal of Family Law* 487 (1987)

Brown, Thomas. "The Miscegenation of Richard Mentor Johnson as an Issue in the National Election Campaign of 1835–1836," 39 *Civil War History* 5 (1993)

Burma, John. "Interethnic Marriage in Los Angeles, 1948–1959," *Social Forces* 42 (December 1963): 156–65

———. "Research Note on the Measurement of Interracial Marriage," *American Journal of Sociology* 57 (May 1952): 587–89

———. "The Measurement of Negro 'Passing,'" *American Journal of Sociology* 52 (July 1946): 18–22

Burma, John, Gary Crester, and Ted Seacrest. "A Companion of the Occupational Status of Intermarrying and Intermarrying Couples: A Research Note," *Sociology and Social Research* 54 (July 1970): 508–19

Burnham, Margaret A. "An Impossible Marriage: Slave Law and Family Law," 5 *Law and Inequality* 197 (1987)

Brynes, Leonard. "Who Is Black Enough for You? The Analysis of Northwestern University Law School's Struggle over Minority Faculty Hiring," 2 *Michigan Journal of Race and Law* 205 (1997)

Calavita, Kitty. "The Paradoxes of Race, Class, Identity, and 'Passing': Enforcing the Chinese Exclusion Acts, 1882–1910," 25 *Law and Social Inquiry* 1 (2000)

Caldwell, Dan. "The Negroization of the Chinese Stereotype in California," 53 *Southern California Quarterly* 123 (1971)

Calmore, John O. "Dismantling the Master's House: Essays in Memory of Trana Grillo: Random Notes of an Integration Warrior," 81 *Minnesota Law Review* 1441 (1997)

Campbell, Suzanne Brannen. "Comment: Taking Race out of the Equation: Transracial Adoption in 2000," 53 *Southern Methodist University Law Review* 1599 (2000)

Carter, Elmer A. "Crossing Over," *Opportunity* (December 1926): 376–78

Chamallas, Martha. "The New Gender Panic: Reflections on Sex Scandals and the Military," 83 *Minnesota Law Review* 305, 344–50 (1998)

Chen, Jim. "Unloving," 80 *Iowa Law Review* 145 (1994)

Chiles, Chip. "A Hand to Rock the Cradle: Transracial Adoption, the Multiethnic Placement Act, and a Proposal to the Arkansas General Assembly," 49 *Arkansas Law Review* 501 (1996)

Chimezie, Amuzie. "Transracial Adoption of Black Children," *Social Work* 20 (July 1985): 296

Chin, Gabriel J. "Segregation's Last Stronghold: Race Discrimination and the Constitutional Law of Immigration," 46 *UCLA Law Review* 1 (1998)

Clark, Maxine, Linda Windley, Linda Jones, and Steve Ellis. "Dating Patterns of Black Students on White Southern Campuses," *Journal of Multicultural Counseling and Development* 14 (April 1986): 85–93

Clark, William Bedford. "The Serpent of Lust in the Southern Garden," *Southern Review* 10.4 (October 1974): 805–22

Clinton, Catherine. "Bloody Terrain: Freedwomen, Sexuality and Violence During Reconstruction," *Georgia Historical Quarterly* (summer 1992)

Davidson, Jeanette. "Black-White Interracial Marriage: A Critical Look at Theories About Motivations of Partners," *Journal of Intergroup Relations* 18 (winter 1991–92): 14–20

Davis, Adrienne D. "The Private Law of Race and Sex: An Antebellum Perspective," 51 *Stanford Law Review* 221 (1999)

Davis, Kingsley. "Intermarriage in Caste Societies," *American Anthropologist* 43 (July–September 1941): 376-95

Destro, Robert A. "Symposium: Law and the Politics of Marriage: *Loving v. Virginia* After 30 Years Introduction," 47 *Catholic University Law Review* 1207 (1998)

Dorr, Gregory Michael. "Principled Expediency: Eugenics, *Naim v. Naim,* and the Supreme Court," 42 *The American Journal of Legal History* 119 (1998)

Durrow, Heidi W. "Mothering Across the Color Line: White Women, 'Black' Babies," 7 *Yale Journal of Law and Feminism* 227 (1995)

Ford, Christopher A. "Administering Identity: The Determination of 'Race' in Race-Conscious Law," 182 *California Law Review* 1231 (1994)

Forde-Mazrui, Kim. "Black Identity and Child Placement: The Best Interests of Black and Biracial Children," 92 *Michigan Law Review* 925 (1994)

Fricke, Harriet. "Interracial Adoption: The Little Revolution," 10 *Social Work* (July 1965)

Gatewood, William B., Jr. "The Perils of Passing: The McCorys of Omaha, Nebraska," *History* (summer 1990)

Getman, Karen A. "Sexual Control in the Slaveholding South: The Implications and Maintenance of a Racial Caste System," 7 *Harvard Women's Law Journal* 115 (1984)

Golden, Joseph. "Patterns of Negro-White Intermarriage," 19 *American Sociological Review* 144 (1954)

———. "Social Control of Negro-White Intermarriage," 36 *Social Forces* 267 (1958)

Gould, L. Scott. "Mixing Bodies and Beliefs: The Predicament of Tribes," 101 *Columbia Law Review* 702 (2001)

Gross, Ariela. "Litigating Whiteness: Trials of Racial Determination in the Nineteenth-Century South," 108 *Yale Law Journal* 109 (1998)

Hanan, Jehnna Irene. "Comment: The Best Interest of the Child: Eliminating Discrimination in the Screening of Adoptive Parents," 27 *Golden Gate University Law Review* 167 (1997)

Hardaway, Rodger D. "Unlawful Love: A History of Arizona's Miscegenation Law," *Journal of Arizona History* 27 (winter 1986): 377–90

Harris, Cheryl. "Whiteness as Property," 106 *Harvard Law Review* 1709 (1993)

Hawkins-Leon, Cynthia G. "The Indian Child Welfare Act and the African American Tribe: Facing the Adoption Crisis," 36 *Brandeis Journal of Family Law* 201 (1998)

Hayes, Peter. "The Ideological Attack on Transracial Adoption in the USA and Britain," 9 *International Journal of Law and the Family* 1 (1995)

Heer, David M. "Negro-White Marriages in the United States," 27 *Journal of Marriage and the Family* 262 (1966)

———. "The Prevalence of Black-White Marriage in the United States, 1960 and 1970," *Journal of Marriage and the Family* 36 (May 1974): 246–58

Hernandez, Tanya Kateri. "Multiracial Discourse: Racial Classifications in an Era of Color-Blind Jurisprudence," 57 *Maryland Law Review* 97, 98 n. 4 (1998)

Hickman, Christine B. "The Devil and the One Drop Rule: Racial Categories, African Americans and the U.S. Census," 95 *Michigan Law Review* 1161 (1997)

Higginbotham, A. Leon, Jr., and Barbara K. Kopytoff, "Racial Purity and Interracial Sex in the Law of Colonial and Antebellum Virginia," 77 *Georgetown Law Journal* 1967 (1989)

Hine, Darlene Clark. "Rape and the Inner Lives of Black Women in the Middle West: Preliminary Thoughts on the Culture of Disemblance," 14 *Signs* 912 (1989)

Howard, Margaret. "Transracial Adoption: Analysis of the Best-Interest Standard," 59 *Notre Dame Law Review* 503 (1984)

Howe, Ruth-Arlene W. "Redefining the Transracial Adoption Controversy," 2 *Duke Journal of Gender Law and Policy* 131 (1995)

———. "Transracial Adoption: Old Prejudices and Discrimination Float Under a New Halo," 6 *Boston University Public Interest Law Journal* 409 (1997)

Hughes, Michael, and Bradley R. Hertel. "The Significance of Color Remains: A Study of Life Chances, Male Selection, and Ethnic Consciousness Among Black Americans," 69 *Social Forces* 1105 (1990)

"Intermarriage with Negroes—A Survey of State Statutes," *Yale Law Journal* 36 (April 1927): 858–66

Isaacs, Asher D. "Interracial Adoption—Permanent Placement and Racial Identity—An Adoptee's Perspective," 14 *National Black Law Journal* 126 (1996)

Jenks, Albert E. "The Legal Status of Negro-White Amalgamation in the United States," *American Journal of Sociology* 21 (March 1916): 666–78

Jennings, Thelma. "'Us Colored Women Had to Go Through Plenty': Sexual Exploitation of African-American Slave Women," 1 *Journal of Women's History* 45 (1990)

Jonas, Lisa, and Marshall Silverberg. "Comment: Race, Custody and the Constitution: *Palmore v. Sidoti*," 27 *Howard Law Journal* 1549 (1984)

Jones, Trina. "Shades of Brown: The Law of Skin Color," 49 *Duke Law Journal* 1487 (2000)

Kang, Jerry. "Cyber-Race," 113 *Harvard Law Review* 1131 (2000)

Kaplan, Sidney. "The Miscegenation Issue in the Election of 1864," *Journal of Negro History* 34.3 (July 1949): 274–343

Karst, Kenneth L. "Myths of Identity: Individual and Group Portraits of Race and Sexual Orientation," 43 *UCLA Law Review* 263 (1995)

Katyal, Neal Kumar. "Men Who Own Women: A Thirteenth-Amendment Critique of Forced Prostitution," 103 *Yale Law Journal* 791, 796–803 (1993)

Kennedy, Randall. "Symposium: Border People and Antidiscrimination Law: Interracial Intimacies: Sex, Marriage, Identity, Adoption," 17 *Harvard Blackletter Journal* 57 (2001)

———. "How Are We Doing With *Loving:* Race, Law, and Intermarriage," 77 *Boston University Law Review* 815 (1997)

Kephart, William M. "The 'Passing' Question," *Phylon* 10 (1948)

Lichter, Daniel, et al. "Race and the Retreat from Marriage: A Shortage of Marriageable Men?," 57 *American Sociological Review* 781, 797 (1992)

Lombardo, Paul A. "Miscegenation, Eugenics, and Racism: Historical Footnotes to *Loving v. Virginia,*" *University of California Davis Law Review* 21.2 (winter 1988): 421–52

Lythcott-Haims, Julie C. "Where Do Mixed Babies Belong? Racial Classifications in America and Its Implications for Transracial Adoption," 29 *Civil Rights–Civil Liberties Law Review* 531 (1994)

Mabry, Cynthia R. "Love Alone Is Not Enough!," 42 *Wayne Law Review* 1347 (1996)

Macaulay, Jacqueline, and Stewart Macaulay. "Adoption for Black Children: A Case Study of Expert Discretion," 1 *Research in Law and Sociology* 265, 266 (1978)

Marcosson, Samuel. "Coloring the Constitutional of Originalism: Clarence Thomas at the Rubicon," 16 *Law & Inequality Journal* 429, 451 (1998)

Margulies, Peter. "The Identity Question, Madeleine Albright's Past and Me: Insights from Jewish and African-American Law and Literature," 17 *Loyola of Los Angeles Entertainment Law Journal* 595 (1997)

McGuire, Hunter, and G. Frank Lydston. "Sexual Crimes Among the Southern Negroes Scientifically Considered: An Open Correspondence," *Virginia Medical Monthly* 20 (May 1893): 105

McHattan, Henry. "The Sexual Status of the Negro—Past and Present," 10 *American Journal of Dermatology and Genito-urinary Disease* 8 (January 1906)

Merton, Robert K. "Intermarriage and Social Structure: Fact and Theory," *Psychiatry* 4 (August 1941): 361

Metteer, Christine M. "A Law unto Itself: The Indian Child Welfare Act as Inapplicable and Inappropriate to the Transracial/Race-Matching Adoption Controversy," 38 *Brandeis Law Journal* 47 (1999)

Metzenbaum, Howard M. "S. 1224—In Support of the Multiethnic Placement Act of 1993," 2 *Duke Journal of Gender Law and Policy* 165 (1995)

Mills, Charles W. "Do Black Men Have a Moral Duty to Marry Black Women?," 25 *Journal of Social Philosophy* 131 (1994)

Mills, Gary B. "Miscegenation and the Free Negro in Antebellum 'Anglo' Alabama: A Reexamination of Southern Race Relations," 68 *Journal of American History* 16 (1981)

Mini, Michelle M. "Note: Breaking Down the Barriers to Transracial Adoptions: Can the Multiethnic Placement Act Meet This Challenge?," 22 *Hofstra Law Review* 897 (1994)

Monahan, Thomas P. "The Occupational Clan of Couples Entering into Interracial Marriages," 7 *Journal of Comparative Family Studies* 175 (1976)

Mullins, Jennifer. "Note and Comment: Transracial Adoption in California: Serving the Best Interests of the Child or Equal Protection Violation?," 17 *Journal of Juvenile Law* 107 (1996)

Mumford, Kevin. "After Hugh: Statutory Race Segregation in Colonial America," 43 *American Journal of Legal History* 280 (1999)

Nelson, William Javier. "Racial Definition: Background for Divergence," *Phylon* 47.4 (1986): 318–26

Note: "Custody Disputes Following the Dissolution of Interracial Marriages: Best Interest of the Child or Judicial Racism?," 19 *Journal of Family Law* 97 (1980)

Note: "Who Is a Negro?," 11 *University of Florida Law Review* 235 (1958)

Nott, Josiah C. "The Mulatto a Hybrid-Probable Extermination of the Two Races if the Whites and Blacks Are Allowed to Intermarry," *American Journal of Medical Sciences* 66 (July 1843)

Pascoe, Peggy. "Miscegenation Law, Court Cases, and Ideologies of 'Race' in Twentieth-Century America," 83 *Journal of American History* 44 (1996)

Painter, Nell Irvin. "Of Lily, Linda Brent and Freud: A Non-Exceptionalist Approach to Race, Class, and Gender in the Slave South," 76 *Georgia Historical Quarterly* 241 (1992)

Pattiz, Davidson M. "Racial Preferences in Adoption: An Equal Protection Challenge," 82 *Georgetown Law Journal* 2571 (1994)

Peets, Lisa. "Racial Steering in the Romantic Marketplace," 107 *Harvard Law Review* 877 (1994)

Perez, Amanda T. "Transracial Adoption and the Federal Adoption Subsidy," 17 *Yale Law and Policy Review* 201 (1998)

Perry, Twila L. "Transracial and International Adoption: Mothers, Hierarchy, Race, and Feminist Legal Theory," 20 *Yale Journal of Law and Feminism* 101 (1998)

Philips, Sloan. "The Indian Child Welfare Act in the Face of Extinction," 21 *American Indian Law Review* 351 (1997)

Phillips, Stephanie L. "Claiming Our Forefathers: The Legend of Sally Hemings and the Tasks of Black Feminist Theory," 8 *Hastings Women's Law Journal* 401 (1997)

Pittman, R. Carter. "The Fourteenth Amendment: Its Intended Effect on Anti-Miscegenation Laws," 43 *North Carolina Law Review* 92, 108 (1964)

Poussaint, Alvin F. "The Stresses of the White Female Worker in the Civil Rights Movement in the South," 123 *American Journal of Psychiatry* 401 (1966)

Pratt, Robert A. "Crossing the Color Line: A Historical Assessment and Personal Narrative of *Loving v. Virginia*," 41 *Howard Law Journal* 229 (1998)

"The Rape Myth of the Old South Reconsidered," 61 *Journal of Southern History* 481 (1995)

Robinson, Amy. "It Takes One to Know One: Passing and Communities of Common Interest," 20 *Critical Inquiry* 715 (1994)

Rosettenstein, David S. "Trans-Racial Adoption and the Statutory Preference Schemes: Before the 'Best Interests' and After the 'Melting Pot,'" 68 *St. John's Law Review* 137, 142 (1994)

Rothman, Joshua D. "'Notorious in the Neighborhood': An Interracial Family in Early National and Antebellum Virginia," 67 *Journal of Southern History* 273 (2001)

———. "To Be Freed from That Curse and Let at Liberty: Interracial Adultery and Divorce in Antebellum Virginia," 106 *The Virginia Magazine of History and Biography* 443, 457 (1998)

Ruchames, Louis. "Race, Marriage, and Abolition in Massachusetts," originally published in 40 *Journal of Negro History* 250 (1955), reprinted in *Race, Law, and American History, 1700–1990 (Race and Law Before Emancipation)* 448, Paul Finkelman, ed. (1992)

Saks, Eva. "Representing Miscegenation Law," *Raritan* 8.2 (fall 1988): 39–69

Sanjek, Roger. "Intermarriage and the Future of Races in the United States," in *Race,* Steven Gregory and Roger Sanjek, eds. (1994)

Schuhmann, George. "Miscegenation: An Example of Judicial Recidivism," *Journal of Family Law* 8 (1968): 69–78

Sealing, Keith E. "Blood Will Tell: Scientific Racism and the Legal Prohibitions Against Miscegenation," 5 *Michigan Journal of Race and Law* 559 (2000)

Seidelson, David E. "Miscegenation Statutes and the Supreme Court: A Brief Prediction of What the Court Will Do and Why," 15 *Catholic University Law Review* 156 (1966)

Seltzer, Richard, and Robert L. Smith. "Color Differences in the Afro-American Community and the Differences They Make," 21 *Journal Black Studies* 279 (1991)

Sherman, Richard B. "'The Last Stand': The Fight for Racial Integrity in Virginia in the 1920s," 49 *Journal of Southern History* 69 (1988)

Simon, Rita J. and Howard Altstein. "The Relevance of Race in Adoption and Social Practice," 11 *Notre Dame Journal of Law, Ethics, and Public Policy* 171 (1997)

Strasser, Mark. "Symposium Topic: Loving in the New Millenium: On Equal Protection and the Right to Marry," 7 *University of Chicago Law School Roundtable* 61 (2000)

Townsend, Jacinda T. "Reclaiming Self-Determination: A Call for Interracial Adoption," 2 *Duke Journal of Gender Law and Policy* 173 (1995)

Van Tassel, Emily Field. "Freedom: Personal Liberty and Private Law: 'Only the Law Would Rule Between Us': Antimiscegenation, the Moral Economy of Dependency, and the Debate over Rights After the Civil War," 70 *Chicago-Kent Law Review* 873 (1995)

Varan, Rebecca. "Desegregating the Adoptive Family: In Support of the Adoption Antidiscrimination Act of 1995," 30 *John Marshall Law Review* 593 (1997)

Wadlington, Walter. "The *Loving* Case: Virginia's Anti-miscegenation Statute in Historical Perspective," 52 *Virginia Law Review* 189 (1966)

Wallenstein, Peter. "Law and the Boundaries of Place and Race in Interracial Marriage: Interstate Comity, Racial Identity, and Miscegenation Laws in North Carolina, South Carolina, and Virginia, 1860–1960s," 32 *Akron Law Review* 557 (1999)

———. "Race, Marriage and the Law of Freedom: Alabama and Virginia, 1860–1960s," 70 *Chicago-Kent Law Review* 371 (1994)

Walters, Ronald G. "The Erotic South: Civilization and Sexuality in American Abolitionism," 25 *American Quarterly* 177 (1973)

Wardle, Lynn D. "*Loving v. Virginia* and the Constitutional Right to Marry," 41 *Howard Law Journal* 289 (1998)

Wartenberg, Thomas E. "'But Would You Want Your Daughter to Marry One?' The Representation of Race and Racism in *Guess Who's Coming to Dinner?*," 25 *Journal of Social Philosophy* 99 (1994)

Weinberger, Andrew. "A Reappraisal of the Constitutionality of Miscegenation Statutes," 42 *Cornell Law Quarterly* 208 (1957)

Weinstock, Robert B. "*Palmore v. Sidoti*: Color-Blind Custody," 34 *American University Law Review* 245 (1984)

Westley, Robert. "First Time Encounters: 'Passing' Revisited and Demystification as a Critical Practice," 18 *Yale Law & Policy Review* 297 (2000)

Woodhouse, Barbara Bennett. "'Are You My Mother?': Conceptualizing Children's Identity Rights in Transracial Adoptions," 2 *Duke Journal of Gender Law and Policy* 107 (1995)

Woods, Karen M. "A 'Wicked and Mischievous Connection': The Origins of Indian-White Miscegenation Laws," 23 *Legal Studies Forum* 37, 54–55 (1999)

Woodson, G. Carter. "The Beginnings of Miscegenation of the Whites and Blacks," *Journal of Negro History* 3.4 (October 1918): 335–53.

Wriggins, Jennifer. "Rape, Racism, and the Law," 6 *Harvard Women's Law Journal* 103 (1983)

Wright, Luther, Jr. "Who's Black, Who's White and Who Cares: Reconceptualizing the United States' Definition of Race and Racial Classifications," 48 *Vanderbilt Law Review* 513 (1995)

Yoshino, Kenji. "Assimilationist Bias in Equal Protection: The Visibility Perception and the Case of 'Don't Ask, Don't Tell,'" 108 *Yale Law Journal* 485 (1998)

———. "Covering," 111 *Yale Law Journal* 769 (2002)

Zrecny, Myriam. "Race-Conscious Child Placement: Deviating from a Policy Against Racial Classification," 69 *Chicago-Kent Law Review* 1121, 1125 (1994)

## Articles in Newspapers and Magazines

"13-year-old Daughter of Mixed Marriage in Chicago, Promised Her Negro Father to Stay Negro," *Jet*, July 1959

"60 Negro Soldiers of U.S. 10th Infantry Division Married to German Women Request Transfers—Unit Is Returning to Georgia," *Jet*, 20 February 1958

"200 Interracial Marriages Take Place in Chicago," *Baltimore Afro-American*, 3 September 1949

"242-year-old Maryland Law Making It a Crime for White Woman to Bear Children Fathered by a Negro, Declared Unconstitutional," *Jet*, May 1957

"1,000 Witness Interracial Marriage in Chicago," *Jet*, 17 July 1952

"A Marriage of Enlightenment," *Time*, 29 September 1967

"Actress Diahann Carroll Discusses Mixed Marriage," *Jet*, 15 March 1973

Adams, Jacqueline. "The White Wife," *New York Times Magazine*, 18 September 1994

Adams, Russell. "The Meaning of Mixed Marriages," *Washington Post*, 5 October 1991

Albrecht, Brian. "Being Biracial: It's No Big Deal to Children of Mixed Color," *Cleveland Plain Dealer*, 11 April 1993

Albright-Creque, Tracy. "Success Story #9," *Interrace* 39, December/January 1995

"Alfonso Kyles (Negro) and Enid Kyles (White) Fight for Custody of Their Baby in Washington, D.C. Court," *Jet*, 8 November 1956

Anderson, Nicholas. "Success Story #8," *Interrace*, October/November 1994

Anderson, Trezzvant. "Police Arrest Mixed Couples Interracial Romance 'Shake Up' Arkansas," *Pittsburgh Courier*, 4 October 1958

"Anna's Sin: Italian Film About Interracial Romance Is First to Allow Negro Lover to Win Girl," *Ebony*, March 1954

Anson, Robert Sam. "Black and White Together: Can Love Really Be Color Blind?," *Mademoiselle*, February 1981

"Anti-Miscegenation Statutes: Repugnant Indeed," *Time*, 23 June 1967

April, S. "Miscegenation Is a Phony Issue," *Negro Digest*, October 1962

"Are Interracial Homes Bad for Children?," *Ebony*, March 1963

"Are Interracial Whites America's Shunned People?," *Cleveland Call and Post*, 27 July 1989

"Are the Children of Mixed Marriages Black or White?," *Jet*, 21 May 1990

"Are Mixed Marriages Increasing?," *Jet*, 9 July 1953

"Are White Women Stealing Our Men?," *Negro Digest*, April 1951

Askew, Rev. C. Eugene. "Yes, I Would Want My Daughter to Marry a Negro," *Negro Digest*, July 1964

Autrobus, Edmund. "Englishwoman in Dixie," *Negro Digest*, June 1948

"Baha'i Faith: Only Church in World that Does Not Discriminate," *Ebony*, October 1952

Bailey, Pearl. "This Time It's Love: Singer-Actress Pearl Bailey Tells Story of Her Marriage to White Louis Bellson," *Ebony,* May 1953

Baldwin, James. "On Being White . . . And Other Lies," *Essence,* April 1984

"Bedroom Issues: Interracial Marriage in Florida," *Newsweek,* 21 December 1963

Belafonte, H. "Why I Married Julie," *Ebony,* July 1957, 90–95

Bennetts, Leslie. "Interracial Couples' View of Life as Mixed Marriages Increase," *New York Times,* 23 February 1960

Berry, Bill. "Interracial Marriages in the South," *Ebony,* June 1978

Besharov, Douglas J. and Timothy S. Robinson. "One Flesh," *The New Democrat,* July/August 1996

Biddle, Frederic M. "When Color Lines Are Drawn Within a Family," *Boston Globe,* 26 November 1996

Bird, Robert S. "Integration—and a Campus Romance," *U.S. News and World Report,* 22 February 1960

Black, Doris. "How Passing Passed Out," *Sepia,* December 1972

"Black and White Dating," *Time,* 19 July 1968, pp. 48–49

"Black Children, White Parents," *New York Times,* 27 November 1993

"Black Telephone Worker Who Dated White Woman, Files Suit to Keep His Job," *Jet,* 24 November 1986

"Black Women Prefer to Remain Single Rather than Marry Outside of the Race," *Jet,* 18 July 1988

"Black Women/White Men: The Other Mixed Marriage," *Ebony,* August 1982

"Blacks More Uptight About *Roots* Interracial Marriage than Whites," *Jet,* 29 March 1979

Booker, Simeon. "A Challenge for the Guy Smiths: Peggy Rusk, Negro Husband Face Their Future with Smile," *Ebony,* December 1967

Booker, Simeon. "The Couple That Rocked the Courts," *Ebony,* September 1967

Borgese, G. A. "A Bedroom Approach to Racism," *Negro Digest,* December 1944

Bouchet, Nicole, "On the Contrary," *Interrace,* vol. 9, no. 43, 1998

"Boy, Girl, Black, White," *Time,* 6 April 1970

Braxton, Greg. "TV Finds Drama in Interracial Dating," *Los Angeles Times,* 22 March 2000

"Britain's Brown Babies," *Ebony,* November 1946

Britt, Donna. "Even on 'ER,' Race and Love a Touchy Mix," *Washington Post,* 9 April 1999

———. "Hard to be Colorblind About Love," *Washington Post*, 11 June 1999

Britt, May. "Why I Married Sammy Davis, Jr." *Ebony*, January 1961

Buck, Pearl S. "Should White Parents Adopt Brown Babies?," *Ebony*, June 1958

Buckley, Gail Lumet. "When a Kiss Is Not Just a Kiss," *New York Times*, 31 March 1991

Burke, Ruth. "Handle with Care: How to Protect a Mixed Marriage," *Negro Digest*, May 1964

Burroughs, Nannie H. "Church Leader Argues Against Mixed Marriage," *Ebony*, November 1950

Calloway, Nathanial. "Mixed Marriage Can Succeed," *Negro Digest*, March 1949

Campbell, Bebe Moore. "Brothers and Sisters," *New York Times Magazine*, 23 August 1992

———. "Is It True What They Say About Black Men?," *Ebony*, July 1987

———. "Staying in the Community," *Essence*, December 1989

Campbell, Jeanne. "This Is My Daughter (White Mother, Negro Child)," *Negro Digest*, June 1965

———. "Can a Nigger Love a Honky?" *Look*, 7 January 1969

Cannon, Poppy. "Can Interracial Marriage Work?," *Ebony*, June 1952

———. "How We Erased Two Color Lines," *Ebony*, July 1952

———. "My Life as an Ambassador in Two Worlds," *Sepia*, January 1961

———. "The Love That Never Died," *Ebony*, January 1957

Carter, Lloyd H. "The Other Cheek," *Interrace* 7, March/April 1991

"Case Against Mixed Marriage," *Ebony*, November 1950

"Case History of an Ex-White Man," *Ebony*, December 1946

Chase, Ilka. "The Hazards of Mixed Marriage," *Negro Digest*, September 1948

Cheers, D. M. "A Visit with Unusual Twins . . . One Is Black, the Other White" *Jet*, 2 June 1986

Chennault, L. "How I Face the World with My Negro Child," *Ebony*, December 1960

"Chicago Mixed Couples United Against White, Negro Hostility," *Jet*, 17 November 1960

Childs, C. W. "Black and White Couples: Have Attitudes Changed?," *Redbook*, September 1969

China, Mary, "Success Story #2," *Interrace*, September/October 1993

"Chubby Checker and Dutch Beauty Queen Catherina Lodders," *Jet*, 30 April 1964

"Church Wedding for Mixed Couple; British Girl and Ex-Soldier Defy Taboos to Get Married in Cleveland's Biggest Negro Church," *Ebony*, December 1951

"College Drops Name of Donor Who Sent Hate-Mail to Interracial Couples," *Jet*, 7 March 1988

"College Famed for Liberalism Sends White Student Home for Deciding to Marry Negro Coed," *Associated Negro Press*, 5 May 1952

Collins, Glenn. "Children of Interracial Marriage," *New York Times*, 20 June 1984

Coombs, O. "Black Men and White Women: 13 Years Later," *Essence*, May 1983

"Court Takes 8-year-old Son of White Beauty Who Wed Negro Dentist," *Jet*, 9 August 1956

Courtland, Milloy. "Black Men and White Women: My Memories of Thinking the Unthinkable in Louisiana in 1968," *Washington Post*, 23 February 1986

Creary, Herman J. "Are Americans Afraid to Be Free?: A Consideration of Interracial Marriage," *Catholic World*, November 1963

"The Crime of Being Married," *Life*, 18 March 1966

"Crime of Interracial Marriage," *America*, 8 April 1967

Cross, Farrell, and Wilbur Cross. "World Report on Intermarriage," *Negro Digest*, August 1961

Cross, Kathleen. "Trapped in the Body of a White Woman," *Ebony*, October 1990

"Crosses Burn Near Home of Negro, White Woman," *Jet*, 15 April 1953

"Crown of *Porgy* Cast Weds White Girl," *Jet*, 7 May 1953

Cunningham, Evelyn. "Gotham Citizens Express Opinions of Mixed Unions," *Pittsburgh Courier*, 4 December 1954

"Current Comment: Miscegenation Test Case," *America*, 6 February 1965

Dabney, V. "Is a Mixed Race Inevitable?," *U.S. News & World Report*, 10 May 1965

Davis, Sammy, Jr. "Is My Mixed Marriage Mixing Up My Kids?," *Ebony*, October 1966

———. "Why I Became a Jew," *Ebony*, February 1960

"Davis Knight, White," *Newsweek*, 28 November 1949

"Daytime TV's First Interracial Marriage Set for 'General Hospital,'" *Jet*, 29 February 1988

"Deep Freeze Woman Reports Her White Fiancé Committed Suicide," *Jet*, 4 September 1952

DeFeder, Jim. "How Much for a White Baby?," *Talk,* December 1999/January 2000

"Denise Nicholas and Carroll O'Connor Wed on TV Drama 'In the Heat of the Night,'" *Jet,* 9 May 1994

"Detroit White Woman Marries Negro, James Riggins; Fights to See Her White Son by Former Marriage," *Jet,* 23 July 1959

"Detroit's Most Discussed Mixed Marriage," *Ebony,* April 1953

"Do Negro Stars Prefer White Husbands?," *Ebony,* May 1954

"Do Negroes Want to Vanish?," *Jet,* 25 August 1955

Dobbs, J. Wesley, and Murdock, C. "My Daughter Married a White Man," *Ebony,* January 1954

"Does Mixed Marriage Hurt Race Relations?," *Jet,* 3 July 1952

"Does Mixed Marriage Produce Better Babies?," *Jet,* 19 March 1953

Downs, Joan. "Black/White Dating," *Life,* 28 May 1971

"Dr. Peale's Advice: Give Up White Boyfriend, Girl Told," *Pittsburgh Courier,* 6 November 1954

DuBois, W. E. B. "Intermarriage," *The Crisis* (February 1913): 181–2

———. "Sex and Racism," *The Independent,* 6 (March 1957)

———. "Social Equality and Racial Intermarriage," *World Tomorrow* 5 (March 1922): 83

Duffy, Edna. "The Mailbag: Troubles of a Mixed Couple," *Negro Digest,* February 1950

Duke, Lynn. "Still the Rarest of Wedding Bonds," *Washington Post,* 12 June 1992

Evers, Mrs. M. "Why Should My Child Marry Yours?," *Ladies' Home Journal,* April 1968

"Ex-Alabama Principal Who Ousted Mixed-Race Dating Banned from Visiting School District," *Jet,* 30 January 1995

"Famous Negroes Married to Whites," *Ebony,* December 1949

Feinstein, Herbert. "Lena Horne Speaks Freely on Race, Marriage, Stage," *Ebony,* May 1963

Fernandez, Carlos A. "United We Stand!," *Interrace* 59 (November/December 1989)

Fisher, L. "America's Most Controversial Marriage," *Sepia,* February 1961

Fosdick, Franklin. "Is Intermarriage Wrecking the NAACP?," *Negro Digest,* June 1950

Furlong, W. B. "Interracial Marriage Is a Sometime Thing," *New York Times Magazine,* 9 June 1968

George, Lynell. "Cross Colors: Interracial Dating Is Not New, but How

Couples Get Together Has Changed," *Los Angeles Times*, 27 March 1994

Gitlin, Thyra Edwards, and Murray Gitlin. "Does Interracial Marriage Succeed?," *Negro Digest*, July 1945

Glazer, Nathan. "Black and White After Thirty Years," *The Public Interest*, September 1995

Greene, Leonard. "Is History Repeating Itself in Army Rape Allegations?," *Boston Herald*, 17 March 1997

Gross, Jane with Ronald Smothers. "In Prom Dispute, a Town's Race Division Emerges," *New York Times*, 15 August 1994

"Growing Concern for Interracial Children," *Jet*, 23 July 1984

"Guess Who's Coming to Dinner?," *Ebony*, January 1968

Haizlip, Shirlee Taylor. "Passing," *American Heritage* 46.1, February/March 1995

Hall, Elizabeth. "A Raw Power Question," *Psychology Today*, January 1974

Halsell, Grace. "Mixed Marriage in Mississippi," *Sepia*, January 1973

Haney, Marie. "We Faced the Unseen: Interracial Marriage," *Negro Digest*, June 1964, 69–70

Hart, Newell. "Direct Action," *Negro Digest*, September 1964

"Harvard U. Teacher Weds Negro Socialite," *Jet*, 1 November 1953

"Has Integration Increased Mixed Marriage?," *Jet*, 20 June 1957

"He Won't Bring White Bride Home," *Pittsburgh Courier*, 11 October 1958

Heim, Oskar. "Why I Want a Negro Wife," *Negro Digest*, July 1954

"Homes Needed for 10,000 Brown Orphans: Deserted Tots Find Few Would-be Parents to Adopt Them," *Ebony*, October 1948

Horne, Lena. "My Life with Lennie," *Ebony*, November 1965

"How Campus Reacts to Interracial Romance of Basketball Star Warren Sutton and Dorothy Lebohner," *Jet*, 25 February 1960

"How Connecticut Mixed Family Faces Bigotry," *Jet*, 7 November 1963

"How the NAACP Stands on Intermarriage," *U.S. News & World Report*, 2 September 1963

"I Want to Marry a Negro," *Negro Digest*, August 1948

"I'm Through with Passing," *Ebony*, March 1951

"Integration Won't Boost Race Mixing," *Pittsburgh Courier*, 4 October 1958

"Intermarriage and the Race Problem: Interviews with Leading Authorities," *U.S. News & World Report*, 18 November 1963

"Interracial College Marriage," *Ebony*, July 1954

"Interracial Couple in N.Y. Get Damages from Landlord," *Jet*, 4 May 1987

"Interracial Marriage: A Christian View," *Christian Century*, 14 June 1967

"Interracial Romance," *Sepia*, December 1964

"Is Mixed Marriage a New Society Fad?," *Ebony*, September 1951

Jackson, Jacquelyne J. "Where Are the Black Men?," *Ebony*, March 1972

"Jail for Marriage," *Newsweek*, 27 December 1948

Johnson, Jack. "Does Interracial Marriage Succeed?," *Negro Digest*, May 1945

Johnson, R. E. "Bill Cosby Tells Why There Is No Interracial Dating on His TV Show," *Jet*, 11 November 1985

Jones, Isaac. "Interracial Couples Setting Pattern for Real Democracy," *Baltimore Afro-American*, 15 May 1948

Jones, Lisa. "Reckless Igging," *Village Voice*, 14 June 1992

Kantrowitz, B. "Color Blind Love," *Newsweek*, 7 March 1988

———. "The Ultimate Assimilation," *Newsweek*, 24 November 1986

Karkabi, Barbara. "Love, Marriage, Race and Kids," *Houston Chronicle*, 11 October 1992, Lifestyle, p. 1

Kauffmann, Stanley. "LeRoi Jones and the Tradition of the Fake," 12 *Dissent* 207, 1965

Keedoja, E. "Children of the Rainbow," *Newsweek*, 19 November 1984

Keith, Harold. "Who Wants Intermarriage," *Pittsburgh Courier*, 23 August 1958

———. "Who Wants Intermarriage: Most Courier Readers Stand Against Interracial Unions," *Pittsburgh Courier*, 20 September 1958

Kennedy, Randall. "My Race Problem—And Ours," *Atlantic Monthly*, May 1997

———. "Orphans of Separatism: The Painful Politics of Transracial Adoption," *The American Prospect*, spring 1994

Khama, Seretse. "Why I Gave Up My Throne for Love," *Ebony*, June 1951

Killens, John. "Would You Want One of Them to Marry Your Daughter?," *Negro Digest*, August 1965

King, Charles H., Jr. "Memo to White Supremacists: 'I Don't Want to Marry Your Daughter,'" *Negro Digest*, April 1964

King, Colbert. "The Fuss over Mixed Marriages," *Washington Post*, 24 September 1991

Kingslow, Janice. "I Refuse to Pass," *Negro Digest*, May 1950

Kunerth, Jeff. "U.S. Laws, Social Taboos Unkind to Mixed Couples," *Orlando Sentinel Tribune*, 14 January 1990

Kuttner, Nanette. "Women Who Pass as White," *Liberty*, March 1949

"The Last Taboo? Does Wave of Interracial Movies Signal a Real Change?," *Ebony*, September 1991

Lawrence, D. "And What About Intermarriage?," *U.S. News & World Report*, September 1958

"Leading Sociologists Discuss Sex Fears and Integration: Symposium," *U.S. News & World Report*, 19 September 1958

Lester, Julius. "White Woman—Black Man," *Evergreen Review*, September 1969

———. "White Woman—Black Man (Part II)," *Evergreen Review*, October 1969

Lewin, Tamar. "Two Views of Growing Up When the Faces Don't Match," *New York Times*, 27 October 1998

Lewis, Sharon D., and R. Cousin. "Black Women/White Men: The 'Other' Mixed Marriage," *Ebony*, January 1978

Lipton, Michael A., and Stephen Sawicki. "White Lie: June Cross Exposes the Skeleton in Her Mother's Closet—Herself," *People*, 2 December 1996

"The Loneliest Brides in America," *Ebony*, January 1953

"Love Writes a Happy Ending to Chubby Checker's Romance," *Sepia*, June 1964

Malveaux, Julianne. "Sex Scandal Shows Racism, Stupidity," *USA Today*, 9 May 1997

"Man Abducts Children from Wife Who Wed Negro," *Jet*, 25 June 1953

Margolick, David. "A Mixed Marriage's 25th Anniversary of Legality," *New York Times*, 12 June 1992

"Marriage Bias Scored," *New York Times*, 10 October 1969

"The Marriage of Eartha Kitt," *Ebony*, September 1960

"Marriage of Enlightenment: D. Rusk's Daughter Marries a Negro," *Time*, 29 September 1967

"The Marriage That Could Not Work," *Ebony*, July 1967, pp. 119–22

"Marriages That Criss-Cross the Color Line," *Chicago Defender*, 29 July 1950

Mayer, Milton. "The Issue Is Miscegenation," *The Progressive*, September 1959

McCarthy, Sheryl. "A Grown Child Tries to Untangle Her Roots," *Newsday*, 28 November 1996

McGrady, Charlene. "Success Story #1," *Interrace*, spring/summer 1993

McQueen, Michel. "Black Woman, White Man," *Washington Post*, 25 January 1981

Mehlinger, K., L. Gant, and D. K. Davis. "Sister Debates a Brother on that Black Man–White Woman Thing," *Ebony*, August 1970

Merida, Kevin. "In Defense of Love Beyond Race," *Washington Post,* 14 December 1997

Mills, Candy. "The Christians," *Interrace* 11, May/June 1992

———. "Goodnight Aunt Pearl, We'll Miss You," *Interrace* 23, September/October 1990

———. "Messengers of Truth," *Interrace* 28, December 1993

———. "A Star Is Reborn," *Interrace* 38, November 1993

Mills, Patrice, and Audrey Edwards, "Black Women and White Men," *Essence,* October 1983

"Minnesota Bible College Jock Says He Was Expelled for Dating White Girl There," *Jet,* 11 May 1987

"Mississippi Allows a Mixed Marriage," *New York Times,* 3 August 1970

"Mississippi: The Children's Children," *Time,* 27 December 1948

"Mississippi: Jail for Marriage," *Newsweek,* 27 December 1948

"Mississippi's First Mixed Marriage Since 1890," *Jet,* 20 August 1970

"Mixed Couple in Massachusetts Can Adopt Black Child," *Jet,* 11 August 1986

"Mixed Couple Ordered to Give Up 3-Year-Old They Have Reared Since Birth," *Jet,* 12 August 1985

"Mixed Couple Ordered to Stay Out of Indiana," *Jet,* 7 May 1953

"Mixed Couple Skips Louisiana Jim Crow, Weds in Minnesota," *Jet,* 25 June 1953

"Mixed Marriage Woes of Negro GIs in Georgia," *Jet,* 13 June 1963

"Mixed Marriages Doomed by Racism, College Students Say," *Jet,* 20 May 1971

"Mixed Marriages—and an Exception," *Newsweek,* 22 December 1958

"Mixed Marriages in D.C. on Increase," *Baltimore Afro-American,* 23 July 1949

"Mixed Marriages: Next Trend in Race Problem?," *U.S. News & World Report,* 28 June 1965

"Mixed Weddings Big Social News for New Englanders," *Ebony,* July 1954

Monroe, Sylvester. "Love in Black and White: The Last Racial Taboo," *Los Angeles Times Magazine,* 9 December 1990

"National Affairs: We Fell in Love," *Newsweek,* 16 September 1963

"Negro GIs of 2nd Armored Division Stationed in Germany Choose Between Their White Wives and the Army," *Jet,* 19 September 1957

"Negro Merchant Seaman Jean A. Brown Says Bigotry Forced His White Wife and Three Children to Flee His Home in Norwood, NJ," *Jet,* 21 May 1959

"Negro Ph.D. Candidate Samuel Harris at Michigan State University Marries Wren Crawford, Wealthy White Student," *Jet,* 13 April 1961

"Negro Teacher Weds White Coed," *Jet,* 10 January 1952

"Negro Woman Gets 2-year Prison Term in Alabama for Marrying White Man," *Jet,* 7 October 1954

"Negro Women with White Husbands," *Jet,* 21 February 1952, pp. 24–29

"Negroes Are Found to Be Uninterested in Mixed Marriage," *New York Times,* 25 May 1964

Nemy, Enid. "Numbers of Black Women Say They Will Not Date White Men," *New York Times,* 23 November 1970

Nevins, Allan. "Intermarriage of the Races Will Be Inevitable," *U.S. News & World Report,* 14 November 1958

Nix, Shann. "When Love Was a Crime," *San Francisco Chronicle,* 17 September 1992

Norment, Lynn. "Am I Black, White, or in Between?," *Ebony,* August 1995

———. "Black Men/White Women: What's Behind the New Furor," *Ebony,* November 1994

———. "Guess Who's Coming to Dinner Now? The Sudden Upsurge in Black Women/White Men Celebrity Couples," *Ebony,* September 1992

———. "A Probing Look at Children of Interracial Marriage," *Ebony,* September 1985

"North Carolina's Strangest Mixed Marriage," *Jet,* 25 October 1956

"Now That Mixed Marriage Is Legal," *U.S. News & World Report,* 26 June 1967

"Number of Interracial Couples Increased Dramatically in U.S. Within Recent Years," *Jet,* 1 March 1979

"Numbers Increase in Interracial Marriages," *Jet,* 30 July 1984.

Otley, Roi. "Five Million U.S. White Negroes," *Ebony,* March 1948

Owen, David. "The Straddler," *The New Yorker,* 30 January 1995

"Palmore Couple Hit Rocks: She Charges Hubby Hit Her; Gets a Restraining Order," *Jet,* 14 January 1985

Parker, Everett C. "New York City: Negro-White Marriages," *Christian Century,* 6 November 1963

"Part Negro Held White by Court, Set Free," *Chicago Sun-Times,* 15 November 1949

Patterson, Orlando. "Race Over," *The New Republic,* 10 January 2000

Peters, William. "We Dared to Marry," *Redbook,* August 1954

———. "We Weren't Supposed to Marry," *Redbook,* September 1960

———. "Are There Boundary Lines in Love?" *McCall's,* June 1968

"Pinky: Story on Girl Who Passes Will be Most Debated Film of the Year," *Ebony,* September 1949

Piper, Adrian. "Passing for White, Passing for Black," *Transition* 58, 1992

Pitts, George. "Who Wants Intermarriage: Intermarriage Favored but Non-Skilled Females Object," *Pittsburgh Courier,* 6 September 1958

———. "Who Wants Intermarriage: Majority Would Not Object to Children Marrying Whites," *Pittsburgh Courier,* 13 September 1958

Pitts, Leonard. "Is There Room in This Sweet Land of Liberty for Such a Thing as 'Cablinasian'? Face It, Tiger: If They Say You're Black, Then You're Black," *Baltimore Sun,* 29 April 1997

Podhoretz, Norman. "Confessions of a Liberal," *Negro Digest,* July 1963

Poe, Janita. "When Your Heritage Doesn't Fit a Preset Category," *Philadelphia Inquirer,* 7 July 1993

Poussaint, Alvin F. "The Black Male—White Female: An Update," *Ebony,* August 1983

———. "The Price of Success: Remembering Their Roots Burdens Many Blacks to Mainstream with Feelings of Either Guilt or Denial," *Ebony,* March 1988

Powledge, Fred. "Negro-White Marriages on Rise Here," *New York Times,* 18 October 1963

Pressley, Sue Anne. "The Color of Love," *Washington Post,* 22 August 1994

"Prominent Negro Leaders Answer Question: Does Interracial Marriage Hinder Integration?," *Ebony,* July 1957

Randolph, Laura B. "Black Women/White Men: What's Goin' On?," *Ebony,* March 1989

Reeves, Richard. "Race Colors Love and Marriage in America," *Atlanta Journal and Constitution,* 11 December 1991

Robinson, Lori. "I Was Raped," *Emerge,* May 1997

Robinson, Louie. "Death of Actress Inger Stevens Reveals Marriage to Black Man," *Jet,* 21 May 1970

Roosevelt, Eleanor. "Should a Negro Boy Ask a White Girl to Dance?," condensed from *Ladies' Home Journal* in *Negro Digest,* December 1947

Ross, Michelle. "Is Mixed Marriage Jinxed?," *Ebony,* August 1953

Sass, Herbert Ravenel. "Mixed Schools and Mixed Blood," *Atlantic Monthly,* November 1956

Schreiber, A. "Case for Intermarriage," *Harper's Weekly,* January 1916

Schuyler, George S. "Do Negroes Want to Be White?," *American Mercury,* 55 June 1956

Schuyler, George S., and Josephine Schuyler. "Does Interracial Marriage Succeed?," *Negro Digest,* June 1945

Schuyler, George S. "An Interracial Marriage," 62 *American Mercury* 277, March 1946

————. "When Black Weds White," *Modern Monthly,* February 1934

————. "Who Is 'Negro'? Who Is 'White'?," *Common Ground* 1, autumn 1940

"She Left Her Race for a Zulu Lover," *Ebony,* October 1955

Shepherd, Elizabeth. "Adopting Negro Children: White Families Find It Can Be Done," *New Republic,* 20 June 1964

"Should Churches Back Mixed Marriages?," *U.S. News & World Report,* 2 December 1963

Siegel, Ed. "Of TV, Race, and Romance," *Boston Globe,* 17 November 1991

————. "On Film, Stage and TV, Love Is Becoming Colorblind," *Boston Globe,* 25 June 2000

Sim, Jillian A. "Fading to White," *American Heritage,* March 1999

"A Sister Debates a Brother on 'That Black Man–White Woman Thing,'" *Ebony,* August 1970

Smith, Maurice. "Success Story #7," *Interrace,* August/September 1994

Smolowe, Jill. "Intermarried . . . with Children," *Time,* fall 1993, Special Issue

Smothers, Ronald. "Principal Causes Furor on Mixed-Race Couples," *New York Times,* 16 March 1994

Sokolsky, George E. "My Mixed Marriage," *Atlantic Monthly,* August 1933.

"Spike Lee Falls Out with Jazzman Dad Bill Lee over Mixed Marriage," *Jet,* 19 May 1994

Staples, Brent. "The White Girl Problem," *New York Woman,* March 1989

Stewart, Ted. "Why Interracial Marriage Is Increasing," *Sepia,* May 1971

————. "Why So Many Intermarriages?," *Sepia,* June 1977

Still, William Grant, and Mrs. William Grant Still. "Does Interracial Marriage Succeed?," *Negro Digest,* April 1945

Sverdlik, Alan. "Marriage in Black and White," *Atlanta Constitution,* 25 July 1988

"T.V.'s 'Golden Girls' Clash over Race and Age Differences in Interracial Romance," *Jet,* 21 March 1988

Taylor, Charles. "Black and Taboo All Over," Salon.com, 14 February 2000

Taylor, Lloyd. "Interracial Romance on Campus," *Crisis,* January 1953.

Taylor, Robert, "Interracial Couples Form Organization for Mutual Benefit," *Pittsburgh Courier,* 7 August 1948

"Test-Tube Moms Deliver Black Babies After Error," *Jet,* 28 April 1986

"The Trials of an Interracial Couple," *Ebony,* October 1965

Trillin, Calvin. "American Chronicles Black or White," *The New Yorker,* 24 February 1986

Tucker, Dorothy. "Guess Who's Coming to Dinner Now?," *Essence,* April 1987

Turner, Renée. "Interracial Couples in the South," *Ebony,* June 1990

"Twins: One Black, One White, Born to Interracial Pair," *Jet,* July 1989

Uggams, Leslie. "Why I Married an Australian: Young Singer Tells of Her Marriage Across Color Lines," *Ebony,* May 1967

"Unusual Dating Service Helps Build Bridges Among Cultures," *Atlanta Journal and Constitution,* 8 August 1989

"U.S. Interracial Marriages Have More Than Doubled Since the 1968 U.S. Supreme Court Decision," *Jet,* 30 July 1984

Walters, Ronald. "The Meaning of Mixed Marriages," *Washington Post,* 5 October 1991

Watkins, Mel. "Sexism, Racism, and Black Women Writers," *New York Times,* 15 June 1986

Watts, Robert Anthony. "Not Black, Not Whites, But Biracial: Mixed People Questioning Labels," *Atlanta Journal and Constitution,* 1 December 1991

"We Fell in Love," *Newsweek,* 16 September 1963

Weathers, Diane, ed. "White Boys," *Essence,* April 1990

Webster, Yehudi O. "Twenty-one Arguments for Abolishing Racial Classification," *The Abolitionist Examiner,* June/July 2000, www.multiracial.com

"Weddings: Mr. and Mrs. Smith," *Newsweek,* 2 October 1967

Weisman, Al. "He Passed as a Negro," *Negro Digest,* October 1951

"When Negroes and White Intermarry—The Problems," *U.S. News & World Report,* 7 October 1963

"Where Integration Led to Intermarriage," *U.S. News & World Report,* 16 September 1963

"Where Mixed Couples Live: Finding a Home Is Trying Problem for Bi-Racial Families Throughout the Entire Country," *Ebony,* May 1955

"White by Day . . . Negro by Night," *Ebony,* April 1952

"White Drummer Defies Father to Wed Pearl Bailey," *Jet,* 27 November 1952

"White Man Kills Parents over His Black Girlfriend," *Jet,* 17 October 1988

"White Man, Negro Woman Jailed for Living Together in South Carolina," *Jet,* 3 November 1957

"White Mom Upsets 242-year-old Race Law in Maryland, Seeks Her Negro Baby," *Jet,* 9 May 1957

White, Walter. "Why I Remain a Negro," *Saturday Evening Post,* 11 October 1947

"White Women in Negro Society," *Jet,* 5 June 1952

"Why Being Called 'Nigger Lover' Doesn't Offend Me," *Interrace* 10, July/August 1991

"Why I Never Want to Pass," *Ebony,* June 1959

"Why More White Men Are Marrying Negro Women," *Jet,* 3 December 1953

"Why Musicians Choose White Wives," *Jet,* 8 January 1953

"Why People Choose to Date Outside Their Race," *Jet,* 3 February 1992

Williams, Lena. "After the Roast, Fire and Smoke Follow Danson and Goldberg," *New York Times,* 13 October 1993

Wilmot, Cynthia. "My Baby Is Half Negro," *Negro Digest,* February 1949

Winchester, Brenda-Jean. "More Than a Pretty Face," *Interrace* 3, April/May 1995

"Would You Want Your Daughter ... ? Symposium on Mixed Marriages," *U.S. News & World Report,* 9 May 1964

Wright, Lawrence. "One Drop of Blood," *The New Yorker,* 25 July 1994

"You Can't Join Their Clubs: Six Mixed Couples Talk About Love, Marriage and Prejudice," *Newsweek,* 10 June 1991

### Court Cases

*Alfred (a slave) v. State,* 37 Miss. 296 (1859)

*Audat v. Gilly,* 12 Rob. 323 (La. 1845)

*Bell v. State,* 25 S.W. 684 (Tex. Crim. App. 1894)

*Burns v. State,* 48 Ala. 195 (1872)

*Cline v. City of New Orleans,* 207 So. 2d 856 (La. Ct. App. 1968)

*Commonwealth ex rel. Meyers v. Meyers,* 360 A. 2d 587 (Pa. 1976)

*Commonwealth v. Wright,* 27 S.W. 815 (Ky. 1894)

*Compos v. McKeithen,* 341 F. Supp. 264 (E.D. La. 1972)

*Dallas v. State,* 79 So. 690 (Fla. 1918)

*Davis v. Gately,* 269 F. Supp. 996 (D.C. Del. 1967)

*Dees v. Metts,* 17 So. 2d 137 (Ala. 1944)

*Dred Scott v. Sandford,* 60 U.S. 393 (1857)

*Eberheart v. State,* 206 S.E. 2d 12 (Ga. 1974), *vacated,* 433 U.S. 917 (1977)

*Ex parte Francois*, 9 F. Cas. 699 (C.C.W.D. Tex. 1879)

*Farmer v. Farmer*, 439 N.Y.S. 2d 584 (N.Y. Sup. Ct. 1981)

*Farr. v. Thompson*, 25 S.C.L. (Chev.) 37 (S.C. 1839)

*Ferrall v. Ferrall*, 69 S.E. 60 (N.C. 1910)

*Fields v. State*, 132 So. 605 (Ala. Ct. App. 1931)

*Gilbert v. State*, 23 So. 2d 22 (Ala. Ct. App. 1945)

*Gober v. Gober*, 1 N.C. 188 (1802)

*Green v. City of New Orleans*, 88 So. 2d 76 (La. Ct. App. 1956)

*Green v. State*, 58 Ala. 190 (1877)

*Henggeler v. Hanson*, 510 S.E. 2d 722 (S.C. Ct. App. 1998)

*Holt v. Chenault*, 722 S.W. 2d 897 (Ky. 1987)

*Hudgins v. Wright*, 11 Va. (1 Hen. & M.) 134 (1806)

In re *Adoption of Gomez*, 424 S.W. 2d 656 (Tex. Civ. App. 1967)

In re *Adoption of a Minor*, 228 F. 2d 446 (D.C. Cir. 1955)

In re *Adoption of Vito*, 712 N.E. 2d 1188 (Mass. App. Ct. 1999)

In re *Bridget R.*, 49 Cal. Rptr. 507 (Ct. App. 1996), *cert. denied* 117 S.Ct. 693 (1997).

In re *Hobbs*, 12 F. Cas. 262 (C.C.N.D. Ga. 1871)

In re *Marriage of Brown*, 480 N.E. 2d 246 (Ind. Ct. App. 1985)

In re *Marriage of Burton*, 1990 WL 127277 (Ill. App. Ct. 1990), *vacated*, 580 N.E. 2d 208 (Table) (Ill. App. Ct. 1990)

In re *Marriage of Mikelson*, 299 N.W. 2d 670 (Iowa 1980)

In re *Rhinelander's Will*, 36 N.Y.S. 2d 105 (N.Y. App. Div. 1942), *order reversed*, 47 N.E. 2d 681 (N.Y. 1943)

In re *T.J.*, 666 A.2d 1 (D.C. 1995)

In re *Welfare of D.L.*, 486 N.W. 2d 375 (Minn. 1992)

*Isom v. Isom*, 538 N.E. 2d 261 (Ind. Ct. App. 1989)

*Jackson v. State*, 72 So. 2d 114 (Ala. Ct. App. 1954)

*Jones v. Jones*, 542 N.W. 2d 119 (S.D. 1996)

*Keith v. Commonwealth*, 181 S.E. 283 (Va. 1935)

*Kinney v. Commonwealth*, 71 Va. (30 Gratt.) 858 (1878)

*Kirby v. Kirby*, 206 P. 405 (Ariz. 1922)

*Knight v. State*, 42 So. 2d 747 (Miss. 1949)

*Lenora v. Scott*, 10 La. Ann. 651 (1855)

*Locklayer v. Locklayer*, 35 So. 1008 (Ala. 1903)

*Lonas v. State*, 50 Tenn. (3 Heisk.) 287 (1871)

*Loving v. Virginia*, 388 U.S. 1 (1967)

*Malone v. Haley*, No. 88-339 (Sup. Jud. Ct. Suffolk County, Mass., July 25, 1989)

*Marie v. Avart's Heirs*, 10 Mart. (o.s.) 25 (La. 1821)

*McLaughlin v. Florida,* 379 U.S. 184 (1964)

*McPherson v. Commonwealth,* 69 Va. (28 Gratt.) 939 (1877)

*McQuirter v. State,* 63 So. 2d 388 (Ala. Ct. App. 1953)

*Miller v. Lucks,* 36 So. 2d 140 (Miss. 1948)

*Moon v. Children's Home Society,* 72 S.E. 707 (Va. 1911)

*Moore v. Tangipahoa Parish School Board,* 304 F. Supp. 244 (E.D. La. 1969)

*Murphy v. Murphy,* 124 A. 2d 891 (Conn. 1956)

*Naim v. Naim,* 87 S.E. 2d 749 (Va. 1955), *vacated,* 350 U.S. 891 (1955)

*Pace v. Alabama,* 106 U.S. 583 (1883)

*Palmore v. Sidoti,* 466 U.S. 429 (1984)

*Parker v. Parker,* 1996 WL 557816 (Tenn. Ct. App.)

*People v. Cahan,* 282 P. 2d 905 (Cal. 1955)

*Perez v. Lippold,* 198 P. 2d 17 (Cal. 1948)

*Plessy v. Ferguson,* 163 U.S. 537 (1896)

*Roldan v. Los Angeles County,* 18 P. 2d 706 (Cal. Dist. Ct. App. 1933)

*Schexnayder v. Schexnayder,* 371 So. 2d 769 (La. 1979)

*Scroggins v. Scroggins,* 14 N.C. (3 Dev.) 535 (1832)

*Smith v. DuBose,* 3 S.E. 309 (Ga. 1887)

*State v. Bell,* 66 Tenn. (7 Baxt.) 9 (1872)

*State v. Brown,* 108 So. 2d 233 (La. 1959)

*State v. Canley,* 20 S.C.L. (2 Hill) 614 (S.C. 1835)

*State v. Harris,* 716 A. 2d 458 (N.J. 1998)

*State v. Mann,* 13 N.C. (2 Dev.) 263 (1829)

*State v. Pass,* 121 P. 2d 882 (Ariz. 1942)

*State v. Ross,* 76 N.C. 242 (1877)

*State v. Tackett,* 8 N.C. (1 Hawks) 210 (1820)

*State ex rel. Treadway v. Louisiana State Board of Health,* 56 So. 2d 249 (La. Ct. App. 1952)

*Stone v. Jones,* 152 P. 2d 19 (Cal. Dist. Ct. App. 1944)

*Stroman v. Griffin,* 331 F. Supp. 226 (S.D. Ga. 1971)

*Sunseri v. Cassagne,* 195 La 19 (1940).

*Toledano v. Drake,* 161 So. 2d 339 (La. Ct. App. 1964)

*Tucker v. Blease,* 81 S.E. 668 (S.C. Sup. Ct. 1914)

*Tucker v. Tucker,* 542 P. 2d 789 (Wash. Ct. App. 1975)

*Turman v. Boleman,* 510 S.E. 2d 532 (Ga. Ct. App. 1998)

*United States v. Brittain,* 319 F. Supp. 1058 (N.D. Ala. 1970)

*Vail v. Bird,* 6 La. Ann. 223 (1851)

*Van Houten v. Morse,* 38 N.E. 705 (Mass. 1894)

*Von Buelow v. Life Insurance Co. of Virginia,* 9 Teiss. 154 (La. Ct. App. 1912)

*Wambles v. Coppage,* 333 So. 2d 829 (Ala. Civ. App. 1976)
*Ward v. Ward,* 216 P. 2d 755 (Wash. 1950)
*Watson v. City of Memphis,* 373 U.S. 526 (1963)
*Wood v. Commonwealth,* 166 S.E. 477 (Va. 1932)

## Unpublished Papers

Daniel, Tia L. "An Overview of Historical Amalgamationists and the Modern Amalgamationist Impulse," Third-Year Paper, Harvard Law School, 1998

Martyn, Byron Curtis. "Racism in the United States: A History of the Anti-Miscegenation Legislation and Litigation," Ph.D. Dissertation, University of Southern California, 1979

Press, Marcia. "That Black Man–White Woman Thing: Images of an American Taboo," Ph.D. Dissertation, University of Indiana, 1989

Roberts, Robert Edward Thomas. "Negro-White Intermarriage: A Study of Social Control," MA Thesis, University of Chicago, 1940

Romano, Renée Christine. "Crossing the Race Line: Black-White Interracial Marriage in the United States, 1945–1990," Ph.D. Dissertation, Stanford University, 1996

Sharstein, Daniel Jacob. "In Search of the Color Line: *Ferrall v. Ferrall* and the Struggle to Define Race in the Turn-of-the-Century American South," Senior Thesis, Harvard University, 1994

Wacks, Jamie L. "Reading Race, Rhetoric and the Female Body: The Rhinelander Case and 1920s American Culture," Senior Thesis, Harvard University, 1995

Williams, Diana Irene. "New Orleans in the Age of *Plessy v. Ferguson:* Interracial Unions and the Politics of Caste," Senior Thesis, Harvard University, 1995

# Acknowledgments

I take pleasure in acknowledging that in writing this book I have been helped by a wonderful community of people, many of whom are based at Harvard Law School, my institutional home. Dean Robert Clark has been unstintingly supportive. I cannot say that I have been overburdened by teaching or that I could have done better had I simply been able to obtain the resources to review this or that set of documents. Harvard Law School, particularly its staff of excellent librarians, has done its part, and for this I am deeply grateful.

Scores of students have improved this book by offering corrections, suggestions, and, at times, objections. The comments of Leslie Ballentyne, Kami Chavis, Edward K. Cheng, Justin Driver, Brian Fitzpatrick, Ben Glassman, Ketan Jhaveri, Aaron Katz, Walter Mosley, Brian Privor, David Solet, and Jim Trilling have been particularly instructive. David Gallagher gave me the benefit of his splendid research and judgment during the final stage of manuscript preparation.

Peers have been very generous with their time, energy, and knowledge. I hasten to add that although some of them are sharply critical of what I have written, all of them have afforded me collegial respect and assistance. For this I thank Angela Kennedy Acree, Anita Allen, Barbara Ann Atwood, R. Richard Banks, Lawrence Blum, Sissela Bok, Scott Brewer, Laura A. Cecere, Eric Foner, Charles Fried, Sally Goldfarb, Janet Halley, Phillip Heymann, Joan H. Hollinger, Duncan Kennedy, Henry Kennedy Jr., Andrew Koppelman, John Lamb, Sanford Levinson, Ken Mack, Christine Metteer, Martha Minow, Robert Mnookin, Kevin Mumford, Nell Newton, Martha Nussbaum, George Packer, Joshua Rothman, Renee C. Romano, Jed Rubenfeld, Vickie

Schultz, Rita J. Simon, Joseph Singer, Werner Sollors, Tania Tetlow, Detlev Vagts, Michael S. Wald, Lucie White, and David E. Wilkins.

Several people influenced me greatly not only through their sharing of information and criticism but also through their exemplary conduct as political activists who have striven to enlarge the possibilities for interracial intimacy in America. I have in mind here three people in particular: Professor Elizabeth Bartholet of the Harvard Law School, William L. Pierce, formerly the president of the National Council for Adoption, and Carol Coccia, formerly the President of the National Coalition to End Racism in America's Child Care System.

Over the years, I have encountered scores of people who have dealt with me personally in ways that have nurtured the hope that animates this volume. Particularly significant have been my associations with John F. McCune and the St. Albans School family, my teachers and classmates at Princeton University and Yale Law School, Robert Kuttner and the American Prospect, Annique Caplan, David Prather, Dana Zed, the Foner-Garafola family, the Bowen Family, the Lamb family, the Levinsons, the McCorkles, the Riordans, the Vorenbergs, the Boks, the Shapiros, the Rudenstines, Daniel Bell, Robert K. Merton, Rodney Johnson, Jack Cogan, Mary L. Cornille, Michael Sandel, and Kiku Adatto.

Erroll McDonald, my editor at Pantheon Books, displayed his usual patience and, as always, his colleague Altie Karper deftly shepherded the manuscript through the rigors of publication. Susan Norton and Dorothy Straight offered scores of excellent suggestions that ranged far beyond their duties as copyeditors. Benjamin Sears typed and retyped the manuscript and, almost as importantly, prevented me from losing it. Andrew Wylie, my literary agent, has consistently offered sage advice.

My wife, Dr. Yvedt Matory, has been unfailingly supportive, as have our wonderful children: Henry William, Thaddeus, and Rachel.

Finally, I would like to express my heartfelt admiration for the couple to whom this book is dedicated—my extraordinary parents: Rachel Spann Kennedy and Henry Harold Kennedy Sr.

Please bring to the attention of Randall Kennedy corrections, suggestions, or objections: rkennedy@law.harvard.edu.

# Index

# ALSO BY RANDALL KENNEDY

## RACE, CRIME, AND THE LAW

In this groundbreaking, powerfully reasoned, lucid work that is certain to provoke controversy, Randall Kennedy takes on a highly complex issue in a way that no one has before. Kennedy uncovers the long-standing failure of the justice system to protect blacks from criminals, probing allegations that blacks are victimized on a widespread basis by racially discriminatory prosecutions and punishments, but he also engages the debate over the wisdom and legality of using racial criteria in jury selection. He analyzes the responses of the legal system to accusations that appeals to racial prejudice have rendered trials unfair, and examines the idea that, under certain circumstances, members of one race are statistically more likely to be involved in crime than members of another.

Current Affairs/Law/0-375-70184-2

## NIGGER

It's "the nuclear bomb of racial epithets," a word that whites have employed to degrade African Americans for three centuries. Paradoxically, among many black people it has become a term of affection and even empowerment. The word, of course, is nigger, and in this candid and lucidly argued book, Kennedy traces its origins, maps its multifarious connotations, and explores the controversies that rage around it. Should blacks be able to use nigger in ways forbidden to others? Should the law treat it as a provocation that reduces the culpability of those who respond to it violently? Should it cost a person his job? With a range of reference that extends from the Jim Crow South to the O. J. Simpson trial, Kennedy takes on not just a word, but our laws and culture with bracing courage and intelligence.

Current Affairs/Cultural Studies/0-375-71371-9

VINTAGE BOOKS
Available at your local bookstore, or call toll-free to order:
1-800-793-2665 (credit cards only).